Th(

MW01077838

Privilege and the

Work-Product

Doctrine

The Attorney-Client Privilege and the Work-Product Doctrine

FIFTH EDITION
VOLUME II

Edna Selan Epstein

SECTION *of*
LITIGATION
AMERICAN BAR ASSOCIATION

Defending Liberty
Pursuing Justice

Cover design by Richard Laurent.

© 2007 American Bar Association. All rights reserved.
Printed in the United States of America.

16 15 14 13   6 5 4 3

Library of Congress Cataloging-in-Publication Data

Epstein, Edna Selan.
    The attorney-client privilege and the work-product doctrine / by Edna Selan Epstein.—5th ed.
        p. cm.
    Includes bibliographical references.
    ISBN 978-1-59031-1-804-1
    1. Confidential communications—Lawyers—United States.   2. Attorney and client—United States.   3. Corporate legal departments—United States.   I. Title.

    KF8959.A7 E67 2007
    347.73'504—dc22

                                                    2007011254

Discounts are available for books ordered in bulk. Special consideration is given to state bars, CLE programs, and other bar-related organizations. Inquire at Book Publishing, ABA Publishing, American Bar Association, 321 North Clark Street, Chicago, Illinois 60610.

www.ShopABA.org

Contents

PART 3
**Factors Common to Both the Attorney-Client Privilege
and the Work-Product Protection**   **1123**

The Work-Product Protection **2**

I. PURPOSE AND SCOPE OF WORK-PRODUCT PROTECTION

The protection given to "work product" arises from a common assumption—that an attorney cannot provide full and adequate representation unless certain matters are kept beyond the knowledge of adversaries. The foci of the two doctrines are different, however. With the attorney-client privilege, the principal focus is on encouraging the client to communicate freely with the attorney; with work-product, it is on encouraging careful and thorough preparation by the attorney. As a result, there are differences in the scope of the protection. For example, the privilege extends only to client communications, while work product encompasses much that has its source outside client communications. At the same time, the privilege extends to client-attorney communications seeking legal advice, but the work-product protection is limited to preparation for litigation.

    The nature of the protection also differs. The attorney-client privilege is absolute. If all four requisite elements are present and the privilege has neither been waived nor does any exception apply, the privilege will be applied without any weighing of the need for disclosure in the particular case. By contrast, whether work-product protection will be afforded depends on both the type of matter being sought and the adversary's need for it.

The words "doctrine," "immunity," and "privilege" (among others) have been used in naming the protection given work product. Any of the terms is probably appropriate. Some resist use of the term "privilege," because the protection is qualified, unlike the traditional communications privileges. In respect to both waiver and exception issues, how the work-product protection will be treated is quite similar to how the privilege is treated.

Although the title of this book still retains the term "doctrine," which was in widespread use at the time of the first edition, the text increasingly speaks in terms of the "work product protection."

- *Hickman v. Taylor*, 329 U.S. 495, 509–10 & n.9 (1947). In recognizing the work-product protection, the Court said that it was not a "privilege" as that term is used in the law of evidence or the civil procedure rules, but noted that the English treat it as a privilege.

The particular nomenclature is only rarely significant. Nevertheless, there are occasions when the fact that the work-product protection is not regarded as a "privilege" has become significant.

- *Railroad Salvage of Conn., Inc. v. Japan Freight Consolidators (U.S.A.) Inc.*, 97 F.R.D. 37, 39–40 (E.D.N.Y. 1983). The work-product protection is not a "privilege" within the meaning of the Federal Rule of Evidence 501, which applies state privileges to state law claims and defenses. Federal law applies as to whether work-product protection will be granted to a particular document.

- *United States v. Nobles*, 422 U.S. 225, 242–54 (1975). Although the majority suggested that the work-product protection was an evidentiary privilege applicable at trial, they held that the defendant had waived any protection in this particular case by making affirmative use of the work product. Justice White said that it was not necessary to reach the waiver issue and that he would have rested the decision solely on the ground that work product was protected in discovery but had no evidentiary privilege.

A. *History and Policy of Work-Product Protection*

Discussion of work-product protection must begin with the Supreme Court's seminal decision in *Hickman v. Taylor*, 329 U.S. 495 (1947). Although parts of the protection have been codified in provisions such as Federal Rules of Civil Procedure 26(b)(3), *Hickman* continues to be the standard by which courts interpret those provisions and protect work product when those provisions do not apply. *See generally* K. Clermont, *Surveying the Work Product*, 68 CORNELL L. REV. 755 (1983); Note, *The Work Product Doctrine*, 68 CORNELL L. REV. 760 (1983).

■ *Hickman v. Taylor* arose from a wrongful death action against the owners of a tugboat that sank. In the course of discovery, attorneys representing the family of one of the deceased crew members filed interrogatories on the tug owners seeking written statements made by survivors or witnesses concerning the accident; the exact provisions of any oral statements; and any records, reports, or other memoranda made concerning the incident. The owners, through their attorney, admitted that statements had been taken, but refused to summarize or set forth their contents.

The district court held that the matters were not protected from disclosure and ordered production of all written witness statements, as well as answers stating the substance of any facts learned through oral witness statements. The court also ordered production of the attorney's memoranda regarding oral statements in order for the court to determine which parts should be disclosed to the plaintiffs. The defendants and their attorney refused to comply and were held in criminal contempt. 4 F.R.D. 479 (E.D. Pa. 1945) (*en banc*).

The Third Circuit reversed, holding that even though the material was not privileged under the rule of evidence because it did not contain communications between client and attorney, as "work product of the lawyer," it should be treated as privileged from disclosure under the discovery rules. Like the evidentiary privilege rule and the rules of protection associated with legal proceedings, a protection from compelled disclosure for work product furthers the public policy "to aid people who have lawsuits and prospective lawsuits." 153 F.2d 212, 223 (3d Cir. 1945) (*en banc*).

The Supreme Court affirmed the court of appeals, holding that the material "falls outside the arena of discovery and contravenes the public policy underlying the orderly prosecution and defense of legal claims. Not even the most liberal of discovery theories can justify unwarranted inquiries into the files and the mental impressions of an attorney." *Hickman*, 329 U.S. 495 at 510 (1947). On examining the role of an attorney within our system of adjudicating disputes, the Court concluded that the attorney's mental processes must, to some extent, be protected from invasion by and disclosure to the opposing side.

A lawyer, as an officer of the court, is bound to work for the advancement of justice, while faithfully protecting the rightful interests of the client. In performing various duties, however, it is essential that a lawyer work with a certain degree of privacy, free from unnecessary intrusion by opposing parties and their counsel. Proper preparation of a client's case demands that the attorney assemble information, sift what the attorney considers to be the relevant from the irrelevant facts, prepare legal theories, and plan a strategy without undue and needless interference. That is the historical and the necessary way in which lawyers act within the framework of our system of jurisprudence to promote justice and to protect their clients' interests. *Id.* at 510–11.

The Court qualified an attorney's work-product protection from discovery. An attorney's file cabinet could not be used to obtain blanket protection from discovery for all otherwise discoverable materials. "Where relevant and non-privileged facts remain hidden in an attorney's file and where production of those facts is essential to the preparation of one's case, discovery may properly be had." *Id.* at 511. Thus, production might be justified when witnesses are no longer available. Consonant with the general policy against invading the privacy of an attorney's course of preparation, however, the burden to establish adequate reasons for requiring discovery rests on the one who would invade that privacy.

Were such materials open to opposing counsel on mere demand, much of what is now put down in writing would remain unwritten. An attorney's thoughts, heretofore inviolate, would not be immune from invasion. Inefficiency, unfairness, and sharp practices would inevitably develop in the giving of legal advice and in the preparation of cases for trial. The effect on the legal profession would be demoralizing. And the interests of the clients and the cause of justice would be poorly served.

To summarize, *Hickman v. Taylor* established three propositions that are still important in this area:

(1)   Material collected by counsel in the course of preparation for possible litigation is protected from disclosure in discovery.

(2)   That protection is qualified, in that the adversary may obtain discovery on showing sufficient need for the material.

(3)   The attorney's thinking—theories, analysis, mental impressions, beliefs, etc.—is at the heart of the adversary system, and privacy is essential for the attorney's thinking; thus, the protection is greatest, if not absolute, for materials that would reveal that part of the work product.

The last point gives rise to a distinction frequently noted in the cases between "opinion" and "ordinary" work product. *Hickman* implies, and Federal Rule of Civil Procedure 26(b)(3) prescribes, that the work product entitled to protection may be divided into two categories: "opinion" work product, which reflects or reveals an attorney's mental processes, and "ordinary" work product. Under the rule, ordinary work product is subject to discovery upon a showing of need and hardship, but the court "shall protect against disclosure the mental impressions, conclusions, opinions, or legal theories of an attorney or other representative of a party concerning the litigation." This distinction, which is not susceptible to any bright-line test, is discussed at length in Part 2, Section V.

B. *Codification of Work-Product Protection*

The principles established in *Hickman* have been codified for certain applications in federal rules. Both Federal Rule of Civil Procedure 26(b)(3) and Federal Rule of Criminal Procedure 16(b)(2) limit pretrial discovery of materials prepared in anticipation of litigation. Neither rule provides the same protection as *Hickman*, however; nor do they each provide the same protection. For example: (1) their application is limited to pretrial discovery; (2) they protect materials prepared by a party's representative other than the party's attorney; (3) the criminal rule strictly limits disclosure regardless of any good cause showing; (4) the civil rule speaks only to discovery of documents and tangible things. Thus, *Hickman's* principles remain the benchmark when a court is faced with work-product questions such as whether the privilege applies at trial or to oral statements, as well as when the court is interpreting the codified rules.

The codification of the work-product protection governs all cases tried in the federal courts. It is to the rules and the interpretations given to the rules by the courts that one must now look for guidance with respect to the contours and scope of the work-product protection.

State formulations of the work-product protection, unlike state formulations of the attorney-client privilege, even in cases based on diversity, do not apply to federal proceedings. It is Rule 26(b)(3) of the Federal Rules of Civil Procedure that prevails.

- *United Coal Cos. v. Powell Constr. Co.*, 839 F.2d 958, 966 (3d Cir. 1988). The district court erred in not applying Federal Rule of Civil Procedure 26(b)(3) when it erroneously held that the work-product protection did not apply to documents containing mental impressions of anyone other than an attorney.

- *Pete Rinaldi's Fast Foods Inc. v. Great Am. Ins. Co.*, 123 F.R.D. 198, 201 (M.D.N.C. 1988). "In determining questions involving work-product protection, federal courts apply federal law, even in diversity cases. [Citations omitted] Decisions concerning work product are not governed by the Federal Rules of Evidence 501 which mandates the application of state law with respect to determination of testimonial or evidentiary privileges in diversity cases."

1. Civil Discovery Rule

Rule 26(b)(3) of the Federal Rules of Civil Procedure provides in pertinent part:

> [A] party may obtain discovery of documents and tangible things otherwise discoverable . . . and prepared in anticipation of litigation for trial by or for another party or by or for that other party's representative (including the other party's attorney, consultant, surety, indemnitor, insurer, or agent) only upon a showing that the party seeking discovery has substantial need of the materials in the preparation of the party's case and that the party is unable without undue hardship to obtain the substantial equivalent of the materials by other means. In ordering discovery of such materials when the required showing has been made, the court shall protect against disclosure of the mental impressions,

conclusions, opinions, or legal theories of an attorney or other representative of a party concerning the litigation.

The second paragraph of the rule permits a person making a statement to obtain it without the required showing. Rule 26(b)(4) states special rules for trial-preparation materials of experts.

Rule 26(b)(3) thus provides a *qualified* protection from discovery in a civil action when materials are

(1)　documents and tangible things otherwise discoverable,
(2)　prepared in anticipation of litigation or for trial, and
(3)　by or for another party or by or for that other party's representative.

To overcome the qualified protection, the party seeking discovery must make a showing of

(1)　substantial need for the materials and
(2)　inability to obtain the substantial equivalent of the information without undue hardship.

Even upon such a showing, however, the court is required to protect the attorney's mental processes from disclosure to the adversary. Thus, the policy underpinnings of the work-product protection enunciated by the Supreme Court in *Hickman v. Taylor* retain all their vitality.

2. Criminal Discovery Rule

Rule 16 of the Federal Rules of Criminal Procedure includes provisions codifying the work-product protection for pretrial discovery in criminal proceedings. That rule provides in pertinent part:

(a) Disclosure of Evidence by the Government.

. . .

(2) Information Not Subject to Disclosure. Except as provided [for defendant's statement, defendant's prior record, and reports of examinations and tests], this rule does not authorize the discovery or inspection of reports, memoranda, or other internal government documents made by the attorney for the government or other government agents in connection with the investigation or prosecution of the case, or of statements made by government witnesses or

prospective government witnesses except as provided in 18 U.S.C. § 3500 [which prohibits any discovery of a Government witness's statement until after the witness's direct testimony].

(b) Disclosure of Evidence by the Defendant.

(2) Information Not Subject to Disclosure. Except as to scientific or medical reports, this subdivision does not authorize the discovery or inspection of reports, memoranda, or other internal defense documents made by the defendant, or the defendant's attorneys or agents in connection with the investigation or defense of the case, or of statements made by the defendant, or by government or defense witnesses, or by prospective government or defense witnesses, to the defendant, the defendant's agents or attorneys.

Significantly, the criminal rule does not authorize the discovery of any portion of "reports, memoranda, or other internal . . . documents" that may contain an attorney's mental impressions, conclusions, opinions, or legal theories. The criminal practice rule thus is more categorical in its prohibition against disclosure than is the equivalent civil practice rule. The courts have accordingly recognized that although the work-product protection originated in a civil action, it has an even more important role to protect an attorney's mental impressions and any statements taken of defense witnesses in the context of a criminal charge.

- *United States v. Nobles*, 422 U.S. 225, 238 (1975). "Although the work product doctrine most frequently is asserted as a bar to discovery in civil litigation, its role in assuring the proper functioning of the criminal justice system is even more vital. The interests of society and the accused in obtaining a fair and accurate resolution of the question of guilt or innocence demand that adequate safeguards assure the thorough preparation and presentation of each side of the case."

3. Availability of Work-Product Protection in Other Proceedings

Criminal Rule 16 and Civil Rule 26 apply only to the discovery procedures established under the respective rules. There are numerous other circumstances in which one party may seek disclosure of an adversary's work product; the courts have generally recognized the protection in those instances as well, using the principles of *Hickman v. Taylor.*

a. Grand Jury

Federal Rule of Criminal Procedure 16 posits a pretrial proceeding in which there is a known defendant; it thus does not expressly apply to the investigatory procedures of a grand jury. Nonetheless, it is clear that discovery by the government in grand jury proceedings is subject to the work-product protection.

- *In re Grand Jury Subpoena*, 599 F.2d 504, 509 (2d Cir. 1979). "The Federal Rules of Evidence now specifically make reference to rules of privilege in grand jury proceedings. Rule 1101(c) declares that the 'rule with respect to privileges applies at all stages of all actions, cases and proceedings'. . . . Thus, the attorney-client privilege, as a true 'privilege,' is applicable to grand jury subpoenas. And even if the work product protection is not strictly a 'privilege,' as applied to interviews with nonparty witnesses, the rule has been applied to grand jury proceedings."

- *In re Grand Jury Proceedings (Duffy)*, 473 F.2d 840, 845 (8th Cir. 1973). An attorney was excused from testifying before a grand jury with respect to his memoranda and recollections of conversations with nonemployees of his corporate client. The court held that the work-product protection limited the scope of a grand jury's power because there are "vital public policy considerations which dictate that the need for protection of an attorney's work product outweighs the public interest in the search for truth."

- *In re Grand Jury Investigation*, 412 F. Supp. 943, 947 (E.D. Pa. 1976). A grand jury witness may resist questioning or a subpoena on grounds that it calls for the production of work product.

- *In re Rosenbaum*, 401 F. Supp. 807, 808 (S.D.N.Y. 1975). The work-product protection prevented a grand jury from compelling a defense attorney to testify, in effect, against a former client concerning a conversation with a witness who was being investigated for perjury in connection with the trial of the client.

■ *United States v. Mitchell*, 372 F. Supp. 1239, 1245 (S.D.N.Y.), *appeal dismissed sub nom. Stans v. Gagliardi*, 485 F.2d 1290 (2d Cir. 1973). Statements that the defendant prepared for his attorney's use in a grand jury proceeding and the attorney's notes of interviews with witnesses and third parties were encompassed by the work-product protection, although the witnesses' statements would not have been protected by the attorney-client privilege.

■ *In re Terkletoub*, 256 F. Supp. 683, 684–86 (S.D.N.Y. 1966). A defense attorney preparing for a criminal trial did not have to testify before a grand jury as to the existence, time, place, or content of an interview with a witness.

b. *Other Investigations*

Work-product protection is also available in investigations that occur outside the grand jury context.

■ *Upjohn Co. v. United States*, 449 U.S. 383 (1981). In an administrative investigation, the IRS sought, by means of an investigatory summons, material that was work product. Quoting *Hickman v. Taylor* and noting that IRS summons-enforcement proceedings are governed by the federal rules, the court held that work-product protection applied.

c. *Trials*

The Supreme Court has indicated that work-product protection extends to the trial stage of the litigation process, as well as to the pretrial stages.

■ *United States v. Nobles*, 422 U.S. 225, 239 (1975). "[T]he concerns reflected in the work product protection do not disappear once trial has begun. Disclosure of an attorney's efforts at trial, as surely as disclosure during pretrial discovery, could disrupt the orderly development and presentation of the case."

d. *State Court Proceedings*

Most states have adopted discovery procedures similar to those applied in the federal courts, and they tend to provide similar protection for attorney work product.

e. *Arbitrations*

Because arbitrations are adversary proceedings, documents created for submission in such proceedings have been accorded subsequent work-product protection.

- *Samuels v. Mitchell*, 155 F.R.D. 195 (N.D. Cal. 1994). Since arbitrations are adversarial in nature, documents prepared for use in arbitrations are accorded work-product protection.

C. *Scope of Work-Product Protection*

The work-product protection is broader in scope and reach than is the attorney-client privilege.

- *In re Grand Jury Investigation (Sun Co.)*, 599 F.2d 1224, 1232 (3d Cir. 1979). The scope and reach of work-product protection is broader than that of attorney-client privilege.

Opinion work product enjoys a protection that is almost as absolute as that of the privilege and broader in scope of coverage.

- *Upjohn Co. v. United States*, 449 U.S. 383, 401 (1981). "[S]uch work product (attorney's opinions and mental impressions) cannot be disclosed simply on a showing of substantial need and inability to obtain the equivalent without undue hardship."

- *In re Sealed Case*, 676 F.2d 793, 810 (D.C. Cir. 1982). "However, to the extent that work product reveals the opinions, judgments, and thought processes of counsel, it receives some higher level of protection, and a party seeking discovery must show extraordinary justification." Thus, even though the court of appeals cut a wide swath in the crime/fraud and implied waiver formulations in this leading work-product protection case, nonetheless a substantial number of the documents were not ordered produced because opinion work product (the musings of investigative counsel) were not intended for any further dissemination. The court of appeals opined that the opinion work product was nearly as absolute as the attorney-client privilege and more extensive in its reach.

It may thus be poor practice not to assert the protection separately from the privilege, where there is a likelihood that the protection will cover materials that the privilege would not.

Although the scope of the attorney work-product protection is broad, merely labeling a document as such will not do the trick, any more than sending a document to an attorney for safekeeping or for cursory review necessarily invests that document with the attorney-client privilege.

- *Ledgin v. Blue Cross & Blue Shield*, 166 F.R.D. 496, 498–99 (D. Kan. 1996). Merely placing an attorney work product stamp on a document is insufficient to make that document subject to the attorney work-product doctrine.

D. *Discovery of Underlying Facts*

Just as the attorney-client privilege protects from discovery the *communication* between client and attorney, but not the underlying facts, so too, the work-product protection cannot be asserted to prevent disclosure of the underlying facts, which are discoverable in any adversary proceeding. A document may be protected from compelled disclosure. An attorney may not be forced to take the stand and testify as to that attorney's mental impressions. That does not, however, mean that the underlying facts thereby are absolutely protected from discovery, either by way of interrogatories or by way of depositions of other knowledgeable witnesses, discovered through interrogatories.

- *ECDC Envtl. LC v. New York Marine & Gen. Ins. Co.*, 1998 U.S. Dist. LEXIS 8808, at *44 (S.D.N.Y June 4, 1998). "If a document constitutes protected work product, the party possessing the document generally need not produce it—even if the document contains only factual information. However, because the work product privilege does not protect the facts in that document (the privilege protects documents, not facts), the party seeking those facts may obtain them through other means of discovery, such as through depositions and interrogatories."

- *Casson Constr. Co. v. Armco Steel Corp.*, 91 F.R.D. 376 (D. Kan. 1980). A default judgment was entered against a party that stonewalled discovery. The refusal to respond was based on a faulty raised and unsupported claim of attorney-client privilege and work-product protection from discovery. The work-product protection served as no shield from discovery as to facts that the attorney had learned, persons from whom the facts had been learned, or the existence of documents, even though the documents in which the attorney may have set down that knowledge might be protected from discovery by virtue of the work-product doctrine.

A party may not use the fact that relevant information sought is work product to block discovery. Courts will generally order production of the information sought, in any form in which the producing party can gather it, reserving the right to claim work-product protection for a particular document. They will not countenance refusal to provide factual information on the grounds that it purportedly exists only in work-product form. Interrogatories can always be posed and must be answered even if the particular work-product document need not be produced.

- *Koch Materials Co. v. Shore Slurry Seal, Inc.*, 208 F.R.D. 109, 121 (D.N.J. 2002). "The plaintiff may choose in what form it produces relevant factual information. But, it cannot withhold relevant information on the basis of attorney work product."

II. PROCEDURAL MATTERS

A. *Applicable Law*

Although in diversity cases courts will apply the law of the forum state to determine issues of attorney-client privilege, they do not do so when making rulings on work-product doctrine protection. When work product is at issue in diversity cases, the federal common law is deemed to apply. In most cases, the distinction may be one without a difference, yet it is hard to understand the logic behind the distinction. Granted Rule 501 of the Federal Rules of Evidence expressly governs the issue of applicable law with respect to the privilege but not the protection accorded by the doctrine, which is deemed to be a "federal doctrine" in the federal courts albeit the various states also recognize the existence of the doctrine and accord it protection under their various case precedents.

- *Pyramid Controls, Inc. v. Siemens Indus. Automations*, 176 F.R.D. 269 (N.D. Ill. 1997). "Unlike the attorney-client privilege, in diversity cases, federal law governs issues concerning the work-product doctrine."

- *Dawson v. New York Life Ins. Co.*, 901 F. Supp. 1362, 1366 (N.D. Ill. 1995). "Although neither party has addressed the issue, the Court must first determine whether federal or state law applies. Under *Federal Rule of Evidence 501*, in civil actions in which state law provides the rule of decision, state law privileges apply. Because this is a diversity action in which Illinois law supplies the rule of decision, the Court finds that Illinois law on the attorney-client privilege governs."

- *Insurance Corp. of Ireland, Ltd. v. Bd. of Trustees of Southern Illinois Univ.*, 937 F.2d 331, 334 n.3 (7th Cir. 1991). Plaintiff waived both the attorney-client privilege and work-product protection by putting at issue its state of mind when it claimed it paid its attorneys "under duress."

Because work-product protections are predicated on Federal Rule of Civil Procedure 26(b)(3), federal law applies even in diversity cases, even though the law of the state in which the forum sits is applied to attorney-client privilege issues.

- *Abbott Labs. v. Alpha Therapeutic Corp.*, 200 F.R.D. 401, 405 (N.D. Ill. 2001). "The work-product doctrine has its origins in Federal Rule of Civil Procedure 26(b)(3) which, unlike Federal Rule of Evidence 501, contains no requirement that federal courts in diversity suits apply the privilege law of the state in which the federal court sits. [Fed. R. Civ. Proc. 26(b)(3)] We therefore hold that Illinois law is the law to be applied when discerning Alpha's claims of attorney-client privilege over the documents and federal law is to apply to Alpha's claims under the work-product doctrine."

B. *Standing to Assert or to Waive Protection*

In a sense, the work-product protection is a "privilege" accorded to the attorney, just as the attorney-client privilege is the "privilege" of the client. Thus, there is some dispute among the courts as to whether the attorney alone, or the client as well, has standing to assert the existence of the protection to preclude compelled disclosure.

Clearly, a lawyer may assert the existence of the work-product protection for documents authored by or whose creation was supervised by the attorney. Usually, however, it is ultimately the client's interest that is being protected. A lawyer rarely has as much to lose from such disclosure as a client at whose behest or for whose benefit the work product was generated.

Obviously, a client may invoke the work product doctrine, if it applies, but given that the work product protection seeks in part to protect the attorney's interest in the attorney's own intellectual product, many courts have given the attorney standing to invoke the work product independently at least when the attorney's interests are not adverse to the client's.

- *In re Grand Jury Proceedings*, 43 F.3d 966, 972 (5th Cir. 1994). The law firm was retained to represent various interests. Even though that retention had been terminated and the clients had voluntarily waived any attorney-client privilege, the law firm asserted work product claims as to certain documents including third-party interviews it had prepared in the course of that prior representation. The law firm resisted the District Court's order that production was warranted and prevailed on appeal to the extent that the appellate court reversed and remanded to the district court for a determination of whether the government had sustained a requisite showing of need. There is no indication in the opinion of why the law firm would have had any interest whatsoever in protecting its work product in this instance when the clients had waived any attorney-client privilege which might have attached to their communications with the attorneys. The underlying case involved narcotics and money charges. The law firm had filed a suggestion of death in order to obtain a release of investment funds which had been frozen. The government conceded that the law firm was not suspected of any wrongdoing.

- *In re Grand Jury Proceedings, Thurs. Special Grand Jury, Sept. Term*, 33 F.3d 342, 348 (4th Cir. 1994).

- *In re Sealed Case*, 676 F.2d 793, 809 n.56 (D.C. Cir. 1982). "Hickman v. Taylor, . . . the leading case on work-product protection, identifies a complex of interrelated interests that the work product doctrine seeks to protect. They range from clients' interests in obtaining good legal advice, undistorted by mechanisms to avoid discovery, to the interests of attorneys in their own intellectual product. Courts have often recognized that the interests of attorneys and those of their clients may not always be the same. To the extent that the interests do not conflict, attorneys should be entitled to claim privilege even if their clients have relinquished their claims." (Citation omitted.)

■ *In re Special Sept. 1978 Grand Jury (II)*, 640 F.2d 49, 63 (7th Cir. 1980). The court said that both the client and the attorney could assert the work-product protection, but that no reason existed to allow the protection at the behest of the client when there was a *prima facie* showing of fraud. The attorney, however, had an independent claim to his work product. The court concluded that fact work product was not protected but "opinion" work product was. The notion that the work product of an attorney—whether fact or opinion—which has been bought by a fraudulent client and used to advance his fraudulent cause—is still somehow independently sacrosanct is bizarre and not explained. It is merely asserted, without more.

"We conclude that the client cannot assert the work-product doctrine any more than he can assert the attorney-client privilege when there has been a showing of ongoing client fraud. Therefore, we hold that the Association cannot invoke the work-product doctrine as to the subpoenaed documents because of its prima facie fraud in the filing of the reports.

"Where it is the attorney who asserts the work-product doctrine, the fact of prima facie client fraud is not our only consideration. As we have noted one of the purposes of the work-product doctrine is to protect the work of the attorney from disclosure for the benefit of the attorney. Jenner & Block argues that even if its client was engaging in fraud, the law firm should be able to claim the doctrine on its own behalf. As we perceive the problem, the policy in favor of insulating the attorney's work product for the sake of the attorney must be weighed against the policy which favors disclosure where the client has used his attorney to engage in fraud. We reach different conclusions depending on the type of information subpoenaed.

"With respect to all information furnished to the attorney, whether transmitted in written form or communicated orally and recorded verbatim or in summary form, we conclude that the scale tips in favor of disclosure. We reach this result because we are persuaded that the strong policy disfavoring client fraud requires that the client relinquish the benefit he would gain from the work-product doctrine, which benefit is just as real although it is his attorney, rather than he, who asserts the doctrine. We are persuaded, however, that the attorney's mental impressions, conclusions, opinions, and legal theories must still be protected in order to avoid an invasion of the attorney's necessary privacy in his work, an invasion not justified by the misfortune of representing a fraudulent client. We therefore hold that the work-product doctrine is waived for client fraud even when asserted by the attorney except that it is assertable to protect the attorney's mental impressions, conclusions, opinions, and legal theories about the case."

- *In re Grand Jury Proceedings (FMC Corp.)*, 604 F.2d 798, 801, n.4 (3d Cir. 1979). "We do not intend any implication that the work product material may be divulged on the client's waiver alone. The concern of the lawyer in maintaining the confidentiality necessary to proper preparation of a case must be recognized. For example, an intrafirm memorandum commenting adversely on a client's credibility may be a crucial part of the preparatory process that, if revealed, and especially if later found to be untrue, might be destructive of the attorney-client relationship. This aspect of the privilege is a factor the trial court must consider in determining whether work product should be divulged. It is not necessary to expand upon that issue here because counsel's interests asserted in the district court are in harmony with his client's, nor do we find after an examination of the challenged documents any indication that the problem exists in this case."

- *In re Grand Jury Subpoena (Zerendow)*, 849, 853 (D. Mass. 1995). "While the attorney-client privilege belongs to the client alone, the work-product doctrine may be asserted by either the client or the attorney. 'The general policy against invading the privacy of an attorney's course of preparation is so well recognized and so essential to an orderly working of our system of legal procedure that a burden rests on the one who would invade that privacy to establish adequate reasons to justify production thorough a subpoena or court order.'" (Citations omitted.)

- *Catino v. Travelers Ins. Co., Inc.*, 136 F.R.D. 534, 539 (D. Mass. 1991). The court held that when the client waives work-product immunity, the attorney can only seek protection of opinion work product, albeit not for fact work product.

- *In re Grand Jury Proceeding (Duffy)*, 473 F.2d 840, 848 (8th Cir. 1973). The attorney attempted an interlocutory appeal that was dismissed as such. He attempted a mandamus action, which writ was denied. Finally, he accepted a contempt citation to have the matter appealed. The attorney then prevailed and the production order for the work product was denied. "It is clear that Duffy's personal recollections, notes, and memoranda pertaining to his conversations with non-employees of his client are within the rubric of the work-product definition. . . . The work product sought in this case is absolutely, rather than conditionally, protected."

Suggestion has been made that an attorney alone has standing to assert the existence of the protection to prevent compelled disclosure of such a document. Other courts have said they are not prepared to go so far and have accorded a client standing to assert the existence of the work-product protection.

- *In re Grand Jury Proceedings (FMC Corp.)*, 604 F.2d 798, 801 (3d Cir. 1979). "It is not realistic to hold that it is only the attorney who has an interest in his work product or that the principle purpose of the privilege—to foster and protect proper preparation of a case—is not also of deep concern to the client, the person paying for the work. To the extent a client's interest may be affected, he, too, may assert the work product privilege." Thus, the court expressly held that a client had standing to assert the protection.

- *In re Grand Jury Proceeding (Sun Co.)*, 599 F.2d 1224 (3d Cir. 1979). A client's objections to production of work-product protected documents were considered extensively, without, however, any express holding that the client had standing.

And those who have standing to assert generally have standing to waive as well. What happens where the client and the attorney have divergent views as to whether work-product protection should be asserted or waived? One court has held that the attorney then retains protection only for opinion but not for ordinary work product. It is not clear that in the event of dispute between a client and the attorney all courts would follow this reasoning. Since the client has employed, and presumably paid, the attorney to produce the work product, be it ordinary or opinion, as the "principal" in the production, the client ought perhaps logically have the trump card in any such divergence of interest. Which is precisely what the Fourth Circuit then did when it held that there was no waiver where the "client," an agency of the United States government, had not authorized disclosure.

- *Hanson v. United States Agency for Int'l Dev.*, 372 F.3d 286 (4th Cir. 2004). The court of appeals affirmed the district court's decision that the USAID had the right to assert a work-product protection in response to a FOIA request. It moreover also held that the producer of the work-product report had not waived the protection when he sent a draft to the plaintiff without having been authorized to do so.

The court did not consider to what an extent such a holding flies in the face of an extensive body of case law which holds that unauthorized and even inadvertent disclosure by the government of third-party work product entrusted into its keeping constitutes a waiver of that party's work product, even in the face of a confidentiality agreement entered into and breached by the disclosure. Surely what is sauce for the goose should be sauce for the gander. Or if good enough to protect the government why is it not good enough to protect similarly situate private parties?

- *Catino v. Travelers Ins. Co., Inc.*, 136 F.R.D. 534, 539 (D. Mass. 1991) (Collings, Mag. J.). When the client waives work-product immunity, the attorney can only seek protection of opinion work product, not ordinary work product.

The government's right to work-product protection exists in litigation just like that of any other party and more generally in FOIA requests under exemption 5. *See Hanson v. United States Agency for Int'l Dev.*, 372 F.3d 286 (4th Cir. 2004). The government has as much right to assert the work-product protection as does any private party.

It would seem self-evident that a party on whose behalf work product was not prepared, absent a common interest, can assert a third-party's work-product protection on their behalf.

- *Green v. Sauder Mouldings, Inc.*, 223 F.R.D. 304 (E.D. Va. 2004). Plaintiff, injured in a forklift accident hired as a consulting expert, the individual who had conducted an examination of the forklift that caused the accident. The consulting expert had written the report on behalf of plaintiff's employer and the employer's workman's compensation carrier. The defendant, the rental company from whom the forklift had been obtained, served a subpoena for the investigative report on the company which had produced it. Apparently, that third party interposed no objection to its production. Instead plaintiff attempted and failed to quash the subpoena on third-party grounds. The court held that the work-product claim was not his and thus he had no standing to assert it.

C. Burden of Proof

In the federal courts where the federal common law of privilege applies, the proponent of a privilege has the burden of proving its applicability.

- *Logan v. Commercial Union Ins. Co.*, 96 F.3d 971, 976 (7th Cir. 1996). The burden of proof is on the proponent of the work-product doctrine.

- *Coastal States Gas Corp. v. Department of Energy*, 617 F.2d 854, 862 (D.C. Cir. 1980). The court found that the federal agency failed to sustain its burden of proof for its various claims of privilege. "We remind the agencies, once again, that the burden is on them to establish their right to withhold information from the public and they must supply the courts with sufficient information to allow us to make a reasoned determination that they were correct."

A party relying on the work-product protection to forestall discovery must demonstrate the applicability of the protection, just as the proponent of the attorney-client privilege must do so. And, as is the case when the attorney-client privilege is invoked, the work-product protection must be specifically raised and demonstrated, rather than asserted in a blanket fashion.

- *Shiner v. American Stock Exch.*, 28 F.R.D. 34, 35 (S.D.N.Y. 1961). On a motion to vacate a notice of deposition of plaintiff's attorney as a witness, the court held that the attorney could not assert the work-product protection from discovery until specific questions were asked. Only in ruling on specific objections would the court decide whether the work-product protection applied. An attorney cannot claim "that everything he knows is either privileged or part of his 'work-product.'"

The burdens of proof shift from one party to another. The party asserting the protection must show that the matter in dispute was prepared in anticipation of litigation. Once a *prima facie* showing is made that the material sought to be discovered is indeed work product, the burden of proof shifts to the party seeking discovery. The discovering party must then affirmatively show both a substantial need for the material and an inability to obtain it by other means without undue hardship.

- *Kent Corp. v. NLRB*, 530 F.2d 612, 623–24 (5th Cir.), *cert. denied,* 429 U.S. 920 (1976). When the prospect of litigation exists because a potential claim has been identified, the claim of work product is prima facie valid, and the burden shifts to the party seeking discovery to show substantial need and an inability to obtain the material by other means.

- *In re Natta*, 410 F.2d 187, 193 (3d Cir.), *cert. denied,* 396 U.S. 836 (1969). The burden of demonstrating good cause is on the proponent of disclosure.

- *Republic Gear Co. v. Borg-Warner Corp.*, 381 F.2d 551, 558 (2d Cir. 1967). Discovery of work product was denied where the materials sought were not essential, but merely helpful to the adverse party in the thorough preparation of the case.

Moreover, the more the documents sought reveal an opposing attorney's mental processes and theories, the greater the burden on the party seeking disclosure to demonstrate both great need and substantial hardship.

- *Upjohn Co. v. United States*, 449 U.S. 383 (1981). Work product that reveals the attorney's mental processes cannot be disclosed "simply on a showing of substantial need and inability to obtain the equivalent without undue hardship." The Supreme Court concluded that a "far stronger showing" is required than was made in that case.

- *In re Murphy*, 560 F.2d 326, 336 (8th Cir. 1977). Work product containing an attorney's opinions and theories enjoys "nearly absolute protection" and may be discovered only in "rare and extraordinary circumstances."

In some cases, however, the court has ordered production of opinion work product when it was impossible to redact the documents in such a way as to allow production of the needed facts without disclosing an attorney's mental impressions, opinions, or legal theories.

- *Xerox Corp. v. International Bus. Machs. Corp.*, 64 F.R.D. 367, 381 (S.D.N.Y. 1974). Those portions of an attorney's notes containing the attorney's thoughts, impressions, views, strategy, conclusions, and other similar information would be excised where possible; if it was not possible to separate such information, the entire document must be produced because an attorney's work product is not entitled to protection "at the expense of hiding the non-privileged facts from adversaries or the courts."

The proponent of the privilege cannot assert a Fifth Amendment privilege to prevent disclosure of privileged communications and then do nothing further to demonstrate that the privilege in fact exists.

- *In re Bevill, Bresler & Schulman Asset Mgmt. Corp.*, 805 F.2d 120, 126 (3d Cir. 1986). "A party asserting a privilege bears the burden of proving the applicability of the privilege. [Citation omitted.] The district court's decision simply held that by refusing to answer any questions or submit any evidence. Bevill did not bear his burden of proof. A party cannot invoke a privilege by remaining silent."

D. *Client's Right to Work Product*

Since a client generally is the individual or entity for whom work product is created, a client generally is held to have a right to obtain the work product. Such a right extends to a former client as well.

- *Reiff v. Much Shelist Freed Denenberg, Ament & Rubenstein, P.C.*, 2003 U.S. Dist. LEXIS 18888 (N.D. Ill. Oct. 23, 2003.). In a malpractice action by a former client "[t]he work-product privilege would not apply to documents that Reiff now seeks that were prepared by his attorney on his behalf in the previous case."

- *Spivey v. Zant*, 683 F.2d 881 (5th Cir. 1982). An attorney had no right to refuse to respond to a habeas corpus subpoena served on him by a former client or to refuse to disclose documents in his personal possession on the ground of work-product protection. "[T]he work product doctrine does not apply to the situation in which a client seeks access to documents or other tangible things created or amassed by his attorney during the course of the representation." The court noted but did not decide whether an attorney's mental impressions and opinions were likewise subject to turn over to a former client, although no principled reason would seem to exist why they would not be.

Thus, the fact that a subsequent adversity of interests may exist between an attorney and a former client does not preclude the former client from discovering work-product protected materials.

Similarly, a corporate board of directors may assert a right to work product. That right has been upheld even if the former board member is now adverse to the corporation. The deciding question is whether the work product was created at a time that predates the current adversity. However, any such case contradicts a substantial number of cases in the attorney-client privilege area which holds that a former officer or board member loses any right to waive the privilege.

- *Gottlieb v. Wiles*, 143 F.R.D. 241 (D. Colo. 1992). The former chairperson of a corporate board and chief executive officer of a company was entitled to examine work-product protected documents created during his tenure even though, at present, his position is adverse to that of the corporation. He was not, however, entitled to examine work-product protected materials prepared after his tenure for use in the adverse proceeding itself. Thus, interview notes and summaries prepared by counsel during the time that the former director had been a director were ordered produced.

- *Roberts v. Heim*, 123 F.R.D. 614 (N.D. Cal. 1988). Work-product protection could not extend to preclude production of documents to limited partners in a lawsuit brought by them against the general partners.

The law firm would necessarily have represented both and, thus, could not avoid production to one client at the behest of another.

But see:

- *First Wis. Mortgage Trust v. First Wis. Corp.*, 86 F.R.D. 160, 167 (E.D. Wis. 1980). At one point in time, the Milwaukee law firm Foley and Lardner ("Foley") represented all four parties involved in litigation. A dispute arose among the parties, and First Wisconsin Mortgage Trust ("the trust") terminated its relationship with Foley and brought a claim against the other three parties. The court disqualified Foley from representing the remaining parties but granted its motion to preclude the trust from obtaining documents prepared by Foley in the course of its representation of the four parties. In its decision, the court said that Foley had "some interest at least in the privacy of its own work product, independent of its client's position," and that a "lawyer's interest in the confidentiality of his own work product . . . is in itself protectible," even possibly from his client. The gravamen of the holding, however, may well have been not that the attorney necessarily has a protectible interest in work product as against a client, but that it would be unseemly to allow attorney work product to be used by one client of an attorney against other clients of that attorney.

Accordingly, the successor-in-interest to the client, such as a trustee in bankruptcy will also have a right to obtain work product, even over the objection of attorneys by whom or on whose behalf it was prepared.

- *In re ANR Advance Transp. Co.*, 302 B.R. 607, 617, 620 (E.D. Wis. 2003). Chapter 7 trustee given work product over objection of attorneys, both inside and outside counsel, of debtor in bankruptcy. There is no indication in the opinion why the attorneys were resisting the magistrate's turnover order or appealing from his decision. "I conclude that the law firms may not interpose the work-product doctrine to deny the trustee access to the material he seeks. To grant the law firms work-product immunity under the circumstances present here would not serve the purpose of the work-product doctrine. Clients are not adversaries of their lawyers, and the zone of privacy that the work product rule protects was designed to shield lawyers from their opponents, not their clients. . . . [T]he work product doctrine protects the attorney but does so only because such protection is necessary to enable the attorney to serve his or her client well and function effectively in an adversary system." The attorneys were resisting the turnover since the advice which they had given their clients regarding a merger and attendant withdrawal liability of the debtor corporation was potentially at issue.

III. ELEMENTS OF WORK-PRODUCT PROTECTION

Because most work-product issues arise in the context of civil discovery, the following discussion of the elements of the protection tracks the organizational structure of Federal Rule of Civil Procedure 26(b)(3).

ELEMENT 1: Documents and Tangible Things Otherwise Discoverable

Because Rule 26 applies only to matter otherwise discoverable, if the matter is privileged, one ordinarily need go no further. If some other privilege such as the attorney-client or trade-secrets privilege applies, the material is not discoverable regardless of whether it also constitutes attorney work product. Therefore, the analysis of whether a communication is within the attorney-client privilege or some other testimonial or substantive privilege should precede any inquiry into whether the work-product protection applies. It is only when a document is *not* otherwise privileged from discovery that the question of whether it is protected work product becomes significant.

Rule 26 applies only to tangibles; thus, whether a deponent may be required to disclose work product in her answers is governed not by the rule, but by *Hickman*. One type of non-tangible work product *Hickman* specifically addressed was requiring an attorney to report on an oral statement of a witness.

- *Hickman v. Taylor*, 329 U.S. 495, 512–13 (1947). "Under ordinary conditions, forcing an attorney to repeat or write out all that witnesses have told him and to deliver the account to his adversary gives rise to grave dangers of inaccuracy and untrustworthiness. . . . Such testimony could not qualify as evidence; and to use it for impeachment or corroborative purposes would make the attorney much less an officer of the court and much more an ordinary witness."

- *In re Grand Jury Proceedings*, 473 F.2d 840, 848 (8th Cir. 1973). The attorney's recollections of a witness's conversations were absolutely protected against discovery.

Requiring the attorney to recount witnesses' statements raises concerns about inaccuracy; the *Hickman* Court was also concerned that the discovery rules not give one party a "free ride" at the expense of another, which is inconsistent with the adversary system. The Court's strong adherence to that policy clearly suggests that requiring a party or attorney to disclose unwritten trial strategy is impermissible.

- *Ford v. Philips Elec. Instruments Co.*, 82 F.R.D. 359, 360 (E.D. Pa. 1979). An attorney's discussions with a third-party witness of the attorney's evaluation of the case and his mental impressions, although not within the rule, were nonetheless not discoverable at the deposition of the third-party witness.

Rule 26(b)(3) applies to all kinds of tangible things. It includes not only written memoranda, but also photographs, diagrams, drawings, and computer-generated data.

- *Hickman v. Taylor*, 429 U.S. 495, 511 (1947). Work product encompasses "interviews, statements, memoranda, correspondence, [and] briefs" of attorneys.

- *Parker v. Carroll*, 20 Fed. R. Serv. 2d 698, 700–701 (D.D.C. 1975). Diagrams and drawings are statements subject to Rule 26(b)(3).

- *Galambus v. Consolidated Freightways Corp.*, 64 F.R.D. 468, 473 (N.D. Ind. 1974). "Photographs, diagrams and the like made at or about the time of the occurrence giving [rise] to the suit, should be held discoverable under Rule 26(b)(3)."

- *Peterson v. United States*, 52 F.R.D. 317, 320 (S.D. Ill. 1971). Discovery of the "contents" of a document by means of an interrogatory is the equivalent of discovering a tangible thing, so it is subject to Rule 26(b)(3).

Regardless of the form of the work product, the critical question is the extent to which it discloses attorney thought processes. The more it does so, the more protection it will be given. For example, if a witness gives a statement to an attorney, it may be possible to infer the direction of the attorney's thinking from the witness's answers to the questions posed. If the statement is a verbatim transcript of the witness's answers or has been adopted by the witness, that inference is the only intrusion of the attorney's thinking, and the level of protection is relatively low. If, however, the "statement" is in the form of the attorney's notes of the witness's answers, the attorney's thinking as an observer and recorder is involved to a greater extent, and there is a correspondingly higher level of protection.

- *In re Grand Jury Subpoena Dated Dec. 19, 1978*, 599 F.2d 504, 512 (2d Cir. 1979). Although a lesser degree of necessity may have to be shown to justify disclosure, written answers to questionnaires set out in the witness's own words are as entitled to work-product protection as notes and memoranda based on oral interviews.

- *Harper & Row Publishers Inc. v. Decker*, 423 F.2d 487, 492 (7th Cir. 1970), *aff'd by an equally divided Court*, 400 U.S. 348 (1971). Memoranda of witness interviews prepared by or under the supervision of the attorney are protected; "of course, the less the lawyer's mental processes are involved, the less will be the burden to show good cause" for disclosure.

- *Ross v. Bolton*, 106 F.R.D. 22, 24 (S.D.N.Y. 1985). Transcripts of unsworn depositions taken by the staff attorney of a third party in the investigation were held protected under analogy to *Hickman* because the witnesses deposed, as well as the questions asked, would reveal the nature and direction of the investigation.

- *In re Grand Jury*, 106 F.R.D. 255, 257 (D.N.H. 1985). Notes of a witness's interviews are the attorney's "reduction of [witness's] oral responses to skilled questions posed by" the attorney, which may bring those notes within the work-product protection.

Since the Rule covers tangible things and *Hickman* covers an attorney's mental processes, whether written or oral, neither covers matters which an attorney may actually have done—namely actions which the attorney might have taken for whatever reason.

- *Abels v. JBC Legal Group, P.C.*, 2005 U.S. Dist. LEXIS 41176 (N.D. Cal. Oct. 21, 2005). "Defendants object to numerous deposition questions posed to attorney Boyajian during his May 5, 2005 deposition on the grounds that the information sought is privileged and constitutes attorney work product. They also object that the questions call for a legal opinion or are not relevant to this action. The objections based on work product and legal opinion are not proper, however, as the questions posed seek facts about attorney Boyajian's conduct rather than his operational strategy, thoughts, or impressions. Fed. R. Civ. Pro. 26(b)(3)."

In one reported case, a court protected as work product the process of conducting an inspection of a vessel that was to be done by one side's experts.

- *Mancuso v. D.R.D. Towing Co.*, 2006 U.S. Dist. LEXIS 9672 (E.D. La. Mar. 10, 2006). Court ordered that one side's experts stay on the stern while the other side's were on the bow (both agreed they could view the wheelhouse simultaneously. No joke). The purpose of keeping the two inspection teams separate was so neither would poach on the other's work product and each could discuss matters freely. Since the Rule only protects "documents and tangible things" presumably the work-product protection here accorded to the process of conducting an inspection fell within the penumbra of *Hickman*.

The large computer databases that have become a staple of litigation in the federal courts can also pose work-product problems. Putting full-text copies of all the documents on a computer really involves nothing of the lawyer's distinctive skills or mental processes. An indexing or abstracting scheme, or a selection of particular documents, however, may reveal the direction of an attorney's thinking regarding the case. The same thing is true, of course, of any selection or arrangement of documents by an attorney.

- *National Union Elec. Corp v. Matsushita Elec. Indus. Co.*, 494 F. Supp. 1257, 1258–60 (E.D. Pa. 1980). By means of a computer-generated paper printout, the plaintiff produced substantial financial data in answer to interrogatories. The defendant sought the data in computer-readable form, but the plaintiff argued that the database had been compiled under counsel's direction. The court held that because the defendant was asking for only the same material in the same arrangement as the printout, there was no work product involved. The court noted that the litigation support system that had been created out of the database would have been given protection. *See In re IBM Peripherals EDP Devices Antitrust Litig.*, 5 Computer L. Serv. Rep. 878 (N.D. Cal. 1975).

- *United States v. AT&T*, 642 F.2d 1285, 1288–89, 1296–1301 (D.C. Cir. 1980). In earlier litigation between AT&T and MCI, MCI had copied 1.5 million pages of the approximately 7 million pages AT&T had produced. In this litigation, MCI turned over that material to the government, together with a "database" of computerized abstracts of the materials it had received from AT&T during the earlier discovery and "database documents" describing the structure of the database and explaining how information can be entered and retrieved. AT&T sought to discover the database and the database documents from the government, not because they might be admissible as evidence, but because they "might well enable AT&T to determine which documents a plaintiff's counsel would consider important, why counsel might consider them to be important, and what portions of those documents counsel might think are most important for the issues in this suit." The database and database documents were protected as work product.

- *Sporck v. Peil*, 759 F.2d 312, 315–17 (3d Cir.), *cert. denied*, 474 U.S. 903 (1985). The plaintiff's lawyer had selected for copying over one hundred thousand documents out of the "hundreds of thousands" the defendant had produced. In preparation for the defendant's deposition, his attorney selected an unknown number of the documents that had been produced. The majority held that the selection and compilation of documents by counsel in preparation for pretrial discovery falls within the highly protected category of opinion work product. The dissenting judge thought that, on these facts at least, the inference from the selection to the attorney's litigation strategy was too attenuated.

- *James Julian, Inc. v. Raytheon Co.*, 93 F.R.D. 138, 144 (D. Del. 1982). A party sought a binder containing discoverable documents that the opponent had used for preparing witnesses. The court said that the selection and ordering of a few documents out of the thousands involved in the case "could not help but reveal important aspects of [counsel's] understanding of the case. Indeed, in a case such as this, involving extensive document discovery, the process of selection and distillation is often more critical than pure legal research."

- *Montrose Chem. Corp. v. Train*, 491 F.2d 63, 67–71 (D.C. Cir. 1974). The court denied discovery under the Freedom of Information Act (FOIA) of staff summaries of evidence presented in administrative agency hearings because "[t]o probe the summaries of record evidence would be the same as probing the decision-making process itself. To require disclosure of the summaries would result in publication of the evaluation and analysis of the multitudinous facts made by the Administrator's aides and in turn studied by him in making his decision."

- *City Consumer Servs., Inc. v. Horne*, 100 F.R.D. 740, 745–47 (D. Utah 1983). Eighty thousand business records of a bankrupt financial corporation were made available to the parties in this consolidated securities-fraud case for review and copying. Claiming that the records were haphazardly stored and organized, defendants sought to discover the documents copied and compiled by plaintiffs' counsel. The plaintiffs objected on work-product grounds, but the court held that the defendants were entitled to exchange their discovery material with the records retained by the plaintiffs, in order to "avoid duplication, surprise, and prejudice." The court noted that there was no protection for preexisting business records, but apparently did not recognize, or did not hear, the argument that selection within equally available records indicates the attorney's mental processes.

The obvious danger in shielding from judicially compelled disclosure any selection of documents made by an attorney is that the potential for abuse is enormous. All an attorney would have to do to protect any document from compelled disclosure would be to attach it to an otherwise privileged document and contend that it formed the basis for the legal opinion reached. To ask judges to wade through the reasoning involved to see if that claim is credible is to place even more of a decisional burden on them than *in camera* inspection of documents already does. Accordingly, the best procedure in most cases is the one followed by Magistrate Judge Facciola in *Willingham, infra,* treating each of the documents relied upon by counsel independently for any privilege or protection which might apply.

- *Willingham v. Ashcroft,* 228 F.R.D. 1, 7 (D.D.C. 2005). "It is certainly true that, in preparing his legal opinion, Associate Chief Counsel Goldman selected certain documents to review and use as support for his legal conclusions. However, this is not a case involving the selection and reliance upon a few documents, from a sea of thousands of documents produced in discovery, and it is no secret that the documents upon which Goldman relied are important to the litigation. Even more importantly, via the privilege log, counsel has already identified the documents upon which Goldman relied in drafting his legal memorandum. Accordingly, ordering production of the supportive documents, even though they were attachments to a document that is clearly privileged, will not violate the work-product doctrine. Indeed, if attaching a non-privileged document to a privileged one would automatically prevent it from being discoverable, the liberal discovery contemplated by the federal rules would be obviated. With that in mind, I have reviewed the attachments individually, without regard to their status as attachments, and have determined that none of them is independently protected by the work-product privilege."

Work-product protection does not shield *information* from disclosure; it only protects a party against having to turn over particular documents containing the information. Interrogatories can be addressed to obtain the sought-after information. Once witnesses are located, their depositions can be taken.

- *Brock v. Frank V. Panzarino, Inc.,* 109 F.R.D. 157, 160 (E.D.N.Y. 1986). "By denying defendants access to the statements [because of the work-product privilege], the court is not limiting defendants from taking further discovery." Rather, it is just denying them the less expensive method to discover the information they seek.

- *Eoppolo v. National R. Passenger Corp.,* 108 F.R.D. 292, 294 (E.D. Pa. 1985). The defendant was required to respond to an interrogatory asking it to state "the information you or any of your representatives have or are aware of relating to the accident," as it did not elicit information going beyond the underlying facts of the accident. The interrogatory did not call for, and could not require, the defendant to supply counsel's view of the case, identify the facts counsel found significant, or specify the questions asked by the defendant's agents in obtaining the information.

Thus, the fact that information is included in a protected document does not mean that the information may not be discovered. For example, a witness who has given a statement to an attorney may be deposed regarding the information that was the subject of the statement.

- Fed. R. Civ. P. 26(b)(3) Advisory Comm. Note, 48 F.R.D. 487, 501 (1970). "No change is made in the existing doctrine, noted in the *Hickman* case, that one party may discover relevant facts known or available to the other party, even though such facts are contained in a document which is not itself discoverable."

The witness may even be asked by opposing counsel what was told to the attorney or investigator in an interview. Although that may incidentally reveal the attorney's line of inquiry, it does not cause the problem noted in *Hickman* of making the attorney a potential witness against the client.

- *Delco Wire & Cable, Inc. v. Weinberger*, 109 F.R.D. 680, 691–92 (E.D. Pa. 1986). The witness could be questioned as to what he told the attorney in preparing for his deposition, as that was not protected work product.

- *United States v. International Bus. Machs. Corp.*, 79 F.R.D. 378, 380 (S.D.N.Y. 1978). "The Supreme Court did not hold or even intimate that opposing counsel could not subsequently inquire of the witnesses themselves what they said at the interview."

Similarly, a party may be required to disclose the sources of information, even though the information the party has received from those sources is protected as work product. Thus, the identity of occurrence witnesses and the existence and description of relevant documents are discoverable matters.

- *United States v. Exxon Corp.*, 87 F.R.D. 624, 638 (D.D.C. 1980). The court said that a party cannot invoke work-product protection to shield itself from answering whether protected documents even exist.

- *Lauritzen v. Atlantic Greyhound Corp.*, 8 F.R.D. 237, 238 (E.D. Tenn. 1948), *aff'd*, 182 F.2d 540 (6th Cir. 1950). The defendants were ordered, over work-product objection, to turn over lists of bus passengers and other witnesses to a bus accident.

- *Butler v. United States*, 226 F. Supp. 341, 343 (W.D. Mo. 1964). The court held that the discovering party was entitled to know the "existence, description, nature, custody, condition or location" of relevant documents.

Discovery requests calling for revelation of attorney thought processes, such as the "summary" of a document or the list of witnesses who will be called at trial, are protected under the rule, however.

- *Bell v. Swift & Co.*, 283 F.2d 407, 409 (5th Cir. 1960). A party is not required to state the names and addresses of the witnesses the party proposes to introduce at trial.

The decisions conflict as to whether discovery will be permitted of the names and addresses of witnesses who were interviewed in preparation for litigation.

- *Castle v. Sangamo Weston, Inc.*, 744 F.2d 1464, 1467 (11th Cir. 1984). "The law is clear that [names and addresses of the witnesses the plaintiffs already interviewed are] subject to discovery."

- *In re Grand Jury Impanelled Oct. 18, 1979*, 633 F.2d 282, 289 (3d Cir. 1980). The court said that a list of the persons interviewed by an investigator for the attorney was work product because it revealed the attorney's strategy of investigation in preparing a defense; however, disclosure could be ordered on a relatively low showing of need. The decision may be explained by the fact that the government was apparently asking the questions more to find out if interviewees were being intimidated than to get information about the facts they knew.

- *Board of Educ. v. Admiral Heating & Ventilating, Inc.*, 104 F.R.D. 23, 32 (N.D. Ill. 1984). The court said that to go beyond identifying persons who have knowledge of relevant events "to tell plaintiffs whom defendants have interviewed, where and when such interviews took place and whether or not a record was made—is to give plaintiffs no more knowledge of substantive relevant facts, but rather to afford them the potential for significant insights into the defense lawyers' preparation of their case (and thus their mental processes)." The court also held it was inappropriate to require identification of persons who "participated in" rather than just "furnished information utilized in" interrogatories.

Attorneys have tried, generally without success, to contend that the work-product designation does not cover conversations and nontangible matters.

Restatement (Third) of the Law Governing Lawyers § 87. "Intangible work product is equivalent work product in unwritten, oral or remembered form. For example, intangible work product can come into question by a discovery request for a lawyer's recollection derived from oral communications." Comment (f).

- *United States ex rel. [Redacted] v. [Redacted]*, 209 F.R.D. 475 (D. Utah 2001). The argument that conversations between government and realtors was not work product because they were not a document nor were they "tangible" material was not successful.

ELEMENT 2: Prepared in Anticipation of Litigation or for Trial

The *Hickman* decision was concerned with "[p]roper preparation of a client's *case*" and the protections needed for "materials obtained or prepared . . . with an eye toward *litigation*." The work-product privilege that has developed consequently applies not to all materials in an attorney's files, but only to those materials that were prepared in anticipation of litigation or for trial.

- *Jordan v. United States Dep't of Justice*, 591 F.2d 753, 775 (D.C. Cir. 1978) (*en banc*). "The work-product rule does not extend to every written document generated by an attorney; it does not shield from disclosure everything that a lawyer does. Its purpose is more narrow, its reach more modest. . . . [T]he purpose of the privilege is to encourage effective legal representation *within the framework of the adversary system* by removing counsel's fears that his thoughts and information will be invaded by his adversary. In other words, the privilege focuses on the integrity of the adversary trial process itself. . . . This focus on the integrity of the trial process is reflected in the specific limitation of the privilege to materials 'prepared in anticipation of litigation or for trial.'"

- *Hercules Inc. v. Exxon Corp.*, 434 F. Supp. 136, 151 (D. Del. 1977). "The rationale is restricted to 'in anticipation of litigation' on the theory that an attorney who does not envision litigation (except as a remote contingency of any legal action) will not anticipate discovery requests, and therefore the fear of disclosure will not deter fully an adequate consideration of the client's problem."

- *Coastal States Gas Corp. v. Department of Energy*, 617 F.2d 854, 865 (D.C. Cir. 1980). Agency memoranda regarding audits of the corporation were not protected by the work-product privilege because they were not prepared in anticipation of litigation. "[A]t the very least, some articulable claim, likely to lead to litigation, must have arisen." The court did not decide "whether litigation need be consciously contemplated by the attorney; the documents must have been prepared with a specific claim supported by concrete facts which would likely lead to litigation in mind." Although every audit potentially could lead to litigation, this possibility was too insubstantial to support a claim of privilege.

Thus, two factors must be present for the work-product protection to apply: there must be a threat of litigation and there must be a motivational component. The document must have been prepared because of that threat. One of the best formulations is that of Judge Rushfelt:

- *Marten v. Yellow Freight Sys.*, 1998 U.S. Dist. LEXIS 268, 1998 WL 13244, at *10 (D. Kan. Jan. 7, 1998). "The work product standard has two components. The first is what may be called the 'causation' requirement. This is the basic requirement of the Rule that the document in question be produced because of the anticipation of litigation, i.e., to prepare for litigation or for trial. The second component is what may be termed a 'reasonableness' limit on a party's anticipation of litigation. Because litigation can, in a sense, be foreseen from the time of occurrence of almost any incident, courts have interpreted the Rule to require a higher level of anticipation in order to give a reasonable scope to the immunity.

"The court looks to the primary motivating purpose behind the creation of the document to determine whether it constitutes work product. Materials assembled in the ordinary course of business or for other non-litigation purposes are not protected by the work product doctrine. The inchoate possibility, or even the likely chance of litigation, does not give rise to work product. To justify work product protection, the threat of litigation must be 'real and imminent.' To determine the applicability of the work product doctrine, the court generally needs more than mere assertions by the party resisting discovery that documents or other tangible items were created in anticipation of litigation."

The timing factor seems so self-evident that it is often mistakenly overlooked in resisting a claim that a particular document is work-product protected. It is worthwhile to inquire whether, although the document predates the commencement of an adversary proceeding or claim, it was in fact produced before or after the likelihood of that adversary proceeding became manifest.

- *Helt v. Metropolitan Dist. Comm'n*, 113 F.R.D. 7 (D. Conn. 1986). A proponent of the work-product protection failed to establish that the documents had been created after notice of the ERISA sex discrimination claim and, thus, did not meet the prerequisite for the application of the protection.

A. What Constitutes Litigation?

What constitutes "litigation" for the purpose of giving rise to the work-product protection?

The Federal Rules do not define the term *in anticipation*, nor do they define what is meant by *litigation*.

The Special Masters' Guidelines for the Resolution of Privilege Claims contain a detailed discussion of the phrase. *See United States v. AT & T*, Civ. No. 74-1698 (D.D.C. Feb. 28, 1979). The special masters, Paul R. Rice and Geoffrey C. Hazard, Jr., defined "litigation" as including "a proceeding in court or administrative tribunal in which the parties have the right to cross-examine witnesses or to subject an opposing party's presentation of proof to equivalent disputation."

By focusing on the cross-examination aspects of a proceeding, the special masters defined "litigation" as an adversary proceeding. That definition implements the *Hickman* policy of protecting the special place of the attorney in the adversary process. Its reach, given the nature of the American adversarial process, is broad indeed, and reaches criminal as well as civil matters in a broad range of possible proceedings. The definition given to *litigation* by the special masters has been extended judicially to such proceedings as the grand jury, where no cross-examination generally takes place.

- *United States v. Nobles*, 422 U.S. 225 (1975). The work-product protection applies to materials prepared for defense in a criminal case, as well as in civil litigation.

- *Natta v. Zletz*, 418 F.2d 633, 637–38 (7th Cir. 1969). Documents prepared in connection with patent interference proceedings were work-product protected from discovery.

The proceeding for which documents are prepared need not actually take place in a court of record, as long as the proceeding is adversarial in nature.

- *Willingham v. Ashcroft*, 228 F.R.D. 1 (D.D.C. 2005). Any documents prepared after plaintiff filed agency appeals of her indefinite suspension were made in anticipation of litigation even though no judicial proceeding was as yet in the offing. However, a synopsis of agency actions taken against other similarly situated employees (i.e., lawyers) seems to have been done for personnel purposes. Absent any declaration that they were created for litigation purposes they were not work-product protected. Similarly memos which recount events which occurred were not given work-product protection where there was no indication as to for what purpose they had been created.

- *Kent Corp. v. NLRB*, 530 F.2d 612, 615, 623 (5th Cir.), *cert. denied*, 429 U.S. 920 (1976). Investigatory reports compiled by the NLRB in preparation for agency determination as to whether unfair labor charges had sufficient merit to justify instituting formal proceedings were prepared in anticipation of litigation.

- *Hercules Inc. v. Exxon Corp.*, 434 F. Supp. 136, 151–52 (D. Del. 1977). In a patent interference hearing, the court allowed work-product protection for documents prepared in anticipation of a proceeding before the Board of Patent Interferences, although that tribunal is not a court of record. The court also found that a document from one patent attorney to another requesting a law search was protected work-product material, as it primarily reflected a concern with future litigation. Other documents, however, prepared with a view to claims arising in an ex parte prosecution of a patent application were not work-product material. The court explained the distinction: "The prosecution of an application before the Patent Office is not an adversary, but an ex parte proceeding. Although the process involves preparation and defense of legal claims in a quasi-adjudicatory forum, the give and take of an adversary proceeding is by and large absent."

- *Burlington Indus. v. Exxon Corp.*, 65 F.R.D. 26, 42 (D. Md. 1974). The court explained that work-product protection would not protect documents "relating to research tests, and experiments which are to be disclosed to the Patent Office at the time of an application for a patent since the documents do not constitute the results of an attorney's efforts to represent his client in a potentially adversary legal proceeding."

- *United States v. Brown*, 478 F.2d 1038 (7th Cir. 1973). Materials prepared for a proceeding seeking enforcement of an Internal Revenue Service summons were work product in nature.

Preparation of documents for agency filings, such as under the securities, tax and other regulatory laws are generally not deemed to be in anticipation of litigation, unless there is an adversarial component to the proceeding.

The case law in this area is far from reassuring in terms of either predictability or analytic clarity. As an example of adjudication heaving and bringing forth a mouse after laboring for dozens of pages if you can bear to plow through, take a look at:

- *Pacific Gas & Elec. Co. v. United States*, 69 Fed. Cl. 784, 799, 805, 808 (Fed. Cl. 2006). At issue were whether documents related to public regulatory proceedings, including, but not limited to, PG&E's

rate proceedings before the California Public Utilities Commission [(CPUC)], proceedings before the California Coastal Commission [(CCC)], and licensing proceedings before the Nuclear Regulatory Commission [(NRC)] were work-product protected. The court concluded that "Adversarial Aspects of CPUC and NRC Proceedings Constitute 'Litigation' for the Purposes of the Work Product Doctrine, but CCC Proceedings do [sic!] Not."

That unfortunately did not resolve the matter in any functional way. Instead, many pages later, the court stated: "Having determined that only the truly adversarial aspects, if any, of proceedings before the CPUC and NRC constitute "litigation" for the purposes of the work product doctrine, n11 and that CCC permit proceedings do not constitute 'litigation,' the court turns to provide guidance to the parties as to what kinds of documents created in preparation of the CPUC and NRC proceedings were created 'in anticipation of litigation" and therefore may be protected from discovery under the work-product doctrine. The fundamental inquiry that must be made is "the purpose for which a party created a document." And after all of that, do we finally get to find out which documents are and which are not work-product protected? Not on your life. Instead the parties are exhorted: "Using the guidance provided in this Opinion, the parties shall confer with each other to determine whether there continue to be any disputes regarding work-product protection of documents related to public regulatory proceedings."

If this be adjudication, something has gone desperately wrong. Would not a bright-line test, applicable by all without the need for such unproductive labor, serve the judicial process far more? Would not much be gained and little lost were judges simply to hold that documents prepared for filing in any agency proceeding where private adversarial parties do not contend with one another are simply not privilege protected? Is the cost in judicial resources and legal resources really worth this alternative result before the Federal Court of Claims? Or have we not totally lost sight of what is to be protected and for that matter why it should be protected in the first place?

■ *Biddison v. Chicago*, 1989 U.S. Dist. LEXIS 3991, at *2 (N.D. Ill. Feb. 3, 1989). Documents prepared at an accountant's request to allow the preparation of financial reports required by the federal securities laws were not accorded work-product protection, although the court noted that the case presented a close question. On the other hand the court granted work-product protection to an Environmental Impact Statement because it said that it was prepared at a time that there was a virtual certainty that litigation would result.

- *In re Grand Jury Subpoena*, 220 F.R.D. 130, 156 (D. Mass. 2004). It took a treatise and a 109-page opinion for the court to conclude that notes taken by an attorney of a conference call with a regulatory agency [the Food and Drug Administration] regarding the failure rate of a medical device that his clients were manufacturing and knowingly shipping despite a high failure rate although unquestionably work product in nature, since it would show the attorney's mental processes, were neither taken in anticipation of litigation nor taken because of the prospect of litigation. No investigation was pending. The conference call was seeking clarification and guidance from the regulators. The work-product protection holders made a judicial admission which one would have thought dispositive. It was: "it is true, of course, that neither [XYZ] nor [Attorney] anticipated or even imagined that their efforts to seek guidance from the FDA would be the subject of a criminal investigation." Nonetheless, the court plowed on addressing, dismissing, arguing with all other possibilities, demonstrating yet again that when it comes to opinion writing, more is invariably less.[1] The grand jury subpoena was enforced; the protective order sought by the attorney and his client was denied. The Court stated that it had found no authority suggesting that a government investigation itself constitutes litigation. But hedging its bets also said that once one is undertaken, litigation often does result.

---

1. This case is a prime example of the new style in opinion writing. It is intended less to resolve a specific litigated issue than it is designed to showcase the law-review writing competence of the judge, or perhaps it is merely his law clerk, with an eye perhaps to a Supreme Court clerkship. Here is one small example: the Court expressly declines to rest its no work-product protection holding on the crime/fraud exception; it nonetheless plows on for no less than 10 full pages describing the ample contours of case law precedent that the Court has stated is irrelevant to its holding. Would that someone were able to tell us just what is the point! And would that the courts would spare us such judicial opinions decked out like law review articles which are hardly the acme of cogent or terse legal writing.

Do governmental investigations rise to the status of "litigation" sufficient to give rise to a work-product protection for matters prepared in anticipation of such investigations? Apparently not. Thus documents prepared in anticipation of a government investigation are not accorded work-product protection.

- *Guzzino v. Felterman*, 174 F.R.D. 59, 63 (W.D. La. 1997). "Counsel have not cited, and this Court's research has not revealed any, cases which hold that documents prepared in anticipation of a federal agency's investigation are protected by the work-product doctrine." But by the same token, "[f]ederal courts have concluded that once an investigation by a federal agency has commenced, that a corporation may reasonably be said to anticipate litigation."

Yet once a government investigation is begun, many courts concede that litigation may not be far behind. And therefore documents that are prepared after a government investigation is already underway may well be accorded work-product protection.

If that distinction makes logical sense to you, dear reader, more power to you.

- *Martin v. Bally's Park Place Hotel & Casino*, 983 F.2d 1252, 1261 (3d Cir.), *amended*, 15 O.S.H. Cas. (BNA) 2224 (3d Cir. 1993). The court held that materials prepared after an OSHA investigation had commenced were in anticipation of litigation.

- *Briggs & Stratton Corp. v. Concrete Sales & Servs.*, 174 F.R.D. 506, 509 (M.D. Ga. 1997). The court held that materials prepared after the EPA had identified potentially responsible parties in an environmental cleanup were work-product protected.

- *Garrett v. Metropolitan Life Ins. Co.*, 1996 U.S. Dist. LEXIS 8054, at *11–12 (S.D.N.Y. June 12, 1996) (Bernikow, Mag. J.), *adopted*, 1996 U.S. Dist. LEXIS 14468 (S.D.N.Y. Oct. 3, 1996). "Regulatory investigations by outside agencies present more than a mere possibility of future litigation, and provide reasonable grounds for anticipating litigation. Moreover, a document does not have to be created in anticipation of the current litigation. . . . MetLife notes that three class actions, 25 individual actions, and eight regulatory investigations were pending at the time it retained MMR to conduct the survey. All of these claims and investigations raised the same issues—MetLife's allegedly improper sales practices. Thus, a substantial probability existed that future litigation would arise that asserted these same claims. But more than that, plaintiffs agree that MetLife undertook the survey in response to these claims and investigations. Yet they have not argued that the work-product privilege did not apply in those cases. In the absence of such an argument, and without any evidence that the privilege would not apply in those cases, the documents retain their protection." (Citations omitted.)

- *Pacamor Bearings, Inc. v. Minebea Co.*, 918 F. Supp. 491, 513 (D.N.H. 1996). "Although investigations by government agencies are not 'litigation' as that term is generally understood, in the context of Rule 26(b)(3), however, courts recognize that 'investigation by a federal agency presents more than a remote prospect of future litigation, and provides reasonable grounds for anticipating litigation sufficient to trigger application of the work product doctrine.'" (Citations omitted.)

- *Martin v. Monfort, Inc.*, 150 F.R.D. 172, 173 (D. Colo. 1993). In an affidavit, corporate general counsel averred that the time and motion studies that were the subject matter of the motion to compel were conducted only after the corporation had been contacted by the Department of Labor. The court held them to be work-product protected because after such investigatory contact by a federal agency there was a likelihood of litigation. Nor was there any indication that but for the contact the studies would have been conducted in the ordinary course of business. Moreover, the corporation represented to the court that it had no intention of using the information at trial or making them available to a testifying witness to form an expert opinion thereon. Accordingly, the studies did not have to be produced.

- *Bituminous Cas. Corp. v. Tonka Corp.*, 140 F.R.D. 381, 390 (D. Minn. 1992). The court held that materials prepared after a state pollution control agency began investigating a company were in anticipation of litigation.

- *In re LTV Sec. Litig.*, 89 F.R.D. 595, 612 (N.D. Tex. 1981). The court held that documents generated during the pendency of an SEC investigation were generated in anticipation of litigation.

However, since administrative proceedings not infrequently lead to litigation, work product issues relating to documents prepared in connection with administrative filings frequently go both ways. Although once again the distinction between administrative proceedings and governmental investigations in terms of likelihood of litigation is at best elusive.

- *Hodges, Grant & Kaufmann v. United States*, 768 F.2d 719, 722 (5th Cir. 1985). Documents prepared by accountant for the client's use in dealing with the IRS may well have been prepared in anticipation of an administrative *dispute* and hence may constitute work product.

In the securities regulation context, some courts have held that documents prepared for an independent auditor in connection with a publicly held corporation's efforts to comply with the federal securities laws do not constitute attorney work-product because they are created primarily for (or because of, depending on the standard used) the business purpose of preparing financial reports that would satisfy the requirements of the federal securities laws.

- *McEwen v. Digitran Sys., Inc.*, 155 F.R.D. 678, 684 (D. Utah 1994). After reviewing documents *in camera*, the court concluded that the defendants had not sustained the burden of proof that the documents were protected by the work-product privilege because the "primary motivating purpose" behind the creation of the documents appeared to be to enable the re-issuance of defendants's financial statements in order to relist its stock, not to assist attorneys in connection with pending or anticipated litigation.

- *Independent Petrochemical Corp. v. Aetna Cas. & Sur. Co.*, 117 F.R.D. 292, 298 (D.D.C. 1987). The court refused to extend work-product protection to audit letters prepared by an attorney where Magistrate Judge's *in camera* examination of the letters revealed that they were not prepared to assist company in present or reasonably anticipated litigation but rather to assist accounting firms "in the performance of regular accounting work done by such accounting firms."

- *United States v. Gulf Oil Corp.*, 760 F.2d 292, 296–97 (Temp. Emer. Ct. App. 1985). "These documents were not created to assist Cities in the litigation of its declaratory judgment action against the

D.O.E. Rather, they were created, at Arthur Young's request, in order to allow Arthur Young to prepare financial reports which would satisfy the requirements of the federal securities laws."

■ *United States v. El Paso Co.*, 682 F.2d 530, 543–44 (5th Cir. 1982), *cert. denied*, 466 U.S. 944 (1984). The court found that documents "written ultimately to comply with [Securities Exchange Commission (SEC)] regulations" were prepared "with an eye on its business needs, not on its legal ones" and do not "contemplate litigation in the sense required to bring it within the work product doctrine."

The patent application process has also produced a number of cases that analyze what constitutes attorney work product created in anticipation of litigation.

■ *McCook Metals L.L.C. v. Alcoa, Inc.*, 192 F.R.D. 242, 260 (N.D. Ill. 2000). The court stated that the preparation of a patent application has generally not been held to be in anticipation of litigation, as it is primarily an *ex parte* administrative, not an adversarial, proceeding. Specific items relating to the patent application process that were not deemed work product included memoranda discussing which specifications to include in the patent application, discussion of which terms in the original patent application, and technical information from the client to attorney used for the purpose of preparing a patent application.

However, the court distinguished documents prepared in preparation for a patent reexamination proceeding when related litigation was subsequently initiated in the federal courts and accorded work-product protection to them, reasoning that, regardless of whether the reexamination proceeding was initiated by a competitor or the patent holder were adversarial in nature. So too documents prepared for an interference proceeding were also held to be protected.

The Southern District of New York has taken an approach similar to that of the Northern District of Illinois with respect to patent application proceedings. Under this approach, even if the document was prepared to address issues in an *ex parte* patent proceeding, any portions of it that explicitly address the prospect of future litigation or offer an analysis of issues principally pertinent to such a proceeding will be protected.

- *Golden Trade v. Lee Apparel Co.*, 143 F.R.D. 514 (S.D.N.Y. 1992). Documents prepared in contemplation of *ex parte* proceedings before the [Patent and Trade Office (PTO)] are not, on that basis alone, entitled to work-product protection. In contrast, if a document is prepared in anticipation of or with an eye to future adversarial administrative proceedings or future litigation, it will be protected, subject of course to the discovering party's ability to show a pressing need for the document. *In re Gabapentin Patent Litig.*, 214 F.R.D. 178, 184–85 (D.N.J. 2003). ("Generally, work performed by an attorney to prepare and prosecute a patent does not fall within the parameters of the work-product protection . . . since the prosecution of [a] patent is a non-adversarial, ex parte proceeding. Thus, work done to that end is not "in anticipation of" or ["]concerning" litigation. This rule does not, however, preclude application of the work product protection to work performed to prosecute a patent application if it was also performed in anticipation of or concerning litigation."

Accord:

- *In re Application of Minebea Co.*, 143 F.R.D. 494 (S.D.N.Y. 1992). The court held that generally work product prepared to prosecute a patent application was not work-product protected but that did not preclude the possibility that it was also prepared for another in anticipation of litigation context. The court then went on to protect "opinion" work product created in the process of pursuing the patent applications as of a specific date at which time the patent holder claimed to have anticipated litigation, without however identifying the litigation.

- *Oak Indus. v. Zenith Elec. Corp.*, 687 F. Supp. 369, 373–75 (N.D. Ill. 1988). The preparation of a patent application for prosecution was not in anticipation of litigation because the filing was primarily an ex parte administrative, not an adversarial, proceeding. However, documents prepared for a reexamination proceeding at the request of a party challenging the patent were deemed to be in anticipation of litigation because the proceeding was adversarial in nature.

- *Electronic Memories & Magnetics Corp. v. Control Data Corp.*, 1975 U.S. Dist. LEXIS 11757 (N.D. Ill. 1975). Documents prepared in anticipation of an interference proceeding are adversarial in nature and hence work-product protected.

When the legal representation has been provided in the course of something that a court determines not to have been an adversarial proceeding, the work-product protection will not be extended.

- *In re Grand Jury Subpoenas dated March 9, 2001*, 179 F. Supp. 2d 270 (S.D.N.Y. 2001). Subpoena issued by United States Government against Marc Richard's attorneys was not quashed on work-product or privilege grounds. The court concluded that the lobbying effort to obtain a pardon for Marc Richard involved no adversarial proceeding, but partook instead of a lobbying effort.

- *Harper-Wyman Co. v. Connecticut Gen. Life Ins. Co.*, 1991 U.S. Dist. LEXIS 5007, No. 86 C 9595, 1991 WL 62510, at *3 (N.D. Ill. Apr. 17, 1991). The court held that documents prepared in connection with the insurance industry's lobbying efforts were not protected by work-product doctrine because lobbying efforts do not constitute litigation and documents in question were not used in an adversarial context, even though lobbying efforts might have been sparked by lawsuits against insurers.

B. *What Constitutes "Anticipation?"*

At the risk of stating the obvious, which generally becomes obvious only after it has been stated, the concept "in anticipation of litigation" contains within it two related, but nonetheless distinct, concepts. One is temporal. The other is motivational. To be "in anticipation of" litigation a document must, obviously, have been prepared before or during the litigation. That temporal element, standing alone, however, is not sufficient. The document or material must also have been prepared *for* litigation and not *for* some other purpose. It is the second concept that is determinative for the work-product protection. Thus, materials may be prepared before or when litigation is imminent or pending without necessarily having been in the least prepared "in anticipation" of litigation from a motivational point of view.

1. Time When Work Product Is Prepared

"In anticipation" was defined by the Special Masters Rice and Hazard in *United States v. AT & T*, Civ. No. 74-1698 (D.D.C. Feb. 28, 1979), as meaning:

> Any time after initiation of the proceeding or such earlier time as the party who normally would initiate the proceeding had tentatively formulated a claim, demand, or charge. When the material was prepared by a party who normally would initiate such a proceeding, that person must establish the date when the claim, demand, or charge was tentatively formulated. When the material was prepared by a potential defendant or respondent, that person must establish the date when it received a demand or warning of charges or information from an outside source that a claim, demand, or charge was in prospect.

Case law also makes clear that no lawsuit need already have been filed for the "in anticipation of litigation" requirement to be met.

- *Occidental Chem. v. OHM Remediation Servs. Corp.*, 175 F.R.D. 431, 439 (W.D.N.Y. 1997). The court examined as to what date litigation could be considered to be "imminent" and accorded protection from that date forward. It did conclude that in many respects the work product claims were not well founded, not so much on that grounds but because the expert was in fact hired to do remedial work on the construction project which was the subject of the litigation.

- *Upjohn Co. v. United States*, 449 U.S. 383, 386–87, 397–402 (1981). The Supreme Court applied the work-product protection even though no proceedings against the company were threatened when the documents were prepared. Thus, the Court appears to have construed the "in anticipation of litigation" requirement quite broadly, perhaps suggesting that a corporation's attempts to ferret out instances of wrongdoing may be sufficient to satisfy the requirement. Realistically, however, the corporation could expect regulatory or shareholder litigation when the suspected "questionable payments" came to light.

- *In re International Sys. & Controls Corp. Sec. Litig.*, 693 F.2d 1235, 1239 n.4, 1239 (5th Cir. 1982). A Securities and Exchange

Commission investigation into "sensitive payments" necessarily implies there will be shareholder litigation. "From the moment management learned of the SEC investigation, it could almost count on some form of shareholder's derivative or class action suit." Since the adversarial relationship was predictable, the work product was prepared "in anticipation of litigation" and could be protected. "It is not reasonable to indulge in the fiction that counsel, hired by management, is also constructively hired by the same party counsel is expected to defend against."

But see:

- *SEC v. National Student Mktg. Corp.*, 18 Fed. R. Serv. 2d (CBC) 1302 (D.D.C. 1974). Materials prepared during the Securities and Exchange Commission's investigative phase were not in anticipation of litigation. Materials prepared after a draft memorandum recommending suit be brought by the SEC were in anticipation of litigation.

- *Augenti v. Cappellini*, 84 F.R.D. 73, 79–80 (M.D. Pa. 1979). Notes made at the suggestion of counsel while contemplating some legal action, though not necessarily a particular suit, are made in anticipation of litigation.

- *Rodgers v. U.S. Steel Corp.*, 22 Fed. R. Serv. 2d (CBC) 324 (W.D. Pa. 1975). Materials prepared after the enactment of Title VII of the Civil Rights Act of 1964 concerning validation of the defendant's personnel policies were prepared in anticipation of litigation, even though not prepared for the instant suit. They were prepared with an eye to possible litigation.

- *Burlington Indus. v. Exxon Corp.*, 65 F.R.D. 26, 42 (D. Md. 1974). "In order to satisfy the requirement that documents be prepared in anticipation of litigation, it is not necessary that the documents be prepared after litigation has been commenced. The work-product doctrine applies to material prepared when litigation is merely a contingency."

The converse also applies. Merely because litigation is already pending does not transform everything done by an attorney representing a litigant into work product worthy of the protection. What the attorney does must be related to the pending litigation.

- *Sandberg v. Virginia Bankshares, Inc.*, 979 F.2d 332 (4th Cir. 1992), *amended*, LEXIS Slip Op. (4th Cir. Nov. 17, 1992), *unopposed mot. to vacate granted*, 1993 U.S. App. LEXIS 33286 (4th Cir. Apr. 7, 1993). Notes taken by general counsel at a shareholder's meeting, even though litigation was pending, were not necessarily taken in anticipation of that litigation. The proponent of the work-product protection did not sustain its burden of proof and demonstrate either the capacity in which the notes were taken or their purpose. "The mere fact that a lawsuit is pending does not transform an attorney's notes into material prepared in anticipation of litigation. Moreover, while a general counsel may be involved in litigation strategy and oversight, it is also possible that her involvement in the litigation is no different from that of other corporate officers. In either case, her purpose in taking the notes is not self-evident and we find that Bankshares has failed to satisfy its burden of proof on this issue."

2. Likelihood of Litigation

There is no clear test as to what constitutes a likelihood of litigation. So too, courts have used a variety of phrases to describe the requisite nexus that must exist between the prospect of litigation and the preparation of the document at issue for the work-product protection from compelled disclosure on the document sought to be discovered.

- *Home Ins. Co. v. Ballenger Corp.*, 74 F.R.D. 93, 101 (N.D. Ga. 1977). There must be a "*substantial* probability that litigation will occur and that commencement of such litigation is *imminent*." (Emphasis added).

- *In re Grand Jury Investigation (Sturgis)*, 412 F. Supp. 943, 948 (E.D. Pa. 1976). The threat of litigation must be both "real and imminent."

- *Stix Prods., Inc. v. United Merchants & Mfr.*, 47 F.R.D. 334, 337 (S.D.N.Y. 1969). The prospect of litigation must be "identifiable."

Thus, the case-created formulations, by implication, suggest that a mere prospect of litigation, without a specific threat thereof, would not be sufficient.

- *International Ins. Co. v. Lloyd's of London*, 1990 WL 205461, at *4 (N.D. Ill. 1990). The claim likely to lead to litigation must pertain to this particular opposing party, not the world in general.

Nor would too distant a time nexus be sufficient to accord work-product protection.

Some circuits have adopted the formulation set forth in 8 CHARLES ALAN WRIGHT AND ARTHUR R. MILLER, FEDERAL PRACTICE AND PROCEDURE § 204, at 198 (1970):

> Prudent parties anticipate litigation and begin preparation prior to the time suit is formally commenced. Thus, the test should be whether in light of the nature of the document and the factual situation in the particular case, the document can fairly be said to have been prepared or obtained because of the prospect of litigation.

Other circuits have approved implicitly the formulation of 4 JAMES WM. MOORE ET AL., FEDERAL PRACTICE ¶ 26.63[2.-1], at 26-349 (1970), that the litigation must "reasonably have been anticipated or apprehended." Intention—only implicit in some of the other formulations—is here made explicit. Thus, the fact that litigation did fortuitously follow upon the creation of the document, would not be sufficient for the work-product protection to attach, absent a requisite component of intentionality. Namely, the document had to have been created with the prospect of litigation in mind.

- *In re Special Sept. 1978 Grand Jury (II)*, 640 F.2d 49, 61–62 (7th Cir. 1980). Documents prepared to comply with board of elections reporting requirements were found to have been prepared in anticipation of litigation, where circumstances indicated imminent litigation with respect to the reports.

- *In re Grand Jury Proceedings (FMC Corp.)*, 604 F. 2d 798 (3d Cir. 1979). Identity, at least in part, of subject matter and overlap in time, is sufficient to meet the "in anticipation" test, even though prepared for different proceedings, one civil and the other criminal.

- *In re Grand Jury Proceedings*, 601 F.2d 162, 171–72 (5th Cir. 1979). Financial analysis prepared by an accountant employed by a broker's lawyer to assist the lawyer in assessing the broker's potential criminal liability was protected, even though no indictment had issued at the time it was prepared.

- *In re Grand Jury Investigations (Sun Co.)*, 599 F.2d 1224, 1229 (3d Cir. 1979). Documents produced in the course of a self-investigation into illegal foreign payments met the criteria for being deemed work product where the prospect of litigation was "real enough" and "sufficiently strong."

- *In re LTV Sec. Litig.*, 89 F.R.D. 595, 612 (N.D. Tex. 1981). Documents that were generated during the pendency of a Securities and Exchange Commission investigation are work product because the investigation presents more than a remote prospect of future litigation.

The threat of litigation has to be both real and imminent for the "in anticipation of litigation" requirement to be present.

- *McCoo v. Denny's Inc.*, 192 F.R.D. 675, 683 (D. Kan. 2000). "The inchoate possibility, or even the likely chance, of litigation does not give rise to the privilege." (Internal citations and quotations omitted.)

- *Allen v. Chicago Transit Auth.*, 198 F.R.D. 495, 498 (N.D. Ill. 2001). Internal documents prepared after an internal complaint is made do not qualify as work product where there is no showing that litigation always ensues and no showing of why in this particular instance litigation was anticipated.

- *Lewis v. UNUM Corp. Severance Plan*, 203 F.R.D. 615, 623 (D. Kan. 2001). "While litigation can result from any fiduciary act, the Plan Administrator's acts of securing legal advice for the plan, and the advice rendered, prior to the plan's decision regarding benefits cannot be said to be in anticipation of litigation. Such acts occurred before the 'objected to' decision was final and the divergence of interests occurred. The fact that litigation later resulted does not change the ordinary business nature of the attorney's legal advice into advice rendered in anticipation of litigation." (Citations omitted.) Thus minutes of Benefit Plan Committee and communications between in-house counsel, plan administrator, and the company's human resource personnel were not work-product protected.

- *Zenith Elecs. Corp. v. WH-TV Broad. Corp.*, 2003 U.S. Dist. LEXIS 13816, at *19 (N.D. Ill. Aug. 7, 2003). Failure to prove in other than a conclusory fashion when the corporation first anticipated litigation resulted in the court applying the date that suit was filed. That made many arguably work-product-protected documents discoverable.

An area of the law where litigation is often attendant upon a business decision is reduction in work force cases. There, obviously, the facts underlying the proposed reduction are not protected from discovery and use. Accordingly, by and large any work papers reflecting the proposed reduction given to counsel to review are likely not to be deemed work-product protected.

- *Freiermuth v. PPG Indus., Inc.*, 218 F.R.D. 694 (N.D. Ala. 2003). Reduction in force work sheets were not work-product protected.

But see:

- *Maloney v. Sisters of Charity Hosp. of Buffalo, New York*, 165 F.R.D. 26 (W.D.N.Y. 1995). Worksheet and computer printout reviewed by counsel to determine whether reduction in force was legal were protected from disclosure under the work-product doctrine.

When insurance coverage is denied, litigation is highly likely to result by the insured against the insurance company. And it then follows as the night unto the day that the insured will seek documents, reports, claim investigations, witness interviews from the insurance company's files. That request presents a special problem for the application of the work-product rule because it is the very nature of an insurer's business to investigate and evaluate the merits of claims. Accordingly, most courts hold that documents constituting any part of a factual inquiry into or evaluation of a claim, undertaken in order to arrive at a claim decision, are produced in the ordinary course of an insurer's business and, therefore, are not work-product protected. On the other hand documents created after the claim has been denied are most likely to be created to defend the decision to deny the claim and are generally given work product protection.

- *Cellco P'ship v. Certain Underwriters at Lloyd's London*, 2006 U.S. Dist. LEXIS 28877 (D.N.J. May 11, 2006). Defendants denied coverage for a claim in excess of $21 million arising out of the theft of PIN numbers by an employee. The court used the date that coverage was denied as a dividing line for the production of work-product documents. Work product generated before the claim was filed was denied was producible; that generated after was not.

- *Tudor Ins. Co. v. McKenna Assocs.*, 2003 U.S. Dist. LEXIS 10853, No. 01 Civ. 0115, 2003 WL 21488058, at *3 (S.D.N.Y. June 25, 2003). Investigations conducted prior to a decision to deny coverage cannot be considered "in anticipation of litigation," because no litigation could be anticipated until a determination was made not to pay the claim.

- *Cutrale Citrus Juices USA, Inc. v. Zurich Am. Ins. Group*, 2004 U.S. Dist. LEXIS 22487, at *8 (M.D. Fla. Sept. 10, 2004). "While there is no bright-line rule in the insurance context marking the boundary between documents protected under the work-product privilege and documents produced in the ordinary course of business, the date coverage is denied by the insurer has been recognized by a number of courts as the proper date after which it is fairly certain there is an anticipation of litigation and thus documents generated after that date would be protected as work product."

Accord:

- *Ring v. Commercial Union Ins. Co.*, 159 F.R.D. 653, 656 (M.D.N.C.) (1995). "[I]n general, only documents accumulated after the claim denial will be prepared in anticipation of litigation."

- *Harper v. Auto-Owners Ins. Co.*, 138 F. R. D. 655, 662 (S.D. Ind. 1991). Only documents created after claim denial were work-product protected.

- *Schmidt v. California State Auto. Assoc.*, 127 F.R.D. 182, 184 (D. Nev. 1989). The case was brought by a passenger in the insured's vehicle against the insured's insurance company. The court used the actual filing of the passenger's claim as the demarcation date for purposes of assessing the work-product claims, because only then did it become "sufficiently choate to bring materials created by the defendant within the purview of Rule 26(b)(3)."

- *Pete Rinaldi's Fast Foods, Inc. v. Great Am. Ins. Cos.*, 123 F.R.D. 198, 202 (M.D.N.C. 1988). The case involved a bad faith claim of failure to settle against the insurance company by the insured. "The federal cases determining whether insurance companies claims files constitute work product have not been entirely consistent. On one extreme lie the decisions which do not grant protection unless the insurance company has turned the matter over to an attorney for the purpose of litigation. On the other extreme, some courts have determined that the insurance company's initial investigation of an accident or claim is almost always done with one eye focused on a probable prospect of litigation. This Court agrees with those increasing number of courts which reject these extremes and decide the matter on a case-by-case basis."

  The court went on to say that the insurance company could not say with a straight face that it sold its policies intending not to provide coverage and thus its entire file was prepared in anticipation of litigations with its insured. The court therefore concluded that the dividing line for determining "anticipation of litigation" with its insured would be set by the time at which the insurance company offered the policy limits, after the plaintiff went into bankruptcy, presumably after an adverse judgment. Prior to that time the insurance company had not written to the insured actually declining coverage. Documents created before that were not created in anticipation of litigation with the insured and were discoverable; those created thereafter, the insurance company would have to sustain the burden of proving that they were work-product protected and why that was the case. The insurance company could not just dump the documents on the court and expect the court to do its work for it by way of an *in camera* review.

- *Mission Nat'l Ins. Co. v. Lilly*, 112 F.R.D. 160, 164 (D. Minn. 1986). "The vast majority of the documents submitted under claim of privilege here constitute pure factual investigation of the claim, some of it described as being required by the terms of the policy itself . . . such investigation is the 'routine business of an insurance company.'"

- *Tejada Fashions Corp. v. Yasuda Fire & Marine Ins. Co.*, 1984 U.S. Dist. LEXIS 15815, 1984 WL 500 (S.D.N.Y. June 18, 1984). "From the face of the documents it is clear that Investigative Services, Inc. was carrying out an investigation to determine whether to honor the insured's claim and, if there was doubt as to its validity, to determine how much money to offer, if any, in partial satisfaction of the claim. It also appears that all three reports were prepared before any decision by defendant to reject the claim. * Finally, although not explicitly stated by defendant, it is apparent that the reports were not prepared by or at the request of or under the supervision of an attorney. Rather, the documents bear all the indicia of a routine investigation conducted for the insurance company to enable it to dispose of the claim, if possible, without reference to a lawsuit."

3. Requisite Specificity of Claims

An additional factor that courts often look for and confound with the imminence of litigation is whether some specific claim is in the offing.

- *Herbert v. Lando*, 73 F.R.D. 387, 402 (S.D.N.Y.), *remanded on other grounds*, 568 F.2d 974 (2d Cir. 1977), *rev'd on other grounds*, 441 U.S. 153 (1979). In a defamation action based on alleged malicious publication, the plaintiff moved for an order compelling discovery of communications among the defendant, its counsel, and others discussing possible responses to a letter sent by the plaintiff after publication listing "discrepancies" in the defendant's article. The documents were held to be protected work product—even though suit had not yet been filed—because the plaintiff's communication of discrepancies "clearly gave rise to the 'prospect of litigation,' and it would have been imprudent for [defendant] to conclude otherwise."

- *Eoppolo v. National R. Passenger Corp.*, 108 F.R.D. 292, 294–95 & n.1 (E.D. Pa. 1985). The court said that "'the anticipation of the filing of a claim against a railroad, when a railroad employee has been injured or claims to have been injured on the job, is undeniable, and the expectation of litigation in such circumstances is a reasonable assumption.'" The court rejected the contrary view that statements routinely secured by a claims adjuster or railroad accident department are not prepared in anticipation of litigation, saying that when the plaintiff, early in the litigation, makes a broad request for all statements and reports, "the better position is to require a showing of hardship and need."

- *Sylgab Steel & Wire Corp. v. Imoco-Gateway Corp.*, 62 F.R.D. 454, 457 (N.D. Ill. 1974), *aff'd without op.*, 534 F.2d 330 (7th Cir. 1976). In a patent infringement action, discovery was sought of opinion letters prepared by defendant's attorney several years before the formal commencement of litigation. The court found that the documents were prepared "with an eye toward litigation." "If the prospect of litigation is identifiable because of specific claims that have already arisen, the fact that, at the time the document is prepared, litigation is still a contingency has not been held to render the [work-product] privilege inapplicable."

- *Fontaine v. Sunflower Beef Carrier, Inc.*, 87 F.R.D. 89, 92–93 (E.D. Mo. 1980). Statements taken from the defendant's driver by the defendant's safety director, insurer, and investigator immediately after an accident were in anticipation of litigation—even though taken prior to the time that suit was filed—where it was apparent who would be the plaintiff and what claims would be asserted.

- *American Optical Corp. v. Medtronic, Inc.*, 56 F.R.D. 426, 431 (D. Mass. 1972). Documents prepared by an attorney commissioned to study the validity of the patent prior to a licensing agreement being reached were protected work product. The documents concerned the question of whether the plaintiff should risk litigation or accept a license.

- *Arney v. Geo. A. Hormel & Co.*, 53 F.R.D. 179, 181 (D. Minn. 1971). Documents interpreting pension plan provisions that were exchanged between the company's officers and attorneys after the plaintiff gave a work-termination notice were work product because suit was foreseeable at that time, even though no suit was filed for almost two years. Documents prepared before the plaintiff notified the company he was resigning were not work product.

Some courts have indicated that litigation need not be "imminent" as long as the prospect of litigation motivated the creation of the material being sought.

- *United States v. Davis*, 636 F.2d 1028, 1040 (5th Cir.), *cert. denied*, 454 U.S. 862 (1981). "We conclude that litigation need not necessarily be imminent, as some courts have suggested, . . . as long as the primary motivating factor behind the creation of the document was to aid in possible future litigation."

Other courts, however, have noted that a "remote prospect" or a "mere possibility" of litigation is insufficient.

- *Bituminous Cas. Corp. v. Tonka Corp.*, 140 F.R.D. 381 (D. Minn. 1992). Before party was designated a "responsible party" under CERCLA, the prospects of litigation were too remote to invoke the work-product doctrine. After such designation there is a strong prospect of future litigation and the protection of the work-product doctrine will be accorded.

- *In re Special Sept. 1978 Grand Jury (II)*, 640 F.2d 49, 65 (7th Cir. 1980). Documents prepared by counsel when dealing with an association's tax-exempt status and tax deficiency were not protected: "a remote prospect of future litigation is not sufficient."

- *Detection Sys., Inc. v. Pittway Corp.*, 96 F.R.D. 152, 155 (W.D.N.Y. 1982). "Although the work-product immunity applies to materials prepared when litigation is merely a contingency, . . . more than the mere possibility of litigation must be evident."

Particularly in the criminal context, the courts have shown a reluctance to accept government objections to discovery on work-product grounds unless the document in question was prepared by trial counsel and reflects trial preparation strategy. The reluctance stems from a judicial concern lest exculpatory Brady materials be kept from the defense by the prosecutorial authorities under the guise of work-product privilege. Thus, in the context of criminal prosecutions, documents may not be accorded work-product protection, even if in the civil context they might well have been protected from compelled disclosure. The issue is rarely addressed in terms of Brady material principles. Instead, courts turn to concepts of the imminence of litigation, albeit it is dubious that such are the grounds on which the decisions are in fact based.

- *Peterson v. United States*, 52 F.R.D. 317, 321 (S.D. Ill. 1971). The court rejected the government's assertion that internal IRS memoranda that were prepared during the investigatory and settlement phases of a tax audit were work-product protected. "Litigation cannot be anticipated in every case when relatively few result in litigation."

In the civil context, work product claims made by the government have failed even when the likelihood of litigation was "very strong." Again, a sub rosa principle may be informing the decision, namely that the actions of government should be open to public scrutiny.

- *Coastal Corp. v. Duncan*, 86 F.R.D. 514, 522 (D. Del. 1980). The Department of Energy failed to establish the work-product privilege where it could only state that the documents at issue were prepared when litigation was "considered likely" and that, in the context of its regulatory activities, the likelihood of litigation was "very strong."

- *Spaulding v. Denton*, 68 F.R.D. 342, 343–46 (D. Del. 1975). Immediately after the sinking of a yacht, the insurer directed a marine surveyor to discover all facts as soon as possible. The resulting report was found not to have been prepared "in anticipation of litigation" because, although the insurers knew there would be some sort of claim, litigation was "only a possibility," and acquiring knowledge of the unusual circumstances was the purpose of the investigation. However, a report prepared by the surveyors after the claim was several months old and each side was represented by attorneys was held to have been prepared in anticipation of litigation.

Thus, the requirement that the document has been prepared in anticipation of litigation to be work-product protected is sometimes formulated as that the document must have been prepared with an eye to some *specific* litigation.

- *Resident Advisory Bd. v. Rizzo*, 97 F.R.D. 749, 754 (E.D. Pa. 1983). "[T]he privilege is not applicable unless some specific litigation is fairly foreseeable at the time the work product is prepared."

- *James Julian, Inc. v. Raytheon Co.*, 93 F.R.D. 138, 143 (D. Del. 1982). "[L]itigation must be at least a real possibility at the time of preparation or, in other words, the document must be prepared with an eye to some specific litigation."

- *Coastal Corp. v. Duncan*, 86 F.R.D. 514, 522 (D. Del. 1980). The failure to specify the litigation for which documents were purportedly created was fatal to the Department of Energy's claim of work-product protection.

In other cases the touchstone is a specific claim, rather than a specific lawsuit.

- *Resident Advisory Bd. v. Rizzo*, 97 F.R.D. 749, 754 (E.D. Pa. 1983). "However, the privilege is not applicable unless some specific litigation is fairly foreseeable at the time the work product is prepared. . . . The abstract possibility that an event might be the subject of future litigation will not support a claim of privilege." The court did not discuss how the facts of the case applied to its formulations.

- *Coastal States Gas Corp. v. Department of Energy*, 617 F.2d 854, 865 (D.C. Cir. 1980). Memoranda from regional counsel to auditors in Department of Energy field offices, issued in response to requests for interpretations of regulations by firms then being audited by the department were held not to have been prepared in anticipation of litigation, except when the opinion was issued after identification of a specific claim by or against a specific firm being audited.

- *Fustok v. Conticommodity Servs., Inc.*, 106 F.R.D. 590, 591–92 (S.D.N.Y. 1985). Work-product protection was denied because "at the time the report was commissioned or prepared the prospect of litigation was not 'identifiable' because 'specific claims' [had not] already arisen."

- *Hercules Inc. v. Exxon Corp.*, 434 F. Supp. 136, 151 (D. Del. 1977). "The fact that litigation may still be a contingency at the time the document is prepared has not been held to render the privilege inapplicable, if the prospect of litigation is identifiable because of specific claims that have already arisen."

- *SCM Corp. v. Xerox Corp.*, 70 F.R.D. 508, 515 (D. Conn.), *appeal dismissed*, 534 F.2d 1031 (2d Cir. 1976). "A specific claim must have arisen to make the prospect of litigation identifiable in order for the work product rules to apply."

Some courts have gone so far as to recognize the protection only when the documents were created with the current litigation in mind.

- *United States v. International Bus. Machs. Corp.*, 71 F.R.D. 376, 378 (S.D.N.Y. 1976). Only documents prepared for use in this particular litigation are given work-product protection.

In other cases, however, material prepared with no specific litigation in mind has been protected.

- *Founding Church of Scientology of Washington, D.C., Inc. v. Director, FBI*, 104 F.R.D. 459, 464 (D.D.C 1985). Work-product protection does not require the party invoking the doctrine to provide information as to exactly what litigation was contemplated.

- *United States v. Capitol Serv., Inc.*, 89 F.R.D. 578 (E.D. Wis. 1981). Documents prepared in anticipation of *any* litigation, rather than just the particular suit in question, are work product.

- *Rodgers v. U.S. Steel Corp.*, 22 Fed. R. Serv. 2d (CBC) 324 (W.D. Pa. 1975). The court held that materials concerning an in-house review of defendant's personnel procedures, which were prepared after the enactment of Title VII of the Civil Rights Act of 1964, were prepared in anticipation of litigation even though the documents had not been prepared for use in the instant suit.

The absence of any bright line as to what constitutes the likelihood of litigation or whether specificity of a given claim is a necessary prerequisite for the work-product protection to become operative makes predictability elusive. The reason why it is so elusive is that courts are reluctant to sweep under the work-product protection any and all investigative reports prepared in what may well be the ordinary course of business or any and all assessments of possible claims.

4. Time as Continuum

At the risk of stating the obvious, time is a continuum. Thus, when the temporal aspect of the "in anticipation" element is analyzed, a court may wish to determine whether the litigation is embryonic, inchoate, remote, or whether it has ripened and assumed a discernable shape. We have seen that most times, this aspect is assessed from the point of view of form—the question being whether there is a cognizable claim in the offing. At times, however, the cases may look at the same question more directly from a temporal perspective. They then seek to identify a specific event that served as the crystallizing event making litigation "imminent." Obviously, a letter from the other side's attorney would be all but dispositive.

- *Reavis v. Metropolitan Prop. & Liab. Ins. Co.*, 117 F.R.D. 160 (S.D. Cal. 1987). Litigation was imminent when the plaintiff's attorney contacted the defendant and advised the defendant of that fact.

Other cases will push back the time substantially, yet still look for a rational linkage between the claim and the prospect for litigation. In cases where coverage is wrongfully denied, the natural temporal point is the denial of the claim.

- *APL Corp. v. Aetna Cas. & Sur. Co.*, 91 F.R.D. 10, 21 (D. Md. 1980). Until the insurance company had conducted an investigation and denied the claim for indemnification did the likelihood of litigation become manifest. "And it was not until that determination was made that 'there was a substantial probability that litigation would occur and that commencement of such litigation was imminent'." (Citations omitted.)

Although most work-product-protected materials are prepared sometime before the commencement or during the pendency of litigation, on rare occasions such materials may be prepared after the litigation has terminated, whether by way of settlement or presumably even an adjudicatory disposition. Such materials have also been accorded work-product protection.

- *eSpeed, Inc. v. Board of Trade*, 2002 U.S. Dist. LEXIS 7918, at *5 (S.D. N.Y. May 1, 2002). "While no case appears to have squarely addressed the issue, I do not think that inherently privileged quality is dissipated by the fact that the case against Cantor had been settled before Bollinger committed his oral opinions to writing. A leading commentator has said that 'just as litigation need not have been commenced for work-product protection to apply, a document does not necessarily lose its protection when the litigation ends.' 6 *Moore's Federal Practice* (3d ed. 2001) at Sec. 26.70[3], p. 26–214."

5. Facts Indicative of "Anticipation"

Facts considered relevant to and sometimes dispositive of the "anticipation" inquiry include: a party's consultation with a lawyer. Obviously, the list is not exhaustive.

- *Woodard v. Schmidt-Tiago Constr. Co.*, 108 F.R.D. 731, 734 (D. Col. 1986). "The tests run from 'some possibility of litigation' to a 'substantial probability that litigation will occur'. Courts have considered factual information to make that determination. One of the facts considered has been whether an attorney was consulted prior to the information being obtained by the party for the attorney prior to the suit being filed [sic!]."

A party's retention of a lawyer. Although for larger corporations which have many lawyers both in-house and on litigated matters this may be less compelling. Yet entering into an engagement letter to represent the client on some possible matter entailing litigation should definitely suffice.

- *EEOC v. Lutheran Soc. Servs.*, 186 F.3d 959, 968 (D.C. Cir. 1999). The court considered unrebutted affidavits that counsel was hired to assess potential claims against it in anticipation of litigation dispositive and reversed the trial court, finding that the investigative report created by counsel thereafter warranted work product protection.

A party's receipt of correspondence from the other party's lawyer stating the existence of some claim or making some demand.

- *McNulty v. Bally's Park Place, Inc.*, 120 F.R.D. 27, 29 (E.D. Pa. 1988). Where a statement was given by an eyewitness to an insurance adjuster after the insured was put on notice by plaintiff's attorney that he was considered to have been negligent and the cause of plaintiff's injury, the statement was accorded work product protection.

Notice from the government that it believes a party is not in compliance with legal obligation.

- *Bernardo v. Commissioner*, 104 T.C. 677, 688 (1995), *amended*, 95 TNT 140-27 (T.C. 1995). "Respondent contends that only documents prepared after the notice of deficiency was issued to petitioners were prepared in anticipation of litigation. We disagree. Once the IRS informed petitioners that its Art Advisory Panel concluded that Omphalos had a fair market value that was substantially less than the charitable contribution deduction petitioners claimed on their 1986 Federal income tax return, it was reasonable for petitioners and their representatives to anticipate litigation concerning those deductions."

Even press articles have been deemed sufficient to sound warning bells that litigation was likely.

- *Wsol v. Fiduciary Mgmt. Assocs.*, 1999 U.S. Dist. LEXIS 19002, at *6–7 (N.D. Ill. Dec. 7, 1999). "The court concludes the report and letter are protected work product. The report was created in anticipation of litigation. Plaintiffs retained Coffield to produce the report following publication of articles in the press, receipt of certain correspondence, and issuance of federal subpoenas from a Boston grand jury, all suggesting irregular and improper practices connected with the fund's investments. Litigation arising from these practices could be anticipated. That plaintiffs did in fact anticipate litigation is shown by the fact they retained Coffield not only to review and investigate these practices, but also to assess legal consequences and analyze various allegations raised against the fund. Consequently, the court rejects FMA's arguments that the report was merely a routine investigation into the business practices of the fund, its trustees, and employees."

The issuance of a federal grand jury subpoena is obviously notice that litigation may be in the offing.

The commencement of litigation in foreign countries makes it likely that litigation may be commenced here as well. Documents prepared for that on-going foreign country litigation retain their work-product protection in litigation in the United States courts as well.

- *SmithKline Beecham Corp. v. Apotex Corp.*, 2000 U.S. Dist. LEXIS 13606, at *12 (N.D. Ill. Sept. 13, 2000), *mandamus denied without op.*, 243 F.3d 565 (Fed. Cir.), *reported in full*, 2000 U.S. App. LEXIS 29637 (Fed. Cir. Nov. 1, 2000). On an appeal from the Magistrate's ruling, the district court said: "Plaintiffs do not challenge the criteria articulated by [Magistrate] Judge Bobrick for evaluating claims of work product. They do, however, contend that the record before the magistrate judge clearly indicated that litigation was ongoing in Canada and Spain prior to May 1998 and that litigation was anticipated as early as 1992. In support of this argument, Plaintiffs cite various log entries stating that litigation was either ongoing or anticipated, as well as the affidavit of Brian Russell, one of Plaintiffs' UK patent agents. In his affidavit, Russell testifies that, "since 1992, SB has anticipated litigation with respect to paroxetine patents." He then lists numerous documents which, he states, "are, or reflect, confidential internal SB communications prepared primarily for the purpose of aiding in future litigation.

  "We agree with Plaintiffs that those log entries which expressly indicate that a document was prepared in aid of *ongoing* litigation, in combination with the Russell affidavit, clearly meet the standard adopted by Judge Bobrick. Neither the original May 26 order or the June 27 order on Plaintiffs' motion for reconsideration acknowledges the existence of such entries or of the corresponding testimonial evidence. We hold that this oversight was clear error and find the elements of the work-product doctrine satisfied as to those documents described as having been prepared in connection with ongoing paroxetine patent litigation."

C. Causation: In Anticipation of Litigation from a Motivational Perspective

Until fairly recently courts have tended to assess whether the *primary* motivation for the preparation of a document was in anticipation of litigation. But documents often have multiple purposes. Thus, gradually, courts have started to speak instead in terms of a "*because of*" standard. They ask whether the document was prepared *because of* the fact that litigation was anticipated. If the document was prepared *because of* the anticipated litigation, it warrants protection. If it was not prepared *because of* the anticipated litigation, it does not. It is not in the least self-evident that this new formulation is a material aid to the analysis or that this formulation changes the end result. Nonetheless, courts seem increasingly to speak in such terms. Although some courts still require that the *primary* purpose for the preparation of the work product be anticipation of litigation. Others seem content to find work-product protection if anticipation of litigation is one of its purposes.

Looking at the cases, it is not evident that either the *primary purpose* language or the *because of* or even the *but for* language are material aids to the analytic process. Perhaps the only distinction that can be applied with any assurance of a fairly consistent result is to ask whether the document would have been prepared regardless of whether litigation was also in the offing. If it would have been prepared regardless of whether litigation was in the offing, then there is generally no reason to accord the document work-product protection. If, however, the document would not have been prepared in the ordinary course of business or for any other *independent business purpose*, which would not necessarily come within the compass of in the *ordinary* course of the client's usual business, then there is generally no reason to accord the document work-product protection.

Thus it is suggested that the analysis ask two questions:

(1) Were the documents prepared in the ordinary course of business, such as an insurance company's investigatory files?

(2) Was there an independent business purpose for which the document would have been prepared even if there had been no litigation anticipated?

If the answer to either question is yes, then there is no need to accord the document work-product protection.

- *De Beers LV Trademark Ltd. v. Debeers Diamond Syndicate Inc.*, 2006 U.S. Dist. LEXIS 6091 (S.D.N.Y. Feb. 15, 2006). Documents prepared by a consulting firm were more indicative of strategic business decisions that should be taken were not prepared in anticipation of litigation but with a business purpose in mind.

- *Mims v. Dallas County*, F.R.D. 479 (N.D. Tex. 2005). After lawsuit was filed complaining of conditions in the county jail hospital, the county hired a consultant to undertake an investigation and make recommendations. The local newspaper obtained a copy thereof by undisclosed means and published a series of articles, including the recommendations made in the report. The county argued that the report was prepared in anticipation of litigation. Stuff and non-sense said the court in effect. It was hard to conceive that the investigation had not been undertaken with a remedial purpose in mind. Disclosure to the plaintiffs was ordered. The court did not discuss what analytic impact if any the fact that the local paper had obtained a copy and that the findings were in all events totally public had on its decision. The county was obviously concerned not that the other side discover the conclusions in the report but that it use them at trial on the underlying claim.

The issue of what is the underlying purpose of documents in the context of insurance litigation is raised with great frequency. Usually the insurance company urges that the document was prepared in antic-ipation of litigation and with very great frequency the courts hold that it was prepared either in the insurance company's ordinary course of business of investigating and thereafter adjusting the claim.

- *Guidry v. Marine LLC*, 203 U.S. Dist. LEXIS 15272 (E.D. La. Aug. 25, 2003), *aff'd*, 2003 U.S. Dist. LEXIS 18930 (E.D. La. Oct. 22, 2003). The insurance company urging work-product protection had not shown that documents were generated for the purpose of adjusting the claim rather than litigating it.

- *Stalling v. Union Pac. R. R. Co.*, 2003 U.S. Dist. LEXIS 15454, at *2–3 (N.D. Ill. Sept. 4, 2003). The magistrate's finding that a guide to claims agents was not work-product protected was sustained. "The UP claims operations reference guide is a comprehensive ref-erence tool for UP claims representatives. It discusses the claims representatives' duties, which include investigating and settling most of the claims asserted against UP, in great detail. Of course, any claim asserted against the railroad may ripen into litigation, so the manual discusses that contingency. But that does not transform what is essentially a training manual for UP risk management em-ployees into attorney work product. Absent evidence that the prospect of this or some other litigation motivated UP to create the guide, and it has provided none, the work-product doctrine does not exempt it from discovery. (Citations omitted.)

- *Auto Owners Ins. Co. v. Totaltape, Inc.*, 135 F.R.D. 199, 202–03 (M.D. Fla 1990). The court held that insurer's claims manual and guidelines for business interruption claims were not work product because they were created in and also used in the ordinary course of the insurer's business.

- *In re Grand Jury Subpoena*, 357 F.3d 900, 907, 908 (9th Cir. 2004). "[A] document should be deemed prepared in anticipation of litigation' and thus eligible for work product protection under *Rule 26(b)(3)* if in light of the nature of the document and the factual situation in the particular case, the document can be fairly said to have been prepared or obtained *because of* the prospect of litigation." The court specifically stated that the "because of standard does not consider whether litigation was a *primary or secondary motive* behind the creation of a document." Rather, it considers the totality of the circumstances and affords protection when it can fairly be said that the "document was created because of anticipated litigation, and would not have been created in substantially similar form but for the prospect of that litigation." (Emphasis added.)

In so holding, the Ninth Circuit has thus followed the lead of the Second Circuit in the *Adlman*, widely cited and considered as authority on the issue of whether a document was prepared "in anticipation of litigation" and thus should be accorded work-product protection. The document had to be clearly prepared *because of* litigation and generally not according such protection where the primary purpose is other and the prospect of litigation merely a subsidiary reason.

- *United States v. Adlman*, 134 F.3d 1194, 1202–03 (2d Cir. 1998). The party seeking to withhold a document must demonstrate that the document it seeks to withhold was created *because of* the anticipation of litigation. The court expressly rejected the requirement that a document must be prepared exclusively in anticipation of litigation to be work-product protected. As long as a credible prospect of litigation existed, documents would be work product protected even if the primary purpose for their creation was a business one. "The formulation of the work-product rule used by the Wright & Miller treatise, and cited by the Third, Fourth, Seventh, Eighth, and D.C. Circuits, [where a document] should be deemed prepared 'in anticipation of litigation' and thus within the scope of the Rule, if 'in light of the nature of the document and the factual situation in the particular case, the document can fairly be said to have been prepared or obtained because of the prospect of litigation." (Citations omitted.) That formulation is a tautology if ever there was one.

The court's statement, however, that if documents "would have been created in essentially similar form irrespective of the litigation[,] . . . it [cannot] fairly be said that they were created 'because of' actual or impending litigation," provides the greatest assistance in determining when a document should be deemed to have been prepared *in anticipation of litigation*. Like most felicitous formulations they seem self-evident only after the fact.

- *In re Grand Jury Subpoena*, 357 F.3d 900, 909–10 (9th Cir. 2004). The court noted that, if certain documents were prepared for both litigation and non-litigation purposes and "the two purposes cannot be discretely separated from the factual nexus as a whole," the documents may be protected under the work-product doctrine.

- *Jumpsport, Inc. v. Jumpking, Inc.*, 213 F.R.D. 329, 347–48 (N.D. Cal. 2003). The court refined the "because of" standard articulated in *Adlman* to protect documents when litigation was a substantial factor in their creation and disclosure would offend the policies animating the work-product doctrine.

Thus the prior holdings, certainly in the Second and Ninth Circuits, that a document had to be prepared *exclusively* with a litigation purpose in mind, are no longer applicable, although no doubt litigants will continue to cite them for some time if they are urging such a proposition., *e.g.*,

- *Occidental Chem. Corp. v. OHM Remediation Serv. Corp.*, 175 F.R.D. 431, 435 (W.D.N.Y. 1997). The court concluded that a document must be prepared exclusively for litigation in order to constitute work product.

The Second Circuit had in the past utilized the analytic framework we suggest, considering whether there was an independent business purpose for the preparation of the document, regardless of whether litigation was in the offing and when it determined that there was accorded no work product protection.

- *In re Kidder Peabody Sec. Litig.*, 168 F.R.D. 459, 463, 466 (S.D.N.Y. 1996). Kidder's outside counsel investigated a fraud by one of the firm's traders. Thereafter Kidder issued a press release indicating that it had hired a prominent attorney who was a former head of enforcement at the SEC "to lead a comprehensive investigation into what went wrong and to recommend steps to prevent a recurrence." The public statements and "Kidder's unique public profile and its vulnerability to market opinion and to losing business to its competitors if its traders were suspect to the trading public, made it imperative that the internal investigation be well publicized and viewed as the inquiry of and 'independent' and incorruptible outsider." Thus the court concluded that business and not litigation purposes were the driving forces behind the conduct of the internal investigation and the publicity that Kidder gave to it.

  An alternative and equally satisfactory analysis, were theories of affirmative reliance and waiver of confidentiality by putting into the public domain the purported conclusions of the independent investigation while wishing to preserve the details upon which it rested as work product. There is no doubt, however, that the public trumpeting of the conclusions of the report, even had it been prepared initially only with an eye to defending potential litigation, would have and should have acted to vitiate any otherwise available work-product protection.

  Nonetheless the court only ordered production of factual summaries and continued to accord work-product protection to opinion work product.

The language used by the *Kidder* court. that the documents must be created *principally or exclusively* to assist in contemplated litigation has been criticized. It is also not the applicable legal standard in the Seventh Circuit and has since been rejected by the Second Circuit. *United States v. Adlman*, 134 F.3d 1194, 1198 and n.3 (2d Cir. 1998). The result in *Kidder*, however, on whatever analytical basis one uses, surely was not.

Contrast the *Kidder* facts and conclusion with that of:

- *Hollinger Int'l Inc. v. Hollinger Inc.*, 230 F.R.D. 508 (N.D. Ill 2005). The Board of Directors formed a Special Committee, which hired an attorney to conduct an investigation after the Board had received letters from a minority shareholder demanding that it investigate and take corrective action in respect to payments made to executives under non-compete contracts. The Special Committee had as its mandate to initiate litigation, if warranted. The court concluded that the primary purpose for the report was anticipation of litigation and that it was therefore work product protected.

- *Banks v. Office of the Senate Sergeant-at-Arms*, 228 F.R.D. 24, 26–27 (D.D.C. 2005). "Hence, *if the same or essentially similar documents would have been created whether or not litigation was foreseen,* 'it [cannot] fairly be said that they were created because of' actual or impending litigation." (Internal quotation marks removed. Emphasis added). The court concluded, after an *in camera* review of the documents that they contained attorney's mental impressions and litigation strategy and hence were "highly protected opinion work product." Other documents contained no indication on their face of when or why they were created and hence warranted no work-product protection.

    Assessing whether the documents would have been prepared in substantially similar form even without the litigation which ensued, is a more felicitous, albeit perhaps backdoor, way of getting at the issue of whether they were prepared "in anticipation of litigation" as the Rule requires to accord work-product protection.

- *Anderson v. Sotheby's Inc. Severance Plan*, 2005 U.S. Dist. LEXIS 9033, at *23–24 (S.D.N.Y. May 13, 2005). No work-product protection accorded to assessment of severance plan payments. "All of the Withheld Documents appear to be documents that Defendants would have created in the ordinary course of assessing an employee's beneficiary's claim for a large severance benefit. They would have investigated the claim by conducting interviews to see whether the claimant's new responsibilities and new compensation were comparable to those at his old job. Also, Defendants would have run some numbers to assess the value of the severance, and they would have negotiated with Cendant about the possibility of indemnification. As Plaintiff points out, if the work-product doctrine protected these documents, 'no ERISA plan beneficiary could ever obtain discovery into records of an Administrator's investigations of the claim' because an administrator could almost always claim that it anticipated possible litigation."

During an *in camera* inspection of the withheld documents the court noted a possible settlement figure on one e-mail. It determined this to be opinion or "core" work product and ordered the settlement figure redacted.

- *Willingham v. Ashcroft*, 2005 U.S. Dist. LEXIS 5431, 2005 WL 873223, at *2 (D.D.C. Apr. 4, 2005). "[T]o be protected by the work-product doctrine, a document must have been created for use at trial or because a lawyer or party reasonably anticipated that specific litigation would occur and prepared the document to advance the party's interest in the successful resolution of that litigation. Motivation is key. In ways that cannot often be foreseen when they are created, documents may prove useful in litigation because they record an event or memorialize an occurrence. But, their creation at a time when litigation was anticipated does not automatically render them privileged. The purpose of preparing for the anticipated litigation is critical, lest the rule be interpreted to protect everything a lawyer or party does when litigation is anticipated even though the lawyer or party did not create the document to advance the client's interest in the litigation."

- *In re Grand Jury Subpoena*, 357 F.3d 900, 910 (9th Cir. 2004). The court found that litigation purpose so permeated any non-litigation purpose that the two purposes could not be separated and thus accorded work-product protection.

The fact that litigation eventually does occur is not sufficient justification for making every document prepared before litigation work-product protected. To do so would be to insulate from discovery all possibly embarrassing matters from subsequent discovery merely by involving in-house or outside counsel in the process of product development or self-assessment.

To preclude that result, courts often go to great lengths to determine whether the primary motivation for the creation of the document was with an eye to fairly specific and likely litigation, or whether some other business purpose was the motivating factor. Where the primary motivation is not directly related to litigation, work-product protection will often be denied lest in a litigious society everything becomes subsumed within the work-product protection.

Gradually, courts seem to have developed a tacit "but for" test for determining whether the motivation that prompted the creation of a document was litigation or some other reason. If the document would have been likely to have been prepared regardless of whether litigation was also expected to ensue, it will not be deemed to have been prepared in anticipation of litigation and no work-product protection will attach.

- *Willingham v. Ashcroft*, 2005 U.S. Dist. LEXIS 22258, at *12 (D.D.C. Oct. 4, 2005). The court found that one of the documents as to which work-product protection was claimed was "a synopsis of adverse actions taken by the DEA against attorneys. It was drafted by the Office of Attorney Personnel Management for personnel purposes and, without a declaration indicating that these entries were crafted in anticipation of litigation, they cannot fairly be read to have been created for that purpose. Indeed, the document would have been created in 'essentially similar form irrespective of the litigation.'" (Footnotes and citations omitted.)

- *In re OM Group Sec. Litig.*, 226 F.R.D. 579 (N.D. Ohio 2005). Report prepared by attorneys for the audit committee of a public company held not to be work-product protected since it led to a restatement of earnings and although there was a possibility that litigation would ensue, such an investigation would have had to be done for a business reason in all events. Although not work-product protected, the court found much of the documents to have been attorney-client privileged, but that the privilege was waived when a summary Power Point presentation based on much of the privileged documents was prepared and presented to the Board of Directors and then turned over during discovery. The court concluded that: "There is no reason Defendants, who voluntarily disclosed substantial information about an investigation that led to a public announcement that OMG anticipated a restatement of earnings, should now be able to withhold information that would allow Plaintiff to review the whole picture. For these reasons, Plaintiff is entitled to the documents relating to and/or underlying the presentation. (493, 43)." The privilege holder had contended that it would forgo any reliance on the Audit Committee report in its case. It is not clear whether the document was produced inadvertently or tactically.

Query should a privilege holder be entitled to recoup a privilege if it is willing to forgo reliance on the privilege for any aspect of its case? And were that to be the law where would it leave all the cases of waiver for inadvertent disclosure? On the other hand, in patent cases at least courts are beginning to allow parties to retain the privilege by forgoing an "advice of counsel" defense. In the above cited case, it is hard to ferret out just what were the strategic and tactical issues in play.

- *First Pac. Networks, Inc. v. Atlantic Mut. Ins. Co.*, 163 F.R.D. 574 (N.D. Cal. 1995). Communications between client or its counsel and the insurance carrier were not accorded work-product protection. "When it is clear that documents would have been prepared independent of any anticipation of use in litigation" (i.e., because some other purpose or obligation was sufficient to cause them to be prepared), no work product can attach.

- *Fox v. California Sierra Fin. Serv.*, 120 F.R.D. 520 (N.D. Cal. 1988). Legal opinion letters regarding securities issued and tax liabilities that the defendant was required to provide in conjunction with a public offering could not be deemed to have been prepared in anticipation of litigation and, therefore, were not subject to work-product protection.

Courts look to the following types of factors to determine whether a document was prepared "in anticipation of litigation."

(1) Was counsel retained with an eye toward litigation?
(2) Was counsel involved in the preparation of the document?
(3) Was it a routine practice to prepare that type of document or was the document instead prepared in response to a particular circumstance?
(4) Would the document have been created in substantially the same form even had no litigation ensued or been in the offing?

Despite the fact that some courts now speak in terms of an inquiry as to whether the document was prepared *because of* or *but for* the anticipation of litigation, others continue to speak in terms of *primary* and *secondary* motivations.

Some circuits view the phrase as encompassing documents prepared "primarily or exclusively to assist in litigation"—a formulation that would potentially exclude documents containing analysis of expected litigation if their primary, ultimate, or exclusive purpose is to assist in making some business decision. Other circuits ask whether the documents were prepared "because of" existing or expected litigation—a formulation that would include such documents, despite the fact that their purpose is not to "assist in" litigation.

- *Resolution Trust Corp. v. Massachusetts Mut. Life Ins. Co.*, 200 F.R.D. 183 (W.D.N.Y. 2001). The opinion follows *Adlman* in granting work-product protection where a memorandum was drafted for the RTC discussing options available for handling the underfunding of a pension plan where a considerable portion of the options included potential litigation, even though at the time the memorandum was written, litigation was neither in the offing nor determined as the option to be pursued.

  Courts will not only assess whether the attorney preparing the work product subjectively believed that litigation would ensue, but also whether, given the facts, that belief was a reasonable one. *Maertin v. Armstrong World Indus., Inc.*, 172 F.R.D. 143, 149 (D.N.J. 1997). The court found that the party asserting the work-product privilege had demonstrated that the documents at issue were prepared with a subjective belief that litigation might ensue, and that the subjective belief was objectively reasonable.

1. Internal Investigations or Business Audits

Particularly problematic is when a company conducts an internal audit. Since such internal audits are usually done when there is some problem and in our society problems often result in litigation, the attempt is usually made to protect such audit either on privilege or work-product grounds. The attempt generally fails, unless the proponent of the protection can show that the audit was conducted only with an eye to preparing for prospective litigation, rather than for some subsidiary purpose. This is particularly difficult. When there are problems, not only does litigation often result but a well-run business may well wish to take some prophylactic measures, including but not limited to personnel decisions regarding responsible employees and changes of procedures. It may be easier to obtain attorney-client privilege protection if such audits are structured as an attempt to obtain legal advice, than it would be to obtain work-product protection.

As a general rule, courts seem to find internal audits and accident investigations not to be work-product protected unless litigation is clearly the *primary* motive. The reasoning is that to do otherwise would be to give virtually all investigations work product protection since there is always the *possibility* that litigation may ensue. The work product protection was clearly not intended to reach so far. In principle the *because of* analysis should protect a larger array of documents than the *primary* motive analysis. Time will tell whether the change in formulation from *primary* and *secondary* motives to *because of* and *but for* will in any way change the actual result and extend work product protection to a larger cachement of situations.

- *Electronic Data Sys. Corp. v. Steingraber*, 2003 U.S. Dist. LEXIS 11818 (E.D. Tex. July 9, 2003). Work-product protection was not accorded to certain documents where the court found the primary purpose of a legal audit to be to determine whether an employee was committing fraud and thus should be fired. Although it was foreseeable that litigation might result from that act, the primary purpose was a human resources decision, not the prospect of potential litigation. On the other hand, the court determined a date when litigation became a "near certainty" and accorded work-product protection to any documents created after that date.

- *Seibu Corp. v. KPMG LLP*, 2002 U.S. Dist. LEXIS 906, at *12 (N.D. Tex. Jan. 22, 2002). Work-product protection was not accorded to an internal audit conducted by an accounting firm following the bankruptcy filing of the audit client. The court concluded that the primary purpose of the documents was to make personnel decisions, not to prepare for litigation. "Rather, it appears that the primary purpose of the internal investigation was to make personnel decisions regarding the termination of partners responsible for the Q-ZAR audit. This is insufficient to bring the documents within the ambit of the work-product doctrine."

- *Caremark, Inc. v. Affiliated Computer Servs., Inc.*, 195 F.R.D. 610, 614 (N.D. Ill. 2000). The court concluded that "simply because a company's internal investigation was coexistent with a present or anticipated lawsuit that was the same subject matter of the litigation did not render that internal investigation work-product-protected."

- *Long v. Anderson Univ.*, 204 F.R.D. 129, 136 (S.D. Ind. 2001). No work-product protection was accorded to an investigation undertaken by an insurance carrier.

- *In re Kidder Peabody Secs. Litig.*, 168 F.R.D. 459, 463 (S.D.N.Y. 1996). The general counsel for the securities firm Kidder Peabody ("Kidder") hired outside counsel within days of discovering that one of Kidder's major traders had misappropriated funds, which had caused it to overstate its earnings substantially. Outside counsel immediately undertook an intensive fact-finding investigation to determine what had occurred and why. Despite affidavits by Kidder's general counsel and outside counsel that the investigation's purpose was to permit outside counsel to defend Kidder's legal interests in future legal proceedings and that outside counsel had indeed defended the firm in subsequent legal proceedings, the court found that anticipation of litigation was not the primary purpose of Kidder's retention of outside counsel and counsel's conduct of employee interviews. "On this issue, Kidder's affiants offer no meaningful evidence. Instead, Kidder simply parrots the legal standard that the interviews were conducted principally as an aid to litigation." While the court believed that Kidder's investigation was conducted, in part, to prepare for anticipated litigation, the court found that Kidder also hired outside counsel in part "for the specific purpose of having him conduct an internal inquiry in order (1) to find out what [its trader] had done and why it had taken so long to discover the wrongdoing, and (2) to prepare a report summarizing his factual conclusions in detail and making recommendations for corrective action by Kidder." *Id.* at 465. Most important, the court concluded that "Kidder would have hired outside counsel to perform such an inquiry even if no litigation had been threatened at the time. . . . It is painfully evident that the . . . scandal presented Kidder not only with a serious legal problem, but with a major business crisis," and that hiring outside counsel was designed to handle that business crisis.

But see:

- *United States v. ChevronTexaco Corp.*, 241 F. Supp. 2d 1065, 1082, 2002 U.S. Dist. LEXIS 24970, at *43 (N.D. Cal. Mar. 25, 2002), *amended in part*, 241 F. Supp. 2d 1065, 2002 U.S. Dist. LEXIS

24971 (N.D. Cal. June 18, 2002), *adopted*, 2002 U.S. Dist. LEXIS
20010 (N.D. Cal. Sept. 12, 2002). "Thus we agree with the
Second Circuit that, except where a document would have been
generated in the normal course of business even if no litigation
was anticipated, the work product doctrine can reach documents
prepared 'because of litigation' even if they were prepared in connection with a business transaction or also served a business
purpose." The upshot was that many documents prepared by the
outside auditors were deemed work-product protected even though
they would not have been attorney/client privilege protected and
even though no litigation was actually pending. An affidavit was
submitted to demonstrate why the "anticipation of litigation" was
reasonable.

The claims of insurance companies to work-product protection,
even when they hire outside attorneys to investigate the claims, are
regarded with a particularly jaundiced eye. The business of insurance
companies is to investigate and to pay insurance claims. That ordinary course of business cannot and should not be protected merely
because litigation often results and merely because attorneys are
often hired to conduct the investigations either on an in-house or
outside counsel basis.

- *SEC v. Credit Bancorp, Ltd.*, 51 Fed. R. Serv. 3d (Callaghan) 1429
  (S.D.N.Y. 2002). "Because the Insurers have not submitted evidence
  which establishes that Pattison & Flannery created the challenged
  documents in the course of providing legal advice, as opposed to its
  investigation of the facts surrounding the prior claims, the documents
  will be produced."

2. Tax and Business-Related Documents

- *United States v. El Paso Co.*, 682 F.2d 530 (5th Cir. 1982), *cert. denied*, 466 U.S. 944 (1984). A tax pool analysis designed to set forth
  the contingent tax liability of a corporation was not work-product
  protected because its primary function was purportedly to comply
  with accounting and therefore business needs, even though there
  was some likelihood that litigation with the IRS over the tax returns might result.

At least in this respect, however, courts have been evenhanded and have required the IRS to turn over its own assessments of the strengths and weaknesses of its case to taxpayers as well, according such documents no more work-product protection than was accorded to the taxpayer's assessments of its contingent tax liability.

- *Abel Investment Co. v. United States*, 53 F.R.D. 485 (D. Neb. 1971). Work-product protection was not accorded to IRS documents prepared in response to a tax refund claim where the sought-after documents impartially evaluated the strengths and weaknesses of the IRS's and the taxpayer's positions because the documents were routinely prepared before any lawsuit began and were not developed by the attorney who would be trying the case in the event that litigation did ensue.

- *United States v. Gulf Oil Corp.*, 760 F.2d 292, 296 (Temp. Emer. Ct. App. 1985). "If the primary motivating purpose behind the creation of the document is not to assist in pending or impending litigation, then a finding that the document enjoys work product immunity is not mandated." Documents were prepared at the request of auditors to allow for the preparation of financial reports that would satisfy the requirements of the securities laws and not primarily with an eye to potential litigation with the Department of Energy.

- *United States v. Davis*, 636 F.2d 1028, 1040 (5th Cir.), *cert. denied*, 454 U.S. 862 (1981). Litigation need not be imminent "as long as the primary motivating purpose behind the creation of the document was to aid in possible future litigation." Here that was not the motivation. The disputed work papers were prepared to aid in the filing of tax returns and not primarily to help litigate over those returns. Thus, the work-product protection did not apply.

Where the primary purpose for preparing a document is not litigation but some other business purpose, work-product protection is not accorded.

- *Bank Brussels Lambert v. Fiddler, Gonzalez & Rodriguez*, 2003 U.S. Dist. LEXIS 9108 (S.D.N.Y. June 2, 2003), *aff'd & summ j. granted in part, denied in part*, 2005 U.S. Dist. LEXIS 5484 (S.D.N.Y. Apr. 1,

2005), *adhered to on recons.*, 2005 U.S. Dist. LEXIS 12983 (S.D.N.Y. June 29, 2005). Due diligence was done to conform conduct with legal obligations and not in anticipation of litigation, and hence was not work-product protected.

- *Fox v. California Sierra Fin. Serv.*, 120 F.R.D. 520, 528–29 (N.D. Cal. 1988). Legal opinion letters regarding securities offering that defendant was required to provide were not prepared in anticipation of litigation.

So merely adding in-house counsel to a distribution list where business matters are addressed in conjunction with statements about possible litigation is not likely to provide the work-product protection.

- *Amway Corp. v. Procter & Gamble Co.*, 2001 U.S. Dist. LEXIS 4561, at *27 (W.D. Mich. Apr. 3, 2001). "*In camera* inspection of each shows that the context of the Category II documents was public relations and other business strategizing and was not legal in nature, even when lawsuits or the prospect of lawsuits were under discussion. Procter & Gamble has not sustained its burden to show that these documents were generated in connection with the request for or the rendering of legal advice. . . . Disclosure of these documents exposes Procter & Gamble's public relations strategies, not its litigation strategy." Thus the fact that in-house counsel was on the distribution list of the documents was not sufficient to make them privileged and to protect them from compelled disclosure.

2. Implementation-of-Policy Documents

Parties often seek the work product protection for documents which may outline or set forth how a particular policy, such as one governing affirmative action, for example, will be implemented. There is no reason why such an attempt should succeed.

- *Hardy v. New York News, Inc.*, 114 F.R.D. 633 (S.D.N.Y. 1987). The court concluded that documents prepared to implement an affirmative action policy were not prepared in anticipation of litigation, but to fulfill a management function. The court said that the fact that documents prepared for a business purpose were also determined to be of potential use in pending litigation did not turn these documents into work product or confidential communications between client and attorney.

3. Settlement Documents

It may surprise some attorneys to discover that documents or other materials prepared looking toward, or in implementation of, a settlement often have been held not to be in anticipation of litigation. The tacit assumption may also be that such materials are prepared with an eye to disclosure in all events.

- *Scott Paper Co. v. Ceilcote Co.*, 103 F.R.D. 591, 596 (D. Me. 1984). Attorney's memoranda reporting on the defendants' perceptions of a contractual dispute and exploring the possibility of settling the dispute through commercial rather than legal means were not generated in anticipation of litigation.

- *Binks Mfg. Co. v. National Presto Indus., Inc.*, 709 F.2d 1109, 1118, 1120 (7th Cir. 1983). No error occurred in requiring the production and subsequently permitting the admission at trial of two memoranda dealing with the very dispute at issue in the litigation. "Remote prospect of litigation" does not mean that the memoranda were "prepared . . . *because* of the prospect of litigation." The court concluded that the documents, despite their threatening tone, were produced with an eye toward negotiation and a business accommodation of the claim and not with an eye to litigation, even though litigation did indeed result.

- *Grumman Aerospace Corp. v. Titanium Metals Corp.*, 91 F.R.D. 84, 89–90 (E.D.N.Y. 1981). A consultant's report prepared for settlement negotiations could be discovered. First, although settlement negotiations presuppose the existence of identifiable claims and adversarial preparation, the report at issue was a study of objective economic facts, drawn from the files of self-acknowledged antitrust violators against whom the report could not be used pursuant to confidentiality agreements. Second, the report did "not embody an adversary's competing view of the effects" of the antitrust violations.

- *Osterneck v. E.T. Barwick Indus.*, 82 F.R.D. 81, 86–87 (N.D. Ga. 1979). Pursuant to a Securities and Exchange Commission (SEC) consent decree, the defendant agreed to appoint a special review committee to report to its board of directors on matters alleged in the SEC's complaint. The attorneys preparing a report were providing investigatory—not legal—assistance, so it was clearly not prepared "in anticipation of litigation."

- *Delco Wire & Cable, Inc. v. Weinberger*, 109 F.R.D. 680, 690 (E.D. Pa. 1986). Counsel's memoranda regarding steps to be taken to comply with the court's order made during litigation are not materials prepared in anticipation of litigation.

There is countervailing authority, however, that does consider documents prepared for settlement of existing or potential litigation to be work-product protected. Obviously, to settle actual or potential litigation, the litigation itself must be a fairly real prospect.

- *Boss Mfg. Co. v. Hugo Boss AG*, 1999 U.S. Dist. LEXIS 987, at *4–5 (S.D.N.Y. Feb. 1, 1999). Where renegotiation of an existing contract was undertaken lest settlement of litigation violate that contract, documents created by attorneys reflecting those negotiations were privileged both because of ongoing litigation and in contemplation of prospective litigation if the renegotiation failed.

- *N.V. Organon v. Elan Pharms., Inc.*, 2000 U.S. Dist. LEXIS 5629 (S.D.N.Y. May 1, 2000), *recons. denied*, 2000 U.S. Dist. LEXIS 15394 (S.D.N.Y. Oct. 23, 2000). Drafts of settlement documents were protected on work product and privilege from disclosure in a suit about failure to abide by the oral settlement agreement.

4. Routine Investigatory Documents

As a general rule, ordinary investigations that a business may conduct, even if there is a small prospect of litigation, will not be accorded work-product protection. Courts generally find that there was a business reason for the conduct of the investigation and that the investigation would have been conducted in substantially the same manner even without any possibility of litigation.

- *Benton v. Brookfield Props. Corp.*, 56 Fed. R. Serv. 3d (Callaghan) 46 (S.D.N.Y. 2003). The case arose out of two deaths on a construction site. At the time the insurance company had a representative on site who immediately conducted an investigation. The court found that the facts did not support a claim of work product protection made by the insured and would not have supported such a claim even if made by the insurer. The operative facts are worth repeating. They are instructive for others seeking or resisting discovery of similar investigative reports. "Soules was present on the work site as a risk engineer for Zurich, not as a representative of defendants. When an accident occurred on a site assigned to him, his role was to start the investigative process, secure evidence, and determine, if possible, the cause of the accident.

When the accident at issue in this case occurred, he immediately went to the site, investigated and prepared a report, which he sent to Zurich's underwriting and claims representatives. He did so, by his own testimony, in the ordinary course of his employment by Zurich, and, at least in part, to assist Zurich in determining whether to offer coverage to the insured. . . . Moreover, although an attorney for defendants was present at the site at the time, Soules neither spoke to that attorney nor operated under his instructions, and he did not provide that lawyer a copy of the report when he e-mailed it to Zurich."

- *Janicker v. George Washington Univ.*, 94 F.R.D. 648, 650 (D.D.C. 1982). Because the work-product protection does not extend to "more or less routine investigation[s]" conducted "in the ordinary course of business," there must be "objective facts establishing an identifiable resolve to litigate prior to the investigative efforts resulting in the report. . . . While litigation need not be imminent, the primary motivating purpose behind the creation of a document or investigative report must be to aid in possible future litigation."

A *fortiori*, when a business is required to keep or to make accident reports pursuant to some agency rule, no work-product protection will be accorded to the investigative reports, however likely it may also be that the accident or event reported will lead to litigation.

- *Rakus v. Erie-Lackawanna R. Co.*, 76 F.R.D. 145 (W.D.N.Y. 1977). Accident reports generated as required by ICC regulations are generated in the company's ordinary course of business and are discoverable even if there is a reasonable prospect that litigation may result as a consequence of the accident.

The question of whether a particular document will be accorded work-product protection arises with particular frequency in the investigation of claims. Courts have generally shown an enormous reluctance to grant work-product protection to investigations of possible claims when an investigation is conducted by an insurance company, for instance, reasoning that it is the routine and ordinary course of business of an insurance company to investigate a claim. To obtain protection, one must identify the moment at which that general purpose shifts and becomes locked into a resolve to litigate the claim. However, routine investigative reports will not be protected.

- *Fine v. Bellefonte Underwriters Ins. Co.*, 91 F.R.D. 420 (S.D.N.Y. 1981). Reports of three outside investigators hired by an insurance company to investigate a fire were ordered produced because it was not clear that the reports were created with a fixed resolve to litigate, rather than as a routine investigation of a possibly resistible claim; no outside counsel had been retained and the claim had not been denied coverage.

Once an insurance company or other corporate entity retains specific counsel to defend against a particular, identifiable claim, work-product protection will generally be accorded to investigative reports and/or similar reports. To accord such documents work-product protection merely by virtue of the fact that litigation counsel has been retained, would cloak ordinary business activities with protection from discovery. It would also invite excessive resistance to the settlement of claims and the automatic engagement of outside counsel to supervise the conduct of all business affairs once litigation was in the offing.

- *Spaulding v. Denton*, 68 F.R.D. 342, 345 (D. Del. 1975). Reports prepared by outside investigators at the behest of an insurance company into the circumstances surrounding a ship sinking, after each side was represented by counsel, would not be made work-product immune from discovery where the investigation was not directed by counsel.

- *Thomas Organ Co. v. Jadranska Slobodna Plovidba*, 54 F.R.D. 367, 372–73 (N.D. Ill. 1972). Investigative reports of claims prepared months before an attorney was retained to represent the insurance company were prepared in the ordinary course of business and were not work-product immune from discovery. The case interpreted Rule 26(b)(3) shortly after its adoption.

■ *Hardy v. New York News, Inc.*, 114 F.R.D. 633 (S.D.N.Y 1987). Even after labor counsel was retained to represent the defendant with respect to its labor policies, that fact did not accord work-product protection to documents written by the defendant's manager of Equal Employment Opportunity Programs.

■ *Atlanta Coca-Cola Bottling Co. v. Trans America Ins. Co.*, 61 F.R.D. 115, 118 (N.D. Ga. 1972). The court ordered the insurance claim file produced, despite defendant's contention that it was prepared in anticipation of litigation. "[I]t can hardly be said that the evaluation of a routine claim from a policyholder is undertaken in anticipation of litigation, even though litigation often does result from denial of a claim. The obviously incongruous result of the position urged by defendant would be that the major part of the files of an insurance company would be insulated from discovery."

5. Assessments of Litigation as Work Product

Few materials are as likely to be accorded an unquestioning work-product protection as assessments of ongoing litigation. An attorney's mental impressions are clearly incorporated into such work product. This is the case even if and when public disclosure is intended of that assessment. Only if some cover-up were alleged would the work-product protection be stripped.

■ *Carey-Canada, Inc. v. California Union Ins. Co.*, 118 F.R.D. 242 (D.D.C. 1986). Drafts describing ongoing litigation by in-house counsel are inevitably drafted with an eye to that litigation and, therefore, do not constitute part of the normal business of the corporation and are not discoverable.

6. Patent Filings

Patent office filings are by their very nature public filings and moreover non-adversarial in nature. It is hard to imagine how anything prepared for such purposes could be given work-product status. Yet some courts have suggested that litigation lurks in patent office filings and that they are willing to countenance an assessment of the purpose with which the documents have been prepared.

- *Hercules, Inc. v. Exxon Corp.*, 434 F. Supp. 136, 152 (D. Del. 1977). "[A] responsible patent attorney always anticipates the possibility of future litigation involving the patent. It is possible that, during the ex parte prosecution, certain memoranda or recordings, etc. prepared by the attorney may reflect concerns more relevant to future litigation than to the ongoing prosecution. If the primary concern of the attorney is with claims which would potentially arise in future litigation, the work product immunity applies; if the attorney's primary concern is claims which have arisen or will arise during the ex parte prosecution of the application, however, the work-product rule does not apply."

  The court's holding thereby makes inevitable a document-by-document assessment and invites dispute and litigation.

D. *Indicia of Primary Motivation*

It is often not possible to determine directly the primary motivation for the preparation of a document. Thus, certain indicia have evolved as more likely than not to lead to a finding that the primary motivation for the creation of a document was in anticipation of litigation.

Conversely, a party seeking to obtain work-product documents needs to realize that merely because an opponent claims that a document was created in anticipation of litigation and is deserving of work-product protection does not necessarily make it so.

The inquiry may be very fact specific and therefore vary from case to case. For instance, where an attorney is promptly hired upon the occurrence of an accident, where the attorney then hired the investigator (and pays the bill) for the conduct of witness interviews, where the witnesses are informed that the interviews are being conducted for an attorney with a possibility that litigation may result and where the investigatory includes personal assessments of the quality (and credibility) of the witnesses, there is a very good likelihood that the resulting report will be deemed work-product protected rather than an insurance investigation conducted in the ordinary course of an insurance business.

- *Gator Marshbuggy Excavator L.L.C. v. M/V Rambler*, 2004 U.S. Dist. LEXIS 16090, at *10 (E.D. La. Aug. 13, 2004). "The statements in Hoerner's [the attorney] and Benfield's [the investigator] affidavits that they obtained Naquin's [a witness] statement in anticipation of litigation are merely conclusory. However, other factors indicate that the primary motivating purpose behind the taking of Naquin's statement was to aid in future litigation. ARTCO [the ship's owner] knew that its captain had been criminally charged with careless operation of a watercraft and that the June 3, 2003 incident had allegedly caused property damage to plaintiffs' marshbuggy. ARTCO promptly hired counsel, who obtained the Sheriff's reports that named Naquin as a witness. ARTCO's attorney promptly retained Benfield to investigate Naquin's knowledge of the accident. Benfield's handwritten notes taken during the interview, the transcript of his interview with Naquin, his handwritten summary of the interview and his typed report to Hoerner contain indicia that he was aware that Naquin's statement was being obtained in anticipation of litigation. For example, Benfield advised Naquin that the recording was being made for an attorney because Naquin was a witness to the incident. In his typed report to Hoerner, Benfield provided his opinion concerning Naquin's credibility and the value of Naquin's information to Hoerner's client in terms of causation and liability. Finally, Benfield closed his file and billed Hoerner for his services after finishing his typed report. Benfield did not participate in any attempts to adjust or settle any potential claim, as other insurance adjusters have done in cases in which courts have found that the investigation was not performed in anticipation of litigation but in the ordinary course of business before counsel was retained."

The court pointed out that Naquin was available for deposition and that the party seeking to know what his testimony would be could proceed in that manner. If there was any doubt as to whether his testimony at deposition conformed to what he had initially told the investigator, the court would review statement and deposition testimony *in camera.*

Here are certain indicia that occur with some frequency and assist in having a document deemed work-product protected.

1. Designating Documents as Work-Product Protected

Indicating on the face of the document that it is being created for use in litigation provides direct (though not conclusive) evidence of why it was created. It is like chicken soup. It may not be a surefire cure, but it generally cannot hurt.

- *United States v. International Bus. Machs. Corp.*, 71 F.R.D. 376, 379 (S.D.N.Y. 1976). The court treated as outside the privilege "[a]ll documents which do not disclose that they were prepared for use in this litigation."

Obviously, however, document designation alone cannot possibly be dispositive. If it were, all any party would ever need to do to avail itself of the work-product protection would be to label each and every document it did not wish to have produced as "work product."

2. Participation of Attorney

Clearly, the mere fact that an attorney is involved in the preparation of some document is hardly sufficient standing alone to make it work-product protected. Indeed with the enormous increase in the number of attorneys filling an increasingly broad range of roles in a corporation, that indicator standing alone is hardly dispositive. Small wonder that courts are, as they should be, wary of according work product protection merely because a person, corporate or individual, had the foresight to engage a lawyer in some process. Nonetheless, there are times when courts have stated that the participation of attorneys was a clear indicia that litigation was expected to follow. Since engaging the lawyer, however, often follows upon the heels of some identifiable threat, it is hard to know what is the real indicator that litigation is anticipated: the threat or the fact that an attorney has been engaged to meet that threat.

- *In re Woolworth Corp. Sec. Class Action Litig.*, 1996 U.S. Dist. LEXIS 7773, 1996 WL 306576 (S.D.N.Y June 7, 1996). After Woolworth's Treasurer made allegations of accounting irregularities, the Audit Committee of the Board of Directions and a Special Committee of independent directors retained the law firm of Paul, Weiss to investigate. The law firm and its accounting expert gathered and analyzed relevant information and documents, interviewed forty-five Woolworth employees, and prepared a report that plaintiffs "used as a roadmap for their litigation." The district judge rejected plaintiffs' argument that the notes and memoranda were not prepared in anticipation of litigation because "all participants knew when Paul, Weiss became involved that litigation—civil, and possibly criminal—as well as regulatory action were virtually certainties. Applying a distinction between 'anticipation of litigation' and 'business purposes' is in this case artificial, unrealistic, and the line between is here essentially blurred to oblivion."

- *Janicker v. George Washington Univ.*, 94 F.R.D. 648, 650–51 (D.D.C. 1982). The fact that a party may anticipate the contingency of litigation resulting from an event does not automatically qualify an in-house report as work product. Because the investigative report was prepared without involvement of an attorney and for routine administrative reasons, the court ordered the report to be produced.

Participation of an attorney in the preparation of the sought-after documents does not confer an automatic work-product protection. This is particularly true in the context of materials prepared for submission to third parties, including governmental agencies.

- *Burlington Indus. v. Exxon Corp.*, 65 F.R.D. 26, 42 (D. Md. 1974). "The work-product doctrine, however, cannot be used to protect documents relating to research, tests and experiments which are to be disclosed to the Patent Office at the time of the application for a patent since the documents do not constitute the results of an attorney's efforts to represent his client in a potentially adversary proceeding, but instead, result from a legal duty to produce the total information for the Patent Office."

- *Thomas Organ Co. v. Jadranska Slobodna Plovidba*, 54 F.R.D. 367, 372–74 (N.D. Ill. 1972). Documents prepared by marine surveyors hired by the insurer of the damaged goods before an attorney first became involved were made in the ordinary course of business and were not protected by work-product protection.

Widely followed, the *Thomas Organ* seeming black-letter law ruling that no attorney involvement meant no work-product protection being accorded has also occasionally been criticized. However, the courts that followed *Thomas Organ* far outnumbered those that did not. *Accord:*

- *Universal Vendors, Inc. v. Candimat Co. of Am.*, 16 Fed. R. Serv. 2d (CBC) 1329 (E.D. Pa. 1972). A document reflecting chronology of the parties' pre-suit contractual dealings was not work-product immune when there was no indication that it had been prepared or requested by counsel.

- *McDougall v. Dunn*, 468 F.2d 468, 473 (4th Cir. 1972). Statements given to a claims adjuster shortly after an automobile accident were discoverable.

But see:

- *Fontaine v. Sunflower Beef Carrier*, 87 F.R.D. 89 (E.D. Mo. 1980). The court took an extreme opposing position to that of *Thomas Organ* and declared that any investigative report prepared in the wake of an accident was necessarily prepared in anticipation of litigation and was, therefore, work-product protected under Rule 26(b)(3).

- *Almaguer v. Chicago, Rock Island & Pac. R. Co.*, 55 F.R.D. 147, 148–49 (D. Neb. 1972). "[S]tatements taken by a claim agent immediately after an accident are taken in anticipation of litigation. . . . The anticipation of the filing of a claim against the railroad, when a railroad employee has been injured on the job, is undeniable, and the expectation of litigation in such circumstances is a reasonable assumption."

Most courts take a case-by-case analysis. Nonetheless, the general result is that disclosure will be allowed more often than not.

- *Basinger v. Glacial Carriers, Inc.*, 107 F.R.D. 771 (M.D. Pa. 1985). An investigative report conducted by the defendant's insurance company would not have to be produced and a deposition subpoena issued would be quashed. It is apparent that the investigation was done with the potential for litigation in mind. In all events, alternative means existed to obtain the sought-after information: police reports could be obtained directly and witnesses interviewed by the insurance company could be directly interviewed or deposed.

- *APL Corp. v. Aetna Cas. & Sur. Co.*, 91 F.R.D. 10 (D. Md. 1980). After conducting a thorough review of the case law starting with *Thomas Organ* and its progeny both pro and con, and doing an exhaustive analysis of the conditions under which the insurance investigative report was produced, the court concluded that work product-protection did not apply to an insurance company investigation of an employee dishonesty claim and ordered the investigative report produced because it was not prepared in "anticipation of litigation" after all.

If a similar analysis to that conducted by the *APL* court were to be undertaken in each case that insurance investigative reports are sought, the inefficiency would be monumental. It may be preferable to have a bright-line test, such as suggested by Judge Will in *Thomas Organ*. Preparing investigative reports is certainly in the ordinary course of business of an insurance company. Accordingly, those reports should be ordered produced, absent some extraordinary showing that an investigation was done not to assess the claim, but to prepare to defend on the very case *sub judice*, under the direction of trial counsel.

Some courts will grant work-product protection to investigative reports prepared at the behest of trial counsel, but not to investigative reports otherwise prepared.

- *Tejada Fashions Corp. v. Yasusa Fire & Marine Ins. Co.*, 1984 U.S. Dist. LEXIS 15815 (S.D.N.Y. June 18, 1994). The court found an investigation into fire with the possibility of litigation to be within the routine work of the insurance company and required by the policy. The court also expressly found that the investigation was not prepared at the behest of counsel. The work-product claim was denied.

- *Spaulding v. Denton*, 68 F.R.D. 342, 345 (D. Del. 1975). "*Thomas's* flat requirement of a lawyer's involvement raises a bump which the 1970 Amendments [to the Federal Rules of Civil Procedure] had smoothed over. . . ." Nonetheless, the court found that the insurance investigation conducted immediately after the accident was not done in anticipation of litigation, but that the report, done after each side was represented by counsel, was work-product immune. Thus, having sought to smooth away the bump, the *Spaulding* court merely moved it further down the anticipation-of-litigation road, recognizing clearly that otherwise the danger would be that an insurance company would conform its investigative practices "so as to make all documents appear to be prepared 'in anticipation of litigation.'"

Courts seem to be more willing to extend work-product protection to consultants who, at first glance, would not appear to be assisting attorneys directly with litigation preparation. Most noteworthy is the case of a public relations firm whose work and communications with attorneys was granted work-product protection.

- *In re Copper Market Antitrust Litig.*, 200 F.R.D. 213 (S.D.N.Y. 2001). Public relations law firm specialized in litigation crisis management and, based on that and other indicia, the court was persuaded to accord work-product protection to its communications with litigation counsel.

3. Commentary on Ongoing Litigation

Once litigation has in fact been initiated, any commentary on the course of that litigation by an attorney is most likely to be accorded work-product protection. Not only does it meet all the criteria of ordinary work product, but necessarily encompasses an attorney's mental impressions on the very litigation at issue. Indeed, few types of work product are as likely to be accorded so absolute a protection from discovery. This is so, even if the attorney is drafting a disclosure statement commenting on the litigation for public consumption. Only if a claim were to be made that the disclosure itself was intended as a cover-up might the prior drafts become discoverable.

- *Carey-Canada, Inc. v. California Union Ins. Co.*, 118 F.R.D. 242 (D.D.C. 1986). Because drafts describing ongoing litigation by in-house counsel are inevitably drafted with an eye to that litigation and do not constitute part of the normal business of the corporation, they are not discoverable.

4. Routine Business Practice

It is clear that documents which are prepared in the ordinary course of business, even if some litigation then results concerning that business practice, are not work-product protected.

- *Naquin v. Unocal Corp.*, 2002 U.S. Dist. LEXIS 15722, 2002 WL 1837838, at *7 (E.D. La. Aug. 12, 2002). "If a party or its attorney prepares a document in the ordinary course of business, it will not be protected from discovery even if the party is aware that the document may also be useful in the event of litigation." (Internal quotation marks omitted.)

Courts may therefore be called upon to determine whether a document was prepared in anticipation of litigation or for some other business purpose.

- *Navigant Consulting, Inc. v. Wilkinson*, 220 F.R.D. 467, 476 (N.D. Tex. 2004). Needless to say, a work-product protection claim, claimed wherein one of the emails, the author of the document, a lawyer, said: "I don't think we need any further legal research for now, we have a difficult *business decision* to make."

Absent such, shall we call them, admissions against interest, the courts determine what the primary purpose for the creation of the document is. They inquire whether it was a routine practice to prepare that type of document. If it was, work product protection will not be accorded. If it was the routine practice of the business to prepare such documents, they will often ask what event sparked the preparation of that particular document and how imminent was the prospect of litigation. The mere fact that a document was not routinely prepared or was prepared after an accident, with an eye to possible litigation, does not thereby confer work-product protection.

- *Whitney Nat'l Bank v. Karam*, 2004 U.S. Dist. LEXIS 8245, at *9 (S.D. Tex. Feb. 20, 2004). "To the extent that the documents in issue here were not prepared for litigation, but rather to satisfy a contractual obligation to provide claim information to Lloyds or to try to persuade Lloyds to provide full coverage under the fidelity bond, the attorney work-product protection does not apply. When documents would have been prepared independent of any anticipation of use in litigation, but because some other purpose or obligation was sufficient to cause them to be prepared, no work-product protection attaches." The motion to reconsider was denied.

- *Celmer v. Marriot Corp.*, 2004 U.S. Dist. LEXIS 15394 (E.D. Pa. July 16, 2004). The court concluded that it was routine business practice for Marriott to prepare an "incidence" report whenever there was an accident which was based upon an interview with the injured party and any witnesses. Indeed the court concluded that the claim of privilege and work-product protection was so lacking in substance that it awarded costs and attorney's fees in the amount of $1,500 to the plaintiff obliged to litigate the issue.

- *Logan v. Commercial Union Ins. Co.*, 96 F.3d 971, 977 (7th Cir. 1996). The court held the insurance company's investigative file to be work-product protected because all the documents were written after the claim was processed, investigated, and denied; it was gathered after litigation was filed; and it reflected the company's plan of defense. In so holding, the court said: "[W]hile much of the paperwork generated by insurance companies is prepared with an eye toward a possible legal dispute over a claim, it is important to distinguish between 'an investigative report developed in the ordinary course of business' as a precaution for the remote prospect of 'litigation' and materials prepared because 'some articulable claim *likely* to lead to litigation . . . has arisen.'"

But see:

- *Prisco Serena Sturm Architects v. Liberty Mut. Ins. Co.*, 1996 U.S. Dist. LEXIS 2216, 1996 WL 89225, at *2 (N.D. Ill. Feb. 27, 1996). In the context of an insurance post-loss investigation, we have previously recognized that an insurance company's claim file is not entitled to blanket work-product protection.

- *Garfinkle v. Arcata Nat'l Corp.*, 64 F.R.D. 688, 690 (S.D.N.Y. 1974). The court held that opinion letters regarding whether the sale of shares without SEC registration might result in liability were prepared as a routine procedure and were not prepared with litigation in mind.

The fact that an investigation is routinely conducted, even in circumstances frequently giving rise to litigation, suggests that the matters would be investigated and committed to writing even without work-product protection, so the *Hickman* policies are not implicated.

- *Miles v. Bell Helicopter Co.*, 385 F. Supp. 1029, 1033 (N.D. Ga. 1974). The court held that accident reports prepared immediately following a helicopter crash were not prepared in anticipation of litigation simply because such crashes usually gave rise to litigation. The reports were routinely prepared, not "in response to a particular claim advanced by any individual, but merely on the contingency that litigation might well arise from the helicopter crash."

Thus, for work-product protection from discovery to attach to a particular document, the probability of litigation must be substantial and the commencement of litigation must be imminent. It should be borne in mind, however, that even if work-product protection does attach to a given document, that does not make the investigators and their conclusions immune from discovery through interrogatories and depositions.

Insurance company investigations are the prime example of routine practices in circumstances frequently resulting in litigation where the resulting reports are generally denied work-product protection. Any claim gives rise to an investigation as a precondition for determining whether the claim will or will not be accorded coverage. The investigative reports are virtually always discoverable, unless done after the actual commencement of litigation and at the direct behest of the trial attorney.

- *Westhemeco Ltd. v. New Hampshire Ins. Co.*, 82 F.R.D. 702, 708–9 (S.D.N.Y. 1979). Documents generated by an insurance company during a routine investigation of plaintiff's claim were not prepared in anticipation of litigation even though litigation eventually resulted and even though litigation would have been a likely event if the claim could not be resolved.

- *Atlanta Coca-Cola Bottling Co. v. Transamerica Ins. Co.*, 61 F.R.D. 115, 118 (N.D. Ga. 1972). An insurer's evaluation of a claim by policy holders was not in anticipation of litigation because most claims result in payment; thus, evaluation of the claim is routine and part of the ordinary business practice of the defendant.

Similarly, agency rule making documents are usually discoverable.

- *Heaton v. Monogram Credit Card Bank*, 2004 U.S. Dist. LEXIS 4065, at *18 (E.D. Pa. Mar. 16, 2004). "Reviewing applications for deposit and creating regulations are clear examples of work done by the agency in the ordinary course of business." Accordingly, the court allowed work-product protection only for memos written about the instant litigation and required production of historical ad hoc approvals of special banks and historical interpretations of what "engaged in the business of receiving deposits" meant, an issue in the litigation.

So too, documents prepared by government agencies in an investigatory phase are frequently discoverable even though the investigatory phase often will be followed by litigation.

- *Abel Inv. Co. v. United States*, 53 F.R.D. 485, 489 (D. Neb. 1971). Reports and memoranda prepared by employees of the Internal Revenue Service relating to a particular taxpayer were not "in anticipation of litigation," although they contained mental impressions, conclusions, and legal theories of the IRS employees. The court noted that such documents were prepared routinely by the IRS, that they had not been prepared under the direction of an attorney, and that they were not designed to be used in an adversary context. The court rejected the position that a tax dispute begins whenever an individual return is selected for audit.

- *SEC v. National Student Mktg. Corp.*, 18 Fed. R. Serv. 2d (CBC) 1302, 1310–11 (D.D.C. 1974). In a fraud action brought by the SEC, some memoranda prepared by SEC staff in the course of an investigation of the defendants were held not in anticipation of litigation if they were prepared during the time the agency accumulated and evaluated factual materials; however, documents prepared after a draft memorandum to the commission recommending that suit be filed were within the privilege.

5. Dual Purpose Documents: For Business and Litigation

Courts are increasingly inclined to accord work-product protection to dual purpose documents provided one of the purposes is litigation motivated, provided that the documents would not have been prepared in substantially identical form even had there been no litigation purpose.

- *In re Grand Jury Subpoena (Torf)*, 357 F.3d 900 (9th Cir. 2004). The Ninth Circuit reversed the district court and vacated the contempt citation of a consultant who had prepared reports that the court of appeals found had a clear litigation purpose. The government had argued, successfully in the district court and unsuccessfully in the court of appeals, that since they would have been prepared for the purpose of entering into a consent agreement, they were not litigation motivated. The court said it was the first time that it was considering the availability of the protection for dual purpose documents and was also joining many sister circuits in adopting the "because of" standard, specifically following the reasoning of the Second Circuit in *Adlman*. Except that to the extent that *Adlman* might be read to state that no dual purpose documents could be work-product protected, it believed that the Seventh Circuit got it right in holding that they could.

- *In re Special September 1978 Grand Jury (II)*, 640 F.2d 49 (7th Cir. 1980). The court extended work-product protection to materials that were produced both in anticipation of litigation and for the filing of Board of Elections reports required under state law. When the law firm's client received the Board's request for the required reports, the client had already received a subpoena from a federal grand jury. The so-called "independent" purpose of complying with the Board's request was grounded in the same set of facts that created the anticipation of litigation, and it was the anticipation of litigation that prompted the law firm's work in the first place.

But see:

- *United States v. Frederick*, 182 F.3d 496, 501–02 (7th Cir. 1999), *cert. denied*, 528 U.S. 1154 (2000). The Seventh Circuit held that "a dual-purpose document—a document prepared for use in preparing tax returns *and* for use in litigation—is not privileged." The court said that were it to hold otherwise, people in or contemplating litigation would be able to invoke an accountant's privilege, provided that they used their lawyer to fill out their tax returns.

Doubtlessly the court considered that filing tax returns is something people do all the time. If a document is prepared for something that people do all the time then it should not be given work-product protection just because litigation is also a possibility.

The one all-encompassing context in which accident reports and witness statements are taken for a dual purpose—both the conduct of a business and in anticipation of possible, nay often probable litigation—is in the insurance context.

There are other contexts as well when a document is not routinely prepared in the course of a business, but when the document nonetheless has a dual purpose: one litigation-based; the other business-based. In such instances it is clear that, regardless of its possible use in litigation, the information acquired is important for other purposes in the party's business. Thus, in a variety of contexts—hospital review committees, defective product reviews, analysis of business disputes, claims adjustment investigations, contingent tax liability analysis—where a dual purpose exists: possible litigation and a business purpose.

In all of these contexts, even though litigation may be foreseeable, courts have not hesitated to make investigative documents discoverable on the ground that there was a business purpose separate and distinct from the prospect of possible litigation that led to the investigation.

Then courts follow the admonition of 8 CHARLES ALAN WRIGHT & ARTHUR R. MILLER, FEDERAL PRACTICE AND PROCEDURE ¶ 2024, at 198–99 (1970):

> But the converse of this is that even though litigation is already in prospect, there is no work-product protection for documents prepared in the regular course of business rather than for purposes of the litigation.

Thus the cases are legion where accident reports are prepared and witness statements taken after an accident have been found to be discoverable. So too have expert reports prepared to assess the causes of the accident- or insurance-triggering event. Usually the time frame established to determine discovery is that anything which transpires up to the time that coverage is being investigated and until such time as coverage is declined by the insurance company is discoverable by the insured. Matters which occur thereafter or documents prepared thereafter are as a general rule considered to be in anticipation of the insurance company's probable status as defendant in an action brought by the insured for wrongful denial of coverage.

- *Calabro v. Stone*, 225 F.R.D. 96 (E.D.N.Y. 2004). No showing was made that witness statements taken 3 weeks after the accident occurred and long before litigation commenced were taken in anticipation of litigation rather than in the ordinary course of the insurance's business of evaluating possible claims. The end result is that generally, courts have found accident reports generated for the investigation and evaluation of claims to be part of the regular, ordinary and principal business of insurance companies. Likewise, investigative reports sent by an insured to an insurance company are generally considered to have been created in the ordinary course of business rather than in anticipation of imminent litigation. Accordingly, witness statement provided by defendant to its insurance carrier ordered produced.

- *Goodyear Tire & Rubber Co. v. Kirk's Tire & Auto Servicenter of Haverstraw, Inc.*, 2003 U.S. Dist. LEXIS 15917, 2003 WL 22110281 (S.D.N.Y. Sept. 10, 2003). Plaintiff served a subpoena on the company hired by defendant to investigate an insurance claim. Defendant's motion to quash the subpoena was denied. The court held that the results of the investigation were neither privileged nor work-product protected. "Work-product protection may be extended to reports generated by insurers and adjusters because they are party representatives. . . . However, "application of the work-product doctrine to documents prepared by insurance companies has been particularly troublesome because it is the routine business of insurance companies to investigate and evaluate claims and to defend their insureds against third-party claims." . . . The question of whether insurer and adjuster reports were created "because of" impending litigation depends on whether the moving party can point to a definite shift made by the insurer or adjuster from acting in its ordinary course of business to acting in anticipation of litigation." (Case citations omitted.) The court concluded that none of the "benchmarks" which would have indicated that the investigation had proceeded from one conducted in the routine course of business to one conducted "in anticipation of litigation" were present.

- *Willis v. Westin Hotel Co.*, 1987 U.S. Dist. LEXIS 524, at *1 (S.D.N.Y. Jan. 30, 1987). "Material prepared by non-attorneys in anticipation of litigation, such as accident reports, is immune from discovery only where the material is prepared exclusively and in specific response to imminent litigation."

- *Whitman v. United States*, 108 F.R.D. 5, 8–9 (D.N.H. 1985). The record of a hospital peer-review hearing held one or two months after the operation that was the subject of the litigation was not protected from discovery as work product. The court found that the primary purpose in the preparation of the report was a retrospective analysis done to advance medical treatments, rather than in anticipation of litigation.

- *Scott Paper Co. v. Ceilcote Co.*, 103 F.R.D. 591, 596 (D. Me. 1984). Notes made by counsel of a meeting held to discuss a business problem were discoverable because the purpose of the meeting was to prevent "a fledgling business dispute from leading to legal action." Therefore, the notes were not prepared in anticipation of litigation.

- *Tejada Fashions Corp. v. Yasuda Fire & Marine Ins. Co.*, 1984 U.S. Dist. LEXIS 15815, 1984 WL 500 (S.D.N.Y. June 18, 1984). Documents prepared by an investigator employed by an insurance company were not work-product protected, even if litigation was expected.

- *525 Fulton St. Holding Corp. v. Mission Natl Ins. Co.*, 1984 U.S. Dist. LEXIS 15402, 1984 WL 591 (S.D.N.Y. June 29, 1984). Plaintiff/insured brought a claim against the insurance company for failure to provide coverage. The ostensible reason for the failure was that the insurance company claimed that the business interruption was wilfully caused by the insured. The insurance company had hired an independent metallurgist to conduct an investigation prior to declining coverage. The court held that the investigation had not been conducted in the ordinary course of business and not in anticipation of litigation.

Although the court did not consider the expert witness aspect of the case, since neither party raised it as a possible grounds, it is much like a party asserting advice of counsel and then refusing to permit discovery of that advice. If the expert concluded that the insured event was caused by the insured, it is perfectly extraordinary to claim that the basis for that determination are not discoverable or for matter would not form the very gravamen of the litigation over coverage. What was the insurance company thinking? Was the insurance company thinking?

- *Fine v. Bellefonte Underwriters Ins. Co.*, 91 F.R.D. 420, 422 (S.D.N.Y. 1981). Whether the document was created "because of" impending litigation depends on "whether the moving party can point to a definite shift made by the insurer or adjuster from acting in its ordinary course of business to acting in anticipation of litigation." Since the party seeking to protect the accident reports from discovery could not, they were ordered produced.

Even if no insurance company is involved and another type of business conducts an internal investigation, no work-product protection will necessarily result.

- *Heavin V. Owens-Corning Fiberglass*, 2004 U.S. Dist. LEXIS 2265 (D. Kan. June 3, 2004). Investigative file opened when workman's compensation claim was made was not done in anticipation of litigation, even though litigation was a possibility. The file was not protected from discovery.

- *Soeder v. General Dynamics Corp.*, 90 F.R.D. 253, 255 (D. Nev. 1980). An in-house airplane accident investigation was found to be motivated by a desire to improve the product, guard against adverse publicity, and otherwise protect the company's economic interests—as well as for use in any litigation—such that the report was prepared in the ordinary course of business and was not work-product protected.

Thus, the investigative report was found to fall under the compass of Rule 26(b)(1) and, because produced in the ordinary course of business for business motivations, it was discoverable.

- *Hensel Phelps Constr. Co. v. Southwestern Roofing & Sheet Metal Co.*, 29 Fed. R. Serv. 2d (CBC) 1095 (D. Colo. 1980). Documents prepared by the plaintiff regarding a defective roof supplied by the defendant were discoverable because the primary purpose for preparing the documents was to determine what the roofing problems were and how the building could be made usable.

One non-litigation purpose of conducting an investigation and preparing reports is to comply with regulatory requirements. Even though the resulting documents may be prepared with a high probability of litigation in mind, they generally will not be found to be encompassed within work-product protection from discovery at the behest of a potential claimant who has become an actual adversary.

- *United States v. El Paso Co.*, 682 F.2d 530, 542–44 (5th Cir. 1982), *cert. denied*, 466 U.S. 944 (1984). Tax-pool analyses prepared by accountants were discoverable because the primary motivation for preparing the analysis was compliance with public reporting requirements, and not possible litigation over tax returns filed by the company.

- *Galambus v. Consolidated Freightways Corp.*, 64 F.R.D. 468, 472 (N.D. Ind. 1974). "Statements of a truck driver to his employers and to the carrier using his services made pursuant to ICC regulations are made in the ordinary course of business under those regulations and were not work products."

It is clear that courts are leery of the attempt of prospective clients to sweep all types of investigations into the discovery-protected category by virtue of employing attorneys to conduct investigations that could equally as well have been conducted by non-attorneys. When that is the case, courts have not accorded the work-product protection, rejecting it on the grounds that the client has created an illusory screen for discoverable material that would be "unfair" to withhold from an adversary in search of the truth.

- *Mission Nat'l Ins. Co. v. Lilly*, 112 F.R.D. 160, 163 (D. Minn. 1986). The fact that counsel was employed in a concurrent capacity—to investigate an insurance claim and to defend against that claim—will not insulate from discovery the investigative report. "It would not be fair to allow the insurer's decision in this regard to create a blanket obstruction to discovery of its claims investigation."

Some courts will deny all protection to insurance reports generated after an accident, even though it is clear that the accident may result in litigation. Most of the federal courts do not regard accident reports and witness statements taken after an accident to be work product because these were not prepared *exclusively* and in *specific response* to litigation.

- *Weber v. Paduano*, 2003 U.S. Dist. LEXIS 858, 2003 WL 161340, at *4 (S.D.N.Y. Jan. 22, 2003). "[T]he very business of the producing party is to evaluate claims that may ultimately ripen into litigation.'"

Accord:

These courts have suggested that any distinction is meaningless and have ordered production of all accident reports and witness statements even when counsel prepared, or was involved in, the preparation of the report.

- *Mission Nat'l Ins. Co. v. Lilly*, 112 F.R.D. 160, 163 (D. Minn. 1986). The identity of the person or entity requesting an insurance investigation report should have, and has, no bearing on whether the report is discoverable.

- *Fine v. Bellefonte Underwriters Ins. Co.*, 91 F.R.D. 420, 422–23 (S.D.N.Y. 1981). Reports of three outside inspectors investigating a fire were ordered produced even though they were produced after counsel was retained to defend the claim through litigation and were therefore "prepared under the general guidance of counsel in anticipation of litigation." The court did not clearly articulate the basis for its conclusion: "on balance, I find that the sought-after reports were produced in the ordinary course, and not pursuant to a clear decision, based on substantial bona fide reasons, to reject the claim and to litigate."

Certain of the state courts may grant greater protection to accident reports and witness statements. A thorough review of these is beyond the scope of this compendium. Suffice it to say that in the federal courts, even in diversity actions, federal law not the various state rules apply to the production of work-product protection. New York is one state that tends to follow federal law in this regard, allowing discovery of virtually all accident reports and witness statements taken by any agent of an insurance company after an accident.

Yet another limitation on the scope of discovery of witness statements taken after an accident has occurred by a potential adversary is the elapse of time between the event and the taking of the witness statement. The closer in time to the event, the more likely will the statement be ordered produced. The longer in time since the event and the taking of the witness statement, the more likely will the court tell the party seeking the witness statement to go take its own deposition or interview the witness on its own.

- *Breneisen v. Motorola, Inc.*, 2003 U.S. Dist. LEXIS 11485 (N.D. Ill. July 7, 2003). Documents reflecting a factual summary and a chronology of significant events prepared under direction of human resources department providing for use of inside and outside counsel after suit was filed were deemed to be largely work-product protected even though plaintiffs argued that policy manual required an investigation that was thus conducted in "ordinary course of business." The opinion does not clarify what facts determined that neither privilege nor work-product protection applied to certain documents.

- *Ramsey v. NYP Holdings, Inc.*, 2002 U.S. Dist. LEXIS 11728, at *33 (S.D.N.Y. June 27, 2002), *clarified*, 2002 U.S. Dist. LEXIS 18186 (Sept. 27, 2002). Where documents were prepared at the behest of parents for the dual purpose of anticipating their own possible criminal prosecution for the child's murder and to find the real killer, the parents have not sustained the burden of proving that the primary purpose was in anticipation of litigation. "[D]ocuments that would have been created even absent the prospect of litigation are not protected. . . . [The parents] are necessarily required to demonstrate that the contested documents would not have been created but for the concern about prosecution, that is, that they would not have been created simply to serve the parents' desire to find their daughter's murderer."

- *Hamilton v. Canal Barge Co.*, 395 F. Supp. 975 (E.D. La. 1974). Five eyewitness statements taken by an insurance adjuster the day after an accident were ordered produced, even though the court found they had been taken in anticipation of litigation. The court also included an extended discussion of the diminution of the reliability of memory with time, including psychological studies, as a predicate for ordering production of these statements taken so soon after the event sub judice.

- *Tinder v. McGowan*, 15 Fed. R. Serv. 2d (CBC) 1608 (W.D. Pa. 1970). Witnesses statements taken nearly contemporaneously with the occurrence of the accident would be ordered produced when counsel for the requesting party did not have an opportunity to similarly question witnesses contemporaneously to the event, but the entire investigative file would not, since neither substantial need nor undue hardship had been demonstrated.

6. Avoidance of Litigation

If the motivation for the creation of a document was to assure a client's compliance with the law and thus the avoidance of litigation, courts have generally said that does not constitute "in anticipation of" litigation. Were it to do so, all legal advice, which presumptively is designed to assure that a client is in compliance with the law, would be subsumed under the work-product doctrine.

- *In re Derienzo*, 1998 Bankr. LEXIS 635, at *15–16 (Bankr. M.D. Pa. Apr. 28, 1998). "The fact that Sears and/or Sears National Bank assert that they attempted to comply with all laws and regulations in the transfer of these credit card accounts is commendable. It is also an approach expected from any organization, business, corporation, partnership, etc., which is making business decisions which will impact not only itself, but also its customers. To say, however, that all the actions taken by Sears and Sears National Bank were done in an effort to comply with the law to avoid litigation is, at best, convenient. If the Court would accept that blanket assertion, then the veil of the work-product doctrine could represent an insurmountable barrier to normal discovery. To the extent that any of the documents contain legal analysis going to the heart of rendering legal opinions and advice to a client, they are hereby protected below in certain documents which the Court finds are covered by the attorney-client privilege."

E. *Review of Preexisting Documents*

It should be apparent that documents *prepared* for other purposes do not become protected as work product by being *examined* in anticipation of litigation.

- *In re Grand Jury Subpoenas dated March 19 & Aug. 2, 2002*, U.S. Dist. LEXIS 17079 (S.D.N.Y. Sept. 12, 2002), *aff'd*, 318 F.3d 379 (2d Cir. 2002). Law firm that had obtained a multitude of documents regarding foreign bank accounts of its clients was required to hand them over pursuant to the subpoena when the court refused to accept its claim of work-product privilege. The court stated that these were preexisting documents not subject to any work-product protection claims before collection by the attorneys. The collection by the attorneys did not reveal any attorney mental processes. Thus the *Sporck v. Peil*, 759 F.2d 312 (3d Cir. 1985) exception that does protect an attorney's selection process where a great multitude of documents are screened was not applicable.

- *In re Grand Jury Proceedings*, 601 F.2d 162, 171–72 (5th Cir. 1979). Documents prepared by an accountant to assist the lawyer were protected, but the privilege "does not shield documents turned over to [the accountant] that would have been subject to production if kept in [the attorney's] hands."

- *City Consumer Servs., Inc. v. Horne*, 100 F.R.D. 740, 747 (D. Utah 1983). A bankrupt corporation's business records that had been reviewed by counsel were not records prepared in anticipation of litigation.

- *Brown v. Hart, Schaffner, & Marx*, 96 F.R.D. 64, 68 (N.D. Ill. 1982). "An attorney may not bring a document within the scope of the work-product rule simply by reviewing it if it was not originally prepared in anticipation of litigation."

F. *Attorney's Non-Litigation Activity*

When attorneys act as legal advisors outside the litigation context, the work-product protection from discovery generally does not apply. In those circumstances, protection from discovery will have to be based on the attorney-client privilege.

- *F. H. Krear & Co. v. 19 Named Trustees*, 90 F.R.D. 102, 103–04 (S.D.N.Y. 1981). In-house counsel's negotiations with a long-time business acquaintance with respect to procuring computer services and counsel's investigation into whether the seller was complying with the contract were of a business nature unrelated to litigation and were therefore not protected from discovery.

- *In re Fischel*, 557 F.2d 209, 212–13 (9th Cir. 1977). Summaries of business transactions prepared by an attorney to assist a client in tax planning were not work-product protected as they were not prepared in anticipation of litigation.

- *In re Penn Cent. Commercial Paper Litig.*, 61 F.R.D. 453, 468 (S.D.N.Y. 1973). A printer's proof of the draft of a debenture offering circular is not protected even if the draft was prepared by an attorney. The documents were prepared in connection with a proposed debenture offering and not in anticipation of litigation.

- *Jordan v. United States Dep't of Justice*, 591 F.2d 753, 775–76 (D.C. Cir. 1978). A manual that was prepared to guide U.S. attorneys in the exercise of their prosecutorial discretion and that set forth standards for determining whether to bring individuals to trial was held not covered by the work-product doctrine. The court reasoned that because of its subject matter, the manual was not generated in anticipation of a particular action, or even in anticipation of trials in general. It did not disclose any attorney strategy or thought processes relevant to trial preparation.

Work-product protection has been given under FOIA's Exemption 5, which is the equivalent of the work-product protection in the governmental rule making and administrative context.

- *Hanson v. United States Agency for Int'l Dev.*, 372 F.3d 286, 293 (4th Cir. 2004). A report written by an attorney hired not by an agency of the United States government, but by a construction company to assist in the resolution of construction claims between the construction company and an agency of the Egyptian government was given work-product protection. The project was apparently funded by USAID, an agency of the United States government. The court found first that USAID and the construction company that hired the consultant/attorney shared a common legal interest in resolving the disputes.

  The court then addressed plaintiff's claim that the attorney/consultant disclaimed that he was acting as a lawyer. The court emphasized the nature of attorney/consultant's tasks which involved legal skills. "He monitored settlement negotiations, exercised legal judgment in assessing the positions of the parties, recommended a settlement amount for the dispute, and advised USAID on how it should change the dynamics of the negotiation process." He reviewed contract documents and signed his report with a J.D.—all indicia of acting as a lawyer, concluded the court.

The analysis is unusual. Work product does not have to be prepared by an attorney to be so protected. But it must be prepared *in anticipation of litigation.* And that issue is slid over with remarkable rapidity by the court. "Roy's legal analysis was also plainly performed in anticipation of litigation, a prospect not unknown to the construction industry." If that were the generalized law of work product then all the insurance industry files which are not work product protected would *in pari passu* suddenly become protected.

Finally, the court dispatched the question of whether a waiver occurred when the attorney/consultant provided a draft of his own report, namely his work product to the plaintiff. The court concluded that no waiver had occurred because the work product belongs to both client and attorney and the attorney could not waive the client's right therein or the protections afforded thereby without the client's authorization.

The opinion is nothing short of remarkable to the extent that it undoes in a most airy fashion and without any real discussion reams of work-product protection cases, most particularly on the issue of waiver where case after case has held that the government's unauthorized disclosure of work-product-protected documents, even when they are subject to a confidentiality agreement, nonetheless constitute a waiver as to one and all, authorized or not authorized. Moreover, no other case has ever suggested that the work-product protection can not be waived by the attorney whose product it is or even if waived can be recaptured by the client.

G. *Extent of Protection*

1. If No Litigation Ensues

The work-product protection applies if the material was prepared in anticipation of litigation, even if no litigation actually ensues.

- *Jackson v. United States Attorneys Office*, 293 F. Supp. 2d 34 (D.D.C. 2003). The court, relying on *Grolier*, did not order disclosure of work-product-protected material under FOIA even though no prosecution (i.e., presumably prosecution of plaintiff's perjury complaint) ensued.

- *Kent Corp v. NLRB*, 530 F.2d 612, 623 (5th Cir.), *cert. denied*, 429 U.S. 920 (1976). Reports prepared by staff attorneys to assist the agency's decision on whether to pursue formal charges were work-product protected regardless of whether there was ultimately a decision to dismiss. "Insofar as the privilege is meant to promote candid expressions of an attorney's theories and perspectives, it cannot properly be made to turn on whether litigation actually ensued."

Of course, if there is no litigation, it may be more difficult to establish that the motivation to litigate was present when the document was created.

And if the litigation for which the work product was prepared does not ensue and the documents are then sought in some other context by other parties, Rule 26 (b)(3) may not avail. It only prevents discovery of materials prepared by or for *a party* or his representative; courts can nevertheless issue protective orders under Rule 26(c) to prevent discovery, or to prohibit the party seeking discovery from disclosing the discovered information to any non-participant in the litigation.

2. In Current Litigation Only

A decided minority of the courts has held that the work-product protection is available only in the adversary proceeding for which the work product has been prepared. With good reason, most courts have rejected that interpretation.

- *Lawrence v. Cohn*, 2002 U.S. Dist. LEXIS 1222 (S.D.N.Y. Jan. 25, 2002). Party claiming work-product protection instructed to determine "provenance" of handwritten attorney notes. If prepared in conjunction with current litigation would be privilege; if for prior litigation, would not.

- *Frontier Ref., Inc. v. Gorman-Rupp Co., Inc.*, 136 F.3d 695, 703 (10th Cir. 1998). "[W]e conclude that the work-product doctrine extends to subsequent litigation. This court need not, however, determine whether the subsequent litigation must be closely related because this indemnity action is unquestionably "closely related" to the underlying suit between Frontier and the injured contractors."

Yet the concept had a certain logical consistency. Intended to protect the adversarial process, once the dispute is over what remains to be protected indefinitely? Nonetheless, the concept of any kind of protection seems to come with an aura of "immortality." Once protected, always protected seems to be the overriding rationale, as indeed it is in English law when it comes to professional privilege, which is close to our concepts of work product. Thus most of the cases which held that work-product protection extended only to the case for which it was prepared, are now somewhat long in the tooth, and the ones that do not apply it rarely articulate an understandable rationale which one could then apply next time a similar set of circumstances presented themselves for adjudication.

- *Southern Union Co. v. Southwest Gas Corp.*, 205 F.R.D. 542, 549 (D. Ariz. 2002). "Thus, the proponents of the privilege have not established that the documents, which were purportedly prepared in anticipation of the proceedings before the ACC [Arizona Corporation Commission], can be protected in this litigation because it is not proceedings before the ACC."

- *Commonwealth of Puerto Rico v. S.S. Zoe Colocotroni*, 61 F.R.D. 653, 658–59 (D.P.R. 1974). The court discussed the two theories, one which protects work product only if the other litigation is not yet completed and reasonably related and the broader protection accorded by the *Duplan* case concluding that it should not here be applicable where the party seeking discovery had shown both substantial need and substantial hardship (the other parties with knowledge were located in Europe) to warrant piercing the work-product protection in all events. It thus instructed the magistrate to confine work-product protection to trial preparation in the instant case in the course of his *in camera* review of the documents to determine discoverability.

- *United States v. International Bus. Machs. Corp.*, 66 F.R.D. 154, 178 (S.D.N.Y. 1974). The court rejected the Magistrate Judge's conclusion that "[e]ven though such a document was not prepared for the present litigation, the document is privileged as work product if it was prepared for a lawsuit involving substantially identical issues." The court followed *Honeywell, infra.*

■ *Honeywell, Inc. v. Piper Aircraft Corp.*, 50 F.R.D. 117, 119 (M.D. Pa. 1970). "An attorney's memorandum in a prior case involving different parties does not have the protection of the 'work product" principle.' One should note that most of the cases for which the documents had been prepared had occurred decades ago in a different sort of proceeding.

■ *Republic Gear Co. v. Borg-Warner Corp.*, 381 F.2d 551, 557 (2d Cir. 1967). The deposition of an attorney who did not represent any of the parties of the litigation was sought. The attorney claimed work product for some of the documents sought, even though they were not prepared for the litigation at issue. The court did not like the notion that by bringing an action a party might go fishing in the files of an attorney stranger to the litigation, although its way of stating that proposition is a bit hard to follow. "[W]e have found little authority as to whether the "work product" protection is restricted to materials prepared in connection with the very litigation in which the discovery is sought. The few lower court decisions in which disclosure was compelled dealt with material prepared for use in prior proceedings which had been fully completed before discovery was requested. Those cases are thus clearly distinguishable from the present case, for here the broad purpose of the rule which is designed to encourage effective legal representation by removing counsel's fear that his thoughts and information will be invaded by his adversary if he records them would be defeated if Republic could gain access to Nattier's [the attorney whose work product was sought] files by proceeding against a party Nattier did not professionally represent but nevertheless a party involved in the same transaction in which Nattier's former clients were involved. Here, of course, Nattier's former clients remain suable."

3. In Subsequent Litigation

The United States Supreme Court has provided work-product protection to material prepared in anticipation of concluded litigation in the FOIA context.

- *FTC v. Grolier, Inc.*, 462 U.S. 19, 25 (1983). The court held that FOIA's exemption 5, which is coextensive with the federal work-product rule, protects work-product materials without regard to status of litigation for which it was prepared and thus in dicta suggested the same rule would apply for work-product protection. The issue in the case was whether work product from another litigation was protected from disclosure under the Freedom of Information Act by Exemption 5, which turns on whether the documents would be "'routinely' or 'normally' disclosed upon a showing of relevance." Because all the courts of appeals and the overwhelming majority of the district courts that decided the issue gave some protection to work product prepared in another litigation, the Court held that the materials came within the exemption. In the course of its discussion, the majority noted: "[T]he literal language of the Rule protects materials prepared for *any* litigation or trial so long as they were prepared by or for a party to the subsequent litigation."

Justice Brennan concurred, rejecting the reference to "routine" disclosure and grounding his decision solely on an interpretation of Rule 26(b)(3). He strongly rejected any notion that work-product protection is in any way diminished once the litigation for which the work product was prepared has ended. The risk that disclosure in any litigation will inhibit careful and thorough preparation requires that work product be protected beyond the occasion for its creation. 462 U.S. at 29–31.

The difficulty with the Court's "literal" reading of the rule is that the provision also extends the protection only to documents prepared by or for "another party." If read literally, that means that a person not a party to the litigation has no protection at all, regardless of how closely connected his suit is to the one in which discovery is being sought. 8 CHARLES ALAN WRIGHT & ARTHUR R. MILLER, FEDERAL PRACTICE AND PROCEDURE § 2024, at 201–02 (1970).

Clearly, however, the policy of the work-product doctrine calls for giving both parties and non-parties protection in both related and unrelated cases. However, that is not the way many courts are interpreting either the rule or *Grolier*.

The Fourth, the Sixth, the Seventh and the Eighth, extend the privilege to all subsequent litigation, related or not.

- *Duplan Corp. v. Moulinage et Retorderie de Chavanoz*, 487 F.2d 480, 483–84 (4th Cir. 1973). The Fourth Circuit reversed the trial court's conclusion that the work-product privilege did not carry forward to subsequent litigation. "[T]he thrust of the [*Hickman*] decision was the qualified protection of the professional effort, confidentiality and activity of an attorney which transcends the rights of the litigants. . . . [W]e find no indication that the Court intended to confine the protection of the work product to the litigation in which it was prepared or to make it freely discoverable in a subsequent law suit. . . . On balance, we think the legal profession and the interests of the public are better served by recognizing the qualified immunity of work-product materials in a subsequent case as well as that in which they were prepared."

- *United States v. Leggett & Platt, Inc.*, 542 F.2d 655, 660 (6th Cir. 1976), *cert. denied*, 430 U.S. 945 (1977). The court decided that the doctrine protects work product from disclosure in other litigation since the protection is not absolute in all events and can be breached on a showing of need. The court did not discuss the issue, but recognized the work-product protection where the subsequent litigation was closely related to underlying litigation.

- *Union Pac. R. Co. v. Crew Transp. Servs., Inc.*, 2003 U.S. Dist. LEXIS 21753 (N.D. Ill. Dec. 3, 2003). A non-party insurance carrier was served with a subpoena for documents which were indisputably work product. The party seeking production argued that they had not been prepared for the current litigation. That argument, without more ado by the court, went nowhere.

On the other hand the Seventh Circuit has also noted that work-product issues are very fact specific and prone to a balancing of the factors involved.

- *Velsicol Chem. Corp. v. Parsons*, 561 F.2d 671, 676, n.3 (7th Cir. 1977), *cert. denied*, 435 U.S. 942 (1978). The Seventh Circuit noted that *Rule 26(b)(3)* itself shows that "the [work product] doctrine is not an absolute one and must be weighed against the exigencies of the situation."

- *In re Murphy*, 560 F.2d 326, 334–35 (8th Cir. 1977). "If work product is protected in related, but not unrelated, future cases, an attorney would be hesitant to assemble extensive work-product materials because of the concern that the materials will not be protected in later, unrelated litigation. The fact that the subsequent litigation is not related does not provide a sufficient basis for disregarding the privilege articulated in *Hickman* and incorporated in Rule 26(b)(3). The mischief engendered by allowing discovery of work product recognized in *Hickman* would apply with equal vigor to discovery in future, unrelated litigation."

The Second and the Fifth Circuits have recognized that the work-product doctrine extends to subsequent litigation, but have either declined to decide or have failed to discuss whether the doctrine extends only to subsequent litigation that is "closely related" to the underlying proceedings.

- *Republic Gear Co. v. Borg-Warner Corp.*, 381 F.2d 551, 557 (2d Cir. 1967). The purpose of the rule that protects the attorney's trial preparation would be defeated here if disclosure were allowed, since the attorney whose files were sought represented parties in the same transaction.

- *Cellco P'ship v. Nextel Commun., Inc.*, 2004 U.S. Dist. LEXIS 12717 (S.D.N.Y. July 9, 2004). Protection accorded to work product even though not prepared for current litigation. The court did not discuss whether the two litigations were or were not related although it cited the *Garrett* case, *infra*. which accorded protection to substantially similar litigation.

- *Garrett v. Metropolitan Life Ins. Co.*, 1996 U.S. Dist. LEXIS 8054, 1996 WL 325725, at *4 (S.D.N.Y. June 12, 1996) (Bernikow, Mag. J.), *adopted*, 1006 U.S. Dist. LEXIS 14468 (S.D.N.Y. Oct. 3, 1996). The court held that: "[d]ocuments prepared for one litigation that would have been shielded from discovery in that prior action retain the protection in a second litigation if the two actions are closely related in parties or subject matter."

- *Bruce v. Christian*, 113 F.R.D. 554, 561 (S.D.N.Y. 1986). Memoranda prepared by attorneys recommending a course of litigation or settlement to the client are protected both on privilege grounds, because they are based on interviews with employees and on work-product grounds.

The Fifth Circuit recognized that the work-product doctrine extends to subsequent litigation, but it refused to resolve whether the subsequent litigation must be closely related to the prior litigation.

- *In re Grand Jury Proceedings*, 43 F.3d 966, 971 (5th Cir. 1994). The court explicitly recognized the two approaches [protection in only related or all subsequent litigation] and refused to choose between the two on the ground that it was not necessary to do so in the particular case before it because the documents were protected under either approach. "We need not choose between these two alternative theories at this time because the documents sought to be discovered in this case satisfy both."

- *S. Scrap Material Co. v. Fleming*, 2003 U.S. Dist. LEXIS 13558, 2003 WL 21474516, at *6 (E.D. La. July 31, 2003) (Knowles, Mag. J.). The Court stated, "work product immunity extends to documents prepared in anticipation of prior, terminated litigation, regardless of the interconnectedness of the issues and facts."

- *Levingston v. Allis-Chalmers Corp.*, 109 F.R.D. 546, 552–53 (S.D. Miss. 1985). The court held that non-opinion work product retained its protection only in "related" subsequent litigation, while opinion work product was protected unless the contents were "at issue." After noting the three views, the court gave the following as a rationale for why the protection should not extend to subsequent unrelated litigation: "Where the work-product materials were prepared for a distinct and prior . . . litigation, long completed, the policies underlying the work-product privilege have already been achieved."

At least one circuit, the Third Circuit, has suggested that the doctrine should only apply to closely related subsequent litigation, although it has declined to expressly so hold.

- *In re Grand Jury Proceedings*, 604 F.2d 798, 803–04 (3d Cir. 1979). At issue was whether a corporation's attorneys had made false statements to Environmental Protection Agency officials, thereby vitiating any right both to assert attorney-client and work-product protection for certain documents. Tangentially, the Third Circuit said: "During some stages, moreover, both the civil and grand jury matters were proceeding at the same time and, therefore, a temporal connection between the civil and criminal litigation was established as well. In these circumstances, we conclude that the documents subpoenaed covering the period from July, 1975 to September, 1978 qualify for consideration of the work product privilege even though they may not have been prepared specifically in connection with the grand jury investigations. We therefore need not decide whether the work product privilege applies to all litigation, related or not."

Thus the district courts in the Third Circuit still look to the degree of relationship between the issues and facts of the present case and the prior litigation, whether real or anticipated. *Leonen v. Johns-Manville*, 135 F.R.D. 94 (D.N.J. 1990). A corporation sued with respect to asbestos-related products could not extend claim of work-product protection prior to 1966, when the first suit was initiated. The corporation had claimed awareness of fiberglass products dating as early as 1939, with the first complaint received in 1941. The court implied that was too long a reach with respect to time and subject matter. Documents prepared for related worker's compensation cases filed by three asbestos claimants, however, were protected.

- *Jaroslawicz v. Englehard Corp.*, 115 F.R.D. 515, 517 (D.N.J. 1987). "The SEC investigation and this litigation focused on the same corporate transactions and thus, are related." Moreover, the SEC investigation was an "adversary" proceeding, and thus the protection attached in the first instance. Then, because of the relatedness of subject matter, the protection carried over to the subsequent civil action between private parties.

In the patent context, a district court in the Third Circuit has established a distinction with respect to materials submitted during or prepared in anticipation of, a submission before the Board of Patent Interferences. Those materials submitted with an eye to future patent litigation are work-product protected. Those documents submitted, however, that reflect issues that have or might arise during the ex parte prosecution of the patent application itself are not protected.

- *Hercules Inc. v. Exxon Corp.*, 434 F. Supp. 136, 152 (D. Del. 1977). "If the primary concern of the attorney is with claims which would potentially arise in future litigation, the work product immunity applies; if the attorney's primary concern is claims which have arisen or will arise during the ex part prosecution of the application, however, the work product rule does not apply."

And district courts in Circuits where the Circuit Court of Appeals has not pronounced itself on the subject tend to follow suit and hold that the work product protection extends, but generally in related litigation.

- *FDIC v. Cherry, Bekaert & Holland*, 131 F.R.D. 596, 605 (M.D. Fla. 1990). "A third, intermediate, group of cases holds that subsequent or other litigation must involve closely related issues for the work product doctrine to apply. Although the Eleventh Circuit Court of Appeals has evidently not taken a position on this issue, one Middle District of Florida case has taken the intermediate approach in considering whether the work-product doctrine extends to suits other than the action for which the documents were originally created." (Citations omitted). The court thus used that standard.

- *In re Grand Jury Subpoena*, 220 F.R.D. 130, 150 (D. Mass. 2004). After an extensive and rather pointless review of all the case law on whether work-product protection extends to subsequent litigation and after detailing all the cases where it did not, the district court determined it would not be so extended in a grand jury proceeding. The review of case law helps not a whit to understand the court's rationale, on which it is markedly silent other than on what would seem vague public policy notions that one must ferret out wrongdoing. The court did not consider whether the fraud/crime exception might be applicable, although a dicta statement suggests it might. "We are dealing here, however, with a criminal grand jury investigation into documents prepared in earlier administrative proceedings. The documents prepared by the Sellers firm were not prepared in anticipation of a potential criminal litigation. Moreover, the focus of inquiry is to determine if their preparation was attended by misconduct. Under these circumstances, we believe that the Government has shown adequate grounds to acquire the documents. The criminal dimension of the instant suit makes it clear to us that the policy considerations in the Duplan Corp. case cannot be analogized to cover this situation."

Not all state courts give work-product protection in unrelated cases. New York law does not necessarily protect work-product materials from compelled disclosure in subsequent litigation.

- *Bennett v. Troy Record Co.*, 25 A.D.2d 799, 801 (N.Y. App. Div. 1966). Previous similar claims asserted against an insurance company were not work-product protected. "In our opinion, the phrase 'in preparation for litigation' refers exclusively to the instant litigation and does not grant immunity from disclosure to material prepared for prior litigation." The *ratio decidendi* of the case is far broader than necessary. Comparable holdings in other cases have gone on the decision that such documents are prepared in the ordinary course of business, irrespective of litigation.

Accordingly, federal courts hearing state claims do not do so either.

- *Doubleday v. Ruh*, 149 F.R.D 601 (E.D. Cal. 1993). A federal district court held that the district attorneys' prosecution files were discoverable in a subsequent civil action for malicious prosecution.

4. Protection After Litigation Has Terminated

It may seem self-evident, but it is nonetheless worth stating: the protection of the work product does not necessarily terminate by virtue of the termination of the litigation, even if the materials are not necessarily sought to be discovered in the context of subsequent litigation. One may well wonder when such a situation is likely to arise. It arises in the context of Freedom of Information Act requests. In that context, the claim can and has been successfully made that work-product protection continues and that such materials are not subject to disclosure, unless, that is, the work product has been incorporated in a final agency decision. Then the principle that whatever is incorporated into a final agency decision, be it in the nature of materials which would otherwise be subject to the attorney-client privilege or be they work-product protected, cease by virtue of such incorporation to be privilege or work-product protected.

- *Manna v. United States Dept. of Justice*, 815 F. Supp. 798 (D.N.J. 1993). Department of Justice legal research, trial notes, intra-agency memoranda, analyses, charts, tables, drafts of court filings, and notes prepared by Justice Department personnel are not subject to a convicted organized crime figure's FOIA request on the grounds that such documents remain work-product protected, even after termination of the prosecution of the individual filing the FOIA request.

But see:

- *Niemeier v. Watergate Special Prosecution Force*, 565 F.2d 967, 974 (7th Cir. 1977). "Where litigation is foreclosed as an option and the agency expressly chooses to make use of legal memoranda in its final decision, this choice eliminates any claim of attorney work-product privilege. . . . Under these circumstances, such documents are not the ideas and theories which go into the making of the law, they are the law itself, and as such should be made available to the public.") (Footnotes and internal quotation marks omitted.)

H. *Insurance Company Files*

A frequently litigated sub-set of cases where the question invariably comes up as to whether the investigation was conducted in anticipation of litigation or as a part of the company's on-going business is in the insurance area. In a sense one might say that since insurance companies are in the business of providing insurance and often only after fault is determined in an adjudicatory proceeding, they are virtually always conducting investigations of accidents that have occurred "in anticipation of litigation." Nonetheless, generally speaking, when an insurance company conducts an investigation as to whether it will cover a claim, the courts hold that it is engaged in its ordinary course of business and what it creates by way of documents in the process is generally not work-product protected. Once an insurance company declines coverage, then the courts consider litigation inevitable and generally accord work-product protection to what comes thereafter. Thus in this context a bright line is usually defined as a function of time. And usually the analysis—either explicit or tact—is that until the moment in time that the insurance company declines coverage, the interests of the insured and the insurer are common and not yet divergent.

On the other hand, if it is a third party to the insurance contract that seeks to obtain access to those insurance companies' investigatory files, then those are generally work-product protected.

- *Safeguard Lighting Sys. Inc. v. North Am. Specialty Ins. Co.*, 2004 U.S. Dist. LEXIS 26136 (E.D. Pa. Dec. 30, 2004). The court conflated privilege and protection but held that each protected the files of an outside law firm and of a claims adjuster hired to investigate an accident.

The situation is quite other when the request for insurance company files arises in the context of a bad faith claim brought by the insured, after a denial of coverage. In that instance, the insurance company has put its decision to deny coverage into issue and the contents of its file, at least up to the date of the denial of coverage, become crucial evidence both for the insurance company to substantiate the *bona fides* of its denial and for the insured to challenge it. In that context, an insurance company cannot shield its investigatory file from its insured by having attorneys or even outside counsel conduct the investigation. Nor can insurance companies shield any opinions received from counsel as to why the coverage was not warranted.

Courts sometimes state that more than a mere allegation of bad faith denial of coverage may be necessary to invade the work product privilege. Yet does not the insurance company inevitably put the validity of both its investigation and its legal analysis into issue whenever it declines coverage?

- *Country Life Ins. Co. v. St. Paul Surplus Lines Ins. Co.*, 2005 U.S. Dist. LEXIS 39691, at *23 (C.D. Ill. Jan. 31, 2005). Although the court suggested that something more than a mere allegation of a bad faith denial of coverage would be necessary to invade the work product privilege of the insurance company, nonetheless the court found that the insurance company could not shield its investigative file from disclosure by having outside counsel conduct the investigation or to make the coverage/no coverage determination. "To the extent that these attorneys were opining about whether the relevant facts fit within the various terms of the policy, they were doing exactly what a claims adjuster does. As noted in the case law discussed above, an insurer cannot delegate its obligation to make a coverage determination, which is after all its business, to an attorney and then claim 'work product privilege.'"

I. *False Claims Act Disclosure Statements to Government*

False Claims Act cases are pursued by a party on behalf of the United States government to recoup monies paid to private parties by the government. Section 3730 (b)(2) of the False Claims Act requires that the realtor disclose to the government the basis of the suit.

Courts that have addressed the issue of how the work product doctrine applies to disclosure statements have come to at least four different conclusions:

(1)   the disclosure statement should be produced in its entirety;

(2)   the disclosure statement is not discoverable because the whole statement is opinion work product;

(3)   the disclosure statement is not discoverable because the defendant cannot demonstrate substantial need and undue hardship; and

(4)   the disclosure statement should be produced with the opinion work product withheld.

Those courts which hold that the disclosure statement needs to be produced in its entirety to the adversary do so because these courts interpret the statutory requirement that the relator disclose to the government substantially all material evidence and information he or she possesses as indicative of the fact that the disclosure statement should contain only facts and evidence, not the mental impressions, conclusions, opinions, or legal theories of the relator's attorney. Nonetheless, in each instance, there is a suggestion that had the party resisting complete disclosure made the proper showing, by seeking *in camera* review or redaction, some relief from complete disclosure might have been accorded.

- *United States ex rel. Burns v. A.D. Roe Co.*, 904 F. Supp. 592, 594 (W.D. Ky.1995). In a motion to unseal the court file, the United States government objected only to the unsealing of the statement of material evidence. The court granted the motion to unseal, finding that in a *qui tam* action, the statement of material evidence was discoverable. The court only considered the statement as fact work product and found substantial need and no reason to protect.

- *United States ex rel. Robinson v. Northrop Corp.*, 824 F. Supp. 830 (N.D. Ill. 1993). The court required disclosure of the entirety of the disclosure statement given to the United States government. The court noted, however, that while other courts have ordered the redaction of attorneys' opinions and analysis, the plaintiffs in *Robinson* never asked the court to perform such an act. Thus by implication, had such a request been made, the court might have granted it.

- *U.S. ex rel. Stone v. Rockwell Intern. Corp.*, 144 F.R.D. 396 (D. Colo. 1992). Plaintiff was required to provide defendant with copy of confidential disclosure statement served on government in *qui tam* action.

- *Grand ex rel. U.S. v. Northrop Corp.*, 811 F. Supp. 333 (S.D. Ohio 1992). Written disclosure of substantially all material evidence and information provided to government was not protected by attorney work product or attorney-client privilege

- *United States ex rel. O'Keefe v. McDonnell Douglas Corp.*, 918 F. Supp. 1338, 1346 (E.D. Mo. 1996). The court held that the disclosure statement was discoverable because it was ordinary work product, the defendant demonstrated substantial need and undue hardship, and the relator never provided the court with the disclosure statement for an *in camera* review and thus the court could not determine if there was any opinion work product. Again, by implication, less than full disclosure may have been accorded had the litigant made the proper showing.

At the other extreme, some courts have ruled that the disclosure statement is not discoverable in any form. The rationale given is one of predictability. Making everything work-product protected encourages the preparation of statements which are more than bare minimums and which will operate to persuade the government that a valid case exists, warranting the government's intervention. At least one court held that the whole disclosure statement is opinion work product and thus protected from discovery based on such a rationale.

- *United States ex rel. Bagley v. TRW, Inc.*, 212 F.R.D. 554, 564 (C.D. Cal. 2003). The court noted that the statutory requirement that "relators disclose 'substantially all material evidence and information' does not mean that disclosure statements are 'kitchen sink' documents that indiscriminately catalogue the universe of facts known to the relator (and which therefore could not possibly reveal opinions, theories, or mental impressions)." Instead, the court found that the entire disclosure statement (excluding pre-existing documents attached as exhibits thereto) was opinion work product because the relator and his or her counsel "must engage in a process of selecting and winnowing from the totality of information known to the relator only those facts and evidence that are material to the relator's legal claims." And in so doing "encourages relators to include everything that might help the government in evaluating the case, secure in the knowledge that whatever is written will not be seen by the defendant" and thus advancing the objectives of Section 3730(b)(2). *Id.*

Still other courts do not reach a decision on whether the statement is or is not opinion work product and instead conclude that the work-product privilege is not breached because substantial need has not been established.

- *United States ex rel. Hunt v. Merck-Medco Managed Care, LLC*, 2004 U.S. Dist. LEXIS 7152, 2004 WL 868271 (E.D. Pa. Apr. 21, 2004). The court concluded that defendants could not establish substantial need and undue hardship and thus the disclosure statements were not discoverable. The court saw no need to conduct an *in camera* review.

- *United States v. Medica-Rents Co.*, 2002 U.S. Dist. LEXIS 14249, 2002 WL 1483085, at *2 (N.D. Tex. June 21, 2002). The court concluded that defendants could not establish substantial need and that the information contained in the documents could have been readily obtained through other means.

Still other courts make work for themselves by conducting *in camera* reviews and redacting out that portion of the disclosure statements which contains opinions work product.

- *United States ex rel. Cericola v. Ben Franklin Bank*, 2003 U.S. Dist. LEXIS 15451, 2003 WL 22071484, at *3 (N.D. Ill. Sept. 4, 2003). The court noted that ordinary work product is discoverable if the defendant can establish substantial need and undue hardship but opinion work product is not discoverable. Therefore, the court held that "the more prudent means of determining if the disclosure statement, in whole or in part, is discoverable is by reviewing the disputed document *in camera* to determine what materials may be discoverable as ordinary work product as followed by the majority of courts that have addressed this issue."

- *United States ex rel. King v. F.E. Moran, Inc.*, 2002 U.S. Dist. LEXIS 16277 (N.D. Ill. Aug. 29, 2001). The court ordered the relator to produce the disclosure statement to the court for an *in camera* review and redactions of work product or opinions of counsel by the court.

- *U.S. ex rel. Stone v. Rockwell Int'l Corp.*, 144 F.R.D. 396, 401–402 (D. Colo. 1992). The court found after an *in camera* review that the disclosure statement contained no opinion work product but stated it would allow plaintiff's counsel to submit what they thought constituted opinion work product and the court would consider the propriety of any suggested redactions.

- *Grand ex rel. United States v. Northrop Corp.*, 811 F. Supp. 333, 337 (S.D. Ohio 1992). The court concluded that the disclosure statement should be produced after an *in camera* review and the redaction of the opinions and analysis of the relator's counsel by the court.

J. *Mechanisms for Enhancing Likelihood That Work Protection Will Be Granted*

Are there ways of enhancing the likelihood that if discovery is sought, one can take steps to enhance the likelihood that a court will find the investigation conducted or documents prepared work-product protected because they were prepared in anticipation of litigation?

Yes. And perhaps unfortunately in our litigation prone society, the answer seems to be more rather than less writings.

Have your client enter into an engagement letter with the attorney or other agent that is to conduct the investigation.

Identify whenever possible the nature of the litigation expected, feared, anticipated with as much specificity as possible.

State that the investigation is being conducted, the reports of studies done to assist counsel in preparing for that foreseeable litigation.

Often that is in fact the case. But why try to reconstruct the motivation after the fact? Spell it out before the process begins.

Courts have themselves suggested that such mechanisms will fly and indeed may be seen as indicia of the primary motivation.

- *Pacamor Bearings, Inc. v. Minebea Co., Ltd.*, 918 F. Supp. 491, 513 (D.N.H. 1996). "When a party or the party's attorney has an agent do work for it in anticipation of litigation, one way to ensure that such work will be protected under the work-product doctrine is to provide 'clarity of purpose in the engagement letter. . . .' Otherwise stated, 'clearly the most effective way to guard against inadvertent loss of the protection offered by the work-product doctrine is to ensure that management's written authorization to proceed with the investigation identifies, as specifically as possible, the nature of the litigation that is anticipated.' An affidavit from counsel indicating that such work was done at his direction in anticipation of specified litigation will also help a party meet its burden under Rule 26(b)(3) of establishing that the work was done in anticipation of litigation." (Citations omitted).

ELEMENT 3: By or For Another Party or That Party's Representative

The central theme of the *Hickman* decision was that the essential role of the *attorney* in the adversarial process needed to be protected from intrusion by the adversary. In modern litigation, much of the attorney's role is performed by non-lawyers acting on the attorney's behalf and at the attorney's direction. In many cases, to disclose material prepared by these non-lawyers in effect discloses the attorney's thought processes; in order to encourage careful preparation by the attorney and the attorney's representatives, therefore, it is necessary to assure protection of these materials against disclosure.

In addition to work-product protection being extended to documents prepared by others for an attorney, everyone on the attorney's staff, whether they happen to be lawyers or not, may share the work-product documents without vitiating the existence of the protection.

- *Allendale Mut. Ins. Co. v. Bull Data Sys.*, 152 F.R.D. 132, 136 (N.D. Ill. 1993), *appeal dismissed*, 32 F.3d 1175 (7th Cir. 1994). Non-lawyer employees may exchange or collaborate on work product without waiving the work-product privilege, as long as the work product will eventually assist in litigation.

- *United States v. Nobles*, 422 U.S. 225, 238–39 (1975). The Court extended work-product protection to include the work product of agents for the attorney. "[T]he doctrine is an intensely practical one, grounded in the realities of litigation in our adversary system. One of those realities is that attorneys often must rely on the assistance of investigators and other agents in the compilation of materials in preparation for trial. It is therefore necessary that the doctrine protect material prepared by agents for the attorney as well as those prepared by the attorney himself."

- *Sterling Drug Inc. v. Harris*, 488 F. Supp. 1019, 1026–27 (S.D.N.Y. 1980). Documents prepared by a federal agency staff member under the supervision of attorneys preparing for litigation were held to be work product.

Once the protection is given to the work product of non-lawyers on the theory that they are assisting in the attorney's trial preparation, the practical question arises in each case whether the non-lawyer was acting as the lawyer's representative. Settling a controversy that had always divided the courts, Rule 26 was amended in 1970 to avoid that question; under the amended rule, materials prepared in anticipation of litigation by *any* representative of the client are protected, regardless of whether the representative is acting for the attorney. This change goes beyond the central rationale of *Hickman*, but it is at least consistent with a subsidiary theme of the case, protecting against one party's "free-riding" on another's trial preparations.

- *Garrett v. Metropolitan Life Ins. Co.,*. 1996 U.S. Dist. LEXIS 8054 (S.D.N.Y. June 11, 1996) (Bernikow, Mag. J.), *adopted*, 1996 U.S. Dist. LEXIS 14468 (S.D.N.Y. Oct. 2, 1996). Outside consulting firm was acting as agent of defendant's attorney when consultant's reports were generated under the direction and control of defense counsel.

- *Martin v. Bally's Park Place Hotel & Casino*, 983 F.2d 1252, 1260–62 (3d Cir. 1993). The work-product doctrine was applied to documents prepared by an environmental consultant.

- *Bituminous Cas. Corp. v. Tonka Corp.*, 140 F.R.D. 381, 387–89 (D. Minn. 1992). Work-product protection applied to the report of an environmental consultant.

- *Westhemeco Ltd. v. New Hampshire Ins. Co.*, 82 F.R.D. 702, 708 (S.D.N.Y. 1979). Work-product protection applied to documents prepared by the defendant's investigator. The court noted that it was irrelevant whether the investigator was hired by the defendant or by the defendant's attorney.

- *Spaulding v. Denton*, 68 F.R.D. 342, 345–46 (D. Del. 1975). Reports prepared by a marine surveyor investigating the sinking of a yacht were work product under the Rule 26(b)(3) provision that such materials may be prepared by non-lawyers.

Under the current version of Rule 26(b)(3), then, whether a document is protected as work product depends on the motivation behind its preparation, rather than on the person who prepared it.

- *Sprague v. Director, Office of Workers' Compensation Programs*, 688 F.2d 862, 698–70 (1st Cir. 1982). A letter from a physician to a lawyer in response to the latter's request for information to prepare for litigation was held within the privilege.

- *Eoppolo v. National R. Passenger Corp.*, 108 F.R.D. 292, 295 (E.D. Pa. 1985). Memoranda of meetings held by defendant's officials regarding plaintiff's accident were protected, even though attorneys were not present: "It is not necessary for an attorney to be involved in the proceeding to bar discovery."

- *Carver v. Allstate Ins. Co.*, 94 F.R.D. 131, 133 (S.D. Ga. 1982). The mental impressions of the defendant insurer's claims investigators were protected from discovery.

- *Fontaine v. Sunflower Beef Carrier, Inc.*, 87 F.R.D. 89, 92 (E.D. Mo. 1980). The court protected statements by defendant's driver to defendant's safety director, insurer, and investigator.

- *United States v. Chatham City Corp.*, 72 F.R.D. 640, 642–43 (S.D. Ga. 1976). Statements taken for the United States by FBI agents were held within the protection.

- *Almaguer v. Chicago, Rock Island & Pac.R. Co.*, 55 F.R.D. 147, 148–49 (D. Neb. 1972). The privilege protected statements to the defendant railroad's claim agent.

Despite the broad reach of the rule, a practical problem can occur when the materials have been gathered or prepared by non-lawyers. Unless an attorney directs the effort, a greater danger exists that the court will find the documents or other materials to have been prepared in the ordinary course of business rather than in anticipation of litigation. In that practical sense, the presence of an attorney may be particularly helpful in obtaining work-product protection for the investigatory documents that are being prepared.

- *APL Corp. v. Aetna Cas. & Sur. Co.*, 91 F.R.D. 10, 16 (D. Md. 1980). "[T]he standard to be applied in determining whether the material is protected from discovery because prepared in anticipation of litigation is the same whether the document is prepared by an attorney, or by a non-attorney, either with or without prior consultation with counsel. The fact that the non-attorney did or did not consult with counsel during the preparation of the document in question is, however, relevant, though not conclusively determinative, as to whether the document was prepared in anticipation of litigation."

A leading case has gone as far as to treat the absence of an attorney's participation as giving rise to a conclusive presumption that the investigation and report were in the ordinary course of business and not in anticipation of litigation.

- *Thomas Organ Co. v. Jadranska Slobodna Plovidba*, 54 F.R.D. 367, 372 (N.D. Ill. 1972). "[A]ny report or statement made by or to a party's agent (other than to an attorney acting in the role of counselor), which has not been requested by nor prepared for an attorney nor which otherwise reflects the employment of an attorney's legal expertise must be conclusively presumed to have been made in the ordinary course of business."

- *Scott Paper Co. v. Ceilcote Co.*, 103 F.R.D. 591, 594 (D. Me. 1984). "It is clear from the Supreme Court's articulation of the policy of the work product immunity that it is the work product of the *attorney* preparing for litigation that requires protection from discovery. . . . It is not necessary that a document be prepared by an attorney in order for the immunity to apply. *See* FED. R. CIV. P. 26(b)(3); *United States v. Nobles*, 422 U.S. 225, 238–39 (1975) (materials prepared by agents of the attorney are protected)."

- *Sterling Drug, Inc. v. Harris*, 488 F. Supp. 1019, 1026 (S.D.N.Y. 1980). Communications between federal agency staff members and communications between medical personnel were held not to be work product because they were not "prepared by or at the request of an attorney to prepare for the upcoming litigation."

That view may be justified when work-product issues are not governed by Rule 26(b)(3), for example, in criminal cases.

- *United States v. Nobles*, 422 U.S. 225, 238–39 (1975). The Court applied the work-product doctrine derived from *Hickman* in a criminal case and said, "At its core, the doctrine shelters the mental processes of the attorney," so it protects "material prepared by agents for the attorney as well as those prepared by the attorney himself."

- *In re Grand Jury Proceedings*, 658 F.2d 782, 784–85 (10th Cir. 1981). "Such mental impressions [of the attorney] are a prerequisite to the invocation of the work product doctrine."

It is, however, contrary to the expansive intent behind the 1970 amendment to Rule 26(b)(3).

- FED. R. CIV. P. 26(b)(3) Advisory Comm. Note, 48 F.R.D. 487, 502 (1970). "Subdivision (b)(3) reflects the trend of the cases by requiring a special showing, not merely as to materials prepared by an attorney, but also as to materials prepared in anticipation of litigation or preparation for trial by or for a party or *any* representative acting on *his* behalf" (emphasis added).

- *Fontaine v. Sunflower Beef Carrier, Inc.*, 87 F.R.D. 89, 92 (E.D. Mo. 1980). The *Thomas Organ Co.* decision was strongly criticized, and the Advisory Committee Note was cited.

Few issues are litigated more extensively than when and whether insurance company investigations are deemed attorney work product. The tendency seems to be to find that most accident investigations conducted by insurance companies are done not in anticipation of litigation but in the insurance company's ordinary course of business.

- *Guidry v. Jen Marine LLC*, 2003 U.S. Dist. LEXIS 15272, at *15 (E.D. La. Aug. 25, 2003), *aff'd*, 2003 U.S. Dist. LEXIS 18930 (E.D. La. Oct. 22, 2003). The testimony was that the investigation was done and witness statements were taken with an eye toward settling the matter with the insurance adjuster and that litigation was not anticipated. "The information provided to the Court does not satisfy the defendant's burden of demonstrating that the primary motivating purpose in securing the witness statements was in furtherance of a sufficiently identifiable resolve to litigate, rather than a more or less routine investigation of a possibly resolvable claim." Hence the claim of work-product protection was not sustained.

Where a document has been prepared immediately after an accident by an insurance company that is not directly a party to the litigation, a claim of work product in respect to the investigation or any witness statements is not likely to be successful.

- *Benton v. Brookfield Props. Corp.*, 2003 U.S. Dist. LEXIS 13020 (S.D.N.Y. July 29, 2003). A claim of work-product protection by insured in respect to the investigation and statement of a non-defendant insurance company did not succeed. The court also suggested that claim that no privileged or work-product-protected documents existed had absolved the defendant of a need to prepare a privilege log and that the belated claim of work-production protection might well be considered waived thereby. It is not in the least clear from the opinion why a document prepared by the insurance company would not have fallen into the express wording of Rule 26(b)(3)—namely, a document prepared "by or for another party or by or for that other party's representative (including the other party's attorney, consultant, surety, indemnitor, insurer, or agent)."

- *United Coal Cos. v. Powell Constr. Co.*, 839 F.2d 958, 966 (3d Cir. 1988). The work-product protection extended beyond materials reflecting an attorney's mental impressions to encompass materials prepared in anticipation of litigation by a party's insurer.

Another situation is posed when documents are subpoenaed from a third party. Although they may conceivably be work product of the third party, they are not work product prepared in anticipation of the current litigation. If the subpoenaed party does not resist production, the party to the litigation who attempts to resist the production on work product grounds is not likely to be successful. This is in effect a standing issue, but often the court rules on the basis of a work product analysis.

- *Ricoh Co. Ltd., v. Aeroflex Inc.*, 219 F.R.D. 66, 69 (S.D.N.Y. 2003). Third party sent defendant matters that were work product in the third party's hands. No work product protection was accorded to them. The court said: "Courts have routinely held that documents prepared by one who is not a party to the case at bar are not protected by Rule 26(b)(3), even if the non-party is itself a party to a closely related lawsuit in which he will be disadvantaged if he must disclose in the instant suit."

- *Ramsey v. NYP Holdings, Inc.*, 2002 U.S. Dist. LEXIS 11728, at *19, 22–23 (S.D.N.Y. June 27, 2002), *clarified*, 2002 U.S. Dist. LEXIS 18186 (Sept. 27, 2002). Here the plaintiffs, suspects for the murder of the unsolved murder of their daughter, sued a newspaper for alleged defamation of their infant son. The newspaper sought all the investigative files produced by the plaintiffs' lawyers in anticipation of a possible criminal defense. For purposes of this litigation, the Ramseys were merely nominal parties, suing on behalf of their son, a minor. Rule 26(b)(1) governs material prepared on behalf of a party and thus work product protection was not available to them, claimed the newspaper.

"In light of this wording, the federal courts have repeatedly held, when confronted with the issue, that a non-party witness may not invoke work-product protection under this [*19] rule to preclude production of materials prepared by or for that witness, even if created in contemplation of the witness's own pending or anticipated litigation. Thus, 'documents prepared by one who is not a party to the present suit are wholly unprotected by Rule 26(b)(3) even though the person may be a party to a closely related lawsuit in which he will be disadvantaged if he must disclose in the present suit.' 8 C. Wright, A. Miller & R. Marcus, Federal Practice & Procedure: Civil § 2024 at 354–56 (2d ed. 1994). Accord, 6 *Moore's Federal Practice* § 26.70[4] at 26-218.3." The court went on to collect all the cases so holding.

The court therefore adhered to that precedent, concluding: "If a non-party and his counsel have engaged in such preparation for their own litigation or anticipated litigation, then permitting the resultant work product to be discovered by a party in a separate lawsuit involves a somewhat comparable invasion of the attorney's work-space. Moreover, in some circumstances it could create a competitive distortion in the non-party's own litigation, since the trial preparation materials that he and his attorney created could ultimately end up in the hands of his adversary in his own lawsuit.

"Notwithstanding this concern, the potential harm from treating Rule 26(b)(3) as inapplicable to non-party witnesses is far less acute than the adverse effect of compelling disclosure of work product between adversary parties. First, disclosure from a non-party does not distort the competitive balance between a plaintiff and a defendant, since neither is reaping the benefits of the other's labors; rather, both may obtain the fruits of the labors of the non-party's litigation team. n6 Second, even if such poaching from a non-party is deemed undesirable—and the courts have recognized that the result may involve some potential for harm to the non-party—there is an alternative approach to deal with that concern."

Accordingly, the court entered a protective order limiting production to defendant's counsel lest documents not already proffered to the prosecutor by the Ramseys to avoid prosecution fall into the hands of that potential adversary.

- *Ramsey v. NYP Holdings, Inc.*, 2002 U.S. Dist. LEXIS 11728 (S.D.N.Y. June 27, 2002) (collecting cases), *clarified*, 2002 U.S. Dist. LEXIS 18186 (Sept. 27, 2002).

- *Polycast Tech. Corp. v. Uniroyal, Inc.*, 1990 U.S. Dist. LEXIS 12444 (S.D.N.Y. Sept. 20, 1990). "The work product rule has no application to a document prepared by and in the hands of a third person who is neither a party to nor interested in the action."

IV. QUALIFICATIONS ON WORK-PRODUCT PROTECTION

Work-product protection is not absolute, as is the privilege. Work product receives only a qualified protection. That is to say that even if a document is found to conform to all the definitions of work product, it may nonetheless be ordered produced, after a balancing of two factors. Under both *Hickman* and Rule 26(b)(3), disclosure of work-product materials will be ordered when the party seeking discovery has demonstrated a substantial need for the work-product material and a hardship in obtaining the needed material by alternative, less intrusive means. The quantum of need and hardship that must be demonstrated before the work-product protection will be stripped from materials sought to be produced in discovery varies according to the nature of the material sought. The greatest protection, indeed almost absolute protection, is given to an attorney's mental opinions, trial strategy, and mental impressions.

As a general principle, the names and addresses of witnesses will generally be discoverable. The content of statements they have made to an adversary generally will not be on the theory of that if an attorney is given the identity and location of witnesses, he can go do his own work without poaching on the work already done by the other attorney.

- *Boyd v. City & County of San Francisco*, 2006 U.S. Dist. LEXIS 27647 (N.D. Cal. May 1, 2006). The case involved a shooting death by police officers. Plaintiff had subpoenaed the files of the district attorney and negotiations narrowed the area of continuing dispute to whether the district attorney would produce 1) documents which revealed the identity and contact information of witnesses, including "reluctant witnesses," to the events which are the subject of the lawsuit; and 2) statements or narratives describing what those witnesses observed. The court refused to quash the subpoena on the grounds that substantial need had been shown and that the plaintiff had no alternative means of obtaining the same information.

- *Garnier v. Illinois Tool Works, Inc.*, 2006 U.S. Dist. LEXIS 28370 (E.D.N.Y May 4, 2006). "Certification" (presumably some kind of statement made to counsel) of defendant's employee were not ordered to be produced where the defendant stated a willingness to make the employee available for deposition. Magistrate judge had reviewed the certification *in camera* and determined that it was fact not opinion work product. Nonetheless, plaintiff's claim that he did not have the financial resources to take the deposition was not a showing of substantial hardship.

Thus where alternative means exist at getting the work product information sought—whether by interviews, depositions, subpoenas for the depositions or documents of third parties, generally substantial need will be found wanting.

- *Castle v. Sangamo Weston, Inc.*, 744 F.2d 1464, 1466–67 (11th Cir. 1984). The court of appeals concluded that the trial court had actually abused its discretion when it compelled production of otherwise privileged documents where party had not demonstrated that it could not obtain the information it sought by deposing witnesses whose statements were contained in the documents.

- *In re Int'l Sys. & Controls Corp. Sec. Litig.*, 693 F.2d 1235, 1241 (5th Cir. 1982). The court noted that although expense may be considered in determining undue hardship, "in the ordinary case, the cost of one or a few depositions is not enough to justify discovery of work product." (Citation omitted.)

- *Gay v. P.K. Lindsay Co.*, 666 F.2d 710, 713 (1st Cir. 1981), *cert. denied*, 456 U.S. 975 (1982). "[I]t seems well-settled that there is in general no justification for discovery of the statement of a person contained in work-product materials when the person is available to be deposed." Accordingly, plaintiff's motion to compel production of a witness's certification was denied.

- *Tribune Co. v. Purcigliotti*, 1998 U.S. Dist. LEXIS 5155, 1998 WL 175933, at *4 (S.D.N.Y. Apr. 14, 1998). "'Substantial need' cannot be shown where persons with equivalent information are available for deposition."

- *Atlantic Richfield Co. v. Current Controls*, 1997 U.S. Dist. LEXIS 13082, 1997 WL 538876, at *3 (W.D.N.Y. Aug. 21, 1997). The court noted that the party seeking facts in a privileged document may obtain those facts through other means of discovery, such as through depositions.

- *EEOC v. Carrols Corp.*, 215 F.R.D. 46, 52 (N.D.N.Y. 2003). The court concluded that substantial need was not shown where information contained in questionnaires mailed by the E.E.O.C. to defendant employer's employees could be obtained through other discovery devices.

A. *Substantial Need*

The courts usually address the question of the discovering party's "need" for the information in a conclusory fashion, or only by implication. In *Hickman*, for example, the Court said:

> Where relevant and non-privileged facts remain hidden in an attorney's file and where production of those facts is *essential* to the preparation of one's case, discovery may properly be had. Such written statements and documents might, under certain circumstances, be *admissible in evidence* or *give clues as to the existence* or location of relevant facts. Or they might be useful for purposes of *impeachment* or *corroboration*.

Hickman v. Taylor, 329 U.S. 495, 511 (1947) (emphasis added).

Nonetheless, there are certain circumstances that recur with sufficient frequency that substantial need is usually found. These circumstances generally involve situations in which the adverse party has obtained statements from witnesses who are now unavailable, either because they are deceased, have faulty memories (either brain injury, children, lapse of time), or can no longer be readily found or subpoenaed.

Thus, by implication not only must need be shown, but it is better practice to show and explain why alternative less intrusive means are not available for obtaining the sought-for work-product material. If the witnesses can readily enough be found and interviewed or deposed, generally the work-product protection will not be stripped.

1. Nature of Substantial Need Must Be Specifically Articulated

The nature of the substantial need, however, must be articulated with specificity. When it is not, then work-product protection will prevail.

- *In re Grand Jury Investigation (Sun Co.)*, 599 F.2d 1224 (3d Cir. 1979). Counsel's arguments that documents were necessary "to help prepare himself to examine witnesses, to make sure he overlooked nothing," however, was an insufficient showing of need.

- *Delco Wire & Cable, Inc. v. Weinberger*, 109 F.R.D. 680, 689–90 (E.D. Pa. 1986). The plaintiffs' assertion that they could prove their case only through information in the defendant's possession did not establish substantial need; they were required to show a need for specific documents or information at issue.

- *United States v. Chatham City Corp.*, 72 F.R.D. 640, 644 (S.D. Ga. 1976). "Defendants have shown a general, not a particularized, need for the materials they seek. The claim of necessity for the intrusion into the investigative file appears to be little more substantial than a desire to learn what kind of a case the Government has."

- *Rodgers v. United States Steel Corp.*, 22 Fed. R. Serv. 2d (CBC) 324 (W.D. Pa. 1975). In this employment discrimination case, the court said that discovery of work product to satisfy counsel's hope of finding some "'smoking gun' of culpability, some incontrovertible statement of intent to discriminate" is not permitted under the federal rules.

2. Cost Alone Does Not Constitute Substantial Need

Courts vary in the extent that they will allow a plaintiff (usually) with inadequate resources to have access to the work product of the adversary based on the concept of "substantial need."

- *Garnier v. Illinois Tool Works, Inc.*, 2006 U.S. Dist. LEXIS 28370 (E.D.N.Y May 4, 2006). Plaintiff's lack of financial resources to conduct alternative discovery did not constitute substantial need for work product.

3. Unavailable Witness

As a general rule, witness statements are obtainable by going to the source. Thus, access to witness statements gathered by counsel or at the behest of counsel are work-product protected and need not be turned over because, in the run-of-the-mill situation, no showing of special need can be made. The court's response is generally: "Do your own work. Go and interview the witness yourself or go and take the deposition of a party witness or subpoena a recalcitrant witness."

- *Marshall v. Vermont Food Indus., Inc.*, 23 Fed. R. Serv. 2d (CBC) 1511 (D. Vt. 1977). The defendant was not given access to statements gathered by the plaintiff from witnesses other than the defendant's employees when no showing of substantial need or inaccessibility to defendant's counsel was made.

- *Boyce v. Visi-Flash Rentals Eastern, Inc.*, 22 Fed. R. Serv. 2d (CBC) 1445 (D. Mass. 1976). No access to eyewitness statements was given when they were available for deposition.

But see:

- *DeGiacomo v. Morrison*, 57 Fed. R. Serv. 3d (Callaghan) 87. (D.N.H, 2003). Witness statements taken of two of the defendants by an insurance adjuster employed by their insurance companies shortly after a fatal accident were ordered turned over to plaintiff on grounds that these would be more reliable than memories years after the event if their depositions were now taken by plaintiff's counsel.

Clearly there was no "substantial need" for the witness statements since an alterative means of obtaining the information existed. The court was more concerned with veracity and therefore the integrity of the adjudicative process. It reasoned, without expressly so stating, that the defendants were probably more truthful to the claims adjuster of their insurance company than they might be years later in a deposition taken by plaintiff's counsel. The court further ordered that the statements be submitted to it with the motions for summary judgment that were to be filed.

There are situations, however, when one party has interviewed witnesses who, for a multiplicity of reasons, are no longer available to the adverse party. In such instances, the requisite need may be shown. Certain situations recur with particular frequency. Each is separately considered.

a. *Dead Witness*

It is impossible to interview a deceased witness. Thus, a showing that a witness is deceased is usually sufficient to require the production of work-product materials.

Circumstances where substantial need is found include deceased witnesses, even if protection would be accorded to interview memoranda and a questionnaire completed by still-living witnesses.

- *In re Grand Jury Investigation (Sun Co.)*, 599 F.2d 1224 (3d Cir. 1979). When a memorandum set forth the content of an interview with a deceased employee, sufficient need was shown to overcome the work-product protection. Before the government would be permitted access to an attorney's files regarding interviews with living witnesses, however, it would have to make a significant effort to secure the information directly.

- *Copperweld Steel Co. v. Demag-Mannesmann-Bohler*, 578 F.2d 953, 963 n.14 (3d Cir. 1978). The trial court acted within its discretion in ordering production of plaintiff's counsel's memorandum regarding an interview with a crucial witness whom the defendant did not have an opportunity to depose prior to the witness's death.

- *Hamilton v. Canal Barge Co.*, 395 F. Supp. 975 (E.D. La. 1974). Where the plaintiff was no longer alive to give his own account of the accident, the defendant was ordered to produce five eyewitness statements taken the day after the accident by the defendant's insurance adjuster, even though the statements were taken in anticipation of litigation.

b. Witness Beyond Court's Reach

Absence of the witness from the reach of the court's subpoena power may constitute substantial need as well.

Because a witness beyond the court's subpoena power cannot be compelled to provide information, the party seeking information from an absentee witness is usually treated as having shown inability to obtain the information.

- *Hamilton v. Canal Barge Co.*, 395 F. Supp. 975, 976–78 (E.D. La. 1974). The court ordered production of a statement given by an eyewitness on the day of the accident because the witness was in Scotland during pretrial discovery.

  Usually, a distant jurisdiction will enforce a foreign subpoena; it is just more cumbersome to have it do so. Thus, a party who wishes to strip the work-product protection will usually have to resort to an argument based on undue hardship and its attendant costs instead.

c. Witness Who Claims Privilege

A witness who claims a privilege not to testify is, in effect, unavailable, such that if the witness has essential information, the statement given in anticipation of litigation will be ordered produced.

- *Carter-Wallace, Inc. v. Hartz Mountain Indus., Inc.*, 553 F. Supp. 45, 50–51 (S.D.N.Y. 1982). Because the defendant corporation's principal executives all claimed their privilege against self-incrimination at deposition, the plaintiff was unable to obtain needed information about the case. The court ordered the corporation to disclose the factual findings of an internal investigation that was work product.

d. Witness with Faulty Memory

Substantial need has been found when a witness is brain injured.

- *State Farm Fire & Cas. Co. v. Perrigan*, 102 F.R.D. 235, 238–39 (W.D. Va. 1984). Where the plaintiff had suffered brain injuries and amnesia that prevented him from remembering the accident, he had shown substantial need for an investigative report; in any event, the court held that the report was made in the ordinary course of business.

Substantial need has been shown when a witness has suffered from amnesia.

- *McDougall v. Dunn*, 468 F.2d 468, 474 (4th Cir. 1972). When the plaintiff suffered amnesia in an accident and did not engage counsel for two years, he showed sufficient need and inability to obtain equivalent information justifying discovery of statements taken by the defendant's insurer shortly after the accident.

Substantial need has been shown when the nature of the "faulty memory" is that a key witness is a child. Contemporaneous statements obtained by an adverse party will be ordered produced because of their substantially greater reliability.

- *Chaney v. Slack*, 99 F.R.D. 531, 534 (S.D. Ga. 1983). Necessity would be shown for contemporaneous statements by child witnesses in proceedings seven months later.

Substantial need may or may not exist because of memory loss by virtue of the passage of time. The party seeking discovery in such a situation, however, had best be prepared to show that the delay was not caused by avoidable negligence in failing to proceed with dispatch.

- *United States v. Murphy Cook & Co.*, 52 F.R.D. 363, 364 (E.D. Pa. 1971). A party seeking to discover witnesses' statements taken by the opposing party immediately after an accident met the "substantial need" requirement of Rule 26(b) by showing that witnesses had forgotten details of the events in the five years that had elapsed. "The mere lapse of time is in itself enough to justify production of material otherwise protected as work product where there was no allegation that party seeking discovery had unreasonably delayed his attempts to interview these witnesses."

- *Xerox Corp. v. International Bus. Machs. Corp.*, 64 F.R.D. 367, 375, 381–82, 389 (S.D.N.Y. 1974). The defendant's attorney took notes of his interviews with twenty-three witnesses. The notes were ordered to be produced because the recollection of the witnesses was so poor that they were unable to furnish any information to the plaintiff. The court reviewed the documents and excised privileged information. "A party should not be allowed to conceal critical, non-privileged, discoverable information, which is uniquely within the knowledge of the party and which is not obtainable from any other source, simply by imparting the information to its attorney and then attempting to hide behind the work-product doctrine after the party fails to remember the information."

- *Harper & Row Publishers, Inc. v. Decker,* 423 F.2d 487, 492 (7th Cir. 1970), *aff'd by an equally divided Court,* 400 U.S. 348 (1971), *reh'g denied,* 401 U.S. 950 (1971). The Seventh Circuit let stand an order to produce an attorney's memoranda of interviews because of the failure of witnesses' memories because of lapse of time.

Occasionally, a court will order production of interview notes—even without an affirmative showing that the witness cannot recollect the facts—if sufficient time has elapsed for the court to believe that the interviews, taken at the time of the event, are bound to be more reliable than present recollection.

- *Southern R. Co. v. Lanham,* 403 F.2d 119, 127–31 (5th Cir. 1968), *reh'g denied,* 408 F.2d 348 (5th Cir. 1969). The statements of the train crew involved in a railroad accident were taken by counsel immediately after the accident. The court ordered the notes of the interviews produced because the depositions of these witnesses, taken well after the accident had occurred, would be less reliable than their immediate impression of the facts that was contained in the prior statements.

- *Hamilton v. Canal Barge Co.,* 395 F. Supp. 975, 976–78 (E.D. La. 1974). Eyewitness statements taken the day of the accident by the defendant's insurance adjuster were ordered produced.

Many courts, however, consider that the mere passage of time is not sufficient to require production when the requesting party has not shown due diligence in attempting to obtain the information directly from other sources.

- *Fidelity & Deposit Co. v. S. Stefan Strauss, Inc.*, 52 F.R.D. 536 (E.D. Pa. 1971). The plaintiff's motion for production of the statement of the defendant's former employee concerning his activities on the day of the fire in question was denied. There had been no attempt to interview or depose him until 30 months after the fire and 16 months after commencement of the suit. Nor was there reason to believe that the statement would be materially different from the deposition testimony taken.

- *Almaguer v. Chicago, Rock Island & Pac. R. Co.*, 55 F.R.D. 147, 149–50 (D. Neb. 1972). More than mere passage of time between an eyewitness's statement of the events to the defendant's claim agent and the taking of the witness's deposition were required to show need. The fact that the witness was an employee of the defendant at the time of the accident and at the time the statement was taken was not sufficient to show either a need for the statement given to the employer or an inability to get the substantial equivalent by other means—namely, taking the deposition of the eyewitness.

- *Guilford Nat'l Bank v. Southern R. Co.*, 297 F.2d 921, 927 (4th Cir. 1962). The plaintiff's interviews taken six-to-nine days after the accident would not be appreciably less reliable than those taken by the defendant the day after, such that the plaintiff's showing was insufficient.

The faulty memory of witnesses is not a sufficient predicate of "substantial need" to obtain discovery of work product.

- *Cardiac Pacemakers, Inc. v. St. Jude Med., Inc.*, 2001 U.S. Dist. LEXIS, 8322, at *6 (S.D. Ind. Apr. 26, 2001). "Defendants have deposed all four people who attended the meetings, and they have obtained non-privileged documents relating to the meetings. Defendants might be able to piece together a more complete picture of events in the meeting by piercing the privilege, but the same could be said in almost any case. That showing does not rise to the level of a substantial need."

e. Hostile Witness

A witness who is hostile may effectively deprive the discovering party of the opportunity to obtain the information needed.

- *In re Grand Jury Subpoena*, 81 F.R.D. 691, 695 (S.D.N.Y. 1979). Witnesses whose testimony was sought were "hostile" because they refused to testify without immunity, such that the disclosure of work product was properly required.

One cannot show "substantial need" or "inability to obtain the information by less intrusive means" however, only by alleging potential interest or bias of the witness; there must be some factual showing that the witness has changed his or her story or is holding back information.

- *Guilford Nat'l Bank v. Southern R. Co.*, 297 F.2d 921, 927 (4th Cir. 1962). The plaintiff could not show an inability to obtain equivalent information merely because the witnesses were the defendant's employees who would not want to fix blame for the accident on their employer.

- *Eoppolo v. National R.R. Passenger Corp.*, 108 F.R.D. 292, 295 (E.D. Pa. 1985). Although in many cases statements made at the time by the defendant and its employees may be more accurate and truthful than information sought after litigation is under way, the plaintiff must offer more than mere surmise and conjecture and must show that this is so in the particular instance in order to obtain discovery.

4. Disclosure at Trial Likely

A substantial probability that the party would have to disclose the matter at trial may constitute sufficient need for the information so that a court will order pretrial discovery of work product.

- *Wheeling-Pittsburgh Steel Corp. v. Underwriters Labs., Inc.*, 81 F.R.D. 8, 11–12 (N.D. Ill. 1978). Even if it were work product, the methodology used to calculate plaintiff's damage claim from statistical data would have to be disclosed at trial, and there is no reason to delay disclosure until then.

5. Work Product Probative of Key Issue in Litigation

At times the work product, even work product involving an attorney's mental impressions, is a key issue in the litigation. When either party expressly or tacitly puts an attorney's mental processes into issue, generally, the work-product protection will be stripped. One cannot use work product as a sword and refuse to reveal it at one and the same time. This concept is examined in greater extent under the section dealing with "waiver" and is also examined below in the discussion of when even opinion work product may be ordered produced. There is clearly a "substantial need" for the work product when it is put into issue in litigation.

It should be clear, however, that the opinions sought to be produced generally arose in contexts other than the present litigation. Thus, it is rare that a fact pattern presents itself that would make discoverable to an adversary the opinion work product and trial strategy of the other side's lawyer in the very litigation in which the opinion work product was being sought. A close approximation of such a situation, however, exists when a claim is made that an insurance company has acted in bad faith in refusing to settle a claim against its tortfeasor insured. Virtually the entirety of the claims file, including any attorney's mental impressions thereby becomes discoverable and the only protection against discovery left in such an instance is that which is encompassed under the privilege.

- *Reavis v. Metropolitan Prop. & Liab. Ins. Co.*, 117 F.R.D. 160, 164 (S.D. Cal. 1987). The entirety of the claims review file became discoverable at the instance of an injured plaintiff in a suit alleging a bad faith refusal by the insurance company to settle the claim against its insured.

For example, when the action or knowledge of an attorney, other than trial counsel in the litigation at issue, may be dispositive of the case, pretrial discovery of the attorney's work product is often ordered. When, for instance, an investigation was conducted by an attorney and a party defends on the ground that it conducted a reasonable investigation of a claim for sexual harassment, a substantial need has been adequately demonstrated to require the production of the attorney's notes and memoranda regarding the investigation that, but for that defense, would remain protected from compelled disclosure.

- *Peterson v. Wallace Computer Servs.*, 984 F. Supp. 821, 826 (D. Vt. 1997). A magistrate's ruling protecting investigative notes and memoranda of an attorney were ordered produced when the party defended on grounds of adequacy of investigation.

- *Bird v. Penn Cent. Co.*, 61 F.R.D. 43, 46–47 (E.D. Pa. 1973). In an action to rescind an insurance policy to which the defendant interposed a laches defense, the plaintiffs' knowledge of the grounds for the action is a central issue, creating a substantial need for discovery in the files of the attorney who acted as the plaintiffs' investigator.

- *Kockums Indus., Ltd. v. Salem Equip., Inc.*, 561 F. Supp. 168, 172–73 (D. Or. 1983). When the defendant's ability to succeed on its counterclaim depended on a showing that the plaintiff had pursued its suit knowing it would be unsuccessful on the merits and the opinions of the plaintiff's attorneys regarding the merits of the plaintiff's action were directly at issue, the defendant showed a specific and compelling need for the documents. Because the documents involved were opinion work product, however, the defendant was also required to show "extraordinary circumstances." The defendant satisfied this requirement by making a prima facie showing of unfair competition.

- *Byers v. Burleson*, 100 F.R.D. 436, 439 (D.D.C. 1983). When the plaintiff sued her former attorney for legal malpractice and the issue was whether the plaintiff's suit was barred by the statute of limitations, the documents would reveal exactly when the plaintiff anticipated litigation against the defendant and, thus, when the statute of limitations began to run. Because the plaintiff could not obtain the information in any other way, the attorney was ordered to produce the records.

- *Panter v. Marshall Field & Co.*, 80 F.R.D. 718, 725–26 (N.D. Ill. 1978). The defendants' reliance on counsel's advice as a justification for their challenged actions created a "compelling need" for disclosure and overcame the work-product privilege.

- *Handgards, Inc. v. Johnson & Johnson*, 413 F. Supp. 926, 931 (N.D. Cal. 1976), *remanded on other grounds*, 601 F.2d 986 (9th Cir. 1979), *cert. denied*, 444 U.S. 1025 (1980). The principal issue in the case was "the good faith of defendants in instituting and maintaining a prior patent litigation against plaintiff." The attorneys who managed and supervised the former litigation for the defendants were called as witnesses to express their opinions of the merits of the prior suits. The court concluded that the attorneys' work product was discoverable because such information was directly at issue and the need for production was, therefore, compelling.

- *Truck Ins. Exch. v. St. Paul Fire & Marine Ins. Co.*, 66 F.R.D. 129, 133–36 (E.D. Pa. 1975). Work-product protection will not be accorded when the activities of counsel in the underlying lawsuit are the basis of a defense in the second lawsuit.

- *American Standard, Inc. v. Bendix Corp.*, 80 F.R.D. 706, 709 (W.D. Mo. 1978). When the plaintiff claims that it discovered fraud through its attorney, the attorney becomes the most important witness on when the fraud was discovered and whether the statute of limitations bars the claim. Therefore, the attorney's work product is discoverable.

6. Possible Rebuttal and Possible Impeachment

A distinction has sometimes been drawn between information a party needs to make its case in chief and information that might be used to cross-examine an opponent's witness.

- *Breedlove v. Beech Aircraft Corp.*, 57 F.R.D. 202, 205 (N.D. Miss. 1972). "Plaintiffs have made no showing whatsoever that they need the materials to prepare their case; . . . [they] assert that they need the reports to cross-examine [defendant's] experts whom the defendant may put upon the stand, but there is no assertion that the plaintiffs need the materials to make out their own case in chief."

Sufficient need is not shown by the mere possibility that the documents could assist in the examination or impeachment of witnesses.

- *Stephens Produce Co. v. NLRB*, 515 F.2d 1373, 1376–77 (8th Cir. 1975). There was no justification for ordering disclosure of an investigator's notes of statements when there was no inconsistency between written statements given the investigator and the witness's testimony.

- *Gay v. P.K. Lindsay Co.*, 666 F.2d 710 (1st Cir. 1981), *cert. denied*, 456 U.S. 975 (1982). No need was shown for a work-product statement when the witnesses said the same thing in their depositions and the depositions could be, and were, used to impeach them at trial.

- *In re Grand Jury Investigation (Sun. Co.)*, 599 F.2d 1224, 1233 (3d Cir. 1979). "We do not believe . . . that the desire to impeach or corroborate a witness' testimony, by itself, would ever overcome the protection given" an attorney's memorandum of a witness's statement.

- *Brock v. Frank v. Panzarino, Inc.*, 109 F.R.D. 157, 159 (E.D.N.Y. 1986). Even when the defendant would be entitled to the witness's statements for impeachment purposes at trial in a labor case, "the possibility of locating impeachment material in a potential witness' prior statement does not amount to substantial need."

When, however, there are indications beyond mere surmise that impeaching material will be found in the work product, the requisite need may be shown.

- *Augenti v. Cappellini*, 84 F.R.D. 73, 80 (M.D. Pa. 1979). Indications in depositions that allegations in the complaint were inconsistent with the party's prior statements constituted the need for the work product.

- *Tinder v. McGowan*, 15 Fed. R. Serv. 2d (CBC) 1608 (W.D. Pa. 1970). The defendant's statements to a claims adjuster were not ordered produced when the defendant was deposed and had answered interrogatories on the mere suppositions that contradictions might occur in the prior statements.

Of course, it may be necessary for the court to make an *in camera* inspection to determine if the work product contains material for which a substantial need has been shown.

- *Kennedy v. Senyo*, 52 F.R.D. 34, 37 (W.D. Pa. 1971). The court ordered an *in camera* inspection of the insurer's file to determine whether it contained materials bearing on an alleged misrepresentation regarding the limitations period.

7. Most Reliable Available Information

Some courts will grant access to eyewitness or even defendant statements taken soon after an accident, for instance, even if those witnesses are available for deposition, on the tacit grounds that such statements, made closer to the time of the accident and to an individual acting as an insurance adjuster for their insurance company, are more likely to be more reliable than depositions taken by an adverse attorney long after the fact.

- *DeGiacomo v. Morrison*, 57 Fed. R. Serv. 3d (Callaghan) 87 (D.N.H. 2003). Witness statements of two defendants given to the claims adjustor of their insurance companies were ordered produced as more reliable.

When the sole source of the necessary information is in the possession and control of the adverse party, it will be assumed that no available alternative means exist and the party seeking production will not necessarily have to embark on much costlier, and more cumbersome deposition discovery, interrogatories, and document requests.

- *In re Sunrise Sec. Litig.*, 130 F.R.D. 560, 569, 1989 U.S. Dist. LEXIS 6288 (E.D. Pa. 1989). A party does not necessarily have to show that no alternative means of obtaining the information exists as long as the "information is within the exclusive control of the party from whom discovery is sought, regardless of whether the information might also be obtained from that party through depositions, interrogatories or document production."

8. Substantial Need Not Shown

When an alternative source of information or rebuttal testimony exists, substantial need is generally not shown.

- *Baker v. General Motors Corp.*, 209 F.3d 1051, 1056 (8th Cir. 2000), *reh'g denied*, 2000 U.S. App. LEXIS 11721 (8th Cir. May 24, 2000). When an alternative witness exists to rebut the testimony, substantial need has not been shown. Dissents to appellate opinions dealing with privilege issues are rare. Here there was one, with the dissenting judge urging that "[t]he district court correctly held that this is an abuse of evidentiary privilege because it permits a party to adhere to what appears to be an unequivocal position when contradictory evidence is available but inadmissible. I find fault with the majority's legal reasoning and with the policy implications of its opinion." The dissenting judge argued that by disavowing a harmful memorandum as having been authorized or used by the corporation, GM placed into issue any investigation its attorneys conducted on the issue. The dissent goes too far. If the dissenting judge's position was an accurate reading of attorney-client privilege law or attorney opinion work product, any time a client makes any contention, the attorney's files would become discoverable in the hope of finding rebuttal evidence for the client's contention. Evidence that is merely corporative of other evidence already in the possession of, or readily available to, a party generally does not meet the standards of "substantial need."

- *Director, Office of Thrift Supervision v. Vinson & Elkins, LLP*, 124 F.3d 1304, 1308 (D.C. Cir. 1997). Substantial need was not shown when documents sought would merely reinforce known inconsistencies.

- *A.I.A. Holdings, S.A. v. Lehman Brothers, Inc.*, 2002 U.S. Dist. LEXIS 20107, at *16 (S.D.N.Y. Oct. 21, 2002). The claim was that work-product documents were not otherwise available because originals had burned. The court did not accept the argument, concluding that the underlying information sought was available in other forms. In addition, the court refused to make available a work-product tape, finding that the key witness had been deposed and admitted sufficient impeachment information.

B. *Unable to Obtain Substantial Equivalent by Other Means Without Undue Hardship*

1. No Readily Available Alternative Means

So too, courts, at least tacitly, tend to require an explanation of why or how alternative sources for obtaining the equivalent information do not exist before the work-product protection will be lifted.

- *In re Grand Jury Subpoena Dated Nov. 8, 1979*, 622 F.2d 933, 935 (6th Cir. 1980). When a party does not make any showing that other witnesses were unknown to it or unavailable to testify, it is merely "on a general fishing expedition" into the attorney's files "to satisfy itself that nothing has been overlooked." The work-product protection forbids such excursions.

- *Reavis v. Metropolitan Prop. & Liab. Ins. Co.*, 117 F.R.D. 160 (S.D. Cal. 1987). In a lawsuit by an injured party against the insurance company of the insured tortfeasor, alleging a bad faith failure to settle the claim, the court found that even if the claims adjuster was available for deposition, that is not the substantial equivalent of the claims file to prove the underlying claim.

- *APL Corp. v. Aetna Cas. & Sur. Co.*, 91 F.R.D. 10, 14 (D. Md. 1980). A claim that an insurance company wrongfully denied the full amount of the claim will make the claims file discoverable. "While plaintiffs could conduct their own interviews of the people in question, and might learn what they have previously stated to Aetna, it is not unlikely that the documents from Aetna's files reflecting investigation of plaintiffs' claim will themselves be capable of establishing in the most effective way what information Aetna had available when Aetna decided to deny plaintiffs' claim." The court concluded that the file constituted importance evidence, both of Aetna's diligence in its investigation and good faith in denying the claim.

The tacit need to show that no readily available alternative means exist is sometimes subsumed into a showing of substantial need. Better practice would suggest that the issue should be dealt with, whenever possible, as a separate component of the requisite showing if work product materials are sought. The "inability" factor was suggested in

- *Hickman v. Taylor*, 329 U.S. 495, at 511–12 (1947). "[P]roduction might be justified where the witnesses are *no longer available or can be reached only with difficulty*. Were production of written statements and documents to be precluded under such circumstances, the liberal ideals of the deposition-discovery portions of the Federal Rules of Civil Procedure would be stripped of much of their meaning." (Emphasis added.)

- *Valve Corp. v. Sierra Entm't Inc.*, 2004 U.S. Dist. LEXIS 29618 (W.D. Wa. Dec. 6, 2004). Where plaintiff demonstrated that it had sought revenue information by interrogatories and in depositions and was unable to obtain it, court allowed production of work product materials instead. The documents which dealt with ongoing internal discussions among defendant's executives concerning distribution of plaintiff's products and the business impact in giving up some distribution rights. The court found the documents.

When discovery of witness statements is sought, a key consideration is whether the party seeking discovery can interview the witnesses himself or herself. 4 MOORE'S FEDERAL PRACTICE 26.64[3], at 362–69 & n.8 (2d ed. 1984).

- *In re Grand Jury Investigation (Sun Co.)*, 599 F.2d 1224, 1232 (3d Cir. 1979). Interview notes of a deceased witness can be obtained. Those of living ones may not because they are subject to subpoena power. Even with respect to a nonresident alien, "the government should make a reasonable effort to secure his testimony before attempting to invade an attorney's files."

- *In re Federal Copper of Tennessee, Inc.*, 19 B.R. 177, 182–83 (Bankr. M.D. Tenn. 1982). An accountant and an attorney did not have to turn over interview notes to the trustee because the trustee could interview these potential witnesses just as the accountant had interviewed them. However, the names of the witnesses did have to be disclosed.

- *United States v. Chatham City Corp.*, 72 F.R.D. 640, 643–44 (S.D. Ga. 1976). A substantial equivalent of the witness's statements can be obtained by personal interview, by deposition, or by written deposition.

- *Gilhuly v. Johns-Manville Corp.*, 100 F.R.D. 752, 755–56 (D. Conn. 1983). The defendants could not compel the plaintiff to answer questions about meetings with coworkers where asbestos exposure was discussed. Because the discussions related to the case, they were work product, and the defendants could obtain the same information by questioning the coworkers.

- *Boyce v. Visi-Flash Rentals E., Inc.*, 22 Fed. R. Serv. 2d (CBC) 1445, 1446 (D. Mass. 1976). Statements taken by the plaintiff's attorney from eyewitnesses to a fatal accident were not discoverable. "A party seeking documents that allegedly are subject to the work-product doctrine has a heavy burden of establishing they are essential for the preparation of its case. . . . [W]ork-product material will be denied if the party seeking discovery can obtain its equivalent by other means [such as] taking the depositions of witnesses."

- *Miles v. Bell Helicopter Co.*, 385 F. Supp. 1029, 1032 (N.D. Ga. 1974). Immediately after the crash of a helicopter in which the plaintiff's husband died, employees of the defendants prepared reports that consisted largely of experts' findings on the cause of the crash and the condition of the helicopter. The plaintiff made no showing that she could not obtain the substantial equivalent of these reports by taking the depositions of the employees who prepared them.

- *Dingler v. Halcyon Lijn N.V.*, 50 F.R.D. 211, 212 (E.D. Pa. 1970). The plaintiff's motion to produce a statement made by a longshoreman to an agent of the defendants' counsel was denied. Because there was no showing that the longshoreman was unavailable for deposition, the plaintiff had not established that he was unable to obtain the information without undue hardship by means other than the work product.

The principle of available alternative means is not restricted to the situation where witness statements by the adverse party are sought. A comparable principle applies to any documents prepared by the adverse party, which might be helpful to or short-circuit discovery and preparation for the adversary. If available alternative means exist for obtaining the information, in all likelihood the work product will not be ordered produced.

- *In re Dayco Corp. Derivative Sec. Litig.*, 99 F.R.D. 616, 620 (S.D. Ohio 1983). The plaintiffs were not permitted to discover a special report submitted to a board of directors because alternative means of discovering the information existed. They had possession of the documents that formed the predicate of the report and depositions of the company's employees could be taken. Thus, the court was not impressed with the cost argument that depositions would cost $5,000 each, given the magnitude of the class claims asserted in the litigation. Nor was the court convinced by the argument that a deponent might assert a Fifth Amendment privilege.

Sometimes the discovering party has access to equivalent information in other proceedings.

- *Sprague v. Director, Office of Workers' Compensation Programs*, 688 F.2d 862, 870 (1st Cir. 1982). After an *in camera* inspection of a letter from a doctor that was work product, the court decided that it contained no significant information that did not already come out in testimony before the administrative law judge, nor did it contain anything to effectively impeach the doctor's testimony before the judge; thus, the plaintiff had the "substantial equivalent" of the letter in the testimony.

- *Eoppolo v. National R. Passenger Corp.*, 108 F.R.D. 292, 295 (E.D. Pa. 1985). The plaintiff could not obtain statements of the defendant's witnesses taken in anticipation of litigation immediately after an accident unless the plaintiff showed an inability to obtain the information by first deposing the defendant's witnesses and finding them unable to recollect the events.

2. Cost as a Factor of Undue Hardship

The concept of "undue hardship" generally devolves into an issue of how much it will cost to obtain comparable information by other less intrusive means. Nonetheless, the additional cost of obtaining the information by means other than the production of the documents at issue is not in itself a sufficient showing of undue hardship in obtaining discovery of work-product materials.

- *In re LTV Sec. Litig.*, 89 F.R.D. 595, 616 (N.D. Tex. 1981). But when there is a significant extra cost entailed in obtaining substantially equivalent information, the courts will weigh the relative resources of the parties.

- *Jarvis, Inc. v. AT & T*, 84 F.R.D. 286, 293 (D. Colo. 1979). When a plaintiff would have to depose 1,500 witnesses to obtain information equivalent to the material he sought to discover, "undue hardship" was shown.

- *Allen v. Denver-Chicago Trucking Co.*, 32 F.R.D. 616, 618 (W.D. Mo. 1963). Good cause was shown for producing in Missouri a statement by a California resident who could be "reached only with difficulty and unnecessary expense."

But litigants should nonetheless be aware that however little sense it may make to require each party to undergo their own costly discovery rather than make them share in the costs of discovery already done, by one party by and large, costs alone do not necessarily a case for undue hardship make any more than they make a case for substantial need.

- *Pine Top Ins. Co. v. Alexander & Alexander Servs., Inc.*, 1991 U.S. Dist. LEXIS 14610, 1991 WL 221061, at *2 (S.D.N.Y. Oct. 1, 1991). "The undue hardship test is generally not satisfied merely by the expense of obtaining the materials."

Potential duplication of cost and effort is implicit in every application of the work-product rule. And it is rare that cost alone will be a basis for invading work-product protection unless the additional cost is truly prohibitive. Or so a long line of earlier cases suggested. A question arises regarding whether, in today's litigation climate with increased sensitivity to the costs of litigation, such a cavalier attitude toward duplicative costs will persist. There are hints in the decided cases that such an attitude will soften.

- *Connelly v. Dunn & Bradstreet, Inc.*, 96 F.R.D. 339, 343 (D. Mass. 1982). To defeat the qualified work-product protection, a party must show that the substantial equivalent is not available through other means, such as when a witness is unavailable or when contemporaneous statements were made that cannot be reproduced. Mere inconvenience or expense will not defeat the effect of the doctrine.

- *Marshall v. Vermont Food Indus., Inc.*, 23 Fed. R. Serv. 2d (CBC) 1511 (D. Vt. 1977). The defendant was not given access to statements gathered by the plaintiff from witnesses other than the defendant's employees, absent a showing of substantial need or inaccessibility to defendant's counsel.

- *Boyce v. Visi-Flash Rentals Eastern, Inc.*, 22 Fed. R. Serv. 2d (CBC) 1445 (D. Mass. 1976). No access to eyewitness statements was given when they were available for deposition.

- *United States v. Chatham City Corp.*, 72 F.R.D. 640, 644 (S.D. Ga. 1976). "The cost or inconvenience of taking depositions 'is not in itself' sufficient to meet the 'undue hardship' requirements of the rule."

- *Arvey v. Geo. A. Hormel & Co.*, 53 F.R.D. 179, 181 (D. Minn. 1971). The court denied production of various letters and documents transmitted between executives of the defendant and its law firm and legal opinions or memoranda from one attorney of the firm to another. The information the plaintiff sought could be obtained by other discovery methods, and the "costs or inconvenience" of doing so was "not in itself a sufficient showing to meet the 'undue hardship' requirements."

In today's litigation environment with its far greater awareness of litigation costs, presumably a claim of undue or duplicative cost will have greater impact than it would have in the past. Therefore, counsel seeking work-product protected documents would be well advised to consider such an assertion in seeking work product that is easily enough obtainable through traditional, but more costly, discovery.

C. *Balancing Need for Information Against Work-Product Protection Policies*

Application of the work-product doctrine requires a weighing of the respective parties' interests. The court must determine if the need of one party for the information outweighs the interest of the other party in protecting its work product from disclosure. If an adverse party can make a sufficient showing of need for the information and inability to obtain the material from other sources without undue hardship, disclosure of work-product protected material will be ordered. Whether the party seeking discovery has shown the requisite need will depend on available alternative sources of the needed information, the relative resources of the parties, and the need to protect an expectation that confidentiality would be preserved.

- *In re Grand Jury Subpoena Dated Nov. 8, 1979*, 622 F.2d 933, 935 (6th Cir. 1980). The court set out the following six factors that should be evaluated when a movant asserts that it has shown "good cause" for disclosure:

  (1) the nature of the information sought;

  (2) the extent to which the information would reveal the attorney's mental processes;

  (3) the likely reliability of the information;

  (4) the degree of danger that the attorney-client relationship would be disrupted;

  (5) the availability of other sources for the information; and

  (6) whether the letter or spirit of the Fifth and Sixth Amendments would be infringed.

The court concluded that when a party does not make any showing that other witnesses were unknown to it or unavailable to testify, it is merely "on a general fishing expedition" into the attorney's files "to satisfy itself that nothing ha[d] been overlooked." The work-product privilege forbids such excursions.

- *United States v. Amerada Hess Corp.*, 619 F.2d 980 (3d Cir. 1980). When the work product has minimal substantive content and presents none of the dangers that the rule is designed to avoid, the federal government's need to avoid time and effort in obtaining the information elsewhere was sufficient to defeat the effects of the doctrine precluding disclosure.

- *Stout v. Norfolk & W. R. Co.*, 90 F.R.D. 160, 161 (S.D. Ohio 1981). Contemporaneous statements by witnesses to an accident are unique and cannot be duplicated so "there is always a showing of undue hardship."

But when a document as to which work-product protection is claimed is a good evidentiary source for proving issues in dispute, it will be ordered produced.

- *Klein v. FPL Group, Inc.*, 2003 U.S. Dist. LEXIS 19979, 2003 WL 22768424 (S.D. Fla. Sept. 26, 2003). Witness notes ordered produced to allow a determination of whether the outside directors who made the decision to terminate the lawsuit were independent, acted in good faith, and reached their decision after conducting a reasonable investigation.

V. PROTECTING ATTORNEY'S MENTAL IMPRESSIONS

A. *Rule Implies Absolute Protection Is to Be Accorded*

Rule 26(b)(3) states that a court shall protect against disclosure of the mental impressions, conclusions, opinions, or legal theories of an attorney when discovery is ordered. This material is generally referred to as "opinion work product," as distinguished from ordinary work product. Materials that are merely gathered by or compiled at the request of an attorney in anticipation of litigation are referred to as "ordinary work product."

The language of the rule seems absolute and indeed courts do bend over backwards to protect an attorney's mental impressions in virtually all situations.

Though Rule 26(b)(3) seems to give absolute protection for the mental impressions and opinions of an attorney, in fact the Supreme Court a half a century ago, in 1946, rejected a proposed amendment to Rule 30(b) that would have given opinion work product an absolute protection. *See* Report of Proposed Amendments to Rules of Civil Procedure, 5 F.R.D. 433, 456–57 (1946); Order dated December 27, 1946, 329 U.S. 843 (1946) (omitted any reference to the proposal in the enumeration of the adopted rules).

The greater protection given opinion work product in Rule 26(b)(3) follows from the concern expressed in *Hickman* to protect the special role of the attorney in the adversary process.

- *Hickman v. Taylor*, 329 U.S. 495, 510–13 (1947). "Were [an attorney's 'statements, memoranda, correspondence, briefs, mental impressions, personal beliefs'] open to opposing counsel on mere demand, much of what is now put down in writing would remain unwritten. An attorney's thoughts, heretofore inviolate, would not be his own. Inefficiency, unfairness and sharp practices would inevitably develop in the giving of legal advice and in the preparation of cases for trial." The Court said that although discovery might be had of written statements and documents containing relevant and nonprivileged facts essential to the preparation of one's case, "[u]nder ordinary conditions, forcing an attorney to repeat or write out all that witnesses have told him and to deliver an account to his adversary gives rise to grave dangers of inaccuracy and untrustworthiness."

- FED. R. CIV. P. 26(b)(3) Advisory Committee Note, 48 F.R.D. 487, 502 (1970). "The *Hickman* opinion drew special attention to the need for protecting an attorney against discovery of memoranda prepared from recollection of oral interviews. The courts have steadfastly safeguarded against disclosure of lawyers' mental impressions and legal theories, as well as mental impressions and subjective evaluations of investigators and claim-agents."

Thus, a mere showing of need and an inability to obtain the work product by other means is not sufficient to pierce the protection accorded to opinion work product.

The Supreme Court in *Upjohn* explicitly declined to rule on the question of whether opinion work product, like materials protected by the attorney-client privilege, should be absolutely immune from discovery. It did, however, indicate that a higher standard of need would be applied to discovery of opinion work product than to discovery of ordinary work product.

- *Upjohn Co. v. United States*, 449 U.S. 383, 400–402 (1981). The work product at issue consisted of attorney's notes and memoranda incorporating oral statements of witnesses that went beyond the mere recordation of the witness's responses. "While we are not prepared at this juncture to say that such material is always protected by the work-product rule, we think a far stronger showing of necessity and unavailability by other means than was made by the Government or applied by the magistrate in this case would be necessary to compel disclosure." To show "substantial need" and "undue hardship," the government had shown that the interviewees were scattered across the globe and that Upjohn had forbidden its employees to answer "irrelevant" questions. The Court remanded the case to the court of appeals to reconsider what showing the IRS could make to support its request for the documents.

Although all the circuits will protect "core" or opinion work product more zealously than they protect "mere" fact work product, the extent of the protection, or at least the way courts speak about it and therefore presumably act upon their words, varies from one circuit to another.

The Fourth Circuit and the Eighth Circuit are among the courts that have held that protection for opinion work product is absolute.

- *Duplan Corp. v. Moulinage et Retorderie de Chavanoz*, 509 F.2d 730, 733–34 (4th Cir. 1974), *cert. denied*, 420 U.S. 997 (1975). "[N]o showing of relevance, substantial need or undue hardship should justify compelled disclosure of an attorney's mental impressions, conclusions, opinions or legal theories. This is made clear by the Rule's use of the term 'shall' as opposed to 'may.'" The court reasoned that the modifying clause in Rule 26(b)(3) operates as an absolute, and not a qualified, limitation on the production of such materials.

Thereafter the Fourth Circuit has stepped back from its categorical formulation that opinion work product is never discoverable. It too has recognized the theoretical possibility that opinion work product might, in the proper situation, be discoverable without as yet having held it to be in any specific situation.

- *In re Martin Marietta Corp.*, 856 F.2d 619, 626 (4th Cir. 1988), *cert. denied*, 490 U.S. 1011 (1989). "We think *generally* such opinion work product is not subject to discovery."

So too has the Eighth Circuit which began with a more categorical stand from which it backed off slightly.

- *In re Grand Jury Proceedings*, 473 F.2d 840, 848 (8th Cir. 1973). Opinion work product is "absolutely, rather than conditionally, privileged."

- *In re Murphy*, 560 F.2d 326, 336 (8th Cir. 1977). "In our view, opinion work product enjoys a nearly absolute immunity and can be discovered only in very rare and extraordinary circumstances."

So has the occasional district court in the First Circuit which if unwilling to pronounce itself for absolute core work-product protection has come close to it.

- *In re Grand Jury Subpoena*, 220 F.R.D. 130 (D. Mass. 2004). "Regardless of what the proper rule may be in the civil discovery context, the appropriate standard in grand jury proceedings is that opinion work product protection can only be overridden in 'rare circumstances,' upon 'a highly persuasive showing.' In other words, protection for opinion work product should be "nearly absolute." Affording absolute protection would improperly limit courts' power to supervise the truth-seeking process in cases that involve both the compelling public interest in the prosecution of criminals and a criminal suspect's fundamental right to due process."

But see:

- *Ferrara & DiMercurio, Inc. v. St. Paul Mercury Ins. Co.*, 173 F.R.D. 7, 13 & n.8 (D. Mass. 1997) (Bowler, Mag. J.) (*citing Micron Separations, Inc. v. Pall Corp.*, 159 F.R.D. 361, 364 (D. Mass. 1995) (Collings, Mag. J.)). The court stated that opinion work product "is not absolutely immune from discovery."

Most courts have accorded core work product a heightened, protection even when they have not been willing to give it absolute protection.

- *United States v. Adlman*, 134 F.3d 1194, 1204 (2d Cir. 1998). The court said that "at a minimum, . . . a highly persuasive showing" is needed to overcome protection for opinion work product.

- *Director, Office of Thrift Supervision v. Vinson & Elkins, LLP*, 124 F.3d 1304, 1307 (D.C. Cir. 1997). "Opinion work product . . . is virtually undiscoverable."

- *Holmgren v. State Farm Mut. Auto Ins. Co.*, 976 F.2d 573, 577 (9th Cir.), *aff'd, remanded on other grounds*, 1992 U.S. App. LEXIS 29008 (9th Cir. Nov. 9, 1992). The court stated that opinion work product "may be discovered and admitted when mental impressions are at issue in a case" and the need for the material is "compelling."

- *In re Grand Jury Investigation*, 599 F.2d 1224, 1231 (3d Cir. 1979). The court suggested that interview memoranda "will be discoverable only in a 'rare situation.'"

- *Harper & Row Publishers, Inc. v. Decker*, 423 F.2d 487, 492 (7th Cir. 1970), *aff'd by an equally divided Supreme Court*, 400 U.S. 348 (1971), *reh'g denied*, 401 U.S. 950 (1971). ("Of course, the less the lawyer's 'mental processes' are involved, the less will be the burden to show good cause.").

It seems fairly clear, therefore, that protection of opinion work product is not absolute, but that consideration is given to such factors as the extent to which the attorney's mental processes are involved, the inhibiting effect that disclosure would have, and the extent to which the discovering party is seeking a free ride on the attorney's thinking.

The types of attorney opinion work product that are accorded absolute or nearly absolute protection are assessments of the merits of the claims and defenses asserted, assessments of the credibility and usefulness of witnesses, proposed settlement options and possible settlement amounts.

- *Willingham v. Ashcroft*, 2005 U.S. Dist. LEXIS 22258, at *10-12 (D.D.C. Oct. 4, 2005). "[T]he documents that were prepared in anticipation of litigation clearly reflect the DEA's or its attorneys' mental processes because they contain counsel's analysis of the merits of the agency's imposition of indefinite suspension, their assessment of the importance of the case from an agency-wide point of view, or their thoughts regarding possible settlement. Thus, these materials constitute opinion work product because they reflect the DEA's or the attorneys' "mental impressions, conclusions, opinions, or legal theories," and they are entitled to almost absolute protection." *See* Fed. R. Civ. P. 26(b)(3). Therefore, in order to justify the production of these documents, plaintiff would have to make a stronger showing of need than is normally required of ordinary work product. *See Byers*, 100 F.R.D. at 439. After reviewing the documents, I am confident that plaintiff can make no showing that would be strong enough to justify the release of the DEA attorneys' pure legal analysis of this case, and these documents need not be produced. Indeed, she has made no such showing in Plaintiff's Second Motion to Compel the Production of Documents. To rule otherwise and order production of the documents would violate a cornerstone of our adversarial system: the ability of an attorney to prepare his case "with a certain degree of privacy, free from unnecessary intrusion by opposing parties and their counsel." *See Hickman*, 329 U.S. at 510–11. Accordingly, defendant need not produce these materials.

- *In re Allen*, 106 F.3d 582, 608 (4th Cir.), *reh'g denied*, 119 F.3d 1129 (4th Cir. 1997), *cert. denied*, 522 U.S. 1047 (1998). The selection and ordering of documents by an attorney constitutes opinion work product because it reveals the attorney's "thought processes and theories regarding the litigation."

- *Petersen v. Douglas County Bank & Trust Co.*, 967 F.2d 1186, 1189 (8th Cir. 1992). The district court held a nonparty in civil contempt of court for failing to produce certain documents with respect to which a claim of work-product protection had been made. The court of appeals affirmed, except to the extent the order required production of documents that were selected and compiled by the third party in anticipation of litigation.

- *Shelton v. American Motors Corp.*, 805 F.2d 1323, 1329 (8th Cir. 1986), *reh'g denied*, 1987 U.S. App. LEXIS 2002 (8th Cir. Jan. 30, 1987). The court of appeals reversed the trial court's grant of a default judgment based on an attorney's repeated refusal to answer deposition questions on privilege and work-product grounds. The court held that an adversary is precluded from forcing an attorney to identify documents relied on by the client to develop its legal theories of the case. "The issue on appeal is whether a deponent's mere acknowledgment of the existence of corporate documents is protected by the work-product doctrine or the attorney-client privilege. We hold that where, as here, the deponent is opposing counsel and has engaged in a selective process of compiling documents from among voluminous files in preparation for litigation, the mere acknowledgment of the existence of those documents would reveal counsel's mental impressions, which are protected as work product. . . . We believe Burns' selective review of AMC's numerous documents was based upon her professional judgment of the issues and defenses involved in this case. This mental selective process reflects Burns' legal theories and thought processes, which are protected as work product." The court of appeals concluded that other means existed and had indeed been either used or offered to obtain the information sought in the course of the deposition of in-house counsel.

- *In re Murphy*, 560 F.2d 326, 336–39 (8th Cir. 1977). In an action by the government for patent invalidity and antitrust violations, the government sought to discover the files of the defendants' attorneys in prior litigation because the prior actions of the defendants and their attorneys were at issue. Nonetheless, discovery was denied because the court believed that opinion work product enjoys a "nearly absolute immunity." The court suggested that opinion work product could be discovered only in rare situations where "weighty considerations of public policy and a proper administration of justice would militate against the non-discovery of an attorney's mental impressions."

- *Federal Election Comm'n v. Christian Coalition*, 178 F.R.D. 456 (E.D. Va. 1998). An attorney's opinions about the merits of a case are protected from compelled disclosure.

The mere transfer to an attorney of documents that a client deems important is obviously not work-product protected, although it may conceivably be protected under the attorney-client privilege, since no mental impressions of the attorney would be revealed by their disclosure.

- *Shelton v. American Motors Corp.*, 805 F.2d 1323, 1328 (8th Cir. 1986), *reh'g denied*, 1987 U.S. App. LEXIS 2002 (8th Cir. Jan. 30, 1987). Documents are not protected under the work-product doctrine, however, merely because the other party transferred them to their attorney, litigation department, or insurer.

There is clearly a substantial burden on the party seeking opinion work product to show need and inability to obtain the information without undue hardship. It is a burden that can rarely be met. Almost the sole occasion when the burden is met is when an effective "waiver" has occurred by virtue of putting the attorney's mental impressions at issue in the litigation itself. (*See* discussion of substantial need under Heading A of this section, and discussion of waiver in Section VII.)

- *Guideline No. 18, Special Masters' Guidelines for the Resolution of Privilege Claims, United States v. AT & T*, Civ. No. 74-1698 (D.D.C. Feb. 28, 1979). "Disclosure will not be required of the mental impressions, conclusions, opinions, or legal theories of the attorney or his agent in the absence of a showing of extreme necessity by the party seeking discovery."

Occasionally, the court will order production of opinion work product. This may be because the information is essential to a fair resolution of the controversy and the harm to the adversary process is relatively insignificant.

- *United States v. Brown*, 478 F.2d 1038, 1040–41 (7th Cir. 1973). The court ordered production of a memorandum that summarized notes and legal judgments made by the defendant's attorney at a meeting attended by the client's aide and an associate of the client's accounting firm. The court held that even assuming the defendant had a valid work-product claim, the government showed "good cause" for production of the memorandum, since the information contained in the memorandum was necessary for a correct determination of the taxpayer's liabilities and could not be obtained from any other source.

- *Central Nat'l Ins. Co. v. Medical Protective Co.*, 107 F.R.D. 393, 395 (E.D. Mo. 1985). The plaintiff had shown the "good cause" necessary to defeat the qualified privilege of the work-product doctrine where the documents at issue went to the heart of the plaintiff's claim.

- *Byers v. Burleson*, 100 F.R.D. 436, 429 (D.D.C. 1983). When a plaintiff was suing her former attorney for legal malpractice and the issue was whether the plaintiff's suit was barred by the statute of limitations, the documents would reveal exactly when the plaintiff had anticipated litigation against the defendant and, thus, when the statute of limitations began to run. Because the plaintiff could not obtain the information in any other way, the attorney was ordered to produce the records.

Although the protection accorded to even opinion work product and the mental impressions of an attorney is not as absolute as the rule would seem to imply, nonetheless, as a practical matter in most instances, the presence of an attorney's mental impressions in the document operates to make the document less readily discoverable and raises the quantum of "substantial need" and "undue hardship" that must be shown to obtain the document. It does not, however, guarantee protection from discovery, since courts have and can excise or edit out the attorney's mental impressions and order production of the remaining materials.

- *Xerox Corp. v. International Bus. Machs. Corp.*, 64 F.R.D. 367, 381 (S.D.N.Y. 1974). The court would, if possible, distill out those portions containing the attorneys' "thoughts, impressions, views, strategy, conclusions and other similar information." If it was not possible to redact such information, however, the entire document would be produced. "It is . . . apparent that the basic thrust of *Hickman* and its progeny is that documents containing the work-product of attorneys which contain the attorneys' thoughts, impressions, views, strategy, conclusions, and other similar information produced by the attorney in anticipation of litigation *are to be protected when feasible, but not at the expense of hiding the non-privileged facts from adversaries or the court*" (Emphasis added.)

Frequently, the court can provide needed information from work product and still protect the attorney's mental processes by ordering production of redacted documents. An *in camera* review of the documents may be required for the redaction.

However, an attorney cannot render an innocuous document work-product protected by scribbling mental impressions on the document. Such flights can be excised without allowing the scribbles to become an occasion of work-product protection.

1. Prior Drafts

It is hardly surprising that drafts of documents, which so clearly reflect and disclose an attorney's mental processes and reasoning, are protected from compelled disclosure.

- *Banks v. Office of the Senate Sergeant-at-Arms*, 2006 U.S. Dist. LEXIS 33912, at *8 (D.D.C. May 23, 2006). Prior drafts were work product protected as were requests for attorney comments and editorial changes since they were intended as "confidential." "Where counsel was involved in drafting and editing these documents, the drafts are clearly work product because the edits and commentary tend to reveal counsel's opinions and mental impressions."

- *Simmons, Inc. v. Bombardier, Inc.*, 221 F.R.D. 4 (D.D.C. 2004). Prior drafts of an attorney opinion letter in a patent infringement suit were protected from disclosure. The court was critical of the broad subject matter waiver for attorney work product in patent infringement suits where the defense of wilful infringement is raised since it implicitly seems to believe that clients and their attorneys are mendacious, stating something to the client in the formal opinion letter while in fact believing something else.

- *SEC v. Yuen*, 2004 U.S. Dist. LEXIS 29417 (C.D. Cal. Nov. 10, 2004). No disclosure of a prior draft of a settlement memo was ordered. It remained work-product protected.

- *Nesse v. Pittman*, 202 F.R.D. 344, 351 (D.D.C. 2001). "If [counsel] modifies the draft, comparing the draft with the modified final discloses her mental processes if the changes are more than typographical. If [counsel] files the draft and never sends it, the draft discloses her mental processes in the most obvious way."

- *Niagara Mohawk Power Corp. v. Stone & Webster Eng'g Corp.*, 125 F.R.D. 578, (N.D.N.Y. 1989). Draft answers to interrogatories were protected by work-product privilege.

- *Alexander v. FBI*, 198 F.R.D. 306, 312 (D.D.C. 2000). "The final letter is not protected by attorney-client confidentiality because it was disclosed to third parties. Plaintiffs argue that the release of the final draft waives the attorney-client privilege as it applies to prior drafts of the document. Drafts of documents that are prepared with the assistance of counsel for release to a third party are protected under attorney-client privilege."

- *Blumenthal v. Drudge*, 186 F.R.D. 236, 243 n.8 (D.D.C. 1999). "Because a draft of a legal document contains insights into the mental processes of defendant's attorney, and because plaintiffs have not shown a substantial need for the document, it is properly shielded from disclosure as attorney work product."

Where a court decides that the underlying primary motivation for the creation of a document had a business purpose rather than having been created in anticipation of litigation, the document is not work-product protected and therefore no reason exists to protect the prior drafts either.

- *Visa U.S.A., Inc. v. First Data Corp.*, 2004 U.S. Dist. LEXIS 17117 (N.D. Cal. Aug. 23, 2004). Where drafts of risk assessment for a private payment agreement had primarily a business purpose they were not work-product protected nor privilege protected although circulated to counsel for their comments and input. Other documents prepared at the request of counsel that had no other business purpose were at least work-product protected.

2. Assessment of Litigation

Any assessments of the litigation at hand or evaluations of alternative options to the litigation at hand are work-product protected.

- *Newport Pacific Inc. v. County of San Diego*, 200 F.R.D. 628, 634 (S.D. Cal. 2001). "To the extent that the information at issue here is County Counsel's analysis of issues for presentation to the Board at closed session where the Board makes policy and strategy choices on litigation, the information is attorney work product, and therefore protected from disclosure."

- *LaSalle Bank N.A. v. Mobile Hotel Props., LLC*, 2004 U.S. Dist. LEXIS 7293 (E.D. La. Apr. 23, 2004), *modified on other grounds*, 2004 U.S. Dist. LEXIS 10185 (E.D. La. June 4, 2004). Budgets, alternative options to litigation, assessment of legal rights, status reports of status of loan up to litigation, litigation committee agendas and documents entitled "business plans" which an *in camera* review indicated were an assessment of status of loan and options other than litigation were all work-product protected and not discoverable. In the modification, the court held that communications ruled to be privileged as documents could not then be inquired into via a Rule 30(b) deposition, but also noted the distinction between facts, which could be inquired into, but privileged communications which could not.

3. Attorney's Notes

Production of an attorney's notes, whether it is in the course of witness interviews, consultations with a client or opposing party or third parties with peripheral interest in potential litigation should be and generally are protected. Few things are as likely to disclose an attorney's mental process as the conscious choice made as to what aspects of the conversation or of the rambling thoughts about issues and strategy as an attorney chooses consciously or not to set down in notes made about the litigation.

- *Baker v. GMC (In re GMC)*, 209 F.3d 1051, 1054 (8th Cir. 2000), *reh'g denied without op.*, 2000 U.S. App. LEXIS 11721 (May 24, 2000). "Forcing an attorney to disclose notes and memoranda of witnesses' oral statements is particularly disfavored because it tends to reveal the attorney's mental processes."

- *United States v. Paxson*, 861 F.2d 730, 735 (D.C. Cir. 1988) (applying the same principle).

- *In re San Juan Dupont Plaza Hotel Fire Litig.*, 859 F.2d 1007, 1015 (1st Cir. 1988). "[D]isclosure creates a real, nonspeculative danger of revealing the lawyer's thoughts."

Attorneys often take notes in the course of a meeting or even during interviews with witnesses. Generally, it is held that such notes are likely to contain an attorney's mental processes and be work-product protected. Indeed, they are usually regarded as "core" or "opinion work product" and they are given almost absolute work-product protection.

- *United States v. Arias*, 373 F. Supp. 2d 311 (S.D.N.Y. 2005). An attorney's notes taken during a proffer session with United States attorneys and his client were work-product protected. There is no explanation as to why the prosecutors would have any need for such notes since they too were present at such meetings.

That is not to say that the situation will never arise where attorney notes will be ordered produced. They may become necessary where doubt is raised to some extent about the bona fides of crucial evidence.

■ *Reliance Ins. Co. v. Keybank U.S.A.*, 2006 U.S. Dist. LEXIS 12002 (N.D. Oh. 2006). Where an expert witness gave inconsistent testimony and the attorneys conceded that they had assisted in the writing of the expert's report, the court said assistance in writing was not tantamount to ghost writing but production of attorney notes was ordered to determine the extent of the assistance given.

Where, however, the notes are made in the context of a normal business enterprise or the routine course of a client's business, they will not be work-product protected. Generally, courts do not consider regulatory processes to be adversarial in nature and thus not a "litigation" proceeding. On occasion courts will go through elaborate analysis to assess whether a particular regulatory proceeding would or would not be considered to be "in anticipation of litigation."

■ *In re Grand Jury Subpoena*, 220 F.R.D. 130 (D. Mass. 2004). Notes made by an attorney in the course of conversations with the FDA about possible recall of a defective product were the type of normal course of business communications between a regulating agency and the companies it regulates. They can not be said to have been in anticipation of prospective products liability litigation over the product and hence were discoverable.

The opinion contains an extensive review of the near totality of work product protection law. Useful for readers of this book, but hardly necessary to the decision reached. Unfortunately most legal opinions are getting longer and longer, unnecessarily so. Is it because they are written by law clerks acting as if they are still writing those compendiums of the law articles for law review? More increasingly is less.

B. *Exceptions to Absolute Protection Given to Opinion Work Product*

The primary exception that courts have carved out to the virtually absolute prohibition against invasion of an attorney's mental processes and opinions and trial strategy, is when the litigation itself or a litigant puts those opinions into direct issue either by virtue of an "advice of counsel" claim or by designating an attorney as an expert witness. In each instance, the attorney's opinions and mental processes are thereby placed into issue and necessarily must become discoverable under the legal rule: You Can't Have Your Cake and Eat It Too.

4 J. MOORE, FEDERAL PRACTICE 26.64[4], at 26-447 states:

> [W]hen the activities of counsel are inquired into because they are at issue in the action before the court, there is cause for production of documents that deal with such activities, though they are "work product."

An attorney's activities may be at issue in the action before the court either because those activities form a key factor in the claim or a defense asserted against that claim, and/or because the attorney will be a witness in the litigation.

1. Attorney as Expert Witness

Clearly, when a party designates an attorney as a potential witness, if the testimony is to be other than as a fact witness, any and all opinion work product is put into issue and that attorney should be no more entitled to work-product protection for his opinions and mental processes than would any other expert witness.

- *Vaughan Furniture Co. Inc. v. Featureline Mfg., Inc.,* 156 F.R.D. 123 (M.D.N.C. 1994). When the attorney is designated as an expert witness, no more protection will be accorded to his or her mental processes than would be to those of any other expert witness, and the attorney's opinions thereby become discoverable.

- *Mushroom Assoc. v. Monterey Mushrooms, Inc.,* 1992 U.S. Dist. LEXIS 20629, 25 U.S.P.Q. 2d (BNA) 1304, 1992 WL 442914 (N.D. Cal. Aug. 21, 1992). An attorney was named as an expert in patent litigation.

- *Handgards, Inc. v. Johnson & Johnson,* 413 F. Supp. 926 (N.D. Cal. 1976), *remanded on other grounds sub nom. Handgards, Inc. v. Ethicon, Inc.,* 601 F.2d 986 (9th Cir. 1979), *cert. denied,* 444 U.S. 1025 (1980). A plaintiff brought an antitrust action against a competitor, claiming that patent infringement actions were instituted in bad faith. Once the defendant indicated an intention to call its three attorneys as witnesses, the totality of the litigation files became discoverable.

2. Attorney's Opinion Relevant to Prove Issue in Dispute[2]

When a defense of "advice of counsel" is raised, then even opinion work product becomes fair game for discovery because a predicate for the validity of the defense may well be what was the information given to the attorney that became the predicate of the advice.

Obviously there is substantial overlap in this category and the one where an attorney is designated as a witness.

- *Coleco Indus., Inc. v. Universal City Studios*, 110 F.R.D. 688, 690 (S.D.N.Y. 1986). The plaintiff claimed that the defendant had wrongfully threatened suit to coerce a settlement. When the defendant raised an "advice of counsel" defense, opinion work product became discoverable. "A consistent line of cases has developed an exception to the work-product privilege where a party raises an issue which depends upon an evaluation of the legal theories, opinions and conclusions of counsel."

- *Handgards, Inc. v. Johnson & Johnson*, 413 F. Supp. 926 (N.D. Cal. 1976), *remanded on other grounds sub nom. Handgards, Inc. v. Ethicon, Inc.*, 601 F.2d 986 (9th Cir. 1979), *cert. denied*, 444 U.S. 1025 (1980). In a patent infringement suit, defendants raised an "advice of counsel" defense. Thus, the opinion of counsel was crucial to determining the defendant's good faith.

3. Attorney's Actions Relevant to Issue in Dispute

At times it is not the advice of counsel that is raised as a defense by one of the existing parties, but the actions of counsel that form the gravamen of the claim itself. In such an instance, namely just about any situation where the actions of counsel are claimed to constitute some type of malpractice or legal violation, opinion work product is likely to be discoverable.

---

2. An entire subset of this issue arises in the context of patent litigation when an advice of counsel defense is raised to a claim of wilful infringement. That subset has been dealt with in Part I under the designation of waiver since there is no logical way of separating the spillover between privilege waiver and attorney work-product waiver in that category of case and the full lay of the land would not be comprehensible to the reader were any attempt made to divide the cases between attorney-client privilege waiver and attorney work-product waiver.

■ *SEC v. Nat'l Student Mktg. Corp.*, 18 Fed. R. Serv. 2d (CBC) 1302, 1305 (D.D.C. 1974). A law firm was accused of negligence and other misconduct in the provision of legal services in failing to disclose relevant financial data. This placed into issue what the law firm did and did not know, thereby vitiating any opinion work-product protection. When the production requests are made on attorneys as defendants—that is, where the activities of counsel are being inquired into because they are at issue in the action before the court—a rare exception to the rule of non-disclosure applies. "[W]hile Rule 26(b)(3) provides that protection against discovery of the attorney's or representative's 'mental impressions, conclusions, opinions or legal theories' shall be provided, such protection would not screen information directly at issue."

Should there perhaps be some distinction made, or at least considered, in view of the fact that courts are far more prone to permit privileges as shields than as swords? Should the plaintiff be at a greater disadvantage by virtue of having had the option of bringing the action, than the defendant who presumably did not "choose" to be sued? Probably not and, to date, no court has so held. It is sufficient that courts be alert to manipulative uses sought to be made or claims not asserted in good faith. Albeit, it seems unlikely that a party would assert either a claim or a defense merely to get access to opinion work product.

4. Obtaining Work Product of Plaintiff's Attorney to Prove Defendant's Defense

Generally speaking, when an attorney's activities are instrumental in proving an issue in dispute, discovery of even opinion work product is accorded. The courts do not seem to distinguish in that regard as to whether it is the plaintiff's claim that will be proved by invasion of the defendant's attorney's opinion work product, or whether it is the defendant who will be permitted to prove his or her defense by invading the plaintiff's attorney's opinion work product.

There are two types of frequently recurring litigation when a plaintiff may be fairly assured that the opinion work product of prior counsel will be discoverable. Those two types of litigation are in a patent infringement suit when the defendant may seek to defend based on the claim that the patent was improperly obtained, and in a suit for insurance contribution or indemnity when the underlying settlement, if not negotiated by the insurance company being asked to pony up, will be discoverable, including all legal opinions of the settling attorney.

- *Bio-Rad Labs., Inc. v. Pharmacia, Inc.*, 130 F.R.D. 116 (N.D. Cal. 1990). In a patent infringement action, the defendant was entitled to discover the opinion work product of the plaintiff's patent attorney, who also was retained as an expert consultant to plaintiff's trial counsel on the infringement action. The fact that the patent attorney would not be called as a witness was not dispositive.

- *Charlotte Motor Speedway, Inc. v. International Ins. Co.*, 125 F.R.D. 127 (M.D.N.C. 1989). The defendant insurance company was permitted to discover material relating to the settlement of an underlying securities appraisal claim when the plaintiff brought an action to recover the cost of the settlement and the cost of the litigation from its directors and officers of the insurance company. When the actions of counsel are key to determining whether an insured lived up to his her contractual obligations of good faith settlement under the insurance policy, opinion work product will be discoverable.

- *Truck Ins. Exch. v. St. Paul Fire & Marine Ins. Co.*, 66 F.R.D. 129 (E.D. Pa. 1975). In an indemnity and/or contribution action brought by one insurance company against another, the defendant company was entitled to discovery of the settlement documents and other work product prepared by the plaintiff's attorney in the underlying settled action for which indemnity/contribution was sought.

- *Kearney & Trecker Corp. v. Giddings & Lewis, Inc.*, 296 F. Supp. 979 (E.D. Wis. 1969). The defendant asserted in a patent infringement suit that the patent being litigated had been improperly obtained. The defendant thus was given access to opinion work product of the plaintiff's patent attorney to prove the defense.

So too, in malpractice claims, the entirety of an attorney's file is likely to become discoverable even if raised in the context of a defense to a claim.

- *Rutgard v. Haynes*, 185 F.R.D. 596 (S.D. Cal. 1999). In a malpractice claim, the entirety of a subsequent attorney's file was discoverable to assist the defendant in the proof of his defense that the subsequent attorney contributed to the damages claimed by the plaintiff in a malpractice action.

5. Obtaining Work Product of Defendant's Attorney to Prove Plaintiff's Claim

The fact that a defendant is given access to plaintiff's counsel's work product to defend against a claim is not as surprising as the fact that plaintiffs, in the right circumstances, are also given access to the work product of defendant's counsel in some prior proceeding. After all, a defendant does not choose to be sued and greater latitude may therefore be deemed necessary to defend when one is not the instigator. However, certain claims that our system of jurisprudence recognizes as meritorious can only be proved with access to defendant's counsel's work product. That is clearly the case in the context of malpractice actions against attorneys.

- *Pappas v. Holloway*, 787 P.2d 30, 38 (Wash. 1990). "[T]he mental impressions and opinions of the attorneys involved in the underlying litigation in an attorney malpractice case are an 'integral part of the malpractice issue' and hence are discoverable."

Another type of claim where a plaintiff has a good chance of obtaining opinion work product from defendant's counsel is when a claim is made that an insurance company wrongfully refused to settle an insurance claim, or when a claim is made that an action was prosecuted maliciously. In each instance, what the attorney knew, when the attorney knew it, and how the attorney knew is likely to be a crucial issue in contention and to form the basis of the proof of the claim. Thus, the nature of the claim itself puts work product often necessarily into play.

- *Holmgren v. State Mut. Auto. Ins. Co.*, 976 F.2d 573 (9th Cir.), *aff'd, remanded on other grounds*, 1992 U.S. App. LEXIS 29008 (9th Cir. Nov. 9, 1992). A third-party tort victim suing an insurance company for failure to settle a claim is entitled to discovery of the insurer's attorney's opinion work product.

- *Bird v. Penn Cent. Co.*, 61 F.R.D. 43, 47 (E.D. Pa. 1973). The context was a suit by an insurance company to rescind the issuance of an insurance policy acquired on the basis of false statements and material omissions in the application. The defendant raised a laches defense, thus putting into issue what the plaintiff knew and when the plaintiff knew it, thereby obtaining the work product of plaintiff's counsel. "Because the nature of this defense concerns knowledge, legal theories and conclusions of plaintiff's attorneys . . . , such 'advice of counsel' evidenced in these documents is discoverable when it is directly relevant to a possible rescission action or suggests reasons to indicate the propriety of such an action."

In the malicious prosecution case, rulings go both ways as to whether discovery will be given of the attorney's work product. If alternative modes of proof exist, the holding may be that necessity has not been demonstrated. When no alternative proof modes exist, however, discovery may be granted.

- *Kockums Indus. Ltd. v. Salem Equip., Inc.*, 561 F. Supp. 168, 172 (D. Or. 1983). When the defendant's ability to succeed on its counterclaim depended on a showing that the plaintiff had pursued its suit knowing it would be unsuccessful on the merits, and the opinions of the plaintiff's attorneys regarding the merits of the plaintiff's action were directly at issue, the defendant showed a specific and compelling need for the documents. Because the documents involved were opinion work product, however, the defendant was also required to show "extraordinary circumstances." The defendant satisfied this requirement by making a prima facie showing of unfair competition.

- *Walker v. United Parcel Servs.*, 87 F.R.D. 360, 362 (E.D. Pa. 1980). Absent a strong showing of necessity, prejudice, or hardship, the plaintiff could not depose the defendant's attorney who allegedly had retaliated against the plaintiff for filing this suit, when the attorney's testimony would serve only to buttress other witnesses' testimony. The deposition inevitably would probe into the attorney's mental impressions, opinions, and legal strategy.

- *Kirkland v. Morton Salt Co.*, 46 F.R.D. 28, 30 (N.D. Ga. 1968). In an action for malicious prosecution, the plaintiff was entitled to discovery of work product as to the underlying collection action to demonstrate that the suit had been filed when the debt was paid. The court, without explanation, stated that "[t]here are no such mental impressions or conclusions as are most closely protected in *Hickman*." Despite the court's statement, it would seem probative to inquire as to what the attorney knew and how the attorney knew it to prove the plaintiff's case.

C. *Specific Categories of Documents*

1. Litigation Reserves

Litigation reserves established by companies which are not insurance companies as well as historic and budgeted litigation costs and expenses sometimes have and sometimes have not been accorded work product protection.

The only apparent principle is that litigation reserves established by public companies seem to be more likely to be held to be discoverable, presumably on the theory that financial matters must be transparent in such publicly held companies.

- *Frank Betz Assocs., Inc. v. Jim Walter Homes, Inc.*, 226 F.R.D. 533 (D.S.C. 2005). Protected. Disclosure of reserves not required. Disclosure to auditors did not constitute waiver. The underlying claim was one of copyright infringement brought by an architectural firm.

- *SEC v. R.J. Reynolds Tobacco, Holdings, Inc.*, 2004 U.S. Dist. LEXIS 24545 (D.D.C. June 29, 2004). Not protected. Historic litigation costs and expenses associated with tobacco litigation as well as budgeted or forecast costs and expenses even when case specific were not accorded work product protection. The rationale for the holding is not clearly set forth. It may well be that as a publicly held company such matters are intrinsically disclosable

- *Simon v. G.D. Searle & Co.*, 816 F.2d 397, 401 (8th Cir.), *cert. denied*, 484 U.S. 917 (1987). Some protected. Some not protected. Aggregate reserves established in assessing claims were not work-product protected, because they are "in the nature of business planning documents. . . . The risk management department was not involved in giving legal advice or mapping litigation strategy in any individual case." But to the extent that any individual case reserve was calculated by a Searle attorney, such might be work-product protected. "The individual case reserve figures reveal the mental impressions, thoughts and conclusions of an attorney in evaluating a legal claim. By their very nature they are prepared in anticipation of litigation and, consequently, they are protected from discovery as opinion work product."

■ *In re Pfizer Inc. Sec. Litig.*, 1994 U.S. Dist. LEXIS 7454 at *3, 4 (S.D.N.Y. June 6, 1994), *adhered to*, 1994 U.S. Dist. LEXIS 16746 (S.D.N.Y. Nov. 21, 1994). The court reiterated that aggregate case reserves were not work-product protected while individual case reserves, which would demonstrate the attorney's assessment of the strengths and weaknesses of particular cases were work-product protected. Similarly any documents dealing with the methodology of how individual case reserves were to be calculated were accorded work-product protection. "This is because the methodology reflects an attorney's thoughts, conclusions, and mental impressions as to the value of a tort claimant's suit." But those that reflected how aggregate ones were calculated was not. The court did not explain how logically aggregate ones could be calculated in any way other than adding up individual ones. It did conclude, however, that "These documents focus on a business issue, namely how much money Pfizer must hold in reserve consistent with generally accepted accounting principles and SEC reporting requirements. In order to determine the appropriate level of aggregate reserves, the documents make broad projections and analyses regarding the extent of Pfizer's financial exposure, without revealing the specifics as to any individual case. The projections tend to be actuarial in nature, based on statistical averages. The names of individual claimants are not identified. We conclude, therefore, that because "the primary motivational purpose" behind the creation of the documents was a business and not a legal one, they do not receive work product protection."

2. Insurance Reserves[3]

Insurance reserves are not attorney-client privileged. But they generally are work-product protected. Therefore here is an example of

---

3. To some extent insurance is a subset of litigation reserves. Nonetheless, they are handled separately here since this discovery request comes up with great frequency in litigation.

an instance where it would be foolish to rely on one theory and overlook the other.

- *Allendale Mut. Ins. Co. v. Bull Data Sys.*, 152 F.R.D. 131, 138 (N.D. Ill. 1993). "[I]insurance reserves are the regular business of insurance companies, not a part of legal advice"

Reserves for litigation drawn up by insurance companies are generally discoverable unless established by the attorney called on to defend the particular case *sub judice*. They may also be discoverable in a bad faith denial of coverage claim as evidence of bad faith. The setting of a large loss reserve while denying coverage would tend to substantiate the bad faith claim.

- *Country Life Ins. Co. v. St. Paul Surplus Lines Ins. Co.*, 2005 U.S. Dist. LEXIS 39691 (C.D. Jan. 31, Ill. 2005). The amount of loss reserves established on the claim would be discoverable, probably on a counsel's eyes only basis, assuming that the bad faith claim survived a motion to dismiss.

- *Nicholas v. Bituminous Cas. Corp.*, 2006 U.S. Dist. LEXIS 13271 (N.D. W. Va. Feb. 24, 2006). The case involved a bad faith failure to settle by an insured against the insurance company. The insurance company raised an "advice of counsel" defense. Reserves were established by the claims adjusters without input from counsel. Hence the advice of counsel defense did not waive the work-product protection with which such reserves were invested. There is a West Virginia statute which requires the establishment of reasonable reserves and generally makes the amount not discoverable.

- *Safeguard Lighting Sys., Inc. v. North Am. Specialty Ins. Co.*, 2004 U.S. Dist. LEXIS 26136, at *10 (E.D. Pa. Dec. 30, 2004). "[A]ny material which pertains to instructions and procedures for adjusting claims and which was given to the adjusters who worked on plaintiffs' claim may be relevant to the action and must be produced."

Information regarding the reserves allocated by an insurance company to cover a particular claim sometimes have and sometimes have not been accorded work-product protection. The result seems to turn on whether a court deems it to be in the ordinary course of business to establish such loss reserves or whether instead the establishment of the loss reserves is found to turn upon a lawyer's assessment of the value of a particular claim which entails an evaluation of the nature of those claims and potential defenses thereto.

- *Caliber One Indem. Co. v. Millard Chi. Window Cleaning, LLC*, 2006 U.S. Dist. LEXIS 12995 (N.D. Ill. Mar. 6, 2006). Where plaintiff produced without objection certain historic reserves, the court ordered production of all such under a theory of waiver, while protecting from disclosure current ones.

- *Bondex Int'l, Inc. v. Hartford Accident & Indem. Co.*, 2006 U.S. Dist. LEXIS 6044 (N.D. Ohio Feb. 14, 2006). Protected. Loss reserves are not relevant to any issue in litigation and in all events work product protected.

- *Nicholas v. Bituminous Cas. Corp.*, 2006 U.S. Dist. LEXIS 13271 (N.D. W. Va. Feb. 24, 2006). Protected. Found that loss reserves were protected work product.

- *Rhone-Poulenc Rorer, Inc. v. Home Indem. Co.*, 139 F.R.D. 609 (E.D. Pa. 1991). Protected. Reserves contain mental assessments by lawyers of value of claims and hence are work-product protected.

- *Champion Int'l Corp. v. Liberty Mut. Ins. Co.*, 128 F.R.D. 608 (S.D.N.Y. 1989). Not protected. Defendants failed to show that documents reflecting the amount of reserves established were prepared principally to assist in the litigation.

3. Fee Arrangements in Multiple Party Cases

Since fee arrangements are generally discoverable, no self-evident reason exists why they should not be discoverable in a multiple party context other than one. Sometimes the division of fees among defendants, for instance, may reflect counsel's assessment of the relative culpability, liability and validity of defenses of the various defendants.

Fee arrangements in class actions are not work-product protected nor are they attorney-client privileged.

- *Porter v. Nations Credit Consumer Disc. Co.*, 2004 U.S. Dist. LEXIS 13641 (E.D. Pa. July 9, 2004). Fee arrangements with plaintiff's counsel discoverable in class actions.

4. Litigation Assessments

Direct litigation assessments, other than such as may be reflected in insurance and litigation reserves, are the archetype of attorney work product which would reveal attorney mental impressions and opinions and should in virtually all situations be given absolute protection.

- *Bush Dev. Corp. v. Harbour Place Assocs.*, 632 F. Supp. 1359, 1363 (E.D. Va. 1986). Counsel's statements, even when transcribed by the client, are prime examples of opinion work product entitled to nearly absolute protection from compelled disclosure.

5. Reduction in Force Work Papers

Another type of document that parties often seek to have work product protected is work papers prepared in connection with reductions in work force. Such attempts usually do and should fail since they have little to do with litigation and much to do with running a business.

- *Freiermuth v. PPG Indus., Inc.*, 218 F.R.D. 694 (N.D. Ala. 2003). Reduction in force work papers were not granted work product protection.

But see:

- *Maloney v. Sisters of Charity Hosp.*, 165 F.R.D. 26 (W.D.N.Y. 1995). Where counsel had articulated his reasonable belief, formulated at the time the documents were prepared, and based on his experience in the area of employment and labor law, that the large scale reduction in force proposed by defendant would likely result in litigation, the work papers were granted work-product protection. Happily this precedent has not been much followed, since were it to be all that would be necessary would be such a lawyer's imprimatur to make virtually any document prepared for a business decision to be work product protected.

6. Document Organization, Selection, Indexes

Although the attempt has been made to claim work-product protection for selections and organization of documents on the grounds that such selection would reflect an attorney's mental processes, by and large the attempt has not been successful where the underlying documents are not themselves work-product protected.

- *In re Grand Jury Subpoenas Dated March 19, 2002 and August 2, 2002*, 318 F.3d 379, 385, 386 (2d Cir. 2003). "[N]ot every selection and compilation of third-party documents by counsel transforms that material into attorney work product."

7. Insurance Company Files

Insurance company files are usually discoverable at the instance of the insured in a bad faith case and also when one company seeks indemnity from another. The party from whom indemnity is sought, is usually given access to the files of the party seeking the indemnity.

- *American Cas. Co. v. Healthcare Indem., Inc.*, 2002 U.S. Dist. LEXIS 952 (D. Kan. Jan. 21, 2002). Work-product protection was not accorded to the insurance company's claim file.

- *Audiotext Communications Network, Inc. v. U.S. Telecom, Inc.*, 164 F.R.D. 250, 252 (D. Kan. 1996). "The selecting and grouping of information does not transform discoverable documents into work product."

- *Mead Corp. v. Riverwood Natural Res. Corp.*, 145 F.R.D. 512, 520 (D. Minn. 1992). The court distinguished the *Sporck* and *Shelton* cases and ordering production of certain documents, stating: "[N]ot everything which may give inkling of a lawyer's mental impressions, conclusions, opinions or legal theories is protected as the lawyer's work-product. Almost every adversarial position adopted can, through deduction, give some indication of thought processes or strategy."

- *Washington Bancorp. v. Said*, 145 F.R.D. 274, 276 (D.D.C. 1992) The issue was whether an attorney-created index cataloguing 2400 boxes of documents constituted fact or opinion work product. The court recognized that the index was a hybrid of fact and opinion work product. Although the index was a compilation of factual information, it "also arranged that information in a way that could reveal the preparing attorney's opinions about the information indexed and how it relates to the underlying case." The court concluded that unlike the attorney's compilation of documents in *Sporck,* which involved singling out a few documents out of thousands, the index compiling facts about 2400 documents was "not selective enough to qualify for 'opinion' status under *Sporck [infra.].*" It also concluded that the costs entailed in recreation of the database posed an undue hardship.

- *Bohannon v. Honda Motor Co.,* 127 F.R.D. 536, 539–40 (D. Kan. 1989). The court held "collecting and organizing discoverable documents in a notebook does not make the notebook protected work product."

But see:

Where one party gave the other notice that documents had been gathered and collected by their attorneys from the public domain for cross-examination purposes, they may be able to avoid either producing them or even listing them in a privilege log because to do so would give the adversary too much of an insight into the mental processes of the attorney.

- *ASPCA v. Ringling Bros. & Barnum & Bailey Circus,* 233 F.R.D. 209, 213 (D.D.C. 2006). "[D]efendants have repeatedly explained that their attorneys gathered publicly available documents about Rider in the course of this litigation, which they assert were not previously in the possession of defendants, for the purpose of cross-examining and impeaching him. I do not see how additional information would better enable plaintiffs to evaluate the applicability of work-product protection to the documents at issue. Moreover, plaintiffs have not argued that the documents are not work product or that they have a sufficient need for the documents so as to overcome the documents' work-product protection. Accordingly, I will not order the Rider documents gathered by defendants' counsel for the purpose of cross-examination and impeachment produced or included on a privilege log."

Also those documents selected which counsel selects to prepare a witness do not usually have to be produced unless of course they are used to refresh the witnesses' recollection, at which point Rule 612 of the Federal Rules of Evidence tends to trump any work-product protection which would otherwise inhere in the selection process. Thus if a party wishes to discover what those viewed documents were, it is advisable to get the deponent to confess that they helped refresh his recollection.

■ *Stone Container Corp. v. Arkwright Mutual Ins. Co.*, 1995 U.S. Dist. LEXIS 2400 at *4, 1995 WL 88902 (N.D. Ill. 1995). A party sought documents selected by his adversary's attorney to help his client (rather than a neutral witness) to prepare for a deposition. The documents themselves had already been produced. What was at issue was a designation of those documents which had been presented by the attorney to a deponent in preparation for his deposition. The district court found that information to be protected by the work product doctrine. "[T]he selection process itself represents defense counsel's mental impressions and legal opinions as to how the evidence in the documents relates to the issues and defenses in the litigation." Thus the court found a substantive distinction between selection of specific documents from a larger group, and production of the documents in a context that did not reveal the selection. Had the witness, in the course of the deposition, conceded that the documents had been helpful in refreshing his recollection there is little doubt that thereafter they should have become discoverable.

■ *Aguinaga v. John Morrell & Co.*, 112 F.R.D. 671, 683 (D. Kan. 1986). The court held that the selection and compilation of documents *used to refresh a witness's memory* were protected by work-product doctrine pursuant to Fed. R. Evid. 612. (Emphasis added.)

The *Sporck* case is the one which most courts rely upon to protect document selections and compilations under work product theories.

■ *Sporck v. Peil*, 759 F.2d 312, 316 (3d Cir. 1985) The issue was whether an attorney's selection and compilation of documents for the client to review in preparation for his deposition constituted opinion work product. The Third Circuit concluded that it was because "in selecting and ordering a few documents out of thousands counsel could not help but reveal important aspects of his understanding of the case."

Third-party documents which have been obtained by one side or another also generally are not accorded work-product protection. Indeed if obtained by subpoena, notice must be given to an adversary who may thereby obtain its own copy. Based on that analogy, no doubt, absent unusual circumstance the fact that one side may have compiled third-party documents does not necessarily make what was compiled work-product protected.

- *Hunter's Ridge Golf Co., Inc. v. Georgia-Pacific Corp.*, 233 F.R.D. 678 (M.D. Fla. 2006). "It is well settled that ordinarily, the work-product doctrine does not shield from discovery documents created by third parties."

- *Matter of Grand Jury Subpoenas Dated Oct. 22, 1991, and Nov. 1, 1991*, 959 F.2d 1158, 1166 (2nd Cir. 1992). The court of appeals affirmed the district court's holding that telephone records in the possession of a law firm were not invested with any work-product protection where a subpoena asked for all of them and not a compilation or selection which might have been made by the law firm. There was thus no intention or possibility of getting at the mental processes of an attorney.

However, an exception to this general rule exists "where a request is made for documents already in the possession of the requesting party, with the precise goal of learning what the opposing attorney's thinking or strategy may be."

- *Gould Inc. v. Mitsui Mining & Smelting Co., Ltd.*, 825 F.2d 676 (2nd Cir. 1987). This exception has been described as narrow and requires the showing of a real, rather than speculative, concern that the thought processes of counsel in relation to pending or anticipated litigation would be exposed.

Where party has not made an index of documents produced, it need not do so nor does it have to produce an index that was produced for its own use.

- *Braun v. Agri-Sys.*, 2006 U.S. Dist. LEXIS 25185 (E.D. Cal. 2006). The court concluded that a document index, prepared by the party's document production firm, need not be produced. The litigation purpose so pervaded any subsidiary business purpose that work-product protection was warranted.

8. Data Compilations

Where one side has compiled data, often at substantial cost, access is often given to the adversary under theories that there is a substantial need for the data and that to recreate it yet again would entail an undue hardship. Often when that is the holding, the court will order the costs of producing the data compilation to be shared. The reasoning is that if one party is going to use the data to prove its case, the other is entitled to it eventually in all events. Why not sooner rather than later? But also it would hardly be fair to allow the adversary to piggyback in terms of cost and proof on work done by the data compiler.

- *Portis v. City of Chicago*, 2004 U.S. Dist. LEXIS 12640 (N.D. Ill. 2004). Plaintiff's compilation of arrest records of some 20,000 individuals did not warrant opinion work-product status, but was ordered produced on substantial need and undue hardship grounds, but with the costs of creation to be shared by defendants The underlying Monell claim was a "widespread and systemic practice in the City of Chicago of detaining individuals arrested on minor ordinance offenses for an extended period of time after all administrative steps have been completed." Plaintiffs' database showed the period of time each potential class member was detained, and was thus highly relevant to that claim.

  Plaintiffs maintained that the database was a research project that would not be a basis for expert testimony and that unless and until that happened the court should not compel its production. The court said it was "hard pressed to believe" that the plaintiffs who had spent $90,000 in having the database compiled did not intend to use it to prove their case.

  Moreover, since the database would be used for class notices, it would prove an invaluable tool for both sides to assess the merits of the litigation to assure and would make it easier for the City to confirm the proposed class list, expedite the class-notice process considerably and thereby move the case forward.

Indeed plaintiffs originally wanted the City to collaborate with them in creating the database, and thus would not prejudice plaintiffs while it would be an undue hardship for the City to independently recreate what already existed.

- *Williams v. E.I. DuPont de Nemours & Co.*, 119 F.R.D. 648, 651 (W.D. Ky. 1987). The defendant was ordered to pay the plaintiff a fair portion of the fees and expenses incurred for the work of the plaintiff's expert in encoding the requested data and creating a database that was ordered to be produced.

- *Fauteck v. Montgomery Ward & Co., Inc.*, 91 F.R.D. 393, 398 (N.D. Ill. 1980). The court compelled production of a database that would eventually be discoverable, even if arguably not presently discoverable, on grounds that doing so would advance litigation without prejudice to defendants.

9. Witness Statements[4]

Few aspects of work-product protection are as tangled as whether witness statements are or are not work product and even if work product under what circumstances will they be ordered produced. Generally speaking, substantially verbatim statements may become discoverable in order to test the veracity of a testifying witness. An attorney's annotated rendition of such statements generally are not.

Often production of the verbatim statements may be withheld until after the witness has testified.

But even a signed or verbatim statement may expose the attorney's line of approach while notes or summaries taken by an attorney or even an attorney's agent of a witness statement pose serious work-product difficulties. How reliable is what was taken down? Is the attorney being transformed from an advocate into a potential witness? How much of an inevitable selection process and thus the attorney's mental processes would be disclosed by granting disclosure? But most of all, if

---

4. *See also* Witness Statements under the Section on Exemptions to Work Product *infra*.

the witness is available for deposition, the courts then reason, why does one party to the litigation have to piggyback on preparatory work done by its adversary?

The United States Supreme Court erected a substantial zone of privacy around such notes even though the lower courts have somewhat eroded it in certain circumstances.

- *Hickman v. Taylor*, 329 U.S. 495, 511 (1947). "But as to the oral statements made by witnesses to [opposing counsel], whether presently in the form of his mental impressions or memoranda, we do not believe that any showing of necessity can be made under the circumstances of this case so as to justify production. Under ordinary conditions, forcing an attorney to repeat or write out all that witnesses have told him and to deliver the account to his adversary gives rise to grave dangers of inaccuracy and untrustworthiness. No legitimate purpose is served by such production. The practice forces the attorney to testify as to what he remembers or what he saw fit to write down regarding witnesses' remarks. Such testimony could not qualify as evidence; and to use it for impeachment or corroborative purposes would make the attorney much less an officer of the court and much more an ordinary witness. The standards of the profession would thereby suffer."

Thus absent special circumstances, witness interviews are by and large deemed to be work-product protected, unless done by an insurance company before it decides to adjust or deny the claim, in which case witness statements are generally deemed to have been done in the ordinary course of business.

- *O'Connor v. Boeing N. Am., Inc.*, 216 F.R.D. 640, 643 (C.D. Cal. 2003). The court held that "[n]otes and memoranda of an attorney from a witness interview are opinion work-product entitled to almost absolute immunity."

- *Sr Int'l Bus. Ins. Co. Ltd. v. World Trade Ctr. Props. LLC*, 2002 U.S. Dist. LEXIS 10919, at *19–20 (S. D. N.Y. June 19, 2002). "Clearly, much more can be learned about a lawyer's strategy and tactics from documents that the lawyer prepares than can be gained from general questioning concerning a witness's recollection of conversations with an attorney concerning the events about which the witness is expected to testify. Thus, to the extent that the work product privilege is to be extended to verbal communications between a lawyer and a witness, it should be limited to questioning that is either specifically designed to discover the attorney's work product or for some other reason presents a substantial likelihood that a response to the question will result in a significant disclosure of counsel's legal strategy and thought processes."

- *Long v. Anderson Univ.*, 204 F.R.D. 129, 138 (S.D. Ind. 2001). Witness statements taken by an insurance carrier in a sexual harassment suit were protected. The party seeking the statements "may discover the names of the individuals Adrian interviewed and either conduct their own witness interviews or take depositions of any relevant witnesses."

- *Goodyear Tire and Rubber Co. v. Chiles Power Supply, Inc.*, 190 F.R.D. 532, 536–37 (S.D. Ind. 1999). In that case, the district court held that witness statements taken by an insurance company in regard to a third-party claim were in anticipation of litigation, since their primary motivation for taking the statements was to prepare for litigation.

- *In re Grand Jury Subpoena (Zerendow)*, 849, 854 (D. Mass. 1995). An attorney refused to testify before the grand jury as to the content of his recollection of conversations he sat in on between his client and federal agents. That refusal to testify as to the *content* of those conversations or to produce his notes was sustained by the court on work-product grounds. The attorney, however, waived any immunity from disclosure as to the *fact* of whether he had any independent recollection when he filed an affidavit stating he did not. "Here, the government does not seek production of the attorney's notes of the interview of his client, but his testimony as to his recollection of that conversation. These attorney recollections fall squarely within the contours of the work-product doctrine. The fact that the testimony concerns an interview between Zerendow's client and government agents, rather than an interview of a nonparty witness does not defeat, but rather enhances, defendant Phelan's and Zerendow's arguments. If it were otherwise, a defense attorney who sought to protect his client's rights by being present at an interview between his client and government agents would risk being required to expose his thought process to opposing counsel, and even worse, risk becoming a witness against his client. This would have a chilling effect on effective representation by defense counsel. . . .

"This court need not walk the difficult lines here of determining whether an attorney's recollection of a conversation between his client and a government agent is opinion or ordinary work product, or is entitled to absolute or only qualified protection. Even under the more lenient standard of qualified protection, the government has not met its burden of establishing good cause for production of the testimony. As both AUSA Jonathan Chiel and Special Agent DeAngelis were present during the conversation, the testimony, if consistent with their memory, will only be cumulative or corroborative. If Attorney Zerendow's memory of the conversation were inconsistent, and he testified at trial as an exculpatory witness, his notes, which he used to refresh his recollection, would have to be produced pursuant to Fed. R. Evid. 612."

- *Miles v. M/V Mississippi Queen*, 753 F.2d 1349, 1351–53 (5th Cir. 1985). Although the court has some latitude in determining when the statements must be produced—for example, permitting the party's deposition to be taken first—the party's right to his or her statement is not diminished when the court suspects duplicity. Failure to order production in this case, however, was held (two to one) to be harmless error.

- *Sherrell Perfumes, Inc. v. Revlon, Inc.*, 77 F.R.D. 705 (S.D.N.Y. 1977). An antitrust plaintiff's interest in obtaining the defendants' unrefreshed recollection justified postponing the disclosure of tape recordings the plaintiff had made of conversations with the defendants until after they had been deposed.

When an attorney for one party questions or prepares witnesses who are not employees of his own client, blanket work-product protection will not be given to such interviews, and general inquiry into the substance of what was asked and what the witness said may be permitted.

- *Metzger v. Francis W. Parker Sch.*, 2001 U.S. Dist. LEXIS 12492 (N.D. Ill. 2001). Attempt to shield notes of a fact witness on the

grounds that although he was the plaintiff's father, he was also acting as his attorney, and that the notes he took were in anticipation
of litigation, was not successful. The court said, in effect, if you are
going to testify, any notes you may have taken are fair game for
cross-examination purposes.

But see:

Counsel may use notes taken of witness interviews during examination of the witnesses without thereby losing work-product protection for
them. As long as no "testimonial" use is put to the notes they can remain
work-product protected. The reasoning is that the witness is available and
is responding to questions and subject to cross-examination. In a sense
the notes are irrelevant for any testimonial purpose in the context, serving merely as an *aide memoire* for the attorney doing the questioning. If,
however, the notes themselves are used to impeach the witness, obviously
they would have to be tendered to the adversary as well.

- *SEC v. Talbot*, 2005 U.S. Dist. LEXIS 12603 at *6–7; Fed. Sec. L.
  Rep. (CCH) P93,272 (C.D. Cal. 2005). Witness interview notes
  taken by SEC in the pre-litigation investigation phase were deemed
  work product protected. "In the present case, the SEC attorney
  asked questions that clearly referred to notes that were made during
  witness interviews. The witnesses were asked to confirm or deny
  whether certain statements were made. It is the witnesses' responses
  that are evidence, not the questions. Had the attorney who had
  taken the notes been called upon to impeach the witnesses—i.e., to
  say that the witnesses' testimony is inconsistent with what the witnesses previously said—then the situation would be like that presented in *Nobles*, and production would be required."

Surprisingly courts do not address the seeming contradiction between Rule 26(b)(3) and their holdings denying production. Indeed,
even where the statements are verbatim, they are often regarded as
work product. The courts reason that if an adversary is provided with
the names of potential witnesses, as is now mandatory even without interrogatories being posed to that effect, they can do their own leg work.
Thus there must be some extra showing of either unavailability or special
need to obtain witness statements.

- *Gator Marshbuggy Excavator L.L.C. v. M/V Rambler*, 2004 U.S. Dist. LEXIS 16090 at *10 (E.D. La. 2004). Witness statement taken by an investigator hired by counsel for the insured was deemed work-product protected. Take a deposition was the suggestion of the court that stated it would review the statement and deposition testimony *in camera* for inconsistencies.

- *American Federal Bank, FSB v. United States*, 60 Fed. Cl. 493;2004 U.S. Claims LEXIS 106 (C. Fed. Cl. 2004). Voluntary interviews conducted of former federal employees by plaintiff would be work-product protected nor did counsel for the United States have to be present at such interviews.

- *EEOC V. Rose Casual Dining, L.P.*, 2004 U.S. Dist. LEXIS 1983 (E.D. Pa. 2004). A reasonable investigation defense was raised to a discrimination lawsuit. The court found that two investigations were conducted. One in-house before litigation was threatened and in the course of which no witness statements were taken and one after litigation was threatened. This second one was conducted by counsel and did generate witness statements which were held to be work-product protected.

- *Hertzberg v. Veneman, United States Dept. of Agriculture*, 273 F. Supp. 2d 67 (D.D.C. 2003). Where Department of Forestry did a mass firing, the witness statements of 13 were taken. The court found them to be work-product protected under Exemption 5 of FOIA where the Department demonstrated that they were taken in anticipation of litigation over the firings.

- *In re General Motors Corp.*,209 F.3d 1051 (8th Cir. 2000). The Eighth Circuit granted a writ of mandamus from a magistrate judge's ruling and reversed the ruling that interview notes of GM counsel of an engineer who had conducted a cost/benefit study of repairing fuel tanks were discoverable.

- *Harper & Row Publishers Inc. v. Decker*, 423 F.2d 487, 492 (7th Cir. 1970), *aff'd by an equally divided Court*, 400 U.S. 348 (1971). Memoranda of witness interviews prepared by or under the supervision of the attorney are protected; "of course, the less the lawyer's mental processes are involved, the less will be the burden to show good cause" for disclosure.

■ *Ford v. Philips Elec. Instruments Co.*, 82 F.R.D. 359, 360–61 (E.D. Pa. 1979). At a deposition of a third-party witness, inquiring counsel asked the witness about his conversations with the opposing party's attorney prior to the deposition. The court ruled that the attorney's opinions as conveyed to the witness were protected from inquiry, but that the version of the *facts* conveyed by the attorney were not. "Insofar as defendant's question attempted to elicit from the witness the specific questions that plaintiff's counsel posed to him, or even the area of the case to which he directed the majority of his questions, it exceeds the permissible bounds of discovery and begins to infringe on plaintiff's counsel's evaluation of the case. However, insofar as it was directed to the substance of the witness's knowledge of relevant facts, it is clearly an acceptable line of inquiry. . . . Defendant's counsel shall be given free rein to inquire into the substance of the witness's knowledge concerning matters relevant to the subject matter of this action. . . . Such inquiry may not, however, include questions that tend to elicit the specific questions posed to the witness by plaintiff's counsel, the general line of inquiry pursued by plaintiff's counsel, the facts to which plaintiff's counsel appeared to attach significance, or any other matter that reveals plaintiff's counsel's mental impressions concerning this case."

Thus, the personal recollections of an attorney are generally immune from discovery under the work-product doctrine. This is so particularly when the original witnesses are available.

■ *Computer Assocs. Int'l, Inc. v. Quest Software, Inc.*,2003 U.S. Dist. LEXIS 16378, at *5–6 (N.D. Ill. 2003). "We decline, however, to order CA to turn over additional information relating to these interviews. Such information does have the possibility of giving defendants a significant insight into the litigation strategy of CA. Moreover, such disclosures are unnecessary as defendants will have a fair opportunity to contact and interview these witnesses regarding any statements that they have made to CA. We see no reason why plaintiff should be forced to assist defendants in their own witness interviews." While the names of witness-employees interviewed by a party were deemed discoverable, the content of the interviews was not.

- *United States v. Bonnell*, 483 F. Supp. 1070, 1078–79 (D. Minn. 1979). An attorney's recollections of a meeting in response to an IRS tax summons would be privileged from production.

- *In re Grand Jury Proceedings (Duffy)*,473 F.2d 840, 848 (8th Cir. 1973). An attorney was not required to produce summaries of witness interviews or to testify before a grand jury with respect to his personal recollections of the interviews, or any conclusions that he drew with respect to these interviews. The party seeking disclosure failed to establish that the desired information could not be obtained through further witness interviews.

Obviously, where an attorney's witness interview notes in fact contain far more of his own observations, questions and mental impressions than they do any kind of verbatim transcription of the witness's statement, work product protection will be granted.

- *United States v. Dayan*, 2004 U.S. Dist. LEXIS 25503 at *4 (S.D.N.Y. 2004).The Government contended that defendant's attorney's notes were witness statements within the contemplation of *Fed. R. Cr. P. 26.2.* The court conducted an *in camera* review of the notes and concluded that they were not a substantially verbatim recital of a witness's oral statement but instead "contain what appear—so far as they are legible at all—to be mental impressions, notes, and questions for counsel, and hence were work-product protected and not discoverable."

- *United States v. Marcus Schloss & Co., Inc.*, 1989 U.S. Dist. LEXIS 6271, 1989 WL 62729 at *3 (S.D.N.Y. June 5, 1989). The court found that these notes could not fairly be deemed to reflect fully and without distortion what had been said and therefore could not be used to impeach the witness's testimony at trial.

- *United States v. Sainato*, 29 F. Supp. 2d 116, 118 (E.D.N.Y. 1998). The court ruled that the notes in question were "rough, choppy, disjointed, scattered jottings full of sentence fragments," were not "exact recordings of the witnesses' statements" and thus not subject to disclosure under *Rule 26.2.*

- *Brownell v. Roadway Package Sys., Inc.*, 185 F.R.D. 19 (N.D.N.Y. 1999). The court found that an at-issue waiver occurred where defendant claimed to have conducted an investigation into employee complaints regarding sexual harassment prior to firing the employee. The court further found that outside counsel merely continued the investigation commenced by the human resource department and therefore the investigation was not work-product protected.

But see:

- *EEOC v. Rose Casual Dining, L.P.*, 2004 U.S. Dist. LEXIS 1983(E.D. Pa. 2004). Witness statements made at the behest of litigation counsel, after an employee had been fired and after a letter had been written by the employee suggesting a sexual harassment cause of action, were work-product protected while any statements taken before firing and before engagement of outside counsel were not. The court found that two separate investigations had been conducted and that therefore there was no at-issue waiver in respect to the latter investigation although there was one in respect to the one conducted prior to the firing by the human resource department.

Witness statements taken for purposes other than in anticipation of litigation are not protected as word product since one of the key elements for the finding of work-product protection is then not present.

- *In re Royal Ahold N.V. Sec. & ERISA Litig.*, 230 F.R.D. 433 (D. Md. 2005). The court found that many of the notes and memoranda prepared by outside counsel of witness interviews were taken to satisfy the company's outside auditors and thus were not work-product protected.

Occasionally, a party will make tape recordings of conversations with individuals to prove its case. Such tape recordings may take place in the work place. They are generally not work-product protected and surely the recording party can not make some but not others available on a selective basis.

- *Gray v. Oracle Corp.*, 2006 U.S. Dist. LEXIS 33439 (C.D. Utah 2006). The district court sustained the magistrate judge's ruling that tape recordings made by the plaintiff of conversations with other employees were not work-product protected. There was no discussion of the rationale for the holding. In all events the plaintiff had disclosed some but not all and the court said that such selective waiver was not permissible.

As amended in 1970, Rule 26(b)(3) gives a person—either a party or a nonparty witness—a right to obtain a previously made statement by that person about the action or its subject matter. No special showing is necessary to obtain production. This provision applies to written statements signed, adopted, or approved by the maker, as well as to "substantially verbatim" recordings or transcriptions of oral statements.

A party's own statement is discoverable because when the party does not already have a copy, it is usually because the party was not represented by counsel. Although in such circumstances the party was functioning at a disadvantage, the party's statement is nevertheless admissible against him or her at trial, where, by "springing" it on the party, inadvertent discrepancies may be given disproportionate prominence. The Advisory Committee believed that similar considerations were also operative with statements of nonparty witnesses. When there are substantial concerns about the maker's truthfulness, the court may delay production of the statement until after the witness has been deposed.

- *Frank v. L.L. Bean, Inc.*, 2005 U.S. Dist. LEXIS 19722 at *6–7 (D. Me. 2005). The court, in what is surely bizarre reasoning, stated that supplying a witness with merely a transcript of his answers, but not of the questions was sufficient. The questions were work-product protected. The witness was a former employee of the defendant and had given a statement to plaintiff's counsel. Later the witness agreed to be represented for his deposition by defendant's counsel who sought a transcript of what he had told plaintiff's counsel. "The distinction between narrative statements and information garnered by an attorney through 'skillful questioning' has long supplied the divining line between what is, and what is not, protected work product where witness statements are concerned. In my view, the language of Rule 26(b)(3) adheres to this line by defining 'statement' as, for present purposes, a 'recording[] or a transcription [of] a substantially verbatim recital of an oral statement by the person making it.' Fed. R. Civ. P. 26(b)(3) (emphasis added). Disclosure of plaintiff counsel's questions would exceed the scope of the right afforded to Allen under this language." (Citations omitted.)

10. Witness Identities

Potential witnesses and individuals with possible knowledge must now be voluntarily identified by each party. Rule 26(b)(1) requires parties, as a matter of course and before any discovery requests have been exchanged, to disclose "the name and, if known, the address and telephone number of each individual likely to have discoverable information that the disclosing party may use to support its claims or defenses." That does not mean that counsel must identify who among them has been interviewed or will be relied upon to formulate a claim or defense. That, some courts have held, remains work-product protected, although in light of Rule 26(b)(1) the courts which are so holding may well be creating a distinction without any meaningful difference.

a. *Identities of Witnesses Interviewed Work-Product Protected*

In all events and despite Rule 26(b)(1) some courts have applied work-product protection to certain inquiries into "the identity of persons contacted and/or interviewed during an investigation in anticipation of litigation or for trial."

Many district courts in the Ninth Circuit have held such information to be work-product protected albeit there are Ninth Circuit district court cases which go the other way. *See infra.*

- *In re Ashworth Sec. Lit.*, 213 F.R.D. 385, 389 (S.D. Cal. 2002). The court held that the names of individuals who provided information to plaintiff's counsel that was used in the complaint were work-product protected.

- *In re MTI Tech. Corp Sec. Litig.*, 2002 U.S. Dist. LEXIS 13015, at *18–*19 (C.D. Cal. 2002). The court ruled that the identity of six individuals referenced in the complaint was work-product protected and thus not discoverable.

- *In re MTI Tech Corp. Sec. Litig. II*, 2002 U.S. Dist. LEXIS 13015 (C.D. Cal. June 14, 2002). Plaintiffs produced a list of 71 witnesses as part of their Rule 26 initial disclosures. Defendants moved to compel plaintiffs to reveal which of those 71 individuals had been interviewed by counsel and provided anonymous source material for the complaint. The Court denied the motion, holding that the opinion work-product doctrine protected plaintiffs from having to identify which of the 71 witnesses were the anonymous sources.

- *In re Ashworth Secs. Litig.*, 213 F.R.D. 385 (S.D. Ca. 2002). The court rejected an interrogatory that asked which of the individuals, identified in plaintiffs' initial disclosure, provided information used in framing the complaint.

- *Schbley v. Gould*, 1994 U.S. Dist. LEXIS 4082, at *4 (D. Kan. Mar. 29, 1994). "A party is entitled to discovery from another party of the identity and location of persons having knowledge of any dis-coverable matter. However, the work-product rule does protect against inquiry of the identity of persons contacted and/or inter-viewed during an investigation of the incident in anticipation of litigation or for trial." Thus the court did not require an answer to an interrogatory which sought whether defendants had any com-munication with a list of 54 persons, and the substance of those communications. *BASF Corp. v. Old World Trading Co.*, 1992 U.S. Dist. LEXIS 951, at *10 (N.D. Ill. 1992). The court ruled that a list of persons interviewed by counsel during investigation was work-product protected.

- *Stokes v. Renal Treatment Centers-Illinois, Inc.*, 1998 U.S. Dist. LEXIS 21022 (E.D. Mo. Sept. 16, 1998). The dispute centered on whether the plaintiff's counsel had to reveal contacts with employ-ees and former employees of the defendant, together with the in-formation she obtained from them. Defendant served plaintiff with an interrogatory requiring her to "state whether you or anyone act-ing on your behalf is aware of and/or has obtained a statement from defendant or any of its employee(s), agent(s) or representative(s) concerning matters alleged in the complaint." The plaintiff's coun-sel admitted that she had obtained signed statements from five of defendant's current and former non-managerial employees, but she refused to specifically identify these employees on the grounds that this information was protected from disclosure by the attorney work-product doctrine. However, in response to other interrogatories, plaintiff identified all persons whom she believed have knowl-edge of the matters alleged in the complaint and described with particularity all facts supporting her allegations. In opposing the motion to compel, plaintiff's counsel also disclosed the job titles of the employees who were interviewed, the person who interviewed them, and the dates upon which the statements were obtained and signed. The defendant, nonetheless, maintained that plaintiff should be required to specifically identify the five current and former employees that plaintiff's counsel selected to interview.

Since none of the statements made by the individuals interviewed could be deemed admissions against interest, no further disclosure was required and the motion to compel was accordingly denied. Moreover, since that was the case the interviews did not violate ethical rules prohibiting *ex parte* communications with an adverse party's current and former non-managerial employees.

b. *Identities of Witnesses Interviewed Not Work-Product Protected*

Ninth Circuit courts go both ways, on occasion refusing discovery *see supra* and on others declaring quite similar information not to be work-product protected without any principle which would allow for prediction as to how they will go and thus a sure source of additional discovery disputes.

- *Miller v. Ventro Corp.*, 2004 U.S. Dist. LEXIS 6913, at *6 (N.D. Cal. Apr. 21, 2004). The court held that the identity of individuals referenced in the complaint was not protected from disclosure.

- *In re Theragenics Corp. Sec. Litig.*, 205 F.R.D. 631, 636 (N.D. Ga. 2002). The court ruled that the names of witnesses interviewed by counsel who had knowledge of the facts alleged in the complaint were not work-product protected from disclosure.

Other courts have it both ways, calling such information work product, but then also ruling it is not protected from disclosure because the other side has "substantial need" for the information. One can not help wondering why such contortions are necessary and why Rule 26(b)(1) is not dispositive.

- *In re: Priceline.Com Inc. Sec. Litig.*, 2005 U.S. Dist. LEXIS 11142 at *10–12 (D. Conn. 2005). "The court holds that the identity of witnesses with whom plaintiffs or their counsel have had contact and individuals referenced in the complaint is attorney work product but that this information is not immune from discovery. Because this information was accumulated during the course of plaintiffs' attorney's investigation, it is attorney work product. Discovery of this information would reveal aspects of plaintiffs' counsel's investigation, and, through this information, defendants could possibly gain insight into counsel's thought process. Although this information is attorney work product, however, it is subject to disclosure under *Rule 26* if 'the party seeking discovery has substantial need of the materials in the preparation of the party's case and that party is unable without due hardship to obtain the substantial equivalent of the materials by other means. . . .' *Fed. R. Civ. P. 26(b)(3)*. In this case, forcing defendants to ferret through the substantial list of individuals who have information relevant to plaintiffs' claims in order to discover those individuals upon whose knowledge plaintiffs have framed their allegations would be an undue hardship. *Rule 26* provides unqualified protection for the 'mental impressions, conclusions, opinions, or legal theories of an attorney'; in this case the information sought does not impinge upon the zone of unqualified protection. The courts in the cases cited herein have taken different views on this position according to the particular facts of each case, and this court finds that the defendants' need for the information substantially outweighs the potential for an intrusion into plaintiffs' counsel's case preparation."

Still other courts finesse the question of whether the information sought is or is not work product in nature and basically state there is no harm in the disclosure and that in fact it will expedite the discovery process which seems by far the most felicitous approach.

- *Computer Associates Internat'l, Inc. v. Quest Software, Inc.*, 2003 U.S. Dist. LEXIS 16378 at *5 (N.D. Ill. 2003). Disclosure of names of interviewed witnesses was required. "[W]e find that CA must turn over the names of the current and former Quest employees it has interviewed in connection with this litigation. While it is true that defendants have an opportunity to interview these employees on their own, we believe that the disclosure of the names is extremely unlikely to have a prejudicial effect on CA or give defendants any insight into its preparation for litigation. . . . Instead, it

will serve only to expedite the gathering of relevant information."
(Citations omitted.)

- *In re: Initial Public Offering Sec. Litig.*, 220 F.R.D. 30; 2003 U.S.
Dist. LEXIS 19340 (S.D.N.Y. 2003). The court found that the
identity of individuals with knowledge of tie-in arrangements in a
public offering were not work-product protected.

The Third Circuit courts have fairly uniformly followed their court of
appeals in concluding that Rule 26(b)(1) warrants disclosure of the identity of witnesses who have been interviewed. When they do so the court's
determination to allow the discovery of the identities of witnesses interviewed is based on the extent to which the information disclosed an
attorney's thought processes and whether the disclosure would reveal the
attorney's mental impressions, conclusions, opinions, or legal theories, usually concluding that the identity alone does not do so and thus holding the
information not work-product protected and therefore discoverable.

- *United States v. Amerada Hess Corp.*, 619 F.2d 980, 988 (3d Cir.
1980). The Court of Appeals found that a list of persons interviewed by defendant's counsel did not directly or indirectly reveal
the mental processes of defendant's attorneys and furnished no information as to the content of any statement. Therefore the court
found that a list of interviewees was "of rather minimal substantive
content, and presents none of the classic dangers to which the
Hickman v. Taylor rule is addressed." The court held that work
product did not preclude its production.

- *In re: Automotive Refinishing Paint Antitrust Litig.*, 2006 U.S. Dist.
LEXIS 34129 at *15–16 (E.D. Pa. 2006). The court held that the
identity and location of persons having knowledge of any discoverable matter" are explicitly within the scope of permissible discovery
under the Federal Rules, *Fed. R. Civ. P. 26(b)(1)*. "The interrogatories found objectionable by Plaintiffs seek the identities of persons who provided Plaintiffs with certain information at certain
times. . . . While these lists may provide a remote clue as to the nature and scope of Plaintiffs' investigation, their substantive work
product content is minimal. In producing this information, Plaintiffs need not reveal any of the details of the interactions that

occurred or the mental impressions, conclusions, legal theories, or opinions drawn therefrom. Defendants merely seek 'specific subcategor[ies] of all potential fact witnesses,' a permissible subject for discovery."

- *In re Aetna Inc. Sec. Litig.*, 1999 U.S. Dist. LEXIS 8038, at *6–7 (E.D. Pa. 1999). The court found that the names of individuals interviewed by Plaintiffs' counsel and referenced in the complaint had minimal work product content and were not protected under *Hickman*.

- *In re Towner Petroleum Co. Sec. Litig.*, 1986 U.S. Dist. LEXIS 29067, at *32–34 (E.D. Pa. 1986). A request to identify persons interviewed by opposing counsel did not seek the substance of any conversations and hence was not work product protected or attorney-client privileged.

- *Electronic Data Sys. Corp. v. Steingraber*, 2003 U.S. Dist. LEXIS 11818, 2003 WL 21653405 (E.D. Tex. 2003). The court did not require answer to an interrogatory that asked defendant to identify individuals who had been interviewed concerning the relevant allegations in the case.

- *American Floral Services, Inc. v. Florists' Transworld Delivery Ass'n.*, 107 F.R.D. 258 (N.D. Ill. 1985). The court ruled that the identity of witnesses having knowledge of the relevant facts is discoverable information.

11. Witness Preparation

Deposition questions regarding witness preparation raise problems of infringing upon the attorney's mental processes. The principles enunciated in *Hickman* are invoked to protect an attorney's intangible work product as it may be reflected in conversations the attorney has with a witness who is not the attorney's client. If a witness is instructed not to testify as to certain matters in the course of the deposition, courts will review the questions asked and sort out those areas of inquiry that are protected as opinion work product from those that are not protected. The matter can be brought to the attention of the court either by the proponent of questions on a motion to compel answers or as a protective motion by the party objecting to the questions.

- *Delco Wire & Cable, Inc. v. Weinberger*, 109 F.R.D. 680, 689–92 (E.D. Pa. 1986). At the deposition of a staff attorney for a Department of Defense procurement office, several categories of questions were asked regarding the preparation given to a prior deponent. The court ruled as follows on various categories of questions that purportedly sought to explore attorney work product:

  (1) The advice the attorney gave to a prior deponent concerning how that witness should testify in the course of his deposition was protected opinion work product.

  (2) What the prior deponent told the staff attorney was not protected opinion work product.

  (3) Inquiries regarding the role of another attorney in representing the prior deponent were not protected opinion work product.

  (4) The nature of the discussions held between the attorney and the prior deponent was not sufficiently spelled out to permit the court to rule on whether such discussions were protected work product.

  (5) Opponents of the question had not borne the burden of showing that work done by attorneys in relation to events leading up to the litigation was done *in anticipation* of litigation. Therefore, answers to the questions posed would be compelled.

  (6) Questions relating to an attorney's settlement recommendations necessarily delved into that attorney's legal opinion concerning the strengths and weaknesses of claims made in the litigation and, hence, were protected.

- *Phoenix Nat'l Corp., Inc. v. Bowater United Kingdom Paper Ltd.*, 98 F.R.D. 669, 671 (N.D. Ga. 1983). The defendant's employees did not have to answer questions dealing with the defendant's attorney's view of the case and the specific questions counsel's agent asked in investigations. Although these questions did not deal with documents or tangible things, they still concerned the attorney's "mental impressions" and, therefore, were protected work product.

Protection has been accorded for documents shared with a jury consultant who assists counsel with "wood-shedding" a witness.

- *In re Cendant Corp. Sec. Litig.*, 343 F.3d 658 (3d Cir.) The jury consultant was provided with documents prepared by the party's counsel reflecting counsel's mental impressions, opinions, conclusions, and legal theories. In addition, the jury consultant's notes of these discussions may reflect the mental impressions, opinions, conclusions, and legal theories of counsel; hence "core" work-product protection was accorded under the theory that if similar wood-shedding had been done directly by counsel, the issue would never have even arisen. The magistrate so ruled. The district court reversed. The circuit court in turn reversed and reinstated the magistrate's ruling, holding that the discussions with the jury consultant were work-product protected.

If, on the other hand, documents are provided to a witness to assist the witness in formulating his testimony, they may be ordered produced.

- *Auscape Int'l. v. Nat'l Geographic Society*, 2002 U.S. Dist. LEXIS 19428 (S.D. N.Y. 2002). Where the attorney prepared a summary of the complaint to assist in preparation of witnesses, the summary was ordered produced. Although the summary contained attorney opinions, it did not contain anything that had not already been made public in another form, namely the complaint. Thus it is hard to use this case as precedent that all such work product would be discoverable even if the information had not already been made public in some form.

And if in the course of the deposition, a witness concedes that his memory was refreshed by documents shown to him in preparation of his deposition, those documents will then be ordered produced.

12. Settlement Negotiations

Settlement negotiations often entail an exchange of information. Does such exchange necessarily entail a waiver of work product? Not necessarily. The waiver usually does not reach the legal theories that may have been formulated by counsel and shared in the course of settlement negotiations. Such waiver, however, will reach any information expressly shared in the course of the settlement discussions.

- *Burlington Indus. v. Exxon Corp.*, 65 F.R.D. 26, 46 (D. Md. 1974). The court held that waiver of attorney work product during settlement negotiations was limited to information disclosed during negotiations and explained that a legal position taken at settlement negotiations does not make opinion work product discoverable unless the settlement agreement itself is directly at issue.

■ *American Optical Corp. v. Medtronic, Inc.*, 56 F.R.D. 426, 432 (D. Mass. 1972). Detailed contention in pre-litigation negotiating session that the patents at issue were invalid and therefore not infringed by defendant did not waive work-product protection upon which those contentions were based. "As to this contention, I reject the notion that a party waives its privilege if its lawyer, bargaining on its behalf, contends vigorously and even in some detail that the law favors his client's position on a point in issue— whether that point is the contested validity of a patent, the contested validity of a contract, or some other matter. Bargaining, like litigation itself, partakes of the adversary procedure. Negotiated settlements are to be encouraged, and bargaining and argument precede such settlements. Clients and lawyers should not have to fear that positions on legal issues taken during negotiations waive the attorney client privilege so that the private opinions and reports drafted by an attorney for his client become discoverable."

VI. EXCEPTIONS TO THE WORK-PRODUCT PROTECTION

A. *Witness Statements*

When a witness testifies, any previously made verbatim statements or statements otherwise adopted by the witness are discoverable for impeachment purposes. Rule 26(b)(3) makes these discoverable, but as we have seen in the Section of Witness Statements, *supra* generally, courts will protect witness statements from compelled disclosure if they are not substantially verbatim and/or contain attorney commentary, impressions and the like.

B. *Experts*

1. Testifying Experts

The 1970 amendments to Federal Rule of Civil Procedure 26(b) added the following subdivision governing discovery from experts:

(4) Trial Preparation: Experts. Discovery of facts known and opinions held by experts, otherwise discoverable under

the provisions of subdivision (b)(1) of this rule and acquired or developed in anticipation of litigation or for trial,
may be obtained only as follows:

(A)(i) A party may through interrogatories require any
other party to identify each person whom the other party
expects to call as an expert witness at trial, to state the
subject matter on which the expert is expected to testify,
and to state the substance of the facts and opinions to
which the expert is expected to testify and a summary of
the grounds for each opinion. (ii) Upon motion, the court
may order further discovery by other means, subject to
such restrictions as to scope and such provisions, pursuant
to subdivision (b)(4)(C) of this rule, concerning fees and
expenses as the court may deem appropriate.

(B) A party may discover facts known or opinions held by
an expert who has been retained or specially employed by
another party in anticipation of litigation or preparation
for trial and is not expected to be called as a witness at
trial, only as provided in Rule 35(b) or upon a showing of
exceptional circumstances under which it is impracticable
for the party seeking discovery to obtain facts or opinions
on the same subject by other means.

(C) Unless manifest injustice would result, (i) the court
shall require that the party seeking discovery pay the expert a reasonable fee for time spent in responding to discovery under subdivisions (b)(4)(A)(ii) and (b)(4)(B) of
this rule; and (ii) with respect to discovery obtained under
subdivision (b)(4)(A)(ii) of this rule the court may require, and with respect to discovery obtained under subdivision (b)(4)(B) of this rule the court shall require, the
party seeking discovery to pay the other party a fair portion
of the fees and expenses reasonably incurred by the latter
party in obtaining facts and opinions from the expert.

The rule implicitly divides discovery of experts into four categories: routine discovery of experts to be called at trial, further discovery of trial experts, discovery of experts not expected to be called at

trial, and discovery of experts not specially retained. It treats the facts learned and opinions formed by all experts in anticipation of litigation as work product and prescribes the showing needed for pretrial discovery, depending on the use to be made of the expert. *See generally* 8 CHARLES ALAN WRIGHT & ARTHUR R. MILLER, FEDERAL PRACTICE AND PROCEDURE §§ 2029-33 (1970 & Supp. 1987).

The underlying assumption of the rule is that adequate presentation of the expert's testimony at trial, including presentation of its weaknesses through cross-examination, requires pretrial discovery. Thus, under Rule 26(b)(4)(A) a party is entitled, without further showing of need, to discover the identity of experts to be called at trial, the facts and opinions on which they are expected to testify, and the grounds for those opinions.

- *Beverage Mktg. Corp. v. Ogilvy & Mather Direct Response, Inc.*, 563 F. Supp. 1013, 1014–15 (S.D.N.Y. 1983). Disclosure of reports prepared by experts is governed by Rule 26(b)(4), not 26(b)(3), given the purpose of allowing an opponent to meet expert testimony effectively.

The distinction between the first two categories is that subdivision (A)(i) provides for such discovery ordinarily to be by means of interrogatories, while (A)(ii) permits the court to provide for further discovery of the expert by other means. The rule does not suggest any factors bearing on whether discovery other than by interrogatory should be permitted, and in practice, the courts frequently allow deposition discovery of trial experts as a matter of routine. *See generally* Graham, *Discovery of Experts under Rule 26(b)(4) of the Federal Rules of Civil Procedure: Part Two, An Empirical Study and a Proposal,* 1977 U. ILL. L.F. 169, 172.

Thereafter Rule 26(a)(2)(B) of the Federal Rules of Civil Procedure was amended in 1993 to require that reports be prepared for each testifying expert containing, among other things, "the data or other information *considered* by the witness in forming the opinions." (Emphasis added.)

The Advisory Committee Notes to the 1993 Amendment, explain this requirement as follows:

> The [expert] report is to disclose the data and other information considered by the expert and any other exhibits or

charts that summarize or support the expert's opinions. Given this obligation of disclosure, litigants should no longer be able to argue that materials furnished to their experts to be used in forming their opinions—*whether or not ultimately relied upon by the expert*—are privileged or otherwise protected from disclosure when such persons are testifying or being deposed. (Emphasis added.)

Increasingly, the tendency seems to be to require the production of all materials, including pure opinion work product, given to experts who will be testifying, as opposed to consulting experts. It is strongly urged that this is the correct decision for a multiplicity of reasons.

An opposing party should be entitled to discover everything that went into an expert's opinion, whether consciously so or not, particularly in light of the extraordinarily expanded role experts play in modern litigation.

If the party employing and proffering the expert as a witness wishes to preserve the work-product privilege, the remedy could hardly be simpler. Don't show the work product to the expert. If the work product is necessary to allow the expert to reach the conclusion which the party is paying him to reach, clearly the opposing party and ultimately the fact finder must be entitled to know whatever went into his conclusion—be it money or documents. Only so can the opinion be subject to adequate cross examination.

If full discovery is not allowed, there will be endless litigation over whether or not the expert "considered" a particular document in reaching his opinion.

If full discovery is not to be allowed, there will be far less predictability over what will or won't be discoverable and far less uniformity in the results.

Simplicity of litigation is always devoutly to be wished, particularly in light of contemporary standards of cumbersome, protracted and costly pre-trial litigation and motion practice which absorbs untold hours of court and litigation attorney time. Why add yet another area of muddled law and contradictory decisions begging for more litigation?

Thus it is urged that the rule should always be: If you disclose it to a testifying expert witness, you must disclose it to the other side. Happily more courts are recognizing that is the only sensible way to proceed. The day may even come when objections interposed thereto are deemed frivolous. Where the roles of consulting and testifying expert are held by the same individual, full disclosure must prevail because otherwise considerable gamesmanship as to what was learned in which role and endless litigation as to in what capacity matters had been disclosed will follow.

- *Wilson v. Wilkinson*, 2006 U.S. Dist. LEXIS 32113, at *13 (S.D. Oh. 2006). Where it is impossible to distinguish between the role of consulting and testifying expert everything must be disclosed. "[D]isclosure of material "considered," allows discovery of all communications between counsel and a retained testifying expert, even if those communications contain the attorneys' mental impressions or trial strategy or is otherwise protected by the work product privilege."

- *Synthes Spine Co., L.P. v. Walden*, 232 F.R.D. 460, 464 (E.D. Pa. 2005) The court collected cases. Recognizing that some courts still did not require disclosure of all documents be they otherwise privilege or opinion work-product protected which were considered by an expert disclosed, but also noted that it was increasingly a minority position. It opted for full disclosure, trying once again to formulate that all does indeed mean all. "The Court finds that plaintiff must disclose all materials, regardless of privilege, that plaintiff's expert generated, reviewed, reflected upon, read, and/or used in formulating his conclusions, even if these materials were ultimately rejected by plaintiff's expert in reaching his opinions. This includes disclosure, in whatever form the expert received them, of materials that plaintiff's counsel supplied to plaintiff's expert, including e-mails, summaries of lost sales, summary spreadsheets, pleadings, corporate information, sales charts and breakdowns, time analyses, retainer letters and invoices, and draft expert reports."

The court included all oral communications, including any such communications between the attorney and the client to which the testifying expert was privy and which he "considered" in formulating his opinion, but excluded those which the expert did not "consider" in formulating his opinion. Thereby leaving precisely the wriggle room and scope to litigate what was and what was not "considered" for disclosure purposes.

And here we thought that the court meant *all* when it said all. Besides since oral communications leave no trace one will never know whether this aspect of the order was or was not complied with.

- *In re Omeprazole Patent Litig.*, 2005 U.S. Dist. LEXIS 6112 (S.D.N.Y. 2005). Motion to compel a testifying expert to answer deposition questions as to conversations with counsel regarding why he dropped certain portions from his report was granted.

- *Zheng v. Liberty Apparel Co., Inc.*, 2004 U.S. Dist. LEXIS 15026 (S.D.N.Y. 2004). With a long line of string citations, the court simply and happily without much discussion concluded that Rule 26(a)(2)(B)'s expert disclosure requirements were paramount over any work product protection concerns and accordingly overruled all objections to full disclosure.

- *In Re: McRae*, 295 B.R. 676; 2003 Bankr. LEXIS 837; 41 Bankr. Ct. Dec. 172; 16 Fla. L. Weekly Fed. B 166 (N.D. Fla. 2003). Where inter-office memoranda from one attorney to another were provided to the testifying expert, they must be provided to the opposing side even if they contain legal theories.

- *Lugosch v. Congel*, 219 F.R.D. 220, 280 (N.D.N.Y. 2003). "For a host of reasons, particularly overall functionality, predictability, litigation certainty, truth seeking, and eventual testimonial use, this Court embraces those precedents that support the bright-line rule that expert disclosure of all data and information considered by the expert should be disclosed notwithstanding the presence of work-product consideration. Indeed, we agree with the reasons postulated in support of a bright-line rule of disclosure especially in light of modern day litigation practice . . ."

- *Western Resources, Inc. v. Union Pac. R. R. Co.*, 2002 U.S. Dist. LEXIS 1911 at *14, 2002 WL 181494 at *9 (D. Kan. 2002). The court held that even documents considered but rejected by a testifying expert may be necessary for effective cross-examination. "To determine whether an expert 'considered' materials, *as that term is commonly used*, would require the court to explore the expert's subjective mental processes and risks the creation of an unwieldy rule that would provide uncertainty as to the protected status or work product or other privileged materials. The court believes it is important for practitioners to have a more definitive rule under which they can determine whether waiver has occurred. This is so even if the testifying expert avers under oath that he did not actually consider such materials in formulating his opinion."

- *In re Pioneer Hi-Bred Int'l Inc.*, 238 F.3d 1370, (Fed. Cir. 2001). All documents shown to an expert were discoverable regardless of their nature.

- *Energy Capital Corp. v. United States*, 45 Fed. Cl. 481, 494 (Fed. Cl. 2000). All documents given to testifying experts were ordered produced, including those containing work product and opinion work product. "Complete disclosure promotes the discovery of the true source of the expert's opinions and the detection of any influence by the attorney in forming the opinion of the expert. In addition, the attorneys can minimize how much the other side learns of their opinion work product by monitoring what information is provided to the expert. If the expert does not have the attorney's opinion work product, then neither will the other side's attorney. Lastly, a clear line is easier to administer and a predictable result helps the litigants plan their strategy."

- *TV-3, Inc. v. Royal Ins. Co. of Am.*, 193 F.R.D. 490, 492 (S.D. Miss.), *aff'd*, 194 F.R.D. 585 (S.D. Miss. 2000). The court required disclosure of all documents and oral communications reviewed by experts in connection with formulating opinions, even those ultimately rejected or not relied upon.

- *B.C.F. Oil Refining, Inc. v. Consolidated Edison Co. of New York, Inc.*, 171 F.R.D. 57, 67 (D.D.N.Y. 1997). "There does not seem to be a principled difference between oral and written communications between an expert and an attorney insofar as discoverability is concerned."

- *Oneida, Ltd. v. United States*, 43 Fed. Cl. 611, 618–19, 82 A.F.T.R.2d (RIA) 99-2346, at *23–24, 28 (Fed. Cl. 1999). The court reviewed cases under comparable Federal Rule 26(b)(2) and required disclosure of factual and core work product provided to testifying experts. "Having reviewed these precedents, the court is persuaded that core work product information provided to a testifying expert witness should be discoverable, unless such materials bear no probative relationship to the opinion or testimony the expert is likely to give. This construction of RCFC 26(b)(2) arguably proceeds directly from the language of the rule itself, which provides that the protections afforded trial preparation materials are 'subject to the [expert discovery] provisions of subdivision (b)(3).' However, the welter of conflicting decisions construing this language suggests that it is neither clear on this point nor determinative. Nonetheless, several reasons counsel in favor of construing this language to allow considerable discovery of core work-product information provided to a testifying expert."

The court concluded that the following policy reasons urged full disclosure. 1) The integrity of the truth-finding process depended on effective cross-examination, which in turn requires the ability to determine the source of the expert's opinions. 2). Disclosure in such circumstances would cause no harm to the principles underlying the work-product doctrine. 3). Adoption of a bright-line test promotes litigation efficiency and certainty. "In sum, the court is not persuaded that the rule it embraces—that core work-product information provided to a testifying expert witness should be discoverable, unless such materials bear no probative relationship to the opinion or testimony the expert is likely to give—poses a serious threat to the principles underlying the work-product doctrine. At the same time, this court is convinced that this rule promotes the truth-finding process as it was intended to be promoted by paragraph (3) of Rule 26(b) of the RCFC and by *Rules 702, 703 and 705 of the Federal Rules of Evidence*." Most assuredly.

- *Karn v. Ingersoll-Rand Co.*, 168 F.R.D. 633, 638 (N.D. Ind. 1996). At issue in this personal injury action was a medical history report prepared by plaintiff's counsel as fact word product and forwarded to testifying experts who although they reviewed the entire report contended they had only relied on the post-injury portions of the document. The court, looking at the 1993 amendments to Rule 26(a)(2), found that the term "considered" meant something different than and more than "relied upon" and thus ordered production. "In this Court's view, new Rule 26 and its supporting commentary reveal that the drafters considered the imperfect alignment between 26(b)(3) and 26(b)(4) under the old Rule, and clearly resolved it by providing that the requirements of (a)(2) 'trump' any assertion of work product or privilege." The court went on to remark that the balancing test used by certain courts even after the 1993 amendments, however seemingly erudite, was totally superfluous. "The 'bright-line' interpretation expressed here also makes good sense on several policy grounds: effective cross-examination of expert witnesses will be enhanced; the policies underlying the work-product doctrine will not be violated; and, finally, litigation certainty will be achieved—counsel will know exactly what documents will be subject to disclosure and can react accordingly."

Indeed the *Karn* case has become somewhat of a touchstone for those courts which follow it in holding that the 1993 amendments to Rule(a)(2) mandate full disclosure any work-product materials shown to a testifying expert.

Some cases, which are surely wrongly decided, have continued to accord work-product protection to work-product materials disclosed to experts where such materials contained an attorney's legal theories. Rule 26(a)(2)(B) makes no such distinction. The Committee commentary makes clear that no such distinction should be made. Nonetheless, some courts seem awfully reluctant to let go of what they are familiar with regardless of rule changes to the contrary.

- *Smith v. Transducer Tech., Inc.*, 197 F.R.D. 260 (V.I. 2000). Documents shown to expert which contained the attorney's legal theories were not ordered produced.

- *Haworth v. Herman Miller, Inc.*, 162 F.R.D. 289 (W.D. Mich. 1995). Work-product protection accorded to documents shown to expert where they contained an attorney's legal theories.

2. Non-Testifying Experts

When the expert employed in anticipation of litigation is not expected to be called as a witness at trial, subdivision Rule 26(a)(2)(B) provides that discovery is available only on terms generally applicable to other work product: "exceptional circumstances under which it is impracticable for the party seeking discovery to obtain facts or opinions on the same subject by other means."

- *Lugosch v. Congel*, 219 F.R.D. 220, 244 (N.D.N.Y. 2003). Financial audits conducted of partnership assets when concern arises as to mismanagement need not be shared with the defendant managers, despite having been shared with other partners with a common interest, unless they were considered by a testifying expert.

- *Delcastor, Inc. v. Vail Assocs., Inc.*, 108 F.R.D. 405, 408–09 (D. Colo. 1985). Even if the defendant's expert, who would testify only to facts observed, was not a 26(b)(4)(A) expert, the plaintiff showed the "exceptional circumstances" required under Rule 26(b) (4)(B). The defendant's expert witness had observed the site of a mudslide only one day after the occurrence, but the plaintiff's expert had not been able to observe the site until five days after the mudslide, when conditions had changed a great deal; besides, another of the defendant's expert witnesses had relied on the "fact" expert's report.

- *Heitmann v. Concrete Pipe Mach.*, 98 F.R.D. 740, 742–43 (E.D. Mo. 1983). The report of a non-testifying expert was ordered produced when it was given to and relied on by a testifying expert.

The rule thus implements the anti-free-rider policy expressed in *Hickman.*

- *Grindell v. American Motors Corp.*, 108 F.R.D. 94, 95 (W.D.N.Y. 1985). The plaintiffs could not depose the defendants' expert witness regarding tasks he had performed as a consultant when they could obtain the information from another source and when they could have hired their own experts to rebut any opinions he held.

- *Pearl Brewing Co. v. Joseph Schlitz Brewing Co.*, 415 F. Supp. 1122, 1138 (S.D. Tex. 1976). Plaintiffs voluntarily made available a printout of the computer program that utilized their trial expert's design and information. The defendant was unable to understand this printout because the coded symbols used in the computer's program were not known to him. The defendant's request for discovery of computer information and depositions of the plaintiffs' non-trial computer-programming experts was granted. The court reasoned that the defendant was not seeking to "avoid the expense of compensating expert witnesses or to develop its own case entirely out of the mouth of its adversary's expert witness." Rather, the defendant was only attempting to vindicate its legitimate need to examine the "mechanical methods, tests, procedures, assumptions and comparisons" that underlay the testimony of the opposing party's trial expert.

A category implicit in the rule is the expert who has not been "retained or specially employed . . . in anticipation of litigation." No special provision is made regarding discovery of facts known and opinions held by such an expert, so the other discovery provisions apply. Thus, the expert who is an actor (e.g., the defendant doctor in a malpractice case) or viewer with respect to the events has no protection from discovery of relevant information. Likewise, the regular employee of the defendant who investigated an accident and formed conclusions about it in the ordinary course of business is subject to discovery. When the expert is regularly employed by the party but formed opinions in anticipation of litigation, the better (but not universal) view is that "exceptional circumstances" should be required before permitting discovery. *See generally* 8 CHARLES ALAN WRIGHT & ARTHUR R. MILLER, FEDERAL PRACTICE AND PROCEDURE § 2033 nn.91–92 (2d ed. 1970 & Supp. 1987), and authorities cited therein. Essentially, an expert in this last category has prepared work product to which the *Hickman* policies apply.

C. *Surveillance Tapes*

In personal injury litigation, it has become common to do covert surveillance tapes of plaintiffs to disprove the extent of the alleged injury. Although seemingly classically "work product," and intended essentially as impeachment of the plaintiff, courts have generally made such tapes discoverable on the grounds either of avoiding "surprise" or that such tapes go to a fundamental fact in dispute. The rationale may be foggy. The result by and large is not.

- *Chiasson v. Zapata Gulf Marine Corp.*, 988 F.2d 513, 517 (5th Cir. 1993). The Fifth Circuit addressed the discoverability of videotape surveillance. The court held that regardless of whether the surveillance video has impeachment value, it must be disclosed prior to trial if it is at all substantive evidence as opposed to solely "impeachment evidence." *Id.* at 517–18 n.44.

- *Forbes v. Hawaiian Tug & Barge Corp.*, 125 F.R.D. 505, 507–08 (D. Haw. 1989). Surveillance tapes were discoverable.

- *Snead v. American Export-Isbrandtsen Lines, Inc.*, 59 F.R.D. 148, 150–51 (E. D. Pa. 1973). Surveillance tapes were discoverable.

The principle of discoverability has been applied in cases other than personal injury litigation.

- *Southern Scrap Material Co. v. Fleming* 2003 U.S. Dist. LEXIS 10815 (E.D. La. 2003). Videos done by defendant attorneys who were being sued by a company alleging that lawsuits had been fraudulently filed against it were discoverable to demonstrate whether the attorneys had any basis for the filing of the suits. The court concluded that the videos were "substantive in nature" and probative of issues in dispute.

D. *Attorney's Conduct in Issue*

If the attorney's conduct is a central issue in the case, the work-product protection does not apply. This rare situation is to be distinguished from those in which the attorney's files provide a particularly probative and virtually irreplaceable source of information about issues in the case.

- *Charlotte Motor Speedway, Inc. v. International Ins. Co.*, 125 F.R.D. 127 (M.D.N.C. 1989). Where the "activities and advice of counsel" are a crucial issue in resolving a claim of bad faith settlement under an insurance contract, the attorney's work product, including the opinion work product, became discoverable.

- *In re John Doe*, 662 F.2d 1073, 1080 (4th Cir. 1981), *cert. denied*, 455 U.S. 1000 (1982). When the attorney's prior representation was a target of the grand jury's investigation, his work product in that case was not protected from discovery.

- *SEC v. Nat'l Student Mktg. Corp.*, 18 Fed. R. Serv. 2d (CBC) 1302, 1305 (D.D.C. 1974). When the production requests are made upon attorneys as defendants—that is, where the activities of counsel are being inquired into because they are at issue in the action before the court—a rare exception to the rule of nondisclosure applies. "[W]hile Rule 26(b)(3) provides that protection against discovery of the attorney's or representative's 'mental impressions, conclusions, opinions or legal theories' shall be provided, such protection would not screen information directly at issue."

E. *Crime or Fraud*

Because the standards of what constitute a *prima facie* showing are generally comparable in the context of the work-product protection and in the context of the attorney-client privilege, the reader is referred to the comparable crime/fraud exception under the discussion of attorney-client privilege for a more extensive discussion. *See* Part 1, Section B, "Crime or Fraud Exception to Attorney-Client Privilege," *supra*, for a more thorough treatment of the case law.

The crime/fraud exception was slower to evolve as an exception to the work-product protection than it was in the attorney-client privilege context.

- *In re Grand Jury Subpoenas Duces Tecum*, 773 F.2d 204, 206 (8th Cir. 1985). The question of whether the crime or fraud exception applies to the work-product privilege was left unresolved, but for purposes of reviewing the trial court's determination that a *prima facie* case was not made, the court assumed the exception exists.

Denying the work-product protection when the disputed materials have been prepared in furtherance of crime or fraud is certainly consistent with the policies of the doctrine. Protection is given to promote the adversary process, not to pervert it.

- *In re Special Sept. 1987 Grand Jury (II)*, 640 F.2d 49, 63 (7th Cir. 1980). "When the case being prepared involves the client's ongoing fraud, however, we see no reason to afford the client the benefit of this doctrine. It is only the 'rightful interests' of the client that the work product doctrine was designed to protect."

- *In re John Doe Corp.*, 675 F.2d 482, 491–92 (2d Cir. 1982). The court noted that when the work product is part of the criminal scheme, "all reason for protecting it from judicial examination evaporates." On the contrary, the fear of disclosure serves a useful deterrent purpose.

Accordingly, the question of whether the crime/fraud exception is applicable in the work-product context is no longer in serious dispute. Courts generally hold that the exception applies to the work-product doctrine as much as it does to the attorney-client privilege. When a document has been prepared in anticipation of litigation to *further* a fraud, the work-product protection will generally not be available.

- *In re Grand Jury Proceedings (FMC Corp.)*, 604 F.2d 798, 802 (3d Cir. 1979). "The work-product privilege is perverted if it is used to further illegal activities as is the attorney-client privilege, and there are no overpowering considerations in either situation that would justify the shielding of evidence that aids continuing or future criminal activity."

In order for the work product to be discoverable, the same two-pronged test is generally applied as we have seen in the attorney-client privilege context. First, there must be a prima facie showing of a crime/fraud. Second, there must be a showing that the work product sought and the crime/fraud alleged are reasonably related. The two-pronged test for disclosure was clearly enunciated by Judge Wright.

- *In re Sealed Case*, 676 F.2d 793, 815 (D.C. Cir. 1982). "The government's showing is sufficient if it proffers evidence that, if believed by a trier of fact, would establish the elements of some violation that was ongoing or about to be committed when the work product was prepared."

The same discussion as to how a *prima facie* case is to be defined that we saw at length in the privilege context is equally a matter for discussion in the work-product context. The criteria that any given circuit chooses to apply does not differ with respect to the privilege and the protection. Therefore, for a more detailed discussion, the reader is again referred to the parallel section under the attorney-client privilege. Although some courts use Black's definition of what constitutes a *prima facie* case, as seen in the parallel section (Part 1, Section V, Heading C, "Crime or Fraud Exception to Attorney-Client Privilege"), each circuit tends to have its own manner of addressing the issue. There is more linguistic distinction rather than substantive difference in the formulations used.

- *In re Int'l Sys. & Control Corp.*, 693 F.2d 1235, 1242 (5th Cir. 1982). At issue was whether binders created by a corporation to investigate the payment of bribes were discoverable. The district court had used Black's Law Dictionary definition of a *prima facie* case, namely, evidence that unless contradicted would support a finding. The court of appeals did not criticize the standard applied, but reversed the district court's finding that the standard had been met where there was no showing of specific intent by management to continue the fraud when the documents as to which a work-product protection claim was made were created.

There is, however, some divergence as to how much will be revealed of work product and under what conditions in at least the Fourth Circuit, which requires continuing protection for attorney opinion work product even if the crime/fraud exception applies. Only if it is found that the attorney was himself a knowing participant in the crime/fraud will the protection for opinion work product be stripped away. The distinction that the Fourth Circuit makes does not necessarily make much sense although it has a surface appeal. The work product doctrine was essentially evolved to protect an attorney's mental processes from an adversary. What interest does an attorney have in protecting his mental processes from the government when his client, who has paid for the work product and for whose benefit it was prepared, made an illegal use of it?

- *In re Grand Jury Proceedings*, 33 F.3d 342, 349 (4th Cir. 1994). The court held that while the attorney-client privilege may be vitiated without showing that the attorney knew of the fraud or crime, those seeking to overcome the opinion work-product privilege must make a *prima facie* showing that the "attorney in question was aware of or a knowing participant in the criminal conduct." If the attorney was not aware of the criminal conduct, a court must redact any portions of subpoenaed materials containing opinion work product. Thus only the attorney-client privilege and fact work product was here vitiated because the attorneys did not know to what use their legal opinions and work were being put.

Created in the grand jury context, the crime/fraud exception has been applied in the context of civil litigation with respect to work-product immunity, as much as it has with respect to the attorney-client privilege.

- *In re Int'l Sys.*, 693 F.2d 1235, 1242 (5th Cir. 1982). Although such an exception has been carved out in the grand jury context, the precedent is persuasive and can be applied in the civil context as well. "First, there must be a *prima facie* showing of a violation sufficiently serious to defeat the work-product privilege. Second, the court must find some valid relationship between work product under subpoena and the *prima facie* violation." Here, there were only allegations of such fraud. Those allegations were insufficient, however detailed. The district court erred in requiring production of opinion work product. Although a showing of illegal payments could be made, the party seeking discovery had not shown any specific intent by management to cover up those payments when the work product was generated.

If the lawyer's legal representation is deemed knowingly fraudulent in its nature it will be stripped of work-product protection which would otherwise be accorded.

- *In re Impounded Case*, 879 F.2d 1211, 1213–14 (3d Cir. 1989). The court noted that the work-product doctrine did not limit discovery into matters where a law firm allegedly acted criminally.

- *In re Doe*, 662 F.2d 1073 (4th Cir. 1981). The Fourth Circuit affirmed a district court order that allowed disclosure of opinion work product where the government presented a *prima facie* case of subordination of perjury by the attorney during his representation of clients in criminal trials.

The principle that communications between attorneys and their clients that are designed to commit some future crime or fraud are not privileged is not confined to the federal courts. The state courts have also recognized such an exception as not worthy of the protections generally accorded to legal advice that lawyers give to their clients.

- *Moskovitz v. Mt. Sinai Med. Ctr.,*69 Ohio St. 3d 638, 660, 635 N.E.2d 331, 349, *cert. denied,* 513 U.S. 1059 (1994). "That is to say, the mere relation of attorney and client does not raise a presumption of confidentiality of all communications made between them. . . . Moreover, it is beyond contradiction that the privilege does not attach in a situation where the advice sought by the client and conveyed by the attorney relates to some future unlawful or fraudulent transaction. Advice sought and rendered in this regard is not worthy of protection, and the principles upon which the attorney-client privilege is founded do not dictate otherwise."

1. Protection Can Be Claimed by Either Attorney or Client

A significant difference between the crime/fraud exception in the attorney-client privilege context from its operation in the work-product protection context is that, in the latter, the actions of two parties are to be considered in determining whether the crime/fraud exception exists. The client's intention and the attorney's intention at the time the disputed document was created are both relevant areas of inquiry. If either party had an intent to commit or to conceal an ongoing crime or fraud at the time the document was created, that may be sufficient to strip away the protection.

- *In re Sealed Case,* 676 F.2d 793, 815 (D.C. Cir. 1982). "The *prima facie* violation may also be the attorney's, since attorney misconduct negates the premise that the adversary system furthers the cause of justice." This is dicta in this case because no actual wrongdoing by the attorney conducting the in-house investigation was demonstrated.

When a court determines that the law firm doing the legal work can be deemed a "co-conspirator" then even opinion work product is not immune from discovery. One appellate court has suggested that an inquiry regarding whether the law firm can be found to have been a "co-conspirator" may become apparent from a review of the documents, even when the government has made no such claim.

- *In re Antitrust Grand Jury*, 805 F.2d 155, 168 (6th Cir. 1986). "The government has not implicated any of the law firms in any illegal conduct. This fact does not, however, give them an absolute shield to protect their opinion work product. Should the district court review the documents and find that the law firms were knowing and willing conspirators in the alleged crime, then all opinion work product made in furtherance of the alleged crime should also be produced."

Because both the attorney and the client have an independent interest in the work-product protected materials, each have standing to assert the protection. Thus, the "innocence" of each party may also serve to protect the disputed document. The innocent client may continue to claim the protection of the doctrine even when the work product was prepared by the fraudulent attorney, and an innocent attorney may continue to protect his or her thought processes on behalf of a criminal client. Only if the disputed document was itself created to further or to conceal a fraud will the protection be stripped away.

- *In re Doe*, 662 F.2d 1073, 1079 (4th Cir. 1981), *cert. denied*, 455 U.S. 1000 (1982). "[T]he ability to protect work product normally extends to both clients and attorneys . . . and the attorney or the client, expressly or by conduct can waive or forfeit it, but only as to himself, and the fraud exception applies to both attorneys and clients."

- *Moody v. Internal Revenue Serv.*, 654 F.2d 795, 800, 800–01 (D.C. Cir. 1981). "[A]t least in some circumstances, a lawyer's unprofessional behavior may vitiate the work-product privilege." "[T]he client's interest in preventing disclosures about his case may survive the misfortune of his representation by an unscrupulous attorney."

- *In re Special Sept. 1987 Grand Jury (II)*, 640 F.2d 49, 63 (7th Cir. 1980). "We conclude that the client cannot assert the work-product doctrine any more than he can assert the attorney-client privilege when there has been a showing of ongoing client fraud. . . . As we perceive the problem, the policy in favor of insulating the attorney's work product for the sake of the attorney must be weighed against the policy which favors disclosure where the client has used his attorney to engage in fraud."

- *In re Sealed Case*, 676 F.2d 793, 812 (D.C. Cir. 1982). "In some circumstances the attorney may be innocently involved in the client's crime or fraud. But a guilty client may not use the innocence or ignorance of its attorney to claim the court's protection against a grand jury subpoena. Unless the blameless attorney is before the court with an independent claim of privilege, the client's use of an attorney's efforts in furtherance of crime or fraud negates the privilege."

- *In re Murphy*, 560 F.2d 326, 331 (8th Cir. 1977). Work product created by antitrust counsel is too tangential for the protection to be stripped when the fraud was committed by the client on the Patent Office.

Sometimes, a distinction is drawn according to whether the client or the attorney is the one planning or engaging in the crime or fraud. If it is the client, the exception may extend only to "ordinary" work product, and "opinion" work product will retain its protection.

- *In re Special September 1978 Grand Jury (Jenner & Block Subpoena)*, 640 F.2d 49 (7th Cir. 1980). The work product of a law firm was ordered to be produced to a grand jury after a showing by the government that the material was unwittingly generated in furtherance of a client fraud on the state board of elections. The court concluded that no protection could attach to any information conveyed by the client to the attorney, whether that information had been communicated in written form or orally or whether the communicated information was then transcribed in summary fashion by the attorney. "[T]he strong policy disfavoring client fraud requires that the client relinquish the benefit he would gain from the work-product doctrine, which benefit is just as real although it is his attorney, rather than he, who asserts the doctrine." Only the attorney's mental impressions, conclusions, opinions, and legal theories would continue to be protected. "We are persuaded, however, that the attorney's mental impressions, conclusions, opinions, and legal theories must still be protected in order to avoid an invasion of the attorney's necessary privacy in his work, an invasion not justified by the misfortune of representing a fraudulent client."

On the other hand, the attorney's participation in the fraud will act to deny protection to the opinion work product in which the attorney has a particular interest.

- *In re Doe*, 662 F.2d 1073, 1079–80 (4th Cir. 1981), *cert. denied*, 455 U.S. 1000 (1982). The fraud exception, allowing discovery of opinion work product, applies to an attorney who is a target of a grand jury investigation regarding his illegal activity while representing a client in a former litigation.

- *In re Murphy*, 560 F.2d 326, 336 n.19 (8th Cir. 1977). "[A] court may conclude that opinion work-product is not immune if it contains inculpatory evidence of the attorney's own illegal or fraudulent activity."

- *In re Grand Jury Subpoena*, 524 F. Supp. 357, 363 (D. Md. 1981). The court would not allow discovery of opinion work product unless the government established *in camera* that the target was "engaging in illegal conduct in connection with his representation of his former client." Suggesting that it was not treating the problem as one of waiver, the court also said that the government would have to show need and undue hardship in order to obtain the opinion work product.

In one frequently cited case, however, the court sustained the claim of protection for opinion work product, even though the matter was the subject of a grand jury investigation into an alleged obstruction of justice.

- *In re Terkletoub*, 256 F. Supp. 683 (S.D.N.Y. 1966). An attorney justifiably asserted the work-product protection and refused to answer grand jury questions as to who he had interviewed and what was said in preparing the defense of a perjury case in a subsequent investigation for obstruction of justice arising out of the defense of the initial case.

The client's independent claim of work-product protection may survive a claim of crime or fraud even if the claim of the attorney, standing alone, could not.

- *Moody v. IRS (Moody I)*, 654 F.2d 795, 801 (D.C. Cir. 1981), *on remand* 527 F. Supp. 535 (D.D.C. 1981). "Because the client has an interest in preventing disclosures" about his or her case, the client's privilege (even with respect to opinion work product) "may survive the misfortune of his representation by an unscrupulous attorney."

On remand, the court was to determine two questions: "(a) whether a government attorney violated professional standards applicable to members of the bar, and (b) if so, whether the unprofessional behavior vitiates the attorney work-product privilege incorporated in Exemption 5 of FOIA, 5 U.S.C. § 502(b)(5). It determined each in the negative, reviewed the documents *in camera* for work-product protection and granted summary judgment for the IRS."

- *Moody v. IRS (Moody II)*, 682 F.2d 266 (D.C. Cir. 1982). Believe it or not, the case was appealed yet again and remanded yet again, even though the summary judgment was affirmed. The court of appeals was still not content with the disposition of both the work-product protection issues and the attorney misconduct issues. As to the former issue, the court noted that work-product protection did not extend to subsequent adversary proceedings. It also wished the district court to reconsider whether the government attorney's "conduct may have vitiated the work-product privilege. In our view, Liken's [the government attorney] unsworn and possibly self-serving memoranda are inadequate to make this determination. The determination of the facts and of whether professional standards may have been violated may require affidavits from Liken and others and perhaps testimony and legal argument to be had *in camera*. However, we do not believe that a full adversary hearing is required since such a hearing might disclose information that is otherwise privileged."

To determine whether the work product deals with the defense of a *completed* fraud and thus is protected, or whether it was prepared to further and assist a *planned or ongoing* fraud, the courts often refer to two criteria: whether the attorney's assistance was sought to further a scheme, and how close the relationship is between the work product and the scheme.

- *In re Murphy*, 560 F.2d 326, 338 (8th Cir. 1977). Two showings must be made to obtain opinion work product: (1) that the client was engaged in or planning a criminal or fraudulent scheme when the client sought the advice of counsel to further the scheme and (2) that the document sought bears a close relationship to the client's existing or future scheme to commit a crime or fraud. In this case, the work product was not ordered to be produced.

2. Considering Actions of Attorney and Client

Most courts apply a different test to determine whether work-product material is protected from compelled discovery in the light of a crime or fraud. They separate the intent of the client and the attorney and protect work-product material when the attorney is "innocent" of any intent to assist in the commission or cover-up of a crime or fraud. The innocence of the attorney is irrelevant for purposes of protecting attorney-client privileged materials from compelled disclosure. It is the key to a determination of whether work-product materials will nonetheless be protected. However, in order to be protected in the face of a crime or fraud by the client, the work-product protection must be raised by the attorney on his or her own behalf. If raised by the client, it will not be protected.

- *In re Grand Jury Proceedings*, 43 F.3d 966, 972 (5th Cir. 1994). The trial court's enforcement of a subpoena served on attorneys was reversed and a stay was ordered of any further release of privileged work-product documents to the government pending a determination by the trial court regarding whether the government had made the requisite showing of attorney knowledge of the client's intended fraud to negate the work-product privilege.

- *United States v. Under Seal (In re Grand Jury Proceedings, Thursday Special Grand Jury September Term 1991)*, 33 F.3d 342, 349 (4th Cir. 1994). "The record in the case does not indicate that the attorney engaged in . . . misconduct . . . and, therefore, the attorney may not be said to have waived his right to assert the work product privilege."

- *In re Sealed Case*, 676 F.2d 793, 812 (D.C. Cir. 1982). The court noted that the crime/fraud exception applies "unless the blameless attorney is before the court with an independent claim of privilege."

- *In re Special September 1978 Grand Jury*, 640 F.2d 49, 63 (7th Cir. 1980). The court commented that when the work-product privilege is asserted by an innocent attorney, the invasion of the attorney's privacy occasioned by divulging the attorney's work product is "not justified by the misfortune of representing a fraudulent client."

- *In re Grand Jury Proceedings*, 604 F.2d 798, 802 n.5 (3d Cir. 1979). The court stated that an "attorney, without knowledge of his client's illegal activity, might nevertheless properly claim and prevail in asserting a work product privilege."

- *In re Grand Jury Proceedings*, 604 F.2d 798, 802–03 (3d Cir. 1979). The crime/fraud exception is applicable to attorney work product and can be raised by the client as well as by the attorney. The appellate court held that here the trial court did not adequately delineate at what time the client consulted the attorney. If the client consulted the attorney after the completion of the crime/fraud, then the attorney's assistance was not being sought to implement the crime/fraud and the work product would not be discoverable. If the crime/fraud was a continuing one, then the exception would apply to the work-product doctrine and such materials would be discoverable. The court focused not on the knowing involvement of the attorney in helping to implement the crime/fraud, but entirely on the intention of the client, in effect applying the identical test to determine the discoverability of attorney-client privileged and work-product protected material.

Although most courts allow an innocent attorney to protect his or her work product even when the client had a culpable intent in using the attorney's services, not all courts do so, even if the attorney had no knowledge of the client's fraudulent intent.

- *In re Carter*, 1998 U.S. Dist. LEXIS 19497 (D.D.C. 1998). A motion to quash a subpoena served on Monica Lewinsky's lawyer was denied on the ground that a facial showing had been made on the client's intention to file a perjurious affidavit in a court proceeding. The attorney's lack of awareness of the client's fraudulent intention was deemed not relevant to protect from compelled disclosure even the attorney's work product.

3. *Prima Facie* Case in Work-Product Protection Context

The party seeking to discover work-product protected materials must make a *prima facie* showing of the illicit scheme. Naked assertion in pleading, however detailed, may not be sufficient to meet the requisite prima facie showing.

- *In re Int'l Sys. & Controls Corp. Sec. Litig.*, 693 F.2d 1235, 1241–42 (5th Cir. 1982). Pleadings alone, no matter how detailed, do not meet the requisite of a *prima facie* showing of a violation sufficiently serious to defeat the protection accorded by the doctrine.

- *In re Grand Jury Investigation*, 599 F.2d 1224 (3d Cir. 1979). A naked assertion of corporate cover-up was insufficient to overcome the work-product doctrine on the basis of a purported ongoing crime or fraud. The government's unsupported assertion that a company's internal investigation of questionable payments might involve a cover-up was insufficient to justify breaching work-product protection.

- *Miller v. Haulmark Transp. Sys.*, 104 F.R.D. 442, 446 (E.D. Pa. 1984). A decision to plead one set of facts instead of another plausible set of facts did not rise to the level of intent to commit a crime or fraud justifying inquiry into work product regarding a meeting at which the decision was made.

Unsubstantiated assertions, however detailed the allegations in the pleadings may be, do not constitute a *prima facie* case.

- *In re Int'l Sys. & Control Corp. Sec. Litig.*, 693 F.2d 1235, 1242 (5th Cir. 1982). The case law development in grand jury proceedings was applied for the basic principle that a crime/fraud exception exists that will trigger disclosure of work product. "While the pleadings in this case are unusually detailed, they are not evidence to make a *prima facie* case."

In private civil litigation it may be necessary to show the client's specific intent to engage in illegal conduct before the protection will be breached. Indeed, but for such a showing, disclosure of work product might well impede the self-scrutiny and house cleaning that government policy otherwise seeks to accomplish. Thus, even if a *prima facie* case has been established, the relationship between the work product and the crime/fraud must also be established. Not all self-investigations done by counsel will come into this compass. If the corporate motive was "pure" in conducting the self-investigation, the work product is more likely to be protected than if an attorney was engaged to assist in, perpetuate, or cover up a fraud. Public policy clearly favors the former motive. Engaging an attorney to cover up the fraud, however, is but a continuation of a fraudulent scheme, and hence the protection will and should be stripped under the crime/fraud exception.

- *In re Int'l Sys. & Controls Corp. Sec. Litig.*, 693 F.2d 1235, 1243 (5th Cir. 1982). In this shareholder derivative suit, the court suggested that some "specific intent" to perpetuate a fraud was required before the protection of the work product would be stripped from documents produced by counsel at the behest of management. The court noted that it was clear that the plaintiffs could show fraudulent practices were going on, but it was not clear that they could show that the purpose of the investigation was to cover up the illegal payments. In fact, the purpose in commencing the internal investigation (from which the plaintiffs sought work product) could have been "entirely pure. For the modern corporate world with multiple subsidiaries and hundreds of employees, shady practices may occur without the directors' and officers' knowledge. An attempt by the management to investigate past and present questionable practices should not be discouraged by guaranteed disclosure."

When it can be shown that the purpose for creating the work product was to perpetuate or to disguise the existence of the underlying crime or fraud, clearly the protection will not be available.

- *In re John Doe*, 675 F.2d 482, 492 (2d Cir. 1982). When an attorney deleted information from an internal review to hide from auditors and underwriters the fact that a payment had been made to a politically connected attorney to effect a bribe, the document wherein the deletion occurred was not protected by the work-product doctrine. "[W]here so-called work-product is in aid of a criminal scheme, fear of disclosure may serve a useful deterrent purpose and be the kind of rare occasion on which an attorney's mental processes are not immune."

When the documents are sought in a criminal investigation, however, it is not necessary to show specific criminal intent in preparing the documents as long as a *prima facie* showing of the connection to the scheme is made.

- *In re Sealed Case*, 676 F.2d 793, 815 (D.C. Cir. 1982). Requiring a specific showing of illicit intent when work product was sought by a grand jury would lead either to involving the grand jury in "minitrials" on preliminary issues or to near evisceration of the exception.

There must also be a specific showing that the documents sought were prepared in furtherance of a fraud. Logically, courts may never reach the issue as to whether there has been a *prima facie* showing of a fraudulent scheme because a facial examination of the documents may be able to demonstrate that even if there be such a scheme, the documents sought were not prepared in furtherance of the scheme. Timing alone may preclude a finding of "in furtherance." Thus, documents created after the termination of the purported fraudulent scheme, by definition, could not have been prepared in furtherance thereof, other than perhaps a continuing cover-up.

- *In re Murphy*, 560 F.2d 326, 338 (8th Cir. 1977). The court failed to rule whether there was a crime or fraud exception to the work-product rule since no relationship between the document sought to be discovered and the purported fraud was found to exist. To be discoverable under this exception, the court held that there must be a "close relationship" between the document and the fraud. The nature of the engagement of each law firm was analyzed to reach the conclusion.

- *Hercules Inc. v. Exxon Corp.*, 434 F. Supp. 136, 155–56 (D. Del. 1977). Where discovery was denied on dual grounds that the documents sought were prepared subsequent to purported fraud, and on the basis of review, the court determined that the documents did not "relate to the alleged instances of fraud or reflect information, opinion or advice relevant to the issues of scienter or intent."

- *W. R. Grace & Co. v. P. Ballantine & Sons, Inc.*, 175 U.S.P.Q. (BNA) 464 (D.N.J. 1970). Documents dated after the issuance of the patent claimed to have been fraudulently procured would not lose protection on the ground of the fraud exception.

At times, rather than use language that speaks of the document being prepared "in furtherance" of the fraud, courts suggest that the document must be "reasonably related" to the fraud.

- *In re Intl Sys. & Control Corp.*, 693 F.2d 1235, 1243 (5th Cir. 1982). The document sought must be "reasonably related" to the fraud to be discoverable.

F. Garner *Doctrine in Work-Product Context*

In the attorney-client privilege context, the privilege is not absolute in the fiduciary context. This principle is usually referred to as the *Garner* doctrine. Some courts have held that the *Garner* exception does not carry over into the work-product context on multiple grounds.

The *Garner* doctrine has been held not to apply to the work-product doctrine by some courts because the two are conceptually inconsistent. The *Garner* doctrine is predicated on an underlying commonality of ultimate interest between the attorney for the corporation and the minority shareholder. It is the commonality of interest that permits the shareholder to invade the privilege.

The predicate for determining whether work-product protection will be accorded is based on the existence of an adversarial position. The protection only comes into play when materials or documents, created in anticipation of litigation, are sought to be discovered. Thus, the documents to which work-product protection attaches were necessarily created after an adversarial relationship between the shareholder and corporate management existed.

To be logically consistent, the analysis of whether the work-product protection is available necessarily should proceed based on two factors. Did an adversarial relationship exist between the party on whose behalf the document with respect to which a work-product claim is asserted was created and the seeker of the document? Did that adversarial relationship exist at the time that the document was created? Logically, only if both questions are answered in the affirmative should the work-product protection be accorded. If the adversarial relationship came into existence only after the document was created, then the work-product protection should not be available.

In addition there is a separate party—the attorney—who may have an independent claim to work-product protection for the attorney's mental impressions and opinions. At least there are cases that have so held, although it is suggested that the preferable and more logically rigorous analysis would be to merely determine the existence of an adversarial relationship and the time of its inception in relation to the creation of the work-product doctrine. If the client would be given access to the work-product protected document, is there any good reason why a party with a common interest or to whom the client owed a fiduciary duty should not similarly be accorded access to the work-product protected document?

- *Donovan v. Fitzsimmons*, 90 F.R.D. 583, 588 (N.D. Ill. 1981). "Shareholders or beneficiaries, however, do not stand in the same position with respect to the *attorney*, for whom the work-product rule is designed to benefit, as they do to their own trustees. And as a result, the *Garner* analysis cannot be readily applied to defeat the work-product rule." Nonetheless, discovery was ordered at the behest of the Department of Labor, which had brought an ERISA action against trustees for breach of fiduciary duty when they entered into a series of questionable investments. In a case such as this, the "advice of counsel" is likely to be of crucial significance such that production should be made of any documents provided to or relied on by the trustees.

Moreover, the work-product protects an attorney's mental processes in preparing his or her client's case. The assumption is that if there is already an adversarial litigated situation between fiduciary and beneficiary, the former is entitled to legal counsel and legal counsel's mental impressions are entitled to protection from forced disclosure on the same terms and conditions as any other assertion of the doctrine, which is a qualified one in all events, subject to invasion on a proper showing or on the failure of the proponent to demonstrate the essential elements.

- *In re Int'l Sys. & Control Corp.*, 693 F.2d 1235, 1239 (5th Cir. 1982). The suit involved a derivative action arising out of illegal payments. The *Garner* doctrine was held not to apply to work product. The court reasoned that the *Garner* doctrine is predicated on a mutuality of interest between management and shareholders. Once there is an expectation of litigation between management and shareholders, that mutuality of interest is destroyed. "The work-product privilege is based on the existence of an adversarial relationship, not the quasi-fiduciary relationship analogized to in *Garner*. . . . It is not reasonable to indulge in the fiction that counsel, hired by management, is also constructively hired by the same party counsel is expected to defend against." Management could readily foresee from the time it first learned of the existence of illegal payments and determined to investigate whether such payments had occurred that litigation at the behest of shareholders could result. Thus, an adversary relationship, rather than a commonality of interests, existed and the predicate for the application of the work-product protection was established.

Other courts are increasingly applying the *Garner* doctrine to work-product materials, finding it illogical to make any distinction between the privilege and the doctrine in that regard. It is this book's position that it is the more logically consistent course to make the *Garner* doctrine equally applicable in the work-product area as it is in the area of attorney-client privilege. This should be particularly so when a commonality of interests existed at the time the document, for which work-product protection is claimed, was created.

- *Aguinaga v. John Morrell & Co.*, 112 F.R.D. 671, 682 (D. Kan. 1986). Documents produced by union counsel, with an eye to some future litigation, were discoverable. "This Court specifically rejects a work product 'exception' to *Garner*, since *Garner* itself makes clear that whether the documents consisted of advice pertaining to the pending litigation was only one idicium of good cause."

- *Nellis v. Air Line Pilots Ass'n*, 144 F.R.D. 68 (E.D. Va. 1992). Documents labeled as work-product materials containing mental impressions and legal opinions of counsel for a union were not protected from disclosure in litigation brought by union members. The burden of demonstrating that the documents were prepared in anticipation of litigation was not met by the union as the proponent of nondisclosure.

When there is a doubt, however, that a common interest in fact exists between parties at the time that the work-product documents were created, access will not, and should not, be given to such documents.

- *Remington Arms Co. v. Liberty Mut. Ins. Co.*, 142 F.R.D. 408 (D. Del. 1992). An insurer was not granted access to work-product documents created in the underlying action against the insured for environmental damage. The zone of privacy afforded to an attorney's mental impressions cannot be breached to compel access to work product of an attorney working for another party on the ground that an identity of interests exists.

G. *Work Product When Common Interest Exists*

In civil litigation involving the president of the United States, the president and his wife had asserted a common interest exception to waiver of the privilege with respect to conversations in which their respective attorneys partook. The claim was denied on the ground that the president's wife had an interest in avoiding proceedings against Mr. Clinton, as her husband, but that these did not extend to the Office of the President.

- *In re Grand Jury Subpoena Duces Tecum*, 112 F.3d 910, 922–23 (8th Cir.), *cert. denied sub. nom, Office of the President v. Office of Independent Counsel*, 521 U.S. 1105, 138 L. Ed. 2d 991, 117 S. Ct. 2482 (1997). The president's wife, in her personal capacity, was attempting to assert the attorney-client privilege with regard to a meeting she had with the White House lawyer. Mrs. Clinton did not allege that she was either an agent of the White House or acting in her official capacity as First Lady. Both the White House and the president's wife moved to block production of the notes on the basis of the attorney-client privilege. They relied, in part, on the common-interest doctrine, which expands the coverage of the attorney-client privilege when two or more clients with a common interest in a matter are represented by separate lawyers and agree to exchange information concerning the matter. Writing for a divided panel, Judge Bowman rejected the assertion of the privilege, in part, because of disparity of interest between the White House and the president's wife. Judge Bowman noted that the common interest necessary to invoke the privilege under such circumstances may be "either legal, factual, or strategic in character," but held that the standard had not been satisfied. He concluded that while the primary interest of the president's wife was in the criminal conviction, the White House, as an institution, faced no such threat.

When work product is prepared for litigation in which multiple parties have an interest, such as an insurance company and its insured or an indemnitor and indemnitee pursuant to contract, the work product is not protected from discovery in a subsequent adversary proceeding between the parties that, at the time of the underlying litigation, had a common interest. Since the work-product protected documents were prepared for each party to the common interest, how could one preclude the other from access thereto?

- *LaSalle National Trust v. Schaffner*, 1993 U.S. Dist. LEXIS 4410, at *19–20. The court found that the common-interest doctrine abrogated *opinion* work-product protection between an insurer and insured "with respect to documents prepared solely for the underlying litigation."

- *Abbott Labs. v. Alpha Therapeutic Corp.*, 200 F.R.D. 401, 410 (N. D. Ill. 2001). "Alpha is under a contractual obligation to cooperate with Abbott regarding claims asserted against Alpha for which Alpha may seek indemnification from Abbott. . . . This broad duty undertaken by both parties cannot be ignored simply because the parties are now attempting to hash out which party should shoulder the liability incurred in the underlying litigation."

- *Tudor Ins. Co. v. Kenna Assocs.*, 2003 U.S. Dist. LEXIS 10853 (S.D.N.Y. 2003). A declaratory judgment action was brought by the insurance company against the insured and the injured party after a denial of coverage. The court concluded that the insurance company could not assert a privilege in respect to files of the attorney it hired to defend insured after it denied coverage. "[T]o the extent that the interests of the insured and the insurer collide with respect to the assertion of the attorney-client privilege for communications with counsel retained for the insured, the insured necessarily prevails." On the other hand, although the interests of the insured and the injured party were aligned in the litigation, the privileged document need not be disclosed to the injured party.

H. *Insurance Company Files*

Whenever an insured sues an insurance company for bad faith the insurance company files become a subject for discovery. Claims of work product by the insurance company against the insured are likely to fail, usually on the ground that because the insurance company is in the business of investigating claims such investigatory files are prepared in the ordinary course of the insurance company's business even though litigation is often foreseeable.

- *Kidwiler v. Progressive Paloverde Ins. Co.*, 2000 U.S. Dist. LEXIS 4915 (N.D. W. Va. 2000). Work-product protection was not accorded to witness statements taken by the insurance company when sought by insured in a bad faith case.

- *Video Warehouse of Huntington, Inc. v. Boston Old Colony Ins. Co.*, 160 F.R.D. 83, 85 (S.D. W. Va. 1994). "As has been observed, discovery of documents by an insured from its insurer 'presents a special problem for application of the work-product rule because it is the very nature of an insurer's business to investigate and evaluate the merits of claims.'"

- *Harper v. Auto-Owners Ins. Co.*, 138 F.R.D. 655, 663–664 (S.D. Ind. 1991). The insured brought a bad faith denial of coverage claim where the reason given for the denial was arson. "It is presumed that a document or thing prepared before a final decision was reached on an insured's claim, and which constitutes part of the factual inquiry into or evaluation of that claim, was prepared in the ordinary and routine course of the insurer's business of claim determination and is not work product. Likewise, anticipation of litigation is presumed unreasonable under the Rule before a final decision is reached on the claim. The converse, of course, is presumed for documents produced after claims denial. To overcome these presumptions, the insurer must demonstrate, by specific evidentiary proof of objective facts, that a reasonable anticipation of litigation existed when the document was produced, and that the document was prepared and used solely to prepare for that litigation, and not to arrive at a (or buttress a tentative) claim decision."

- *Pete Rinaldi's Fast Foods, Inc. v. Great Am. Ins. Cos.*, 123 F.R.D. 198, 202 (M.D.N.C. 1988). "Because an insurance company has a duty in the ordinary course of business to investigate and evaluate claims made by its insureds, the claims files containing such documents usually cannot be entitled to work-product protection."

- *State Farm Fire & Cas. Co. v. Perrigan*, 102 F.R.D. 235, 237 (W.D. Va. 1984). Since "the nature of the insurance business requires an investigation prior to the determination of the insured's claim" no work-product privilege is available.

Although state law does not govern discovery of work product in the federal courts, which is based on Federal Rules of Civil Procedure, nonetheless some state courts have held that in a bad faith claim the entire insurance company file becomes discoverable. Such holdings are impacting on federal rulings as well.

- *Allstate Indem. Co. v. Ruiz*, 899 So. 2d 1121, 1129, 2005 WL 774838, at 8. The Florida Supreme Court held that the nature of the underlying cause of action mandates that the *entire* claim file is discoverable in a bad faith action brought in state court. After *Ruiz*, it is clear that Florida recognizes no privileges or limitation with respect to claim file materials in such an action.

- *Cozort v. State Farm Mut. Auto. Ins. Co.*, 233 F.R.D. 674 (M.D. Fla. 2005). Because the work product was created for litigation in the Florida state courts, the federal court decided to follow the *Ruiz* precedent. It made the entire insurance company file discoverable, including attorney opinion work product, which it held to be directly at issue and encompassed any attorney-client privilege materials as well. It also said that even had it applied only federal law the same result would have obtained.

I. *Right of Trustee-in-Bankruptcy to Attorney Work Product*

Based on *Weintraub*, it would seem to follow without question that a trustee-in-bankruptcy for a corporate entity has a right to the work product of the debtor's attorney. The question is more complex in the case of an individual debtor and in light of bankruptcy code provisions that the trustee is entitled to a turnover of the bankrupt's documents that may be held by attorneys or accountants. Cases that have considered the question have not applied those provisions automatically, but have focused their analysis on the issue of adversity. When there is none between the trustee-in-bankruptcy and the debtor, a turnover will be ordered. Conversely, when such adversity exists, no automatic turnover would be required. *Foster v. Hill (In re Foster)*, 188 F.3d 1259, 1272 (10th Cir.1999). The claim of work product does not entitle an attorney to withhold from a client's trustee-in-bankruptcy work product prepared for the client's prepetition lawsuits, as long as the trustee and the client are not adverse in those suits.

J. *No Protection for Third-Party Work Product*

Many courts hold that work-product protection extends only to the case for which it was prepared or for substantially similar and related adjudications. Thus the work-product claim where such product has been prepared for very different proceedings may not be applicable in a totally new proceeding.

■ *Ramsey v. NYP Holdings, Inc. d/b/a the New York Post*, 2002 U.S. Dist. LEXIS 11728 (S.D. N.Y. June 26, 2002), *clarified*, 2002 U.S. Dist. LEXIS 18186 (S.D.N.Y. Sept. 3, 2002). This case arises in the context of the infamous and mysterious death of JonBenet Ramsey, a six-year-old. Apparently the *New York Post* suggested that her brother, a minor, may have been implicated in the slaying. The minor's parents sued for libel and then asserted the work-product protection in respect to many documents prepared by the parents' attorneys in anticipation of a possible criminal prosecution against them. None was contemplated against the minor brother. Their assertion of the protection was not successful on the grounds that the protection does not extend to non-parties even if the documents are work-product protected as to them, since the policy concerns underlying the protection are not thereby undermined. "This policy [of not giving one party to litigation an unfair advantage at the expense of the other] would not be advanced, however, by protecting a representative's work product that is undertaken in anticipation of the representative's own separate litigation. Indeed, such an approach would create an arbitrary distinction between nonparty witnesses and litigants' representatives, since the non-party witness cannot invoke Rule 26(b)(3) to protect work product created for his own litigation, whereas the representative could invoke 26(b)(3) to protect work product created for his own litigation."

VII. WAIVER OF THE WORK-PRODUCT PROTECTION

A. *Relation to Waiver of Attorney-Client Privilege*[5]

The work-product protection must be separately asserted. It is not automatically subsumed when the attorney-client privilege is raised as an objection to production of a document. In fact, it has been held that failure to separately raise the work-product protection will constitute a waiver should the claim of privilege fail.

- *Carey-Canada, Inc. v. Aetna Cas. & Sur. Co.*, 118 F.R.D. 242, 248 (D.D.C. 1987). Failure to raise work product as an alternative ground for seeking to protect from compelled disclosure a memorandum entitled in the privilege log as "[i]nteroffice memorandum from in-house counsel to client's Insurance Department re: notice letters to insurance companies" constituted a waiver as to that particular objection and the document was subject to disclosure when the court found that the attorney-client privilege, which had been asserted, did not apply because the proponent of the privilege did "not claim that these memoranda are based on or disclose confidential information."

The waiver of the attorney-client privilege for a communication does not automatically waive whatever work-product immunity that communication may also enjoy, as the two are independent and grounded on different policies. Waiver of the privilege should always be analyzed distinctly from waiver of work product, since the privilege is that of the client and the work product essentially protects the attorney's work and mental impressions from adversaries and third parties even when communicated to the client. Occasionally, courts do not separately analyze waiver of the privilege and waiver of work-product protection, but assume that waiver of the privilege necessarily entails waiver of any work-product protection as well.

- *Dunhall Pharms. v. Discus Dental*, 994 F. Supp. 1202, 1204–05 (D.C. Cal. 1998). In a patent infringement action, the defense of reliance

---

5. *See also* the Section of Advice of Counsel in Patent Litigation where this issue is more extensively considered.

on advice of counsel waives protection for work product with respect to the subject matter of the asserted defense, whether or not it was communicated to the client, up to the time of the filing of the lawsuit. The magistrate's ruling that the work product was not waived was reversed in large part for that reason.

"A narrowly circumscribed waiver, at the discovery stage, creates a danger of a defendant utilizing favorable opinion letters while allowing unfavorable evidence to languish in their attorney's files under the protection of the work product doctrine. *Steelcase* over-emphasizes the Federal Circuit's limitations on admissibility, and fails to take into account Rule 26(b)(1)'s broader reach at the discovery phase of litigation. While negative evidence contained in an attorney's files may not ultimately reflect upon the client's state of mind, and will therefore not be admissible as evidence of willfulness, that evidence could very well lead to the discovery of relevant and admissible evidence of the client's state of mind that might not otherwise come to light. If the attorney's files contain evidence contradicting or questioning the opinion relied on by the client, the plaintiff has a right to know about such evidence in order to fully question defendants and their counsel regarding that evidence, disclosure to the client, and other related issues.

"Additionally, focusing solely on whether evidence was clearly communicated by the attorney to the client can obscure the fact that evidence which does not facially reflect communication to the client may nonetheless be relevant to showing the client's state of mind. This is so simply because negative evidence contained in the attorney's files raises the reasonable circumstantial inference that the client was somehow appraised of the negative opinions."

■ *SNK Corp. of America v. Atlus Dream Entm't Co.*, 188 F.R.D. 566 (N.D. Cal. 1999). Waiver of privilege by raising an advice of counsel defense to a patent infringement suit entailed a waiver of all work product as well because that work product might well reflect matters that were orally communicated to the client.

Other courts, however, hold that waiver of the privilege does not necessarily entail waiver of the work-product protection but only to such work product as was actually communicated to the client.

- *Steelcase Inc. v. Haworth, Inc.*, 954 F. Supp. 1195, 1198–99 (W.D. Mich. 1997). Reliance on advice of counsel does not waive protection for work product not communicated to the client.

Separating the waiver issues would seem clearly to be the better approach because the privilege is that of the client while the work-product protection essentially belongs to, and is intended to protect, the attorney's work and mental processes.

It does not follow from the fact that a client waives the privilege, leading to a required deposition of the attorney with respect to the advice given to the client that, therefore, the attorney's mental impressions and opinions have also been waived and the attorney can be deposed on those matters.

- *Nguyen v. Excel Corp.*, 197 F.3d 200, 210 (5th Cir. 1999). Although the appellate court found that there had been a waiver of the attorney-client privilege sufficient to permit depositions to be taken of the attorneys, it concluded that the magistrate judge had gone too far in permitting inquiry into the attorneys' opinions and mental impressions of their client's compliance. "[The magistrate judge's] order permits inquiry into counsels' understanding of defendant's perceptions, and the third sentence of the order permits inquiry into counsels' opinions. These inquiries are impermissible." The appellate court could have, but did not, remark that permitting such inquiry would have placed the attorneys in the untenable spot of testifying not merely to facts, but to their own opinion as to their client's willingness to comply with the law. It also would have, in a sense, allowed "expert" testimony on a matter that ultimately ought to remain within the province of the jury.

- *In re Grand Jury*, 106 F.R.D. 255, 257 (D.N.H. 1985). "[Defendant]'s waiver of the attorney-client privilege does not necessarily mean that the protection afforded by the work-product doctrine is also breached."

- *Hercules, Inc. v. Exxon Corp.*, 434 F. Supp. 136, 156 (D. Del. 1977). "Since the attorney-client privilege is the *client's* privilege, while work-product immunity may be invoked only by the attorney, waiver of attorney-client privilege does not necessarily also waive work-product immunity, as to an attorney's memoranda on the same subject."

- *Handgards, Inc. v. Johnson & Johnson*, 413 F. Supp. 926, 929 (N.D. Cal. 1976), *remanded on other grounds sub nom. Handgards, Inc. V. Ethicon Inc.*, 601 F.2d 986 (9th Cir. 1979), *cert. denied*, 444 U.S. 1025 (1980). While "the deliberate injection of the advice of counsel into a case waives the attorney-client privilege as to communications and documents relating to the advice," such waiver "does not necessarily mean that the protection afforded by the work-product doctrine" is also waived. The court concluded that waiver of the privilege and the protection afforded by the doctrine must be approached separately because they are separate means of protecting communications from compelled disclosure.

B. *Who May Waive the Work-Product Protection*

Work-product is prepared by an attorney but usually for a client's benefit. Presumably either may waive the work-product protection. But is the waiver of either binding on the other? Not necessarily.

- *Hanson v. United States Agency for Int'l Dev.*, 372 F.3d 286, 294 (4th Cir. 2003). "[A]n attorney may not unilaterally waive the privilege that his client enjoys. The ability to protect work product normally extends to both clients and attorneys, and the attorney or the client, expressly or by conduct, can waive or forfeit it, *but only as to himself*."

Were the Hanson case precedent to be applied to every case of disclosure, whether intentional or inadvertent, a whole new area of litigation in all disclosure cases would thereby be opened. In most instances, courts have held that it is the fact of the disclosure that is determinative for purposes of waiver analysis and not the party making the disclosure.

C. *Disclosure*

While the attorney-client privilege is often treated as waived by any voluntary disclosure, only disclosures that are "inconsistent with the adversary system" are deemed to waive work-product protection.

The attorney-client privilege may be nonexistent *ab initio* by virtue of the fact that a communication is made with the intention that the attorney will disclose the communication to third parties, yet an independent work-product protection, susceptible of assertion by the attorney, may nonetheless exist as to the manner in which the attorney has fashioned that communication for purposes of the intended disclosure.

- *Carey-Canada, Inc. v. California Union Ins. Co.*, 118 F.R.D. 242 (D.D.C. 1987). An attorney's drafts of annual report disclosures to be released in an annual report were subject to the protection because they reflected the attorney's assessment of that litigation, were predicated on information provided by the client, and obviously were not in fact disclosed to third parties in the annual report.

Thus, a finding that the qualified work-product protection has been waived by disclosure to others is much less likely than is a finding that the attorney-client privilege has been waived under similar circumstances. That is because the attorney-client privilege is based on the principle of confidentiality, so any disclosure taints the privilege at its very source. Selective and strategic disclosure is entirely consistent with the work-product doctrine, however, because it is concerned with implementing the adversary process, not just encouraging confidential communications.

- *United States v. Gangi*, 1 F. Supp. 2d 256, 266 (S.D.N.Y. 1998). A draft indictment and a prosecution memorandum were inadvertently filed with the clerk's office and then removed from the file by assistant U.S. attorneys. The court found that the filing constituted a waiver. Failure to label documents as privileged and the attorney's lack of review of the document and the fact that the government gave no instructions to FBI agents about the confidential nature of the prosecution memorandum weighed in favor of a finding of waiver by showing that reasonable precautions to protect the privilege were not taken. "If anything, the Government has a higher duty and must take even greater care to protect its privileges than a private litigant in a civil dispute." Ultimately, however, notions of "fairness" required a finding of waiver because the prosecution memorandum was widely distributed and would therefore assist some, but not all, defendants in a finger-pointing defense case.

- *Milford Power Ltd. P'ship v. New England Power Co.*, 896 F. Supp. 53, 58 (D. Mass. 1995). During Rule 26(a) discovery, eight work-product documents were produced to the opposing side. The party making inadvertent production sought a protective order requiring return of the documents, and seeking to have producing counsel disqualified, in part, on conflict-of-interest grounds because he represented both parties at one time. The court refused to disqualify the attorney who received and reviewed the documents, but did order the documents returned, relying on the factors enunciated in the *Hydraflow* and *Hartford* cases and on Formal Opinion 368 (1992) of the ABA's Committee on Ethics and Professional Responsibility. The opinion states that a "lawyer who receives materials that on their face appear to be . . . confidential . . . should refrain from examining the materials, notify the sending lawyer and abide the instructions of the lawyer who sent them."

- *City of Worchester v. HCA Mgmt. Co., Inc.*, 839 F. Supp. 86, 89 (D. Mass. 1993). A third-party accounting firm produced privileged documents inadvertently that were ordered returned upon a motion for a protective order. The court did not explain which factors allowed it to reach the conclusion that the work-product protection had not been waived by the inadvertent production. The court stated that the presumption that an inadvertent production brought in its wake a waiver should instead be to the contrary, that it did not, unless good reason were shown why it should.

- *Fleet Nat'l Bank v. Tonneson & Co.*, 150 F.R.D. 10, 16 (D. Mass. 1993). The court concluded that the appropriate question was "not whether it remains essential to continue to recognize the privilege; the question, rather, is whether there is cause not to do so, such as that recognition might work an injustice or impose an undue burden on the judicial system."

The question of when disclosure to one person should thereafter require disclosure to another is more complex in the context of the work-product protection than it is in the context of the attorney-client privilege. The predicate of the inquiry in the work-product context is not, as it is in the attorney-client context, whether the material was disclosed, but whether the material was disclosed to an adversary.

- *United States v. AT&T*, 642 F.2d 1285, 1299 (D.C. Cir. 1980). The work-product privilege "does not exist to protect a confidential relationship, but rather *to promote the adversary system by safeguarding the fruits* of an attorney's trial preparations from the discovery attempts of the opponent. The purpose of the work product doctrine is to protect information against opposing parties, rather than against all others outside a particular confidential relationship, in order to encourage effective trial preparation. . . . We conclude, then, that *while the mere showing of a voluntary disclosure to a third person will generally suffice to show waiver of the attorney-client privilege, it should not suffice in itself for waiver of the work product privilege.*"

Thus, inadvertent or even intentional disclosure of work-product documents will not necessarily constitute a waiver as to all such documents.

- *Duplan Corp. v. Deering Milliken, Inc.*, 540 F.2d 1215, 1222 (4th Cir. 1976). "We . . . are of the opinion that broad concepts of subject matter waiver analogous to those applicable to claims of attorney-client privilege are inappropriate when applied to Rule 26(b)(3)."

- *In re F.A. Potts & Co.*, 30 B.R. 708, 711–12 (E.D. Pa. 1983). When a letter was written in anticipation of litigation, the mere fact that it was disclosed to an "unrelated third party" did not constitute waiver because the purpose of the doctrine is to protect material from adversaries and not necessarily from the rest of the world. Waiver occurs only if disclosure to a third party substantially increases the possibility that an adversary could get the information.

The essential question with respect to waiver of the work-product doctrine by disclosure is whether the material has been kept away from adversaries. Thus, the protection is retained when there has been disclosure to persons with a common interest, to persons in the course of a business relationship, and to the government. In all cases, the focus of the inquiry is on the extent to which the relationship is an adversarial one and the efforts made to keep adversaries from obtaining the material.

1. Disclosure to an Adversary

Although not all disclosures of work-product protected materials necessarily result in a waiver as to other parties, voluntary disclosure to an adversary generally does result in a waiver. Because the protection is designed to protect an attorney's trial preparation and mental processes from discovery at the behest of an adversary, clearly voluntary disclosure to an adversary would almost invariably be seen as a total waiver.

- *United States v. MIT*, 129 F.3d 681, 687 (1st Cir. 1997). "The prevailing rule (is) that disclosure to an adversary, real or potential, forfeits work-product protection."

- *Salomon Bros. Treasury Litig. v. Steinhardt Partners, L.P.*, 9 F.3d 230, 234–35 (2d Cir. 1993). Disclosure of work-product protected materials to the SEC, with whom the trader stood in an adversarial position, was deemed to constitute a waiver in a subsequent class-action litigation with private parties.

- *In re Sunrise Sec. Litig.*, 130 F.R.D. 593, 597, 1989 U.S. Dist. LEXIS 13880 (E.D. Pa. Nov. 17, 1989). When a law firm voluntarily turns over work-product documents to the Federal Savings and Loan Insurance Corporation (FSLIC), in its capacity as receiver for a failed savings and loan, no claim of protection will withstand a motion to compel brought by the FSLIC in its corporate capacity, suing the saving and loan's former officers and directors. However, when the law firm refused to tender certain documents, predicated on the claim of work product, no waiver occurred. The documents were, nonetheless, discoverable because a claim was made that the law firm was negligent in the legal services provided to the failed savings and loan, thereby assisting in its demise. The law firm itself was charged with securities violations and many defendants raised a defense of "advice of counsel."

If the disclosure is inadvertent and occurs in the context of document production, the same principles as apply to inadvertent disclosure of attorney-client privileged materials would apply in this context. An analysis would be made of the five factors discussed above (*see* Sec. IV,D,7) would generally be applicable here as well. Be aware that any perceived negligence is likely to result in a holding that waiver has occurred, at the very least for the document in question, which obviously will not be as serious in its ramifications as waiver of subsidiary matters, which are less likely to be held waived. The bell can't be "unrung" in respect to the disclosed document and it is generally not admissible evidence at trial in all events. The ramifications are more serious if a waiver in respect to one document is held to entail subject matter waiver. It shouldn't in this context since the same evidentiary reliability issues are not at stake. In all events as always in any inadvertent disclosure the worst harm done is often to the careless attorney's *amour propre*.

- *Caliber One Indem. Co. v. Millard Chicago Window Cleaning, LLC*, 2006 U.S. Dist. LEXIS 12995 (N.D. Ill. Mar. 6, 2006.) Where the Plaintiff inadvertently disclosed historical data on set aside loss reserves, the court required it to also produce documents on what reserves had been set aside current litigation, noting in passing that it might have ordered production in all events on the grounds of substantial need.

There was no discussion of why inadvertent production of historical reserves should entail necessary production of current ones or how such information in the least fell into the category of discoverable or relevant facts in all events rather than invading the attorney's mental assessment of the value of the case. Other cases have so found.

- *SEC v. Cassano*, 189 F.R.D. 83, 85 (S.D.N.Y. 1999). The court held that the Securities and Exchange Commission ("SEC") waived the work product privilege when it accidentally produced to defense counsel an internal action memorandum drafted by SEC staff along with some fifty boxes of documents. The SEC made documents available for inspection by defense counsel in the SEC's New York Regional Office with the understanding that it would copy such documents at the end of the agreed-upon review period. Early on in the inspection period, defense counsel discovered the memorandum in question, and requested that an SEC paralegal copy it immediately. The paralegal telephoned the SEC's lead counsel to obtain clearance. The attorney who received the call did not review his own copy of the memorandum before authorizing the paralegal to provide a copy to the defense. The Court concluded that "any attorney faced with such a request in comparable circumstances should have reviewed the document immediately, if only to find out what the other side thought so compelling."

- *United States v. Gangi*, 1 F. Supp. 2d 256 (S.D.N.Y. 1998). A 69-page memorandum created by the USAO was accidentally attached to the back of a 75-page draft indictment. Together, the two documents were handed to the judge at the defendant's presentment, "publicly filed and widely distributed." In such an instance, "the purpose of the work-product doctrine, that 'opposing counsel should not enjoy free access to an attorney's thought processes,' has already been severely undermined," thereby supporting a finding of waiver.

Where, however, the bell has not been rung because opposing counsel have not yet looked at the work-product-protected document (as when it is produced on a computer disk or to a preparation assistant), courts will find that to hold that a waiver has occurred would be unnecessarily punitive.

- *United States v. Rigas*, 281 F. Supp. 2d 733, 742 (S.D.N.Y. 2003). Work-product materials were tendered on a hard drive. Producing counsel learned of the inadvertent production and advised defense counsel who did not look at the document pending judicial adjudication of the issue. The court held that there was no carelessness in the production and the inadvertent disclosure would be excused without entailing a waiver. "All defense counsel have refrained from reviewing Lee's work product pending resolution of this discovery dispute. As a result, the purpose of the work-product privilege has not been undermined and no one defendant will be prejudiced vis-à-vis any other defendant should the privileged documents in question be returned to the Government."

A potential issue arises in finding waiver of work-product material by inadvertent disclosure where the party guilty of the inadvertence is a governmental agency. The rights, interests and even safety of third parties or witnesses in a criminal context might be compromised. Not yet directly litigated or used as a grounds for decision, it nonetheless has been suggested as a possible concern.

- *United States v. Rigas*, 281 F. Supp. 2d 733, 742 (S.D.N.Y. 2003). "Courts in this district have expressed reservations regarding findings of waiver in cases where disclosure could place victims and witnesses at risk." The statement was dicta in the context of the case since there was no indication that either victims or witnesses would be placed at risk and therefore that factor in no way determined the holding that no waiver had occurred.

- *United States v. Gangi*, 1 F. Supp. 2d 256, 267 (S.D.N.Y. 1998). Same concern expressed.

- *SEC v. Cassano*, 189 F.R.D. 83, 86 (S.D.N.Y. 1999). "The SEC has not suggested that the safety or privacy of any witness would be compromised in any serious way absent the relief it seeks."

Actual disclosure to an adversary need not necessarily have occurred in order for a waiver to occur. It is often enough if a substantial risk of disclosure has been created.

- *Behnia v. Shapiro*, 176 F.R.D. 277, 279 (N.D. Ill. 1997). A waiver of the work-product protection can occur when the protected communications are disclosed in a manner that "substantially increases the opportunity for potential adversaries to obtain the information."

The cases discussed above under the rubric of inadvertent disclosure of the attorney-client privilege should be valid precedent here also. Although, quite obviously, the bell of disclosure cannot be "unrung" here. In the attorney-client privilege area, a court can order that the privileged communication cannot be used as evidence. There is no way for a court, however, to wipe from an adversary's mind any mental impressions or litigation strategy that may have been disclosed.

Any inadvertent disclosure of work product should not ordinarily entail subject matter waiver. Given the purposes that are served by the work-product doctrine such a result would in ordinary circumstances be perfectly extraordinary and entirely punitive for no cognizable judicial purpose.

- *In re Hechinger Inv. Co. of Del., Inc.*, 303 B.R. 18 (D. Del. 2003). The party making inadvertent disclosure in the course of document production of work-product materials waited 5 months to request their return and then abandoned the endeavor. The court therefore concluded that the inadvertent disclosure was not excusable.

The court seems to have overlooked thereby the operative issue. The documents being of a work-product nature were not likely to be usable for evidentiary purposes and the bell could not be unrung. Small wonder that attempts to retrieve the work-product documents was abandoned. The court refused to find that the inadvertent disclosure entailed a subject matter waiver.

- *Carter v. Gibbs*, 909 F.2d 1450 (Fed. Cir. 1990). The government waived work-product privilege by inadvertently appending an internal Justice Department memorandum, containing work product, to the copy of the government brief served on the opposing party.

Actual disclosure to an adversary may not be necessary to constitute a waiver of the work-product privilege. Where disclosure increases the opportunity for even potential adversaries to discover information, a waiver may be deemed to have occurred.

- *Falise v. American Tobacco Co.*, 193 F.R.D. 73, 79 (E.D.N.Y. 2000). Unlike the attorney-client privilege, "the work-product privilege is not necessarily waived by disclosure to any third party; rather, the courts generally find a waiver of the work product privilege only if the disclosure substantially increases the opportunity for potential adversaries to obtain the information." (Citations omitted.)

2. Disclosure to a Party with a Common Interest in Litigation or Business

In the privilege context, the common interest that parties must share has to have a legal component in order for documents shared between them to retain their privileged character. That is not the case with the work-product protection. Parties who share only a business interest may nonetheless share work-product-protected documents without thereby losing the work-product protection. The rational is that such sharing does not make it more likely that an adversary will obtain the work-product-protected materials. Bear in mind that the work-product protection is designed to maintain the integrity of the adversarial process by precluding one party from being able to poach upon the preparation of the other.

For there to be a common interest attorney-client privilege, the parties generally have to share a legal interest. Sharing merely a business interest is not sufficient. That is not the case in respect to sharing work product privilege.

- *Sheets v. Insurance Co. of N. Am.*, 2005 U.S. Dist. LEXIS 27060 (W.D. Va. Nov. 8, 2005). Parties who had a common interest in insurance coverage did not lose the work-product protection by sharing documents on that issue even though their interests in litgation might in other respects have been adverse.

- *Cellco P'ship v. Nextel Communications, Inc.*, 2004 U.S. Dist. LEXIS 12717, 2004 WL 1542259, at *1 (S.D.N.Y. July 9, 2004). The court decided that the defendant and its advertising agency shared a common business interest and therefore disclosure of an e-mail with legal advice did not waive work-product privilege.

- *In re Copper Mkt. Antitrust Litig.*, 200 F.R.D. 213, 221 n.6 (S.D.N.Y. 2001) (holding that there was no waiver of the work-product protection because the business and public relations firm specializing in "litigation-related crisis management" shared a common interest). Thus, the fact that Merrill Lynch and Deloitte & Touche do not share a common litigation interest is of no moment.

- *Blanchard v. Edgemark Fin. Corp.*, 192 F.R.D. 233 (N.D. Ill. 2000). "With regard to the documents transmitted to Mr. Olson, to the extent that they are protected by the work-product doctrine, the existence of a confidentiality agreement between Mr. Olson and EdgeMark militates against a finding of a waiver. The confidentiality agreement is evidence that EdgeMark took steps to ensure that its work product did not land in the hands of its adversaries. Therefore, EdgeMark did not waive work-product protection." However, documents that were transmitted to the attorney for a party with a common financial interest were not thereby made privileged if it has not been demonstrated that the underlying documents were either privileged or work-product protected.

Thus, disclosure between parties that have common financial interests are sufficient to protect the work-product privilege, even if such would not be sufficient to protect the attorney-client privilege. A confidentiality agreement concerning disclosed work product is sufficient to show an intent to protect the work product from actual or potential litigation adversaries.

- *Merrill Lynch & Co. v. Allegheny Energy, Inc.*, 229 F.R.D. 441, 448 (S.D.N.Y. 2004). Merrill disclosed an internal investigation of a theft by one of its employees to its outside auditing firm. The court concluded that "the critical inquiry—to me—must be whether Deloitte & Touche should be conceived of as an adversary or a conduit to a potential adversary." It then concluded: "Thus, any tension between an auditor and a corporation that arises from an auditor's need to scrutinize and investigate a corporation's records and book-keeping practices simply is not the equivalent of an adversarial relationship contemplated by the work-product doctrine. Nor should it be. A business and its auditor can and should be aligned insofar as they both seek to prevent, detect, and root out corporate fraud. Indeed, this is precisely the type of limited alliance that courts should encourage."

It goes without saying that when parties have a common adversary in litigation and are conducting a joint defense, they may share work product, including legal theories, without thereby waiving the protection.

In the case of the privilege, it can only be shared between parties with a common legal interest as opposed to merely a common business interest. That is not the case in respect to sharing work-product materials. Since the operative inquiry as to waiver is whether it enhances the prospect that an adversary would gain possession, sharing work-product materials with a party with a common business interest does not do so and hence does not constitute a waiver.

- *Cellco P'ship v. Nextel Communication, Inc.*, 2004 U.S. Dist. LEXIS 12717 (S.D.N.Y. July 9, 2004). The fact that Nextel shared work product with its advertising agency which was under a contractual obligation to maintain confidentiality did not constitute a waiver since it in no way enhanced the prospect that an adversary would gain access.

- *Hydranautics v. Filmtec Corp.*, 2003 U.S. Dist. LEXIS 25094 (S.D. Cal. Aug. 18, 2003). No waiver of work-product protection occurred when documents regarding a common legal interest, namely a common interest in a patent, were shared with the government.

- *In re Sunrise Sec. Litig.*, 130 F.R.D. 560, 583, 1989 U.S. Dist. LEXIS 6288 (E.D. Pa. May 31,1989). No waiver occurs when work product is shared not with an adverse party, but with one having interests in common.

- *In re Crazy Eddie Sec. Litig.*, 131 F.R.D. 374, 379 (E.D.N.Y. 1990). The defendant moved to obtain interview notes the company had voluntarily submitted to plaintiffs as party to an agreement with the company to cooperate in prosecuting claims against the company's former management. The investigative report and interview notes were disclosed to the company's insurance carrier, accounting consultants, and plaintiff's counsel. Here, the protection was extended because disclosure had been made to parties with common interests.

Often, parties enter into a joint defense agreement. It is likewise advisable to enter into a memorandum of understanding when parties intend to pursue claims jointly. This was done in the *Crazy Eddie* litigation and relied on, perhaps not substantively but certainly cosmetically, by the court in its ruling.

- *Grumman Aerospace Corp. v. Titanium Metals Corp.*, 91 F.R.D. 84 (E.D.N.Y. 1981). The parties' common interest in using the work product in litigation is one of the clearest indications against waiver.

- *Castle v. Sangamo Weston, Inc.*, 744 F.2d 1464, 1466–67 (11th Cir. 1984). In this age discrimination case, the court held that the protection was not waived when the plaintiff turned work product over to the EEOC while they were both engaged in preparing for a joint trial.

- *United States v. AT&T*, 642 F.2d 1285, 1299–1300 (D.C. Cir. 1980). "A disclosure made in the pursuit of . . . trial preparation, and not inconsistent with maintaining secrecy against opponents, should be allowed without waiver of the privilege." The court held that MCI had not waived its privilege when it provided work product it had developed in its litigation against AT&T to the government for its action against AT&T. "*The work product privilege rests on the belief that such promotion of adversary preparation ultimately furthers the truth-finding process.* For MCI to contribute the fruit of its analysis to the Government on those issues common to their two cases will further the Government's preparation for trial and eliminate some duplication of effort." While the truth-finding process might be further enhanced in the short run by ordering disclosure, "[i]n the long run, however, this would discourage trial preparation and vigorous advocacy and would discourage any party from turning over work product to the government."

- *Duplan Corp. v. Deering Milliken, Inc.*, 397 F. Supp. 1146, 1172 (D.S.C. 1974), *aff'd*, 540 F.2d 1215 (4th Cir. 1976). "The sharing of information between counsel for parties having common interests does not destroy the work-product privilege during the course of the litigation."

Moreover, even if one party to a common defense unilaterally tenders work-product materials to an adversary, such tender does not constitute a waiver for the other parties to a common defense.

- *John Morrell & Co. v. Local Union, 304A, United Food & Commercial Workers*, 913 F.2d 544, 556 (8th Cir. 1990), *cert. denied*, 500 U.S. 905 (1991). The court reasserted the principle that neither party to a joint defense agreement can waive the privilege without the other party's consent. Thus the trial court committed no error by refusing to admit a privileged document into evidence where each party to the joint defense had not waived the privilege.

Even in the absence of a common defense or an express agreement, disclosure to related parties assisting each other in litigation will not waive work-product protection.

- *ECDC Envtl., L.C. v. New York Marine & General Ins. Co.*, 1998 U.S. Dist. LEXIS 8808 (S.D.N.Y. June 4, 1998). Disclosure of work product to outside contractors did not waive protection where contractors were either related companies to plaintiff or acted as agent for plaintiff in the litigation.

But see:

Courts are beginning to resist some of the expansion of the common interest exception into new contexts. Plaintiff litigants in shareholder derivative suits have tried to share work-product documents with the corporation on whose behalf suit has been brought without also incurring waiver. They have not been successful.

- *Ferko v.* NASCAR, 219 F.R.D. 396 (E.D.Tex.), *recons. denied,* 219 F.R.D. 403, 406 (E.D. Tex. 2003). The court concluded that antagonism between plaintiff shareholders and corporation is inherent in fact that corporation refused to bring suit against co-defendant and that the fact that both shareholders and corporation would benefit if plaintiffs won suit does not a common interest make in the absence of precedent so holding in the circuit.

On reconsideration and after a review of the documents, the court found them to be work product, but that the the protection had been waived when shared between parties without a common interest—the grounds on which the work-product protection holder had attempted to avoid a finding of waiver. "Plaintiffs claim that a common legal interest exists between Plaintiffs and Speedway because Speedway admitted the truth of Plaintiffs' allegations against NASCAR, because Plaintiffs sued NASCAR on behalf of Speedway, and because Plaintiffs do not allege any wrongdoing by Speedway. Plaintiffs and Speedway would both benefit if Plaintiffs won this lawsuit. Speedway would recover damages; Plaintiffs would recover attorney's fees. It is also true that Plaintiffs and Speedway are nominal, not actual, adversaries in this lawsuit. Plaintiffs claim wrongdoing by NASCAR, not by Speedway. To a limited extent, Plaintiffs and Speedway have similar interests.

"Even added together, however, these similar interests do not constitute a common legal interest." (Record citations deleted.)

Disclosure of documents for legitimate business reasons also does not necessarily constitute waiver of the work product, especially when confidentiality is protected. Courts have held that such common interests exist in the patent field and between an insurance company and its insured but have been reluctant to expand it into other domains. What the rational is for allowing it in the patent and insurance areas but not in other contexts is not self-evident. It may be that both the patent and insurance areas are so prolific in spawning litigation. That is a guess since the cases rarely articulate a rationale beyond a declaration of a legal common interest.

- *Constar Int'l, Inc. v. Continental Pet Techs., Inc.,* 2003 U.S. Dist. LEXIS 21132 (D. Del. Nov. 19, 2003). Cross-licensees of patent rights may share work product between themselves without thereby waiving the protection as to third parties.

- *United States v. Gulf Oil Corp.*, 760 F.2d 292, 296 (Temp. Emer. Ct. App. 1985). The Department of Energy sought to enforce a subpoena for work-product documents that had been disclosed by Cities Service Company in the course of merger discussions with Gulf. The court held the protection had not been waived even though the merger was not consummated and Gulf retained microfilm copies. The parties subsequently became adversaries, but at the time the documents were given to Gulf, the parties had a common, nonadversarial interest in reviewing the work product, and Gulf was at all times under a promise of confidentiality.

- *James Julian, Inc. v. Raytheon Co.*, 93 F.R.D. 138, 142–44 (D. Del. 1982). Neither the attorney-client nor the work-product privilege was waived by placing documents in a general corporate file available to a number of employees, as the files were available only to employees who needed them and the documents had not been broadly circulated or used as training materials. "It is only when facts have been made known to persons other than those who need to know them that confidentiality is destroyed."

- *American Standard, Inc. v. Bendix Corp.*, 71 F.R.D. 443, 446–47 (W.D. Mo. 1976). In an antitrust action, the court held that although the work-product material had been disseminated on a limited basis to third parties who would be witnesses, the work-product privilege was not waived because the parties sharing the documents had intended to maintain confidentiality and had no reason to believe the opponent would have access to the materials.

- *Burlington Indus. v. Exxon Corp.*, 65 F.R.D. 26, 45–46 (D. Md. 1974). Work-product immunity is not lost when parties exchange confidential work product during settlement negotiations between them.

- *Stix Prods., Inc. v. United Merchants & Mfrs. Inc.*, 47 F.R.D. 334, 338 (S.D.N.Y. 1969). No waiver occurred when a customer shared his attorney's legal opinion regarding patent validity with the plaintiff's attorney. The customer had an economic stake in the litigation since he, too, was potentially liable to the defendant for patent infringement. The parties shared a common interest, so the work-product immunity was not waived by the fact of the disclosure.

But work product shared among members of a trade association has not been given work-product protection. The rationale being that anticipation of litigations cannot be an ever-present possibility in all commercial settings.

- *United States v. Duke Energy Corp.*, 214 F.R.D. 383 (M.D.N.C. 2003). Duke Energy contended business groups with general common interests may combine to share information concerning potential legal problems and that all the information and documents exchanged with and from the association's attorney would be protected by attorney-client privilege or work-product protection. The court found that proposition to be a drastic expansion of the law of privilege and work-product protection. The Utility Air Regulatory Group ("UARG"), claiming to be neither a lobbying organization nor a trade association, but a "legal advocacy group," sought to intervene to relitigate the issue. Intervention was denied. However, out of an abundance of caution, the court allowed UARG's papers to be submitted by Duke Energy Corp. as on a motion to reconsider. The court stood by its original ruling and declined to have its mind changed by any *in camera* inspection of the contested documents.

As the "business" cases indicate, the better view is that "common interest" motivating a disclosure should be read broadly.

- *United States v. AT&T*, 642 F.2d 1285, 1299 (D.C. Cir. 1980). "'[C]ommon interests' should not be construed as narrowly limited to co-parties. So long as transferor and transferee anticipate litigation against a common adversary on the same issue or issues, they have strong common interests in sharing the fruit of trial preparation efforts."

Of course, an adversarial relationship previous or subsequent to the time of disclosure should not matter as long as the parties had a common interest *at the time of* the disclosure.

- *United States v. Gulf Oil Corp.*, 760 F.2d 292, 296 (Temp. Emer. Ct. App. 1985). Parties had a common interest in merger prospects when work product was disclosed, so the fact that the merger was not consummated and the parties later became adversaries did not make the disclosure a waiver.

- *In re Int'l Sys. & Controls Corp. Sec. Litig.*, 693 F.2d 1235, 1239 (5th Cir. 1982). Although shareholders and management usually have a common interest, in a derivative action they are adversaries. Therefore, work product created by management attorneys is not subject to disclosure under the *Garner* doctrine (*see* Part I, Section V, Heading B, Subheading 1, "*Garner* Doctrine"), but is discoverable only pursuant to Rule 26(b)(3).

- *United States v. Medica-Rents Co.*, 2002 U.S. Dist. LEXIS 14249, 2002 WL 1483085, at *1 n.6 (N.D. Tex. June 21, 2002). The court concluded that disclosure of documents by relators to co-party, the United States and its representatives, did not result in waiver and that the joint defense privilege, an extension of the attorney-client privilege, was applicable to work product as well.

- *United States ex rel. [Redacted] v. [Redacted]*, 209 F.R.D. 475 (D. Utah 2001). Government and party bringing a *qui tam* action have an identity of legal interest sufficient to preclude waiver if work product is shown to each other.

3. Disclosure to Non-Adversary Third Party

In general, disclosure to a third party waives the attorney-client privilege. The same rule does not necessarily apply to the work-product doctrine, even though courts have not focused much on the distinction or sought to explain it other than stating that since the work product doctrine is designed to create a zone of protection within the adversary process since such disclosure does not necessarily entail disclosure to an adversary no reason exists to find waiver.

- *Bank Brussels Lambert v. Chase Manhattan Bank, N.A.*, 1996 U.S. Dist. LEXIS 18849, 1996 WL 944011, at *3 (S.D.N.Y. Dec. 19, 1996). "Work product immunity is waived only if the party has voluntarily disclosed the work product in such a manner that it is likely to be revealed to his adversary."

- *Bowne of New York City, Inc. v. Ambase Corp.*, 150 F.R.D. 465, 479 (S.D.N.Y. 1993).

Frequently, in the context of litigation, an attorney or a party may disclose work-product material to a non-party without necessarily being required to disclose it also to the adversary.

- *United States v. Johnson*, 378 F. Supp. 2d 1041(N.D. Iowa 2005). A death row inmate mailed a chronology of her life, prepared by a "mitigation specialist" and annotated by the inmate, to a disbarred attorney whom she had befriended. The inmate hoped that the attorney would write a book about her life. The mailing was marked as "privileged" even though it was not mailed to the inmate's attorney. The "fraudulent" mailing was discovered by a suspicious prison guard who opened the mailing and forwarded to the prosecutors in the case. The court found no waiver not really on principled grounds but because it deemed it more advisable to bend over backwards in light of the inmate's status on death row. Thus it is not in the least clear that the case would have any precedential value in a commercial context. It is also not in the least clear what testimonial use the document would have to the prosecutors or what reason the inmate had to protect it from further use or disclosure. Presumably the mitigation specialist's chronology, with the inmate's annotated changes, would be given to the prosecutors in all events.

- *Bamberg v. KPMG, LLP*, 219 F.R.D. 33 (D. Mass. 2003). Plaintiffs obtained documents from a third party. They argued that since they had selected the documents allowing their adversary to get copies would disclose work product. The court held that such selection was not protected core work product and that a waiver had occurred when counsel for the third party which produced the documents was allowed to review them for privilege. The adversary would have to share the costs incurred in obtaining the documents as a condition of obtaining copies.

- *Freeport-McMoran Sulphur, LLC v. Mike Mullen Energy Equip. Res., Inc.*, 2004 U.S. Dist. LEXIS 10048 (E.D. La. June 2, 2004). Showing a work-product-protected document to a former employee did not defeat the availability of the protection.

- *United States v. Stewart*, 287 F. Supp. 2d 461 (S.D.N.Y. 2003). Disclosure by Martha Stewart by e-mail of work-product-protected documents to her daughter did not waive work-product protection, although in a prior ruling the court had held that a like disclosure of attorney-client privileged material did constitute a waiver. *See also United States v. Stewart*, 2003 U.S. Dist. LEXIS 15442 (S.D.N.Y. 2003).

- *GAF Corp. v. Eastman Kodak Co.*, 85 F.R.D. 46, 51 (S.D.N.Y. 1979). Work product may be shown to others, "simply because there was some good reason to show it" without waiving the privilege. Moreover, "even a disclosure to a non-adversary that 'substantially' or 'materially' increases the likelihood that an adversary will obtain the information results in a waiver of the work-product protection."

Any generally public disclosure in contexts such as Internet websites or newspaper advertisements where such announcements have a commercial or competitive purpose will effect a waiver of otherwise work-product-protected materials. The rationale is that such disclosure obviously and necessarily increases the risk that an adversary will become privy to the disclosed work product.

- *Kintera, Inc. v. Convio, Inc.*, 219 F.R.D. 503 (S.D. Cal. 2003). On its website Kintera states Convio's employees reported: "software source codes were being copied and used by Convio to sell products to nonprofit organizations," and Convio "directed its employees to use Kintera's trade secrets for various purposes, including developing software and interactive websites for third parties, and other derivative works in the non-profit sector." The court held that such disclosure for commercial purposes by a sophisticated party wiaved any work product protection for the underlying witness affidavits. The court reasoned that there was no good reason to distinguish between the refusal to allow strategic disclosure of the attorney-client privilege without full waiver thereof but to permit such disclosure of the work product protection. In the litigation context there is precedent for protecting conversations between one party's counsel and third-party witnesses based on work product concepts.

- *Peralta v. Cendant Corp.*, 190 F.R.D. 38, 41 (D. Conn. 1999). The court concluded that to the extent that pre-deposition communications between a former employee and counsel for the former employer revealed counsel's legal theories and opinions, no deposition inquiry would be permitted into what had been revealed of such matters to the former employee, despite the risk that such "wood-shedding" might, consciously or unconsciously, falsify the testimony given.

- *Morales v. United States*, 1997 U.S. Dist. LEXIS 6035, 1997 WL 223080 (S.D.N.Y. May 5, 1997), *recons. denied*, 1997 U.S. Dist. LEXIS 10132 (S.D.N.Y. July 8, 1997). Deposition questions to non-party witnesses regarding conversations with defendant's counsel were protected by work product. The court held that no waiver by disclosure to third persons had occurred, and that a material possibility existed that ordering witnesses to respond to questions would reveal the party's legal strategy.

On the other hand some courts, without expressly so stating, seem concerned that disclosure of work-product-protected materials to a non-party witness increases the opportunity for collusive or shaded testimony from that non-party. In such instances waiver will be held to have occurred by sharing work product. It would be preferable were courts to address this potential concern more openly and directly and preclude sharing of work product with third-party independent witnesses where the only purpose of such sharing would seem to be to influence testimony in line with the sharer's strategy for the case.

- *Ricoh Co. v. Aeroflex Inc.*, 219 F.R.D. 66, 70 (S.D.N.Y 2003). "In this case, the practicalities of litigation suggest that Defendants waived protection for these e-mails under the work product doctrine when counsel shared his observations with a third party who was likely to be an independent witness in the case."

Care should always be taken when any work-product material is disclosed to any party likely to disclose such material to an adversary, even if that party is in no way a governmental agency and even if by virtue of the disclosure the disclosing party is not attempting to get the party to whom the work-product material has been disclosed to act in some manner detrimental to a potential adversary. Such disclosure will constitute a waiver.

- *Verschoth v. Time Warner Inc.*, 2001 U.S. Dist. LEXIS 3174 (S.D. N.Y. Mar. 22, 2001)(Mag. J. Francis), *aff'd in part, modified in part*, 2001 U.S. Dist. LEXIS 6693 (S.D.N.Y. May 21, 2001). Disclosure of privileged information to a former employee who was working sporadically for the defendant but without any managerial responsibility constituted a waiver where the former employee was a good friend of the plaintiff. The court deemed that there was reason to believe that in such circumstances the privileged material might be shared by the former employee with the adverse plaintiff.

Disclosure to a potential consultant, even if the consultant is not subsequently retained, however, does not constitute waiver of the work-product protection.

- *U.S. Information Sys., Inc. v. International Bhd. of Elec. Workers Local Union No. 3*, 2002 U.S. Dist. LEXIS 19363, at *13 (S.D.N.Y. Oct. 10, 2002). The court concluded that one could never safely interview a potential consultant if doing so constituted waiver of work product disclosed in the course of such an interview. Accordingly, it held that showing a potential consultant work-product material as part of the interview process did not result in waiver of such work product.

4. To a Governmental Agency

a. Compelled Disclosure

Most cases hold that compelled disclosure of work-product materials to a governmental agency does not necessarily waiver work product.

One instance of compelled disclosure to the government occurs in the context of the Federal False Claims Act (FCA). The FCA prohibits the knowing presentation of a false claim for payment to an officer or employee of the government. 31 U.S.C. § 3729(a). The FCA authorizes a person, the relator, to file a civil action on behalf of the person and the government. 31 U.S.C. § 3730(b)(1). The FCA requires that the person bringing the lawsuit serve upon the government a "written description of substantially all material evidence and information the person possesses" along with a copy of the complaint. 31 U.S.C. § 3730(b)(2).

The FCA is silent as to whether the mandatory written disclosure to the government to inform the government of the claim and to urge the intervention of the government in the action is protected from discovery and the courts have refused to create an absolute privilege protecting the written disclosure from discovery. The majority of these courts have ruled that a defendant is entitled to obtain the disclosure statements that do not reveal the mental impressions, conclusions, opinions, or legal theories of an attorney or other representative of a party concerning the litigation. In other words, ordinary work product is discoverable if the defendant can demonstrate substantial need of the materials without undue hardship to obtain the substantial equivalent of the materials by other means. However, opinion work product included in the disclosure statement is not discoverable.

- *United States ex rel. O'Keefe v. McDonnell Douglas Corp.*, 918 F. Supp. 1338, 1345–46 (E.D. Mo. 1996). The court held that no reading of the statute would make the mandatory disclosure to the government immune from discovery. That opinion work product would remain absolutely immune from discovery, but that since the government had not provided the disclosure statement for *in camera* review, the court held it to be ordinary work product and thus the ball was now in the court of the party seeking discovery to show substantial need. And undue hardship under Rule 26(b)(3).

- *United States ex rel. Burns v. A.D. Roe Co.*, 904 F. Supp. 592, 593–94 (W.D. Ky. 1995).

- *United States ex rel. Robinson v. Northrop Corp.*, 824 F. Supp. 830, 838–39 (N.D. Ill. 1993).

- *United States ex rel. Stone v. Rockwell Int'l Corp.*, 144 F.R.D. 396, 398 (D. Colo. 1992).

Generally, the court redacts the opinion work product from the written disclosure statement. Thus the disclosure statement was treated just as any other work product would have been.

- *U.S. ex rel. Cericola v. Ben Franklin Bank*, 2003 U.S. Dist. LEXIS 15451 (N.D. Ill. Sept. 3, 2003). After an *in camera* review, the court concluded that work product provided to government under FCA was to be disclosed to defendant in redacted form to take out opinion work product and matters under grand jury investigation which were encompassed in a seal order. The relator provided the disclosure statement for *in camera* review. A review of the disclosure statement discloses that the statement included both ordinary work product and opinion work product. The court held that the opinion work product was not discoverable. However, the ordinary work product was discoverable if the defendants had a substantial need for the disclosure statement, and they would suffer undue hardship in procuring the requested information some other way.

However, at least one court found that the entire disclosure statement was not discoverable as opinion work product because the relator and his or her counsel must engage in a process of selecting and winnowing from the totality of information known to the relator only those facts and evidence that are material to the relator's claims. Therefore, the factual narratives revealed the mental impressions, conclusions, opinions, or legal theories of the relator and his or her counsel. This conclusion sweeps broadly and assumes that the factual narrative contains mental impressions, conclusions, opinions, or legal theories of the relator and his or her counsel without an *in camera* review of the disputed document. Accordingly, the more prudent means of determining if the disclosure statement, in whole or in part, is discoverable is by reviewing the disputed document *in camera* to determine what materials may be discoverable as ordinary work product as followed by the majority of courts that have addressed this issue.

- *U. S. ex rel. Bagley v. TRW, Inc.*, 212 F.R.D. 554 (C.D. Cal. 2003). Disclosure statements usually consist of three parts: a narrative portion, an analytical portion applying the facts to the law and an exhibit portion. The court found that the entirety of the disclosure statement in principle warranted treatment as opinion work product and would generally not be discoverable. To the extent that here portions had been voluntarily tendered to the other side or used by a witness to refresh recollection and thus encompassed within the discoverability scope of Rule 612 of the Federal Rules of Evidence, they were discoverable but not beyond that. The court concluded that such a bright line of non-disclosure would be more in conformity with the purposes of submitting such statements to the government to allow for a determination as to what position the government wished to take in respect to the litigation: joining it or moving to dismiss it.

b. *Voluntary Disclosure*

Voluntary disclosure to a government agency to effect a goal by the disclosing party other than assistance in prospective or ongoing litigation (when a variant of the common-interest exception applies) generally constitutes waiver.

Often such disclosure is undertaken to stave off prosecution or to achieve a desired goal either benefitting the party doing the disclosing or occasionally to harm a competitor. Although courts explain decisions that such disclosure of work-product-protected materials makes it more likely that an adversary will obtain the material, an equal although not as clearly expressed concern is that government actions and their motivating factors be transparent. No star chambers. No confidential informants—other than those that require protection in the criminal context to assure their own safety.

- *Western United Life Assur. Co. v. Fifth Third Bank,* 2004 U.S. Dist. LEXIS 23072, at *17 (N.D. Ill. Nov. 10, 2004). Protective order sought by plaintiff for indubitably work-product-protected documents that were voluntarily supplied to the United States attorney constituted a waiver and thus the protective order was not granted. Thus the proponent's argument that voluntary cooperation with the government, as part of a criminal investigation of an individual that had victimized Western, should not result in the waiver of its work-product protection was not successful in protecting the document from disclosure to the victimizer, one of the defendants in the civil action. The court concluded that the facts indicated a conscious disregard for maintaining the secrecy of the documents. "Western was first unaware—for a two-year period—that it had disclosed the documents at all. Then, it was unaware there had been a subpoena. Finally, it was unaware one of the documents had been made public. Those are simply not circumstances consistent with the maintenance of the secrecy of those documents."

- *Spanierman Gallery v. Merritt,* 2003 U.S. Dist. LEXIS 22141 (S.D.N.Y. Dec. 5, 2003). Disclosure by defendant to FBI of work-product materials in an attempt to obtain assistance of FBI in obtaining return of a disputed painting constituted waiver. No analysis was undertaken by the court to distinguish the breach of confidentiality which occurred in respect to tender of privileged communications, thereby warranting waiver for those, and any waiver for work-product documents.

- *United States v. Bergonzi*, 216 F.R.D. 487, 497 (N.D. Cal. 2003). The court found that voluntary disclosure by a company to the SEC and the USAO of a self-audit constituted a waiver. When the government inadvertently produced the documents in litigation with other defendants, the disclosing company was not able to assert work-product protection.

- *Ramsey v. NYP Holdings, Inc.*, 2002 U.S. Dist. LEXIS 11728, at *37 (S.D.N.Y. June 26, 2002), *clarified without substantive change of result*, 2002 U.S. Dist. LEXIS 18186 (S.D.N.Y. Sept. 3, 2002). By disclosing documents in respect to which work-product protection is asserted to the public and to a prosecuting attorney, the non-party asserting the protection had waived any claim thereto. "Both forms of disclosure are antithetical to the work-product protection that they seek to invoke. In this context, disclosure to the District Attorney is disclosure to their contemplated adversary, and disclosure to the public— whether in the form of books, articles, media interviews, press conferences, press releases or similar public pronouncements—is tantamount to disclosure to the District Attorney."

- *Bank of America, N.A. v. Terra Nova Ins. Co.*, 212 F.R.D. 166, 170 (S.D.N.Y. 2002). Where an insurance company voluntarily provided work product to the New York Insurance Department in the hopes that it would proceed against a rogue insurance agent, work product was waived. The court reasoned that the insurance company was itself in a potentially adversarial position when it provided the work-product-protected materials and provided them in an effort to forestall any proceedings.

- *U.S. Information Sys., Inc. v. International Bhd. of Elec. Workers Local Union No. 3*, 2002 U.S. Dist. LEXIS 19363, at *13 (S.D.N.Y. Oct. 10, 2002). Voluntary disclosure of work-product material to a prosecutor waived any protection. "A well-traveled route to achieving relief in civil litigation has been to persuade the government to take action against a party and thereby gain, if possible, the advantage of collateral estoppel in later civil litigation against that party. The party who travels that route should not be protected from disclosure of its statements. . . . In such circumstances the party asserting work product and the government agency are not allies: they have not agreed on a common strategy, much less commenced joint or even parallel litigation."

■ *In re Columbia/HCA Healthcare Corp. Billing Practices Litig.*, 293 F.3d 289, 307 (6th Cir. 2002), *reh'g denied*, 2002 U.S. App. LEXIS 20212 (6th Cir. Sept. 9, 2002), *cert. denied*, 539 U.S. 977 (2003). The Sixth Circuit, after recapitulating the extensive case law in this area, determined that a selective waiver to government agencies that were effectively adversaries of attorney work product would not be permitted. "Again, like our discussion of the attorney-client privilege above, preserving the traditional confines of the rule affords both an ease of judicial administration as well as a reduction of uncertainty for parties faced with such a decision. These and other reasons persuade us that the standard for waiving the work-product doctrine should be no more stringent than the standard for waiving the attorney-client privilege—once the privilege is waived, waiver is complete and final." (Footnote omitted.)

■ *In re Grand Jury Proceedings*, 350 F.3d 299, 303 (2d Cir. 2003), reversing, 2001 U.S. Dist. LEXIS 2425, at *61–62 (S.D.N.Y. Mar. 2, 2001). The court of appeals held that a target of a grand jury may deliver to the prosecutor a letter stating that he believed his actions were lawful because a federal agent so represented them to him without thereby waiving or forfeiting his attorney's work product on that issue. It thereby reversed a contrary holding by the district court. "[W]e believe there is no basis for concluding that the United States Attorney suffered any unfair prejudice in receiving Doe's letter while Doe continued to assert its privilege with respect to the notes taken by its attorneys. . . .

"The district court believed that Doe inflicted unfairness on the prosecutor and forfeited its privilege merely because it told the prosecutor it believed its actions were within the law. The court explained, "By putting at issue Doe Corp.'s good faith belief . . . , Doe has impliedly waived attorney work-product protection." If the district court's reasoning represented the rule of law, it would follow that whenever a suspect in a criminal proceeding told the prosecutor or an investigating agent that he believed he had done nothing wrong, or whenever a party to a brewing civil dispute made a statement to his adversary to the same effect, he would thereby forfeit his privileges.

"That is not the law. Forfeiture of this type is premised on the *unfairness* to the adversary of *having to defend* against the privilege holder's claim without access to pertinent privileged materials that might refute the claim." (Italics in text.)

- *Sims v. Wyandotte County/Kansas City*, 2001 U.S. Dist. LEXIS 16211 (D. Kan. May 2, 2001). Work-product protection was waived by disclosure of documents to the EEOC.

- *Information Resources, Inc. v. Dun & Bradstreet Corp.*, 999 F. Supp. 591, 593 (S.D.N.Y. 1998). Where plaintiff voluntarily submitted work-product material to government agency to incite it to initiate action against its adversary, work-product protection was waived; "The plaintiff and the government were neither adversaries nor allies when the documents were submitted. . . . [W]ork-product immunity is lost when a party simply makes a voluntary submission of material to a government agency to incite it to attack the informant's adversary. This vindicates the principle of full disclosure, prevents the unfairness of selective revelations, and reflects the common-sense perception that in most such cases the privacy attending creation of the work product had either served its purpose or was of little importance in the first place."

But see:

- *Bullard v. City of New York*, 2004 U.S. Dist. LEXIS 6993 (S.D.N.Y. Apr. 19, 2004). Plaintiff in a case of wrongful arrests made a tape whose video portion alone was tendered to a prosecutor to dissuade prosecution. Defendants sought the audio portion also, which had never been disclosed. The court likened the matter to a "Welles Submission" where a party discloses privileged matter to a governmental agency, often the SEC, to urge that the conduct complained of is not actionable. The court concluded that since the audio portion had never been disclosed no waiver in respect thereto had ever occurred.

- *In re McKesson HBOC, Inc. Sec. Litig.*, 2005 U.S. Dist. LEXIS 7098 (N.D. Cal. Mar. 31, 2005). Even though the court found waiver of privilege because there was no intention of confidentiality *ab initio*, since McKesson had decided it would reveal Skadden Arps report to SEC before the report was even in existence and even though the court also rejected the argument that the report was work-product protected under the common interest exception because it found that McKesson was a potential target of the SEC's investigation and thus the interests were adverse not aligned, nonetheless, the court on public policy grounds concluded that the work-product protection should be accorded to voluntary disclosures to a governmental agency even if a similar disclosure to another private party would not be. "The court finds Judge Boggs's dissent [in Columbia/HCA supra] persuasive with regard to recognizing a distinction between disclosure to a private entity (resulting in waiver) and disclosure to a government entity pursuant to a confidentiality agreement (maintaining work-product protection)." Permitting disclosure to the government under a confidentiality agreement would not undermine the underlying principles of the work-product doctrine. "The work-product privilege rests on the belief that . . . promotion of adversary preparation ultimately furthers the truth-finding process."

Accord:

- *Saito v. McKesson HBOC, Inc.*, 2002 Del. Ch. LEXIS 125, at *40 (Del. Ch. Oct. 25, 2002). McKesson did not waive its work product protection as to all adversaries when it disclosed the Skadden Report and Back-up Materials to the government under the terms of the letter agreements

But see the decisions of two other courts in two other civil cases which did find a waiver.

- *McKesson HBOC, Inc. v. Superior Court*, 9 Cal. Rptr. 3d 812 (Cal. Ct. App. 2004), *review denied*, 2004 Cal. LEXIS 4902 (Cal. June 9, 2004). The California court of appeals, on facts identical to those which the District Court confronted in finding no waiver arising from a selective waiver to the SEC and to the United States Attorney, found that such disclosure entrained waiver in civil litigation under the California Code of Civil Procedure and Evidence Code. It was not necessary for the law firm to share privilege/work-product-protected materials with governmental entities to provide legal advice to clients and the interest of the clients and the federal agencies were not aligned, nor did they share a common interest or goal, nor did the governmental agencies have an interest in maintaining confidentiality merely because they signed a contingent confidentiality agreement to obtain access to the documents. The court of appeals finding the issue to be a mixed fact/law one, reviewed *de novo* and affirmed the trial court.

- *McKesson Corp. v. Green*, 597 S.E.2d 447 (Ga. Ct. App. 2004), *aff'd*, 610 S.E.2d 54 (Ga. 2005). The Supreme court of Georgia affirmed the lower court of appeals by holding that the burden of proving waiver of work product lies with the party asserting it and that the lower court correctly found that voluntary disclosure of documents to the SEC under a contingent confidentiality order constituted such waiver. Selective waiver was thus no more allowed under Georgia law than it is permitted in the federal courts.

- *United States v. Bergonzi*, 216 F.R.D. 487 (N.D. Cal. 2003). The government inadvertently disclosed a party's work-product documents which the party had shared with the government. Where the court found that the government and the disclosing party did not have a common interest, but were in fact in an adversarial stance, such as threatened prosecution, disclosure to the government will operate as disclosure as to all.

In the granddaddy of voluntary sharing of work product between a private party desirous of harming a competitor and a governmental agency bent on the same ends on antitrust grounds, a court allowed work-product sharing on the grounds of a common interest exception without constituting waiver or allowing the adversary access to the work product. In light of the cases cited above, was that the correct decision?

- *United States v. AT&T Co.*, 642 F.2d 1285, 1300 (D.C. Cir. 1980). The D.C. Circuit concluded that there was a common interest between MCI and the government in pursuing parallel antitrust cases. It therefore permitted "MCI to contribute the fruit of its analysis to the Government on those issues common to their two cases will further the Government's preparation for trial and eliminate some duplication of effort."

Courts have held that disclosure when responding to a grand jury subpoena, without testing the validity of that subpoena for privilege issues, constitutes a voluntary disclosure.

- *Westinghouse Elec. Corp. v. Republic of Philippines*, 951 F.2d 1414, 1417 (3d Cir. 1991). The Third Circuit rejected the selective waiver rule, and held that Westinghouse, which voluntarily produced documents to the SEC and DOJ in cooperation with an investigation, waived the attorney-client privilege and the work-product doctrine when it disclosed otherwise protected documents. The Circuit deemed Westinghouse's disclosure "voluntary" even though it was prompted by a grand jury subpoena, distinguishing the production of documents under a court order, which it would not consider voluntary.

- *Wawrzynek v. Gliatech, Inc.*, 2004 U.S. Dist. LEXIS 7751 (E.D. Pa. Mar. 26, 2004). Disclosure pursuant to the government pursuant to a plea agreement was deemed voluntary. "I find that Gliatech's disclosure pursuant to the plea agreement falls within the scope of the term 'voluntary' as defined by Westinghouse Court, and that this disclosure acts as a waiver of both the attorney-client privilege and the work-product doctrine as to all documents disclosed by Gliatech to the FDA and/or DOJ."

Disclosure pursuant to a court order would not be considered voluntary, although even then, some courts hold that the party ordered to disclose must face a contempt citation to obtain an appeal from a disclosure order. *See* Part III, Sections S and T on "Appeals" and "Availability of Mandamus," *infra*.

Needless to say this area of the law would seem to be in some need of greater rationality. In light of the fact that the circuits to date have been so unforgiving of selective waiver of the attorney-client privilege, even when it is shared with the government to dissuade prosecution, does it make sense to treat work product any differently? Does not the public policy of transparent government require that the sources for government actions or inactions when no prosecution is commenced be known? Would not such a bright-line test: you give it to the government, you give it to one and all, be far easier to administer and because more predictable allow private parties to conform their actions accordingly? What would be lost by such a bright line?

C. *Mandated Filings*

1. Securities Law Filings

The securities laws mandate filings but do not necessarily mandate what becomes the content of those filings. That is somewhat discretionary. Nonetheless the cases hold that if information is incorporated into such filings, whatever work-product protection would otherwise perhaps have been accorded to the underlying documents is lost.

- *In re Royal Ahold N.V. Sec. & ERISA Litig.*, 230 F.R.D. 433 (D. Md. 2005). Since content of much of the witness interviews made it into Form 20-F filings, the content of the interviews was deemed waived. The court further concluded since the public reports relied heavily on the witness interviews, "testimonial" use had been made of materials that otherwise might have been work-product protected. Finally the court also said that a confidentiality agreement entered into to protected interview memoranda turned over to the SEC was not sufficient where a public disclosure had been made in the Form 20-F filings. Thus on multiple gounds the court found waiver.

2. To an Independent Auditor

Generally speaking, disclosure of work product to an independent auditor of a publicly held company is considered to waive any protection which would otherwise attach thereto. This is so because the primary duty of the independent auditor is to the shareholders and to the investing public. Further and more generalized dissemination is thus a necessary although not inevitable correlation to such disclosure and it is potentially so broad as to vitiate any meaning to the protection. Most courts have so held. So holding obviates the need for further elaborate discovery of and briefing as to the motivation behind the disclosure and the actual rather than potential likelihood of further disclosure. Any bright line in the privilege and protection area is devoutly to be wished. Whatever minor unfairness may in some individual case inure to the privilege or protection holder is more than offset by the attendant greater efficiency in litigation and the greater ease in assessing the legal consequences of any such disclosure.

- *United States v. Arthur Young & Co.*, 465 U.S. 805, 817–18 (1984). "By certifying the public reports that collectively depict a corporation's financial status, the independent auditor assumes a *public* responsibility transcending any employment relationship with the client. The independent public accountant performing this special function owes ultimate allegiance to the corporation's creditors and stockholders, as well as to investing public. This 'public watchdog' function demands that the accountant maintain total independence from the client at all times and requires complete fidelity to the public trust."

- *In re Diasonics Secs. Litig.*, 1986 U.S. Dist. LEXIS 22750, 1986 WL 53402, at *1 (N.D. Cal. July 15, 1986). The court held that documents disclosed to an accounting firm acting as a public auditor were not entitled to work product protection and when entitled to such protection, the protection was waived by disclosure to the accountants

But see:

- *In re Pfizer, Inc. Sec. Litig.*, 1993 U.S. Dist. LEXIS 18215, 1993 WL 561124, at *6 (S.D.N.Y. Dec. 23, 1993), *clarified but not modified and on an another issue*, 1994 U.S. Dist. LEXIS 7454 (S.D.N.Y. June 6, 1994), *adhered to*, 1994 U.S. Dist. LEXIS 16746 (S.D.N.Y. Nov. 21, 1994). Holding that disclosure to independent auditor is not reasonably viewed as a conduit to a potential adversary.

- *Gutter v. E.I. DuPont de Nemours & Co.*, 1998 U.S. Dist. LEXIS 23207, at *5, 1993 WL 2017926, at *5 (S.D. Fla. May 15, 1998) "Disclosure to outside accountants waives the attorney-client privilege, but not the work-product privilege, since the accountants are not considered a conduit to a potential adversary."

In yet another case, the court was unable to decide as a matter of principle whether disclosure to an independent accountant would have resulted in greater public dissemination, but took the matter under advisement for an *in camera* review of the documents at issue, thereby overruling the magistrate's simpler adjudication that the disclosure had waived the protection.

- *In re Raytheon Sec. Litig.*, 218 F.R.D. 354 (D. Mass. 2003). After an extensive review of the cases, the court dodged the bullet of decision and reserved it for another day, pending *in camera* review of the documents to decide whether disclosure to a public accountant had waived the work-product protection. The court concluded that "the record is inadequate for this Court to determine the scope of litigation information an independent auditor or audited company can reasonably be expected to disclose in public financial reports."

Clearly there are times when public accountants are called upon to perform accounting services for a company that are in no way intended as part of a public audit. In such instances no subsequent public disclosure is necessarily intended or implied in the performance of such services. In that case there is no need to apply any automatic waiver of work-product protection. Indeed the public accountant may have been hired to provide assistance in producing the work product.

- *United States v. ChevronTexaco*, 241 F. Supp. 2d 1065, 1087–88, 2002 U.S. Dist. LEXIS 24970 (N.D. Cal. Mar. 25, 2002), *amended in part*, 241 F. Supp. 2d 1065, 2002 U.S. Dist. LEXIS 24971 (N.D. Cal. June 18, 2002), *adopted*, 2002 U.S. Dist. LEXIS 20010 (N.D. Cal. Sept. 12, 2002). The court concluded that in contrast to the "public watchdog" function of Arthur Young, "Price Waterhouse was not acting remotely as an *independent* auditor with respect to the challenged transaction"

The above case law demonstrates that there is ample scope for costly litigation on the issue of whether disclosure to a public accountant entails a waiver of the work-product protection. Would it not speed adjudication to simply make a bright-line test? We would propose the following: Anything disclosed to a public accountant in conjunction with the preparation of financial statements to be made available to shareholders and the investing public necessarily implies a sufficiently broad dissemination to require a waiver of any work-product protection.

3. To or From a Testifying Expert

The integration of 1993 changes to the Rule 26 discovery rules should have, but apparently have not, definitively answered the question of whether everything shown to a testifying expert, including work-product materials and even "core" work-product materials, such as an attorney's legal opinions and legal theories, thereby become discoverable.

The 1993 amendments to Rule 26 (a)(2)(B) of the Federal Rules of Civil Procedure now require that the testifying expert's report be produced and that it "contain a complete statement of all opinions to be expressed and the basis and reasons therefore; the data or other information considered by the witness in forming the opinions; . . . ."

The accompanying Advisory Committee Note explicitly states that "the report is to disclose the data and other information considered by the expert. . . . Given this obligation of disclosure, litigants should no longer be able to argue that materials furnished to their experts to be used in forming their opinions—whether or not ultimately relied upon by the expert—are privileged or otherwise protected from disclosure when such persons are testifying or being deposed." The revised rule proceeds on the assumption that fundamental fairness requires disclosure of all information supplied to a testifying expert in connection with his testimony.

A major authority has also so concluded.

- 8 CHARLES A. WRIGHT, ARTHUR R. MILLER & RICHARD L. MARCUS, *Federal Practice and Procedure* § 2016.2 at 250–52 (1994). "With respect to experts who testify at trial, the disclosure requirements of Rule 26(a)(2), adopted in 1993, were intended to permit further discussion and mandate disclosure despite privilege."

That certainly would seem to be clear enough. The fly in the ointment, however, has been that some litigants have argued that if the expert did not "consider" or rely on certain documents, then they need not be disclosed. Cases that continue to hold that opinion work product provided to a testifying expert is not discoverable tend to rely on the fact that the wording of Rule 26(b)(3) has been unchanged since 1983 and permits a discovery of work product only upon a showing of substantial need.

Other courts recognize that litigating each instance to determine whether the expert did or did not "consider" or rely on such documents to form his opinion is not only cumbersome and costly but not likely to lead to either predictable or uniform results. At present, however, there is not the uniform clarity that was expected to result from the 1993 revisions. For some litigants and courts, nothing would seem to be clear enough. This is an area of privilege law that would do well with a clarifying opinion, if necessary by the Supreme Court, although the courts of appeal are likely to iron out the problem given time.

Moreover, more and more of the District Courts are concluding that a bright-line test is in every respect more efficient. It does always allow the attorney the choice of whether to disclose a work-product-protected document to a testifying expert and thereby waive the protection or not. But surely a fact finder is entitled to test the validity of an expert's opinion by knowing all the components that may or may not have gone into its formulation. Here is one instance where any search for the perfect equilibrium is indeed an enemy of the "good enough" in most cases. Predictability in the law is always to be preferred to doubt. If you don't want your adversary to see it, don't disclose it to a testifying expert.

a. *Cases Requiring Full Disclosure Even of Core Work Product*

Some cases have held in order for waiver to occur, the work product must have been *considered* by the expert in formulating his opinions. This conclusion is consistent with the language of amended Federal Rule of Civil Procedure 26(a)(2)(B), which, as noted above, requires the expert's report to identify all data or other information "*considered* by the witness in forming the opinions." (Emphasis added.) Most courts have also said that there is no requirement that the testifying expert *relied* upon the work product to arrive at his opinion. It is sufficient if he *considered* the material. In fact, the drafters of the 1993 amendments to Rule 26 rejected a version of subsection 26(a)(2) that would have required the expert's report to identify all data or information "relied upon" by the expert in forming his opinions. *See* August 1991 Proposed Rules. Nonetheless, the end result is usually to mandate disclosure. As courts point out, litigating the issue of whether an expert did or did not in fact *consider* a particular document to which he had access is impractical.

To date the Federal Circuit has pronounced itself for full disclosure.

- *In re Pioneer Hi-Bred Int'l, Inc.*, 238 F.3d 1370, 1375–76 (Fed. Cir. 2001). The Federal Circuit said: "The revised rule proceeds on the assumption that fundamental fairness requires disclosure of all information supplied to a testifying expert in connection with his testimony. Indeed, we are quite unable to perceive what interests would be served by permitting counsel to provide core work product to a testifying expert and then to deny discovery of such material to the opposing party." Accordingly, the court held that based on amended Rule 26(a)(2), any materials disclosed to the testifying expert would constitute a waiver of the work-product protection. "Indeed, we are quite unable to perceive what interests would be served by permitting counsel to provide core work product to a testifying expert and then to deny discovery of such material to the opposing party." Nonetheless, the court determined that since it was not factually clear what had been revealed to the testifying expert, a hearing should be held on that issue.

Many of the various district courts and magistrate judges have done so as well.

- *In re Omeprazole Patent Litig.*, 2005 U.S. Dist. LEXIS 6112 (S.D.N.Y. Feb. 18, 2005). The court did not distinguish between core and fact work product but granted a motion to compel the continuation of the testifying expert's opinion as to conversations with counsel regarding any amendment to his report.

- *American Fid. Assur. Co. v. Boyer*, 225 F.R.D. 520 (D.S.C. 2004). Disclosure compelled of:

  (1) Any and all documents, notes or records relating to the above captioned case and Expert's report[s] . . . including correspondence, electronic correspondence and information provided by Plaintiff's counsel.

  (2) Any and all other materials used, referred to or consulted in preparing the Expert's Report . . . to include any draft reports.

- *Baum v. Village of Chittenango*, 218 F.R.D. 36 (N.D.N.Y. 2003). "While this court does not necessarily share Judge Young's certainty [*Aniero* case, *infra*] that the history and language of Rule 26 *mandate* the conclusion that disclosure is required, it does agree that both the history and language strongly suggest as much. . . . Furthermore, this court agrees with his assessment that policy reasons support a bright-line rule of disclosure; namely: the attorney-expert dynamics in the litigation context, including effective cross-examination; the efficiency of the truth-finding process; and, the maintenance of the integrity of the work-product doctrine fostered by a simple attorney decision not to share such material with the expert." (Citation omitted.)

- *Venn v. McRae*, 295 B.R. 676, 679 (Bankr. N.D. Fla. 2003). The court stated it was not persuaded that any exception should be made to protecting under work-product rubrics any documents provided to the testifying expert given the plain language of the new rule and the Advisory Committee Notes. "Once materials are furnished to the experts to be considered in forming their opinions, regardless of whether or not ultimately relied upon by the expert, privilege or protection from disclosure is waived because the plain meaning of Rule 26(a)(2)(B) trumps protections afforded by the attorney-client privilege and the work-product doctrine. It is fair to require full disclosure of all communications to expert witnesses by attorneys because once communication has been furnished to the expert to be considered in forming their opinion, whether or not the expert relies on the documents, the communication will potentially color the expert's opinion. The disclosure of such materials enables the opposing party to test the expert's opinion through more effective cross-examination."

- *Pioneer Hi-Bred Int'l, Inc. v. Ottawa Plant Food, Inc.*, 2003 U.S. Dist. LEXIS 13963 (N.D. Iowa July 25, 2003) (unpublished). The court found no reason why documents shown to testifying expert needed to be disclosed.

- *Southern Scrap Material Co. v. Fleming*, 2003 U.S. Dist. LEXIS 10815, at *72–73 (E.D. La. June 18, 2003), *recons. denied*, 2003 U.S. Dist. LEXIS 13558 (E.D. La. July 29, 2003). "The Court here notes that if and/or when any one or more of the defendants' or the plaintiffs' experts are designated as trial (i.e., testifying) witnesses, their reports and all of the material furnished to them by counsel or utilized by them in producing their reports shall be produced to opposing counsel forthwith and without any further delay. This ruling obtains whether the designation of such an expert be as either a fact or an expert witness. This is so because any factual testimony elicited from such an expert will necessarily relate to their participation in the underlying case or cases as an expert witness. In other words, their trial testimony will inevitably touch upon matters which the parties, both plaintiffs and defendants, now claim are protected by privilege. Testimony of such experts at trial, even as to factual matters, would necessarily waive both the attorney-client privilege, to the extent such matters were disclosed, and any work product protection that is presently claimed."

- *Vitalo v. Cabot Corp.*, 212 F.R.D. 478, 479 (E.D. Pa. Dec. 23, 2002). The court held that Rule 26(a)(2)(B) of the Federal Rules of Civil Procedure, as amended in 1993, vitiates a claim of attorney work product with respect to any information considered by a party's expert, whether or not relied upon by that expert.

- *United States Fid. & Guar. Co. v. Braspetro Oil Servs. Co.*, 2002 U.S. Dist. LEXIS 111, at *22 (S.D.N.Y. Jan. 4, 2002). The court ordered 60 computer discs that had been made available to testifying experts produced. "Under these circumstances, the Court can only conclude that Defendants voluntarily relinquished whatever confidentiality attached to the contents of those discs, and thereby waived the attorney-client privilege with respect to everything on the discs. Similarly, the privilege has been waived for any hard copies of privileged documents that were provided to the experts." Remanded to a magistrate judge for further discovery, he refused to revisit the discovery order when an attempt was made to distinguish consultative from testifying experts. 2002 U.S. Dist. LEXIS 111, at *22 (S.D.N.Y. Jan. 4, 2002). "There is no evidence supporting Defendants' bare assertion that certain documents were reviewed by the experts solely in a consultative capacity. Rather, the record indicates that at least two of Defendants' experts, and their staffs, had access to the entire universe of Defendants' documents for use in connection with the experts' reports and testimony. Nor is there any evidence that Defendants tried to limit access to the database according to the purpose for which it was being used, much less that any documents for which the privilege is being claimed were considered only for consultative purposes."

- *Aniero Concrete Co., Inc. v. New York City Sch. Constr. Auth.*, 2002 U.S. Dist. LEXIS 2892, at *8, 11 (S.D.N.Y. Feb. 21, 2002) (Young, J.). Defendant school construction authority sought an order compelling its co-defendant surety to produce certain documents containing the mental impressions of the surety's counsel that were supplied to the surety's experts in the course of their preparation of reports under Fed. R. Civ. P. 26(a)(2)(B). The surety argued that the documents in question were protected from discovery as work product, and that the expert had not relied upon them in forming his opinion. The court found that authority in the circuit provided that the Fed. R. Civ. P. 26(a)(2)(B) disclosure requirement should prevail over work product, especially since the expert conceded it was his firm's regular practice to review documents similar to the contested documents to determine if they are relevant, although he testified he did not recall reviewing the documents. "The Rule 26 (a)(2)(B) disclosure requirement trumps the substantial protection otherwise accorded opinion work product under Rule 26(b)(3)." Hence core opinion work-product documents were ordered produced. The case also cites many cases that have so ruled since the adoption of the Rule 26(a) amendments.

- *Western Res., Inc. v. Union Pac. R.R. Co.*, 2002 U.S. Dist. LEXIS 1911, at *37 (D. Kan. Jan. 31, 2002). The court held that documents reviewed during a long period of time by a consulting expert became discoverable once the expert was designated as a testifying expert, since the expert had obviously "considered" those documents during the period of time that he was merely a consulting expert. "[W]ork product protection and privilege are waived with regard to protected materials prepared by or transmitted to a non-testifying expert in anticipation of litigation but subsequently read and reviewed by a testifying expert—even if the testifying expert avers under oath that he did not actually consider such materials in formulating his opinion." As a result, virtually all the documents were ordered produced. Others were ordered produced for in camera inspection. The court relied extensively on the *BFC Oil Refining* case, discussed in detail below.

- *Suskind v. Home Depot Corp.*, 2001 U.S. Dist. LEXIS 1349, at *17 (D. Mass. Jan. 2, 2001). The court engaged in an extensive analysis of the 1993 changes to the various components of Rule 26 and concluded that any core work product provided to a testifying expert was discoverable based both on a textual reading of the amendment and on solid public policy grounds. "Lastly, it is my opinion that the 1993 Amendments mandating the disclosure of all materials considered by an expert, even if the materials are otherwise core attorney work product, rest on sound policy judgments."

- *Weil v. Long Island Sav. Bank FSB*, 206 F.R.D. 38 (E.D.N.Y. 2001). The court found that the 1993 revision to Rule 26(a)(2)(B) did not exempt "core" work product from the disclosure requirement, nor did it limit disclosure to factual material as opposed to mental impressions or opinions of counsel.

- *MCI Communications Corp. v. Dataline, Inc.*, 2001 U.S. Dist. LEXIS 18144, at *1–2 (Oct. 30, 2001). The court stated that even before the 1993 amendments, any documents generated by a testifying expert were to be produced. It also ordered produced all documents considered by the testifying expert and required it to be done before the expert sat for his deposition. The court cited with disapproval the *Magee infra* holding and relied upon *B.C.F., infra, W.R. Grace, infra; Suskind,* and *Pioneer Hi-Bred.*

- *W.R. Grace & Co.-Conn. v. Zotos Int'l, Inc.*, 2000 U.S. Dist. LEXIS 18091, at *11 (W.D.N.Y. Nov. 2, 2000). The court concluded that the 1993 amendment which requires all materials considered by a testifying expert mean exactly what they say. No reason exists to exempt "core" work product from that express change in the Rule, particularly when the Advisory Committee Notes are also taken into account. "It is illogical that such broad language, explicitly directed to privileges and other sources of protection against disclosure, was intended to exclude any form of work product. Nor is the stated purpose of the amendment limited to disclosure of factual material as opposed to mental impressions and opinions of counsel." The court cited a long line of cases which so held.

- *TV-3, Inc. v. Royal Ins. Co. of Am.*, 194 F.R.D. 585, 588 (S.D. Miss. 2000). Correspondence between counsel and expert witness was discoverable, "given plain language of Rule 26(a)(2) and its accompanying Advisory Committee Note." "When an attorney hires an expert, both the expert's compensation and his 'marching orders' can be discovered and the expert cross-examined thereon. If the lawyer's 'marching orders' are reasonable and fair, the lawyer and his client have little to fear. If the orders are in the nature of telling the expert what he is being paid to conclude, appropriate discovery and cross-examination thereon should be the consequence. Such a ruling is most consistent with an effort to keep expert opinion testimony fair, reliable and within the bounds of reason."

- *Johnson v. Gmeinder*, 191 F.R.D. 638, 645–47 (D. Kan. 2000). The court held that an investigative report and other materials prepared by a non-testifying expert in connection with investigation of an automobile accident lose privileged status when disclosed to testifying expert (citing Fed. R. Civ. P. 26(a)(2)(B) and advisory committee notes appended thereto). The court determined that an expert is deemed to have "considered" materials for purposes of Rule 26(a)(2)(B) if such expert "has read or reviewed the privileged materials before or in connection with formulating his or her opinion. . . . [T]o determine whether an expert has 'considered' certain materials, *as that term is commonly used*, would require the court to explore the expert's subjective mental processes and risks the creation of an unwieldy rule that would provide uncertainty as to the protected status of work product or other privileged materials. The Court believes it is important for practitioners to have a more definitive rule under which they can determine whether waiver has occurred."

- *Culbertson v. Shelter Mut. Ins. Co.*, 1999 U.S. Dist. LEXIS 2295, at *3 (E.D. La. Mar. 2, 1999). The argument that a testifying expert was in fact a "fact" expert and that therefore disclosure of work product documents shown to him did not have to be disclosed was unavailing. Plaintiff claimed that the witness was to testify as to facts developed in connection with his provision accounting expertise in connection with the litigation. Sounds very like a damages expert. Perhaps with tongue in cheek, the court in a footnote said: "The Court cannot view Shirley as a 'non-testifying' expert inasmuch as Shirley is going to testify, albeit not as an expert."

- *Lamonds v. General Motors Corp.*, 180 F.R.D. 302, 306 (W.D. Va. 1998). The magistrate judge did not order production of work-product-protected documents shown to a testifying expert because defendant was in possession to the factual material in another form and thus had shown no substantial need. The district court found the ruling clearly erroneous. The court discussed the 1993 amendments and the fact that proper cross-examination requires full disclosure, since experts "occupy a central role in modern litigation," yet are "often less then helpful and sometimes misleading, effective cross-examination by an opposing party is an essential tool for exposing any weaknesses in the expert's opinions. One such potential weakness is the source of information the expert has considered in forming his opinions. It can be important for the trier of fact to know whether the expert arrived at his opinion after an independent review of all relevant facts or whether he relied on 'facts' chosen and presented by an attorney advocating a particular position. This information can only surface on cross-examination where an opposing party has been able to discover the material provided to the expert by the lawyer who retained him."

- *FDIC v. First Heights Bank, FSB*, 1998 U.S. Dist. LEXIS 21506, at *13–14 (E.D. Mich. Mar. 3, 1998). "After a review of the two lines of cases dealing with the tension between expert discovery and opinion work-product protection under Rule 26, I find the reasoning of *Karn* and similar cases to be the correct result under the 1993 amendments to the rule. Opinion work product that is reviewed by an expert in preparation for testimony at trial is discoverable under Rules 26(a)(2)(B) and 26(b)(4)(A).

  "The clear language in the Advisory Committee Notes compels this decision. In its commentary, the Advisory Committee resolved the conflict left open in the previous draft of Rule 26. The new rule specifically states that an expert must disclose the basis for his or her opinion prior to being deposed. The language in Rule 26(b)(3) concerning protection of opinion work product is 'subject to' Rule 26(b)(4). Therefore, it is clear that the work product doctrine does not apply to the report prepared or opinion reached by the expert."

- *Baerga v. Hospital for Special Surgery*, 1998 U.S. Dist. LEXIS 17716, at *1–2 (S.D.N.Y. Nov. 9, 1998). "I accept Judge Motley's opinion in *B.C.F. Oil Refining v. Consol. Edison of N.Y.*, 171 F.R.D. 57 (S.D.N.Y. 1997), as authoritative. I prefer its reasoning to that of *Magee v. Paul Revere Life Ins. Co.*, 172 F.R.D. 627 (E.D.N.Y. 1997)

(Orenstein, Mag. J.), which was issued two months later than *BCF Oil* but did not cite it.

"Judge Motley's opinion gave very clear guidance to attorneys in our District. First, if an attorney wants to keep his mental impressions privileged, he should not communicate them to his expert witness. Second, if the expert has a second role, for example 'as a technical consultant,' then 'any ambiguity as to the role played by the expert when reviewing or generating documents should be resolved in favor of the party seeking discovery.' B.C.F. *Oil*, 171 F.R.D. at 61–62."

- *Baxter Diagnostics, Inc. v. AVL Scientific Corp.*, 1993 U.S. Dist. LEXIS 11798 (C.D. Cal. Aug. 6, 1993). Extensive discovery was allowed of all invoices of trial experts, all documents authored by, all oral statements made by and all documents considered trial experts in a blessedly short and to the point opinion.

- *B.C.F. Oil Refining, Inc. v. Consolidated Edison Co. of New York, Inc.*, 171 F.R.D. 57, 61–62 (S.D.N.Y. 1997). The court divided the types of documents into five categories. Category one consisted of "documents which, though coming from plaintiff's expert (or sent to him), have nothing to do with the preparation of his expert report or his expert testimony[.]" The court concluded that theoretically these would not have to be produced, but that any ambiguity as to the role played by the expert when reviewing or generating documents should be resolved in favor of the party seeking discovery. After the documents were assessed, most were ordered produced because it was not clear whether they were considered in a consultative or testifying capacity.

Category two included documents consisting of material consulted on or generated by the expert in connection with his role as an expert. All these were ordered produced. The court concluded that the party seeking discovery should not have to rely on the [resisting party's] representation that the documents were not considered by the expert in forming his opinion.

Category three consisted of data provided by . . . counsel to the expert for his review, which did not contain the attorney's mental impressions or opinions but merely relay facts that the expert is presumably expected to consider. The court ordered these documents produced on the grounds that "it would strain credulity to maintain that [Rule 26(a)(2)] somehow exempts factual information that counsel gave the expert."

Category four consisted of documents containing the thoughts and mental impressions of the attorney [which] were given to the expert for his consideration. Acknowledging that there was a clear split of authority on how to deal with these, the court ultimately ordered them produced, observing that "the [advisory committee note] evinces an intent to require parties to produce attorney opinions given to the expert and considered by the expert in forming his or her opinion."

Category five were documents consisting of notes taken or memoranda generated by counsel after having had oral conversations with the expert that, however, were never seen by the expert. These alone in their entirety were not ordered produced.

- *Karn v. Ingersoll-Rand Co.*, 168 F.R.D. 633, 639 (N.D. Ind. 1996). Citing the text of new Rule 26(a)(2), the advisory committee notes, and public policy grounds, the court held that Rule 26(a)(2)(B) "mandate[s] disclosure of all materials reviewed by an expert witness," and correspondingly "'trump[s]' any assertion of work product or privilege.'"

- *United States v. City of Torrance*, 163 F.R.D. 590, 593 (C.D. Cal. 1995). The court held that where expert has acquired information relevant to his opinion, defendants should not be bound by his statement that he did not consider it.

- *Eliasen v. Hamilton*, 111 F.R.D. 396, 400 n.5 (N.D. Ill. 1986). The court concluded that "documents considered but rejected by the testifying expert in reaching opinions may be equally necessary for effective cross-examination. . . . In fact, the documents considered but rejected by the expert trial witness could be even more important for cross-examination than those actually relied upon by him." (Citations omitted.)

Even the courts requiring the expert witness to have actually reviewed the materials before they are subject to the discovery rule put the burden on the party resisting discovery to prove that the expert witness did not read or review and that thus the expert could not have "considered" any of the work-product-protected materials.

- *United States Fid. & Guar. Co. v. Braspetro Oil Servs. Co.*, 2002 U.S. Dist. LEXIS 111, 2002 WL 15652 (S.D.N.Y. Jan. 7, 2002). The court was exceedingly critical of defendants' rather cavalier way of asserting and seeking to prove any privilege/work-product protection. Accordingly, it allowed discovery of all the documents "made available" to testifying experts and their staffs on some 60 CD-ROMs where the defendants made no attempt to demonstrate which the testifying experts "reviewed," much less "considered."

The cases that antedated the 1993 amendment to Rule 26(b)(4)(A) are now of historical interest only, but even before the amendments, many courts allowed full discovery of materials shown to a testifying expert.

- *Intermedics, Inc. v. Ventritex, Inc.*, 139 F.R.D. 384, 387 (N.D. Cal. 1991). "Absent an extraordinary showing of unfairness that goes well beyond the interests generally protected by the work-product doctrine, written and oral communications from a lawyer to an expert that are related to matters about which the expert will offer testimony are discoverable, even when those communications otherwise would be deemed opinion work product."

- *Boring v. Keller*, 97 F.R.D. 404, 407 (D. Colo. 1983). "One situation in which opinion work product is not protected is where an expert witness utilizes counsel's opinion work product in order to formulate his or her opinion."

It is hard to imagine that the view that argues for full disclosure of anything shown to a testifying expert will not eventually prevail, since it seems fairly fundamental that it is the sole basis for fully testing the basis of the opinion formulated. Moreover, the expedient of assuring non-disclosure is readily available. Don't show it to a testifying expert. Indeed, if an expert is genuinely such, what need would there be to have his opinion formulated by trial counsel's work product?

In light of that prediction, particular care should be taken before in-house counsel is designated as an expert witness, lest doing so opens a Pandora's box in respect to documents that otherwise would be work-product protected.

- *American Steamship Owners Mutual Prot. & Indem. Ass'n, Inc. v. Alcoa Steamship Co., Inc.*, 2006 U.S. Dist. LEXIS 3078 (S.D.N.Y. Jan. 26, 2006). Where testifying expert had for over twenty years been the representative of several law firms which acted as General Counsel to plaintiffs. In that capacity he had read a letter from a law firm which he did not remember and which he declared he would not reread. Nonetheless the letter was ordered produced. The court concluded that the Rule 26(a)(2)(B) disclosure requirement "trumped" the substantial protection otherwise accorded opinion work product under Rule 26(b)(3). Any other documents authored by him or given to him by the plaintiff were also to be produced.

- *QST Energy, Inc. v. Mervyn's & Target Corp.*, 2001 U.S. Dist. LEXIS 23266, at *13 (N.D. Cal. May 11, 2001). Where in-house counsel was designated as a testifying expert, work product assessing both the terms of the contract and potential damage calculations made by in-house counsel was waived.

- *Musselman v. Phillips*, 176 F.R.D. 194, 202 (D. Md. 1997). Where the party claiming continuing protection for work-product materials conveyed to a testifying expert but made no showing as to which were actually reviewed by the expert, all the materials provided to the expert were ordered produced.

- *Barna v. United States*, 1997 U.S. Dist. LEXIS 10853, 1997 WL 417847 (N.D. Ill. July 28, 1997) (same).

The following cases all allow for discovery of core work product shown to or produced by a testifying expert.

b. *Cases Not Requiring Disclosure of Core Work Product*

Where a party can clearly demonstrate that a testifying expert never actually reviewed privileged material, the work product protection will not be breached.

- *Amway Corp. v. Procter & Gamble Co.*, 2001 U.S. Dist. LEXIS 5317 (W.D. Mich. Apr. 17, 2001). The court found Rule 26 disclosure unnecessary. The party asserting work product and privilege protection had provided the court with affidavits and deposition testimony which clearly established in the court's mind that the testifying expert had never read, reviewed or considered the material in reaching his conclusions.

On the other hand there are cases where even despite the 1993 amendment to Rule 26(b)(4)(A), some courts continue to hold that discovery of factual work product is mandated by the Rule but that discovery of "core" or opinion work product, even if considered by the expert is not. They do so because Rule 26(b)(4)(A) does not expressly state that core work product is discoverable and thus they believe the 1993 amendment to the Rule has not undone the holding of *Hickman* which makes "core" work product nearly, albeit not entirely, absolutely protected.

- *Estate of Chopper v. R.J. Reynolds Tobacco Co.*, 195 F.R.D. 648, 650 (N.D. Iowa 2000). Based on Eighth Circuit's inclination to protect core work product, its disclosure to a testifying expert does not mandate disclosure to adversary.

- *Estate of Moore v. R.J. Reynolds Tobacco Co.*, 194 F.R.D. 659, 663 (S.D. Iowa 2000). Core work product used by a testifying expert does not have to be disclosed to an adversary.

- *Nexxus Prods. Co. v. CVS New York, Inc.*, 188 F.R.D. 7 (D. Mass. 1999). The court relied on the reasoning of Haworth in not requiring disclosure of core work product even where such documents had been disclosed to testifying experts. It thus read the 1993 amendment to Rule 26(b)(4)(A) as requiring disclosure of fact work product only.

- *Ladd Furniture, Inc. v. Ernst & Young*, 1998 U.S. Dist. LEXIS 17345, 1998 WL 1093901, at *12 (M.D.N.C. Aug. 27, 1998). The court relied on the importance the Fourth Circuit attached to the protection of core attorney work product in other contexts to reject the view that the 1993 Amendments permitted disclosure of core work-product materials when shown to an expert.

- *Magee v. Paul Revere Life Ins. Co.*, 172 F.R.D. 627, 642–43 (E.D.N.Y. 1997). At issue was whether a claim file reviewed by an expert witness had to be disclosed. The court said it did not. "[T]he Court holds that 'the data or other information considered by [an expert] witness in forming [his] opinions' required to be disclosed in the expert's report mandated under Rule 26(a)(2)(B) extends only to factual materials, and not to core attorney work product considered by an expert. In so holding, the Court agrees with the *Haworth* court's view that Rule 26(a) should not be construed as vitiating the attorney work-product privilege, and the laudable policies behind it, in the absence of clear and unambiguous authority under the Federal Rules of Civil Procedure."

Having so found, however, the court decided that although it was not its regular policy to review documents *in camera* as to which claims of privilege were made, documents which claimed to contain legal theories fell into the small category of documents warranting such review.

- *Haworth, Inc. v. Herman Miller, Inc.*, 162 F.R.D. 289, 295–96 (W.D. Mich. 1995). In the course of a deposition, plaintiff's attorney instructed plaintiff's expert witness not to testify as to conversations with the attorney regarding plaintiff's product manuals which had been shown to him. Consulted by phone, the magistrate judge stated he believed that defendant had the better part of the argument and allowed the expert not to testify pending a full briefing. Thereupon the magistrate ruled that the questions were proper and should be answered. The district court disagreed with the reasoning of the magistrate judge which would have required disclosure of all work product, both factual and "core." The district court believed that the Rule 26(b)(4)(A) only applied to factual work product, not "core" and that in the Sixth Circuit "core" work product was absolutely protected from disclosure. "This Court reads the words as meaning only that all factual information considered by the expert must be disclosed in the report. . . . The whole of the Committee Notes makes clear that attorneys should no longer be able to make work-product privilege arguments regarding materials containing facts or assemblages of facts because they are obligated to disclose all factual information on their own in a report rather than on motion of opposing counsel. Any failure to so disclose requires that the information may not be used at trial. . . . The new procedure simply eliminates the need to have a judge order redaction of core work product from material that contains discoverable facts and data. In this court's judgment, a more effective cross-examination and impeachment of the opposing party's expert witness in a patent case is not the type of circumstance the Supreme Court contemplated would overcome the strong policy against disclosing an attorney's opinion work product. The risk of an attorney influencing an expert witness does not go unchecked in the adversarial system, for the reasonableness of an expert opinion can be judged against the knowledge of the expert's field and is always subject to the scrutiny of other experts." (Citations omitted.)

The court, however, did not accept the argument that fact work product need not be disclosed unless the expert "relied" upon it to formulate his opinion.

The court also reversed as an abuse of discretion the award of sanctions for failure to supply the work product as an abuse of discretion since reasonable jurists could differ as to whether full disclosure had to be made.

Finally, the case was remanded to assure that the defendant had fully complied with the requirement to disclose factual work-product materials.

- *All West Pet Supply Co. v. Colgate-Palmolive Co.*, 152 F.R.D. 634, 638–39 (D. Kan. 1993). The court held that opinion work-product privilege was not waived by disclosure to testifying expert.

A not too frequent situation when documents would not necessarily be ordered produced even though shown to a testifying expert is where they 1) were otherwise privilege or work-product protected, 2) were inadvertently sent to the expert, and 3) had no connection with the opinion which was to be proffered by the expert. Much will depend on how a particular court views inadvertent disclosure of privileged materials in general. And in general, courts are taking a "balancing" approach in which they take into account several factors, including fundamental fairness to the parties, as we have seen extensively in the Section on Inadvertent Disclosure in Part I, *supra*.

- *Simon Prop. Group, L.P. v. mySimon, Inc.*, 194 F.R.D. 644, 647 (S.D. Ind. 2000). Four documents were inadvertently sent to a testifying expert and listed by the expert as documents that had been reviewed albeit they did not constitute documents "considered" to reach a decision. The court went through the balancing test to determine whether the inadvertent disclosure should be deemed a waiver. When all was said and done, however, the court, after an *in camera* inspection, determined that the documents in fact had nothing to do with the expert's opinion and thus did not order them produced since fundamental fairness did not require a finding of inadvertent waiver or mandate production to allow for effective cross-examination.

c. When a Testifying Expert Is or Was Also a Consulting Expert

Some parties, for whatever reasons, initially hire an expert first as a consultative expert and then at some later point transform that expert into a testifying one. Must documents prepared or reviewed by such an expert while wearing the consultative hat also be disclosed? Remarkably and inexplicably based on any cognizable real-world or policy considerations, some courts have answered that question in the negative. The only explanation is that where a lawyer sees a loophole there seems to be a compelling instinct to take it regardless of any rational considerations. Since most individuals are incapable of erasing from their minds what they have *considered* in their capacity as consulting expert once they are transformed into a testifying expert, such a bifurcation makes precious little sense.

- *In re Air Crash at Dubrovnik, Croatia on April 3, 1996,* 2001 U.S. Dist. LEXIS 14334, at *8 (D. Conn. June 4, 2001). The court adopted the general principle that no work product is immune from production when considered by a testifying expert. But then reviewed once again 599 documents which it had ruled had to be disclosed in a group of some 7,100 to determine which might have been created or reviewed by the consultant while he played merely a consultative role. It thereby accepted that such distinctions can be made.

- *Messier v. Southbury Training School,* 1998 U.S. Dist. LEXIS 23221 (D. Conn. June 29, 1998). As a matter of general principle, court stated all work product consulted by a testifying expert had to be produced. Where an expert first played a consultative role, the work product shown to the expert in that capacity did not. Any doubts as to in what capacity the expert was serving at the time the work-product material was considered was to be resolved in favor of disclosure.

Surely, this approach makes little sense. It is not the timing of when a testifying expert considered certain work product, but the fact that it was considered at all. Otherwise, all that any party would need to do would be to designate an expert initially as a consulting expert only. Show the expert any work product that it never wanted the adversary to obtain access thereto. And only thereafter redesignate the expert as a testifying expert.

■ *B.C.F. Oil Refining Inc. v. Consolidated Edison Co. of New York, Inc.*, 171 F.R.D. 57 (S.D.N.Y. 1997). The court divided the documents in dispute into five categories and exempted from production only those which had no connection with the expert's opinion or testimony or which contained attorney notes and memoranda of discussions with the expert, which, however were never forwarded to the expert.

Alternatively a party may seek to immunize work product from discovery by designating an expert retained as a testifying expert into a consultative expert as well. This ploy should not and has not worked.

■ *Furniture World, Inc. v. D.A.V. Thrift Stores*, 168 F.R.D. 61 (D.N.M. 1996). The court concluded that an expert initially designated as a testifying expert could not be shielded from full discovery by being designated as a consulting expert also. The court allowed the party resisting discovery to withdraw the expert as a testifying expert altogether, but pointed out that the time for designating expert witnesses had passed.

Presumably, redesignating a testifying expert entirely as a consultative expert and hiring a new testifying expert to whom some lesser body of work-product material is forwarded in order to retain their status as immune from discovery should work. It is just that you can't, once again, have your cake and eat it too.

4. To a Non-Testifying Expert

Disclosure of materials shared with or created by non-testifying experts are governed by Federal Rule of Civil Procedure 26(b)(4)(B), which states:

> A party may, through interrogatories or by deposition, discover facts known or opinions held by an expert who has been retained or specially employed by another party in anticipation of litigation or preparation for trial and who is not expected to be called as a witness at trial only as provided in Rule 35(b) or upon a showing of exceptional circumstances under which it is impracticable for the party seeking discovery to obtain facts or opinions on the same subject by other means.

Given the wording of the Rule, courts bend over backwards to protect such materials. Protection has been accorded to materials produced by non-testifying experts which in identical circumstances would have entailed a waiver of the attorney-client privilege.

- *In re PolyMedica Corp. Sec. Litig.*, 235 F.R.D. 28 (D. Mass. 2006). Defendants had retained Price Waterhouse as non-testifying experts to prepare a report which was then turned over to the Securities and Exchange Commission. The court found that the report was prepared essentially for the SEC rather than for the instant litigation but that it was work-product protected because litigation with the SEC was anticipated and would have dealt with substantially similar issues. Moreover, turning over the report to the SEC did not constitute a waiver because the defendant did not propose to use the report as a sword in the instant litigation and thus there was no unfairness to plaintiff in not requiring disclosure.

The finding thus runs counter to the long line of cases which hold that any selective disclosure of attorney-client privilege materials, even if it be to a government agency, operates as a waiver. The court did not even discuss that line of cases. Instead the court reasoned that since the defendants were not going to use any aspect of the report as a sword there was no unfairness to plaintiffs in not requiring disclosure. Logical coherence is somewhat wanting. The case does however suggest a means for challenging the entire line of cases which hold that selective disclosure of attorney-client privileged materials even to a governmental agency necessarily entails a waiver of the privilege. Since, however, conceptual matrices governing privilege and work-product protection tend to exist in separate universes and since the doctrine of selective waiver entailing total waiver is now so entrenched in the law the attempt to rationalize the two strands may come to nought.

The issue has not cropped up with frequency. But if a testifying expert communicates with an attorney in a manner and about issues that would be expected of a consultative non-testifying expert, it is not likely that work product protection will be accorded. Thus the moral seems to be that testifying and consultative experts should not confuse their respective roles if the work-product protection is to be accorded.

- *Colindres v. Quietflex Mfg.*, 228 F.R.D. 567 (S.D. Tex. 2005). Court held that e-mail sent by testifying expert to counsel was discoverable because it simply was not encompassed with the definition of work product provided for by Rule 26(a)(2)(B). The proponent of the work product protection argued, without success, that the testifying expert was acting in merely a consultative fashion when he wrote his opinions to counsel about issues which the court had raised at a hearing and that those observations were not considered or incorporated in his report as a testifying expert. The court reasoned that if counsel had written the e-mail to the testifying expert it would be subject to disclosure. The direction in which the e-mail flowed from expert to counsel rather than the other way around, deemed the court, should not control the result.

5. To Outside Auditors

Two lines of cases exist as to whether disclosure of work-product materials to outside auditors for the purpose of allowing them to assess litigation and its effects on the company's financial statements waives the work-product protection.

- *In re Pfizer Inc. Sec. Litig.*, 1993 U.S. Dist. LEXIS 18215, 1993 WL 561125, at *6 (S.D.N.Y. Dec. 23, 1993), *but not modified and on an another issue*, 1994 U.S. Dist. LEXIS 7454 (S.D.N.Y. June 6, 1994), *adhered to*, 1994 U.S. Dist. LEXIS 16746 (S.D.N.Y. Nov. 21, 1994).

The court held that Pfizer's disclosure of documents to its independent auditor, KPMG Peat Marwick ("Peat Marwick"), did not waive its work-product privilege. The court's decision was based on her observation that "Pfizer and Peat Marwick obviously shared common interests in the information, and Peat Marwick is not reasonably viewed as a conduit to a potential adversary."

Other courts have adopted precisely this analysis, but the analysis, it seems should instead be whether disclosure to an independent auditor is of the type that the independent auditor would in turn have to disclose publicly in its audit report.

- *Gutter v. E.I. DuPont de Nemours & Co.*, 1998 U.S. Dist. LEXIS 23207, 1998 WL 2017926, at *5 (S.D. Fla. May 15, 1998). The court held that disclosure to outside accountants did not waive the work-product privilege "since the accountants are not considered a conduit to a potential adversary."

- *Gramm v. Horsehead Indus., Inc.*, 1990 U.S. Dist. LEXIS 773, 1990 WL 142404, at *5 (S.D.N.Y. 1990) (same).

Still others have applied this approach, but scrutinized the precise role of the accountants.

- *Samuels v. Mitchell*, 155 F.R.D. 195, 201 (N.D. Cal. 1994). Deciding that disclosure did not constitute a waiver of the work-product privilege because the accounting firm was acting as a consultant, not a "public accountant," at the relevant time.

- *Medinol, Ltd. v. Boston Scientific Corp.*, 214 F.R.D. 113, 116 (S.D.N.Y. 2002). Finding a waiver of the work-product privilege, the court emphasized the "public watchdog" role of independent auditors., thus by implication concluding that whatever was disclosed to public accountants might find its way into a public financial report. Judge Hellerstein observed that it "has become crystal clear in the face of the many accounting scandals that have arisen as of late, in order for auditors to properly do their job, they must not share common interests with the company they audit." (Emphasis in original.) While this is a valid policy consideration, the fact is that the determination in Medinol was based on a finding that the auditor's interests were not aligned with that of the corporation and that the disclosure of the documents at issue—the Special Litigation Committee's minutes—did not serve a pertinent litigation interest.

- *United States v. MIT*, 129 F.3d 681, 686 (1st Cir. 1997). The court noted that the Massachusetts Institute of Technology ("MIT") had a common interest with the Department of Defense's ("DOD") audit agency in "the proper performance of MIT's defense contracts and the proper auditing and payment of MIT's bills." However, the First Circuit found that the audit agency—which was responsible for preventing an overcharge for services—was a potential adversary because a review of MIT's billing statements could result in a dispute or even litigation. Thus, MIT was found to have forfeited its work product protection, but only after an analysis of the parties' relationship.

- *In re Raytheon Sec. Litig.*, 218 F.R.D. 354, 360 (D. Mass. 2003). The court recognized that "the pivotal question is whether disclosure of documents protected by the work product doctrine to an independent auditor substantially increases the opportunities for potential adversaries to obtain the information." After a discussion of the public responsibilities of independent auditors, the court noted that "there is no evidence that materials disclosed to an independent auditor are likely to be turned over to the company's adversaries except to the extent that the securities laws and/or accounting standards mandate public disclosure." The court, however, declined to rule as to whether there was or was not a waiver pending an *in camera* review of the documents.

a. *Protection Waived*

- *Medinol, Ltd. v. Boston Scientific Corp.*, 214 F.R.D. 113, 116 (S.D.N.Y. 2002). "Here, Ernst & Young reviewed the minutes of the meetings of Boston Scientific's Special Litigation Committee in connection with its role as outside auditor. As the outside auditor, Ernst & Young's interests were not necessarily united with those of Boston Scientific; they were independent of them. Moreover, the sharing by Boston Scientific's lawyers of selected aspects of their work product, although perhaps not substantially increasing the risk that such work product would reach potential adversaries, see *Verschoth*, 2001 U.S. Dist. LEXIS 6693, at *14, 2001 WL 546630, at *3, did not serve any litigation interest, either its own or that of Ernst & Young, or any other policy underlying the work product doctrine."

b. *Protection Not Waived*

■ *Betz Assocs., Inc. v. Jim Walter Homes, Inc.*, 226 F.R.D. 533 (D.S.C. 2005). Although amount of reserves set aside for potential liability in the litigation *sub judice* had been disclosed to outside auditors, since it consisted of the opinions and assessment of the litigation by counsel, was work-product protected and was not waived by virtue of that disclosure.

■ *In re Pfizer Inc. Sec. Litig.*, 1993 U.S. Dist. LEXIS 18215, 1993 WL 561125 (S.D.N.Y. Dec. 23, 1993), *but not modified and on an another issue*, 1994 U.S. Dist. LEXIS 7454 (S.D.N.Y. June 6, 1994), *adhered to*, 1994 U.S. Dist. LEXIS 16746 (S.D.N.Y. Nov. 21, 1994). Pfizer's disclosure of work product to its outside auditors did not waive privilege.

c. *More Proof Required*

■ *In re Raytheon Sec. Litig.*, 218 F.R.D. 354 (D. Mass. 2003). The court concluded that it was not able to determine whether disclosure of work product to outside auditors made it more likely that an adversary would obtain possession thereof. It therefore ordered additional evidence to be presented by the proponent of the work-product protection as to what public auditors were required to disclose.

6. Inadvertent Disclosure of Work-Product-Protected Documents

When attorney-client protected documents are disclosed, they often can be used as probative evidence on some issue in dispute. It is rare that work-product documents can be used as evidence or that they could be probative as to any issue in dispute even in a defense to a wilful infringement patent claim. Thus inadvertent disclosure of work-product-protected materials has less of a potential direct impact upon the course of the litigation.

Moreover, however important work-product protection of an attorney's preparation for the litigation at hand may be, it is rare that the one side cannot figure out with just a bit of thought what the strategy of its adversary is. Also, a great deal of the theory of a case may be ferreted out with contention interrogatories.

And unlike attorney-client protected materials which can be recaptured for evidentiary purposes, once work-product-protected materials are disclosed, the cat is definitely out of the bag. There is no way of erasing what has been learned from the mind of the opposing side.

For all these reasons, it seems that the issue of the inadvertent production of work-product materials arises with far lesser frequency than does that of work-product materials. There is also another, perhaps most telling reason why that should be the case. It is the client's business documents which are usually reviewed for production to the opposing side. It is in the client's files that attorney-client protected materials are most frequently lodged. Work-product materials are most frequently lodged primarily in the attorney's files, although copies may be forwarded to the client. The attorney's files generally are not sought in discovery and thus are rarely either reviewed for production and even more rarely inadvertently produced.

When inadvertent production of work-product documents is made, the courts seem to apply the *Hydraflow* factors which have such currency in the context of the inadvertent production of attorney-client privileged documents.

- *Fleet Nat'l Bank v. Tonneson & Co.*, 150 F.R.D. 10, 11 (D. Mass. 1993). Volume III of a three-volume work-product document was inadvertently produced out of a screening of some 50,000 documents. "At some point that is not clear from the record, plaintiffs' lead trial counsel retained an organization named Kroll Associates ("Kroll"), an accounting firm, to assist him in analyzing and evaluating the Tonneson audits that are the subject of the complaint. Kroll poured over TGC's financial records and the Tonneson audits and prepared its three-volume report for use by plaintiffs' counsel in this case. There is no dispute that, but for Tonneson's various arguments considered below, the Kroll Report would be protected work product."

The court alluded to, but did not extensively analyze the five *Hydraflow* factors, used by most courts in determining whether inadvertent production of attorney-client privilege documents will be excused. Concluding instead that since the work-product protection protects the integrity of the adversarial process from poaching by the other side and that there could be no testimonial use to which the document could be put in all events. The court also said that no waiver occurred in respect to Volume III although it was inadvertently made available to the other side for review although not actually forwarded to opposing counsel since the fact that it was inadvertently allowed to remain in the production was discovered before the actual photocopying and forwarding to opposing counsel. The conclusion of no waiver when it has been made available to the opposing is a curious one.

7. Attempted Recapture of Work-Product Protection

When inadvertent or even intentional disclosure of work-product protected materials occurs, if one wants to recapture the protection, one cannot sit still and do nothing. Formal attempts must be made to have the work-product protected documents returned. Failing that, a protective order should be sought.

- *DVI Fin. Servs. Inc. v. Florida Heart, LLC*, 2003 U.S. Dist. LEXIS 12205 (E.D. Pa. June 23, 2003). The court found that where all the privileged documents were voluntarily disclosed to a non-adversary third party, where the return of the documents was never sought, where no action was then taken to preclude third-party production of the documents, and where deposition question was allowed regarding the documents, and where no judicial enforcement of the privilege was sought by way of protective order until the privilege cat was well out of the non-disclosure bag, any preexisting privilege was thereby fatally compromised. The court ordered that any documents already produced to the non-adversary third party had to be produced and that a proper motion be brought in respect to any privileged documents that had not been forwarded to that party.

- *In re Grand Jury (Impounded)*, 138 F.3d 978, 981 (3d Cir. 1998). "In the case of inadvertent or involuntary disclosures, the party asserting the work-product doctrine must pursue all reasonable means to restore the confidentiality of the materials and to prevent further disclosures within a reasonable period to continue to receive the protection of the privilege." The party seeking work-product protection sought the return of documents, and when the receiving party refused, turned to the court for protection.

With voluntary disclosure to various agencies of the government, there is the danger that the government may disclose such work product inadvertently in litigation with third parties. Attempts to recapture the work product by the holder thereof, even with the use of theories such as "common interest" to obviate waiver problems attendant upon disclosure to the government, have not been notably successful.

- *United States v. Bergonzi*, 216 F.R.D. 487, 498 (N.D. Cal. 2003). When the government inadvertently produced self-audit documents in litigation with other defendants, the disclosing company, allowed to intervene in the proceedings, was not able to assert work-product protection. "Once a party has disclosed work product to one adversary, it waives work-product protection as to all other adversaries." The company's attempt to characterize its relationship with the government as one of common interest instead of adversarial was notably unsuccessful.

C. Selective Waiver

1. To Governmental Agency

Proposed Rule 502(b)(3) of the Federal Rules of Evidence would allow for selective waiver to an agency of the federal government without thereby entailing waiver as to all third parties as is currently the case law. It also would not make such non-waiver contingent upon a non-contingent confidentiality agreement, as is the current suggestion of some case law. Proposed Rule 502 (b)(3) reads:

> (3) the disclosure is made to a federal, state, or local governmental agency during an investigation by that agency, and is limited to persons involved in the investigation.

Since Proposed Rule 502 has not yet been enacted, litigants have no choice but to be aware of the current case law, which, as we have seen in the attorney-client privilege context, is highly intolerant of selective waivers.

A particular subset of disclosure exists when a party submits work-product materials to a governmental or regulatory agency, hoping by such cooperation to forestall adverse action and expecting thereby that the materials disclosed will nonetheless remain work-product protected. As a general rule they will not. The governmental and/or regulatory agency is generally seen as an adverse party. Disclosure to an adverse party usually entrains generalized waiver. Moreover, courts tend to speak of the attempt to selectively waive work-product materials as manipulative in nature and, thus, do not allow it. Thus the law in respect to selective waiver of either the privilege or work product protection is treated essentially the same. Waiver as to one party will be deemed waiver as to all.

The first court to consider the matter both in the privilege and the work-product context, without reaching the issue of selective waiver of work product, but without a great deal of analysis, suggested it would be inclined to countenance such selective waiver as likely to induce cooperation with governmental agencies.

- *Diversified Indus., Inc. v. Meredith*, 572 F.2d 596, 604 n.1 (8th Cir. 1977) (*en banc*). The waiver issue was not reached because the court found that the contested documents were not prepared in anticipation of litigation; nonetheless in a footnote, the court indicated a prospective reluctance to find waiver where there had been voluntary compliance with a government subpoena. "We would be reluctant to hold that voluntary surrender of privileged material to a government agency in obedience to an agency subpoena constitutes a waiver of the privilege for all purposes, including its use in subsequent private litigation in which the material is sought to be used against the party which yielded it to the agency."

Subsequent courts considering the same issue have been utterly unpersuaded that the judicial recognition of selective waiver was necessary to induce cooperation with governmental investigatory agencies. These courts have all but invariably disallowed selective waiver when work-product materials were disclosed to governmental agencies.

- *United States v. MIT*, 129 F.3d 681, 684 (1st Cir. 1997). The court concluded that disclosure by the university to the Defense Contract Audit Agency constituted disclosure to a potential adversary that waived any work-product protection. The fact that MIT hoped that the potential controversy would not become an actual one if it submitted the requested materials did not change the nature of the relationship between the parties from a potentially adversarial one to something else. The court did not reach the issue of whether protection continued for mental impressions, nor did it address the issue of the scope of the waiver that was not pursued on appeal.

- *In re Steinhardt Partners, L.P.*, 9 F.3d 230, 236 (2d Cir. 1993). Civil suits alleging manipulation of the markets for Treasury securities were brought. Discovery sought all documents tendered to the SEC when it conducted an investigation. Counsel had prepared and submitted a memorandum to the SEC with respect to which work-product protection was claimed in the civil suits. The court found that production to the SEC constituted a waiver of whatever work-product protection might otherwise have existed. The court refused to adopt a per se rule that disclosure to one potential adversary entrained thereafter compelled disclosure for all other adversaries, but was also utterly unpersuaded by the argument that a party could selectively disclose such materials when it suited and refuse to do so when that in turn was to its advantage. "An allegation that a party facing a federal investigation and the prospect of a civil fraud suit must make difficult choices is insufficient justification for carving a substantial exception to the waiver doctrine."

- *Westinghouse Elec. Corp. v. Republic of Philippines*, 951 F.2d 1414, 1429–30 (3d Cir. 1991). The Republic of the Philippines sued Westinghouse on the ground that it bribed the former head of state, Marcos. Discovery sought attorney-client privileged and work-product documents, *inter alia* an investigative report done by outside counsel and tendered to the Securities and Exchange Commission and the Department of Justice pursuant to a grand jury subpoena. The mandamus petition that sought to reverse the district court's order finding of waiver and requiring production was denied. "We hold that Westinghouse's disclosure of work product to the SEC and the DOJ waived the work-product doctrine against all other adversaries. . . . Moreover, an exception for disclosure to governmental agencies is not necessary to further the doctrine's purpose. . . . Creating an exception for disclosures to government agencies may actually hinder the operation of the work-product doctrine. If internal investigations are undertaken with an eye later to disclosing the results to a government agency, the outside counsel conducting the investigation may hesitate to pursue unfavorable information or legal theories about the corporation. Thus, allowing a party to preserve the doctrine's protection while disclosing work product to a government agency could actually discourage attorneys from fully preparing their cases."

Apparently the Third Circuit deemed a response to a grand jury subpoena to be a "voluntary disclosure" while obedience to a court order would have been involuntary.

- *In re Subpoenas Duces Tecum*, 738 F.2d 1367, 1371–75 (D.C. Cir. 1984). Where respondent previously had disclosed the documents to the SEC in its "voluntary disclosure program," respondent waived the work-product privilege for a subsequent private civil action. The court's finding of waiver was based on three factors: (1) respondent had not invoked the privilege in a manner consistent with furthering the adversarial process (because the SEC also was respondent's adversary, and respondent could not choose to whom it would disclose documents); (2) respondent had no reasonable basis for believing the SEC would keep the documents confidential; and (3) a finding of waiver would not undercut any policy elements underlying the privilege (effective preparation would not be discouraged by denying protection to documents selectively disclosed).

- *Hobley v. Burge*, 2004 U.S. Dist. LEXIS 6858, 2004 WL 856439, at *7 (N.D. Ill. Apr. 21, 2004). The work-product protection was waived because City had previously disclosed documents to Special Prosecutor.

- *United States v. Bergonzi*, 216 F.R.D. 487, 494, 496–98 (N.D. Cal. 2003). The company waived its attorney-client and work-product privileges when it disclosed documents to government where the confidentiality agreements were not unconditional. Appeal dismissed as moot, 403 F.3d 1048, 1050 (9th Cir. 2005), without reaching the waiver issue. *In re Bank One Sec. Litig.*, 209 F.R.D. 418, 423–25 (N.D. Ill. 2002). Bank One's voluntary production to governmental investigative body, Office of the Comptroller of the Currency, waived its work product privilege because the relationship was adversarial notwithstanding existing confidentiality agreement.

- *In re Columbia/HCA Healthcare Corp.*, 192 F.R.D. 575 (M.D. Tenn.), *appeal dismissed*, 229 F.3d 1151 (6th Cir. 2000). "The Court finds that Columbia/HCA's disclosure of work product to the government was disclosure of work product to an adversary. Such disclosure contradicted the purpose of the protection of the work-product doctrine. Accordingly, the Court finds that Columbia/HCA thereby waived any protection these documents had under the work-product doctrine."

- *Cooper Hosp./Univ. Med. Ctr. v. Sullivan*, 1998 U.S. Dist. LEXIS 22198 (D.N.J. May 7, 1998), *aff'd*, 183 F.R.D. 119 (D.N.J. 1998). At the request of the United States Attorney, the hospital provided a report that was self-critical, preserving whatever work-product-doctrine privileges might apply in a cover letter. The court enforced a request of the New Jersey Department of Health and Senior Services and the New Jersey Department of Human Services for a copy of the report on the ground that whatever protection might otherwise have been accorded was waived when the report was released to one agency of government.

But see:

- *In re Natural Gas Commodity Litig.*, 2005 U.S. Dist. LEXIS 11950 (S.D.N.Y. June 21, 2005). The court did not require the disclosure of opinion work product which had previously been disclosed to federal agencies subject to strict confidentiality agreements where it did supply the underlying documents from which the opinion work product had been derived, thus allowing its adversary access to underlying facts. The Magistrate Judge claimed to have been following the precedent of *In re Steinhardt Partners, L.P.*, 9 F.3d 230, 236 (2d Cir. 1993). *Steinhardt* said in dicta that it would not apply a *per se* no selective waiver rule. Note, however, that in *Steinhardt* the Second Circuit had held on those facts that selective waiver was not permissible.

- *In re Grand Jury Proceedings John Doe Co. v. United States*, 350 F.3d 299 (2d Cir. 2003). The Second Circuit reversed the district court's holding that supplying an attorney letter to the United States

District Attorney to persuade him not to indict necessarily entailed a waiver of all other word-product-protected notes taken by the attorney of discussions with government personnel cited in the letter. The court in so ruling also commented on the inappropriateness of the broad use given to the terms "waiver" and "implied waiver." In fact, the attorney had expressly reserved any applicable privileges in proffering the letter. Forfeiture, said the court, is a more appropriate term. And the hallmark of whether forfeiture should be deemed appropriate is fairness. Moreover, here, the names of federal agents who had purportedly assured the target of the grand jury that his conduct was lawful were provided to the prosecution by defense counsel. As federal agents, they were readily available for interview by the prosecution to determine whether they had in fact made representations of lawfulness. Without so stating, the appellate court was surely concerned lest any attorney attempt to dissuade prosecution be deemed to encompass a forfeiture of all privileges.

While courts have not given subsequent protection to fact product materials disclosed voluntarily to a government agency, they have nonetheless been inclined to continue protection for opinion work product also disclosed on the ground that opinion work product is afforded greater protection, and that it is less likely to come in as evidence and be utilizable manipulatively as both a sword and a shield. The crucial factor behind the protection accorded to the opinion work product in the two cases cited above is that the underlying facts were provided. That having been provided, the adversary was free to do its own work and reach its own conclusions. In effect no further need existed to not allow selective waiver. Indeed to have held that selective waiver was not available would have been punitive.

Thus any litigant who wishes to continue to preserve opinion work product after selective disclosure to a government agency would be well advised to follow suit. And courts would be well advised to require disclosure of the underlying facts but not of the attorney's opinion. Such a procedure conforms to fundamental fairness, while maintaining intact the protections accorded both to privileged communications and opinion work product protections.

- *In re Martin Marietta Corp.*, 856 F.2d 619, 623–24 (4th Cir. 1988), *cert. denied*, 490 U.S. 1011 (1989). The company tendered opinion and non-opinion work product to the government in a criminal investigation in an attempt to forestall indictment. The non-opinion work-product materials were discoverable by the indicted employee. The opinion work-product materials, however, were not discoverable.

When a party can effectively argue that the disclosure to the government agency was not in an adversary context, some hope exists for protecting the work-product privilege from a finding of generalized waiver by virtue of the attempted selective waiver.

- *Westinghouse Elec. Corp. v. Republic of Philippines*, 951 F.2d 1414, 1431 (3d Cir. 1991). "Thus, had the DOJ and the SEC not been Westinghouse's adversaries, and had we concluded that Westinghouse reasonably expected the agencies to keep the material it disclosed to them confidential, we might reach a different result."

- *United States v. AT&T*, 642 F.2d 1285 (D.C. Cir. 1980). When a party submitted work-product protected materials to assist the government in investigating or prosecuting another, the waiver of the work product did not occur in the context of disclosure to an adversary party, and the selective disclosure was found not to entrain a generalized waiver.

- *In re LTV Sec. Litig.*, 89 F.R.D. 595, 614–15 (N.D. Tex. 1981). Materials generated by a "special officer" appointed by the corporation to implement a consent decree with the SEC were privileged. Disclosure to the SEC did not vitiate the privilege because the corporation and the SEC shared an interest in ensuring an implementation of the consent decree, and thus no waiver occurred when the privileged material was sought by the plaintiff shareholders.

Voluntary disclosure to a government agency while still hoping to protect work product from disclosure to other third parties is fraught with difficulty. One has every reason to cooperate with the government, mainly because one has little choice and such cooperation is the surest way of avoiding worse trouble. But if such cooperation entails waiver of privilege and work-product protection in respect to other parties, the cost of such cooperation is thereby increased. Yet such is often the consequence. Imaginative attempts to circumvent the consequences of selective waiver entailing total waiver by virtue of a claim that a "common interest" existed between the disclosing party and the government in order to make the context in which the disclosure took place a privileged one and thereby to obviate the consequences of the cooperative disclosure have not been notably successful.

- *McMorgan & Co. v. First Cal. Mortg. Co.*, 931 F. Supp. 703, 709 (N.D. Cal. 1996). Disclosure to the Department of Labor in an ERISA matter constituted a waiver. The court found that there was no common interest between McMorgan and the Department of Labor (DOL) despite the fact that they both shared the common interest of protecting the participants and beneficiaries of pension funds. The evidence suggested that McMorgan was the target of DOL investigation; thus it was adversarial to the DOL.

- *United States v. MIT*, 129 F.3d 681 (1st Cir. 1997). MIT's voluntary disclosure of documents to one governmental agency made them subject to compelled disclosure to another. The common-interest gambit failed here when the court found that although both MIT and the government audit agency had a "common interest" in the performance of MIT's defense contracts and the proper auditing and payment of bills, that is not the kind of common interest to which the cases refer in recognizing that allied lawyers and clients who are working together in prosecuting or defending a lawsuit or in certain other legal transactions can exchange information among themselves without the loss of privilege.

2. Disclosure for Settlement Purposes

Often in the course of settlement discussions, the parties discuss what they perceive to be the strengths of their case and the weaknesses of their opponent's case. In the process, to convince one another and to substantiate positions taken, work product may be disclosed. Litigators should be aware that doing so may risk that disclosure will be deemed a waiver and that the work product may become discoverable in other contexts.

- *In re Chrysler Motors Corp. Overnight Evaluation Program Litig.*, 860 F.2d 844, 846–47 (8th Cir. 1988). Work-product protected materials were disclosed to an adversary in the course of settlement discussions and pursuant to a confidentiality agreement. The U.S. Attorney subsequently sought access to the material for a possible criminal prosecution. With little explanation, the Eighth Circuit held that whatever protection attached to the work product had been waived.

- *Grumman Aerospace Corp. v. Titanium Metals Corp.*, 91 F.R.D. 84, 90 (E.D.N.Y 1981). A cost analysis of settlement prepared by a neutral fact finder, even if predicated on privileged materials and a confidentiality agreement, is not immune from subsequent disclosure in litigation with a competitor. Thus, the court concluded that documents prepared for use in settlement alone are not work-product protected "because they were not prepared in an adversary context."

Absent an agreement that disclosure for settlement purposes will not constitute subject matter waiver should settlement fail, such waiver will indeed be held to have occurred. Thus counsel wishing to make use of work-product materials to facilitate settlement is foolish to do so without such an agreement.

- *Eagle Compressors, Inc. v. Hec Liquidating Corp.*, 206 F.R.D. 474, 480 (N.D. Ill. 2002). Client revealed attorney's assessment of the strengths and weaknesses of the case in the course of settlement discussions. Although it was pretty much conceded that any attorney-client privilege had thereby been waived by the client, attempt was made, unsuccessfully, to recapture the lost privilege by asserting work-product protection, arguing in effect that the client could not waive the attorney's work product. "Although the settlement negotiations failed, Defendant intended to impart its attorney's mental impressions and conclusions for the purpose of advancing its settlement posture. It is now too late to put the genie back into the bottle."

- *Khandji v. Keystone Resorts Mgmt., Inc.*, 140 F.R.D. 697, 670 (D. Colo. 1992). A brochure and letter were provided in settlement discussions without first obtaining an agreement that they would not be disclosed to the client and insurance carrier. In effect, the court said a unilateral attempt to limit waiver is ineffective. Such agreement in effect needs to be obtained before privileged documents are turned over even for a laudatory purpose such as settlement. "Such a waiver occurs even when disclosure is made during the course of settlement negotiations. The mere fact that opposing parties may have a common interest in settling claims does not neutralize the fact of disclosure, because that common interest always exists between opposing parties in any attempt at settlement. . . . In addition, a waiver of the privilege occurs despite any agreement between the parties to keep the information confidential. Such an agreement does not alter the fact that the work-product doctrine has been breached voluntarily. . . . *Such an agreement may, however, constitute an enforceable contract between the parties. . . .*" (Italics added.)

3. Partial or Manipulative Disclosure

As a general rule, just as a party will not be permitted to pick and choose which aspects of privileged communications will be disclosed, so too, once partial disclosure of work-product materials is voluntarily made, total disclosure will have to be made, unless there is no prejudice to the adversary arising from the partial disclosure. But the truth cannot be distorted by selecting those facts or those mental impressions that will be disclosed and concealing other damaging facts or mental impressions. Since, however, work product is generally less admissible as evidence, the dangers of partial disclosure as less likely in the case of work-product partial disclosures than they are in the case of partial attorney-client privilege disclosures.

- *Robertson v. Allstate Ins. Co.*, 1999 U.S. Dist. LEXIS 2991 (E.D. Pa. Mar. 10, 1999). When an insurance company relied on an "advice of counsel" defense to defend against a bad faith refusal to settle a claim, all communications on that issue were waived. However, the remainder of the file that contained work-product materials did not have to be disclosed in its entirety.

- *Stratagem Dev. Corp. v. Heron Int'l N.V.*, 153 F.R.D. 535, 542–44 (S.D.N.Y. 1994).

- *United States ex rel. Mayman v. Martin Marietta Corp.*, 886 F. Supp. 1243, 1252 (D. Md. 1995). Disclosure of a privileged communication waived the privilege as to all information related to the same subject matter.

- *In re Sealed Case*, 676 F.2d 793, 804, n.33, 807, 818 (D.C. Cir. 1982). A grand jury investigating the bribery of a multinational corporation was entitled to two out of eight documents produced by in-house counsel. As a result of a voluntary self-disclosure to the SEC of an in-house investigation that uncovered corporate bribery, a prosecutorial referral was made. The court of appeals quoted the finding of the district court that the version set forth in the in-house investigation was an "enchanted tale" and that "[t]his kind of selective waiver is precisely the kind of manipulation and sleight-of-hand that led to the waiver doctrine in the first place." The court went on to formulate and affirm a finding of implied waiver, describing it as an "abuse of the privilege," rather than an abuse of the privileged relationship, concluding: "Where society has subordinated its interest in the search for truth in favor of allowing certain information to remain confidential, it need not allow that confidentiality to be used as a tool for manipulation of the truth[-]seeking process." When documents impeach the veracity of the company's purportedly voluntary disclosure to the SEC, they will be ordered produced on a theory of implied waiver. At that point, "acceptable tactics degenerate into 'sharp practices' inimical to a healthy adversary system."

- *In re John Doe Corp.*, 675 F.2d 482, 491–92 (2d Cir. 1982). Background memoranda for an internal investigation report regarding corporate bribes were ordered produced because there were indications that the investigators had suppressed information regarding the bribes.

- *W. R. Grace & Co. v. Pullman, Inc.*, 446 F. Supp. 771, 775 (W.D. Okla. 1976). A general reservation of work product is negated by the production of that work product.

D. *Effect of "Advice of Counsel Defense" on Attorney's Work Product*[6]

In most contexts, it is deemed that the work product is the attorney's and the attorney is entitled to invoke it independently of the client's

---

6. A more extensive review of the cases has been set forth under the same section in attorney-client privilege since raising such a defense, particularly in a claim of wilful patent infringement, often entrains a waiver of the opinion attorney's work product.

actions. That is not always the case. Where an advice of counsel defense is raised, work product documents in the attorney's hands may become discoverable.

- *RCA Corp. v. Data General Corp.*, 1986 U.S. Dist. LEXIS 23244, 1986 WL 1593 (D. Del. July 2, 1986). Documents withheld on work-product grounds by an accounting firm ordered produced where client relied on an advice of counsel defense.

However, when it is not the client that seeks to inject the advice of counsel defense but the opposing side that tries to make it an issue, courts are increasingly exceedingly reluctant to permit that stretch.

- *In re Gibco, Inc.*, 185 F.R.D. 296 (D. Colo. 1997). The court held that the trustee had not sustained his burden of proof to show how work-product-protected interview notes would be relevant to prove his claim of aiding and abetting a fraudulent transfer when the party whose counsel had prepared the work-product documents had not asserted a "reliance on counsel" defense.

- *Rhone-Poulenc Rorer, Inc. v. Home Indem. Co.*, 32 F.3d 851, 864 (3d Cir. 1994). The case involved a declaratory judgment suit of drug companies against their HIV insurers. The lower court held that because the drug companies had waived their privilege by filing suit— a contention reversed by the court of appeals—they had also necessarily waived the work-product protection. The court of appeals held that: "For a number of reasons, one does not lead to the other. As a factual matter, if the state of mind of the insured is in issue, papers reflecting the work product of counsel that were not shared with or communicated to clients cannot affect the clients' state of mind."

E. Affirmative Use

1. Reliance on Protected Material

When a party relies on work product as a basis for a claim or defense, the protection is waived. This frequently happens when a party asserts that a challenged action was taken on the advice of counsel. In such a case, even opinion work product is subject to discovery.

- *Granite Partners v. Bear, Stearns & Co., Inc.*, 184 F.R.D. 49, 53 (S.D.N.Y. 1999). Where an extensive report was prepared by a bankruptcy trustee based on interviews and other assessments of the nature of claims, such work product was discoverable by defendants on mixed grounds of waiver by virtue of use to prosecute the claims and by virtue of substantial need. "The objective of this investigation is to provide the Bankruptcy Court and the parties with a report describing in detail and explaining the events that precipitated the Funds' filing for bankruptcy. The report will, *inter alia*, facilitate determinations regarding assets and liabilities of the estates, by (i) assessing the validity of various creditor claims and (ii) assessing whether the estates have claims against former management, creditors or other persons." The court determined that the defendants would not be able to defend effectively against the claims asserted and the damages claimed without access to how each had been determined. Moreover, some of the interviews had been conducted four years previously and memories were no longer likely to be as reliable. The court concluded that since the trustee's Final Report relied on selective quotes from interviews, the totality of the interviews and the report should be produced. Thus in effect there were multiple reasons for ordering production, with a sense of underlying fairness being the paramount one.

- *Applied Telematics, Inc. v. Sprint Corp.*, 1995 U.S. Dist. LEXIS 14061, 1995 WL 567436, at *2–3 (E.D. Pa. Sept. 21, 1995). The court addressed whether the reliance on an opinion of counsel to defend against a charge of infringement waived the attorney-client privilege as to all opinions and studies concerning the patent at issue. The court held that the waiver only extended to issues relied on by the defendants in defending against a charge of infringement. In limiting the scope of the waiver, the court noted that the defendants did not challenge the validity, enforceability, scope, or interpretation of the patent. The court limited the waiver to legal opinions regarding infringement.

- *United States v. Western Elec. Co.*, 132 F.R.D. 1, 3 (D.D.C. 1990). Where a party has released a number of work-product documents providing the same version of events testified to by its counsel, it cannot preclude discovery of documents on the same subject matter that might dispute that version of events and undermine its "reliance on advice of council" defense.

- *Panter v. Marshall Field & Co.*, 80 F.R.D. 718, 725–26 (N.D. Ill. 1978). The defendants' reliance on the advice of counsel as a justification for their challenged actions constitutes a waiver, or creates a "compelling need" for disclosure, and overcomes the protection.

- *Handgards, Inc. v. Johnson & Johnson*, 413 F. Supp. 926, 931–33 (N.D. Cal. 1976), *remanded on other grounds sub nom. Handgards, Inc. v. Ethicon Inc.*, 601 F.2d 986 (9th Cir. 1979), *cert. denied*, 444 U.S. 1025 (1980). Although attorneys' work product revealing their mental impressions might well be otherwise protected, once a client decides to call the attorneys as witnesses, the work-product protection must give way to full disclosure on any issue to which they will testify. Anything less would permit manipulation of the truth. Thus, when the defendants' case rested on a showing of their good faith in pursuing prior patent litigation, and they gave notice that they would call lawyers who supervised that prior litigation to testify to its merits, the court ordered production of opinion work product.

It obviously also is the case if a party defends on the basis that it conducted an investigation of the plaintiff's claim and found it unfounded. It hardly needs a rocket scientist to figure out that you can't both rely on such an investigation as a defense against a cause of action but hope to retain work product protection as to the investigation relied upon.

Of course if the party abandons its investigative defense, it will generally be permitted the work-product protection, if the report otherwise meets the criteria of work-product-protected materials. But you obviously can't have both the defense of an investigation and the refusal to disclose that investigation based on privilege or protection claims. It never ceases to amaze that parties try to have both.

- *Walker v. County of Contra Costa*, 227 F.R.D. 529, 536 (N.D. Cal. 2005). Defendants' pre-litigation investigation is relevant to their affirmative defense, but the attorney's intra-litigation analysis of that investigation is not. "Whether the report is or is not subject to attorney-client privilege or work-product protection is immaterial in this case because any protection that may have applied is waived by Defendants' stated intent to rely on the investigation as a defense in this action. As mentioned above, Defendants assert as their twelfth affirmative defense that "plaintiff's claims are barred because CCCFPD took and had taken reasonable steps to prevent and promptly correct any discrimination and/or harassment in the workplace, and plaintiff unreasonably failed to take advantage of the preventative and corrective opportunities provided by the CCCFPD or avoid harm otherwise."

- *Kaiser Foundation Hosps. v. Superior Court*, 78 Cal.Rptr. 2d 543 (Cal. Ct. App. 1998). The employer's investigation was performed by a non-attorney human resources specialist. The employer had turned over the human resources report but withheld some attorney-client communications. The employer produced over 90% of its investigation-related documents, but only after obtaining a written stipulation that this production did not constitute a waiver of the attorney-client privilege. The trial judge granted plaintiffs' motion to compel production of the attorney-client communications. The appellate court held this was error, on grounds that the employer had turned over its files and disclosed the substance of its internal investigation as conducted by non-lawyer employees.

- *Volpe v. US Airways, Inc.*, 184 F.R.D. 672 (M.D. Fla. 1998). An employer that relies on the thoroughness of an internal investigation as a defense against a sexual harassment charge must disclose to plaintiff notes taken during such investigation.

- *Johnson v. Rauland-Borg Corp.*, 961 F. Supp. 208 (N.D. Ill. 1997). Where an employer's attorney who investigated a complaint of sexual harassment would testify at trial the employer waived any privilege for attorney's pre-litigation legal advice by raising its internal investigation as defense to harassment claim.

- *Pray v. New York City Ballet Co.*, 1997 U.S. Dist. LEXIS 6995, 1997 WL 266980 (S.D.N.Y. May 19, 1997). Where an employer's litigation defense counsel also served as the attorney conducting an internal investigation of discrimination complaints, the attorney became subject to a deposition; by asserting thoroughness of investigation as defense in sexual harassment litigation. The employer also waived any attendant work product or privilege claims thereby.

- *Wellpoint Health Networks, Inc. v. Superior Court*, 68 Cal. Rptr. 2d 844 (Cal. Ct. App. 1997). Investigation documents which normally would be covered by attorney-client privilege or work-product protected became discoverable by virtue of defendant having raised adequacy of investigation as a defense to discrimination claim.

- *Payton v. New Jersey Turnpike Auth.*, 691 A.2d 321, 335 (N.J. 1997). The court found no work-product protection when an investigation was begun months before plaintiff filed a sexual harassment suit. Moreover any attorney-client privilege was waived once the employer placed the investigation at issue by asserting it as an affirmative defense.

2. "At Issue"

Where one party seeks to assert a right to either insurance or contractual indemnity, work-product material that might cast any light on the right thereto is deemed to have been put "at issue" by the party seeking recovery and is deemed waived.

- *Abbott Labs. v. Alpha Therapeutic Corp.*, 200 F.R.D. 401, 411 (N.D. Ill. 2001). "Alpha cannot assert a claim for indemnification of costs of defending a lawsuit without providing its indemnitor with documentation that proves the legitimacy of those indemnification claims."

If a criminal defendant alleges that the prosecution withheld exculpatory information, he places at issue whether he and his attorney had effective access to the exculpatory information from another source, thereby giving rise to discovery of the fact work product, albeit not necessarily the opinion work product of his defense counsel.

- *Tennison v. City & County of San Francisco*, 226 F.R.D. 615 (N.D. Cal. 2005). Where defendant becomes plaintiff in a civil rights action for wrongful conviction on the grounds that the prosecution withheld exculpatory evidence, the fact work product of his defense attorney in the criminal prosecution becomes discoverable since any knowledge that he or his criminal defense attorney had from other sources would constitute a defense to the wrongful conviction for withheld evidence.

But in a claim that the insurance company acted in bad faith by refusing to settle a claim, the work product of the insurance company's attorney cannot thereby be swept away. It is the insured not the insurance company that has put the matter into issue.

- *McCrink v. Peoples Benefit Life Ins. Co.*, 2004 U.S. Dist. LEXIS 23990, at *12 (E.D. Pa. Nov. 29, 2004). "Plaintiffs' mere claim of bad faith is not enough to shatter this work-product privilege. . . . Like the standard for waiving the attorney-client privilege, this requires an affirmative step by the client, as opposed to an opposing litigant's bald assertion that such advice is relevant." (Citations omitted.)

If a defendant to a patent infringement case elects to forego a defense of advice of counsel, then that advice is not placed "at issue" and no waiver results.

- *SmithKline Beecham Corp. v. Apotex Corp.*, 2005 U.S. Dist. LEXIS 22228 (E.D. Pa. Sept. 28, 2005). One of the defendants brought a motion requiring one of the plaintiffs to declare whether it proposed relying upon an "advice of counsel" defense. The judge ordered SmithKline Beecham to respond. When SB stated it had no such intention, the court warned that any such evidence would therefore be foreclosed at trial.

3. Attorney as Expert Witness

Even if one does not propose to rely on work-product material directly, if one designates an attorney as an expert, the attorney's work product on the issue that the attorney is expected to testify will become discoverable even if it is opinion work product.

- *Dion v. Nationwide Mut. Ins. Co.*, 185 F.R.D. 288, 295–96 (D. Mont. 1998). The insurance company, in a suit brought by an underinsured motorist, called its attorney as an expert witness thereby waiving any work-product privilege that the attorney might have had with respect to the entirety of the claims file. The court suggested that the file might not be protected in all events because processing the insurance claim was an "internal matter" that did not involve work in anticipation of litigation even after the insured threatened to file a "bad faith claim."

- *Vaughn Furniture Co. v. Featureline Mfg., Inc.*, 156 F.R.D. 123, 128 (M.D.N.C. 1994). A subpoena on a patent law firm designated as an expert witness would not be quashed. "[W]hen a party names its attorney as an expert witness, the witness must produce all documents considered by him or her in the process of formulating the expert opinion, including documents containing opinions." Documents reviewed to help answer discovery requests or to discuss trial strategy need not be produced, except to the extent that it formed a basis for the opinion reached.

- *Mushroom Assoc. v. Monterey Mushrooms, Inc.*, 1992 U.S. Dist. LEXIS 20640, 1992 WL 442914 (N.D. Cal. Aug. 21, 1992). When a patent attorney was named as an expert witness, his work product became discoverable just as do the documents that any expert witness relies on to formulate an opinion.

4. Use at Trial

When a party uses work product in the course of a trial or other proceeding, for example to impeach or cross-examine, any work-product privilege is waived. The basis for the waiver is obvious: you cannot have your cake and eat it too. If an attorney intends to rely on a document in any testimonial fashion, the totality of that document is put into issue and becomes discoverable.

- *United States v. Nobles*, 422 U.S. 225, 239 & n.14 (1975). A criminal defendant sought to impeach the testimony of prosecution witnesses by their inconsistent accounts in interviews with a defense investigator. The trial court permitted defense counsel to use the reports in cross-examining the prosecution witnesses without disclosing the reports to the prosecution, but it ruled that the investigator would not be permitted to testify about the interviews unless his reports of those interviews—inspected and edited *in camera*—were disclosed. Defense counsel refused to produce the reports, and the witness was not permitted to testify. The Supreme Court held that the decision to call the investigator as a witness "waived the privilege with respect to matters covered in his testimony." The Court explained: "What constitutes a waiver with respect to work-product materials depends, of course, upon the circumstances. Counsel necessarily makes use throughout trial of the notes, documents and other internal materials prepared to present adequately his client's case, and often relies on them in examining witnesses. When so used, there normally is no waiver. But where, as here, counsel attempts to make a testimonial use of these materials the normal rules of evidence come into play with respect to cross-examination and production of documents."

- *Chavis v. North Carolina*, 637 F.2d 213, 223–24 (4th Cir. 1980). The defendant waived its work-product privilege when its witness, in defending his credibility at trial, referred to and relied on the evidence the defendant sought to claim as its work product.

- *United States v. Salsedo*, 607 F.2d 318, 320–21 (9th Cir. 1979). When the defendant's counsel referred to his alleged work product in cross-examining the government informant, a DEA agent, any privilege from compelled disclosure was waived.

- *Brown v. Trigg*, 791 F.2d 598, 601 (7th Cir. 1986). Statements by the defendant to an expert hired by the defendant's attorney to conduct a polygraph examination were work product. Testimony by the examiner at a juvenile court waiver hearing regarding those statements waived the privilege.

Where a witness alludes to work product as material that he relied on for reaching a certain conclusion, waiver will also be deemed to have occurred.

Moreover, once waiver has occurred by virtue of reliance on work product or privileged material in one context of an adjudicatory proceeding, such as in support of a motion for summary judgment, it cannot thereafter be undone if one's strategic approach changes and one concludes, for instance, after losing the motion for summary judgment, that the material is no longer necessary at trial.

- *Wells v. Liddy*, 37 Fed. Appx. 53, 66 (4th Cir. 2002). In a libel case, G. Gordon Liddy testified that he relied upon work-product materials prepared by his counsel as the basis for making statements alleged to be libelous. The appellate court reversed the district court and found that such testimonial reliance did constitute a waiver. Virginia law governed the waiver of attorney-client privilege material. The court of appeals nonetheless made a statement in that regard, which would be applicable even in a case where federal common law applied. "Once Liddy decided to reveal these confidential communications [in an affidavit in support of a motion for summary judgment], his decision to disclose became final. He may not reattach the privilege now that the issues in the case have 'shifted.'"

5. Witness Preparation and Rule 612

Showing a witness otherwise protected work-product material to prepare the witness to testify is dangerous if the work product must be protected from compelled disclosure. Courts have frequently held that witness-preparation material is subject to discovery, either because the need and inability requirements of Rule 26(b)(3) have been satisfied or because other disclosure rules—principally Evidence Rule 612 and Civil Procedure Rule 26(b)(4) for experts—require production. Although there is some balancing going on, the courts seem often to treat use of work product in witness preparation as a waiver of the protection.

The issue frequently arises at a deposition, in preparation for which the deponent has seen materials constituting opinion work product, such as an attorney's memorandum describing the case. For some courts, the issue is relatively easy, even when an expert has reviewed opinion work product. Following the view that opinion work product is absolutely privileged, they hold that neither Rule 26(b)(4) nor Rule 612 requires production.

- *North Carolina Elec. Membership Corp. v. Carolina Power & Light Co.*, 108 F.R.D. 283, 286 (M.D.N.C. 1985). The court held that opinion work product was absolutely protected from disclosure even though shown to an expert witness, regardless of the constraints of Evidence Rule 612. The court concluded that the opposing party could determine the basis of the expert's opinion by its extensive discovery requests concerning the expert's opinions without needing direct access to an attorney's opinion work product.

For other courts (the vast majority), the issue is much more complicated. The first problem is the meaning of Rule 612. Subdivision

(1) *requires* production of writings used to refresh recollection *while* testifying. A question may arise whether "testifying" includes being deposed, but the general view is that work-product protection is lost when a witness directly refers to the document in a deposition.

- *S & A Painting Co. v. O.W.B. Corp.*, 103 F.R.D. 407, 409–10 (W.D. Pa. 1984). When a witness during his deposition examined and once referred to a portion of handwritten notes prepared prior to the deposition at the request of his counsel, Evidence Rule 612 effected a waiver of the work-product protection.

The real difficulty comes when the deponent has seen the work product before testifying. Rule 612 gives the court *discretion* to order production of a writing used to refresh recollection *before* testifying "if the court in its discretion determines it is necessary in the interest of justice."

For some courts, Rule 612 does not apply to opinion work product used in preparing a deponent.

- *Omaha Pub. Power Dist. v. Foster Wheeler Corp.*, 109 F.R.D. 615, 616–17 (D. Neb. 1986). The court refused to require production of the particular documents that counsel had used (from among those produced in discovery) to prepare the witness. The selection was opinion work product, but disclosure could be avoided by examining the deponent first on his factual knowledge and then asking him to identify the documents that informed him regarding his testimony. In that way, the questioner did not learn of opposing counsel's selection, which was his work product, but did learn sufficient information to conduct a thorough examination of the deponent. The court also said that Evidence Rule 612 does not apply to discovery of materials used to prepare a witness for deposition testimony. "The word 'testifying' as used in the Rule contemplates the presentation of evidence at a hearing before a judge or magistrate."

Sometimes, the discretion given by Rule 612 may be exercised to continue the protection given opinion work product by Rule 26(b)(3).

- *Al-Rowaishan Establishment Universal Trading & Agencies, Ltd. v. Beatrice Foods Co.*, 92 F.R.D. 779, 780–81 (S.D.N.Y. 1982). The court's discretion under Evidence Rule 612(2) does not require production of notes containing largely opinion work product consulted before testifying at a deposition.

The court's discretion may, however, also be used to order disclosure.

- *United States v. 22.80 Acres of Land*, 107 F.R.D. 20, 25–26 (N.D. Cal. 1985). In the exercise of its discretion under Evidence Rule 612(2), the court ordered production of appraisal reports used to refresh the witness's recollection at a deposition. Disclosure, the court reasoned, created no harm to the proponent, as the reports had been written in preparation for an earlier stage of the proceedings.

In exercising discretion under Rule 612, the courts balance the need for disclosure, in order to examine the witness fully, against the need to protect work product, in order to encourage careful preparation.

- *Aguinaga v. John Morrell & Co.*, 112 F.R.D. 671, 683–84 (D. Kan. 1986). A witness could not be compelled to reveal what documents he had been shown in preparation for his deposition. Distinguishing Rule 612 of the Federal Rules of Evidence, the court concluded that the questioning party already had access to the documents in question and that, therefore, the only purpose behind the question as to which documents had been shown would be to inform the opposing side of "the attorneys' process of selection and distillation of documents. Discovery would reveal nothing more than what documents the attorneys thought were relevant to the transactions."

- *Joseph Schlitz Brewing Co. v. Muller & Phipps (Hawaii) Ltd.*, 85 F.R.D. 118, 120 (W.D. Mo. 1980). Disclosure of work-product documents was not compelled when an attorney, prior to testifying, reviewed his own correspondence file. Without a showing that particular documents had been consulted—and maybe not even then—the court was unwilling to invade opinion work product. The court read the legislative history of Evidence Rule 612 as calling for special discretionary safeguards against disclosure of opinion work product used in preparing to testify.

- *In re Comair Air Disaster Litig.*, 100 F.R.D. 350, 353 (E.D. Ky. 1983). A report made by the defendant's investigator shortly after an airplane crash was not protected from disclosure because the defendant's engineer had reviewed the report before being deposed. The court resolved the seeming tension between Rule 26(b)(3) and Evidence Rule 612 by stating that Rule 612 weighted the balance in favor of finding that "substantial need" exists under Rule 26(b)(3) because of the policy in favor of effective cross-examination. There is no absolute waiver of work-product protection; however, consideration must be given to both the extent to which the documents were used and relied on by the deponent and the extent to which they involve opinion work product.

Some say that Rule 612 expresses a policy always calling for disclosure.

- *Wheeling-Pittsburgh Steel Corp. v. Underwriters Labs., Inc.*, 81 F.R.D. 8, 9–10 (N.D. Ill. 1978). The fact that work-product documents were shown to a former employee to refresh his recollection immediately prior to his deposition waived the protection, pursuant to Evidence Rule 612.

One frequently cited decision extends the notion that when a document is shown to an employee to refresh recollection, all protection from disclosure is waived as to opinion work product.

- *Berkey Photo, Inc. v. Eastman Kodak Co.*, 74 F.R.D. 613, 616–17 (S.D.N.Y. 1977). In ruling on a motion to compel the production of trial notebooks prepared by counsel and shown to expert witnesses before their depositions, the court did not require production of the work-product materials. Judge Frankel warned, however, that if materials were shown to a witness in the future, they would thereby lose their work-product privileged status. "In the setting of modern views favoring broad access to materials useful for effective cross-examination, embodied in rules like 612 and like the Jencks Act . . . it is disquieting to posit that a lawyer may 'aid' a witness with items of work-product and then prevent totally the access that might reveal and counteract the effects of such assistance. There is much to be said for a view that a party or its lawyer, meaning to invoke the privilege, ought to use other and different materials, available later to a cross-examiner, in the preparation of witnesses. When this simple choice emerges the decision to give the work product to the witness could well be deemed a waiver of the privilege."

The basis for the ruling denying production of the work-product trial notebooks was the court's belief that an order compelling production would work an undue hardship on the defendant because counsel had been unaware of the scope of the then-recently adopted Evidence Rule 612. The court was careful to put the practicing bar on notice that in the future a different result might obtain: "[G]iven the current development of the law in this quarter, it seems fair to say that counsel were not vividly aware of the potential for a stark choice between withholding the notebooks from the experts or turning them over to opposing counsel."

Not all documents reviewed by a witness necessarily waive their privileged character. If the witness does not use the document to refresh recollection or to testify concerning the content of the document, then the privilege is not waived.

■ *Laborers Local 17 Health Benefit Fund v. Philip Morris, Inc.*, 1998 U.S. Dist. LEXIS 11158, at *18 (S.D.N.Y. July 22, 1998). The court found the argument that the privilege was waived by the witness consulting a privileged document before his deposition "meritless." "[I]t cannot be said that the privileged portion of the document influenced his testimony, and absent such a linkage, there is no basis for implying a waiver of the privilege." The court did suggest that had the deponent been asked whether review of the privileged document had refreshed his recollection there might have been a basis for deeming the privilege waived, but absent such a foundation, the court refused to infer that to have been the case.

■ *James Julian, Inc. v. Raytheon Co.*, 93 F.R.D. 138, 144–46 (D. Del. 1982). Plaintiff's counsel had collected a small percentage of the documents produced in discovery and placed them in binders for use in preparing witnesses for deposition. The binders were ordered to be produced. Although in a case involving many documents, counsel's process of selection necessarily reflected opinion and strategy, Evidence Rule 612 means that the defendants were entitled to know in what way the witness's testimony had been influenced by the plaintiff's counsel's presentation of evidence.

When the deponent is an expert witness, the situation is further complicated by the provisions in Rule 26(b)(4) regarding discovery of the bases of expert testimony. Under the view taken by Judge Frankel in *Berkey Photo, Inc. v. Eastman Kodak Co.*, showing the expert the work product amounts to waiver of the protection, presumably even for opinion work product. Other courts, however, have had to deal with the relationship between the second sentence of Rule 26(b)(3), protecting the attorney's mental processes, Rule 612, and Rule 26(b)(4). *See generally* Note, *Discovery of Attorney Work Product Reviewed by an Expert Witness*, 85 COLUM. L. REV. 812 (1985); Note, *Discovery under the Federal Rules of Civil Procedure of Attorney Opinion Work Product Provided to an Expert Witness*, 53 FORDHAM L. REV. 1159 (1985).

- *Boring v. Keller*, 97 F.R.D. 404, 407–08 (D. Colo. 1983). Before the expert was deposed, the plaintiff's attorney gave him opinion work-product documents, including both an unedited version of the plaintiff's deposition summary containing the attorney's impressions of the plaintiff as a witness and an "expert witness letter" with suggestions to experts and counsel's impressions of the case. The defendant's order to compel discovery was granted because the information presumably influenced and shaped the expert's testimony. The court justified its decision on both the waiver of Rule 23(b) (3)'s protection for opinion work product and promotion of the policies of Rule 26(b)(4).

In two major opinions, the Third Circuit addressed these issues, holding, first, that the protection given opinion work product is not modified by the provisions allowing disclosure of the basis for an expert's opinion, and, second, that Rule 612 applies only when the expert has relied on the documents and they have influenced the deposition testimony.

- *Bogosian v. Gulf Oil Corp.*, 738 F.2d 587, 590, 593–95 (3d Cir. 1984). The trial court had ordered disclosure of opinion work product shown to the plaintiffs' expert witnesses for two reasons: the depositions of the experts could and likely would be used as trial evidence, and it was important that the defendants be able to examine the experts thoroughly and completely. Such examination required predeposition knowledge of all the information the expert had available. In the trial court's view, the qualified immunity in Rule 26(b)(3) for opinion work product should give way to the provisions in 26(b)(4) on preparing for expert testimony.

The appellate court reversed, holding that the privilege was not waived by showing work product to experts. The provisions for discovery of experts supplant only the first sentence of 26(b)(3), so opinion work product is still protected from disclosure by the second sentence. As the majority saw it, Rule 26(b)(4) only keeps experts' reports from being treated as 26(b)(3) work product; it does not allow inquiry into the lawyer's role.

Judge Becker dissented, calling for a case-by-case balancing, with the trial court to conduct an *in camera* review of the particular need to impeach the expert with the opinion work product. He also said that the majority had totally neglected Evidence Rule 612, which authorizes disclosure of materials used in preparing to testify; in applying that provision, he suggested that a distinction be drawn between using opinion work product to "refresh" a witness's recollection and using it to "create" an opinion. *See* Note, *Interactions Between Memory Refreshment and Work-Product Protections under the Federal Rules*, 88 YALE L.J. 390, 404–06 (1978).

- *Sporck v. Peil*, 759 F.2d 312, 313–14, 316–19 (3d Cir.), *cert. denied*, 474 U.S. 903 (1985). This case involved thousands of documents, some of which the defendants' attorney had selected, compiled, and given to the witness before a deposition. At the deposition, before the attorney asked the witness any substantive questions, the plaintiff's attorney asked the witness whether he had reviewed any documents prior to the deposition. The deposing attorney then requested that those documents be produced. The trial court ordered production under Evidence Rule 612, on the grounds that selection of the documents was not opinion work product and that the principles of Rule 612 mandated access to materials used in preparing witnesses.

  The court of appeals reversed, holding that the defendants' attorney's process of selecting and compiling the documents involved opinions and strategies. The court also said that Rule 612 is a rule of evidence, not of discovery; its purpose is to promote a search of the witness's memory and credibility, not to discover relevant facts. In finding a conflict between Rule 612 and the protection given opinion work product, the trial court had erred in failing to find two of the requisites for application of Rule 612—that the witness used the writing to refresh his memory and that he used it for the purpose of testifying. At the time the questions were asked in this case, the witness had given no substantive testimony, so there could be no showing that he had relied on the documents in testifying or that they had influenced his testimony in any way. If he had first given substantive testimony and then been asked about the materials used to refresh what he said, there would be no need to disclose the over-all selection of documents made by the attorney, which was the protected work product.

Given the current uncertain state of the law, prudent counsel will take precautions not to disclose to a witness work product that they do not wish their adversary to see at a later date.

F. *Extent of Waiver*

The work-product protection is not automatically waived by any disclosure to third parties. The work product protection is not suscepti-ble to the same policy concerns as the privilege. Waiver for one consti-tutes waiver for all for the privilege. That is not the case with respect to the work-product protection, which is intended to protect work product from falling into the hands of an adversary. Thus, the government may have comparable, but not necessarily identical, interests to that of the disclosing party. Disclosure, therefore, will not constitute waiver with respect to the adversary.

- *United States v. AT&T*, 642 F.2d 1285 (D.C. Cir. 1980). No waiver occurred where competitors had disclosed their data to the United States government.

- *GAF Corp. v. Eastman Kodak Co.*, 85 F.R.D. 46 (S.D.N.Y. 1979). Where one party to litigation complies with a government request for information discovered in the course of that private litigation, that compliance will not constitute an automatic waiver of the work-product protection with respect to its adversary.

- *In re Grand Jury Subpoenas*, 561 F. Supp. 1247 (E.D.N.Y. 1982). Disclosure of a document to an individual did not increase the likelihood that the government as an adversary would obtain the document, hence the disclosure did not strip the document of the protection.

But see:

- *D'Ippolito v. Cities Serv. Co.*, 39 F.R.D. 610 (S.D.N.Y. 1965). Where, however, a disclosure occurs that substantially increases the likelihood that potential adversaries will obtain work-product protected materials, it is then deemed that a waiver has occurred.

- *First Pacific Networks, Inc. v. Atlantic Mut. Ins. Co.*, 163 F.R.D. 574 (N.D. Cal. 1995). No claim of work-product protection would lie with respect to third parties where documents had heretofore been sent by the insured to its insurance company—a potentially adverse party—in an attempt to persuade the insurer to afford coverage.

- *Samuels v. Mitchell*, 155 F.R.D. 195, 201 (N.D. Cal. 1994). Work-product immunity is waived when an "attorney cannot reasonably expect to limit the future use of otherwise protected material." Here, work product was disclosed to an accountant acting in the capacity of a consultant not in the capacity of a public accountant with duties of disclosure to others besides the client. Therefore, in disclosing the work-product-protected documents to the accountant, there was no danger of subsequent disclosure to adverse parties and the work-product protection was not lost and no waiver occurred.

Surprisingly, even if an attorney tenders work-product protected documents to a client, that act may constitute a waiver if the attorney and the client have adverse interests at the time the tender is made. Therefore, attorneys need to be aware that if work-product-protected materials are delivered to the client at a time that the interests of the attorney and client are not necessarily coterminous or harmonious, that delivery may constitute a waiver of the work-product protection on the part of the attorney.

- *In re Doe*, 662 F.2d 1073 (4th Cir. 1981), *cert. denied*, 455 U.S. 1000 (1982). When an attorney unconditionally released work-product documents to his client at a time that relations between the two were strained, and made no attempt to control their future use, a waiver will be deemed to have occurred piercing the immunity at the behest of adverse third parties, including U.S. attorneys and grand juries.

Thus, disclosure of *some* work-product materials does not thereby necessarily constitute a waiver permitting discovery of *all* work product prepared in the same litigation. Whether disclosure constitutes waiver will depend on the circumstances and reasons motivating the disclosure.

- *FTC v. U.S. Grant Resources, LLC,* 2004 U.S. Dist. LEXIS 11769, at *33 (E.D. La. June 25, 2004). The FTC agreed to provide its Operating Manual and to provide responses to certain interrogatories. Defendants argued, unsuccessfully, that such voluntary production of certain work-product-protected materials necessarily entailed a subject matter waiver in respect to all the factors which went into the decision to bring the instant case. Not so said the court. "Courts have consistently held that there exists no subject matter waiver for the kind of work product expressly defined in *Fed. R. Civ. P. 26(b)(3)* as 'the mental impressions, conclusions, opinions or legal theories of an attorney or other representative of a party concerning the litigation,' *i.e.,* 'opinion' work product. As to the FTC's agreement to provide responses consisting of factual knowledge only, waiver is not implicated, because the facts alone are not subject to any privilege." No cases were cited by the court.

- *In re Qwest Communications Int'l, Inc. Sec. Litig.,* 2005 U.S. Dist. LEXIS 19129 (D. Colo. Aug. 15, 2005). The court reversed the magistrate judge and concluded that in disclosing a report which summarized the content of witness interviews to outside auditors, the company had not waived any opinion work product in that report but only fact word product. It accordingly instructed counsel for Qwest to redact all opinion work product from the report and to produce those portions which constituted fact word product. The court did not discuss why disclosure to outside auditors would have constituted waiver of work product absent a showing that the content was then incorporated into public filings.

- *Hollinger Int'l Inc. v. Hollinger Inc.,* 230 F.R.D. 508 (N.D. Ill 2005). The party resisting subject matter forfeiture did not contest the right of the adversary to the report which had been given to the

SEC. It was also willing to provide fact opinion work-product materials to its adversary. It contested only that such disclosure entailed a forfeiture of opinion work product protection in respect to the same subject matter. Magistrate Judge Nolan, in her typically finely reasoned opinion, agreed.

- *S & A Painting Co., Inc. v. O.W.B. Corp.*, 103 F.R.D. 407 (W.D. Pa. 1984). When a witness during his deposition referred to and once examined a portion of handwritten notes prepared in anticipation of litigation, he waived the work-product protection *only* for those portions of the notes.

The question of whether disclosure made in one context for a limited purpose will result in waiver with respect to other parties or in other subsequent contexts seems to depend, in large measure, on which overriding purposes are served by the partial or limited disclosure. If the purpose is well intentioned and is one that public policy seeks to promote, the courts will frequently grant protection from subsequent or other disclosure. If the purpose of the initial disclosure was a self-serving one with a purpose that public policy does not necessarily seek to promote, protection from subsequent disclosure will frequently be denied.

For example, disclosure to an adverse party of work-product materials during settlement negotiations does not necessarily constitute a waiver of the protection, given the common interest in reaching a resolution. Thus, in order to implement the public policy encouraging settlements, even when a waiver is found, it may be limited to the particular documents disclosed rather than the entire subject matter.

- *Burlington Indus. v. Exxon Corp.*, 65 F.R.D. 26, 45–46 (D. Md. 1974). "During settlement negotiations, the confidentiality necessary to be present to assert an attorney-client or work-product privilege is not lost by disclosure of pertinent information to opposing counsel or control group members. . . . Any question of waiver of the attorney-client privilege or work-product immunity during settlement negotiations must be considered in light of the importance of facilitating such settlement." The court held that work-product protection was waived only for the particular documents disclosed, not for all the work product on the subject matter.

And disclosure of some investigative report for instance to an adversary during the course of discovery, will not necessarily entrain access to all the work product, memos, notes of interviews and such that went into the production of the investigative report.

- *Ziner v. Cedar Crest College*, 2006 U.S. Dist. LEXIS 34858, at *8 (E.D. Pa. May 30, 2006). Outside counsel conducted an investigation of a discrimination claim by another faculty member which in the course of discovery was given to the plaintiff. The magistrate judge held that act did not waive work-product protection for everything that went into the preparation of the report. The report was not directly at issue in the litigation. It was tangential thereto and no testimonial or other use was apparently being proposed. Given them a hand, and they'll try to eat the arm, may have been the rationale of the court.

There is no clear body of law as to whether a partial waiver of work product is identical in its scope to a partial waiver of the attorney-client privilege. Generally, however, a selective waiver of the privilege will entail waiver for the entirety of the subject matter. A partial waiver of the work-product protection, as in the settlement context, may often be limited to only the document disclosed.

- *Akamai Techs., Inc. v. Digital Island, Inc.*, 2002 U.S. Dist. LEXIS 13515 (N.D. Cal. May 30, 2002). Even assuming that there had been no agreement to limit waiver to the damage calculation document actually disclosed in settlement discussions, the court found there would be no reason to expand waiver beyond that sole document.

- *Ramsey v. NYP Holdings, Inc.*, 2002 U.S. Dist. LEXIS 11728, at *37 (S.D.N.Y. June 26, 2002), *clarified*, 2002 U.S. Dist. LEXIS 18186 (S.D.N.Y. Sept. 3, 2002). Full subject matter waiver was not ordered in absence of a showing of partial disclosure; however, where portion of a document was disclosed, the entirety, to the extent that it dealt with the same subject matter, would have to be disclosed also.

- *Greene, Tweed of Del., Inc. v. DuPont Dow Elastomers, L.L.C.*, 202 F.R.D. 418 (E.D. Pa. 2001). Scope of waiver was not limited to opinions or communications as to whether a patent was infringing pursuant to specific patent law provisions, as asserted in an attorney opinion letter that it did not, but was ordered in respect to the entire infringement subject matter.

- *In re Commercial Fin. Servs., Inc.*, 247 B.R. 828, 848 (Bankr. N.D. Okla. 2000). "Subject matter waiver is narrowly construed [and] applies only where partial waiver confers a tactical advantage."

G. *Anticipatory Waiver*

Louisiana follows what it calls the "anticipatory" waiver rule, rather than the waiver by "injection" of an issue into an adversary proceeding. Thus, even if one party does not propose affirmatively to rely on either privilege or work-product-protected matters, but asserting some claim, that party may have placed work-product-protected materials inherently into issue in fairness to the other side. That is the case, for instance, when indemnity is sought for a matter resolved by settlement, for instance. The issue will invariably be what was the nature of the liability and was the amount paid reasonable. Such issues inject into a case attorney work-product materials of the indemnitee, even if the indemnitee does not intend to rely on such materials to prosecute its claim.

- *Conoco Inc. v. Boh Brothers Constr. Co.*, 191 F.R.D. 107, 110–11 (W.D. La. 1998). The plaintiff sought indemnity for a settlement from the defendant and thereby had anticipatorily waived work-product protection. "This court finds that the mental impressions and analysis by Conoco's attorneys regarding the basis of Conoco's liability and the reasonableness of the amount paid in settlement are at issue in this litigation. By seeking indemnity, Conoco has placed at issue the basis for its liability, its liability analysis and the reasonableness of the settlement paid. This court agrees with the Magistrate Judge that Boh has shown a compelling need and no alternative means of obtaining this information and that Conoco has waived its immunity under the work product."

- *Williams Land Co., LLC v. BellSouth Telecomms., Inc.*, 2005 U.S. Dist. LEXIS 6918 (E.D. La. Apr. 13, 2005). The court said that a litigant's pleading of a claim or defense to which his attorney-client communications are relevant does not waive the privilege unless that pleading must inevitably require the introduction of a privileged communication at trial. BellSouth had not indicated that it intended to use any of the privileged communications to prove its asserted "good-faith" defense or to defend against any of the plaintiffs' claims at trial. Until it did so, the court said, its privilege was not waived.

H. *Disclosure to Client*

As a general proposition, an attorney may not withhold work product from his or her own client. The work product is ultimately produced for the client's benefit and it is the client that pays for the work product. The client is entitled to the benefit of the engagement, including the work product produced.

- *Spivey v. Zant*, 683 F.2d 881, 885 (5th Cir. 1992). An attorney could not refuse to disclose documents to his habeas corpus client on the ground of work product or personal possession. "Thus, the work product doctrine does not apply to the situation in which a client seeks access to documents or other tangible things created or amassed by his attorney during the course of the representation."

- *Gottlieb v. Wiles*, 143 F.R.D. 241 (D. Colo. 1992). In the corporate setting when a corporation is a client, an attorney may not withhold work-product materials from a company's board of directors. Thus, a former director may have access thereto also, because he or she could have obtained the materials during his or her tenure.

- *Roberts v. Heim*, 123 F.R.D. 614, 631 (N.D. Cal. 1988). Limited partners may have access to work product generated by the law firm representing the general partner/promoter. "[N]o public policy considerations have been articulated by defendants which would support an assertion of work-product privilege by any attorney to the detriment of his client."

When the client has failed to pay the attorney, however, the attorney should be entirely within the attorney's rights in refusing to tender work product to the client. In that regard, the work-product protection unfolds in a quite distinct fashion from the attorney-client privilege, which is predicated on an ethical responsibility. Obviously, no attorney could reveal a client's confidences merely because a client has refused to pay an outstanding bill. An attorney, however, should be able to refuse to tender work product to a client who has not paid for the creation of that work product. The work-product protection, with respect to the client, is predicated on a business proposition. If the work is paid for, the client is entitled to the attorney's labor. If it is not, the client may not obtain that for which he or she refuses to pay.

Although there can be dispute as to whether a party is in fact a client and whether the disclosure was necessary to effect a litigation purpose, it is self-evident that disclosure to a client would not waive the work-product protection.

- *Newport Pac. Inc. v. County of San Diego*, 200 F.R.D. 628, 634 (S.D. Cal. 2001). "To the extent that the information at issue here is County Counsel's analysis of issues for presentation to the Board at closed session where the Board makes policy and strategy choices on litigation, the information is attorney work product, and therefore protected from disclosure. The Court sees no reason to question Defendants' assertion of that privilege and is satisfied that the information is work product."

As in so many matters, a great deal will depend on the flexibility of the court and on perceived fairness or unfairness to both parties. A party will be permitted to abandon a privilege claim and assert an advice of counsel claim if it is seen as acting in good faith and if time permits.

- *Granite Partners, L.P. v. Merrill Lynch, Pierce, Fenner & Smith, Inc.*, 2002 U.S. Dist. LEXIS 7290, at *9 (S.D.N.Y. Apr. 26, 2002). Defendants sought to preclude an "advice of counsel" defense by an *in limine* motion. The court refused to do so, finding that defendants had not acted in bad faith and time remained to allow depositions to be taken on the defense. "This dilemma is fortunately not intractable. By permitting limited discovery in the two weeks before trial, the Funds may properly prepare for the advice-of-counsel defense and Merrill will not be punished for what amounts to, at most, a sin of omission in not telling the Funds that its privilege had been waived."

Factors Common to Both the Attorney-Client Privilege and the Work-Product Protection

3

I. UNDERLYING FACTS NOT PRIVILEGE PROTECTED

It bears repeating. Underlying facts regardless of their source are discoverable. It is only the content of communications between attorneys and their agents and clients and their agents where those communications have the purpose of seeking or giving legal advice that is not.

Thus foundational questions which seek to determine who was present or who authored a document or to whom it was sent are simply not encompassed within the privilege.

So too work product protection is accorded to documents and tangible things. Questions in depositions such as who prepared a damage calculation or on what it was based are not and can never be subject to a work-product protection objection. Only documents and tangible things are subject to such protection. Certainly not information surrounding a damage claim. And yet, *mirabile dictu* there are actually counsel, even from supposedly reputable firms, who have been known to proffer objections based on work-product protection to such fundamental foundational questions which would be necessary to test the validity of any purported damage claim in all events.

- *Pacific Gas & Elec. Co. v. United States*, 69 Fed. Cl. 784, 799, 805, 808 (Fed. Cl. 2006). The court ordered the resumption of a deposition when such objections were put forth in the course of depositions in part designed to test the parameters of a damage claim. In so doing the court remarked that a work product protection claim is applicable only to documents and tangible things. Information might possibly be attorney-client privilege protected, but surely could not be work-product protected. Given the nature of the questions which were foundational in nature, any objections based on attorney-client privilege would also have been abusive, although the court did not say so, instead offering to make herself available by telephone in case of future disputes.

In the waiver context, some courts distinguish between revealing the facts within an otherwise privileged communication—which would not entail waiver—from revealing that the facts are contained within a privileged communication—which would entail a waiver. They may be splitting hairs in too fine a manner. Once the facts are known, what is it in the privileged communication that remains to be protected?

- *United States v. El Paso Co.*, 682 F.2d 530, 540 (5th Cir. 1982). The court made a distinction between what it called "mere disclosure of the underlying fact" which would not waive the privilege or protection as to a communication containing that fact.

- *Robinson v. Tex. Auto. Dealers Ass'n*, 214 F.R.D. 432, 448 (E.D. Tex. 2003). The court held that revealing "that a communication contained that fact discloses the substance of the communication and, thus, waives the privilege (or the work-product protection, if disclosed to an adversary) as to that communication." Therefore, the court found that Defendants had waived the privilege as to the entire letter, not because they asserted as a defense that they relied on the Commissioner's opinion, but because they substantiated the defense by telling opposing counsel and the court that the opinion was communicated in the letter.

Why did the court choose to go through such contortions when the simple manner of dealing with the issue would have been to state that having put the opinion into issue, their adversary and the court were entitled to see the letter and judge for themselves?

But it is clear that whatever distinctions are made between underlying facts and privileged communications about those facts, courts have little tolerance for the oft-repeated attempts to hide discoverable facts behind dubious privilege and work-product protection claims.

- *Freiermuth v. PPG Indus., Inc.*, 218 F.R.D. 694, 696 (N.D. Ala. 2003). "The completed worksheet lists for each of the seven employees or former employees their respective job titles, dates of hire, performance ratings for the years 1999 through 2001, success factor ratings for five categories, a computation of the success factor average, overall average, indication of discipline or attendance problems, and a rank. The worksheet also indicates for the first four persons listed—birth dates, race, and gender—characteristics which appear to have been intended to be added *after* the aforementioned ratings.

  "Counsel's choice to describe this document, not by its actual title, but as a 'memo' is questionable at best, and mendacious at worst. The document does not appear to contain any mental impressions or analysis by counsel. It appears to merely contain facts that were accumulated on each individual placed on the worksheet." (Footnote omitted.)

So too, counsel can not object to a deponent testifying as to facts in the deponent's knowledge on the grounds that those facts may have come into the deponent's knowledge through his attorney.

- *Protective Nat'l Ins. Co. of Omaha v. Commonwealth Ins. Co.*, 137 F.R.D. 267, 278 (D. Neb. 1989). "There is simply nothing wrong with asking for facts from a deponent even though those facts may have been communicated to the deponent by the deponent's counsel. But, depending upon how questions are phrased to the witness, deposition questions may tend to elicit the impressions of counsel about the relative significance of the facts; opposing counsel is not entitled to his adversaries' thought processes. Here the effort must be to protect against indirect disclosure of an attorney's mental impressions or theories of the case."

The problem in this type of situation is determining the degree to which a particular deposition question elicits the mental impressions of the attorney who communicated a fact to the deponent.

The answer is simple. Don't ask: "What did the attorney tell you?" Instead ask: "What is your understanding?"

Courts have also suggested that the better approach to obtaining such facts is via interrogatories rather than depositions which carry a greater risk of invading the privilege/protection when the only source of a deponent's knowledge is in fact what he learned from counsel.

II. PROCEDURAL ISSUES

Issues common to the assertion of the attorney-client privilege or the work-product protection are addressed here.

A. *Privilege Applicable in all Proceedings*

Theoretically the attorney-client privilege is applicable in all judicial proceedings without exception, except for one which has developed far beyond what anyone initially imaged, namely *in camera* proceedings, which moreover of an *ex parte* nature. That context alone is one ever expanding area where privilege/protection rules do not apply. Nor do most courts or commentators consider that fact to be in the least problematic although it stands as a glaring exception to the principle that the attorney-client privilege is applicable in *all* judicial proceedings. *See* Part III, Section on "In Camera Inspections," *infra*.

Federal Rules of Evidence Section. 1101(c) is the codified source that governs where the privilege is applicable. It provides:

> "The rule with respect to privileges applies at *all* stages of *all* actions, cases, and proceedings."

Thus the Rules of Evidence make it abundantly clear that the attorney-client privilege stands in all federal judicial proceedings.

Rule 501 of the Federal Rules of Evidence authorizes federal courts to determine the scope of privilege "in the light of reason and experience."

The Rules of Civil Procedure make explicit that the privilege/protection are applicable to discovery. Fed. R. Civ. P. 26(b)(1) in relevant portion provides:

> "Parties may obtain discovery regarding any matter, not privileged, that is relevant to the claim or defense of any party . . ."

Commentators, 31 Charles Alan Wright & Victor James Gold, *Federal Practice and Procedure* § 8076, at 618(2000), have suggested that the applicability of the privilege rules in all proceedings "means that privileges can apply even in situations where the other rules of evidence are not applicable." They have also suggested that "[t]he policy behind extending privilege law to all proceedings is that the values protected by privileges can be destroyed by permitting disclosure of privileged material in any judicial context." *Id.* at 614.

Thus the attorney-client privilege and work product protection should apply in the context of arbitration and mediation proceedings which are not governed by the Federal Rules of Evidence. These concepts are also applicable in each of the fifty United States, each of which has its own attorney-client privilege and work-product protection rules, often codified, but whose contours by and large follow those that have developed in the federal common law for governing the scope and applicability of privilege/protection rules.

- *Odfjell ASA v. Celanese AG*, 380 F. Supp. 2d 297 (S.D.N.Y. 2005). In prior proceedings of this case, the court had remanded the case to the arbitration panel to determine the availability of the privilege as to the subpoenaed testimony of a former counsel of a non-party. In this instance it remanded again, but this time with instructions that the arbitration panel abused its discretion in refusing to allow the privilege holder to bring forth materials in support of his privilege claim as untimely when proffered at the hearing. The court stated that the privilege holder had no reason to believe that the panel would not hear it at the date of the hearing when it was proffered and warned that failure to so permit would jeopardize the enforce-ability of any award.

B. *Applicable Law*

1. Privilege Issues in Non-Diversity Cases

When a federal question is being litigated in the federal courts, the attorney-client privilege is a question of federal common law.

When a claim or defense is governed by state law (e.g., in a diversity action), however, state privilege law is applicable.

Rule 501 of the Federal Rules of Evidence provides:

> Except as otherwise required by the Constitution of the United States or provided by Act of Congress or in rules prescribed by the Supreme Court pursuant to statutory authority, the privilege of a witness, person, government, State, or political subdivision thereof shall be governed by the principles of the common law as they may be interpreted by the courts of the United States in the light of reason and experience. However, in civil actions and proceedings, with respect to an element of a claim or defense as to which State law supplies the rule of decision, the privilege of a witness, person, government, State, or political subdivision thereof shall be determined in accordance with State law.

Although state and federal law are generally the same regarding most aspects of the attorney-client privilege, they are not identical. For instance some states, such as New Jersey, have only a qualified attorney-client privilege, which may be pierced in the appropriate circumstances. There, the privilege is relative and not absolute and subject to a public policy/need analysis which, in the federal courts, one is more accustomed to seeing with respect to the work-product doctrine than in conjunction with the privilege.

So too in Illinois, the privilege in the corporate context tends to be confined to the control group of employees rather than being extended to all corporate employees.

Therefore, the choice-of-law statement in Rule 501 is sometimes important and the result with respect to whether the privilege applies will vary depending on whether the privilege law of a particular state or the federal common law with respect to the privilege is applied.

- *Leonen v. Johns-Manville*, 135 F.R.D. 94 (D.N.J. 1990). The court applied New Jersey's qualified privilege law in asbestos litigation and ordered documents, which under federal law would have been privileged, produced on the ground that New Jersey's tripartite test for piercing the qualified privilege had been met: there was a legitimate need for the evidence sought to be reached; there was a showing of relevance and materiality to the issue in dispute; and the party seeking the information had sustained the burden of proof by a preponderance of the evidence that the information sought could not be obtained by less intrusive means.

- *Upjohn Co. v. United States*, 449 U.S. 383 (1981), developed the federal common law of the privilege and extended the privilege in the corporate context to communications with employees beyond the "control group." That was a decision of federal law.

Not all states follow the federal common law of privileges in certain contexts, although a great deal of overlap conceptually does exist. Most particularly, the scope of the privilege in the corporate context may differ.

- *Consolidation Coal Co. v. Bucyrus-Erie Co.*, 89 Ill. 2d 103, 106, 432 N.E.2d 250, 254–58 (1982) (unable to discern an operative standard in *Upjohn*, the Illinois Supreme Court adhered to the control group test). In such a situation, whether an attorney's communication with a corporate employee is privileged may depend on whether state or federal law governs the claim asserted.

Obviously, where a state has no dispositive law in respect to a privilege issue, a federal court will apply the federal common law. Presumably it could refer the matter to the state's supreme court for decision, but such a course for minor evidentiary matters is not followed. If a party were determined on mere delay, presumably such a course could be suggested although it is dubious whether it would be followed by the federal court.

- *Murray v. Gemplus Int'l, S.A.*, 217 F.R.D. 362 (E.D. Pa. 2003). Federal precedents on inadvertent disclosure and scope of waiver were followed in absence of any discoverable Pennsylvania precedent from an appellate court level on those issues.

The Ninth Circuit in a comparable case and over a vigorous dissent, failed to do so and instead held that where the state's highest court was silent on whether the privilege could be invaded after death in a dispute among heirs, that it could not. I know of no comparable holding that silence means necessarily no in such a context or that the state's highest court rather than one of appellate courts was sufficient to establish the state's law or that in the absence of state law, the federal common law is applicable. On the contrary, federal courts will often "divine" in the absence of a definitive ruling from the State's highest court, what its ruling a particular privilege issue would be.

- *In re Estate of Covington*, 2006 U.S. App. LEXIS 13001 (9th Cir. 2006).[1] The Ninth Circuit reversed the ruling of the lower tribunal which had held that in the absence of a definitive statement from the state's highest court, federal common law applied. Such a testamentary exception exists at federal common law of privilege.

When a case involves both federal and state substantive law, it is difficult to apply Rule 501 literally. The courts' usual response is to apply the federal common law of privilege for both federal question claims and any pendent state law claims. This usually accords with the apparent congressional intent to apply the law favoring reception of the evidence. In a particular case, the state policy behind its own privilege rules may fall by the wayside. 2 J. WEINSTEIN & M. BERGER, EVIDENCE ¶ 501 [02], at 501–22 (1980).

- *Perrignon v. Bergen Brunswig Corp.*, 77 F.R.D. 455, 458 (N.D. Cal. 1978). Because the purpose of the law of privileges is "to protect the confidentiality of certain communications under circumstances where such confidentiality serves broad societal goals," it would be meaningless to apply federal law to the federal claims and state law to the pendent state claims if one law would protect confidentiality and the other would require disclosure. The court noted that "[o]nce confidentiality is broken, the basic purpose of the privilege is defeated." Therefore, in federal question cases in which pendent state claims are raised, the federal common law of privileges governs all claims of privilege raised in the litigation.

---

1. The case is perplexingly, nay, disturbingly wrong headed since had the heirs been Caucasians instead of American Indians, they would have been in the state court rather than before a federal administrative law judge and would have gotten a dispositive ruling on the issue from a state appellate court, for want of which their case could not proceed.

The *Perrignon* rationale may be equally applicable in a diversity case in which elements of the case are governed by the laws of two or more states with differing privilege laws.

Other choice-of-law questions may also arise under Rule 501. For example, early in the discovery process it may not always be possible to identify whether a given claim or defense relates to a state or federal claim. It may therefore be difficult to determine whether state or federal privilege law applies. The situation may be further complicated in a multiple-party context, particularly when cross-claims or third-party claims, based on state law, are brought in an action in which the underlying claim is based on federal law.

2. Privilege Issues in Diversity Cases

In diversity cases, the federal courts, with uniformity albeit not with self-evident logical consistency, have concluded that issues of attorney-client privilege are substantive and thus controlled by the forum state's law, while issues of work-product doctrine are procedural and thus controlled by federal law. The reason for this bizarre distinction is that Rule 501 of the Federal Rules of Evidence requires that the privilege law of the forum state be applied, but is silent as to what law applies to issues of work-product doctrine, which are governed by a Federal Rule of Evidence, codifying a Supreme Court case which created the concept of work-product protection.

- *Frontier Refining Inc. v. Gorman-Rupp Co.*, 136 F.3d 695, 702 n.10 (10th Cir. 1998). The court projected what Wyoming law would be on the privilege waiver issue and applied the federal rules of evidence to the work-product issue.

- *Samuelson v. Susen*, 576 F.2d 546 (3d Cir. 1978). Rule 501 requires a district court exercising diversity jurisdiction to apply the law of privilege that would be applied to the courts of the state in which it sits. The district and appellate courts looked to Pennsylvania's conflict of law rules to determine whether Ohio's or Pennsylvania's privilege law applied, even though it could be argued that the law of the two jurisdictions controlling the resolution of the privilege question was essentially the same.

- *American Med. Sys., Inc. v. Nat'l Union Fire Ins. Co.*, 1999 U.S. Dist. LEXIS 19230 (E.D. La. Dec. 10, 1999), *vacated based on settlement,*

2000 U.S. Dist. LEXIS 1441 (E.D. La. Feb. 10, 2000). The court upheld a magistrate's ruling that a party had placed into issue documents that required their disclosure. In so doing, Minnesota law was applied to the attorney-client privilege issue and federal law to the work-product doctrine issue. However, because Minnesota law was silent on the issue, the distinction was a theoretical one in this case and the same body of federal law was in fact consulted to resolve both the attorney-client and the work product issues.

- *Walsh v. Seaboard Sur. Co.*, 184 F.R.D. 494 (D. Conn. 1999). Federal law, based on *Hearn v. Rhay*, 68 F.R.D. 574, 581 (E.D. Wash. 1975), applied to state privilege law on the issue of whether documents had been placed "at issue" sufficient to defeat the privilege and work-product doctrine that otherwise would have been applicable to preclude disclosure.

- *Pyramid Controls, Inc. v. Siemens Indus. Automations, Inc.*, 176 F.R.D. 269, 276 (N.D. Ill. 1997). Where the state law provides no guidance on a given issue, the federal courts are wont to fall back on the federal law as developed on that particular privilege issue.

Since the federal common law of privilege, as applied in federal causes of action, is rarely substantially different than the state privilege laws often the distinction is one without a difference.

- *ERA Franchise Sys. v. Northern Ins. Co.*, 183 F.R.D. 276 (D. Kan. 1998). "Whether the court applies federal or Kansas law generally makes no difference in determining whether the attorney-client privilege applies."

Even though often the distinction is one without a difference, nonetheless the potential distinction between the federal common law of privilege and that of the various states is ignored at one's peril. There are indeed instances where distinctions with real differences do arise. One such example is Illinois where the privilege is restricted to the control group. Another is New Jersey where a statutory provision allows a qualified privilege to be pierced when sufficient need is shown.

Where there is no federal claim, but jurisdiction is based entirely on diversity and there is a conflict between the privilege law of the forum and the privilege law of the state with the most significant contacts with the claims, usual conflict of law principles may take over. The rule is that the privilege law of a state with the most significant contacts with the action and the claims, and not the privilege law of the state of the forum, is applied.

- *In re Derienzo*, 1998 Bankr. LEXIS 635 (Bankr. M.D. Pa. Apr. 28, 1998). The defendants to an adversary complaint were two Chicago-based companies. Hence, the privilege law of the State of Illinois was applied rather than federal common law or the privilege law of the State of Pennsylvania, the state of the forum. "This Court has reviewed the attorney-client privilege law as codified in Pennsylvania and has compared that to the common law privilege as found in Illinois case law as well as the federal common law on this topic. I have determined that they are relatively the same and foster similar purposes. Nevertheless, for purposes of this Opinion, the Court will apply Illinois law to address the attorney-client privilege inasmuch as its interests appear to predominate. The communications at issue were made between employees of a corporation situate[d] in Chicago, Illinois, with its attorneys, both in house, and outside counsel, also situate[d] in Chicago, Illinois."

A diversity case in federal court can present three choice-of-law problems regarding privileges. The first, choosing between federal common law and state law, is resolved by Rule 501. State law governs privileges related to claims or defenses based on state law. The second, deciding whether federal or state conflict of law rules apply in selecting between conflicting state privilege rules, has received a variety of answers.

- *Credit Life Ins. Co. v. Uniworld Ins. Co.*, 94 F.R.D. 113, 188 (S.D. Ohio 1982). The court applied the privilege rules of the state whose law supplied the rule of decision.

- *Mitsui & Co. v. Puerto Rico Water Resources Auth.*, 79 F.R.D. 72, 77–79 (D.P.R. 1978). The court suggested that federal choice-of-law rules should govern the question.

Most courts, however, determine what privileges the forum state would apply by virtue of the forum state's choice-of-law rules.

■ *Pritchard-Keang Nam Corp. v. Jaworski*, 751 F.2d 277, 281 n.4 (8th Cir. 1984), *cert. dismissed*, 472 U.S. 1022 (1985). The district court stripped away the privilege based on the crime/fraud exception from a report prepared by attorneys on behalf of a corporation to determine whether bribes had been paid to foreign governments. The report was prepared on behalf of a special audit committee of the board of directors in response to an SEC inquiry. The question of its discoverability arose in the context of a lawsuit brought by the purchaser of the company against the law firm that acted as general counsel of the company making the payments and that rendered a legal opinion on the value of the assets. The court concluded that the law of the forum and the federal common law were not materially different in this instance. Had the law been different, however, the law of the forum would have been applied to determine the contours of the privilege and the fraud crime exception. The determination of whether a *prima facie* showing of fraud had been made would be a question of federal law, the court concluded in a footnote. The case demonstrates the possible hybrid application of laws resulting in substantial complexity.

The third choice, then, is between conflicting state privilege rules, and there are several approaches possible here, too. Traditionally, privileges were characterized as "procedural" and governed by the law of the forum.

More recently, the conflicts of law doctrine has called for applying the privilege law of the state with the "most significant contacts" to the communication or has analyzed the "interests" of the contesting states. E. Scoles & P. Hay, Conflict of Laws §§ 12.10–.14 (1982); 22 C. Wright & K. Graham, Federal Practice and Procedure— Evidence § 5435, at 871–85 (1980).

The *Restatement Second, Conflicts of Laws*, § 139(a), however, states that when a conflict exists between the applicable law and the forum law, the latter would prevail if it would favor admission of the evidence:

> Evidence that is privileged under the local law of the state which has the most significant relationship with the communication but which is not privileged under the local law of the forum will be admitted unless there is some special reason why the forum policy favoring admission should not be given.

Cases with international contacts are of growing importance in the federal courts, and they obviously can pose choice-of-law problems, with foreign privilege law coming into question.

- *Golden Trade v. Lee Apparel Co.*, 143 F.R.D. 514 (S.D.N.Y. 1992). This case provides an extensive analysis of three countries' choice of law rules regarding privileges in the patent context. The conclusion reached is that foreign privilege law would apply when the issue was seeking legal advice about foreign patents from foreign patent agents. The litigation, however, involved use of affidavits from three different countries as to the contours of their respective privilege rules to sustain the burden of proof on parties asserting a privilege.

- *Renfield Corp. v. E. Remy Martin & Co.*, 98 F.R.D. 442, 444 (D. Del. 1982). In discovery conducted under the Hague Convention, a person requested to give evidence may refuse on the basis of privileges under either the law of the country where the discovery is taken or the law of the jurisdiction from which the discovery request originates. The treaty is "a privilege creating, rather than a privilege limiting, law." Consequently, United States attorney-client privilege applied to communications with French "in-house" counsel, even though France might not recognize the privilege.

- *In re Ampicillin Antitrust Litig.*, 81 F.R.D. 377, 391–94 (D.D.C. 1978). Comity may apply to privilege questions, except when foreign law is contrary to the public policy of the forum. Consequently, communications relating to patent activities in the United States are governed by American privilege rules, while communications relating to patent activities in Great Britain are governed by the British privilege rules.

Many potentially difficult choice-of-law issues are probably avoided by the courts for the simple reason that most jurisdictions within the United States apply and interpret the attorney-client privilege in a substantially consistent manner. To the extent that inconsistent rules develop, the underlying policies of the privilege may be impaired. If the purpose of the privilege is to encourage certain kinds of communications by reassuring the speaker that disclosure of those communications will not later be compelled, that purpose is clearly weakened if the speaker does not know which set of rules will be used to later test the privileged nature of the communication. Arguably, of course, most speakers do not know the rules safeguarding the privilege. They assume, however, that if they tell their attorney something and ask the attorney to keep it confidential, the attorney is duty bound to do so.

The law of the forum state is applied to attorney-client privilege issues in diversity cases even if the contract between the parties designates the law of another state as applicable to the litigation of issues under the contract.

- *Abbott Labs. v. Alpha Therapeutic Corp.*, 200 F.R.D. 401 (N.D. Ill. 2001). Although the contract between the parties named California as the law that would govern the contract, the court stated that the rule that the law of the forum state of Illinois applied to privilege issues.

It is advisable to check whether the law of the state has codified privilege law because such a statutory scheme will have to be cited if privilege issues are litigated. Although most states rely on common law development of attorney/client privilege, some, Kansas and California, Texas, and New York prominently among them, have codified the privilege law. It is rare, however, that the codified law is markedly different from what prevails in the federal courts. In case after case, the courts state that the law of the state must be applied and then usually further conclude that there is no substantial difference.

- *Flint Hills Scientific, LLC v. Davidchack*, 2002 U.S. Dist. LEXIS 997, at *n.3 (D. Kan. Jan. 21, 2002). "Actually, there is no real conflict between federal and Kansas law regarding the attorney-client privilege. . . . The Kansas statute concerning the attorney-client privilege and its exceptions is typical of the laws of other jurisdictions." (Citations omitted.)

There are occasions, obviously, when the state law may vary from that of the federal privilege common law. Thus Texas law does not require that a lawyer be the author or recipient of a communication in order for it to be privileged. Communications between "representatives of the client" are also protected if they otherwise meet the requirements of Rule 503. *See* TEX. R. EVID. 503(b)(1)(D). A "representative" is any person: (1) who has authority to obtain professional legal services on behalf of the client; (2) who has authority to act on legal advice rendered to the client; or (3) who makes or receives a confidential communication while acting within the scope of the client's employment for the purpose of effectuating legal representation for the client. TEX. R. EVID. 503(a)(2)(A)-(B). *See also In re Monsanto Co.*, 998 S.W.2d 917 at 929 (Tex. App.—Waco 1999, no pet.). Federal common law may mirror this result to the extent that it allows communications between corporate agents regarding the legal advice given by an attorney to remain privileged.

Where there is no state privilege law applicable to a particular situation, the court generally will fall back upon applicable federal law as precedent.

- *Flint Hills Scientific, LLC v. Davidchack*, 2002 U.S. Dist. LEXIS 8472, at *30 (D. Kan. Mar. 21, 2002). State law was silent on an issue, so the court applied federal common law privilege principles.

- *Pritchard-Keang Nam Corp. v. Jaworski*, 751 F.2d 277 (8th Cir. 1984), *cert. dismissed*, 472 U.S. 1022 (1985). Because Missouri state courts had never addressed the choice of law with respect to attorney-client privileges, the Eighth Circuit applied Missouri case law holding that the law of the forum governs. The result was that federal privilege law applied.

In one instance the Ninth Circuit in rather surprising fashion and over a heated dissent refused to do just that, holding that where the state was silent as to whether the decedent's attorney-client privilege was not applicable in litigation among heirs, the silence would be construed as requiring no lifting of the privilege even though federal law would have dissolved the decedent's privilege. There is no doubt that given the vast body of law to the contrary, the Ninth Circuit was wrong and surprisingly so.

- *Restatement (Second) of Conflict of Laws at 139* dealing with privileged communications, provides that:

  (1) Evidence that is not privileged under the local law of the state which has the most significant relationship with the communication will be admitted, even though it would be privileged

under the local law of the forum, unless the admission of such evidence would be contrary to the strong public policy of the forum.

(2) Evidence that is privileged under the local law of the state which has the most significant relationship with the communication but which is not privileged under the local law of the forum will be admitted unless there is some special reason why the forum policy favoring admission should not be given effect.

3. Privilege Issues in Cases Where State and Federal Claims Are Intermixed

The circuits differ on what is to be done in the few cases where the law of privilege differs between the state and the federal common law rule in respect to the same item of evidence.

- *Jaffee v. Redmond*, 518 U.S. 1, 15 n.15 (1996). In cases in which the claim of privilege applies to evidence relevant to both a federal claim and a state claim, and a conflict exists between the applicable federal law of privilege and the applicable state law of privilege, the Supreme Court has noted without deciding "that there is disagreement concerning the proper rule" of decision in those cases.

But see:

Rep. No. 93-1277, at 19 n.17 (1974), *reprinted in* 1974 U.S.C.C.A.N. 7051, 7069 n.17. The Report notes on Federal Rule of Evidence 501 that when conflicting bodies of privilege law apply to the same piece of evidence, "the rule favoring reception of the evidence should be applied."

Most courts addressing the conflict between federal law applicable to a federal claim and to a differing law applicable to a pendent state claim have concluded that they would apply the federal law of privilege for both the federal and pendent state claims. To do otherwise would require determinations in respect to each evidentiary issue to determine as to which claim they were probative of and a further determination as to whether that item of evidence was discoverable and then admissible as to which of the two conjoined claims—a result which would be cumbersome.

- *von Bulow v. von Bulow*, 811 F.2d 136, 141 (2d Cir. 1987). The court cited the Senate Report to Rule 501 for the proposition that federal law dealing with work product was to apply to state pendent claims and then concluded: "The instant case is a federal question case by virtue of the RICO claim; and pendent state law claims arise in the case. Accordingly, we hold that the federal law of privilege controls the question whether the privileges asserted by [the third party witness] should be recognized."

- *Pinkard v. Johnson*, 118 F.R.D. 517, 519-20 (M.D. Ala. 1987). "Before determining whether Mr. Chandler is entitled to any privilege, the Court must decide whether federal or state law controls the Court's extension of First Amendment protection. In this case, the plaintiff has brought a federal claim based on Section 1983 and two state law claims based on pendent jurisdiction. n1 The evidence sought from Mr. Chandler is relevant to both federal and state claims. In such situations, courts have held consistently that the asserted privileges are governed by the principles of federal law.

  "This approach is consistent with the legislative history of *Federal Rule of Evidence 501*. The Senate Report which accompanied *Fed. R. Evid. 501* stated that "it is also intended that the federal law of privileges should be applied with respect to pendent state law claims when they arise in a federal question case." S. Rep. No. 1277, 93rd Congr., 2d Sess., *reprinted in* 1974 U.S. Code Cong. & Ad. News 7051, 7059 n.16." (Citations omitted.)

- *First Fed. Sav. & Loan v. Oppenheim, Appel, Dickson & Co.*, 110 F.R.D. 557, 560 (S.D.N.Y. 1986). "Although not explicitly addressed, the parties appear to concede the applicability of federal law, which they uniformly cite in their papers. This appears to be correct.

  "The pertinent choice-of-law rule is established by *Fed. R. Evid. 501*. It provides that privileges 'shall be governed by the principles of the common law as they may be interpreted by the courts of the United States in the light of reason and experience. . . .' except that, 'with respect to an element of a claim or defense as to which State law supplies the rule of decision, the privilege . . . shall be determined in accordance with State law.'

  "Although plaintiff asserts principally state law claims against OAD [defendant], the information at issue is also pertinent to the federal claims it asserts and to the third-party claims asserted by OAD based upon those federal claims. When evidence that is the subject of an asserted privilege is relevant to both federal and state law claims, the courts have consistently held that federal law governs the privilege." (Citations omitted.)

- *Sirmans v. City of South Miami*, 86 F.R.D. 492, 494-95 (S.D. Fla. 1980). "Thus Rule 501 differentiates between actions involving federal question jurisdiction and those where diversity jurisdiction applies. Since the information that is the subject of the instant motion is relevant for both the federal and the state claims the movant must rely upon a privilege developed by the federal courts and not state law privileges."

The Sixth and Eleventh Circuit Courts of Appeals have gone further, ruling that the federal law of privilege governs determination of all privilege issues raised in a federal question case which involves a pendent state law claims, even where a contrary state privilege law would otherwise apply.

- *Hancock v. Hobbs*, 967 F.2d 462 (11th Cir. 1992).

- *Hancock v. Dodson*, 958 F.2d 1367 (6th Cir. 1992).

The *Hancock* decisions have been expressly followed by certain district courts' opinions.

- *In re Combustion*, 161 F.R.D. 54 (W.D. La. 1995). The district court affirmed the Magistrate Judge's ruling that the federal law of privilege provides the rule of decision with respect to privilege issues affecting the discoverability of evidence in a federal question case involving pendent state law claims.

- *Puricelli v. Borough of Morrisville*, 136 F.R.D. 393, 396 (E.D. Pa. 1991) (same).

4. Comity of Law Principles in Foreign Law Context

When contested communications arise in the context of a foreign patent proceeding, principles of comity will often cause the courts of this country to apply the law of the foreign jurisdiction in order to resolve privilege questions. Moreover, courts follow a traditional "contacts" analysis in determining which law will apply. The analysis becomes quite complex—hardly surprising when a conflicts of law analysis is at issue.

- *Johnson Matthey, Inc. v. Research Corp.*, 2002 U.S. Dist. LEXIS 13560 (S.D.N.Y. July 23, 2002), *recons. granted in part, denied in part*, 2002 U.S. Dist. LEXIS 18802 (S.D.N.Y. Oct. 3, 2002). In assessing the potential availability of foreign privilege law governing communications with patent agents, the court engaged in a form of traditional choice of law "contacts" analysis and looked to whether the client was domestic or foreign, and whether the foreign patent agent was working on foreign patent matters or assisting in efforts to obtain a United States patent. The court therefore concluded that to the extent that documents involved royalty payments, they were governed by New York law and did have to be disclosed. But to the extent that the documents involved the British proceeding, they did not have to be disclosed, because English law extends the privilege to patent agents in much the same way we do to attorneys.

A more curious case is one where the court concluded that foreign law was applicable only if it mirrored U.S. law. Although the holding seems bizarre, when one looks at the context, it becomes more comprehensible. The party seeking disclosure of privileged materials argued that under Argentine law, if an attorney engages in a conflict of interest, he is engaging in a criminal act and thus, under the U.S. crime/fraud exception, any privilege that attached to the representation did not hold. It is not surprising that the court held that the attempt was a bootstrap type of logic, which it was not about to endorse. Nonetheless, the *ratio dicendi* is surprising and may well be broader than necessary.

- *Madanes v. Madanes*, 199 F.R.D. 135, 148 (S.D.N.Y. 2001). "The threshold question in this case is whether the criminal law of Argentina should be incorporated in a crime-fraud analysis under the federal common law of privilege. If the crime-fraud exception were based on the client's expectation of confidentiality, then foreign law would be critical because whatever undermines that expectation would likewise undercut the attorney-client privilege. However, the basis for the crime-fraud exception is not any diminished expectation of confidentiality, but rather the overarching public policy principle that a court will not enforce privilege where to do so would facilitate a crime. . . . Viewed in this light, the exception is forum-specific since what constitutes a crime will vary from one jurisdiction to the next. Accordingly, foreign criminal law should be recognized for purposes of federal common law crime-fraud analysis only when it has an analogue in American jurisprudence. In this case, there is no American equivalent to the Argentine statutes that impose criminal liability for an attorney divulging client confidences or accepting an engagement that creates a conflict of interest. Hence, the 'crime' prong of the crime-fraud exception does not apply."

Conflicts of law issues in the context of attorney-client privilege issues seem to arise with greatest frequency in the patent law context.

5. Privilege Issues in Patent Cases

In the patent area, questions of choice of law take on an added complexity. The reason is that for substantive areas of patent law, the law is established by the Federal Circuit, but for procedural issues—and privilege law is considered to be such—the law of the regional circuit applies. What has resulted is somewhat of a shambles where predictability has flown out of the window. This is particularly the case in the realm of advice of counsel, which is raised so frequently as a defense to a claim of willful infringement. The question then arises as to the extent of the waiver and how far it reaches, which is left to regional law. The consequences of this are discussed at some length in the Section on Waiver Arising from Affirmative Reliance, *infra*.

Basically, the Federal Circuit has said that issues of privilege and privilege waiver are not substantive but procedural and thus the law of the regional circuit applies even in patent cases. Thus, in the patent area litigants cannot argue that some particular assertion of the attorney-client privilege implicates the substantive patent law. Unfortunately what that means is that for consistency across the spectrum of cases consistency within the confines of patent law is thereby abandoned.

What scope of waiver is implicated by asserting an advice of counsel defense to willful infringement thus differs from one circuit to the next.

- *Fort James Corp. v. Solo Cup Co.*, 412 F.3d 1340, 1346 (Fed. Cir. 2005), *reh'g denied*, 2005 U.S. App. LEXIS 20077 (Fed. Cir. Sept. 1, 2005), *cert. denied*, 126 Sup. Ct. 1768 (2006). The Court held that the Federal Circuit "applies the law of the regional circuit . . . with respect to questions of attorney-client privilege and waiver of attorney-client privilege." It accordingly applied the law of the Seventh Circuit.

- *Martin Marietta Materials, Inc. v. Bedford Reinforced Plastics, Inc.*, 227 F.R.D. 382, 391-92 (W.D. Pa. 2005). "Based upon consideration of the positions of the parties, the above-cited relevant case law, and the facts of the case *sub judice*, the Court determines that Bedford's allegation of inequitable conduct and the possible waiver of Plaintiff's attorney-client privilege thereto implicates a substantive patent law issue. Specifically, Bedford claims that the Patents-in-Suit are unenforceable based upon the Plaintiff's failure to disclose material prior art to the United States Patent and Trademark Office. Clearly, the question of possible patent protection and whether a patent is enforceable implicates the jurisprudential responsibilities of the Federal Circuit Court. Accordingly, the Court determines, based upon the patent law issues raised by the parties in the case *sub judice*, that Federal Circuit law applies to Plaintiff's alleged waiver of attorney-client privilege and work-product doctrine."

- *Schofield v. United States Steel Corp.*, 2005 U.S. Dist. LEXIS 30471 (N.D. Ind. Nov. 28, 2005). Seventh Circuit law applied to determine scope of waiver in a patent case when an attorney testified as to privileged matters to rebut defendant's defense of inequitable conduct on the part of plaintiff.

- *Simmons, Inc. v. Bombardier, Inc.*, 221 F.R.D. 4, 9 n.5 (D.D.C. 2004). The court said that "discovery disputes and other procedural issues *unique to patent cases* should be decided pursuant to the law of the Federal Circuit, as opposed to the regional circuit."

- *Rhodia Chimie v. PPG Indus., Inc.*, 218 F.R.D. 416, 419 n.4 (D. Del. 2003). The district court determined that "the better reasoned approach recognizes that questions of waiver are not unique to patent law and are a matter of either state law, as to claims and defenses that arise under state law, or precedent from regional circuits."

- *GFI, Inc. v. Franklin Corp.*, 265 F.3d 1268, 1272 (Fed. Cir. 2001), *reh'g denied*, 2002 U.S. App. LEXIS 13352 (Fed. Cir. June 8, 2002), *cert. denied*, 537 U.S. 1046 (2002). The Federal Circuit said as follows: "We apply regional circuit law to procedural questions that are not themselves substantive patent law issues so long as they do not (1) pertain to patent law, . . ."

- *Flex-Foot, Inc. v. CRP, Inc.*, 238 F.3d 1362, 1365 (Fed. Cir. 2001). "We will apply our own law to both substantive and procedural issues 'intimately involved in the substance of enforcement of the patent right' (citation omitted), (2) bear an essential relationship to matters committed to our exclusive control by statute, or (3) clearly implicate the jurisprudential responsibilities of this court in a field within its exclusive jurisdiction. Because waiver by the disclosure of privileged material does not meet any of these criteria, we apply the law of the Fifth Circuit to our review of the district court's judgment." (Citation omitted.)

- *Midwest Indus., Inc. v. Karavan Trailers, Inc.*, 175 F.3d 1356, 1359 (Fed. Cir.) (*en banc* in relevant part), *cert. denied*, 528 U.S. 1019 (1999). Same.

- *In re Spalding Sports Worldwide, Inc.*, 203 F.3d 800, 804 (Fed. Cir. 2000). The court said: "a procedural issue that is not itself a substantive patent law issue is nonetheless governed by Federal Circuit law if the issue pertains to patent law, if it bears an essential relationship to matters committed to our exclusive [jurisdiction] by statute, or if it clearly implicates the jurisprudential responsibilities of this court in a field within its exclusive jurisdiction." Accordingly, the Federal Circuit determined that whether Spalding's invention record was protected by the attorney-client privilege was "unique to patent law because the invention record relates to an invention submitted for consideration for possible patent protection . . . clearly implicating substantive patent law." Accordingly, the Federal Circuit Court concluded that Federal Circuit law applied to the issue of whether the attorney-client privilege applies to an invention record prepared and submitted to house counsel relating to a litigated patent claim.

- *Midwest Indus., Inc. v. Karavan Trailers, Inc.*, 175 F.3d 1356, 1359 (Fed. Cir.), *cert. denied*, 528 U.S. 1019 (1999). The court concluded that whether the invention record is protected by the attorney-client privilege is unique to patent law because the invention record relates to an invention submitted for consideration for possible patent protection.

- *In re Regents of the Univ. of Cal.*, 101 F.3d 1386 (Fed. Cir. 1996), *cert. denied*, 520 U.S. 1193 (1997). The court applied the law of the regional circuit because the issue in that case, whether a licensor and a licensee are joint clients for purposes of privilege under the community of interest doctrine, was not unique to patent law.

When foreign law is implicated in patent cases, the working standard is:

> Any communications touching base with the United States will be governed by the federal discovery rules while any communications related to matters solely involving [a foreign country] will be governed by the applicable foreign statute.

Communications by a foreign client with foreign patent agents relating to assistance in prosecuting patent applications in the United States are governed by American privilege law.

Communications relating to assistance in prosecuting patent applications in a foreign country or rendering legal advice on the patent law of a foreign country are, as a matter of comity, governed by the privilege law of the foreign country in which the patent application is filed, even if the client is a party to an American lawsuit.

The leading case in this regard may well be:

- *Golden Trade v. Lee Apparel Co.*, 143 F.R.D. 514, 518-19 (S.D.N.Y. 1992). The court adopted the comity or "touching base" approach and applied a traditional choice-of-law "contacts" analysis to determine the law that applies to claims of privilege involving foreign documents.

On occasion, courts have extended privilege and work-product protection even if the foreign forum would not have on the grounds that not to do so would offend our own sense of litigation proprieties.

- *Astra Aktiebolag v. Andrx Pharms., Inc.*, 208 F.R.D. 92, 103 (S.D.N.Y. 2002). "Further, ordering discovery without any protection also offends the public policy of this forum, which promotes full discovery but, at the same time, prevents disclosure of privileged documents. If the court were to rule without taking Korea's discovery practices into account, the court would be required to order complete disclosure of all of the Korean documents, many of which would be protected under either the attorney-client privilege or work-product doctrine as applied in this jurisdiction. . . . [A]pplication of foreign privilege law in this case would require disclosure of many documents (1) that are protected from disclosure under American law and (2) that would not be discoverable under Korean law. Therefore, the court will apply its own privilege law to the Korean documents, even though the communications do not 'touch base' with the United States."

6. Privilege Issues in Bankruptcy Context

Federal law governs privilege issues in the bankruptcy proceeding. However, the specific privilege law of a state may govern claims brought in the form of an adversary petition within the bankruptcy proceeding.

- *In re Tippy Togs of Miami, Inc.*, 327 B.R. 236, 237 (Bankr. S.D. Fla. 1999). "This contested matter arises in the bankruptcy case, not in any adversary proceeding involving state law claims or defenses. Therefore, federal law applies to the privilege issue before the Court."

C. *Raising and Demonstrating Each Element of the Privilege*

The existence of the attorney-client relationship does not automatically shroud a communication in the privilege and preclude disclosure. The privilege must:

> Be raised explicitly and claimed specifically with respect to a particular communication;

Be raised in a timely fashion;

Be predicated on a demonstration that each basic element giving rise to the privilege is present.

- *Zenith Radio Corp. v. Radio Corp. of Am.*, 121 F. Supp. 792, 795 (D. Del. 1954). In patent litigation on application for a pretrial order requiring the production of certain documents, the court stated that first, "[o]f course, the privilege must be claimed—it is here."
- *United States v. United Shoe Mach. Corp.*, 89 F. Supp. 357, 359 (D. Mass. 1950). In upholding in part a claim of privilege, the court began its analysis with the observation that "[t]he defendant reasonably claimed whatever privilege it had."

In current practice, the privilege is raised in response to a document request and a privilege log is today appended listing each document in respect to which privilege is claimed and detailing why the claim is supportable. *See* Part III, Section on "Privilege Logs," *infra*.

In the context of a deposition, the claim of privilege is generally raised by a question-by-question objection on privilege grounds or by a blanket objection as to a particular conversation with an attorney. Most frequently, the party seeking discovery will then bring a motion seeking to compel answers to the questions. If the claim of privilege is not sustained, the court may order a renewed deposition on the questions or issues with respect to which a claim of privilege was asserted. The deposition may be taken telephonically to spare the parties and/or deponent the costs of additional travel, or on the grounds of convenience. Occasionally, a court will make itself available for telephonic rulings.

In an adjudicatory proceeding, a question that seeks to elicit communications which are privilege protected must also be raised. In that context a court or adjudicatory tribunal will rule *instanter*.

But one thing that one can not do is raise no objection and hope that by remaining silent, the privilege will not be held to have been waived.

- *Asset Value Fund L.P. v. Care Group*, 1997 U.S. Dist. LEXIS 17968 (S.D.N.Y. Nov. 12, 1997). A limited telephonic deposition of a chief financial officer who had asserted the privilege on a securities registration issue was allowed.

A party asserting the privilege has the burden of affirmatively raising the privilege and also the burden of proof.

It is not sufficient to show only that an attorney-client relationship existed. Rather, the proponent of the privilege must show that the privilege applies to the specific communications whose disclosure is sought.

- *United States v. Goldfarb*, 328 F.2d 280, 281–82 (6th Cir.), *cert. denied*, 377 U.S. 976 (1964). The attorney-client relationship does not create an automatic "cloak of protection . . . draped around all occurrences and conversations which have any bearing, direct or indirect, upon the relationship of the attorney with his client."

- *United States v. Osborn*, 561 F.2d 1334 (9th Cir. 1977). When proponents of the privilege failed to meet their burden of establishing the existence of the attorney-client relationship with respect to specific categories of documents transmitted to the attorney by a client in the context of an attorney-client relationship, the assertion of the privilege was not sustained with respect to those categories of documents.

Mere assertion of the privilege, without the affirmative showing by a proponent of the privilege that each of the requisite elements for its assertion is present, will not suffice to sustain the privilege.

- *In re Bonanno*, 344 F.2d 830, 833 (2d Cir. 1965). "That burden is not, of course, discharged by mere conclusory or *ipse dixit* assertions, for any such rule would foreclose meaningful inquiry into the existence of the relationship, and any spurious claims could never be exposed."

Second, the privilege must be asserted against giving particular testimony or producing particular documents; ordinarily, it may not be raised against testifying generally or against the production of documents in general.

- *In re Walsh*, 623 F.2d 489, 493 (7th Cir.), *cert. denied*, 449 U.S. 994 (1980). The court of appeals reversed an order quashing grand jury subpoenas directing an attorney to testify in an investigation of the disappearance, under suspicious circumstances, of a former client. The court's rationale was that the privilege could not be invoked globally. Whatever privilege existed would have to be expressly asserted in response to each question.

- *Shiner v. American Stock Exch.*, 28 F.R.D. 34 (S.D.N.Y. 1961). A motion to vacate a notice of deposition because of the attorney-client privilege was premature. The court stated that the privilege should be asserted when specific questions were put to the witness during the deposition.

The privilege must be timely raised, i.e., before any disclosure of the communication is made. If the privilege is not raised to limit disclosure during discovery or the taking of depositions, it usually cannot be asserted subsequently at trial. Thus, it is generally advisable to lay a full basis for the claim of privilege—or to contest its existence—at the deposition.

Similarly, if prompt objection is not made to testimony that would disclose privileged communications, the privilege cannot be raised at a subsequent stage of the proceedings. Once confidentiality is breached by disclosure, there is nothing left for the privilege to protect.

- *United States v. Gurtner*, 474 F.2d 297, 299 (9th Cir. 1973). "[T]he failure to assert the privilege when the evidence was first presented constituted a voluntary waiver of the right. . . . Once the subject matter is disclosed by a knowing failure to object there is nothing left to protect from disclosure."

Each element of the privilege must be demonstrated. Blanket assertions are insufficient. The facts establishing the privilege may be raised by affidavit or in an evidentiary hearing. In the course of a deposition, it may be advisable to lay the basis of the privilege claim or objection during voir dire of one's own client if necessary and if the interrogator fails to do so.

- *People's Bank of Buffalo v. Brown*, 112 F. 652, 654 (3d Cir. 1902). "Therefore it is requisite that in every instance it shall be judicially determined whether the particular communication in question be really privileged, and, in order that such primary determination may be advisedly made, it is indispensable that the court shall be apprised, through preliminary inquiry, of the characterizing circumstances. There is no presumption of privilege, and though its allowance may, in a clear case, be founded upon the voluntary statement of the attorney that his knowledge of the fact to which he is asked to testify was acquired in professional confidence, yet, wherever, as in this case, the circumstances suggest that the sufficiency of the grounds of that statement should be considered, it is the right of the opposing party to demand that the proponent of the privilege shall be submitted to such interrogation as may be necessary to test its validity."

Finally, the question arises of how this is to be done. In present practice the preparation of a document log identifying the elements of the privilege is the *sina qua non* of any hope of establishing privilege protection for documents.[2] Often supporting affidavits will also be advisable although they have not yet become indispensable as have privilege logs.

- *In re John Doe Corp.*, 675 F.2d 482 (2d Cir. 1982). The trial court had held that a submission by way of affidavit, rather than live witnesses, to support a claim of attorney-client privilege was not sufficient when the issue was whether a payment had been made to a lawyer to effect a bribe of a public official. Thereafter, one witness took the stand only to assert a Fifth Amendment privilege, while another affirmed the submitted affidavit.

When a blanket assertion of privilege is raised in a deposition a motion by the proponent of the privilege to supplement the record and thereby to establish the scope of the privilege claimed and to lay

---

2. Believe it or not, at the time that this book first appeared in 1979, privilege logs were not yet in the least common. How did we manage without them? But then privilege claims were far less frivolously made. The innumerable exceptions had not yet evolved. Some practitioners, however, claim that it is extraordinarily costly to prepare privilege logs and then no one looks at them.

a proper predicate for the assertion thereof may be allowed by the court.

- *Savoy v. Richard A. Carrier Trucking, Inc.*, 178 F.R.D. 346 (D. Mass. 1998). The attorney objected on privilege and work-product grounds to questions posed of his client as to why the client would not submit to an independent medical examination. The predicate for the assertion of the privilege was not properly laid in follow-up questions. Accordingly, on a motion to compel answers, the court permitted the party asserting the privilege to hone both the basis of the privilege and its scope.

D. *Sustaining Burden of Proof*

1. No Blanket Assertions of Privilege or Protection

Blanket assertions of the attorney-client privilege or of the work-product protection are frowned on and will not be sustained. The burden of proof as to each requisite element of the privilege or the protection is on the proponent of the privilege or protection.

Conclusory assertions of privilege in a document log will generally not pass muster.

- *In re Search Warrant Executed at Law Offices of Stephen Garea*, 1999 U.S. App. LEXIS 3861 (6th Cir. Mar. 5, 1999) ((cite per Sixth Cir. Rules)"). "Many entries in the log were, at best, [c]onclusory. For instance, with respect to the letter from the Office of Tourism alluded to above, the log simply reads, "Third party document . . . by client to counsel for legal advice." Yet, the contents of the document do not necessarily support a conclusion that it was transmitted in order to secure legal advice. It is devoid of any annotation requesting legal counsel and the privilege log does not point to any related document that would lead one to conclude that the client sought legal, rather than business, advice. In our view, a person seeking to assert the attorney-client privilege must make a minimal showing that the communication involved legal matters. This showing is not onerous and may be satisfied by as little as a statement in the privilege log explaining the nature of the legal issue for which advice was sought. However, the [c]onclusory statements contained in the log before us do not satisfy even this minimal requirement."

- *United States v. Constr. Prods. Research, Inc.*, 73 F.3d 464, 473 (2d Cir.), *cert. denied*, 519 U.S. 927 (1996). "If the party invoking the privilege does not provide sufficient detail to demonstrate fulfillment of the legal requirements for application of the privilege, his claim will be rejected."

- *United States v. White*, 970 F.2d 328, 334 (7th Cir. 1992). "A blanket claim of privilege which does not specify what information is protected will not suffice."

- *United States v. First State Bank*, 691 F.2d 332, 335 (7th Cir. 1982). "A taxpayer need not reveal so many facts that the privilege becomes worthless but he must at least identify the general nature of the document, the specific privilege he is claiming for that document, and facts which establish all the elements of the privilege he is claiming."

- *United States v. Davis*, 636 F.2d 1028, 1044, n.20 (5th Cir.), *cert. denied*, 454 U.S. 862 (1981). The Fifth Circuit warned that in future cases failure to demonstrate how any specific document came within the compass of the privilege would be fatal to the successful assertion of the privilege. In this instance, a showing was to be permitted on remand.

When it is not possible to determine from the face of a document or a tape recording that it is submitted to counsel for the purpose of seeking legal advice, the mere assertion that such is the case will rarely suffice. An affidavit to that effect will be necessary.

- *Ralls v. United States*, 52 F.3d 223, 225 (9th Cir. 1995). "A party asserting the attorney-client privilege has the burden of establishing the relationship and the privileged nature of the communication."

- *Large v. Our Lady of Mercy Med. Ctr.*, 1998 U.S. Dist. LEXIS 1702 (S.D.N.Y. Feb. 17, 1998). When nothing other than a client and attorney's assertion identified a tape recording made by a client as done for the purpose of communicating information to an attorney to seek legal advice, the court refused to find that to be the case.

- *ERA Franchise Sys. v. Northern Ins. Co.*, 183 F.R.D. 276 (D. Kan. 1998). Parties objecting to discovery on the basis of the attorney-client privilege bear the burden of establishing that the privilege applies.

- *Boyer v. Board of County Comm'rs*, 162 F.R.D. 687, 688 (D. Kan. 1995). They must make a "clear showing" that the asserted objection applies.

- *Union Fire Ins. Co. v. Midland Bancor, Inc.*, 159 F.R.D. 562, 567 (D. Kan. 1994). They must provide sufficient information to enable the court to determine whether each element of the asserted privilege is satisfied.

- *Jones v. Boeing Co.*, 163 F.R.D. 15, 17 (D. Kan. 1995). A claim of privilege fails upon a failure of proof as to any element. A "blanket claim" as to the applicability of a privilege does not satisfy the burden of proof.

- *Kelling v. Bridgestone/Firestone, Inc.*, 157 F.R.D. 496, 497 (D. Kan. 1994). Counsel objected to the production and use of bank records on a disqualification motion on vague "privilege" or "confidential grounds." "Plaintiff, beyond making a blanket claim of privilege or confidentiality, has failed to demonstrate how each element of the privilege is satisfied. Blanket claims of privilege or confidentiality are clearly insufficient to protect materials from disclosure."

- *United States v. White*, 970 F.2d 328, 334 (7th Cir. 1992). "A blanket claim of privilege which does not specify what information is protected will not suffice."

To sustain a privilege, it is essential not only that it be raised with specificity, but also that it be raised document by document with sufficient identification being provided in any privilege log so that a court can readily test the validity of the assertion.

- *CSX Transp., Inc. v. Admiral Ins. Co.*, 1995 U.S. Dist. LEXIS 22359, 1995 WL 855421, at *3 (M.D. Fla. July 20, 1995). The standard for testing the adequacy of the privilege log is whether, as to each document, it sets forth specific facts that, if credited, would suffice to establish each element of the privilege or immunity that is claimed. The focus is on the specific descriptive portion of the log, and not on the conclusory invocations of the privilege or work-product rule, since the burden of the party withholding documents cannot be "discharged by mere conclusory or *ipse dixit* assertions" (quoting *Golden Trade v. Lee Apparel Co.*, 1992 U.S.

Dist. LEXIS 17739, at *12–13 (S.D.N.Y. 1992)) (further citations omitted).

■ *United States v. Rockwell Int'l*, 897 F.2d 1255 (3d Cir. 1990). A blanket assertion of the privilege was not permissible. The privilege would have to be asserted document by document.

Absent such identifying indicia, courts will order documents produced, often without bothering to review the disputed document. If a party does not sufficiently value the privilege to prove it, why should a court bother to sustain the assertion of the privilege? Despite this basic requirement, it never ceases to amaze how many lawyers do not seem to know the basic minimum required both to raise and to sustain an assertion of privilege or work product protection.

■ *Beasley v. First Am. Real Estate Info. Servs., Inc.*, 2005 U.S. Dist. LEXIS 34030, at *9 (N.D. Tex. Apr. 27, 2005). "Here, defendant alleges that 'the items identified as withheld on Defendant's First Amended Privilege Log are all items that were prepared in anticipation of litigation and would not have been prepared in such form but for the prospect of litigation.' However, absolutely no evidence is offered to substantiate this conclusory assertion. In particular, defendant wholly fails to prove that the 'primary motivating purpose' behind the creation of the e-mails, memos, and notes at issue was to aid in possible future litigation. Nor has defendant tendered the documents to the court for review. Without such evidence, defendant cannot establish that these items are entitled to work product protection." (Citations omitted.)

Obviously, counsel had no idea that any affidavit needed to be submitted to demonstrate the validity of the work product assertion.

Belatedly trying to bootstrap privilege/protection claims that were inadequately asserted in initial discovery responses is very likely to prove fatal to those claims.

■ *NextG Networks of NY, Inc. v. City of New York*, 2005 U.S. Dist. LEXIS 6381 (S.D.N.Y. Apr. 13, 2005). The City had based its privilege arguments exclusively on a privilege log it had belatedly filed. It submitted no affidavit explaining the context in which any of the communications were made. In some instances neither the author nor the recipient of the supposedly privileged document was identified except by name, making it impossible to determine whether either was an attorney. Even where a communication was identified as having involved a lawyer, there was no evidence presented that it was created for the purpose of providing or obtaining legal rather than business advice, or that it was intended to remain confidential, or that the privilege has not been waived. Accordingly, the court decided that neither the privilege nor the work-product protection had been properly asserted. However, the court did not allow any sanctions (costs, attorney's fees) because opponents of privilege would have had to litigate its availability had the City properly asserted them.

- *Navigant Consulting, Inc. v. Wilkinson*, 220 F.R.D. 467, 474 (N.D. Tex. 2004). The party asserting privileges failed to get it right even with a third amended privilege log, merely asserting privilege in respect to any document that was sent from or to attorneys when an investigation was contemplated. The court's frustration comes through loud and clear. "Stymied by this evidence, the court ordered NCI to produce the challenged documents for *in camera* review. The court has now labored through more than 550 pages of documents in an attempt to glean information that might shed additional light on the privilege issues raised by the instant motion. However, in most instances, the court has been left to speculation and guess-work in interpreting the documents."

- *Christman v. Brauvin Realty Advisors, Inc.*, 185 F.R.D. 251 (N.D. Ill. 1999). "To establish the protection of the attorney-client privilege, descriptions of privileged documents must contain sufficient information for the Court to ascertain the content of the documents. Many of the descriptions in the McDermott and Shefsky privilege logs are too vague to do so. For example, several McDermott documents are described as 'fax cover sheet with note.' Likewise, a letter with handwritten notes from McDermott attorney Ellen Kollar, which does not state to whom it is to or from, is too vague for the objecting parties to satisfy their burden of establishing the attorney-client privilege."

- *ConAgra, Inc. v. Arkwright Mut. Ins. Co.*, 32 F. Supp. 2d 1015 (N.D. Ill. 1999). Conclusory allegations of privilege are insufficient to carry the burden of proof.

- *Doebele v. Sprint Corp.*, 2002 U.S. Dist. LEXIS 1001, at *12 (D. Kan. Jan. 21, 2002). "[T]he Court finds Plaintiff's broad and sweeping claim that the portions of the tapes at issue were prepared in anticipation of litigation fails to meet the burden imposed upon her to establish that fact. Because the privilege log provided by Plaintiff fails to set forth the dates of any of the tape recordings or the names of most of the Sprint employees whose voices are on the tape, the Court is unable to make a determination regarding whether Plaintiff, at the time the tapes were recorded, merely assembled the tapes in the ordinary course of personal business and/or believed there was a 'likely chance of litigation' or whether, at the time the tapes were recorded, 'the threat of litigation' was 'real and imminent.'" Accordingly, the motion for an order of protection in respect to the documents was denied.

Thus a general assertion in response to interrogatories that certain matters are privileged can be considered inadequate with the attendant result that amendment is not a remedy but waiver is.

- *Grill v. Costco Wholesale Corp.*, 2004 U.S. Dist. LEXIS 21400, at *3–4 (W.D. Wa. Oct. 8, 2004). "The Court now finds that plaintiff waived her objections by failing to specifically raise it at the time she answered her interrogatories. Interestingly, plaintiffs counsel does not claim that the failure to disclose the documents was inadvertent or a genuine mistake. Instead, he asserts that the general objection to the production of privileged documents was sufficient. The Court is not persuaded."

The question has arisen: When a detailed privilege log has been provided and only certain but not all requisite elements of the privilege are challenged, must the privilege holder then proceed to prove each element of the privilege, even those not challenged? It is a silly question. Current legal practice has more than its sufficient share of wheel-spinning as it is. Does it really need saying: only the aspect of the privilege that is cast into doubt must then be sustained, by affidavit or other evidentiary proof.

- *ECDC Envtl,. L.C. v. New York Marine & Gen. Ins. Co.*, 1998 U.S. Dist. LEXIS 8808, 1998 WL 614478, at *3–4 (S.D.N.Y. June 4,

1998): "Although it is clear that the proponent of the privilege ultimately bears the burden of proving all essential facts necessary to sustain a claim of privilege, the law is not entirely clear as to how this burden may be discharged where, as here, the proponent has served a detailed index of documents withheld, and the challenger has submitted specific challenges. Apart from the specific challenges made in its motion, defendant does not generally challenge the adequacy of plaintiff's index.

Under these circumstances, it appears that the proponent of the privilege may satisfy its burden by submitting evidentiary material as to the challenged elements only. Requiring the proponent to submit evidentiary material to prove all elements of the privilege in response to a specific challenge unduly burdens and wastes the time of both the Court and the parties. A party asserting a claim of privilege is obligated to prepare an index of withheld documents, which must provide sufficient information "to assess the applicability of the privilege or protection." Fed.R.Civ.P. 26(b)(5). Thus, a party challenging an assertion of privilege is given the information necessary to state the grounds of its challenge and is not left to guess at the nature of what's being withheld and why. Since the challenger is given this information, there is no logic or efficiency in requiring the proponent of a privilege or the Court to address matters which are not contested by the challenger."

- *Kiobel v. Royal Dutch Petroleum Co.*, 2005 U.S. Dist. LEXIS 16514, at *13 (S.D.N.Y. Aug. 3, 2005). "[T]the withholding party's initial obligation is to prepare an index of withheld documents providing the specific information required by *Fed.R.Civ.P. 26(b)(5)* and Local Civil *Rule 26.2.*" If the assertions of privilege are not challenged, the withholding party has no further obligation with respect to its assertions of privilege. If the assertions of privilege are challenged and the dispute cannot be resolved informally, the withholding party then has to submit evidence, by way of affidavit, deposition testimony or otherwise, establishing only the challenged elements of the applicable privilege or protection, with the ultimate burden of proof resting with the party asserting the privilege or protection.

2. Raising Privilege or Protection

When privilege or protection is asserted in the context of a deposition or written interrogatories, each must and should be asserted question-by-question.

Whether with respect to documents sought in discovery or in depositions, neither the attorney-client privilege nor the work-product protection can be globally asserted.

Of course, in practice, assertion of privilege and protection is usually asserted with respect to entire areas of inquiry. Should judicial intervention become necessary, however, the assertion is not likely to withstand judicial scrutiny or be affirmed when globally asserted.

- *United States v. White*, 970 F.2d 328, 334 (7th Cir. 1992). "[T]he privilege must be made [sic] and sustained on a document-by-document basis. A blanket claim of privilege that does not specify what information is protected will not suffice."

- *Matter of Feldberg*, 862 F.2d 622, 628–29 (7th Cir. 1988). Questions before a grand jury relating to a lawyer's production of documents must be answered. Those questions that go to legal advice given need not be answered, unless the crime/fraud exception applies.

While many courts require that any privilege be expressly raised, others will occasionally, *sua sponte*, raise an alternative ground, such as work product, to protect a document from compelled disclosure even if the litigant does not. Obviously, however, it is more prudent not to rely on such assistance from the court, since most will consider any grounds not expressly raised as waived.

- *IBJ Whitehall Bank & Trust Co. v. Cory & Assocs.*, 1999 U.S. Dist. LEXIS 12440 (N.D. Ill. Aug. 10, 1999). "Plaintiff does not assert the work product privilege for this document. Plaintiff has, however, met its burden of proof by submitting the documents for an *in camera* review. While some courts may be inclined to reject any privilege that plaintiff fails to assert, we decline to do so here."

In diversity cases, the burden of proof is placed on the party asserting the privilege. Some state courts, however, shift the burden of proof and require the party seeking discovery to assume the burden of showing that the privilege is not applicable.

- *DiPalma v. Medical Mavin, Ltd.*, 1998 U.S. Dist. LEXIS 1747 (E.D. Pa. Feb. 10, 1998). Under Pennsylvania law, the party seeking disclosure of attorney-client communications bears the burden of showing that the communications are not protected. *See Cedrone v. Unity Sav. Ass'n*, 103 F.R.D. 423, 427 (E.D. Pa. 1984); *Estate of Kofsky*, 487 Pa. 473, 482–83, 409 A.2d 1358, 1362–63 (Pa. 1985).

Where one party asserts the privilege and the other seems in every way to acquiesce in such assertion, it should not be permitted to thereafter argue that an implied waiver has nonetheless occurred.

- *XYZ Corp. v. United States*, 348 F.3d 16, 30-31 (1st Cir. 2003). In making a proffer to ward off indictment, a party revealed the tape of telephone conversation between joint venturers, with counsel for one party present. The tape recording discussed pulling a problematic medical device from the market. No claim of privilege was made in respect to the tape disclosed. Nonetheless, the disclosing party repeatedly asserted privilege in respect to other conversations. The Second Circuit held that the government may not seem to acquiesce in such assertions of privilege and thereafter claim that the disclosure of a non-privileged communication constituted an implied waiver as to all other privileged ones. "In a perfect world, of course, XYZ would have secured a written acknowledgment of its privilege reservation in advance of each and every disclosure. But XYZ did secure one such written acknowledgment, and its failure to do so on subsequent occasions is clearly outweighed by two facts: (i) it repeatedly set forth its position, and (ii) the government failed to question the privilege reservation in a timely manner. Under the circumstances of this case, we find that the proffers were made in the course of ongoing plea negotiations; that XYZ explicitly reserved all claims of attorney-client privilege with respect thereto; that the government effectively acquiesced in these reservations; and that the government is bound by them. Consequently, XYZ reserved the attorney-client privilege by means of its pre-indictment presentations."

Because the burden of proof is on the proponent of the privilege, it is reversible error for a trial court to shift that burden on the opponent.

- *Hawkins v. Stables*, 148 F.3d 379, 381, 384 (4th Cir. 1998). "The law of attorney-client privilege places the burden of proof on the proponent of the privilege. The district court [in the course of a bench trial], however, assumed that the privilege applied and placed the burden of proof on the opponent of the privilege. Because the proponent of the privilege, Stables, testified under oath that no confidential communication had occurred [with her former divorce attorney], it is impossible for her to meet the burden of proof. We, therefore, reverse the decision of the district court and remand for further proceedings consistent with this opinion." The matter arose at trial where the proponent's former divorce attorney refused to answer a question regarding his client's veracity in her prior deposition testimony on the ground that it would violate his ethical duty to his client to maintain her confidences. The opponent of the privilege argued that the privilege had been waived in the course of the deposition when the deponent had testified that no conversations on the subject occurred with her divorce attorney.

  "Although the question asked during the deposition clearly elicited information regarding confidential communications Stables may have had with Diehl, and was objectionable on its face on the ground of attorney-client privilege, neither Stables nor her attorney asserted an objection. In response to the question, Stables simply stated that she never had a discussion of the matter with her attorney. By answering the question as she did, Stables both waived her privilege and provided probative evidence that she had had no conversation with her attorney on the subject of a phone tap. Without a communication, there is nothing to which the privilege can attach. Based on her own testimony, Stables cannot meet her burden of proof."

How extensive is the burden of proof? Generally, the proponent of the privilege must prove each and every element of the privilege. As a practical matter, creation of a document index and submission of requisite affidavits to support certain statements asserting the privilege, which may not be self-evident from the index, generally are sufficient unless challenged on some particular basis.

- *Mount Vernon Fire Ins. Co. v. Try 3 Bldg. Servs.*, 1998 U.S. Dist. LEXIS 16183, at *12–13 (S.D.N.Y. Oct. 14, 1998). "Apart from their specific challenges, [defendants] do not generally challenge the adequacy of plaintiff's index. Under these circumstances, it appears that the party asserting either the attorney-client privilege or work-product protection may satisfy its burden by submitting evidentiary material as to the challenged elements only. Requiring the proponent to submit evidentiary material to prove all elements of the privilege in response to a specific challenge unduly burdens and wastes the time of both the Court and the parties."

The burden is ordinarily on the party claiming the privilege to state specifically and establish to the court's satisfaction the facts supporting each of the requisite elements.

- *FTC v. Lukens Steel Co.*, 444 F. Supp. 803, 806 (D.D.C. 1977). The court held that the burden of establishing confidentiality as an essential element of the attorney-client privilege had been met by the proponents of the privilege upon a showing to whom the documents in question had been distributed. "The party seeking the benefit of the privilege has the burden of demonstrating its applicability."

- *United States v. Covington & Burling*, 430 F. Supp. 1117, 1122 (D.D.C. 1977). An action was brought under the Foreign Agents Registration Act by the Justice Department against a law firm representing a foreign country. Certain documents in the law firm's possession were sought. The court held that the law firm had "the burden of showing with sufficient certainty that the elements [of the privilege] do, in fact, exist." The court concluded that where the firm had not specifically alleged that disclosure would reveal a client's confidence, the document could be discovered.

- *International Paper Co. v. Fibreboard Corp.*, 63 F.R.D. 88, 94 (D. Del. 1974). A protective order preventing disclosure of a patent was denied. "A proper claim of privilege requires a specific designation and description of the documents within its scope as well as precise and certain reasons for preserving their confidentiality. Unless the affidavit is precise to bring the document within the rule, the court has no basis on which to weigh the applicability of the claim of privilege. An improperly asserted claim of privilege is no claim of privilege at all. . . . [A] party resisting disclosure on the ground of the attorney-client privilege must by affidavit show sufficient *facts* as to bring the identified and described document within the narrow confines of the privilege."

Because courts generally require the proponent of the privilege to sustain the burden of proof with respect to each element and because one such element is that the privilege has not been waived, theoretically the proponent of the privilege bears the burden of demonstrating lack of waiver. As a practical matter, however, it is generally assumed that no waiver has occurred unless the party seeking discovery contends that it has.

- *Iron Workers Local Union No. 17 Ins. Fund v. Philip Morris, Inc.*, 35 F. Supp. 2d 582, 585 (N.D. Ohio 1999). The plaintiffs filed a motion for a ruling that the defendants had waived the privilege by selective disclosure to Congress and in other actions. The court concluded that, by their opposition to disclosure, the defendants were seeking to keep highly probative evidence from the fact-finder when the evidence was already in the public domain. "Because the moving tobacco defendants fail to sustain their burden of showing that they had not waived the privilege for tactical advantage in providing materials to the U.S. House of Representatives, and because the defendants fail to sustain their burden of showing that they had not waived the privilege for tactical advantage in settling the Minnesota state court litigation, this Court denies the defendants' motion."

Some courts, however, have shifted the burden of proving the negative—namely that the privilege has not been waived—onto the party claiming that it has. There is substantial logic in this approach because it is far easier to prove that something has occurred than it is to prove that it has not.

- *In re Perrigo Co.*, 128 F.3d 430, 440 (6th Cir. 1997). "Accordingly, the burden of establishing a waiver under the balancing approach rests on the party seeking discovery."

Some state courts have shifted the burden of proof on privilege issues from the proponent to the contestant of the privilege by shifting assumptions. Thus, California law assumes that all communications between a client and attorney are privileged, and the party seeking to pierce the privilege assumes the burden of proving that the privilege does not apply.

- CAL. EVID. CODE ANN. § 917. Whenever a privilege is claimed on the ground that the matter sought to be disclosed is a communication made in confidence in the course of the lawyer-client, physician-patient, psychotherapist-patient, clergyman-penitent, or husband-wife relationship, the communication is presumed to have been made in confidence and the opponent of the claim of privilege has the burden of proving that the communication was not confidential.

In addition, if the party seeking production makes a *prima facie* showing that some exception to the attorney-client privilege applies, an opportunity must, nonetheless, be accorded to the proponent of the privilege to rebut the presumption of an applicable exception. A full evidentiary hearing may be necessary.

- *Haines v. Liggett Group Inc.*, 975 F.2d 81, 97, 1992 U.S. App. LEXIS 21069 (3d Cir.), *reh'g denied*, 975 F.2d 81, 1992 U.S. App. LEXIS 26004 (3d Cir. 1992). The district court erred in finding the existence of a crime/fraud exception to the attorney-client privilege sufficient to order the production of documents detailing scientific investigations conducted by tobacco companies without according the companies an opportunity to rebut. The appellate court also chastised the district court for revealing the contents of some of the documents in its published opinion. "[W]here a factfinder undertakes to weigh evidence in a proceeding seeking an exception to the privilege, the party invoking the privilege has the absolute right to be heard by testimony and argument."

Sometimes the cases produce surprisingly divergent results. Thus, the documents produced by the tobacco companies containing scientific results showing tobacco produced cancer were accorded a privilege and the district court was chastised, surprisingly, for publicly releasing the contents of the documents in an opinion justifying his decision that the fraud/crime exception applied. Yet, in *United States v. White*, 950

F.2d 426 (7th Cir. 1991), 970 F.2d 328 (7th Cir. 1992), an attorney seeking to save his hide was permitted to tender documents to the prosecutor that formed the basis of the indictment of his clients for bankruptcy fraud. To a layperson these results may seem untoward. They demonstrate the infinite resourcefulness of the courts in applying the varied elements of the privilege to the multiform facts that life presents in a court of law.

In other cases, no full hearing has been required and affidavits by prosecuting agencies have been deemed sufficient to invade the privilege. Courts have said that motions to quash subpoenas served on attorneys should not turn into mini-trials.

- *In re Grand Jury Investigation (Schroeder)*, 842 F.2d 1223, 1226 (11th Cir. 1987). "That is not to say, however, that motions in opposition to grand jury subpoenas should turn into mini-trials. If courts always had to hear testimony and conflicting evidence on such matters, the rationale behind the *prima facie* standard—the promotion of speed and efficiency at the grand jury stage—would be lost."

It may be anomalous that far greater protection is accorded to the powerful corporation where the privilege is challenged on the basis of the fraud exception in the context of civil litigation, than is accorded to the individual client threatened with criminal prosecution. Compare *Haines* and *Schroeder supra*. To put a kinder and gentler interpretation on the matter, it may be that the courts deem that the grand jury proceedings standing alone constitute *prima facie* evidence of the commission of a crime and are in all events subject to secrecy themselves even if the jeopardy for the individual is loss of liberty rather than civil damages.

Some courts seem to distinguish between matters that may be revealed to a grand jury and matters that may be used at trial, suggesting that a more detailed inquiry may be appropriate with respect to the privilege before it is invaded at a trial than for presentation to a grand jury.

- *In re Berkley & Co.*, 629 F.2d 548, 555 (8th Cir. 1980). "We emphasize the very limited effect of this decision. The determination that the documents are not privileged pertains only to the grand jury proceedings. If indictments are returned and the matter proceeds to trial, Berkley and any individual defendants are free to reassert their claims of privilege to prevent use of the documents at trial. The ultimate question of relevance and admissibility of the documents at trial may then be determined, but only after all parties have had an opportunity to be heard."

Of course, once the testimonial cat has been liberated from the bag of confidentiality there is little possibility of recapture. What if the privileged evidence was the very basis of the indictment itself? Will the subsequent remedy of inadmissibility at trial undo the harm of the indictment?

In the civil context, documents as to which parties plan on taking interlocutory appeals or bringing a mandamus action may be protected by being placed under seal.

- *Haines v. Liggett Group Inc.*, 975 F.2d 81, 97, 1992 U.S. App. LEXIS 21069 (3d Cir.), *reh'g denied*, 975 F.2d 81, 1992 U.S. App. LEXIS 26004 (3d Cir. 1992). "Because of the sensitivity surrounding the attorney-client privilege, care must be taken that, following any determination that an exception applies, the matters covered by the exception be kept under seal and appropriate court-imposed privacy procedures until all avenues of appeal are exhausted. Regrettably this protection was not extended by the district court in these proceedings. Matters deemed to be excepted were spread forth in its opinion and released to the general public. In the present posture of this case, by virtue of our decision today, an unfortunate situation exists that matters still under the cloak of privilege have already been divulged." Given the appearance of partiality, the court of appeals ordered that the case be reassigned on remand.

There is no equivalent remedy available in the criminal context, other than a renewed motion that the documents disclosed to the grand jury are nonetheless privileged at trial. Such a motion does not undo the indictment.

First and foremost and it goes perhaps without saying, the proponent of the privilege or the protection has the burden of sustaining the proposition that what is sought to be protected from compelled disclosure is in fact subject to either the privilege or the protection. Nothing is more common in litigation than a cavalier expectation that of course some communication or document or report or piece of correspondence is either privileged or protected and that all that is necessary for the claim to be valid is to assert the claim.

- *BG Real Estate Servs., Inc. v. American Equity Ins. Co.*, 2005 U.S. Dist. LEXIS 10330, at *11–12 (E.D. La. 2005). "Despite defendants' burden of proof on their privilege claims, they have submitted no evidence of any kind, by affidavit, deposition testimony or otherwise, which might establish that the requested information is privileged in any way. The mere assertion of a lawyer in defendants' memoranda that responsive materials or information were attorney-client communications, work product, part of a joint defense or prepared in anticipation of litigation is not evidence sufficient to bear the burden."

The practitioner also must be aware that today the burden of proof as to privilege is virtually unsustainable without the preparation of what has come to be known as a privilege log. These are discussed in detail in the following separate section.

No privilege assertion will hold if the author, recipients, and purpose for which the document was prepared can not be explained. In a word, designating any one of these as "unknown" is a sure-fire way of getting that the privilege/protection are not available.

- *Automed Techs., Inc. v. Knapp Logistics & Automation, Inc.*, 382 F. Supp. 2d 1372 (N.D. Ga. 2005). Where a document does not on its face show that it is privileged and no one can testify as to its origin, purpose, author or recipients even though coming from legal department files, the party asserting privilege failed entirely in its burden of proof.

3. Demonstrating Applicability of Each Element

The burden is ordinarily on the party claiming the privilege to state specifically and establish to the court's satisfaction the facts supporting each of the requisite elements.

- *FTC v. Lukens Steel Co.*, 444 F. Supp. 803, 806 (D.D.C. 1977). The court held that the burden of establishing confidentiality as an essential element of the attorney-client privilege had been met by the proponents of the privilege upon a showing to whom the documents in question had been distributed. "The party seeking the benefit of the privilege has the burden of demonstrating its applicability."

- *United States v. Covington & Burling*, 430 F. Supp. 1117, 1122 (D.D.C. 1977). An action was brought under the Foreign Agents Registration Act by the Justice Department against a law firm representing a foreign country. Certain documents in the possession of the law firm were sought. The court held that the law firm had "the burden of showing with sufficient certainty that the elements [of the privilege] do, in fact, exist." The court concluded that where the firm had not specifically alleged that disclosure would reveal a client's confidence, the document could be discovered.

- *International Paper Co. v. Fibreboard Corp.*, 63 F.R.D. 88, 94 (D. Del. 1974). A protective order preventing disclosure of a patent was denied. "A proper claim of privilege requires a specific designation and description of the documents within its scope as well as precise and certain reasons for preserving their confidentiality. Unless the affidavit is precise to bring the document within the rule, the court has no basis on which to weigh the applicability of the claim of privilege. An improperly asserted claim of privilege is no claim of privilege at all. . . . [A] party resisting disclosure on the ground of the attorney-client privilege must by affidavit show sufficient *facts* as to bring the identified and described document within the narrow confines of the privilege."

The method by which the various elements of the attorney-client privilege or of the work-product protection are raised is usually by affidavit, at least in the first instance.

- *RCN Corp. v. Paramount Pavilion Group LLC.*, 2003 U.S. Dist. LEXIS 24004 (E.D. Pa. Dec. 19, 2003). Affidavit of in-house counsel that all information he had was garnered in the course of communications between employees and outside counsel in the course of seeking and providing legal advice deemed sufficient in establishing each element of the privilege. The court found that the party seeking to pierce the privilege had not submitted sufficient evidence to suggest that in-house counsel was acting as a business advisor rather than as legal counsel in respect to the transaction at issue.

Sometimes matters are set down for hearings often before a Magistrate Judge, although it is not always easy to determine whether the hearings entail evidence presented as live testimony or as affidavits.

- *Perkins v. Gregg County*, 891 F. Supp. 361, 362, 1995 U.S. Dist. LEXIS 6898 (E.D. Tex.), *adopted*, 891 F. Supp. 861, 1995 U.S. Dist. LEXIS 13737 (E.D. Tex. 1995). Court recited that a full hearing and *in camera* review of tape recordings at issue was conducted in which proponent of privilege prevailed on contention that notes were not a mere diary of the plaintiff's thoughts and thus discoverable, but rather had been taken on advice of counsel and for the purpose of seeking legal advice. Apparently counsel submitted affidavits in which they set forth their instructions to their client. Curiously, in a sense the lawyers "breached" the privilege to sustain the privilege for the document in dispute. After all, was not their advice to the client to keep a diary in recording form itself "privileged"? Obviously such logical niceties necessarily gave way to protect the underlying document.

Failure to meet that burden may result in summary denial of either the privilege or the protection, without the party necessarily being given another chance to make the assertion stick.

At best, the matter will be remanded to a fact-finder (magistrate judge or special master) to make the requisite finding, either by simple examination of the contested documents or by requiring affidavits. Hearings to determine whether each element of the privilege or the protection has been demonstrated are as rare as hen's teeth. No error is committed in not conducting a hearing to determine the applicability of asserted privilege/protection claims.

- *In re Ampicillin Antitrust Litig.*, 81 F.R.D. 377, 390 (D.D.C. 1978). The master did not commit error by failing to hold an evidentiary hearing as to the factual basis for assertions of privilege.

Affidavits usually suffice. However, failure to supply requisite affidavits may be fatal to the claim.

- *In re Sunrise Sec. Litig.*, 130 F.R.D. 560, 569–70 (E.D. Pa. 1989). When no affidavits were submitted by or on behalf of certain clients asserting a privilege, no privilege claim would necessarily lie. The magistrate was instructed to examine the documents and conduct further fact-finding to determine if a privilege claim had been asserted on each client's behalf.

Absent a thorough documentation of each requisite element, documents with respect to which privilege and protection are claimed are subject to a production order.

- *Jones v. Boeing Co.*, 163 F.R.D. 15 (D. Kan. 1995). When a privilege log provided to substantiate a claim of privilege was inadequate, the documents were ordered to be produced. The log indicated the presence of many people at meetings, thereby calling into question any confidentiality at the time of the communication, and also indicating that many of the communications with respect to which a claim of privilege was asserted occurred prior to the time counsel was retained. No second attempt to demonstrate the applicability of privilege and protection was here accorded.

As with every other element of the attorney-client privilege, courts usually state, without much thought, that the burden of proof that no waiver has occurred rests with the proponent of the privilege.

- *Weil v. Investment/Indicators, Research & Mgmt., Inc.*, 647 F.2d 18, 25 (9th Cir. 1981). "One of the elements that the asserting party must prove is that it has not waived the privilege."

Proof that no waiver occurred, however, would require proving a negative. Thus, what generally occurs in practice is that the party seeking disclosure usually uncovers an instance of disclosure that constitutes a waiver. Then, the burden of proof shifts to the proponent of the privilege to demonstrate why the disclosure was itself in a privileged context that did not entrain waiver.

Some courts, however, have shifted the burden of proving that an exception to the privilege applies, including waiver, to the opponent not the proponent of the privilege.

- *FDIC v. Ogden Corp.*, 202 F.3d 454 (1st Cir. 2000). "If the privilege is established and the question becomes whether an exception to it obtains, the devoir of persuasion shifts to the proponent of the exception."

- *Times Picayune Publ'g Corp. v. Zurich Am. Ins. Co.*, 2004 U.S. Dist. LEXIS 1027, at *26 (E.D. La. Jan. 26, 2004). "Once a claim of privilege has been established, the burden of proof shifts to the party seeking discovery to prove any applicable exception to the privilege, such as waiver."

- *Texaco, Inc. v. Louisiana Land & Exploration Co.*, 805 F. Supp. 385, 386 (M.D. La. 1992), *appeal dismissed*, 995 F.2d 43 (5th Cir. 1993). "The State further argues that Texaco has the burden of proving what documents are at issue as the party moving to compel production.

  "The court disagrees. The burden of establishing the applicability of a privilege rests on the party who invokes it. The attorney-client privilege must be specifically asserted with respect to particular documents. Once a claim of privilege has been established, then the burden or proof shifts to the party seeking discovery to prove any applicable exception to the privilege." (Citations omitted.)

  The case involved the applicability of Louisiana's Public Records Act and whether it did or did not preclude discovery of certain documents. The Magistrate Judge ruled that the documents were discoverable because the State had failed to designate as to which a claim of privilege was being asserted. The State contended that there was never any doubt or uncertainty in the minds of either the parties or the court as to which documents were at issue. The Act exempted from disclosure documents that fit the general definition of either attorney-client privilege or work product doctrine.

  Although the cases generally state that each element of the privilege must be demonstrated by the proponent thereof, as a practical matter once a privilege log has been prepared, courts generally require nothing further other than requisite affidavits to support contentions.

- *ECDC Envtl., L.C. v. New York Marine & Gen. Ins. Co.*, 1998 U.S. Dist. LEXIS 8808, at *8–9 (S.D.N.Y June 4, 1998). "Although it is clear that the proponent of the privilege ultimately bears the burden of proving all essential facts necessary to sustain a claim of privilege, the law is not entirely clear as to how this burden may be discharged where, as here, the proponent has served a detailed index of documents withheld, and the challenger has submitted specific challenges. Apart from the specific challenges made in its motion, defendant does not generally challenge the adequacy of plaintiff's index.

Under these circumstances, it appears that the proponent of the privilege may satisfy its burden by submitting evidentiary material as to the challenged elements only. Requiring the proponent to submit evidentiary material to prove all elements of the privilege in response to a specific challenge unduly burdens and wastes the time of both the Court and the parties."

- *CSC Recovery Corp. v. Daido Steel Co.*, 1997 U.S. Dist. LEXIS 16346 at *nn 7 & 8 (S.D.N.Y. Oct. 21, 1997). "Courts have a degree of discretion in assessing whether a claim of privilege has been adequately supported, and may rely upon privilege logs supplemented by attorney affidavits. Contrary to CSC's assertion, affidavits by the authors and recipients of the documents are not invariably required, particularly where the context in which the documents were created, or the documents themselves, leave little doubt as to whether a privilege has been properly asserted."

a. *Privilege Elements*

- *Navigant Consulting, Inc. v. Wilkinson*, 220 F.R.D. 467, 474 (N.D. Tex. 2004). "The court notes at the outset that NCI has failed to adduce sufficient evidence, other than the documents themselves, to establish its claim of privilege. Initially, NCI produced only the Declaration of Philip P. Steptoe in support of its privilege and work-product claims. While this declaration provides a wealth of information about the facts and circumstances giving rise to the LECG and Wilkinson Investigations, it wholly fails to explain how these facts bring any particular document within the ambit of the attorney-client privilege. Instead, Steptoe seems to assume that all documents relating to these investigations are privileged because they were made by or sent to in-house or outside counsel at a time when NCI was, considering possible litigation. Such a categorical approach to the attorney-client privilege is not proper."

- *Walter v. Cincinnati Zoo & Botanical Garden,* 2006 U.S. Dist. LEXIS 25841 (S.D. Oh. May 3, 2006). Where insufficient evidence existed in the record as to the purpose for which the client notes had been prepared, counsel was ordered to supply such evidence so that the court could rule whether the notes were or were not privilege protected. The question posed was, were the notes created for the client's own use or to be given to an attorney so that legal advice could be given?

How did the court imagine that given the choice the party urging protection would not necessarily state that they were prepared for an attorney? Other courts in such circumstances would simply deny the privilege based on failure to sustain the burden of proof.

The common interest privilege is one which the proponent must demonstrate exists. Failure to do so will mean that no privilege will apply to communications between the two parties or their attorneys.

- *In re Rivastigmine Patent Litig.,* 2005 U.S. Dist. LEXIS 20851, at *14–15 (S.D.N.Y. Sept. 22, 2005), *aff'd,* 2005 U.S. Dist. LEXIS 29674 (S.D.N.Y. Nov. 22, 2005). "Novartis has proffered no agreement with Yissum or the inventors demonstrating a common legal strategy. n2 Nor has it provided any affidavit or deposition testimony describing any such strategy. Nor has it even described facts from which even an implicit common strategy could be inferred." Indeed, Novartis' own designated witness testified that there was no joint defense agreement and no "understanding that Yissum or Hebrew University or the inventors of the 807 patent would provide assistance to Novartis if requested. Novartis has thus failed to carry its burden of demonstrating the applicability of the common interest doctrine." (Internal citations omitted.)

At times parties will argue whether a privilege has or has not been waived without either one providing any information to allow for a determination.

- *Sony Computer Entm't Am., Inc. v. Great Am. Ins. Co.*, 229 F.R.D. 632 (N. Cal. 2005). The proponent of the privilege claimed there was no waiver because the presence of a third-party, "claims analyst" was necessary to assist in the privileged communication, but then failed to provide any affidavit or explanation as to why it was necessary or what his role was.

b. Work-Product Elements

- *Bell v. Pfizer, Inc.*, 2005 U.S. Dist. LEXIS 13174 (S.D.N.Y. July 1, 2005). Where privilege log contained no information regarding when or the circumstances under which the documents as to work-product protection was created, the claim necessarily failed. A feeble attempt to claim such protection was apparently made out of fear that the privilege claim would fail under the fiduciary exception.

- *State Farm Mut. Auto. Ins. Co. v. Metropolitan Family Practice*, 2005 U.S. Dist. LEXIS 32620 (E.D. Pa. Dec. 12, 2005). Upon a showing by the parting claiming the work-product privilege that the documents were created in anticipation of litigation, the burden then shifts to the party seeking to discover the documents. The party disputing the work-product privilege must satisfy two elements. First, the party seeking discovery [*11] must show they have 'substantial need of the materials in the preparation of [their] case.' Fed. R. Civ. P. 26(b)(3). Second, the party seeking discovery must show they are 'unable without undue hardship to obtain the substantial equivalent of the material by other means.' If the party seeking discovery shows both elements, the court will still withhold documents that would disclose 'mental impressions, conclusions, opinions, or legal theories of an attorney or other representative of a party concerning the lawsuit.' "

- *MSF Holding Ltd. v. Fiduciary Trust Co. Int'l*, 2005 U.S. Dist. LEXIS 27811 (S.D.N.Y. Nov. 10, 2005), *recons. denied*, 2005 U.S. Dist. LEXIS 34171 (S.D.N.Y. Dec. 7, 2005). Where proponent of work-product protection failed to show that the document would not have been prepared in substantially identical form but for the anticipation of litigation, the claim of work-product protection for the document was denied.

- *Nationwide Mut. Ins. Co. v. Dimenichi*, 2004 U.S. Dist. LEXIS 25153, at *3 (E.D. Pa. 2004). The court concluded that "the parties have not presented the Court with sufficient evidentiary support to resolve this discovery dispute on the basis of the parties' and lawyers' relationships inter se."

- *Continental Cas. Co. v. Marsh*, 2004 U.S. Dist. LEXIS 76, at *24 (N.D. Ill. Jan. 5, 2004). "Document 14, which is undated, consists of handwritten notes written by an unknown lawyer. The document appears to be notes relating to the claims investigation for TIFCO's fidelity bond claim. It is not evident from the face of the document that there was a reasonable anticipation of litigation at the time the document was created, or that primary reason for creating the document was to prepare for litigation. Nor has Continental provided any additional information that would allow the court to conclude that the work product doctrine is applicable. Continental has failed to meet its burden, so Document 14 must be produced."

- *Clavo v. Zarrabian*, 2003 U.S. Dist. LEXIS 27010, at *6–7 (c). D. Cal. Sept. 24, 2003). "Although there are numerous entries in Ralphs' privilege log asserting that item movement reports are protected by the work-product doctrine, including Plaintiff's Document # 312, Ralphs has failed to provide any basis for its claim that the entries are work product. Ralphs' privilege log does not reveal who created and viewed them or why they were created."

- *Western Res., Inc. v. Union Pac. R.R. Co.*, 2002 U.S. Dist. LEXIS 1911, at *11–12 (D. Kan. Jan. 31, 2002). "The only three elements that must be established by the party seeking to invoke work-product immunity are that (1) the materials sought to be protected are documents or tangible things; (2) they were prepared in anticipation of litigation or for trial; and (3) they were prepared by or for a party or a representative of that party."

Other courts have correctly stated that in addition to those three elements, the party seeking discovery must further show both need and no alternative means of obtaining the information. There is no need and it is inappropriate, one court has suggested, to argue waiver unless neither need nor no alternative means have been demonstrated.

- *In re Lorazepam & Clorazepate Antitrust Litig.*, 2001 U.S. Dist. LEXIS 11794, at *13 (D.D.C. July 16, 2001). "But, leaping to a waiver analysis is unnecessary unless and until plaintiffs fail to defeat the work-product privilege by establishing a substantial need for the documents and an inability to secure their substantial equivalent without undue hardship. Fed. R. Civ. P. 26(b)(3). In this case, if plaintiffs cannot make that showing, they have a right to try to establish that Mylan or Foster waived the work-product privilege by behavior inconsistent with its protections."

- *Vargas v. Palm Mgmt. Corp.*, 2004 U.S. Dist. LEXIS 5256 (E.D. Pa. Mar. 26, 2004). Court stated that plaintiff had not established need for work-product-protected documents, but since proponent of the protection had not established that they were so protected in the first instance, discovery was allowed.

c. Demonstrating Waiver or the Availability of an Exception

Although the proponent of the privilege has the burden of demonstrating the availability of the privilege or protection.

- *Atteberry v. Longmont United Hosp.*, 221 F.R.D. 644 (D. Col. 2004). Where proponent of privilege/protection had proffered no privilege log or any other supporting documents in support of its claim, burden had not been met and discovery was allowed.

Once that burden has been met, the burden of proffering evidence and the burden of persuasion then both shift to the proponent of an exception that would permit the privilege or protection to be pierced.

- *FDIC v. Ogden Corp.*, 202 F.3d 454, 460 (1st Cir. 2000). If the privilege is established, the government bears the burden of showing that the privilege is defeated by an exception.

- *Renner v. Chase Manhattan Bank*, 2001 U.S. Dist. LEXIS 9766, at *5 (S.D.N.Y. July 11, 2001). "By its nature, the crime-fraud exception can only apply, if it applies at all, to instances where the attorney-client privilege itself is first established."

The burden of proof in respect to waiver differs in the case of the attorney-client privilege and the work-product protection. The proponent of the attorney-client privilege bears the burden of proof in demonstrating that the privilege has not been waived. The proponent of the work-product doctrine does not. Instead, it is on the party seeking discovery of the work product to demonstrate that waiver has occurred. Why this distinction exists in respect to the burden of proof is not clear. One can only surmise that it is unusual for a party to share work product but less unusual for attorney-client privileged communications to be shared with third parties, and that the burden reflects probabilities of waiver.

- *Greene, Tweed of Del., Inc. v. DuPont Dow Elastomers, LLC,* 202 F.R.D. 418, 423 (E.D. Pa. 2001). "[W]ith respect to the attorney-client privilege, the dispute turns on whether DuPont Dow [defendant] has demonstrated that it has not waived the privilege. With respect to work product immunity, the issue is whether plaintiff has established waiver."

- *Western Res., Inc. v. Union Pac. R.R. Co.,* 2002 U.S. Dist. LEXIS 1911, at *11 (D. Kan. Jan. 31, 2002). "[T]he burden to establish that waiver has not occurred remains with the party who is asserting the attorney-client privilege. . . . In contrast, a party asserting work product immunity is not required to prove 'non-waiver.'"

- *Johnson v. Gmeinder,* 191 F.R.D. 638, 643 (D. Kan. 2000). "In contrast, a party asserting work-product privilege immunity is not required to prove non-waiver." (Footnote omitted.) Accordingly, the party asserting waiver of work-product protection has the burden of establishing waiver.

- *Aull v. Cavalcade Pension Plan,* 185 F.R.D. 618, 624 (D. Colo. 1998). The party asserting waiver of work-product immunity has burden of establishing waiver.

- *Hatco Corp. v. W.R. Grace & Co.,* 1991 U.S. Dist. LEXIS 6479, 1991 WL 83126, at *7 (D.N.J. May 10, 1991). The party seeking to obtain protected work product bears the burden of proving that the protection has been waived.

So too in the case of the crime/fraud exception, the proponent of the exception has the burden of adducing evidence sufficient to make a *prima facie* showing that the crime/fraud exception exists. If sufficient evidence is adduced, the court can conduct an *in camera* inspection of the contested documents. A lesser standard of proof is requisite to trigger the *in camera* inspection than exists to actually find that the exception is applicable.

- *Haines v. Liggett Group, Inc.*, 975 F.2d 81, 95-96, 1992 U.S. App. LEXIS 21069 (3d Cir.), *reh'g denied*, 975 F.2d 81, 1992 U.S. App. LEXIS 26004 (3d Cir. 1992); *see also United States v. Zolin*, 491 U.S. 554, 572 (1989): "Before engaging in *in camera* review to determine the applicability of the crime-fraud exception, the judge should require a showing of a factual basis adequate to support a good faith belief by a reasonable person that *in camera* review of the materials may reveal evidence to establish the claim that the crime-fraud exception applies." . . . "[T]the decision to engage in *in camera* review implicates a much more lenient standard of proof than the determination to apply the crime/fraud exception, as the intrusion on the asserted privilege is minimal") (citations and quotations omitted). What is meant by the term *prima facie* showing is generally no more or less than a factual basis sufficient "to support a good faith belief by a reasonable person that the materials may reveal evidence of a crime or fraud."

In all events, that any burden needs to be met to trigger an *in camera* inspection is an anomaly left over from the days when *in camera* review was not yet conducted for any reason and no reason at all. It is a carryover from the early days of the jurisprudence of privilege/protection when *in camera* inspections were rare and when courts, quaintly, believed that if one was serious about either the privilege or the protection, then it should not be lightly invaded by anyone, including the court. The persistence of such an elaborate tennis match of proof and counterproof, when in fact *in camera* inspections now occur constantly, is but one example of just how mindless formulaic decision making tends to become over time and to continue long after its original purpose has long since come and gone.

In all events, once the proponent of the crime/fraud exception has made the requisite *prima facie* showing, then the ball shifts back into the court of the privilege/protection proponent to put an innocent construction on the seemingly inculpatory evidence. The cases are not clear whether this must be done before or after the *in camera* inspection, although it is hard to believe that any proponent of the privilege would be foreclosed from doing so even after the *in camera* inspection.

- *Wachtel v. Guardian Life Ins. Co.*, 2006 U.S. Dist. LEXIS 27117, at *4–6 (D.N.J. May 5, 2006). "The Third Circuit has established a multi-step process for determining whether a party's claim of privilege should be pierced by the crime-fraud exception. First, in order to invoke the exception, the party seeking discovery must make a *prima facie* showing that (1) the client claiming the privilege was engaging or intended to engage in a crime or fraud at the time of the attorney-client communication, and (2) that the communication was in furtherance of the continuing or intended crime or fraud. *See In re Grand Jury Subpoena*, 223 F.3d 213 (3d Cir. 2000). The *prima facie* showing requires that the party seeking discovery 'present evidence which, if believed by the fact-finder, would be sufficient to support a finding that the elements of the crime-fraud exception were met.'"

    "This evidentiary showing, which is required before the Court may conduct an in camera review of the contested documents, is a lesser standard than that which is ultimately required for disclosure under the crime-fraud exception. *Zolin*, 491 U.S. at 572 (holding that a lesser evidentiary showing is needed to trigger *in camera* review than is required ultimately to overcome the privilege)."

- *In re Grand Jury Investigation*, 445 F.3d 266 (3d Cir.), *cert. denied*, 127 S. Ct. 538 (2006). The court explained that a client's misuse of communications with her attorney in furtherance of an improper purpose was sufficient to satisfy the second prong of the crime-fraud exception and further said that the burden to make the necessary *prima facie* showing for the crime-fraud exception was not a particularly heavy one.

- *Medical Lab. Mgmt. Consultants v. Am. Broad. Cos., Inc.*, 30 F. Supp. 2d 1182, 1206 (D. Ariz. 1998), *aff'd*, 306 F.3d 806 (9th Cir. 2002). The court held that in order to pierce the attorney-client privilege based on the crime-fraud exception, the district court must determine, by a preponderance of the evidence, whether the exception is justified, taking into account the entire record.

- *Laser Indus. v. Reliant Techs.*, 167 F.R.D. 417, 430 (N.D. Cal. 1996). The court must "permit the holder of the privilege to submit evidence and argument that tends to rebut an inference of any of the necessary elements of the crime/fraud exception." Thereafter the "more likely than not" standard is applied to pierce the privilege veil.

- *In re Feldberg*, 862 F.2d 622, 626 (7th Cir. 1988). The court explained that once a *prima facie* case had been made that the privilege holder, as "the one with superior access to the evidence and in the best position to explain things, come forward with that explanation" which would put an innocent construction on the evidence and adduce information by way of facts and argument as to why the privilege should not be pierced.

4. Submission of Affidavits

It is often insufficient to rely on privilege logs, however completely prepared, to sustain an assertion of privilege. More explanation is often necessary and is usually provided by way of explanatory affidavits.

- *Tilberg v. Next Mgmt. Co.*, 2005 U.S. Dist. LEXIS 36336 (S.D.N.Y. Dec. 28, 2005) After an *in camera* inspection of documents uncovered after a forensic search of defendant's computer, the court concluded that they appeared to be work-product protected, but required a submission of an affidavit by counsel that he had indeed requested the preparation of the documents.

- *IBJ Whitehall Bank & Trust Co. v. Cory & Assocs.*, 1999 U.S. Dist. LEXIS 12440, at *14 (N. D. Ill. Aug. 10, 1999). "Whitehall has not offered any affidavits or other evidence to the contrary, relying on the privilege log to establish its burden of proof. The log fails to satisfy Whitehall's burden with respect to these documents."

- *ConAgra, Inc. v. Arkwright Mut. Ins. Co.*, 32 F. Supp. 2d 1015 (N.D. Ill. 1999). A conclusory assertion of privilege was insufficient to sustain its applicability, despite preparation of a document log.

- *Asset Value Fund L.P. v. Care Group*, 1997 U.S. Dist. LEXIS 17968 (S.D.N.Y. Nov. 12, 1997). The court found there was not a sufficient showing to support a claim of privilege as to certain documents. "The privilege log alone does not provide any explanation of what attorney-client communications might be contained in the documents, or whether the communications were in furtherance of legal advice that was sought, or whether the documents were kept confidential." The affidavit submitted with the privilege log was also deemed insufficient in its explanation as to why the documents were privileged.

- *United States v. Construction Prods. Research, Inc.*, 73 F.3d 464, 473–74 (2d Cir.), *cert. denied*, 519 U.S. 927 (1996). General allegations of privilege were insufficient where descriptions of documents alone did not provide sufficient information to support privilege claim, and no affidavit or other documentation was submitted.

Increasingly, affidavits are expected to support assertions of privilege and provide foundational support for privilege logs. Courts expect recipients to be identified by position and the circumstances under which documents were prepared to be set forth both temporally and in terms of the purpose of the communication. Thus clients and their attorneys are being asked to give testimonial support, under oath and with the potential penalties attended thereto, to privilege assertions.

Although very case-specific, the case cited below is nonetheless a telling example of the effective use of affidavits to obtain privilege and work-product protection in circumstances that at first glance would not seem conducive to such claims.

- *In re Copper Market Antitrust Litig.*, 200 F.R.D. 213, 221 (S.D.N.Y. 2001). "RLM specializes in litigation-related crisis management. The firm was hired shortly after Hamanaka's confession, when it was apparent that the CFTC might commence an enforcement action against Sumitomo. Elizabeth Mather, RLM's principal representative for the Sumitomo engagement, states that "from the outset, RLM knew its representation was litigation-related." Further, it is clear that Sumitomo retained RLM to make sure that its public statements would not result in further exposure in the litigation that grew out of the copper trading scandal. In light of these uncontroverted facts, the Court finds that the materials listed on the Privilege Log were prepared by RLM or delivered to RLM in anticipation of litigation and that such documents are protected by work product immunity. For the same reasons, listed documents prepared by Sumitomo or its counsel also are protected by work product immunity." (Internal citations to affidavits omitted but each factual statement was supported by an uncontroverted affidavit.)

- *Renner v. Chase Manhattan Bank*, 2001 U.S. Dist. LEXIS 17920 (S.D.N.Y. Nov. 1, 2001). The court made any number of provisional rulings in respect to privilege assertions but predicated those rulings on multiple affidavits filed to substantiate various assertions in the privilege log and to spell out details of when and under what circumstances the documents were produced and disseminated.

Affidavits can be used not only to support various privilege claims but also to rebut such claims.

- *Resolution Trust Corp. v. Massachusetts Mut. Life Ins. Co.*, 200 F.R.D. 183 (W.D.N.Y. 2001). The court relied extensively on multiple affidavits submitted by the RTC to rebut various theories propounded by defendants arguing that a waiver of work-product-protected materials had occurred. Based on the rebuttal affidavits, the court concluded that no waiver had occurred.

- *Canal Barge Co. v. Commonwealth Edison Co.*, 2001 U.S. Dist. LEXIS 12988 (N.D. Ill. Aug. 23, 2001). Extensive use of unrebutted affidavits and deposition testimony was made to establish that certain individuals fell within Illinois' "control group" for purposes of the applicability of the privilege when documents are disseminated within a corporation.

It is best not to cut corners when submitting affidavits. Conclusory affidavits, along with a failure to submit the documents as to which privilege or work-product protection is claimed, will often be fatal to sustaining the claim.

- *In re Grand Jury Subpoenas Dated Mar. 19, 2002 & Aug. 2, 2002,* 318 F.3d 379, 386 (2d Cir. 2002). In response to a government-issued subpoena for bank records in its possession, a law firm claimed work-product protection. The claim did not succeed where the affidavits were conclusory in nature and the documents were not submitted for an *in camera* review. "This burden of objective proof cannot be met through conclusory ex parte affidavits, such as those filed by appellants with the district court in this case, which simply assert that Akin Gump possesses only a subset of the materials subpoenaed and that this subset was created pursuant to a carefully orchestrated defense strategy. Akin Gump's failure to disclose that strategy ex parte to the district court made it impossible for Judge Chin to determine—and makes it impossible for us to review—whether the responsive subset indeed reflects Akin Gump's discriminating selection, or, instead, whether the subset is simply the product of document maintenance practices by the various banks, a lack of cooperation from some of the account holders, or some combination of these and other factors. Without such disclosure, no court can decide if Akin Gump's work-product concern is real, or only speculative. Similarly troubling is the firm's failure to identify or submit the responsive documents for *in camera* review, a practice both long-standing and routine in cases involving claims of privilege."

Conversely, failure to supply affidavits to support a position that documents are privilege or work-product protected, particularly in the face of counter-affidavits, will be fatal to the claim.

- *Gulf Islands Leasing, Inc. v. Bombardier Capital, Inc.,* 215 F.R.D. 466, 473 (S.D.N.Y. 2003). "Whether material was prepared 'in anticipation of litigation' requires a determination of the subjective question of whether the party actually thought it was threatened with litigation and the objective question of whether that belief was reasonable. . . . In order to demonstrate such a subjective belief, a party asserting work-product protection will generally submit affidavits or similar evidence establishing that it held such a belief." (Citations omitted.)

- *Campbell v. United States Dep't of Justice*, 164 F.3d 20, 20 (D.C. Cir. 1998). "An affidavit that contains merely a 'categorical description' of redacted material coupled with categorical indication of anticipated consequences is clearly inadequate."

If the court invites submission of materials in support of a privilege claim it is highly unwise not to do so.

- *Freeport-McMoran Sulphur LLC v. Mike Mullen Energy Equip. Res., Inc.*, 2004 U.S. Dist. LEXIS 12183 (E.D. La. June 30, 2004). The court refused to consider an affidavit in support of privilege claims which was not filed until the court had ruled against the claims.

Submitting documents for *in camera* inspections is not necessarily sufficient to relieve a party of the burden of supporting its privilege or protection claims with competent affidavits.

- *Caruso v. Coleman Co.*, 1995 U.S. Dist. LEXIS 8914, 1995 WL 384602, at *1 (E.D. Pa. June 22, 1995). Submitting documents to the court for *in camera* review does not relieve a party from the requirement of submitting affidavits or other evidence in support of the asserted privilege.

On occasion parties defy court orders, failing to produce affidavits in support of asserted privilege claims. Generally, when they do so, the privilege has been improperly asserted. Some courts are patient in the face of such discovery game-playing. Increasingly, many courts are not. It is rarely advisable to risk one's credibility in such a manner, particularly since sanctions may result.

- *Amway Corp. v. Procter & Gamble Co.*, 2001 U.S. Dist. LEXIS 4561, at *10 (W.D. Mich. Apr. 3, 2001). "In violation of this court's order, Procter & Gamble has not submitted any affidavit or other sworn evidence to support its claim of attorney-client privilege or work-product immunity with regard to these documents."

The court reviewed the documents and found them to be mere transmittal letters without substantive content and therefore not subject to the privilege in all events.

5. Proving and Applying Foreign Law

The potential complexity for demonstrating each element of privilege rises exponentially in the context of international litigation. It is advisable to have any documents with respect to which a privilege claim is made translated for the court's *in camera* inspection. Affidavits must also be obtained from individuals knowledgeable about the parties to the privileged communications. Given the complexities, courts will not necessarily discount on the grounds of hearsay affidavits that support the privilege by recounting who has been interviewed and what they conveyed. Affidavits from foreign interlocutors are not necessary to support the privilege. But an affidavit by a person who can recount what has been learned in discussions with foreign interlocutors to support the privilege claim is mandatory in the absence of affidavits from foreign interlocutors.

By and large, the privilege law of the United States is far more restrictive and elaborate, not to say arcane, than is the "professional secrecy" law of most non-common-law jurisdictions. Since that is the case, counsel urging protection may well wish to look to foreign law to do so, and not the applicable United States privilege law. But counsel must go to some lengths to prove foreign law. Merely conclusory statements by a foreign attorney will not be sufficient. In such affidavits, one should cite and translate and attach the text of any statutory law or cases upon which the foreign attorney is basing his conclusions that the professional secrecy law would be applicable.

In addition, counsel has to go to some lengths as well to prove that choice of law rules require the foreign law rather than the law of the forum to be applicable. Particularly where a foreign national has chosen to litigate in the United States courts.

■ *Reino de Espana v. American Bureau of Shipping*, 2005 U.S. Dist. LEXIS 15685 (S.D.N.Y. 2005). The court applied United States and not Spanish privilege law to the claims of Spain since that sovereign nation has decided to avail itself of United States courts to adjudicate its claims.

Failure to prove both that the foreign law is applicable and that it is more protective than the law of the forum will be fatal to the claim of privilege where such a claim cannot be sustained under federal or state law of the United States.

- *In re Avantel*, 343 F.3d 311 (5th Cir. 2003). On a writ of mandamus, the Fifth Circuit refused to reverse the district court's factual finding that an affidavit of a Mexican lawyer which merely stated that Mexican secrecy law was more stringent than privilege law in the United States failed to adequately prove the scope of Mexico's professional secrecy law. And that therefore was no error in applying Texas privilege law.

Foreign privilege law arises frequently in the context of patent litigation. Courts will grant comity to the law of foreign jurisdictions, provided the proponent of the privilege remembers to prove the foreign law. Failure to do so may be fatal to the claim. Affidavits submitted by practitioners in a distant or foreign forum are usually sufficient, unless challenged, of course.

- *Organon Inc. v. Mylan Pharms., Inc.*, 303 F. Supp. 2d 546 (D.N.J. 2004). Where the Netherlands enacted a statute covering as privileged communications of patent agents, the American court vacated its own order that the documents must be produced even though the enactment post-dated both the creation of the documents and its own production order. The court went through a long charade, stating that it was interpreting an aspect of Dutch law that no Dutch court had ruled upon and attempting to do so as the Dutch Supreme court would have. Nonsense. It was a simple act of comity. Properly decided. Our sovereignty should not reach as far as any alternative ruling would have done.

- *Stryker Corp. v. Intermedics Orthopedics, Inc.*, 145 F.R.D. 298 (E.D.N.Y. 1992). When communication did not "touch base" with the United States, foreign privilege law was applied, in this instance that of England.

- *Golden Trade v. Lee Apparel Co.*, 143 F.R.D. 514 (S.D.N.Y 1992). Courts will look at the law of the place where the privileged relationship was entered into. Foreign law may be proved by the submission of affidavits of practitioners practicing in such distant forums.

- *Burroughs Wellcome Co. v. Barr Labs., Inc.*, 143 F.R.D. 611 (E.D.N.C. 1992). This case provides an extensive example of the application of multiple foreign laws, proved by means of affidavit, to the availability of the attorney-client privilege in a patent context.

- *In re Ampicillin Antitrust Litig.*, 81 F.R.D. 377, 391 (D.D.C. 1978). Failure to prove the foreign law was fatal to the claim of privilege. "For communications relating to patent activities in other countries, no privilege will be granted as the defendants have failed to indicate what the applicable privilege is, if indeed it exists."

Where actual demonstration is not made of how complying with a discovery order would violate foreign secrecy law, a United States court will not hold its hand in compelling production.

- *In re Air Crash at Taipei*, 211 F.R.D. 374 (C.D. Cal. 2002). Conclusory statements that production of unspecified documents would in a general way violate Singapore secrecy laws was not persuasive and did not preclude discovery.

6. Providing Translations

If a party asserting a claim of privilege fails to provide the court with a translation of the allegedly privileged document, any hope of sustaining the privilege is likely to be lost although, occasionally, time may be given to provide the missing translations.

- *Advertising to Women, Inc. v. Gianni Versace*, 1999 U.S. Dist. LEXIS 12263 (N.D. Ill. Aug. 3, 1999). Bizarrely, the court placed the burden of proving both privilege and waiver thereof on the plaintiffs, which makes no sense because the proponent of the privilege bears the burden of that proof, with the burden then shifting to the party challenging the privilege to show waiver. The documents had fallen into the hands of the party challenging the privilege by their inadvertent production. But what really made the court irate was that it was being asked to pass on the question of whether certain documents written in Italian were privileged without having been provided a verbatim translation.

7. Marking Documents as Privileged

A custom has developed, arising perhaps out of the protective-order context or perhaps merely to forewarn that the privilege is applicable, of marking documents as such. Occasionally, the assumption is made that such marking is sufficient to make the document privileged. It is not. Nonetheless, the practice makes good sense because it may protect privileged documents from inadvertent circulation and careless disposal. Moreover, the fact of the marking may provide the court with evidence that care was taken in the event of inadvertent disclosure. Despite any such marking, however, courts examine the document to determine the availability of the privilege or of the work-product protection. To do otherwise would be to elevate form over substance and to allow the facile invocation of privileges that courts are studious to avoid.

- *In re Derienzo*, 1998 Bankr. LEXIS 635, (Bankr. M.D. Pa. Apr. 28, 1998). Many documents sought to be protected from compelled disclosure were stamped with a notation that the document was subject to attorney-client privilege and not intended for distribution beyond persons named or that the document was confidential because it was an attorney-client communication. However, those notations had relatively little impact on the court because those documents were reviewed for the substance of the communication, rather than their form, in determining which documents were subject to the attorney-client privilege.

An attendant problem of such marking, is that some lawyers, goodness only knows why, have taken to marking each and every document as privileged. It is surely a bizarre custom, which far from serving to protect privileged documents may, by its very promiscuity, serve to make even such legitimate claims somewhat laughable.

E. *Privilege Logs*

Privilege logs were once rare and only gradually came to be suggested as a means both of asserting privilege or protection for a document and putting an adversary on notice that one had done so.

- *United States v. Exxon Corp.*, 87 F.R.D. 624 (D.D.C. 1980). The party claiming privilege for voluminous documents was required to create an index setting forth various elements of privilege claims.

- *United States v. AT&T*, 86 F.R.D. 603 (D.D.C. 1979). Guidelines were adopted setting forth formal procedures to be followed for the claim of privilege with respect to a large volume of documents. Affidavits were to be submitted, setting forth the basis for each claim of privilege in detail. Hearings by special masters and *in camera* inspections were contemplated.

- *In re Fish & Neave*, 519 F.2d 116, 119 (8th Cir. 1975). Document subpoenas were served on attorneys; they were also required to provide a list containing the author's name, addressee's name, and a brief statement of the subject matter of each document so that the discovering party might have "sufficient information that they may argue against the claim of privilege if it is to be put forth."

Privilege logs have now become ubiquitous and are mandated by a large variety of court and tribunal rules.

1. What Rules Apply and What Do They Require?

A blanket assertion of privilege has for long been unavailing to protect documents from disclosure. Instead the practice of creating document indexes to assert the privilege or the protection, once merely good practice, has now become mandatory.

Rule 26(b)(5) of the Federal Rules of Procedures which requires:

> When a party withholds information otherwise discoverable under these rules by claiming that it is privileged or subject to protection as trial preparation material, the party shall make the claim expressly and shall describe the nature of the documents, communications, or things not

produced or disclosed in a manner that, without revealing information itself privileged or protected, will enable other parties to assess the applicability of the privilege or protection.

Similarly, Fed. R. Civ. P. 45(d)(2), which governs subpoenas served on third parties, requires that when information subject to a subpoena is withheld on privilege grounds, the claim must be expressly made and supported by a description of the documents not produced sufficient to enable the demanding party to contest the withholding.

Both Rule 26 (b)(5) and Fed. R. Civ. Pro 45 (d)(2) require that a party asserting privilege or protection supply sufficient details to permit a court to rule as to the availability of either. It is perfectly astonishing how often lawyers draft privilege logs which do not explain who the authors or recipients of documents are as to which privilege is claimed. Or how often the only description of some documents is a cursory "communication with client." Neither is generally sufficient. The following case provides a detailed example of the types of information which may or may not be considered sufficient.

- *SEC v. Beacon Hill Asset Mgmt. LLC*, 231 F.R.D. 134, 143–44 (S.D.N.Y. 2004). "The index does not identify who prepared the spreadsheets or the attorney to whom each was sent. Thus, the index fails to identify an essential element of the attorney-client privilege, namely the existence of an attorney-client communication. *See Golden Trade S.r.L. v. Lee Apparel Co., supra*, 1992 U.S. Dist. LEXIS 17739, 1992 WL 367070, at *5 ('The standard for testing the adequacy of the privilege log is whether, as to each document, it sets forth specific facts that, if credited, would suffice to establish each element of the privilege or immunity that is claimed.'). The affirmation submitted in opposition to the SEC's motion does nothing to fill this evidentiary void.

  "To the extent that BH relies on work-product protection, its showing is also inadequate. BH offers no specific evidence as to any of the spreadsheets claimed to be protected by work product. It does not identify who prepared the spreadsheets, and it provides no information regarding the circumstances under which each spreadsheet was prepared that would support the assertion of work-product protection. *See Grinnell Corp. v. ITT Corp., supra,* 222 F.R.D. 74, 2003 WL 1824642, at *4 (proponent of privilege must establish elements of the privilege as to each document individually).

"The only evidence BH offers to support its assertion of work-product protection is the following statement by its counsel: 'Between September 26 and October 8, Beacon Hill performed a variety of quantitative analyses to determine whether there had been a loss in the Master Fund in September 2002. The analyses undertaken during this period were clearly in anticipation of litigation' This conclusory and generalized statement is insufficient to discharge BH's burden. . . .

"The vast majority of the remaining documents are identified as correspondence or e-mails seeking, transmitting or reflecting legal advice. I find this description to be sufficient. Although the subject matter of the legal advice is not disclosed, given the circumstances, I presume that the advice related [*145] to potential claims that could be asserted against BH as a result of the precipitous decline in the value of its portfolio and BH's delay in disclosing this diminished value. To require BH to disclose additional information would come perilously close to requiring disclosure of the substance of the privileged communication.

"A number of the documents withheld are described as transmitting or reflecting "communications" with counsel. I find this description to be insufficient to sustain an assertion of privilege. An attorney and client can have many communications which are neither privileged nor subject to work product protection, e.g., correspondence advising of the date and time of meetings, correspondence transmitting documents, etc. A description consisting of "communications" or "communications with counsel" is insufficient to establish even the minimal showing required in a privilege log because it does not permit the adversary to make an intelligent assessment as to the applicability of a privilege. Other documents in this category are insufficiently described because the log does not identify the author and intended or actual recipients— required information under Local Civil Rule 26.2. One document is described as "Attachment-letter to investors"; this description does not even remotely suggest that any privilege or protection is applicable." (Some internal citations omitted.)

An attorney would be well advised to determine whether local rules establish alternative guidelines and deadlines for responses to document requests lest failure to do so with a privilege log in the requisite time be deemed a waiver.

- *Ruran v. Beth El Temple of West Hartford, Inc.*, 226 F.R.D. 165, 168–169 (D. Conn. 2005). Local Rule 37 (a) requires that the party asserting the privilege . . . shall provide the following information in the form of a privilege log:

  (1) The type of document;
  (2) The general subject matter of the document;
  (3) The date of the document;
  (4) The author of the document; and
  (5) Each recipient of the document.

  "Even under this approach, however, if the party invoking the privilege does not provide sufficient detail to demonstrate fulfillment of all the legal requirements for application of the privilege, his claim will be rejected."

- *In re Grand Jury Subpoena Dated Jan. 4, 1984*, 750 F.2d 223, 224–25 (2d Cir. 1984). Where a party fails to perfect a claim of privilege that privilege is deemed waived.

Practitioners should also be aware that many agencies have rules that require listing of documents withheld on privilege grounds, which are comparable to those that apply in the federal courts.

- *FTC v. GlaxoSmithKline*, 202 F.R.D. 8 (D.D.C. 2001). The court held that failure to comply with an applicable FTC rule governing motions to quash subpoenas was controlling and procedurally waived any applicable privilege. Rule 2.7(d) of the Federal Trade Commission's Rules of Practice states that "any petition to limit or quash any investigational subpoena or civil investigative demand shall be filed with the Secretary of the Commission within twenty (20) days after service of the subpoena . . . such petition shall set forth all assertions of privilege or other factual and legal objections to the subpoena." 16 C.F.R. Sec. 2.7(d) (2000).

Thus what was once considered merely good practice to facilitate a ruling on privilege issues is now mandated by multiple rules in virtually all courts. Any claim that such document logs would be too burdensome will go nowhere.

- *Green v. Baca*, 219 F.R.D. 485 (C.D. Cal. 2003). Claim that it would be too burdensome to separate privileged from non-privileged documents dismissed as untenable.

A claim that providing a privilege log would invade work product protection by revealing an attorney's mental processes will also go nowhere.

- *PostX Corp. v. Secure Data Motion*, 2004 U.S. Dist. LEXIS 24869, at *5 (N.D. Cal. June 9, 2004), *aff'd*, 115 Fed. Appx. 72 (Fed. Cir. 2004). "PostX states that it is not making a 'blanket refusal to log all documents that post-date the commencement of this litigation. Post X only refuses to log attorney-client communications and attorney work product concerning and post-dating the filing of the initial complaint.' . . . (emphasis in original). PostX argues repeatedly that "it is not required to reveal in a privilege log information that is itself obviously privileged and protected." Id. at 2. It is not "obvious" to the Court why producing a privilege log would itself reveal PostX's privileged information. PostX has failed to provide any help to the Court in determining exactly what is in jeopardy with the production of a typical privilege log, . . ." The documents were accordingly ordered produced. *Aikens v. Deluxe Fin. Servs., Inc.*, 217 F.R.D. 533 (D. Kan. 2003). The court remarked that providing a privilege log would reveal an attorney's mental processes was not one of the grounds for obtaining a protective order under Rule 26.

When both sides have comparable interests in maintaining the claim of privilege, the burden of creating such indexes may not seem too onerous to either side. When the interests differ and when only one side is making a claim of privilege in respect to many documents, the burdens involved in the creation of the indexes may be considerable. Without such indexes and a clear statement of the basis of the claim of the privilege, document by document, a court may well hold that the burden of proof has not been met and may order production of even privileged documents.

2. Defective Privilege Logs

A whole body of case law has now developed detailing the infinite number of ways in which privilege logs are likely to be defective. The *Hill* case, *infra.*, spells out exactly what that court wished to see in a privilege log. Practitioners who wish to avoid challenges to the sufficiency of their privilege logs would be well advised to follow the advice given by that court in respect to what should be included.

- *Hill v. McHenry*, 2002 U.S. Dist. LEXIS 6637, at *6, 8 (D. Kan. Apr. 10, 2002). "[T]he log does not identify the specific privilege/protection being asserted. Under the heading Privilege Asserted, the log merely states, for each document listed, 'Attorney-Client and/or Work-product Privileges.' (Emphasis added.) The privilege log is also deficient in that it fails to state the purpose for which each document was created. In addition, it fails to fully identify the authors and recipients of the documents so as to allow the Court to determine that the documents are in fact communications between the attorney and client (as required for the attorney-client privilege to apply) and/or that they were prepared by or for Defendants or their representatives (as required for the work-product doctrine to apply). Because of these deficiencies, the Court is without sufficient information to determine whether each element of the asserted privilege/protection is satisfied." The court noted that it had the option of permitting discovery by virtue of the defective log but would nonetheless allow amendment before ruling on the validity of the privilege claims. In the amended privilege log, the party claiming protection from compelled disclosure was to enumerate the following for each document withheld:

  (1) A description of the document (e.g., correspondence, memorandum);
  (2) Date prepared;
  (3) Date of document (if different from # 2);
  (4) Identity of the person(s) who prepared the document, including information sufficient to allow the Court to determine whether the document is a communication from the client's attorney and/or whether it was prepared by or for TCI or Tele-Communications or by or for one of their representatives;

(5) Identity of the person(s) for whom the document was prepared and to whom the document was directed (including all copies), including information sufficient to allow the Court to determine whether the document is a communication to the client;

(6) Purpose of preparing the document;

(7) Number of pages of the document;

(8) Basis for withholding discovery of the document, i.e., the specific privilege or protection being asserted; and

(9) Any other pertinent information necessary to establish the elements of each asserted privilege.

The preparation of privilege logs have become increasingly costly and time consuming. And some practitioners question whether anyone in fact reads them at all. Unfortunately courts do if asked to rule on privilege/work product claims and a "defective" privilege log may result in a summary denial of the privilege or work-product protection claimed for a given document.

Nor does it help that the parties often make privilege and protection claims for documents which don't even come close to meeting the criteria for either.

Statements such as "there were no other recipients" in privilege logs have been criticized on the grounds that there is some ambiguity. Instead each individual who received a carbon copy or was blind copied on the document should be detailed.

- *Minebea Co. v. Papst*, 229 F.R.D. 1, 4 (D.D.C. 2005). "The specific names of all recipients and identifying information about them (including those who were cc'd or bcc'd) must be included in a privilege log. Assuming this rule has been applied to these documents, and that Papst's representation that "there were no other recipients" meant that the communication was never shared with any other person or entity, the Court will accept Papst's representation."

So too if in-house counsel is not attached to the legal department exclusively or performs any business functions in a corporation it will not be sufficient to lay a claim of privilege by merely listing that individual in a privilege log as "in-house counsel." More will have to be shown as to why that document authored or sent to him is in fact privileged.

- *In re Asousa P'ship*, 2005 Bankr. LEXIS 2373, at *6 (Bankr. E.D. Pa. Nov. 17, 2005). Where lawyers had multiple roles within a corporation, the court said: "Simply describing these individuals as "in-house counsel" on the privilege log will be insufficient given their dual roles unless the document establishes the involvement of legal counsel."

Beware of sloughing of the preparation of a privilege log by haphazard or conclusory statements. With many courts such will result in an order to produce the document for failure of having sustained the burden of demonstrating the availability of the privilege or protection.

- *SEC v. Beacon Hill Asset Mgmt. LLC*, 231 F.R.D. 134 (S.D.N.Y. 2004). Many documents were ordered produced which were "Inadequately described" or where the description provided was not sufficient to demonstrate the applicability of the privilege or the work product protection.

Beware also of failing to properly identify who the privileged individuals are, preferably in the form of some cast of characters. Do not expect the judge to ferret out that information.

- *SmithKline Beecham Corp v. Apotex Corp.*, 2000 U.S. Dist. LEXIS 13606 at *10 (N.D. Ill. Sept. 13, 2000). The district court said "We will not find that Judge Bobrick committed clear error in refusing to search a 1500-entry, 386-page document for the specific titles and responsibilities of individuals that Plaintiffs took the time to describe only as 'employees.'"

When the author or recipient of a document is not known or listed in a privilege log, a claim of privilege may not necessarily be sustained, even if the content of the document seems to imply that legal advice is being sought or given. Thus, clear identification of both authors and recipients on documents that are written and received for the purpose of obtaining legal advice is a good practice so that identification in privilege logs will not be challenged. The lack of such identification may be made up by affidavits, but surety of privilege protection is more problematic.

- *In re Derienzo*, 1998 Bankr. LEXIS 635 (Bankr. M.D. Pa. Apr. 28, 1998). "One category of documents which were determined not to be subject to the attorney-client privilege were those in which the author of the document was not known. The Court did accept some of the documents authored by a non-attorney as subject to the attorney-client privilege. For those documents where the author was unknown, however, the Court could not determine whether or not they were documents produced by anyone either representing the Defendants or an agent and/or employee of those Defendants. All documents that had an unknown author were, therefore, found to be outside the attorney-client privilege."

Each item used to identify the document must be done with substantial specificity. For example, when the identity and position of recipients of a purportedly privileged document were not identified with sufficient specificity to allow a determination of whether they were encompassed by the Illinois "control group" test, the burden of proving the availability of the privilege was not met.

- *Medical Waste Techs. v. Alexian Bros. Med. Ctr.*, 1998 U.S. Dist. LEXIS 10069 (N.D. Ill. June 23, 1998). "HLS has failed to specify with particularity who exactly the recipients were and what their respective capacities were at the time of distribution. This information is needed in order to see if the recipients of the documents were contained within the control group for the attorney-client privilege."

When the number of documents is sufficiently limited, courts will on occasion dispense with the requirement that a privilege log be prepared before the documents are submitted for *in camera* inspection.

- *Boca Investerings P'shp v. United States*, 1998 U.S. Dist. LEXIS 11840 (D.D.C. Jan. 20, 1998). When the disputed documents numbered only 11, the court denied a motion for sanctions for failure to supply a privilege log and reviewed the disputed documents without such log having been prepared.

3. Waiver of Privilege Claims If Privilege Log Not Provided

Failure to make a proper privilege claim in proper format may well be deemed a procedural waiver of any privilege claim. Courts seem increasingly inclined to so hold, even though courts of appeal have suggested that there should not be a facile deprivation of privilege/protection. Practitioners, however, should not rely on being able to remedy the failing on subsequent motion.

- *Ayers v. SGS Control Servs.*, 2006 U.S. Dist. LEXIS 10134, at *9 (S.D.N.Y. Mar. 9, 2006), *motion for reconsid. denied*, 2006 U.S. Dist. LEXIS 16372 (S.D.N.Y. Apr. 3, 2006). "An assertion of the work product privilege requires the preparation and production of a privilege log. Rule 26(b)(5); Local Rule 26.2. Defendants have failed to provide a privilege log. Defendants have waived any privilege with respect to the tabulation by failing to properly identify it, and assert the privilege."

- *Goodyear Tire & Rubber Co., v. Kirk's Tire & Auto ServiCenter of Haverstraw, Inc.*, 2003 U.S. Dist. LEXIS 15917 (S.D.N.Y. Sept. 10, 2003). Where parties were in possession of third party documents as to which a claim of privilege was made but no privilege log was supplied, the court found waiver.

- *Breon v. Coca-Cola Bottling Co.*, 232 F.R.D. 49 (D. Conn. 2005). Where defendant failed to "perfect" a claim of privilege and work product in respect to certain documents by failing to provide a privilege log, whatever privilege and work product protection might have been applicable ruled by the court to have been waived. Surprising given the sophisticated nature of the defendant and its access, presumably, to knowledgeable counsel. Perhaps the claims of privilege and work-product protection were in fact frivolous and worthless.

- *John Labatt Ltd. v. Molson Breweries*, 1995 U.S. Dist. LEXIS 507, 1995 WL 23603, at *1 (S.D.N.Y. Jan. 19, 1995), *transf'd sub nom.*

Dorf & Stanton Communs. v. Molsen Breweries, 56 F.3d 13 (2d Cir. 1995), *aff'd*, 100 F.3d 919 (Fed. Cir. 1996). Documents were required to be produced in spite of privilege claims where no log had been provided of withheld documents.

If no privilege log can be filed in timely fashion, attorneys would be well advised either to seek an agreement from opposing counsel that they will not use a late filing as a grounds for objecting to the existence of the privilege. Or better still, get leave of court for an extension of time. If the number of documents to be reviewed are at all extensive, no good reason would seem to exist to deny such a request.

One court has found that there was an implied agreement to extend the time for filing a privilege log to avoid a peremptory denial of privilege or protection.

- *Bell v. Pfizer, Inc.*, 2005 U.S. Dist. LEXIS 13174, at *7 (S.D.N.Y. July 1, 2005). "I find that the conduct of counsel gives rise to an implied-in-fact agreement to extend the date for service of indices of documents withheld." At issue was whether defendant waived any privilege/protection claims by filing a privilege log three months after the due date. Plaintiff also filed her log late. Discovery was suspended to allow a ruling on another matter. Once discovery was resumed, defendant filed a privilege log. Prior to the dispute over the privilege claim, plaintiff had not suggested that the late filing would be taken to operate as a waiver. The last point seems dubious insofar as it implies a "fair warning" by an adversary as to what position they propose to take should the other side violate a time rule established by court rules.

4. Amendment of Privilege Logs Either Granted or Required

- *Ryan v. National Union Fire Ins. Co.*, 2006 U.S. Dist. LEXIS 7366, at *21–22 (D. Conn. Feb. 28, 2006). "Defendants have created a privilege log concerning 26 documents created between 11/4/02 and 4/8/03. In this log, the defendants have technically complied with the requirements laid out by the federal and local rules; however, they have not supplied enough information for the court to make a determination of privilege. The log contains the dates, authors, and recipients of the communications, the document type, the subject, and the applicable privilege or protection. However, the log does not include the titles of the communicating parties, their relationship to one another, or detailed information about the subject of the communications. For purposes of attorney-client privilege, the court is unable to determine either whether the communications made were between attorneys and clients or whether they were communications that tend to reveal client confidences. Alternatively, where the defendants allege the work-product doctrine is applicable, they have not specified whether the communications concern fact or opinion work-product. Without this information, it is unclear which standard the court should apply.

"Defendants' Motion for a Protective Order is **DENIED** on the current record. Defendants are **ORDERED** to provide the court with a supplement to the privilege log containing the deficient information described above."

Many courts will allow amendment or filing of privilege logs where none were filed, deeming the issue of privilege too important for summary disposition and recognizing that compiling the requisite privilege logs for numerous documents that are claimed as privilege is burdensome. The practitioner, however, runs the risk of appearing before a court not inclined to be as lenient as some. *See also* Part III, Section on "Sanctions," *infra.*

Also many will grant motions by adversaries requiring more complete privilege logs where it is difficult to sort out what privilege is being claimed and what the grounds for the claim are.

- *Rhodia Chimie v. PPG Indus., Inc.*, 218 F.R.D. 416 (D. Del. 2003). Plaintiff's motion to require production of privilege/work product documents was denied on the grounds of an inadequate privilege log but plaintiff's request to require defendant to provide a more complete privilege log was granted.

- *Mack v. GlobalSantaFe Drilling Co.*, 2006 U.S. Dist. LEXIS 18437 (E.D. La. Apr. 11, 2006). Although the court found the privilege log useless and waded through the documents to guess who the various individuals were and what their roles were and although none of the documents were marked or Bates-stamped so that they could be compared to the little information given in the privilege log and although no privilege was asserted until that throughly inadequate log was filed, the court nonetheless deemed the privilege too important to find waiver. *BG Real Estate Servs. v. American Equity Ins. Co.*, 2005 U.S. Dist. LEXIS 10330 (E.D. La. May 18, 2005). "In this case, however, because of the importance of the privileges asserted and the substantial burden on defendants of compiling the requisite logs, I have not deemed the privileges waived, either by defendants' failure to comply with *Rule 26(b)(5)* or by their failure thus far to sustain their burden of proof. Instead, I have ordered defendants to submit the necessary materials by dates certain, . . . and I will defer ruling for now and address the privilege objections after defendants make their supplemental submissions."

Since federal rules now mandate producing a log of withheld documents, any failure to do so may result in an order mandating production, without any opportunity to cure. And failure to provide such a log as a basis for any protective motions may result in sanctions.

- *SecureInfo Corp. v. Bukstel*, 2003 U.S. Dist. LEXIS 23688 (E.D. Pa. Dec. 16, 2003). Party was sanctioned and prohibited from filing any more motions dealing with privilege until compliance with Rule 26(b)(5).

- *40 Gardenville LLC v. Travelers Prop. Cas.*, 2004 U.S. Dist. LEXIS 8846 (W.D.N.Y. Apr. 22, 2004). Failure to provide privilege log fatal to any privilege claim to the entire closing file of an attorney in a real estate transaction.

With documents increasingly produced in electronic form, new problems are arising. Computer programs may provide information which is generally referred to in computer lingo as "metadata." These provide a history of the document, containing information such as file names, dates of the file, authors of the file, recipients of the file, printout dates, changes and modification dates, and other information. Often the data can be provided in electronic form with the metadata either "scrubbed" or "locked" from ready access. If that is done, it should be stated in a privilege log, lest failure to do so be deemed a waiver.

- *Williams v. Sprint/United Mgmt. Co.*, 230 F.R.D. 640 (D. Kan. 2005). "For any other metadata Defendant claims is protected by the attorney-client privilege or as attorney work product, the Court finds that Defendant should have raised this issue prior to its unilateral decision to produce the spreadsheets with the metadata removed. *Fed. R. Civ. P. 26(b)(5)* requires a party withholding otherwise discoverable information on the basis of privilege to make the claim expressly and to describe the nature of the documents, communications, or things not produced or disclosed in a manner that, without revealing the privileged information, will enable the other parties to assess the applicability of the privilege. Normally, this is accomplished by objecting and providing a privilege log for 'documents, communications, or things' not produced.

  "In this case, Defendant has failed to object and has not provided a privilege log identifying the electronic documents that it claims contain privileged metadata. Defendant has not provided the Court with even a general description of the purportedly privileged metadata that was scrubbed from the spreadsheets. As Defendant has failed to provide any privilege log for the electronic documents it claims contain metadata that will reveal privileged communications or attorney work product, the Court holds that Defendant has waived any attorney-client privilege or work product protection with regard to the spreadsheets' metadata except for metadata directly corresponding to the adverse impact analyses and social security number information, which the Court has permitted Defendant to remove from the spreadsheets."[3]

The court held a rule to show cause as to why defendant should not also be sanctioned in other ways for failure to supply the metadata

---

3. The court turned to *The Sedona Principles: Best Practices, Recommendations & Principles for Addressing Electronic Document Discovery* (The Sedona Conference Working Group Series, July 2005 Version), available generally at http://www.thesedonaconference .org, and more specifically available at http://www.thesedonaconference.org/content/ miscFiles/7_05TSP.pdf. guidance on these electronic discovery issues.

and concluded that defendant had shown sufficient cause to avoid any sanction other than the requirement that the missing data be supplied.

Parties have sought to have a court punish the failure to submit a privilege log in timely fashion by a denial of the availability of the privilege. Because the sanction is severe, the "fault" must be a grievous one for the sanction to be granted. *See* Section on "Sanctions," *infra* for further examples.

- *Burlington Northern v. United States Dist. Court*, 408 F.3d 1142 (9th Cir.), *cert. denied*, 126 S. Ct. 428 (2005) Ninth Circuit confirmed that it did not believe a *per se* waiver rule for failure to file a timely privilege log was appropriate, but that the sanction of waiver granted was appropriate to the circumstances and thus denied the writ.

- *In re DG Acquisition Corp.*, 151 F.3d 75, 80–81 (2d Cir. 1998). The court considered the number of documents that had to be reviewed and the time available to determine that the subpoena had been responded to have been within a reasonable time. And thus did not order the documents produced.

Minor infractions are generally tolerated without resulting waiver, especially if there is any indicia of good faith rather than purposeful abusiveness of the discovery process.

- *Heavin v. Owens-Corning Fiberglass*, 2004 U.S. Dist. LEXIS 2265 (D. Kan. Feb. 3, 2004). Where privilege log was supplied 23 days after responses to discovery, which generally asserted privileges and where the log was supplement at the request of the adversary in two weeks' time, the failure to supply an adequate, timely log with the responses to discovery did not constitute waiver of the privilege. Even though the privilege log was considered to be seriously deficient—for example, identifications such as: "Discuss Plaintiff's worker's compensation claim"; "Discuss case strategy related to Plaintiff's worker's compensation claim"; or "Discuss advantages and disadvantages related to settlement of Plaintiff's claim" were not sufficient to test privilege claims. Nonetheless, the party submitting the privilege log was allowed to file a second amended log, with the benefit of the court's detailed "advisory" opinion as to what would constitute an adequate privilege log.

Be aware, however that the tolerance of certain courts for failure to submit a timely privilege log is diminishing especially if there is any hint of a cavalier or abusive attitude. In those instances, some courts are increasingly, and in rather draconian fashion, imposing sanctions of waiver and worse. *See also* "Sanctions" *infra.*

- *FG Hemisphere Assocs., LLC. v. Republique du Congo,* 2005 U.S. Dist. LEXIS 3523 (S.D.N.Y. Mar. 7, 2005). The Republic of Congo took a rather cavalier attitude to the court's discovery orders and failed to file any privilege log at all. (Needless to say many foreign countries find our discovery procedures arcane, cumbersome and not binding on them). The court found waiver but imposed no other sanctions since there was no mechanism for enforcement. The same can be said if The Republic of Congo ignored the order to produce privileged documents.

- *Carfagno v. Jackson Nat'l Life Ins. Co.,* 2001 U.S. Dist. LEXIS 1768, at *3–4, 7–8 (W.D. Mich. Feb. 13, 2001). "Jackson National does not attempt to excuse, or even explain, its delay in responding to plaintiffs' discovery requests. Rather, defendant asserts only that its conduct was not egregious or prejudicial, and that a waiver of objections is essentially a sanction for egregious discovery abuse. Although some cases discuss waiver in these terms, this is not an accurate characterization of the waiver doctrine. If the time limits set forth in the discovery rules are to have any meaning, waiver is a necessary consequence of dilatory action in most cases. Any other result would . . . completely frustrate the time limits contained in the Federal Rules and give a license to litigants to ignore the time limits for discovery without any adverse consequences. . . . A second and independent reason supports this result. As a result of 1993 amendments to Rule 26 of the Rules of Civil Procedure, documents withheld on a claim of privilege or immunity must be described in a privilege log. Fed. R. Civ. P. 26(b)(5). Although Jackson National's brief makes vague statements concerning the possible privileged nature of documents called for in requests nos. 6, 11 and 13, it has not submitted to this court a privilege log in support of its objections, as required by Rule 26(b)(5). Defendant's failure to provide the court with information of sufficient specificity to permit the court to determine whether the privilege asserted applies to the withheld documents provides an independent ground for finding a waiver of any privilege or immunity." (Citations omitted.)

Without a complete privilege log, any attempt to overturn a magistrate's ruling or that of the district court is likely to fail on appeal.

- *Stalling v. Union Pac. R. R. Co.*, 2003 U.S. Dist. LEXIS 12419, at *8 (N.D. Ill. July 16, 2003). "Defendants, who have admitted that only some of their lobbying documents are privileged, have not submitted a privilege log or made any attempt to describe which documents are subject to which privilege. Without that information, we have no basis for setting aside the Magistrate Judge's Order." *Sustained*, 2003 U.S. Dist. LEXIS 15454 (N.D. Ill. Sept. 3, 2003).

Failure to provide a *timely* does not necessarily result in a finding that whatever privileges have been waived if the court is not a stickler. But the practitioner ought to be aware that the danger exists.

- *Sanchez v. Matta*, 229 F.R.D. 649 (D.N.M. 2004). Failure to provide privilege log "earlier" not fatal to privilege claims. There was no indication of how late the privilege log was provided or why it was late.

Even before the enactment of Rule 26(b)(5), courts had held that failure to provide a log or index and failure to comply with a more detailed local rule in that regard would be considered presumptive evidence that assertion of privilege or protection was specious.

- *Grossman v. Schwarz*, 125 F.R.D. 376, 386–87 (S.D.N.Y. 1989). "[F]ailure to comply with the explicit requirements of Rule 46(e) will be considered presumptive evidence that the claim of privilege is without factual or legal foundation."

The document index, or "privilege log" must be as specific as possible, both with respect to identifying essential privilege criteria such as recipients and authors, and the content thereof with a clear statement as to the basis of the privilege claim. Absent such specificity, a court is more than likely to order production without bothering to peruse the document. The rationale of such peremptory courts is that they do not care to go to greater lengths to protect a party's privilege than that party is willing to do on its own behalf.

Any claim of privilege which can not or does not specify who the author of the document was and who the recipients were, is bound to fail.

- *Williams v. Sprint/United Mgmt. Co.*, 2006 U.S. Dist. LEXIS 4219, at *76 (D. Kan. Feb. 1, 2006). The attempt to protect a document described as "reallignment & selection process transmitting legal advice re: demographic analysis" under the guise of privilege where both the author and the recipients were designated as "unknown" was, need we say it? Unsuccessful.

The court also found that the various descriptions of the documents failed to demonstrate in any way that they were for the purpose of seeking legal advice and thus ordered virtually all of them produced. When it came to claims of work-product protection, the court said: "[T]he Court finds the descriptions provided ('lists,' 'summaries,' 'calibrations,' and 'ratings') are insufficient to establish work-product protection. There is nothing in the descriptions to persuade the Court that these written materials were created, collected or considered in any context other than the normal course of business."

No *in camera* review was conducted. The descriptions in the privilege log alone were relied upon.

The case provides multiple examples of what will not fly even when done by a supposedly sophisticated client using purportedly sophisticated attorneys to defend it.

- *ConAgra, Inc. v. Arkwright Mut. Ins. Co.*, 32 F. Supp. 2d 1015 (N.D. Ill. 1999). The party's brief and privilege log were deemed insufficient to sustain the privilege claims. "The claims of Arkwright that the documents at issue are privileged contain one serious defect: nowhere in its brief or privilege log is this court given enough information on which to decide whether the documents do in fact contain privileged information and to assess the applicability of the privilege."

- *Christman v. Brauvin Realty Advisors, Inc.*, 185 F.R.D. 251 (N. D. Ill. 1999). Vague and generalized index log descriptions resulted in denial of the privilege. "Many of the descriptions in the McDermott and Shefsky privilege logs are too vague to do so. For example, several McDermott documents are described as 'fax cover sheet with note.' Likewise, a letter with handwritten notes from McDermott attorney Ellen Kollar, which does not state to whom it is to or from, is too vague for the objecting parties to satisfy their burden of establishing the attorney-client privilege."

■ *In re Stern Walters Partners, Inc.*, 1996 U.S. Dist. LEXIS 3041, 1996 WL 115290, at *4 (N.D. Ill. Mar. 12, 1996). When the court could not discern from a description of the documents that a privilege applied, the documents were ordered produced.

■ *Weeks v. Samsung Heavy Indus. Co.*, 1996 U.S. Dist. LEXIS 8554, 1996 WL 341537, at *2 (N.D. Ill. June 19, 1996). The log should allow the parties and the court to assess the applicability of the claimed privilege by stating who was involved in the communications and the subject matter of the communications.

■ *Allendale Mut. Ins. Co. v. Bull Data Sys., Inc.*, 145 F.R.D. 84, 89 (N.D. Ill. 1992). The privilege log should list each document sought to be protected and should provide details describing the documents. Some of the details the log should contain for each document include the following: date, author, and all recipients of the document, subject matter, purpose, and an explanation as to why the document should be privileged and not produced in discovery.

An assertion of one grounds in the document index while failing to assert another may well preclude later assertion of the omitted grounds although courts which take pity on litigants and their counsel may allow for timely amendment where no detrimental reliance by the opposing party has occurred. A peremptory dismissal of the grounds not asserted, however, is not unknown.

■ *In re Honeywell Int'l, Inc. Sec. Litig.*, 230 F.R.D. 293 (S.D.N.Y. 2003). Where a party sought to amend a privilege log to assert work-product as well as privilege protection and thus conform the log to its legal theories, the court refused to permit the belated correction and called it precisely the type of litigation "gamesmanship" that correctly designated privilege logs were designed to prevent. Accordingly, production of the documents as to which work-product protection was claimed in the work papers of the party's accountants was ordered.

■ *Union Pacific R.R. Co. v. Crew Transp. Serv., Inc.*, 2003 U.S. Dist. LEXIS 21753 (N.D. Ill. Dec. 2, 2003). Party that sought to argue that documents were privilege protected precluded from doing so and documents were only considered as work-product protected, which was the sole grounds listed in the document index.

A party seeking to preserve a privilege would do well to be thorough and consistent in its identification of documents. Different characterizations as to the nature of a particular document may make the privilege claim suspect.

- *In re Lernout & Hauspie Sec. Litig.*, 222 F.R.D. 29 (D. Mass. 2004). The producing party claimed that the production of a privileged e-mail was inadvertent. It did not know that the recipient was an attorney. The court found that the individual had been designated as a legal counsel and documents addressed to him had been designated as privileged in a log. Accordingly the court did not believe the excuse given for the allegedly inadvertent production, found it had been purposeful and therefore entailed subject matter waiver, requiring the production of an additional 15 documents that were indisputably otherwise privileged.

- *International Surplus Lines Ins. Co. v. Willis Corroon Corp.*, 1993 U.S. Dist. LEXIS 431, 1993 WL 13468, at *2 (N.D. Ill. Jan. 30, 1993). A privilege log was insufficient where it contained one or two words to describe the nature of the document and where it characterized the same document differently three separate times.

Belated supplementation of a privilege log when new privileged and work-product documents are found need not necessarily be fatal to the assertion of privilege in the light of the often complexity of document retention in the modern corporate context.

- *Heavin v. Owens-Corning Fiberglass*, 2004 U.S. Dist. LEXIS 20099 (D. Kan. Apr. 28, 2004). In addressing privilege issues, the court referred to a "Second Amended Privilege Log" without batting an eyelash.

- *Woodland v. Nalco Chem. Co.*, 2003 U.S. Dist. LEXIS 22305 (E.D. La. Dec. 8, 2003). Supplementation of privilege log when three-page handwritten notes by in-house counsel dealing with matters in litigation and communications with corporate employees were belatedly found was sufficient. No "draconian" waiver was warranted when there was no showing of anything but inadvertence in failure to discover document before.

Similarly, a party seeking to compel documents listed on a privilege log might to do well to request greater specificity by the withholding party when attacking the log on the ground of insufficiency. Some courts will not uphold privileges not clearly established. Others, however, have been known to chide attorneys bringing motions to compel where there is no evidence that the party seeking production has made efforts to obtain greater clarification of deficient logs.

- *Metric Constructors, Inc. v. Bank of Tokyo-Mitsubishi, Ltd.*, 1998 U.S. Dist. LEXIS 18428 (E.D.N.C. Sept. 25, 1998). In denying a motion to compel a production of documents with respect to which assertions of privilege had been made, the district court remarked that not only had the party bringing the motion waited six months to do so but in the interim no correspondence regarding a purportedly insufficient privilege log had been addressed by the party seeking production.

Not all courts, however, even in the face of Rule 26(b)(5), will necessarily require any privilege log if they believe that the challenge to the privilege is without basic merit.

- *In re Muskogee Envtl. Conservation Co.*, 221 B.R. 526 (Bankr. N.D. Okla. 1998). When the court determined that the documents sought were not relevant to matters before the court, that the privilege had not been waived, and that the request was overly broad, it declined to require the cost and burden of preparing a privilege log.

Often, if the court finds that a party has failed to comply with a local rule requiring a privilege/protection log or index, the party will be given an opportunity to cure by creating such a log, provided the failure to do so in the first instance has not been "flagrant."

- *Trzeciak v. Apple Computers, Inc.*,1995 U.S. Dist. LEXIS 428 (S.D.N.Y. Jan. 19, 1995). The defendant was ordered to provide a log that complied with the local rule.

- *In re In-Store Advertising Sec. Litig.*, 163 F.R.D. 452 (S.D.N.Y. 1995). A cure was permitted when the existence of documents was known to the parties. However, when the privilege log does not make a complete listing of withheld documents, no cure by merely revising the privilege log will be permitted in lieu of immediate production of the suppressed document. A document that was not listed in a log was ordered produced without any further inquiry as to its status. (Citation omitted.)

- *Allstate Life Ins. Co. v. First Trust Nat'l Ass'n*, 1993 U.S. Dist. LEXIS 5461, 1993 WL 138844, at *3 (S.D.N.Y. Apr. 23, 1993). A party refused any meaningful compliance with the mandates of a privilege log until faced with sanctions. The court ordered that the withheld documents be produced.

- *Kansas-Nebraska Nat. Gas Co. v. Marathon Oil Co.*, 109 F.R.D. 12, 24–25 (D. Neb. 1985). When a party merely asserted a blanket claim but did not identify documents that were being withheld, no cure by belatedly providing a log would be permitted.

The sanction of immediate production is necessary, lest a party be rewarded for stonewalling.

Counsel should not overlook the possibility that a local rule may govern the manner in which such logs are to be prepared with greater specificity. [*E.g.*, Local Civil Rule 46(e)(2)(ii)(A) in the Southern District of New York.]

- *Jones v. Boeing Co.*, 163 F.R.D. 15 (D. Kan. 1995). The court dismissed the claim that such a log for each withheld document was excessively burdensome. When large numbers of documents are involved, the assertions of privilege and protection may be made by document categories.

- *Metro Wastewater Reclamation Dist. v. Continental Cas. Co.*, 142 F.R.D. 471 (D. Colo.), *recons. denied*, 142 F.R.D. 471 (D. Colo. 1992). Privilege was asserted with respect to thousands of documents that fell into eleven broad categories.

Thus, courts are insisting on usable document indexes, by categories, to facilitate review and are publishing the indexes in their orders.

- *North Carolina Elec. Membership Corp. v. Carolina Power & Light Co.*, 110 F.R.D. 511, 517 (M.D.N.C. 1986). This case provides a useful example of a document index; however, check the current rule and the local rule to make sure that additional information is not required.

On occasion, albeit rarely, a detailed index may be sufficient for the court to rule on a claim of protection without reviewing the documents themselves. Nevertheless, it must be adequate to permit the court to determine whether all elements of the privilege are present in each document.

- *Coastal States Gas Corp. v. Dep't of Energy*, 617 F.2d 854, 861 (D.C. Cir. 1980). In lieu of *in camera* inspection, the agency submitted an index of withheld documents along with affidavits in support of the decision not to release the memoranda. The court held that the index entries showing author, addressee, and brief description, together with conclusory assertions of privilege, were insufficient.

The practice of providing document indexes to identify those documents in respect to which an attorney client privilege or work-product protection is claimed is now subject to federal rule, which merely codifies long-standing practice.

Rule 26(b)(5) requires that the withholding party make the claim of privilege or protection expressly "and describe the nature of the documents, communications, or things not produced or disclosed in a manner that, without revealing information itself privileged or protected, will enable other parties to assess the applicability of the privilege or protection." Fed. R. Civ. P. 26(b)(5).

In addition, check local rules. These may contain more detailed specifications as to what must be revealed in a privilege log. As an example, Local Rule 9(d)(1) of the district court in Connecticut requires a privilege log to contain (1) the type of document, (2) the general subject matter of the document, (3) the date of the document, (4) the author of the document, and (5) each recipient of the document.

Preparing an adequate privilege log is doubtlessly a tiring and taxing endeavor, yet failure to do so may, with a particularly meticulous court, result in a finding of waiver even if a valid claim of privilege would otherwise apply.

- *Haid v. Wal-Mart Stores, Inc.*, 2001 U.S. Dist. LEXIS 10564, at *4, 13–14 (D. Kan. June 25, 2001). "The law is well settled that failure to produce a privilege log or production of an inadequate privilege log may be deemed waiver of the privilege." Affirming the magistrate's holding that waiver of privilege had occurred because no privilege log had been supplied and refusing to grant additional time to remedy the lack thereof. "Defendant made a strategic and tactical decision to remove this case from state to federal court. [A document log is necessary to claim privilege in federal court but not in the state court from where the case was removed.] Yet, for some strange reason, defendant chose not to prepare the privilege log that is plainly required in federal practice. [Fn. deleted] In any event, the Court finds defendant has failed to meet its burden to timely show that the documents it is withholding are privileged attorney-client communications. Defendant's objections, therefore, have been waived. Defendant shall provide all documents responsive to this request within eleven days from the date this Memorandum and Order is filed."

- *Maine v. United States Dep't of the Interior*, 285 F.3d 126 (1st Cir.), *op. withdrawn* (Apr. 5, 2002), *substituted op.*, 298 F.3d 60 (1st Cir. 2002). The court found that the party claiming privilege had submitted an inadequate privilege log because the entries failed to demonstrate that the withheld documents contained or related to information that the client intended to keep confidential and it thus failed to establish an essential element of the privilege. Moreover, where the party failed to submit or request leave to submit an amended log, the ruling of the district court on privilege issues would be permitted to stand.[4]

---

4. After the convoluted appeal history, the court finally held that the district court's rulings on the attorney-client privilege were proper, and that the disclosure of the remaining withheld documents was warranted, with only one negligible exception. Yet another example of litigation run amuck for an end result that the lawyers should have been able to agree to. Many litigating lawyers are making little or no effort to police the discovery claims they bring to courts for adjudication. Courts in turn are making too rare efforts to stop them. The elephants heaved and lo and behold they bring forth a veritable mouse. On the client's quarter.

Short-handed identifications of subject matter that merely indicate a discussion about a "claim" have also come to be regarded as too cursory to be useful.

- *Allen v. Chicago Transit Auth.*, 198 F.R.D. 495, 498 (N.D. Ill. 2001). "Accordingly, descriptions such as 'letter re claim,' 'analysis of claim,' or 'report in anticipation of litigation'—with which we have grown all too familiar—will be insufficient. This may be burdensome, but it will provide a more accurate evaluation of a discovery opponent's claims and takes into consideration the fact that there are no presumptions operating in the discovery opponent's favor. Any failure to comply with these directions will result in a finding that the plaintiff-discovery opponents have failed to meet their burden of establishing the applicability of the privilege."

Even where a court does not impose as harsh a remedy of waiver for failure to supply a timely and adequate privilege log, there is no guarantee that amendment will be allowed or that an *in camera* inspection will not be triggered, which will then find that privileges were improperly and far too broadly asserted. The end result is often a very annoyed judge, compelled disclosure, and even sanctions in the form of footing the costs and legal fees incurred by the other side in fighting the discovery battle.

- *United States Fid. & Guar. Co. v. Braspetro Oil Servs. Co.*, 2002 U.S. Dist. LEXIS 111 (S.D. N.Y. Jan 4, 2002). The court repeatedly chides the party asserting privilege for having ignored the court's order that all documents in respect to which such privilege is claimed be fully identified. Although the court stated that it was not basing its rulings on that grounds, it is hard to imagine that the claim of privilege received less sympathetic treatment by the court because of that failure. "Again, Defendants had a duty to inform this Court what materials they supplied to their experts before offering their view as to why the privilege nonetheless still obtained."

- *SmithKline Beecham Corp. v. Apotex Corp.*, 193 F.R.D. 530, 533–34 (N.D. Ill. 2000). "For each document, this description should include the date of the document, all authors and recipients of the document along with their capacities, a statement of the subject matter of the document, and an explanation of the basis for withholding the document from discovery."

If one document is attached to another, each must appear as a separate item in the document log.

- *Mold-Masters Ltd. v. Husky Injection Molding Sys. Ltd.*, 2001 U.S. Dist. LEXIS 20152, at *8 & 9 (N.D. Ill. Dec. 5, 2001). "It should hardly come as a surprise that an attachment to a document must appear as a separate entry on the privilege log. . . . Courts provide protection against disclosure pursuant to the attorney-client privilege and work-product doctrine on a document-by-document basis. Since a document with an attachment constitutes two separate documents, a party objecting to the disclosure of a document with an attachment must prove that both the document and the attachment individually satisfy the requirements of the applicable privilege or doctrine. Merely attaching a document to a privileged or protected document does not make the attached document privileged or protected."

And even if documents are listed in privilege logs but are not then addressed in briefs filed in support of privilege claims, the court may conclude that the claim of privilege has been abandoned. An indulgent court may allow remedy. But don't count on it.

- *Newport Pac. Inc. v. County of San Diego*, 200 F.R.D. 628, 634 (S.D. Cal. 2001). "Defendants do not address these disks and/or e-mails in the Opposition despite the fact that they are listed on the privilege log as attorney-client communication. Because Defendants did not address these documents, the Court concludes Defendants do not oppose production of said disks and/or e-mails. The Court therefore grants Plaintiffs' Motion to Compel and orders production of these documents to the extent that they are not individually addressed below."

To a certain point, most courts are patient and protect assertions of privilege, often allowing multiple amendments to the document indices instead of compelling disclosure. Depending on the patience of the court, even third amended privilege logs have been permitted. But eventually the patience of even the most forgiving court is exhausted. Immediate production of documents in respect to which a valid assertion of privilege might have been properly if timely asserted may then result.

- *Mold-Masters Ltd. v. Husky Injection Molding Sys., Ltd.*, 2001 U.S. Dist. LEXIS 20152, at *10 (N.D. Ill. Dec. 5, 2001). The third amended privilege log was allowed. "[D]ocuments that are not described at all on Husky's privilege log must be disclosed. This Court has provided Husky with multiple opportunities and sufficient time to comply with Rule 26(b)(5). At this stage of the game, immediate production of any document not described at all on Husky's privilege log is the necessary sanction. So too when the court cannot ascertain what is the basis of the privilege assertion, the document will be ordered disclosed."

- *SmithKline Beecham Corp. v. Apotex Corp.*, 193 F.R.D. 530, 534 (N.D. Ill. 2000). If the description falls below the accepted standard under Fed. R. Civ. P. 26(b)(5) and fails to provide sufficient information for the court and the party seeking disclosure to assess the applicability of the attorney-client privilege or work-product doctrine, then disclosure of the document is an appropriate sanction.

Although a privilege log should demonstrate each element of the privilege, each potential factor that might defeat the privilege does not have to be foreseen and eliminated at the risk of having a technical waiver of the privilege as a sanction.

- *A.I.A. Holdings, S.A. v. Lehman Brothers, Inc.*, 2002 U.S. Dist. LEXIS 20107, at *16 (S.D.N.Y. Oct. 18, 2002). The only issue presented was the facial sufficiency of the privilege log, not the substance of the privilege assertion. Court refused to accept the challenge to the sufficiency of the privilege log on the grounds that if accepted, none could pass muster. The court used the example that one element of the privilege was that the communication was with an attorney, but the proponent of the privilege did not have to demonstrate that the attorney had in fact been admitted to the bar of a given state. Thus evidentiary proof needs to be submitted only if some specific aspect is challenged. "Since the challenger is given this information, there is no logic or efficiency in requiring the proponent of a privilege or the Court to address matters that are not contested by the challenger." In addition, failure to list a tape as privileged was excused where the transcript was so listed.

Since preparing privilege logs is such a tedious and time-consuming endeavor, often it is relegated to a paralegal and/or a junior associate who may be given inadequate directions as to what elements are necessary to constitute a valid privilege assertion. To date, courts have been patient with erroneously asserted privileges, but the potential for sanctions by way of compelled disclosure of even privileged materials and cost shifting, including legal fees, is real.

- *Renner v. Chase Manhattan Bank*, 2001 U.S. Dist. LEXIS 17920, at *14 (S.D.N.Y. Nov. 1, 2001). "Based on a review of these documents, one could plausibly imagine that a paralegal was instructed to review Townsend's notebook and remove as privileged any page that made any reference to Donald Clark. But the proper application of the attorney-client privilege requires a more demanding analysis than that."

Moreover, the costs of bringing the motion to compel, including legal fees incurred, will be shifted to the losing side where the court has come to doubt the bona fides of the proponent of the privilege.

- *B. F. G. of Illinois, Inc. v. Ameritech Corp.*, 2001 U.S. Dist. LEXIS 18930 (N.D. Ill. Nov. 8, 2001). The court correctly excoriated a party for preparing a privilege log that in no way permitted a determination of the impropriety of privilege assertions that were revealed from an *in camera* review of the documents not to be warranted and thus awarded the costs and attorney's fees incurred in bringing the motion to compel.

The burden and expense of preparing a privilege log can always be foregone by a representation that no such documents exist. Woe betide the party who does so if privileged documents come to light in depositions and a belated attempt is then made to claim privilege. Courts are not likely to lend themselves, nor should they, to such discovery "fraud." Absent extraordinary facts, waiver should be found albeit a court may nonetheless address the substance of the claim.

- *Benton v. Brookfield Props. Corp.*, 2003 U.S. Dist. LEXIS 13020 (S.D.N.Y. July 23, 2003). To obviate the burden of preparing a privilege log, defendant claimed that no privileged or work-product-protected documents existed. Thereafter the party tried to raise a claim of work-product protection in respect to documents that came to light in the course of depositions. The court suggested that the prior representations might operate as a waiver but then went on to analyze the claim substantively as well and found that the claim of work product could not be met because the documents were not prepared by the party or a party representative but by the insurance company.

F. In Camera *Inspections*

In camera inspections are now routine. Privilege logs often leave much to be desired in terms of completeness, despite the mandates of Rule 26 (a)(6). Even when the mandates of the rule are technically followed, lawyers seem intentionally or merely through ignorance utterly befuddled about just what it is that the privilege/protections do in fact protect. Often what lawyers believe is that any document where a lawyer is the recipient or author is ipso facto privileged. That is pure hogwash. But the result is that cases where *in camera* reviews are conducted for some reason or another have now become legion. It would take an entire book on that subject alone to compile them all. Indeed, at times it almost seems that courts now believe that they are compelled to conduct *in camera* reviews. That is obviously not the law. Some courts expressly still hold that it is sufficient to review privilege logs. However, since counsel knowingly or unknowingly seek to protect under the privilege/protection documents that by no stretch of the imagination fit, courts are using *in camera* inspections to test the validity of the assertions.

- *Pfizer Inc. v. Ranbaxy Labs. Ltd.*, 2004 U.S. Dist. LEXIS 20948 (D. Del. Oct. 7, 2004). A partial *in camera* review was done of documents that had no attorney author or recipient or where an attorney was only one of many recipients. The document sample was chosen by the party resisting the assertion of privilege/protection. The court concluded that neither applied and granted sanctions—costs and attorney's fees incurred in bringing the motion to compel.

- *Nationwide Mut. Ins. Co. v. Dimenichi*, 2004 U.S. Dist. LEXIS 25153 (E.D. Pa. Dec. 9, 2004). "[B]y undertaking an *in camera* review of each of the 261 withheld documents, the Court has determined that a significant number of the documents, in whole or in part, do not contain information that falls within a conventional interpretation of the attorney-client privilege and/or work product doctrine, largely because so much of the information contained in them is merely factual recitation of pleadings filed, meetings held or conversations had with persons outside even Nationwide's description of the confidential lawyer-client relationship."

Indeed, the use of *in camera* examinations of documents prior to a discovery order issuing has become such a standard judicial practice, that a reviewing court has held it to be plain error for a trial court to have failed to do so.

- *In re Antitrust Grand Jury*, 805 F.2d 155, 168 (6th Cir. 1986). It was plain error for the trial court not to have reviewed documents *in camera* before ordering production based on the crime/fraud exception. "We are a little confounded as to why the district court did not review the documents *in camera* before ordering them produced."

- *EEOC v. Lutheran Soc. Servs.*, 186 F.3d 959, 968 (D.C. Cir. 1999). The court was tacitly critical of the district court for ruling on the issue without examining an investigative report prepared by outside counsel in respect to the client's potential exposure for EEOC claims *in camera* although it is hard to see what more an examination of the report might add to assist in the determination that needed to be made. If the hiring of an attorney to assess claims without any litigation in the offing is sufficient to accord work-product protection to the report generated by such an attorney, it should be irrelevant to look at what the report may conclude or why it so concludes.

Query is it such a good idea to have the courts intrude themselves unnecessarily into the assessments made by counsel in a judicial system such as ours which relies on neutral fact-finders of adversaries free to present their own cases and not to have their thinking intruded upon over much either by opponents or for that matter the adjudicators either?

Query why in the name of some abstract perfection require the district courts to expend more judicial resources than necessary to adjudicate the matter in dispute?

And some courts have dismissed privilege out of hand where the actual documents are not also submitted for *in camera* review, although they have also allowed "cure" by belated submission.

- *Mold-Masters Ltd. v Husky Injection Molding Systems Ltd.*, 2002 U.S. Dist. LEXIS 263 (N.D. Ill. Jan. 10, 2002). Having first dismissed the privilege claim because the documents were not submitted for review, the court conducted a review after a belated submission and found that the documents were not privilege protected.

With increasing frequency, documents as to which either the privilege or the protection are asserted are being submitted under seal for *in camera* review, which moreover is necessarily *ex parte*. The United States Supreme Court held that such *in camera* inspections did not of themselves violate the privilege protection.

- *United States v. Zolin*, 491 U.S. 554, 574–75 (1989). The Supreme Court held that nothing in the Federal Rules of Evidence barred *in camera* review of privileged documents, nor did such review destroy the privilege.

Moreover, the Supreme Court lowered the bar as to what showing was necessary to permit an *in camera* inspection to go forward.

"In sum, we conclude that a rigid independent evidence requirement does not comport with 'reason and experience,' Fed. Rule Evid. 501, and we decline to adopt it as part of the developing federal common law of evidentiary privileges. We hold that *in camera* review may be used to determine whether allegedly privileged attorney-client communications fall within the crime-fraud exception. We further hold, however, that before a district court may engage in *in camera* review at the request of the party opposing the privilege, that party must present evidence sufficient to support a reasonable belief that *in camera* review may yield evidence that establishes the exception's applicability. Finally, we hold that the threshold showing to obtain *in camera* review may be met by using any relevant evidence, lawfully obtained, that has not been adjudicated to be privileged."

The Supreme Court struggled with whether *in camera* review was permissible to determine the availability of the crime/fraud exception, indicating that a *prima facie* showing of crime or fraud needed to be made to justify such review. Yet in actual practice today no showing of any kind is necessary to review all other privileged documents *in camera* other than when a claim of crime or fraud is made, surely an untoward and not expected result, but such is the historic development of the common law.

Following that injunction, many courts find that the requisite quantum of proof has not been adduced of a crime or fraud exception to warrant *in camera* review or to warrant it only in respect to certain documents, while reviewing all other privileged documents *in camera* without so much as a blink of an eye, utterly unfazed by the logical contradiction.

Needless to say by submitting documents for the court's review the claim of privilege is not thereby waived in respect to any discovery by the requesting party or for any testimonial use.

- *United States v. Billmyer*, 57 F.3d 31 (1st Cir. 1995). By submitting documents for an *in camera* review, the holder of the privilege did not thereby waive otherwise available appeal rights.

A predicate for conducting an *in camera* inspection, however, may well be an adequate document index. Courts are increasingly reluctant to uphold claims of privilege when such a claim is not supported by an adequate index and demonstrated by affidavit. In addition, courts have been known to refuse to conduct an *in camera* inspection to salvage a claim not adequately supported by index and/or affidavit. On the other hand, courts have conducted sample *in camera* reviews to test the sufficiency of the privilege log and often found it to be a work of pure fiction.

- *United States v. KPMG LLP*, 237 F. Supp. 2d 35, 44 (D.D.C. 2002). Where a sample test of documents against a privilege log showed that only some 13.3% were supportable as described, the court appointed a Special Master to conduct a document by document review. *United States of America, v. KPMG*, 316 F. Supp. 2d 30 (D.D.C. 2004). The review was conducted without remuneration. Surprising. KPMG could well have offered to pay for it and should have been so required. The court concluded: "Overall, the Special Master accurately found that KPMG is misrepresenting its unprivileged tax shelter marketing activities as privileged communications. The Court has lost confidence in KPMG's privilege log since it has been shown to be inaccurate, incomplete, and even misleading regarding a very large percentage of the documents. The claims of privilege under 26 U.S.C. 7525 are unsupportable for the documents submitted thus far to the Court." Accordingly, the court ordered all of the documents produced other than two attorney opinion letters.

- *Vaughan Furniture Co. Inc. v. Featureline Mfg., Inc.*, 156 F.R.D. 123, 129 (M.D.N.C. 1994). The case contains useful examples of what constitutes sufficient and insufficient document indexes. The court was invited to inspect the documents *in camera* to resolve contested issues of privilege and protection, but refused to do so absent a submission of a comprehensive document index.

Indeed it has now become standard operating procedure to test the validity of the privilege/protection assertion by means of *in camera* review. Were it otherwise there would never be a means for testing a party's assertion of privilege. They would simply have to be taken at their word. As any practitioner who has litigated a privilege or protection issue that prospect would leave much to be desired.

On the other hand, it is inherently problematic to allow judicial review of privilege claims by *in camera* review as a matter of course. However limited an *in camera* review the Supreme Court expected it was countenancing, the ship of generalized *in camera* review has long since sailed. Few and far between are the courts that recognize anything in the least problematic about *in camera* review of privileged documents any longer.

- *Ideal Electric Co. v. Flowserve Corp.*, 230 F.R.D. 603 (D. Nev. 2005). Court pointed out that *in camera* review was disfavored in that district and there was no point in conducting it merely because one party so requested. The context was a holding that draft affidavits prepared for court filing were privilege and work product protected.

Other courts have suggested that *in camera* review should be a last step, assuming a determination can not be made from other submitted materials—privilege logs and affidavits.

- *Navigant Consulting, Inc. v. Wilkinson*, 220 F.R.D. 467, 474 (N.D. Tex. 2004) (Kaplan, J.). "Resort to an *in camera* review is appropriate only *after* the burdened party has submitted detailed affidavits and other evidence to the extent possible."

Most now conduct such reviews as a matter of course in a wide array of situations. The caution still voiced by J. Philip Klingeberger, United States Bankruptcy Judge, almost quaint in light of how wide spread *in camera* reviews have become, is nonetheless well taken.

- *In re Bailey*, 2005 Bankr. LEXIS 1814 (Bankr. N. D. Ind. June 15, 2005). *In camera* review was denied where a party claimed that a document had been revised without adequate notice to him as one of the signatories with the intention of having him believe that there had been no substantive changes in the document. The judge examined the document and found the initial draft and subsequent one sufficiently divergent that he seems to have believed, without stating so bluntly, that carelessness on the part of the signatory in not noticing the changes rather than fraudulent intent upon the part of the other party and its lawyer was the cause in the document being signed in a form other than that desired by the party now alleging fraud. Accordingly, any *in camera* review of privileged documents was denied.

Increasingly, however, courts are finding that despite costly and elaborate privilege logs without examining the contested documents *in camera* they are incapable of reaching a determination as to whether the document is or is not privilege or work-product protected.

- *United States ex rel. Fago v. M & T Mortgage Corp.*, 235 F.R.D. 11 (D.D.C. 2006). The court determined that it could not determine whether an investigative report had been prepared primarily for a business reason (assuring HUD that its procedures were adequate) or to defend against the instant litigation until it had reviewed the documents *in camera.*

- *Drayton v. Pilgrim's Pride Corp.*, 2005 U.S. Dist. LEXIS 18571, at *8 (E.D. Pa. Aug. 30, 2005). The court found defendant's claim that it had engaged its outside auditors to assist with litigation when there was already an audit in process to determine the extent of a *listeria* outbreak in the various plants was less than credible. "To assure that the line between materials prepared in anticipation of litigation and those prepared as part of the ongoing review has not been obliterated," the court ordered defendant to make an *in camera* submission of the documents and to include a redacted version for those portions that it claimed were done in anticipation of litigation.

- *Bray v. United States*, 2005 U.S. Dist. LEXIS 3869 (E.D. Pa. Mar. 14, 2005). The party claiming work-product protection for an accident report adduced information in support thereof, but the court concluded that without itself reviewing the report it could not determine whether it was prepared in anticipation of litigation or for some other purpose.

- *Tri-State Hosp. Supply Corp. v. United States*, 226 F.R.D. 118 (D.D.C. 2005). The court concluded that the plaintiff had demonstrated sufficient evidence for it to conduct an *in camera* review to determine whether the government had consulted lawyers with some tortious end in mind (a variety of malicious prosecution and abuse of process types of claims), but that it could not make such a determination without reviewing the documents at issue.

Indeed in one area of the law, patent infringement claims, a judge will often review advice-of-counsel letters *in camera* as a prelude to a decision as to whether to bifurcate the trial on willfulness and liability issues. Advice-of-counsel is oft a defense against willfulness while it plays no role on a decision as to liability which is premised on whether there was or was not an infringement, regardless of what the opinion, erroneous or not, of a patent lawyer may have been. But as the result of examining the opinions *in camera* to determine whether to bifurcate the trial rather than put the defendant to the choice of relying on advice of counsel and waiving the privilege or waiving the advice of counsel defense to retain the privilege, the judge plays an extended role.

- *Bancorp Servs., LLC v. Sun Life Assur. Co. of Can.*, 2006 U.S. Dist. LEXIS 20737 (E.D. Mo. Apr. 14, 2006). The court concluded it could not reach a determination as to whether to allow a bifurcated trial without reviewing the opinion letter *in camera.*

- *Dentsply Int'l Inc. v. Kaydex*, 1994 U.S. Dist. LEXIS 9838, 1994 WL 376276 (N.D. Ill. July 11, 1994). The court determined that disclosure of attorney's opinions, reviewed *in camera,* would not so substantially prejudice plaintiff that separate trials were warranted.

The reality of discovery "abuse," however, is such that parties assert privilege for communications that don't even come close and given the complex jurisprudence which has evolved over time in privilege law, no practical alternative to judicial *in camera* review of privilege/protection claims seems to exist.

And many courts, even the most meticulous among them, find that privilege logs, even when well prepared do not provide any assurance that the correct determination can be reached.

- *Macintosh v. Building Owners & Managers Ass'n Int'l*, 231 F.R.D. 106, 109 (D.D.C. 2005)(Facciola, Mag. J.). "I therefore take it that BOMA has no objection to my review of all documents on its privilege log. Given the small number of documents at issue and my well-documented problems n3 in attempting to rule on privilege questions solely on the basis of a privilege log, I will order BOMA to produce all documents claimed to be privileged on its privilege log for my *in camera* inspection."

An even more frequent problem is that privilege/protection is asserted for whole categories of documents that don't even come close to warranting such protection. The patience of courts with such either frivolously or blatantly erroneous assertions of privilege seems, at times, to be almost bottomless.

See also:

- *Marshall v. District of Columbia Water & Sewage Auth.*, 214 F.R.D. 23, 25 n.4 (D.D.C. 2003). "As I noted in my previous opinions, I have found privilege logs useless. *Mitchell v. Nat'l R.R. Passenger*

Corp., 208 F.R.D. 455, 461 (D.D.C. 2002); *Avery Dennison Corp. v. Four Pillars*, 190 F.R.D. 1 (D.D.C. 1999)."

Indeed, it has even been suggested on appeal that failure to conduct an *in camera* review of privilege protected documents may constitute reversible error. The court that was presented with that argument did not dismiss it out of hand, but merely noted that the record did not sustain that contention and that such a review seemed to have been duly conducted.

- *Procter & Gamble Co. v. Haugen*, 427 F.3d 727 (10th Cir. 2005). "Notably, however, P&G has not submitted any of these documents to us for review. Instead, P&G's sole argument is that, even though it submitted the five documents to the district court for *in camera* review, the district court failed to conduct such a review before ordering them to be produced.

"After carefully reviewing the record on appeal, we reject P&G's assertion. . . . In light of all these circumstances, we conclude there is no basis for finding that the district court failed to conduct an *in camera* review of the five documents." The order requiring the production of the documents was accordingly allowed to stand.

Nonetheless, all too many courts seem to have overlooked the fact that where detailed summaries of the privileged documents exist and there is no reason to believe that they are inaccurate, a trial court need not conduct an *in camera* review of the documents themselves. Considering the labor and cost involved in the preparation of privilege logs, if courts are going to conclude that they can not be relied upon in all events and that *in camera* review must be conducted regardless then why go through the exercise.

- *In re Grand Jury Proceedings*, 33 F.3d 342 (4th Cir. 1994). The Fourth Circuit upheld a district court's decision that had found the crime-fraud exception to apply after conducting an *in camera* hearing of both the government's submission, which the privilege holder had not seen, and the privilege-holder's submission, which consisted of detailed summaries of the allegedly privileged documents. The trial court did not conduct a review of the documents themselves. The Fourth Circuit found there was no abuse of discretion on the part of the trial court not to have done so where detailed summaries had been provided.

Appellants had urged that *Zolin* should apply. The Fourth Circuit found that "*Zolin* did not provide a general rule applicable to all *in camera* reviews of any materials submitted by parties" and that the government was thus not required to demonstrate an adequate factual basis for support of the crime-fraud exception before making an *in camera* submission to the district court." The court noted that because the district court had access to the grand jury's proceedings from the government's submission as well as the privilege-holder's summaries of the allegedly privileged documents, it was in its discretion to determine whether it was necessary to review the actual documents.

■ *In re Sulfuric Acid Antitrust Litig.*, 2006 U.S. Dist. LEXIS 20086 (N.D. Ill. 2006). The court conducted an *in camera* review of a document in complex anti-trust litigation to determine whether a fraud/crime exception would apply to vitiate the privilege and concluded that it did not.

■ *In re Grand Jury Proceedings # 5*, 401 F.3d 247 (4th Cir. 2005). The trial court abused its discretion in not reviewing either the privileged documents *in camera* or detailed summaries prior to determining that the crime fraud exception vitiated either privilege or work product.

■ *In re Grand Jury Subpoenas*, 144 F.3d 653 (10th Cir.), *cert. denied*, 525 U.S. 966 (1998). An *in camera* ex parte proceeding to make a *prima facie* showing of the crime/fraud exception does not violate any rights of the client seeking to maintain the privilege.

■ *A fortiori*, because the privilege does not protect a document from *in camera* review by a judicial officer, the work-product protection is not protected therefrom either.

■ *In re Murphy*, 560 F.2d 326, 336 n.20 (8th Cir. 1977). "Our ruling that opinion work-product is discoverable only in rare and extraordinary circumstances does not shield these materials from judicial scrutiny."

Thus cases now over thirty years old where parties questioned the right of courts to conduct *in camera* reviews as themselves a violation of privilege protections are indeed ancient history.

- *In re Fish & Neave*, 519 F.2d 116, 117–18 (8th Cir. 1975). The court of appeals ruled that *in camera* review was a proper procedure to assess work-product claims. Trial subpoenas had been issued on the law firm on trial, seeking documents when the only witnesses who could testify on the matters sought to be discovered were either dead or unable to testify. Thus, extenuating circumstances had been shown to require production of the documents for *in camera* inspection. The ruling on the availability of hard-core work-product protection and attorney-client privilege would be made by a special master. It was civil contempt for the law firm to refuse to honor the trial subpoena by refusing to submit the documents for an *in camera* inspection.

In camera review also provides the judicial officer undertaking the review the opportunity of excising those portions of a document that contain privileged communications or an attorney's mental impressions, opinions, and legal theories before ordering production.

If appellate review becomes necessary, the appellate court may in turn conduct an *in camera* review of the disputed documents, which are held and transmitted to the appellate court under seal.

- *United States v. Lawless*, 709 F.2d 485, 487 (7th Cir. 1983). "Following oral argument of this case, we ordered the parties to transmit the documents held sealed by the district court for our examination *in camera*."

- *In camera* review, as we have seen, is almost always necessary when a claim is made that the crime/fraud exception permits stripping away privilege and protection. For a detailed analysis of *in camera* review in that special context, the reader should refer to the analysis of how the courts determine when and if each exception is applicable. Suffice it to say here that the Supreme Court has virtually mandated such *in camera* review in that context once, of course, a *prima facie* showing has been made that the crime/fraud exception is applicable. *United States v. Zolin*, 491 U.S. 554, 572 (1989).

That is not to say that all courts do conduct such *in camera* review after a *prima facie* finding that a crime/fraud has occurred. Indeed some courts have held that once the conclusion has been reached that there has been a *prima facie* showing of crime or fraud sufficient to vitiate the privilege, the court need not examine each document or examine each proposed question, unless some temporal or subject matter limits have been placed on the scope of the exception.

- *In re Grand Jury Proceedings (Vargas)*, 723 F.2d 1461, 1467 (10th Cir. 1983). The court held that "once the trial judge has concluded that the privilege does not apply because the government has made such a prima facie showing, the trial court need only conduct an *in camera* inspection of the documents if there is a possibility that some of them may fall outside the scope of the exception to the privilege."

Indeed, the Tenth Circuit advises to so define the scope of the exception that additional involvement of the district court in assessing either documents or questions for whether they fall within or outside the scope of the exception is not necessary.

- *In re Grand Jury Subpoenas v. United States*, 144 F.3d 653, 661 (10th Cir.), *cert. denied*, 525 U.S. 966 (1998). "[W]e will not require that the district court conduct a detailed review of all questions and answers prior to their presentation to the grand jury. Instead, district courts should define the scope of the crime-fraud exception narrowly enough so that information outside of the exception will not be elicited before the grand jury. . . . However, if, before ordering testimony in front of the grand jury, the district court, within its discretion, believes an *in camera* examination of the witness or the questions to be asked of the witness is needed to ensure the scope of the inquiry will not be too broad, it may do so."

But see:

- *In re Sealed Case*, 754 F.2d 395, 402–03 (Fed. Cir. 1985). The circuit court required the district court to engage in a question-by-question determination of the scope of the crime/fraud exception "given the nebulous distinction in this case between prior acts that remain protected by the attorney-client privilege and prior acts forming the basis of the ongoing cover-up."

The consequences that flow from extensive document discovery in complex litigation, from elaborate document indexes and *in camera* review, is that the court may well be put to the burden of an extensive category-by-category, document-by-document analysis and ruling.

- *United States Postal Serv. v. Phelps Dodge Refining Corp.*, 852 F. Supp. 156 (E.D.N.Y. 1994). The court was obliged to set forth its findings regarding sixty-two documents in a table over six pages in length detailing its findings with respect to each and every contested document.

And occasionally a court, be a district court or a magistrate, may refuse to take on so burdensome a task, stating that if a privilege/protection is to be sustained it must be demonstrable from a perusal of the privilege log alone, which therefore best be accurate and detailed.

- *United Investors Life Ins. Co. v. Nationwide Life Ins. Co.*, 233 F.R.D. 483, 486 (N.D. Miss. 2006). "This court will not grant an *in camera* inspection where, as here, there are potentially hundreds, perhaps thousands, of documents which would require review. To inspect the documents at issue in this action would constitute a great and unnecessary expenditure of judicial resources. Rule 26 is clear in its requirement that the assertion of a privilege contain enough information so that the other party, and by logical necessity the court, can determine its applicability. As in Simmons, this court will enforce the terms of Rule 26. The court orders defendants to revise their privilege log entries to include each element of a claimed privilege or protection so that the court and the plaintiff are able to "test the merits" within the four corners of the privilege log itself. Although this task may seem overly burdensome to defendants at first blush, it does not require expenditures of more time and effort than that which the defendants originally expended. For instance, defendants included the date created, creator, receiver, carbon-copied and/or blind carbon-copied parties where applicable, and a description of the document for each entry. The instant order requires only that the description include each requisite element of the privilege or protection asserted, including but not limited to the identities of persons."

Given the burdens attendant upon *in camera* review of extensive document production, increasingly some courts are designating such laborious work either to magistrates or if the case involves a particularly extensive review, to specially designated masters.

- *United States v. Philip Morris, Inc.*[Referred to Special Master Levie], Redacted for Public Filing, 2004 U.S. Dist. LEXIS 27026 (D.D.C. June 25, 2004). Document-by-document rationale for protection or disclosure set forth for each document.

Courts have also conducted *in camera* reviews to determine whether documents taken by former employees for suits against their employers were privilege protected and hence whether their use as testimonial evidence was barred.

- *United States ex rel. Fields v. Sherman Health Sys.*, 2004 U.S. Dist. LEXIS 7297 (N.D. Ill. Apr. 28, 2004). The only facts defendant cited in support of its privilege claim were that the memorandum included the notation, "Privileged and Confidential—Subject to Attorney-Client Privilege and Attorney Work-Product Doctrines," and that it addressed, among other things, procedures for monitoring government regulations and implementing compliance standards. The court found this insufficient to establish that the document was protected by privilege. "This is insufficient to even begin to establish that the document is protected by privilege. Inclusion of a "privileged" notation tells the Court nothing about the circumstances under which the memorandum was prepared, and it should be self-evident that discussion of regulatory matters does not necessarily imply that a lawyer was in any way involved, let alone that the other requirements for privilege protection are satisfied. Because Sherman has offered no evidence to support its privilege claim, the claim is rejected."

Traditionally, *in camera* inspections have not been a prerequisite for a determination that privileges have been improperly asserted, though that tradition seems to be fast eroding.

- *In re Santa Fe Int'l*, 272 F.3d 705, 709 n.5 (5th Cir. 2001). The court was under no obligation to conduct an *in camera* review of documents to determine whether the common interest privilege applied. On the contrary, the burden of proof was upon the proponent to establish that fact. "The dissent's argument that the district court was obliged to examine each document before ruling is not meritorious. The argument fails to take into account that the claimants of the attorney-client privilege had the burden of demonstrating that each document withheld was entitled to protection. The defendants did nothing to show that the communications to third persons were made in anticipation of a common defense. On the contrary, the age of the communications, the lack of evidence of any common defense agreement, and Santa Fe's answers to plaintiffs' requests for admissions made a strong case against the common interest privilege claim." A dissent strongly disagreed and argued that an *in camera* inspection should have been conducted.

Indeed in the context of determining whether the crime fraud exception applies, several circuits have now held that the district court must conduct an *in camera* review of the documents and may not rely only on written submissions detailing the *prima facie* evidence for crime fraud proposed by the party seeking the privileged documents and the description of the privileged documents by the privilege holder.

- *In re Bankamerica Corp. Secs. Litig.*, 270 F.3d 639, 645 (8th Cir. 2001). The Eighth Circuit held that the district court could not find any case in which it affirmed an order to produce documents under the crime-fraud exception when the district court did not first review the documents *in camera*.

- *In re Antitrust Grand Jury*, 805 F.2d 155, 168 (6th Cir. 1986). The Sixth Circuit found that district court committed plain error by ruling that the government established a *prima facie* case of the crime-fraud exception and ordering documents produced without examining the documents *in camera*.

In another context, the Seventh Circuit reversed the imposition of the waiver sanction for allegedly abusive assertions of privilege in part on the grounds of the methodology chosen to test the validity of the assertion of privilege. Instead of an *in camera* review of 400 documents in respect to which privilege was asserted, the magistrate judge undertook only a sampling of the documents.

- *American Nat'l Bank & Trust Co. v. Equitable Life Assur. Soc'y of the United States*, 406 F.3d 867, 881 (7th Cir. 2005). The Seventh Circuit did not explicitly state that an *in camera* review of each privileged document was necessary, but that is the implication when it deemed the sanction of a global waiver of privilege for 400 documents based on a sampling methodology. It is hard to imagine a more cavalier attitude toward the privilege than the one the Magistrate Judge here chose. The District court dismissed the action for want of jurisdiction without reviewing the sanction imposed. The Seventh Circuit held that it had continuing jurisdiction over the judicially imposed sanction and reversed as an abuse of discretion.

Although not mandated in other contexts, *in camera* inspections of privileged documents to test the validity of the assertion are now exceedingly common.

- *Marshall v. District of Columbia Water & Sewage Auth.*, 214 F.R.D. 23, 25 (D.D.C. 2003). All documents in respect to which either the attorney-client privilege or the work-product protection was claimed were ordered produced for *in camera* protection. After such was conducted by the court, it concluded that in each instance both had been properly claimed.

- *Hill v. McHenry*, 2002 U.S. Dist. LEXIS 66379, at *6, 8 (D. Kan. Apr. 10, 2002). The court ordered a copy of each document for which privilege was claimed to be submitted for *in camera* inspection to verify the validity of the claim.

- *Triple Five of Minnesota, Inc. v. Simon*, 2002 U.S. Dist. LEXIS 15955 (D. Minn. 2002), *aff'd*, 2002 U.S. LEXIS 10646 (D. Minn. June 6, 2002). The court examined the documents *in camera*, although it is difficult to see why that was necessary in light of the absence of requisite proof of an intent not to perform to substantiate the claim of fraudulent inducement.

- *Renner v. Chase Manhattan Bank*, 2001 U.S. Dist. LEXIS 9766, at *12–14 (S.D.N.Y. July 11, 2001). "Use of *in camera* review of documents to determine the applicability of the attorney-client privilege is common practice in circumstances such as this. . . . To clarify, this review will not be for the purpose of deciding whether the crime-fraud exception applies. Instead, it is for the limited purpose of deciding the applicability of the attorney-client privilege. Only if the Court decides that the privilege does apply would the Court consider further examination of the privileged communications on the question of the crime-fraud exception, and only after determining that plaintiff had made the necessary showing, under the standards set forth in *Zolin* and *Jacobs*, to trigger a second *in camera* review."

Some courts now order *in camera* inspections when the court is dubious that a valid claim has been made.

- *DeKalb Genetics Corp. v. Pioneer Hi-Breed Int'l*, 2002 U.S. Dist. LEXIS 3297 (N.D. Ill. Feb. 27, 2002). The court expressed doubts about the validity of the privilege claims because it was not timely made. Rather than denying it altogether, however, the court instead ordered inspection of the documents.

Indeed, some courts have suggested that *in camera* inspections of all work-product documents may be necessary to validate that each of the elements necessary to claim the work-product protection is present. Failure to conduct such an inspection has even been called fatal to a ruling that the claim has been demonstrated to be valid.

- *Gould, Inc. v. Mitsui Mining & Smelting Co.*, 825 F.2d 676, 680 (2d Cir. 1987). The appellate court vacated the district court's order quashing subpoena given its failure to develop record on claim of work-product protection, including failure to conduct *in camera* inspection of subpoenaed documents and to state its findings with sufficient particularity.

- *Chambers v. Allstate Ins. Co.*, 206 F.R.D. 579, 585 (S.D. W. Va. 2002). "It is clear therefore that Courts must proceed on a 'case-by-case' basis in consideration of facts indicating the circumstances under which the requested documents were prepared or created and are sought in litigation and finally, upon *in camera* examination of the documents themselves, in consideration of the purpose and intent of the representatives in preparing or creating them."

Such blanket *in camera* examination of privilege-protected documents, however reassuring to the party demanding production, would seem to be problematic both in terms of efficiency and also as necessarily eroding the sanctity of the presumed attorney-client privilege if not the work-product protection. Thus, although many courts grant *in camera* inspections with great frequency, that does not mean that all courts do and that none require a reasonable showing that the privilege or protection has been erroneously asserted prior to undertaking such an *in camera* inspection. As in many discretionary matters, it is wise to know the proclivities of the court before which you are practicing. Many courts refuse to conduct such blanket *in camera* inspections.

- *United Investors Life Ins. Co. v. Nationwide Life Ins. Co.*, 233 F.R.D. 483 (D. Miss. 2006). The Magistrate Judge refused to conduct an *in camera* review of hundreds, possibly thousands of privileged documents and instead ordered an amended privilege log, strictly conforming to the Rule to be filed.

- *MPT, Inc. v. Marathon Labels, Inc.*, 2006 U.S. Dist. LEXIS 4998 (N.D. Ohio Feb. 9, 2006). The court refused to conduct an *in camera* inspection of the documents where there was no indication that the privilege log listings were in error or that the privilege had been frivolously asserted.

- *Maine v. Norton*, 208 F. Supp. 2d 63, 68 (D. Me. 2002). "Plaintiffs alternatively argue that if the Court does not order disclosure of the documents in the Privilege Log, the Court should review all the withheld documents *in camera* and make a document-specific determination on disclosure. The Court has carefully reviewed the Privilege Log and the affidavits filed in conjunction with this Motion and finds, on the basis of that review, that Defendants have met their burden of establishing that the documents are entitled to either deliberative process or work-product protection."

- *Newport Pac. Inc. v. County of San Diego*, 200 F.R.D. 628, 634 (S.D. Cal. 2001). The court refused to conduct any *in camera* inspection where a reasonable showing had not been made that the protection had been improperly asserted, and even went so far as to chide counsel making the request as "border-line frivolous and indicates a failure to abide by the framework of the rules of discovery as outlined in the Fed. R. Civ. Pro."

Some courts, however, increasingly make short shrift of the basic premise that if material is in fact privileged, then it should not be lightly reviewed even by them *in camera* and are increasingly willing to conduct such reviews to put to rest doubts about the correctness of privilege assertions where the parties have no trust in each other's bona fides.

- *Koch Materials Co. v. Shore Slurry Seal, Inc.*, 208 F.R.D. 109, 121 (D.N.J. 2002). "To ensure that all relevant information is produced, the court shall conduct an *in camera* review of the documents identified by the defendant in the privilege log, as well as the redacted portions of the e-mails for relevance. The court shall then determine whether relevant and not privileged information has been withheld."

- *D.O.T. Connectors, Inc. v. J. B. Nottingham & Co.*, 2001 U.S. Dist. LEXIS 739 (N.D. Fla. Jan. 22, 2001). The court required that all documents the party claimed did not fall into any one of the six categories of documents the court ordered to be produced in a patent infringement case would be subject to an *in camera* inspection based on an amended and resubmitted privilege log.

In camera review has now gone well beyond examination of documents claimed to be privileged, but now have been conducted to see whether the privileged documents may suggest the availability of a defense.

- Genentech, Inc. v. Insmed Inc., 233 F.R.D. 556 (N.D. Cal.), *recons. denied*, 234 F.R.D. 667 (N.D. Cal. 2006). The court decided to review certain privileged documents *in camera* to determine whether a defense of "inequitable conduct" was available to defeat a patent infringement claim.

Courts have also conducted *in camera* examinations by a judicial officer of what would be the testimony of counsel. Often, moreover, such *in camera* examination are on an *ex parte* basis.

- *In re Grand Jury Proceedings*, 417 F.3d 18 (1st Cir. 2005). Counsel served with a subpoena to testify before the grand jury was examined *in camera* and *ex parte* upon the objection of his former client to the attorney's testimony before the grand jury on privilege grounds. The *in camera* hearing was conducted with the consent of both parties. The court determined that the attorney's testimony would deal with financial matters, which were not within the scope of privileged communications.

It is not in the least self-evident why an *in camera, ex parte* hearing was required to determine such a fact.

- *In re Grand Jury Subpoena*, 419 F.3d 329 (5th Cir. 2005). "Based on the AUSA's affidavit, the district court, in language tracking the grand jury subpoena, ordered Former Counsel to appear with all written statements and recordings from Appellant and Witness for an *in camera* examination in chambers." The appellate court stated that since appellant did not argue that the district court abused its discretion by conducting the *in camera* examination of former counsel, that issue was waived.

- *Hanes v. Dormire*, 240 F.3d 694, 696 (8th Cir. 2001). "The District Court held an *in camera* examination of [a co-defendant's] counsel to determine whether it was necessary to abrogate the privilege in order to protect [the *habeas corpus* petitioner's] constitutional rights. The court refused to abrogate the privilege and then sealed the examination transcript. Because we believed this ruling could have had some bearing on the ineffective assistance claims before us, we reviewed the transcript. Having done so, we are convinced that the privilege should remain in force and the transcript remain sealed." An exceedingly detailed dissent was scathing in its critique that the privilege was totally inapplicable to the testimony at issue and had been erroneously applied by counsel and courts. Apparently, the issue was the opinion of co-defendant's counsel as to the adequacy of representation by co-defense counsel. "The above statement repeats the error and misunderstanding of attorney-client privilege law which Sprouse's [co-defendant's] counsel, the post-conviction relief court, and the District Court all mistakenly considered. The law on attorney-client privilege is set out above and it clearly shows that the privilege is a very narrow one and extends only to confidential communications from a client to his or her attorney. Hanes [the *habeas corpus* petitioner] is not looking for any such confidential communications. He only wants an opportunity to depose Sprouse's attorney about matters that she saw and observed while watching the cross-examination of Sprouse at the trial so that her opinion as to how ineffective Mr. G was will be evidence the reviewing court can consider." *Id.* at 718.

The dissent is quite correct that the majority and all the lower courts have misinterpreted the scope of the privilege. The disagreement is really over whether a lawyer's opinion of the effectiveness of co-counsel is probative. It is unfortunate that both majority and defense were derailed in privilege discussions that are both inaccurate and ultimately irrelevant to the issue to be decided.

For a meticulous example of where the magistrate judge not only examined each document to determine whether it was privileged, but also determined which portion of an otherwise privilege or work-product-protected document was not similarly protected, see *Continental Cas. Co. v. Marsh*, 2004 U.S. Dist. LEXIS 76 (N.D. Ill. Jan. 5, 2004).

In many instances, however, it is foolish to expect a busy court to spend the time plowing through documents to determine whether privilege and protection have been frivolously asserted. And even magistrates, to whom discovery disputes are increasingly relegated, do not take kindly to the task. Thus woe betide the litigant who asserts privilege and protection frivolously, providing a privilege log that does not permit a determination of whether these have been properly asserted. An "abrogation" of the entirety of the privilege log and a compelled disclosure of all documents is the likely and correct outcome when a court determines that a litigant has been trying to pull a fast one by incorrectly labeling documents and thereby trying to avoid disclosure.

G. *Appointment of Special Masters*

In cases of particular complexity, involving many categories and total numbers of documents withheld on the basis of the privilege or the protection, the burden of review and fact-finding has been delegated to special masters.

- *In re Sunrise Sec. Litig.*, 130 F.R.D. 560, 583 (E.D. Pa. 1989). After establishing what standards should determine the rulings on a plethora of privilege and protection issues, the matter was remanded to a special master to make requisite fact-findings as to each applicable category and rulings with respect to particular documents.

In the *American Tel. & Tel.* litigation, the special masters established general guidelines as to what would and would not be deemed to be privileged.

- *United States v. AT&T*, 86 F.R.D. 603 (D.D.C. 1979). Guidelines were adopted setting out formal procedures for privilege claims on a large volume of allegedly privileged documents. These guidelines involved affidavits setting forth each element of privilege for each document, exchanges of briefs by parties, potential evidentiary hearings, and *in camera* inspection by special masters.

Special Masters may also be appointed to review documents subject to grand jury subpoena when the subpoenaed party has been foolish enough to assert global privilege without conducting its own review and then submitting a privilege log. Some courts prefer such a procedure to allowing a "taint team" in the prosecutors to conduct such review on the grounds that a Special Master is less likely to have a bias against finding a document to be privilege protected.

- *In re: Grand Jury Subpoenas*, 454 F.3d 511 (6th Cir. 2006). The Court of Appeals reversed and mandated the district court to appoint a Special Master to review for privileges the files of a party to whom a grand jury subpoena had been issued. The court was critical of the subpoenaed party for failing to provide a privilege log which would have allowed the prosecutors to test the privilege claims. It was equally critical of the district court for appointing a taint team to resolve the matter. It allowed the district court to decide whether to assess the costs of the Special Master to the subpoenaed party.

Although there is increasingly a tendency to appoint a Special Master in the complex, multi-document case, ordinarily magistrates are relegated the task of examining documents or witnesses *in camera* in order to test the assertion of the privilege if it is not determinable from the indexes alone, or is not susceptible to counsel resolution.

Nonetheless, in cases where privilege issues are disputed for large numbers of documents, some courts are now appointing Special Masters to make a document-by-document review of whether the privilege or protection is available.

- *United States v. Philip Morris, Inc.*, 2004 U.S. Dist. LEXIS 27026 (D.D.C. June 25, 2004). Document-by-document review conduct of 157 documents. Recommendation made as to how each should be treated for privilege purposes and why.

- *United States v. KPMG LLP*, 2003 U.S. Dist. LEXIS 18476 (D.D.C. 2003). Special Master reviewed scores of documents and made individual findings of whether the privilege claims made were valid or whether the documents needed to be produced.

H. *Filing Privileged Documents Under Seal*

If a pleading contains privileged material, it apparently can be filed in redacted form publicly to protect the privilege allowing the privileged portions to be filed under seal.

- *Siedle v. Putnam Invs.*, 147 F.3d 7, 12 (1st Cir. 1998). The district court's order refusing to maintain the seal order was reversed because the complaint, filed by former in-house counsel of defendant, was based on information derived from that relationship and that was privileged. The district court erroneously believed that the client's objection to lifting the seal was based merely on the potential for public embarrassment that indeed would not have been sufficient grounds for maintaining the seal. "In this instance, we discern no evidence that the district court identified and balanced the interests at stake, or that the court endeavored to determine whether any information contained in Siedle's filings actually fell within the ambit of the attorney-client privilege. In the circumstances at hand, these omissions amount to an abuse of discretion. . . . When an attorney and a former client embroil themselves in adversarial litigation, the right of public access to judicial records stands in sharp contrast to the lawyer's duty to hold information obtained from the client during the course of representation in the strictest confidence. A delicate balance must be struck between these competing concerns. We hold that the court below misgauged this balance. Putnam has made a sufficient showing that various filings contain privileged information, and without either an adjudication of the privilege question or an appropriate seal order, Putnam will lose the entire benefit of the putative privilege. We cannot countenance such a result."

- *Rapkin v. Rocque*, 87 F. Supp. 2d 140, 143 (D. Conn. 2000). General counsel claiming her firing was to punish her for assertions of her First Amendment rights was permitted to file a complaint under seal which set forth legal advice given to a client with only a redacted complaint filed publicly. An action was brought by a newspaper to unseal the complaint. The court found the newspaper's action to have been collusively brought. "We agree with Defendants that the public interest in preserving the attorney-client privilege ordinarily outweighs the presumption of access to judicial documents. If it did not, all that would be necessary in any dispute over whether a matter was protected by the attorney-client privilege would be to find a media outlet that stated it wanted the matter revealed in order to make it available to its audience."

When privileged documents for some reason must be filed with the court (as on appeal), it is advisable to file them under seal and not to make the mistake of automatically serving the other side with a copy.

Motions to unseal such documents despite the over-arching concern for public accessibility and scrutiny of judicial proceedings are and should be generally unsuccessful for the self-same reasons that underlie the existence of the privilege.

Where, however, the report of an Examiner in bankruptcy or a Special Master is asked to be placed under seal because it makes use of privileged materials, such a request usually has and should fail. The presumption in the United States is open proceedings in open courts. The remedy is not sealing reports that rely on arguably privileged material wholesale, but redacting the report and placing only the privileged portion under seal.

- *In re Fibermark, Inc.*, 330 B.R. 480 (Bankr. D. Vt. 2005). The court refused to seal the entirety of the report under seal as an exception to 11 U.S. Sec. 107 which requires that all court documents should be open ones. Instead it said privilege/work-product-protected materials could be redacted.

- *Siedle v. Putnam Invs.*, 147 F.3d 7 (1st Cir. 1998). The court reversed a district court's decision to unseal privileged documents at the request of a newspaper. "Indeed, this is precisely the kind of countervailing concern that is capable of overriding the general preference for public access to judicial records."

- *Crystal Grower's Corp. v. Dobbins*, 616 F.2d 458, 462 (10th Cir. 1980). The court refused to unseal privileged documents, concluding that the public's interest in preserving the attorney-client privilege outweighs the public's more general interest in access to court documents.

- *Diversified Group, Inc. v. Paul Daugerdas*, 217 F.R.D. 152 (S.D.N.Y. 2003). In deciding to unseal a record, the court appointed a special master to determine which documents introduced in support of a motion for summary judgment were privileged and should remain under seal. The magistrate concluded that most of the materials were not privileged because the subject matter was disclosed in the complaint, the advice had been sought for marketing rather than legal purposes, and there had thus been no intention of confidentiality at the time that the communications were entered into. The ruling was sustained by the district court. *The Diversified Group, Inc. v. Daugerdas*, 2003 U.S. Dist. LEXIS 16284 (S.D. N.Y. 2003).

- *Dombrowski v. Bell Atl. Corp.*, 128 F. Supp. 2d 216, 219 (E.D. Pa. 2000). The court found that the failure to maintain privileged materials under seal would cause "a clearly defined and serious injury not only to the parties seeking the seal but also to the public interest which the attorney-client privilege is designed to serve." (Internal quotation marks and citation omitted.)

Where the parties fail to place documents under seal, courts will often deem such failure an "inexcusable neglect" of the privilege and refuse to find non-waiver.

- *MG Capital LLC. v. Sullivan*, 2002 U.S. Dist. LEXIS 11803 (N.D. Ill. June 27, 2002). The court refused to order return of a document inadvertently produced in discovery. The document production was relatively small (only 70 pages). The document was not placed under seal when it was used in the course of a deposition and the opposing side had the opportunity to read the document in its entirety.

Then again, other courts are more tolerant and will at least maintain the status quo pending a factual determination of whether the failure was or was not excusable.

- *In re Avantel, S.A.*, 343 F.3d 311 (5th Cir.2003). Privilege documents were "inadvertently" not filed under seal and the appendix containing privileged documents was inadvertently served upon opposing counsel. The court of appeals concluded that the issue was not "moot" by virtue of the disclosure and entered an order requiring the documents to be placed under seal and opposing counsel to return the appendix pending a determination by the district court of the "inadvertent" disclosure issue on remand.

On the other hand the party requesting that certain documents be placed under seal must demonstrate that there is a valid reason to override the public policy for open proceedings in open courts. Even if the other party has no objection, the court will make an independent determination as to whether it is appropriate to place the documents under seal in the first instance.

- *Hillside Dairy, Inc. v. Kawamura*, 2004 U.S. Dist. LEXIS 29440 (E.D. Cal. July 2 2004). Court refused to place attorney's fee arrangements and billing invoices under seal even though the motion to do so was unopposed.

I. *Production in Redacted Form*

The fact that a document contains some privileged material does not make the entire document immune from discovery. The courts have adopted a policy of severability. In other words a document or a videotape or an audiotape can be redacted to protect from disclosure the privileged portion while producing the non-privileged portion.

Nor is it unusual that after an inspection by the court or magistrate, some documents will be deemed privileged, some not, and some ordered produced in redacted form. In such manner, the privileged portion is not disclosed while non-privileged matter is not clothed with a veil of secrecy merely by virtue of the fact that it was discussed in a context where privileged matter was also discussed.

Instances of judicially ordered redaction have a long history in the courts and appear in innumerable cases.

- *Kodish v. Oakbrook Terrace Fire Prot. Dist.*, 235 F.R.D. 447 (N.D. Ill. 2006). Audiotape of a public meeting ordered redacted so that non-privileged portion which discussed plaintiff's work history and evaluations could be produced. The fact that counsel was present during the entirety of the meeting did not thereby make all that transpired in the course of the meeting privileged.

- *Sanchez v. Matta*, 229 F.R.D. 649 (D.N.M. 2004). Because the investigative file contained innumerable relevant facts but because attorney mental impressions were interspersed therein, it was ordered produced in redacted form. One particular document, entitled an investigative report, was held to be completely work-product protected.

- *United States Postal Serv. v. Phelps Dodge Refining Corp.*, 852 F. Supp. 156 (E.D.N.Y. 1994). The privileged portion of a document not otherwise privileged may be redacted and the document will be produced in redacted form.

- *Mission Nat'l Ins. Co. v. Lilly*, 112 F.R.D. 160, 164–65 (D. Minn. 1986). Large numbers of documents bearing on an investigation of possible arson conducted by the attorneys for the insurance company were ordered produced on the ground that the insurance company could not immunize from discovery investigations that are an integral part of the insurance company's ongoing business. Nonetheless, the court accorded such protection by redaction "[a]s to mental processes and opinions of counsel which truly bear on the anticipated litigation, the court has ruled that such sections of the submitted documents be redacted, and that those areas not be inquired into at deposition."

- *SCM Corp. v. Xerox Corp.*, 70 F.R.D. 508, 518 (D. Conn.), *appeal dismissed*, 534 F.2d 1031 (2d Cir. 1976). When the ultimate corporate decision is based on both a business policy and a legal evaluation, the business aspects of the decision are not protected merely because legal considerations are also involved.

- *United States v. United Shoe Mach. Corp.*, 89 F. Supp. 357, 359 (D. Mass. 1950). "[S]uch parts of [the attorney's documents] are privileged as contain, or have opinions based on, information furnished by an officer or employee of the defendant in confidence and without the presence of third persons. . . . Thus, for example, there is no privilege for so much of a lawyer's letter, report or opinion as related to a fact gleaned from a witness, . . . or a public document such as a patent . . . or a judicial opinion."

On the other hand, if the discoverable portion of the document is thoroughly intertwined with the portion that is protected by the attorney-client privilege or work-product protection, courts may make the whole available to opposing counsel.

- *Xerox Corp. v. International Bus. Machs. Corp.*, 64 F.R.D. 367, 381–82 (S.D.N.Y. 1974). "Where the non-privileged facts are intertwined with information which conceivably is privileged, the critical factor becomes the availability of the non-privileged facts from other sources; and where no other sources exist, then a balance must be struck in favor of distilling, if possible, the non-privileged facts from the attorney's documents. If such a distillation becomes impossible, however, then the entire contents of the documents must be produced. This is especially true where one party has control over the information sought. A party should not be allowed to conceal critical, non-privileged, discoverable information, which is uniquely within the knowledge of the party and which is not obtainable from any other source, simply by imparting the information to its attorney and then attempting to hide behind the work-product protection after the party fails to remember the information."

Generally, a party produces documents in redacted form and so indicates in the privilege log compiled.

Occasionally, a party puts the redaction into issue, by first bringing a motion for leave to produce the document in redacted form, but that would seem to be the more cumbersome procedure.

- *Mount Vernon Fire Ins. Co. v. Try 3 Bldg. Servs.*, 1998 U.S. Dist. LEXIS 16183 (S.D.N.Y. Oct. 14, 1998). The party seeking the protection of privileges made an application or motion to produce documents in redacted form without privileged material being included.

Occasionally, a party seeking the protection of the privilege for certain portions of a document leaves the work of redaction to the court. The work entailed for the court in redacting discoverable from non-discoverable portions of documents is obviously substantial. Yet courts have been willing to assume that burden, rather than declare a document undiscoverable in its entirety based on the existence of some privileged material within the document.

- *In re Derienzo*, 1998 Bankr. LEXIS 635 (E.D. Pa. Apr. 28, 1998). The court redacted documents to carve out and require production of portions of documents that would not be encompassed by the privilege.

- *IBJ Whitehall Bank & Trust Co. v. Cory & Assocs.*, 1999 U.S. Dist. LEXIS 12440, at *14 (N.D. Ill. Aug. 10, 1999). The court reviewed dozens of documents to decide which were to be produced in their entirety, which withheld in their entirety, and which produced in redacted form and what the redaction was to be.

But see:

- *In re Qwest Communs. Int'l, Inc. Sec. Litig.*, 2005 U.S. Dist. LEXIS 19129 (D. Col. Aug. 15, 2005). Work of redaction, *i.e.*, editing out attorney mental impressions from interviews of witness/employees, left to attorney as "officer of the court." If an attorney is not to be trusted to do the redaction properly then he may not provide the work product documents at all.

The court's argument was thus: if you can't trust an attorney, you can't trust them at all, so you may as well trust them.

So too, if matters are placed under seal to protect a privilege, non-privileged information can be made public in redacted form to balance out the competing interest in open judicial proceedings.

- *Siedle v. Putnam Invs.*, 147 F.3d 7, 11 (1st Cir. 1998). "We hold that the district court abused its discretion when it summarily unsealed all the filings in an action brought by a lawyer against his former client." The proper remedy would have been to allow public filing of the privileged matters in redacted form.

Failure to follow the subject matter waiver definition of the court by failing to properly redact documents to conform thereto, may result in advertently expanding the scope of the subject matter waiver, just as any other disclosure would.

- *Fort James Corp. v. Solo Cup Co.*, 412 F.3d 1340 (Fed. Cir. 2005), *reh'g denied*, 2005 U.S. App. LEXIS 20077 (Fed. Cir. Sept. 1, 2005), *cert. denied*, 126 S. Ct. 1768 (2006). "If the additional documents produced by Fort James involved subject matter beyond the applicability of the on-sale bar mentioned in JR0028487, then Fort James should have redacted those portions of the documents produced. A party's failure to protect its privilege can result in a loss of that privilege. . . . 128 F.3d 1122, 1126 (7th Cir. 1997). Although admirable, Fort James's stated desire to avoid court intervention in the discovery process would not entitle it to dodge the consequences of any careless disclosures. The court erred in concluding that the additional documents produced by Fort James were not relevant to its determination of the scope of Fort James's privilege waiver." (Citation omitted.)

J. Agreements to Disclose Privileged Material without Privilege Waiver

It has become increasingly common for parties to enter into agreements to disclose privileged materials provided the disclosure is not taken to entail waiver as to all privileged matters. These agreements are often referred to as "claw back" agreements. Proposed Rule 502(d) of the Federal Rules of Evidence thus seeks to codify what has in fact become common practice.

(d) Controlling effect of party agreements.—

> Notwithstanding subdivision (a) [which states that generally speaking disclosure results in waiver] an agreement on the effect of disclosure is binding on the parties to the agreement, but not on other parties unless the agreement is incorporated into a court order.

Because courts will give effect to such agreements, the parties by contract, so to speak, can avoid the general rule that partial disclosure on a given subject matter will bring in its wake total disclosure.

- *Ames v. Black Entm't TV*, 1998 U.S. Dist. LEXIS 18053 (S.D.N.Y. Nov. 17, 1998). The court enforced an agreement in the course of a deposition providing that the general counsel could answer certain questions without waiving the privilege with respect to all of the same subject-matter communications.

- *Dowd v. Calabrese*, 101 F.R.D. 427, 439–40 (D.D.C. 1984). "Counsel for the parties stipulated in the course of the [witness's] deposition that testimony by the witness would not be deemed to constitute any waiver of the attorney-client [*25] or work-product privileges. In view of that stipulation, plaintiffs cannot now rely on the [witness's] deposition to support a claim of waiver."

- *Eutectic Corp. v. Metco, Inc.*, 61 F.R.D. 35, 42–43 (E.D.N.Y. 1973). The court held that there was no waiver by partial disclosure when parties "executed a protective order . . . and expressly provided there would be no waiver of any privilege unless expressed in writing," because "the Court can perceive no sound reason of public policy to rewrite an agreement which facilitates disclosure, closely protects a legitimate privilege, and contemplates a cooperative effort by both parties."

- *United States v. United Shoe Mach. Corp.*, 89 F. Supp. 357, 359 (D. Mass. 1950). The court held that the defendant "did not waive its privilege by surrendering the exhibits in response to subpoenas, because it was agreed in advance by [plaintiff's] counsel that compliance with the subpoenas should not constitute a waiver."

In a sense, courts are willing to enforce such "partial" waiver between two parties, whereby the waiver of some privileged materials will not constitute waiver of all between the two parties to the contract.

That situation does not apply when a party is willing to disclose privileged information to one party; usually some governmental agency will, thereby retaining the privilege against all other parties. Such "selective" waivers, even when unconditional confidentiality agreements are entered into prior to the disclosure, have been markedly unsuccessful. *See* Part I and Part II, Sections on "Selective Waiver in Privilege" and "Work Product" contexts respectively for extensive review of cases, *supra*.

Although there is some slight suggestion that entering into a unconditional confidentiality agreement might, under certain circumstances, protect the materials from subsequent compelled exposure, do not bank on it. Once a waiver has occurred, all the confidentiality agreements that have been devised give precious little assurance of subsequent protection. Nonetheless, litigants are attempting to push the stated rationale for the no-selective waiver rule by entering into confidentiality agreements. Courts initially stated that no selective waiver would be permitted of work-product material on the grounds that any such waiver made it more likely that the materials would eventually come into the hands of an adverse party—often a circular argument since it was the court itself that most frequently gave that third party access to the work-product-protected material. The selectively disclosing party then reasoned: All right, we'll enter into strict confidentiality agreements which should act as an indicia that by making the selective disclosure we were trying to assure that the work product would not inadvertently fall into the hands of an adversary.

- *In re McKesson HBOC, Inc. Secs. Litig.*, 2005 U.S. Dist. LEXIS 7098, 2005 WL 934331, at *9–10 (N.D. Cal. Mar. 31, 2005). Company's confidentiality agreements with the government were sufficient to preserve work-product privilege since it indicated an intention that disclosure of the protected materials would not reach adverse parties.

- *In re M & L Bus. Mach. Co.*, 167 B.R. 631, 637 (D. Colo. 1994). The court said that the "[p]roduction of documents under a grand jury subpoena does not automatically vitiate the attorney-client privilege, much less in an unrelated civil proceeding brought by a non-governmental entity. This is especially true in a case such as this, where the record demonstrates that the [defendant] has consistently sought to protect its privilege" through production pursuant to a confidentiality agreement. The court held that the defendant had not waived its attorney-client privilege in the bankruptcy proceeding by virtue of a previous disclosure of documents to United States Attorney in connection with grand jury investigation where the defendant had entered into a letter agreement with the government which specifically expressed intention to preserve confidentiality of documents with respect to third parties in subsequent proceedings.

- *Saito v. McKesson HBOC, Inc.*, 2002 Del. Ch. LEXIS 139, 2002 WL 31657622, at *11 (Del. Ch. Nov. 13, 2002), *aff'd*, 2005 Del. LEXIS 106 (Del. 2005). The Magistrate Judge allowed a selective waiver because of a confidentiality agreement, which demonstrated that defendant reasonably expected its privilege would be preserved when it disclosed documents to SEC.

The far more frequent holdings seem to be that any confidentiality agreement is unavailing when subsequent parties seek compelled production of previously selectively disclosed documents.

- *In re Bank One Sec. Litig.*, 209 F.R.D. 418, 423–25 (N.D. Ill. 2002). Bank One's voluntary production to governmental investigative body, Office of the Comptroller of the Currency, waived its work-product privilege because the relationship was adversarial notwithstanding existing confidentiality agreement.

- *United States v. Bergonzi*, 216 F.R.D. 487, 494, 496–98 (N.D. Cal. 2003). Where confidentiality agreement entered into prior to disclosure of privilege and work-product-protected documents was not unconditional, no protection against subsequent compelled protection was accorded.

- *United States v. South Chicago Bank*, 1998 U.S. Dist. LEXIS 17444, No. 97 CR 849, 1998 WL 774001, at *4–5 (N.D. Ill. Oct. 30,

1998). Confidentiality agreement did not protect report produced to government from subsequent compelled disclosure.

Before disclosure of privileged materials, for instance for purposes of settlement discussions, it is advisable to obtain an agreement that in the event the settlement does not occur and litigation proceeds, no subject matter waiver will follow.

- *Akamai Techs., Inc. v. Digital Island, Inc.*, 2002 U.S. Dist. LEXIS 13515 (N.D. Cal. May 30, 2002). Court enforced an agreement that disclosure of a damage memorandum for settlement purposes would not constitute subject matter waiver in the event that settlement failed.

On the other hand, there is dicta in cases where no agreement was in fact obtained that even obtaining such agreement might not be sufficient or effective to protect the privilege. Query whether that judicial stance is advisable given public policy concerns to foster settlement. It is true that the bell cannot be unrung. That does not mean, however, that one side should be able to use privileged materials in a testimonial fashion once it has agreed not to do so in order to engage in settlement discussions.

- *Atari Corp. v. Sega of Am.*, 161 F.R.D. 417, 420 (N.D. Cal. 1994). Defendant hired a former employee of plaintiff to negate a claim of infringement, and in the course of settlement discussions provided a videotape of the expert voicing that opinion. Discovery of all documents upon which that opinion was based was allowed. "Any voluntary disclosure inconsistent with the confidential nature of the work-product privilege waives the privilege. . . . Waiver of a privilege may occur by voluntary disclosure to an adverse party during settlement negotiations, despite any agreement between the parties to keep the information confidential."

The court found that in fact, at the time the tape was turned over, it was a part of voluntary discovery and no attempt was made to mark or assert a privilege; thus the sweeping dicta was totally unnecessary to the court's ruling. Moreover, Rule 26(a)(2) 1993 changes make discoverable any work-product documents upon which the opinion of a testifying expert is based, making the dicta all the more unnecessary and harmful.

See also Part I, Waiver of work-product in the context of settlement discussions, *supra*.

On the other hand, any attempt before the fact to excuse negligent production of privileged or work-product documents by way of "blanket" agreements that such production will not constitute waiver are generally frowned upon and not enforced by courts.

- *Koch Materials Co. v. Shore Slurry Seal, Inc.*, 208 F.R.D. 109, 118 (D.N.J. 2002). The court observed that an agreement to waive negligent production of privileged documents immunized attorneys from negligent handling of documents and therefore could lead to sloppy attorney review and improper disclosure, which could jeopardize the client's case. The court refused to enforce such an agreement.

These claw back agreements are entered into to obviate the effect of fairly draconian rulings regarding the consequence of inadvertently produced documents. Generally speaking both sides tend to have a comparable if not identical interest in entering into such claw back agreements. But there is no way of forcing one side to do so if it is unwilling.

Since courts are not showing any reluctance to enforce such contracts between the litigating parties, with time these agreements to return inadvertently produced privilege documents may come to all but totally replace most of the jurisprudence which had developed around the issue of whether and when inadvertently produced documents constituted a waiver. Those cases may well be on the way of having only a historic interest.

Indeed, arguably it may become malpractice not to enter into such agreements to return inadvertently produced privilege documents since they put a client's privilege at the risk of negligent waiver by attorneys and their paralegal or third-party contractors producing large volumes of documents which must be screened for privilege.

A sample of such a clause in an agreement to return inadvertently produced privilege documents might read as follows:

Agreement for Dealing with Inadvertently Produced Privileged Documents.

(1)   Any inadvertent disclosure or production of documents protected by the attorney-client privilege or work-product pro-

tection shall not constitute a waiver of either any available privilege or protection by the disclosing party.

(2) In the event that the receiving party discovers that it has received either attorney-client privilege or work-product-protected documents, it shall bring that fact to the attention of the producing party immediately upon that discovery.

(3) Upon the request of the producing party, the receiving party shall promptly return any attorney-client privilege or work-product-protected document and any copies which the receiving party may have made thereof to the producing party.

(4) Upon the request of the producing party, the receiving party will promptly disclose the names of any individuals who have read or have had access to the attorney-client privilege or work-product-protected document.

(5) No such inadvertently produced attorney-client privilege or work-product-protected document may be used in evidence against the producing party.

(6) In the event that either party must seek judicial enforcement of this agreement, the costs and reasonable attorney's fees of the party seeking enforcement will be paid by the party against whom such enforcement must be sought, but only in the event that the court finds the existence of a valid privilege and grants enforcement of this agreement by ordering the return and non-evidentiary use of the produced document.

There will no doubt develop a whole new jurisprudence around such agreements to return inadvertently produced privilege-protected documents. Questions such is the claim of privilege a valid one are bound to arise. So too may questions as to whether the document was or was not inadvertently or strategically produced. But widespread adoption of such agreements is growing and is likely to make history of the entire jurisprudence of when inadvertently produced documents should be returned and when such inadvertent production will or will not be excused and does or does not constitute waiver.

- *Coffin v. Bowater, Inc.*, 2005 U.S. Dist. LEXIS 11784 (D. Me. June 14, 2005). Plaintiffs moved for the return of a document pursuant to a return of inadvertently produced documents agreement. The privilege was claimed by a third party not party to the litigation. The document had come into the possession of plaintiffs' attorneys; because they also represented the privilege holder, Defendant argued that plaintiffs had no standing to assert a third-party's privilege. The court said it would be inclined to give effect to Defendant's standing argument but for the fact that the agreement was broadly enough written to permit the assertion of even a non-party's privilege.

However, the court also held that there had been waiver when the document was shared with others who did not have a common defense privilege. The document had been prepared not to represent common legal interests in the current litigation but four years before for use in contract negotiations in an essential adverse not common interest situation.

Although such agreements to return inadvertently produced documents should be valid and enforceable even if not incorporated into a protective order entered by the court, it has become increasingly customary to have them incorporated into a protective order entered into the case and regulating discovery. The practice is certainly one that provides greater comfort to the litigants.

K. *Protective Orders*

It has become commonplace to produce documents, subject to a protective order. Many of them are in fact negotiated by the parties and entered by the court on a stipulated basis. They have become legion and are duly available as reported orders on Lexis. What follows is merely a sampling from a small time segment of 2006 reported decisions. Unfortunately some are beginning to read like billion dollar indenture agreements.

- *Rogers v. Nucor Corp.*, 2006 U.S. Dist. LEXIS 26503 (E.D. Ark. Apr. 27, 2006).

- *Wal-Mart Stores, Inc. v. General Power Prods., LLC*, 2006 U.S. Dist. LEXIS 31315 (W.D. Ark. May 15, 2006).

- *Rushing v. Time Warner, Inc.*, 2006 U.S. Dist. LEXIS 31249 (W.D.N.C. May 12, 2006).

- *Emergis Techs., Inc. v. Midwest Energy, Inc.*, 2006 U.S. Dist. LEXIS 30511 (D. Kan. May 9, 2006)

- *De La Torre v. AE Corp. Servs. Co.*, 2006 U.S. Dist. LEXIS 24591 (D. Kan. Apr. 24, 2006).

- *Sprint Telephony PCS, L.P. v. County of San Diego*, 2004 U.S. Dist. LEXIS 10635 (S.D. Cal. May 31, 2004).

To the extent that the parties can not agree to the wording of the protective order that they wish to have the court enter as a "stipulated" one, they have been known to have recourse to the court for resolving the dispute. No doubt we shall be seeing more of that.

- *AFP Advanced Food Prods. LLC v. Snyder's of Hanover Mfg, Inc.*, 2006 U.S. Dist. LEXIS 426 (E.D. Pa. Jan. 6, 2006). Court selected between contested versions to one provision in the protective order. And then entered one that ran on for some 40 pages!

Many of these confidentiality/protective orders contain what have come to be called "claw back" provisions. These are agreements that an inadvertent production of privilege/protected materials will not constitute waiver but will be returned on request. Yet not all of the confidentiality agreements have such "claw back" provisions in them. It is not clear why not. Did neither party think of inserting such a provision? Did one party have a lighter privilege review burden than the other and therefore saw no need for such reciprocity? Did the court refuse to enter an order with such a provision? In light of the dire consequences which may flow from inadvertent production of privileged documents, can one perhaps say that failure to include such a clause when it is possible to do so is inexplicable?

Some parties now mark each and every document "confidential," apparently on some curious theory of "just in case" or if a little is good, everything has got to be better. Such silliness may be courting trouble. Don't put it past some court to conclude that the privilege/protection has been frivolously raised and thus none of it really deserves any protection.

Technically speaking, stipulated protective orders can only have a prospective in effect. So the parties would be well advised to have them entered prior to the exchange of documents. That is not to say that a court would under no conditions given retrospective effect to the intention of the parties, but don't count on it.

- *Calderwood v. Omnisource Corp.*, 2006 U.S. Dist. LEXIS 29475 (N.D. Ohio May 10, 2006). Court held that a protective order had only a prospective effect. However, the party claiming privilege did nothing for some 10 months during which the party who gained possession of the document made use of it in other proceedings without objection by the privilege holder.

Some courts are now ordering parties to enter into confidentiality agreements which can then be entered as stipulated protective orders, suggesting that stonewalling such a request made by an adversary may not be acceptable.

- *Capital Corp. Mergers & Acquisitions, Inc. v. Arias Co.*, 2006 U.S. Dist. LEXIS 26575, at *6 (M.D. Fla. May 4, 2006). "The Court finds it unacceptable that Capital never responded to Mars' offer to enter into a confidentiality agreement. The Court **ORDERS** the parties' counsel to meet in person **on or before May 19, 2006,** to negotiate and execute a confidentiality agreement."

Three Rules potentially govern the entry of such confidentiality/protective orders. The court can issue scheduling orders under *Fed. R. Civ. P. 16*; protective orders under *Fed. R. Civ. P. 26(c)*; or discovery management orders under *Fed. R. Civ. P. 26(b)(2)*.

Confidentiality/protective orders are all but invariably drafted by the parties and not the court. They in effect constitute a "contract" between them, which is usually reviewed and approved by the court.

Though courts are entering such protective orders with increasing frequency, and probably with precious little review or amendment, the practitioner should be aware that the entry of a protective order is not a matter of right for the litigants but is within the court's sound discretion. Indeed, Rule 26(c) requires a showing of good cause to support the issuance of a protective order and indicates that "the burden is upon the movant to show the necessity of its issuance, which contemplates a particular and specific demonstration of fact as distinguished from stereotyped and conclusory statements."

Proposed Rule 502(c) of the Federal Rules of Evidence also contains a provision governing the entry of orders regarding privilege, which presumably would encompass protective orders of various kinds.

(c) Controlling effect of court orders.—

> Notwithstanding subdivision (a), a court order concerning the preservation or waiver of the attorney-client privilege or work-product protection governs its continuing effect on all persons or entities, whether or not they were parties to the matter before the court.

The committee commentary states that such orders are intended to diminish the costs involved in review for privilege, particularly in the context of electronic discovery and that parties are not likely to avail themselves of foregoing such review if the non-waiver provisions would be ineffective against non-parties. Since most jurisprudence is based on a concept that non-parties cannot be bound by court orders, it remains to be seen whether and how such a provision would be given effect.

If Proposed Rule of Evidence 502(c) is enacted it may do away in its entirety the body of case law which presently holds selective privilege waiver to be ineffective.

> 24 Charles Alan Wright and Kenneth W. Graham, Jr., *Federal Practice and Procedure* § 5507, p. 579 (1986). "It has been held that the parties can stipulate, that a disclosure is not a waiver and some courts have honored non-waiver clauses imposed by a discovery order. . . . But it is questionable whether such agreements should be effective as against third parties. Similarly, since courts cannot change the law of evidence by local rule, it is hard to justify a discovery order that purports to have the effect of altering the law of waiver."

But as a practical matter, orders containing time lines for the conduct of discovery are now often entered and these often contain a clause as to how the inadvertent disclosure of privileged documents will be treated. Such clauses in the discovery order are negotiated between the parties and are entered by the court, usually considering that if the parties are satisfied with the protective order it has no cause for quarrel.

One might call such clauses "request and return" clauses which incorporate the ABA Comm. on Ethics and Professional Responsibility, Formal Op. 94-382 (1994). The Formal Opinion is effectively a "cease, report, return" rule that puts the onus of protecting the privilege on the receiving rather than the producing counsel.

- *Western Fuels Ass'n v. Burlington N. R. Co.*, 102 F.R.D. 201 (D. Wyo. 1984). An order expediting discovery stated that inadvertent production of privileged and protected materials would not constitute a waive.

- *Valve Corp. v. Sierra Entm't Inc.*, 2004 U.S. Dist. LEXIS 29618 (W.D. Wash. Dec. 6, 2004). Magistrate judge properly concluded that documents inadvertently produced were subject to a "request/return" protective order, but after an *in camera* review of the documents, the district court overruled the magistrate's conclusion that they were either privilege or work-product-protected since they dealt with sales figures rather than legal advice. Although they were work-product protected, the party seeking production had demonstrated substantial need.

Increasingly where there is a protective order in place, courts will allow the terms of the protective order to "trump" existing case law. Where case law is often extremely unforgiving in terms of even an inadvertent production of a privileged document constituting a waiver, a protective order may well operate to change the effect of such case law.

- *In re Sulfuric Acid Antitrust Litig.*, 235 F.R.D. 407 (N.D. Ill. 2006) The non-waiver clause in the stipulated protective order required the "recipient party" to be informed within 30 days of the discovery of the inadvertent disclosure. The court enforced the non-waiver provision even though one party tried to argue that the 30-day "discovery" meant constructive not actual discovery. And hence that the disclosing party had not acted promptly to retrieve the privilege.

- *Cardiac Pacemakers, Inc. v. St. Jude Med., Inc.*, 2001 U.S. Dist. LEXIS 8320, 2001 WL 699850, at *1 (S.D. Ind. May 30, 2001). The court concluded that the production of 25,000 documents under the mistaken assumption that they had been reviewed and redacted would ordinarily constitute waiver, but that a protective order foreclosed application of inadvertent production case law.

- *Prescient Partners, L.P. v. Fieldcrest Cannon, Inc.*, 1997 U.S. Dist. LEXIS 18818, 1997 WL 736726, at *4 (S.D.N.Y. Nov. 26, 1997). Parties drafted this provision to provide for the out-of-court resolution of inadvertent production issues and to avoid litigating these issues.

- *Minebea Co. v. Papst*, 370 F. Supp. 2d 297 (D.D.C. 2005). Terms of the protective order were used to excuse an inadvertent production of privileged documents while case law would have required waiver. "Simply put, the language of the Protective Order trumps the case law." The court did state that it appeared that not all assertions of privilege were valid ones.

The existence of a protective order with a non-waiver/return clause does not foreclose litigating whether an inadvertently produced document is in fact privileged or work-product protected. If a court finds that it is, it will generally order its return. But such a clause does not mean that the very issue of privilege is foreclosed and that every document that a party may deem to be privileged or work-product protected is so in fact.

- *Coffin v. Bowater, Inc.*, 2005 U.S. Dist. LEXIS 11784 (D. Me. June 14, 2005). Despite the existence of a no waiver/return clause in a protective order entered by the court, the court did not order return of a document as to which the producing party claimed a common interest work-product protection. The court found that the document was prepared 4 years before any litigation and was prepared for collective bargaining purposes.

On the other hand the existence of a protective order which contains a clause that inadvertent production of privileged documents will not constitute a waiver does not allow a privilege holder to sit on its right to retrieve the privileged document. A cavalier attitude toward further disclosure or a failure to act promptly to retrieve the privileged document will act to nullify any "claw back" or "retain and retrieve" the privilege clauses.

- *Calderwood v. Omnisource Corp.*, 2006 U.S. Dist. LEXIS 29475, at *1–2 (N. D. Ohio May 10, 2006). "[E]ven if the document was privileged and inadvertently disclosed, Plaintiff's use of it in two different public fora, with Defendant's knowledge, during the roughly ten-month period since Defendant learned of the document's disclosure, amounts to waiver of any privilege."

Given the burdens and expense of reviewing the mass of materials now stored in computerized form, voluntary agreements of non-waiver are now more important than ever. There is ample precedent and it is of long-standing for courts to give effect to such agreements at least as between the parties, both in respect to documents inadvertently produced and even in respect to answers given in depositions. What is new is the attempt by Proposed Rule 502(c) to make such stipulations or agreed orders binding on non-parties.

- *VLT Corp. v. Unitrode Corp.*, 194 F.R.D. 8 (D. Mass. 2000). The district court approved a stipulation between counsel governing non-waiver of inadvertently produced privileged documents.

- *Ames v. Black Entm't TV*, 1998 U.S. Dist. LEXIS 18053, 1998 WL 812051, at *1 (S.D.N.Y. Nov. 17, 1998). Where the parties had agreed that certain questions could be answered at a deposition without waiver of the privilege, no waiver resulted.

- *Dowd v. Calabrese*, 101 F.R.D. 427, 439 (D.D.C. 1984). A party could not rely on answers in a deposition to support a claim of privilege waiver where the parties had stipulated that answers would not constitute a waiver.

- *Western Fuels Ass'n v. Burlington N. R. Co.*, 102 F.R.D. 201, 204 (D. Wyo. 1984). Where court entered an order requiring expedited discovery without privilege waiver, inadvertent product of privileged documents did not result in waiver.

- *Eutectic Corp. v. Metco*, 61 F.R.D. 35, 42 (E.D.N.Y. 1973). "Prior to any discovery in this case by defendant, plaintiffs and defendant executed a protective order which contemplated a special method of discovery for the particular case and expressly provided there would be no waiver of any privilege unless expressed in writing. . . . If the language of the protective order is to be applied in the instant case, its requirement of express waiver would seem to preclude any argument of waiver to be implied by a particular course of conduct especially one contemplated in the order itself."

- *United States v. United Shoe Mach. Corp.*, 89 F. Supp. 357, 359 (D. Mass. 1950). "The defendant seasonably claimed whatever privilege it had. It did not waive its privilege by surrendering the exhibits in response to subpoenas, because it was agreed in advance by Government counsel that compliance with the subpoenas should not constitute a waiver."

Some courts have been far more reluctant to give effect to such agreements between parties in respect to non-waiver for inadvertent disclosure.

- *Koch Materials Co. v. Shore Slurry Seal Inc.*, 208 F.R.D. 109, 118 (D.N.J. 2002). The court declined to give effect to an agreement between counsel that production of certain documents would not waive privilege protection because such agreements "could lead to sloppy attorney review and improper disclosure which could jeopardize clients' cases."

- *In re Columbia/HCA Healthcare Corp.*, 192 F.R.D. 575, 577–78 (M.D. Tenn.), *appeal dismissed*, 229 F.3d 1151 (6th Cir. 2000). The court held that an agreement with the government to produce documents without waiving privilege/work-product protection was invalid, rejecting the doctrine of "selective waiver."

There is no doubt, however, that even in the absence of Proposed Rule 502(c) of the Federal Rules of Evidence, the use of voluntary protective orders before turning over documents is a useful method of protecting a party from the danger that inadvertent production will necessarily be deemed a waiver has become exceedingly widespread and indeed is highly advisable to protect both the privilege of the parties and their lawyers from having to explain to the clients how they allowed an inadvertent production to occur which resulted in a waiver of privilege protection. Indeed given today's practice and the existing case law on how draconian some courts are when an inadvertent disclosure does occur, failure to negotiate and enter a stipulated protective order containing a "claw back" agreement would be very ill advised.

- *Cardiac Pacemakers, Inc. v. St. Jude Med., Inc.*, 2001 U.S. Dist. LEXIS 8320, at *7, 10 (S.D. Ind. May 30, 2001). The court noted that absent the provisions of a protective order, it would have been compelled to rule that waiver had occurred when some 3500 pages of privileged documents had been turned over in discovery. "The protective order provides that inadvertent production 'shall be without prejudice to any claim that such material is privileged' . . . . The protective order further provides: 'No party or entity shall be held to have waived any rights by such inadvertent production so long as the Recipient Party is notified within 30 days of the discovery of such inadvertent production.' The record here shows inadvertent production followed by a timely notice." The court therefore concluded that in this case, the non-waiver terms of the protective order were plainly intended to *modify* the otherwise applicable law. "Defendants' argument in this case would effectively turn into a nullity the carefully negotiated non-waiver provision, which defendants themselves originally proposed."

Courts will approve and enforce such protective orders between parties, as they would any other contract, where the court has determined that it was freely negotiated and intended to preclude litigation over whether a production was advertent or inadvertent and thus did or did not constitute a waiver.

- *Prescient Partners, L.P. v. Fieldcrest Cannon, Inc.*, 1997 U.S. Dist. LEXIS 18818, 1997 WL 736726, at *4 (S.D.N.Y. Nov. 26, 1997). "If the provision applied only to documents deemed inadvertently produced under governing case law, then the parties would have to brief that law for the court," which would nullify the efforts of the parties to avoid having to litigate inadvertent production issues.

Even where such protective orders are sought and have been entered, courts have warned that any blanket non-waiver clauses will not necessarily be honored.

- *Ciba-Geigy Corp. v. Sandoz Ltd.*, 916 F. Supp. 404 (D.N.J. 1995). The court's opinion in the case makes clear that, during a hearing leading to issuance of a protective order, the court had rejected "the so-called 'blanket' inadvertent disclosure clause advocated by plaintiff's counsel, and insisted that any such provision would not excuse the parties from conducting a privilege review prior to the production of documents, in accordance with controlling case law."

And even if a court is willing to enforce a non-waiver agreement between the parties, it does not follow that it will be enforced in respect to third parties.

- *Hartford Fire Ins. Co. v. Guide Corp.*, 206 F.R.D. 249 (S.D. Ind. 2001). "Third, the parties are advised that P 3(f) may have a more limited scope than they intend. While the parties might be able to bind themselves by agreeing to limit waivers resulting from inadvertent (or deliberate) disclosures, . . . their agreement cannot limit waivers as to third parties." (Citations and footnote omitted.)

- *Westinghouse Elec. Corp. v. Republic of Philippines*, 951 F.2d 1414, 1426–27 (3d Cir. 1991). An agreement between a litigant and the Department of Justice that documents produced in response to investigation would not waive privilege does not preserve privilege against different entity in unrelated civil proceeding.

- *Bowne of New York City v. AmBase Corp.*, 150 F.R.D. 465, 478–79 (S.D.N.Y. 1993). A non-waiver agreement between a producing party and the recipient of privileged documents in one case was held not applicable to a third party in another civil case.

In all events if for some reason one wishes to disclose some privileged communication to an adversary in the context of litigation, one would do well to bring the matter to a court's attention and seek a protective order before one does so, if one wishes thereafter to have any hope of retaining the privilege either in respect to the party to whom the privileged material will be disclosed or in respect to any potential third parties.

- *DC Comics v. Kryptonite Corp.*, 2002 U.S. Dist. LEXIS 10593 (S.D.N.Y. June 12, 2002). Plaintiff brought a motion seeking a protective order that revealing a portion of the communications with its attorney regarding a negotiated agreement would not constitute waiver of the privilege. The court granted the motion but provided that in the event any privileged documents were introduced, all documents created during the entire period of time that the agreement was being negotiated would have to be produced.

Where parties who may not be before the court are represented by counsel who is, a court has a certain amount of leverage and its order or non-waiver or non-disclosure can reach such parties through their counsel.

- *In re Braniff, Inc.*, 153 B.R. 941 (Bankr. M.D. Fla. 1993). Discovery of some documents provided to former officers of the corporate debtor was subject to a protective order of non-disclosure to other parties represented by the same law firm.

- *Contratto v. Ethicon, Inc.*, 227 F.R.D. 304 (N.D. Cal. 2005), *adopted*, 2005 U.S. Dist. LEXIS 11443 (N.D. Cal. Mar. 22, 2005). A motion to keep documents designated as confidential pursuant to a stipulated protective order was denied where the documents did not fit a protective category, such as a trade secret or an attorney-client privileged document.

Disclosure of work-product or attorney-client privileged documents subject to a protective order may act just like any other contract does. It is binding on the parties thereto, but not necessarily binding on non-parties to the agreement.

- *Chubb Integrated Sys. v. National Bank of Washington*, 103 F.R.D. 52 (D.D.C. 1984). The reservation of the work-product protection was ineffective with respect to third parties when documents were disclosed to an adversary. The reservation was effective only with respect to the party to whom the materials had been disclosed. Only that party could not raise the issue of waiver or use the disclosed materials.

While courts have plenary power to govern proceedings that are part of the litigation before them, they do not, apparently, have the power to limit extra-judicial interviews to non-privileged matters.

- *Wharton v. Calderon*, 127 F.3d 1201, 1205 (9th Cir. 1997). In a *habeas corpus* proceeding filed by a prison inmate against the warden, the district court entered a protective order that precluded the warden from communicating with the prisoner's former counsel except by way of deposition. Surprisingly, the court of appeals held that the district court had no such power. "The attorney-client privilege, like most other privileges, is an *evidentiary* privilege—it protects against the compelled disclosure in court, or in court-sanctioned discovery, of privileged communications. It is not a roving commission to police voluntary, out-of-court communications." Perhaps the court reasoned that former counsel was in all events obliged not to disclose privileged communications and therefore the order was unnecessary, although the court of appeals did not say that was its *ratio dicendi.* Thus, the court could not enter a protective order limiting interviews to non-privileged matters, any more than it could enter protective orders with respect to "after-dinner conversations."

Thus the notion that Proposed Rule 502(c) could give a court the power to decide whether turning over a document in discovery in one case subject to a stipulated protective order would never constitute a waiver in another before another judge is problematic.

In some courts when a protective order is granted, its reach is often considerable and effective even against a government investigation, short of empaneling a grand jury and having the grand jury issue a subpoena.

- *GAF Corp. v. Eastman Kodak Co.*, 85 F.R.D. 46 (S.D.N.Y. 1979). A protective order even barred production of materials discovered in private litigation to the government pursuant to a civil investigative demand issued by the agency with supervisory authority.

A court is not likely to enter such a protective order *sua sponte.* Thus, counsel would be well advised to request such an order. If a protective order is not entered, the only recourse to not having a stay of a discovery order granted, but nonetheless prevailing on the appeal, is that the material that has been ordered disclosed will not be admissible as evidence. Clearly, there is no expunging it from the mind of the opposing counsel and fashioning relief.

Even though a court is not likely to issue a protective order *sua sponte,* there is no doubt that a court can issue protective orders to preclude the use of privileged communications in the course of judicial proceedings. If requested to do so, there is some dispute as to whether a court may do so if there is no judicial dispute pending before the court. In the criminal context, the power to enter such a protective order has been codified in the context of law enforcement wiretaps. According to a federal statute, wiretaps must be minimized to exclude eavesdropping and recording of privileged communications and that if such are recorded, they cannot be introduced into evidence against a defendant (18 U.S.C. § 2515).

- *United States v. Grice*, 37 F. Supp. 2d 428 (D.S.C. 1998). An attorney's motion to intervene to suppress a tape recording of his conversation with his client was granted.

Occasionally, parties will apply for a protective order to postpone discovery of undisputed privileged material in a case when there is a possibility that a party will rely on an advice of counsel defense, for instance in patent infringement cases, but where the decision to rely on such a defense has not yet been made.

- *Flex Prods. v. BASF Corp.*, 1998 U.S. Dist. LEXIS 22028 (E.D. Mich. May 13, 1998). A Rule 26(c)(2) protective order was granted to allow a party not to disclose privileged material pending its determination of whether to invoke an advice-of-counsel defense to a charge of willfulness in a patent infringement case.

Other courts have suggested that permitting such postponement of the production of privileged materials is counterproductive to public policy, which should encourage manufacturers to consult with and heed the counsel of patent attorneys as to whether a proposed product infringes some existing product. If the opinion was that it did not infringe, clearly the defendant would not hesitate to disclose it early on in the litigation.

- *Wright Mfg. v. Great Dane Power Equip., Inc.*, 1998 U.S. Dist. LEXIS 19484 (D. Md. July 20, 1998). "A defendant is most likely to want to suppress an opinion that suggests the proposed product violates a valid patent. Therefore, if defendants knew that they would have to waive privilege at the liability stage in order to use an opinion to contest willfulness, perhaps they would pay greater heed to the advice contained in that opinion. After all, a manufacturer has no reason to suppress a patent opinion that says the proposed product is legitimate." Hence, the court refused either to stay discovery or to bifurcate the trial on the issue of willfulness and treble damages until after liability was tried.

When a protective order is issued in the litigation context, increasingly or as part of a protective order, courts threaten sanctions if assertions of privilege are improperly made, for instance in the deposition context. There are few reported cases of such sanctions, however. Those that have been found are addressed under that heading.

- *DiPalma v. Medical Mavin, Ltd.*, 1998 U.S. Dist. LEXIS 1747, at *12 (E.D. Pa. Feb. 10, 1998). "Any assertion by a witness of a privilege which is unfounded may result in the imposition of appropriate sanctions."

Also, courts have fashioned more imaginative relief such as requiring counsel to reveal improperly obtained privileged information to the opposing side, or they have precluded the use of such information at trial. Disqualification has also been requested but so far has not been granted.

- *In re Bank of Louisiana/Kenwin Shops*, 1998 U.S. Dist. LEXIS 17812 (E.D. La. Nov. 10, 1998). The magistrate was instructed to review documents and determine which were in fact privileged and thus not subject to evidentiary use when obtained by counsel from former corporate employees and subject to a turn-over to the corporate holder of the privilege. A motion to disqualify counsel who had received the privileged documents was denied as well as an injunction prohibiting counsel from speaking with any other former employees, subject to the condition that counsel was not to inquire into privileged matters or receive privileged documents.

Parties also may seek protective orders precluding an opposing attorney from interviewing former employees with respect to privileged communication with the corporation's legal counsel. Generally, because there is no ethical prohibition from contacting the former employees of a company, such a protective order may be necessary, particularly if the former employee bears some ill will toward the former employer and would be more than willing to spill the beans.

- *Dubois v. Gradco Sys., Inc.*, 136 F.R.D. 341, 36 (D. Conn. 1991). In certain circumstances, a court may extend a party's privilege to cover the party's former employees.

- *Concerned Parents v. Housing Auth.*, 934 F. Supp. 406, 409 (M.D. Fla. 1996). The court stated that a former managerial level employee could be interviewed by counsel opposing the employer, provided no inquiry was made regarding privileged communications. The issue arose in the context of a motion to disqualify the attorney on those grounds, which motion was not granted. Presumably, a protective order precluding inquiry into privileged communications would have been granted.

Protective orders may also be sought to quash a deposition notice served upon opposing counsel. Except in highly unusual circumstances, a court will generally hold that such a deposition would intrude upon the work product of opposing counsel.

- *In re Bilzerian*, 258 B.R. 846 (Bankr. M.D. Fla. 2001). The SEC prevailed upon its motion for a protective order in response to Rule 30(b)(6) on the grounds that to comply with the subpoena request for the deposition of a person with the requisite knowledge would entail production of an attorney whose knowledge was entirely based on work product.

Occasionally a court is requested to enter an order to retrieve an inadvertently produced or disclosed privileged document. Where a protective order freezes the status quo pending determination of whether the disclosure was excusable "inadvertence," such orders will be entered, even by courts of appeals.

- *In re Avantel, S.A.*, 343 F.3d 311 (5th Cir. 2003). Privilege documents were "inadvertently" not filed under seal and the appendix containing privileged documents was inadvertently served upon opposing counsel. The court of appeals concluded that the issue was not "moot" by virtue of the disclosure and entered orders requiring the documents to be placed under seal and opposing counsel to return the appendix pending a determination by the district court of the "inadvertent" disclosure issue on remand. Presumably on remand the party seeking to preserve the privilege would argue clerical inadvertence and the district court would consider the level of supervision accorded clerks who are responsible for such filings. As a practical matter, the perfect is the enemy of the good. Busy lawyers can hardly be expected to supervise each judicial filing made and each mailing to opposing counsel. On the other hand, a court might not be tolerant of attorneys who fail to foresee the problem when privileged documents are being filed with a court or served upon opposing counsel.

In *habeas corpus* proceedings alleging ineffective assistance of counsel, attorney files containing both privileged and work-product-protected materials may be turned over. Increasingly, courts are entering protective orders providing both for confidentiality of the material in the *habeas corpus* proceeding and precluding the use of the privileged materials in any subsequent proceeding, including a retrial of the defendant.

- *Bittaker v. Woodford*, 331 F.3d 715, 717 (9th Cir.) (*en banc*), *cert. denied*, 540 U.S. 1013 (2003). The court entered the following protective order: "All discovery granted to respondent pursuant to respondent's motion to discover trial counsels' files and conduct depositions of trial counsel, petitioner's defense team and petitioner, shall be deemed to be confidential. These documents and material (hereinafter "documents") may be used only by representatives from the Office of the California Attorney General and only for purposes of any proceedings incident to litigating the claims presented in the petition for writ of *habeas corpus* pending before this Court. Disclosure of the contents of the documents and the documents themselves may not be made to any other persons or agencies, including any other law enforcement or prosecutorial personnel or agencies, without an order from this Court. This order shall continue in effect after the conclusion of the habeas corpus proceedings and specifically shall apply in the event of a retrial of all or any portion of petitioner's criminal case, except that either party maintains the right to request modification or vacation of this order upon entry of final judgment in this matter."

- *Fears v. Bagley*, 2003 U.S. Dist. LEXIS 15021 (S.D. Ohio Aug. 9, 2003). A no dissemination and no subsequent use protective order was entered in a *habeas corpus* proceeding alleging ineffective assistance of counsel. The court, in an elaborate critique of the rationale of the Ninth Circuit's *Bittaker* opinion, stated that the question of reuse at trial issue would be revisited at the appropriate time.

Similarly, in *habeas corpus* proceedings use of any privilege protected communications has been limited to the *habeas* proceeding.

- *Ghent v. Woodford*, 279 F.3d 1121 (9th Cir.), amended, 2002 Cal. Daily Op. Serv. 2246 (9 th Cir. Mar. 11, 2002). The following order was entered: IT IS HEREBY ORDERED that documents and information protected by the attorney-client privilege or the attorney work-product doctrine revealed by petitioner in this *habeas corpus* proceeding are "Protected Information" and cannot be used for any purpose other than the litigation of petitioner's writ application. The revelation or use of the Protected Information in the writ proceedings will not be considered a waiver of the attorney-client privilege or work-product protection outside of the writ proceedings. However, Protected Information does not include such documents or information if they were obtained by means independent of the writ proceedings or their protection was waived by some conduct other than their revelation in the writ proceedings.

Occasionally a party will seek a protective order to relieve it from the undue burden of filing any privilege log. That burden, however, needs to be adequately "proved" unless the burdensomeness can be determined from the face of the request.

- *Aikens. v. Deluxe Fin. Servs., Inc.*, 217 F.R.D. 533 (D. Kan. 2003). Court declined to enter a protective order relieving a party of the burden of filing a privilege log based on the rather extraordinary claim that "they are not reasonably calculated to lead to the discovery of admissible evidence because, by their express terms, they seek only privileged information and protected work product." It found that although the party contended it would take thousands of hours at the costs of hundreds of thousands of dollars to compile such a log in light of counsel's litigation involvement with that client, the request did not seem burdensome on its face.

And often the protective order takes the form of requesting that privileged documents that may be ordered produced be placed under seal. See cases cited in prior section, "Documents Placed under Seal."

In some instances a court will grant a protective order even where it has found documents are not privilege or work product protected, but deems them sufficiently "confidential" in nature.

- *SEC v. R.J. Reynolds Tobacco Holdings, Inc.*, 2004 U.S. Dist. LEXIS 24545 (D.D.C. June 29, 2004). The court stated that although a broad range of litigation costs incurred by defendant had to be revealed to the SEC, the SEC could not disclose the information to any third parties without seeking leave of court.

L. *Confidentiality Agreements*

Often holders of the privilege or work-product protection will disclose material subject to a confidentiality agreement. Unlike chicken soup which may actually help a cold, generally such confidentiality agreements are not binding upon a court in the least. If the disclosure constitutes a waiver under the case law precedent we have examined extensively, there will be a waiver despite all the confidentiality agreements that ingenious attorneys can dream up and draft.

There is a narrow scope and some limited precedent in the Seventh Circuit for the effective use of confidentiality agreements, when a disclosure is made of work-product to a non-adversary third party. In that instance the confidentiality agreement has been seen as evidence that the party was not oblivious to the danger of substantially greater risk of disclosure to an adversary and attempted to guard against it.

- *Blanchard v. EdgeMark Fin. Corp.*, 192 F.R.D. 233, 237 (N.D. Ill. 2000). The court said that "[t]he confidentiality agreement is evidence that [the defendant] took steps to ensure that its work product did not land in the hands of its adversaries."

- *BASF Aktiengesellschaft v. Reilly Indus., Inc.*, 224 F.R.D. 438 (S.D. Ind. 2004) (*accord*).

Submission of documents to governmental agencies and most recently to the SEC in particular has led to the negotiation of express agreements of confidentiality agreements which often contain non-waiver clauses, namely that turnover of such documents does not constitute a waiver of the privilege in respect to other parties. The extent of future use and confidentiality can be spelled out in these agreements. However, parties need to be aware that where documents are prepared with an eye to subsequent production to the government, a crucial element for the privilege to be applicable is missing *ab initio. See* Part 1, Element 3: In Confidence, C, "Intention to Reveal to Third Parties," *supra.*

In cases of voluntary production to a governmental agency, a number of courts are beginning to give effect to non-waiver agreements, providing they are in writing and non-conditional. *See* Section on "Selective Waiver Does Not Lose Privilege Provided a Confidentiality Agreement Is Entered into Before Disclosure," *supra.* But some courts continue to be very resistant to such a change. Moreover there is substantial dispute as to whether the confidentiality agreement is in fact a unconditional one.

Once again Proposed Rule 502(b)(3) of the Federal Rules of Evidence seeks to make any such disclosure to a governmental agency into an exception to the proposition that disclosure entrains waiver.

> (b) Exceptions in general.—A voluntary disclosure does not operate as a waiver if:

> (3) the disclosure is made to a federal, state, or local governmental agency during an investigation by that agency, and is limited to persons involved in the investigation.

- *United States v. Bergonzi*, 216 F.R.D. 487 (N.D. Cal. 2003). Extensive production to SEC and USAO of documents involved in an internal audit was made subject to an express agreement, which included no provision for either confidentiality or no further use. "Giving discretion to the Government to destroy the privilege is inconsistent with the dicta in cases like *In re Steinhardt Part.*, 9 F.3d 230 (2d Cir. 1993), which contemplated that where disclosure occurs pursuant to a confidentiality agreement, disclosure to the government might not constitute a waiver of the privilege."

If a confidentiality agreement recites that confidential documents will be so marked in some manner and are subject to return if inadvertently produced, a court is unlikely to enforce such a provision—assuming privilege would allow for such enforcement under the circumstances presented—if the documents are not even so marked.

- *Urban Box Office Network, Inc. v. Interfase Managers, LLP*, 2004 U.S. Dist. LEXIS 21229 (S.D.N.Y. Oct. 19, 2004). The court found that voluntary disclosure in a prior arbitration proceeding had in all events constituted waiver, but nonetheless dismissed the privilege proponents argument that the confidentiality agreement which the parties had entered into should govern. How so, wondered the court, when the documents are not marked "confidential" or "for counsel only," as the agreement required.

Some counsel produce all documents with a "confidential" stamp just in case. Marking something confidential does not thereby make it attorney-client privileged. And where every document is so marked the effect thereof may be to undermine and render meaningless the purported intention.

Despite the fact that courts will give little other weight to a confidentiality agreement, it may be a useful device since it theoretically at least binds the recipient not to disclose what is being received—a precaution that has often been unavailing when disclosures are made to the federal government. It also may alert a recipient not to disclose it further or carelessly.

Furthermore, when as is often the case, the confidentiality argument is incorporated into a judicially entered protective order, it does at least provide some protection to the parties in the case at hand, although it is not binding on third parties nor necessarily on other courts in subsequent litigation. *See* preceding section on "Protective Orders."

M. "Chinese Walls" by Prosecutors

It is no longer unusual to see subpoenas issued for law firm files or for the entire hard drive of targets of grand jury proceedings. What is to be done while issues of privilege and crime/fraud or other waivers are litigated? How is the government to have access to the disputed materials to present its case? Should the government have access to the disputed materials to present its case? Courts allow for such subpoenas to be issued and then supervise procedures for winnowing out privileged documents. Increasingly the winnowing out process is resolved by setting up a "Chinese Wall" in the prosecutor's office between the team that is to review the files and the prosecutorial team that will gain access to the files only after disputed privilege issues have been ruled upon by a court.

- *United States v. Grant*, 2004 U.S. Dist. LEXIS 9462 (S.D.N.Y. May 25, 2004). Review of seized documents by a special "privilege team" in the United States Attorney's Office, which was other and distinct from the prosecution team was conducted.

N. In Limine *Motions*

The best way to raise a privilege issue that requires resolution at trial rather than in a discovery stage of litigation may be via the *in limine* motion, which seeks a ruling on a key evidentiary issue before commencement of the trial or in the course of the trial, assuming a long trial. Privilege issues may well require briefing. Thus, having them carefully addressed and disposed of before the commencement of trial is a prudent way of proceeding.

When a party makes a successful claim that attorney-client privilege or work-product protection has not been waived by affirmative reliance on such materials or by injection of such materials into issues being litigated, courts have on occasion made a preemptive ruling that no use of the document that is protected by the privilege can be made.

- *Winton v. Bd of Comm'rs*, 188 F.R.D. 398, 402 (N.D. Okla. 1999). "Defendants have made a choice to seek protection for these documents. As a consequence of that choice, Defendants will not be permitted to use any of these documents at trial for any purpose. Defendants may not offer them into evidence; they may not use them to refresh a witness's recollection; and they may not seek to have the jury draw any inferences from the fact that the *in camera* documents were created or delivered to any particular individual. Defendants will not, therefore, be permitted to use the documents submitted *in camera* as both a shield and a sword."

- *United States v. Skeddle*, 989 F. Supp. 905 (N.D. Ohio 1997). An *in limine* motion brought by an intervenor to determine the scope of cross-examination that would be permitted on privilege issues was granted in part and denied in part.

Assertion of the privilege during the course of discovery may give rise to a motion to bar either a defense or any evidence in any way related to the privilege.

- *Trouble v. Wet Seal, Inc.*, 179 F. Supp. 2d 291 (S.D.N.Y. 2001). A motion *in limine* seeking to bar any reliance on an "advice of counsel" defense in an action against trademark infringement was granted where the defendant had repeatedly asserted the privilege in response to any questions seeking to determine what advice had been given by counsel. Seemingly to keep the matter even-handed, the judge also ordered that should the plaintiff charge that defendant had failed to seek counsel's advice on the infringement issue, such an assertion could be rebutted by defendant, but no details thereof could be offered.

In other words, if a defendant will not use advice of counsel as a defense, then plaintiff cannot bring up the issue as a sword, either. If the ultimate goal is to have clients seek and follow the advice of counsel on matters of trademark infringement, such a ruling does not encourage that result. Instead, it allows a defendant to fail to seek or to ignore advice given and not be called to task. Presumably if advice was sought, and if such advice had been that the use did not infringe, the defendant would surely have availed himself of an "advice of counsel" defense. Arguably, the equal-handed ruling undercuts the ultimate policy basis for the privilege: that it is intended to foster the seeking of legal advice that assists the client in conforming his conduct to the requirements of the law.

Where privileged documents have come into the possession of a party without waiver, an *in limine* motion to preclude use of the document will be granted.

- *Josephson v. Marshall*, 2001 U.S. Dist. LEXIS 10049 (S.D.N.Y. July 18, 2001). Where former employee of company turned over privileged documents to adversary without authorization to take the documents or to waive the privilege, a motion precluding their use at trial was granted.

An increasingly common *in limine* motion where issues of potential waiver of the privilege arise by virtue of the assertion of a reliance on "advice of counsel" defense is to file a motion to bifurcate trials (in the patent or tax context, most particularly) into a liability and a penalty phase. The "advice of counsel" defense would then merely come in on the penalty phase, assuming that liability were to be found. But since the issue only arises not as a defense of liability but as a defense to the penalty, privilege waiver would not have to occur prematurely. Namely, if no liability were to be found, it would not be necessary to raise the reasonable reliance on advice of counsel defense.

- *Quantum Corp. v. Tandon Corp.*, 940 F.2d 642 (Fed. Cir. 1991). A motion to bifurcate the liability from the penalty phase was granted. The unhappy choice between the lawful assertion of the attorney-client privilege and avoidance of a willfulness finding if infringement is found has become known as the *Quantum* dilemma. And the *Quantum* solution is to postpone the choice of the liability from the penalty phase of the trial.

- *Aptargroup, Inc. v. Owens-Illinois, Inc.*, 2003 U.S. Dist. LEXIS 11475 (N.D. Ill. July 1, 2003) (Moran, J.). Bifurcation motion granted.

- *A.L. Hansen Mfg Co. v. Bauer Prods., Inc.*, 2004 U.S. Dist. LEXIS 8935 (N.D. Ill. May 17, 2004). The court did not grant bifurcation on the issues of liability and wilfulness but did on liability and damages, achieving in another fashion avoidance of the *Quantuum* dilemma [i.e., whether to waive privilege or forego a defense based thereon before one knows whether there will be any need to do so] in respect to trial by staying discovery of any counsel opinion.

- *William Reber, LLC v. Samsung Elecs. Am., Inc.*, 220 F.R.D. 533 (N.D. Ill. 2004), *vacated on other grounds*, 2004 U.S. Dist. LEXIS 19291 (N.D. Ill. Sept. 24, 2004). The court denied a bifurcation motion, but stayed discovery as to opinions of counsel until after the liability phase had been decided.

The attempt by way of an *in limine* motion to preclude any testimony by an attorney on the grounds of privilege or work-product protection which might be implicated in such testimony is likely to be denied as overly broad.

- *Green v. Baca*, 226 F.R.D. 624 (C.D. Cal. 2005). Motion to exclude any testimony by Special Counsel hired to conduct an investigation of Los Angeles County's detention policies was denied as overly broad.

O. *Status to Intervene*

Sometimes, albeit rarely, a party may be in possession of certain information that it is prepared to disclose and thereby waive, but that a co-holder of the privilege may wish to protect from disclosure. In such instances, standing to intervene exists.

- *United States v. BDO Seidman, LLP*, 2005 U.S. Dist. LEXIS 12363 (N.D. Ill. 2005). After an *in camera* review of a total of 377 documents of respondents and intervenors, the court found that one was subject to the crime/fraud exception. The court then gave the intervenors, investors in the allegedly abusive tax shelter, an opportunity to rebut that finding. Weighing the submissions of the government against those of the intervenors, the court was not persuaded by the intervenors' submission that the document had been prepared with an eye to taking year-end tax losses instead of with an eye to tax fraud.

- *In re Grand Jury Proceedings*, 156 F.3d 1038 (10th Cir. 1998). The court held that a corporate employee had the right to intervene to protect his individually privileged communications with corporate counsel regarding his own potential criminal liability.

Interesting ethical questions arise at the moment that the confidential communication occurs. Does corporate counsel, whose loyalty is presumably to the corporation, have the duty to inform the corporation of the employee's confidential communications? Does corporate counsel alternatively have a duty to give a type of *Miranda* warning to the corporate employee that anything said may be held against the corporate employee?

The answer is that the corporate attorney has a duty to warn the employee, who is about to confess, of the employee's primary obligation to the corporation. Presumably after such warning, any confession would be at the risk of disclosure to the employer.

P. Sanctions

1. Dismissal of Action or Issue Preclusion

Few sanctions are as definitive as dismissal of an action. Yet such a sanction has been ordered, if sanction it can properly be called, when an action is necessarily predicated on revealing client confidences.

- *Eckhaus v. Alfa-Laval, Inc.*, 764 F. Supp. 34, 37–38 (S.D.N.Y. 1991). A motion to dismiss a former legal counsel's defamation action against his employer was granted where maintenance of the action would have resulted in disclosure of client confidences and secrets in violation of established disciplinary rules.

Sanctions for a groundless assertion of nonexisting privileges also exist. Although the heyday of granting sanctions has passed and although it is rare indeed to have the court grant sanctions for the assertion of privilege, even when that assertion is not sustained, precedent for such sanctions does exist. Courts have suggested that it is best to test the validity of the privilege first than to assert it groundlessly in the context of a deposition for instance.

- *Athridge v. Aetna Cas. & Sur. Co.*, 184 F.R.D. 200 (D.D.C. 1998). The court awarded all expenses, including attorneys' fees, in successfully bringing a motion to compel documents when the court concluded that the assertion of the privilege claim was groundless.

On the other hand, dismissal of an action on such alleged grounds has been deemed too harsh a sanction.

- *Genentech, Inc. v. United States Int'l Trade Comm'n*, 122 F.3d 1409 (Fed. Cir. 1997). Dismissal of suit by an administrative law judge for failure to list a limited number of certain privileged documents in a log was an abuse of discretion and an excessively punitive sanction in light of the extensiveness of the discovery and production undertaken, and in light of the administrative law judge's refusal to give the plaintiff time to determine whether a complete log had in fact been submitted.

Dismissal of an action is the sanction meted out to plaintiffs. The equivalent for defendants is issue preclusion or in an extreme situation, the entry of a default judgment. It has been accorded where a court has found that privileges have not been asserted in timely fashion or frivolously asserted.

Where, because of the size of a corporation, money sanctions would have no deterrent effect, courts will fashion sanctions that preclude claims or make particular findings as established in the case.

- *Heath v. F/V Zolotoi*, 221 F.R.D. 545, 549, 552 (W.D. Wa. 2004). Where the court had warned counsel to provide complete responses to discovery requests, it found that sanctions against the law firm and its clients were appropriate where the law firm "asserted frivolous privileges, failed to disclose the existence of the witness statements despite obligations imposed by the Federal Rules of Civil Procedure and this Court's Order, failed to provide a privilege log, and failed to conduct any investigation into the creation of the statements and the current state of the law on privileges." . . . The outrage of the court is apparent in this further statement: " [The] firm argues that if an attorney subjectively believes a document may be privileged there is no obligation to even disclose the existence of the document much less provide a privilege log. This is not the standard of practice in the Western District of Washington. Even assuming such a practice existed, the Federal Rules of Civil Procedure cannot be replaced by community custom. The Rules place an absolute and unequivocal duty on the party withholding discovery to create a privilege log."

Without disclosing the existence of the witness statements in a privilege log it was difficult to adjudicate whether the witness statements were work-product protected or had to be produced either because created in the ordinary course of the insurance companies business or because of substantial need. Bear in mind that often witness statements are work-product protected and the party is told to go take its own depositions. Other factors the court considered in its award of sanctions were that the case had been pending two and half years. The existence of the witness statements taken by the claims adjuster were not disclosed until one week before the discovery cut-off and less than six months to trial.

Accordingly, the court found liability against the client. The law firm was also assessed $25,000 in sanctions, payable in 10 days Was the court angry? You betcha! In a word, the court, absent reversal on appeal, created a fool proof malpractice liability.

- *In Heritage Bond Litig.*, 223 F.R.D. 527 (C.D. Cal. 2004). Issue preclusion was granted for various discovery abuses, including "stonewalling" in respect to filing of privilege logs and improper privilege assertions. There is no indication in the opinion whether the issue in respect to which preclusion was granted was related in some way to the privilege assertions. Attorney's fees of $4,835 were accorded as well.

- *Hayman v. PricewaterhouseCoopers, LLP*, 2004 U.S. Dist. LEXIS 27296, 2004 WL 3192729 (N.D. Ohio July 16, 2004). The case involved a recommendation by the magistrate judge that a default judgment be entered against the defendant as a sanction for its discovery abuses. One of the discovery abuses involved the defendant's production of electronic files with metadata missing. Telxon and the plaintiffs argued that the missing documents, missing attachments, missing metadata, and hard copies of documents in a version different from the versions on any of the electronic databases produced suggested that the defendant was withholding or had improperly destroyed discoverable information. The magistrate judge found the defendant's explanations for missing documents and metadata and for differences between hard-copy versions of documents and those on the electronic databases less than convincing. Although the case does not directly state that metadata should have been produced, that conclusion can be inferred from the court's holding. The litigation concluded before the district judge issued any ruling on the magistrate judge's Amended Report and Recommendation.

2. Waiver of Privilege/Protection Due to Failure to Assert in Timely Fashion

Committee commentary to the new discovery rules foresees waiver as a sanction for failure to provide timely notice of the assertion of privilege or work-product protection in a log.

Fed. R. Civ. P. 26(b)(5). Advisory Committee's Note (1993). "To withhold materials without [providing notice as described in Rule 26(b)(5)] is contrary to the rule, subjects the party to sanctions under Rule 37(b)(2), and may be viewed as a waiver of the privilege . . ."

The D.C. Court of Appeals has concluded that the sanction of waiver of privilege should not be lightly applied absent some egregious conduct.

- *In re: Grand Jury Subpoenas*, 454 F.3d 511 (6th Cir. 2006). The appellate court was critical of the district court's holding that the privilege was waived when no privilege log was provided. The targeted company which had been served with a subpoena had made no review for privilege. To solve the problem the district court had allowed a "taint team" in the prosecutor's office to review for privilege instead of allowing the target company's attorneys to do so belatedly. The court of appeals reversed and mandated the district court to appoint a Special Master, allowing the district court to decide whether to assess the costs thereof to the subpoenaed company.

- *United States v. British Am. Tobacco*, 387 F.3d 884 (D.C. Cir. 2004). "For the third time, we consider the district court's determination that one of the defendants in the United States' RICO action against cigarette companies waived its attorney-client privilege by failing to log a document sought in discovery. As we emphasized the last time around, "waiver of privilege is a serious sanction" that a court should impose only if a party behaves unreasonably or worse. *See United States v. Philip Morris Inc.*, 358 U.S. App. D.C. 226, 347 F.3d 951, 954 (2003) (quoting *First Sav. Bank, F.S.B. v. First Bank Sys., Inc.*, 902 F. Supp. 1356, 1361 (D. Kan. 1995)) (internal quotation marks omitted). Because the record in this case does not reflect the kind of behavior that would satisfy this demanding standard, we reverse and remand with instructions to allow the defendant to log the document."

The Seventh Circuit rejected as totally arbitrary the bizarre sampling methodology which a Magistrate Judge used to test the adequacy of privilege assertions and which the District Court (Kocoros J.) had sustained. The Magistrate did not review each document to test the validity of the privilege claim. Instead he sampled the documents and when he deemed that too many in the sample were not in fact privilege protected, imposed a blanket sanction of waiver for all documents in respect to which any privilege had been claimed.

- *American Nat'l Bank & Trust Co. v. Equitable Life Assur. Soc'y of the United States,* 406 F.3d 867 (7th Cir. 2005). The Seventh Circuit did not look kindly upon the District Court's affirmance of the Magistrate's reluctance to review the documents *in camera* or in the alternative to appoint a Special Master to do so and his choice of a "sampling" technique to test the validity of the privilege assertion and then to order a blanket waiver when he found some inappropriately asserted privileges. Moreover the Seventh Circuit stated that a difference of opinion as to whether a document was or was not privileged did not constitute evidence of bad faith that in any way warranted a blanket waiver of privilege protection. As a sign of how seriously the Seventh Circuit took the sanctions imposed, it went forward with the appeal even though the underlying action had been dismissed for want to jurisdiction and expressly granted multiple relief, including a return of the privileged documents. "Sanctioning Equitable for having too many good-faith differences of opinion was fundamentally wrong. Moreover, the process for arriving at the sanction was arbitrary. Therefore, the global-disclosure sanction, which forced Equitable to disclose information protected by the attorney-client privilege, constituted an abuse of discretion."

The Ninth Circuit has suggested that a *per se* rule mandating waiver for failure to submit a timely privilege log is not an appropriate sanction, but that it would be if the facts are indicative of conscious stonewalling.

- *Burlington Northern & Sante Fe Ry. v. United States Dist. Court,* 408 F.3d 1142 (9th Cir.), *cert. denied,* 126 S. Ct. 428 (2005). The Ninth Circuit refused to issue a writ of mandamus for a sanction of waiver. "We hold that boilerplate objections or blanket refusals inserted into a response to a *Rule 34* request for production of documents are insufficient to assert a privilege. However, we also reject a *per se* waiver rule that deems a privilege waived if a privilege log is not produced within *Rule 34*'s 30-day time limit. Instead, using the 30-day period as a default guideline, a district court should make a case-by-case determination, taking into account the following factors: the degree to which the objection or assertion of privilege enables the litigant seeking discovery and the court to evaluate whether each of the withheld documents is privileged (where providing particulars typically contained in a privilege log is presumptively sufficient and boilerplate objections are presumptively insufficient); the timeliness of the objection and accompanying information about the withheld documents (where service within 30 days, as a default guideline, is sufficient); the magnitude of the document production; and other particular circumstances of the litigation that make responding to discovery unusually easy (such as, here, the fact that many of the same documents were the subject of discovery in an earlier action) or unusually hard. These factors should be applied in the context of a holistic reasonableness analysis, intended to forestall needless waste of time and resources, as well as tactical manipulation of the rules and the discovery process. They should not be applied as a mechanistic determination of whether the information is provided in a particular format. Finally, the application of these factors shall be subject to any applicable local rules, agreements or stipulations among the litigants, and discovery or protective orders."

The Tenth Circuit let stand the sanction of waiver for the untimely filing of a privilege log, refusing a writ of mandamus.

- *Peat, Marwick, Mitchell & Co. v. West*, 748 F.2d 540, 542 (10th Cir. 1984) (*per curiam*), *cert. dismissed*, 469 U.S. 1199 (1985). Even though "it does not seem seriously disputed that the privilege would have attached if the objection had been timely and adequately asserted," a sanction of waiver was allowed to stand.

A survey of district court discovery rulings reveals a very mixed bag, running the gamut from a permissive approach where *Rule 26(b)(5)* is construed liberally and blanket objections are accepted, to a strict approach where waiver results from failure to meet the requirements of a more demanding construction of *Rule 26(b)(5)* within *Rule 34*'s 30-day limit. A strict *per se* waiver rule and a permissive toleration of boilerplate assertions of privilege both represent minority ends of the spectrum. Nonetheless, the practitioner should be aware that an increasing number of courts seem to be willing to police the privilege log requirement by waiver of the privilege for failure to file one in a timely fashion or for a blanket assertion of ill defined privileges.

- *Smith & Nephew, Inc. v. Federal Ins. Co.*, 2005 U.S. Dist. LEXIS 31309 (W.D. Tenn. Nov. 10, 2005). Failure to assert a work-product protection claim in the first objection to production of requested documents was deemed to constitute a waiver. The court, however, did say that even without the waiver, the work-product claim was misplaced.

- *Breon v. Coca-Cola Bottling Co.*,[5] 232 F.R.D. 49, 55 (D. Conn. 2005). Where defendant provided no privilege log, even though it detailed some of the bases for its privilege/protection claims in a responsive pleading, the court deemed that to be insufficient and thus both were waived. "Preparation of a privilege log is a critical step in discharging one's burden of establishing the existence of a privilege."

- *Sanchez v. Matta*, 229 F.R.D. 649 (D.N.M. 2004). Although no privilege log was filed until the opponent filed a motion to compel, the court said it would suffice to decide the issues and no waiver was entailed thereby.

- *Coastline Terminals of Conn. v. United States Steel Corp.*, 221 F.R.D. 14 (D. Conn. 2003). The court excused a failure to assert work-product protection in a privilege log or to amend for over 2 years and then raise the issue for the first time on oral argument. The

---

5. The case provides but one example of the new style in opinion writing—long treatises on the subject of the privilege/protection where the exposition has little connection with the basis of decision. Why, oh why, are the judges allowing their law clerks to do this? What earthly difference does it make what the privilege or the protection do or do not cover when the judge or his law clerk has determined that the rule requires the preparation of a privilege log; none was prepared; therefore no privilege/protection claim has been perfected. Even in legal writing there is both clarity and aesthetical beauty in brevity. There is none in prolixity.

lawyer pleaded his inexperience. The court took pity, out of consideration for the rights of the lawyer's client. Although the work-product protection is designed to protect the lawyer's mental processes, nonetheless, it's existence inures to the ultimate benefit of the client and thus the result is not as illogical as at first blink it might seem. Most of the work product claims were substantively found to be invalid since they involved by and large factual statements in the ordinary course of the business for which the consultants had been hired—remediation of a polluted site.

- *Public Serv. Co. v. Portland Natural Gas*, 218 F.R.D. 361, 363 (D.N.H. 2003). The District Court reversed the Magistrate's finding of waiver for failure to supply a timely privilege log. "While it is possible to read Rule 33(b)(4) to incorporate Rule 26(b)(5)—the argument supporting this view is that a privilege claim cannot be specifically stated without describing the documents that are the subject of the claim in accordance with Rule 26(b)(5)—a more harmonious reading of the rules as a whole leaves the enforcement of Rule 26(b)(5) to the nuanced sanctioning regime governed by Fed. R. Civ. P. 37 rather than [**6] the nearly automatic waiver process required by Rule 33(b)(4).

"Under Rule 37, most failures to comply with discovery obligations initially expose a recalcitrant party only to an order compelling it to comply and requiring it to pay the requesting party's associated costs and legal fees. See Fed. R. Civ. P. 37(a). Harsher sanctions—such as ordering that the disputed facts be taken as established by the requesting party—come into play only if a party fails to obey a court order compelling a response. See Fed. R. Civ. P. 37(b). This contrasts with Rule 33(b)(4) which requires a court to punish untimely or insufficiently specific objections by finding that the objections have been waived unless the noncompliance is excused for good cause shown."

Beware of general objections on privilege/protection grounds without additional specificity or without details in a privilege log. Such claims will always be inadequate and if you hit upon a court that is a stickler, you may be deemed to have waived either privilege or protection.

- *Sonnino v. Univ. of Kan. Hos. Auth.*, 221 F.R.D. 661 (D. Kan. 2004). General privilege/protection objection to production of such documents "to the extent that" they existed was inadequate to properly assert either. The court refused to reconsider its finding of waiver.

- *Calabro v. Stone*, 225 F.R.D. 96 (E.D.N.Y. 2004). The court held that defendant had waived his right to claim that any such document [a statement by the insured to its insurance company] is privileged in light of his apparent failure to disclose the existence of the information in a privilege log or otherwise to raise the issue earlier.

- *Goodyear Tire & Rubber Co. v. Kirk's Tire & Auto Servicenter of Haverstraw, Inc.*, 2003 U.S. Dist. LEXIS 15917, at *9, 2003 WL 22110281 (S.D.N.Y. Sept. 10, 2003). "Here, Defendant has not provided the Court with a privilege log that would aid it in determining whether the documents are work-product. Parties waive their rights to claim work-product protection for any documents that have been in their control and for which a privilege log has not been presented."

- *Weber v. Paduano*, 2003 U.S. Dist. LEXIS 858, at *12 (S.D.N.Y. Jan. 14, 2003). Failure to provide a privilege log can result in a waiver of privilege.

- *In re Clemente*, 17 Fed. Appx. 968 (Fed. Cir. 2001). The court of appeals refused to issue mandamus to overturn a district court ruling that failure to provide timely log resulted in waiver.

Findings are fact-specific. Minor infractions are usually forgiven. Good-faith efforts at compliance are taken into account. And a variety of mitigating circumstances forestall waiver. Among them, informal notification and lack of prejudice are important factors.

- *Anderson v. Hale*, 202 F.R.D. 548, 553 (N.D. Ill. 2001). "In no way do we suggest that Defendants' method—whichever one of the two is considered—of apprising [sic] Plaintiff of the basis for withholding the tapes constitutes perfect compliance under the Rules. But an express claim of work-product protection was made (actually within a shorter time than required), the basis for that claim was sufficiently articulated to put Plaintiff on notice, and Plaintiff suffered no prejudice by the way in which Defendant communicated the information. For those reasons, Defendants' good faith compliance with the Rules precludes a finding of waiver." At issue was identification of tape recordings of witness statements as work-product protected. The work product was nonetheless held to be inapplicable because the attorney had violated ethical standards in making the tape recordings without the witnesses' knowledge and consent. "In sum, because Defendants' counsel violated the Illinois eavesdropping statute and thereby transgressed Local Rule 83.54.4 by violating the rights of third persons, any work-product protection that would have otherwise applied to the tapes is vitiated."

- *Johnson v. Sea-Land Serv., Inc.*, 2001 U.S. Dist. LEXIS 11447 (S.D.N.Y. Aug. 8, 2001). A privileged document was not listed in a privilege log, which in all events was not due until the day after inadvertent production was made of the document. The excuse given for failure to list was that the document was not encompassed in any of the categories of documents sought. The court found that waiver had not occurred.

- *Strougo v. BEA Assocs.*, 199 F.R.D. 515 (S.D.N.Y. 2001). The court refused to find waiver where there was a two-week delay in identifying work-product privilege, finding no harm and commending the party with showing an admirably cooperative approach toward discovery.

A curious wrinkle arises when the files and computer hard drives of attorneys are seized pursuant to a search warrant and privilege issues are then likely to abound. The practice in the United States Attorney's Offices is now to have a team separate from the prosecutorial one review for privilege. The attorney from whom the documents were seized may have an affirmative obligation to identify privileged documents if their location is not self-evident or risk waiver.

- *United States v. Ary*, 2005 U.S. Dist. LEXIS 21958 (D. Kan. 2005). Privileged documents were allegedly stored in a seized black plastic box. When the attorney said nothing regarding that fact for a year and a half, any privilege which might have attached to the documents in the black plastic box was waived.

3. Waiver of Privilege as Sanction for Discovery Abuse

One court has suggested that parties who inappropriately raise privileges or stonewall discovery could be sanctioned by loss of the attorney-client privilege. Because there was an independent ground for deeming that the privilege had been waived it is difficult to predict whether such a holding would be sustained if there was no such independent ground. The court's *dicta* in that case, however, is far reaching in its potential applicability and is of dubious validity absent unusual circumstances.

- *Government Guar. Fund of Finland v. Hyatt Corp.*, 177 F.R.D. 336, 343; 1997 U.S. Dist. LEXIS 20591; 38 V.I. 227 (D. Virgin Is. 1997). "The Court finds that Hyatt's attempt to use the attorney-client privilege as both a shield and a sword is part and parcel of its overall scheme to stonewall discovery and obstruct the processes of this Court. Just as the use of privilege was part of conduct which the Court has found to be sanctionable, just so the release of these documents from that privilege is an appropriate non-monetary sanction."

It should be pointed out immediately, however, that an independent ground—namely, the placing of the privileged communications at issue in an affidavit in a response to a motion for summary judgment—existed. Nonetheless, in its language the court stated that sanctionable conduct regarding the privileged documents was an "independent" ground for ordering their production.

Does failure to list a document in a privilege log as to which privilege is thereafter claimed constitute such discovery abuse as warrants a waiver of the privilege? Not necessarily. But a good reason best be supplied for that failure.

- *United States v. Philip Morris Inc.*, 358 U.S. App. D.C. 226; 347 F.3d 951; 2003 U.S. App. LEXIS 22629 (D.D.C. 2003). Case remanded for District Court to consider whether waiver was in factor the appropriate sanction for failure to list a privileged document in a log.

4. Monetary Sanctions

Beyond waiver, in appropriate circumstances courts will also allow monetary sanctions where there is no good-faith basis for the assertion of privileges and particularly egregious foot-dragging takes place.

A less extreme sanction is where costs and fees in defending against groundless assertions of privilege are made. Indeed it is surprising how often the assertion of privilege/protection is palpably frivolous, by sophisticated clients represented by supposedly competent counsel. Were such sanctions more frequently imposed the practice, which from the reported cases seems to have become quite widespread, entailing utterly unnecessary litigation and court time and the costs attendant thereupon might be diminished.

- *Neuberger Berman Real Estate Income Fund, Inc. v. Lola Brown Trust No. 1B*, 230 F.R.D. 398 (D. Md. 2005). Court found privilege/ protection objections to be without "substantial justification." The court went on to recount the long history of discovery abuse including utterly unsubstantiated privilege claims. "The defendants have sorely misunderstood the demanding and limited nature of the attorney-client, the common legal interest extension of the attorney-client privilege, and the work product doctrine. While the Court understands the complexity of large document productions, defendants' failure to take seriously their responsibilities under the law here is stunning. Defendants' failure to repeatedly comply with their obligations under the rules and governing law has delayed plaintiff's discovery, slowed down the resolution of the dispute, unnecessarily complicated the discovery process, and resulted in unnecessary cost. Delay can be nearly as effective in the concealment of facts as outright destruction in interfering with the prosecution of a case." Accordingly, the court told the party bringing the motion to compel to submit its costs and fees. Associated with filing two motions to compel.

- *Celmer v. Marriot Corp.*, 2004 U.S. Dist. LEXIS 15394, at *12 (E.D. Pa. July 15, 2004). "[W]e question whether Defendant believed, in good faith, that the attorney-client and work-product privileges actually apply to the instant set of facts. In fact, Defendant fails to provide any analysis as to why the privileges should apply to the instant case. Moreover, it appears that the privileges were asserted because it was Defendant's policy to do so in all cases, not necessarily because the facts warranted doing so." Attorney's fees and costs in the amount of $1,500 were assessed against Marriott.

- *Pfizer Inc. v. Ranbaxy Laboratories Ltd.*, 2004 U.S. Dist. LEXIS 20948 (D. Del. 2004). After a sample review of documents as to which privilege/protection were asserted—documents where an attorney was neither author nor recipient or where an attorney was only one of many recipient—the court concluded that the privilege/protection was frivolously asserted and assessed costs and attorney's fees attendant upon the bringing of the motion.

- *Sine v. Bank of N.Y.*, 323 F. Supp. 2d 831(N.D. OH. 2004). No matter how outrageous, sooner or later it crops up in some case. Here an adversary who had obtained privileged communications from their opponent in a collection case made a totally groundless assertion of privilege, which was shown as bogus indeed when the court conducted an *in camera* inspection of the documents even in the absence of a privilege log.

- *Sonnino v. Univ. of Kansas Hospital Auth.*, 220 F.R.D. 633, 647 (D. Kan. 2004). Plaintiff instructed to submit petition for costs and fees where court found that most objections to discovery, including privilege assertions, were unsustainable.

- *Precision Pine & Timber, Inc. v. United States*, 2001 U.S. Claims LEXIS 181 (Ct. Fed. Cl. 2001). Monetary sanctions, including attorney's fees in the amount of $53,811.88, constituting approximately half the amount sought, were imposed on United States for dilatory and overly broad objections to discovery, including improper general assertions of privilege and failure to provide a factual basis for its assertion of privilege and work-product immunity.

- *Amway Corp. v. Procter & Gamble Co.*, 2001 U.S. Dist. LEXIS 4561, at *36 (W.D. Mich. 2001). The court found that Proctor & Gamble's assertions of privilege were knowingly meritless and that it ignored court orders to substantiate its claims. It thus determined that the appropriate sanction was to make a preclusive finding regarding a key issue in the litigation that had been revealed by the withheld but not privileged documents. "The withheld documents disclose that, well before Procter & Gamble had any basis to believe that Amway was in any way involved with the spreading of the Satanism rumor, Procter & Gamble had determined to target competitors for lawsuits involving the rumors, in order to further its public relations and competitive goals. The least punitive sanction in the circumstance is an order taking the foregoing fact as admitted for purposes of this litigation. This fact, although relevant to the present case, is not claim-dispositive of either Amway's complaint or Procter & Gamble's counterclaim." Since the order was entered by a magistrate judge out of an abundance of caution, the sanction portion was entered as a recommendation to the district court. No citation has been found to any ruling by the district court on this issue.

The practitioner who seeks to have sanctions imposed or the one who seeks to avoid such sanctions even for the most egregiously frivolous of privilege assertions or discovery abuse, may sometimes rely on the existence of local rules which require parties to consult in person on discovery issues before motions to compel are brought.

- *Rambus, Inc., v. Infineon Techs. AG.*, 220 F.R.D. 264, 273 (E.D. Va. 2004). After recounting a remarkably tortuous legal history of the case, the court refused to impose sanctions on the grounds that no consultative meeting, as required by local rules, had been held prior to the bringing of the otherwise totally justified motion to compel. Here is what the court had to say about Rambus's discovery shenanigans: "Notwithstanding the Court's repeated admonitions and the terms of the relevant rules and orders, the privilege list filed by Rambus on December 15, 2003 is so sparse, in significant part, on its face, as to be inadequately compliant with the rules and orders. Many of the entries on Rambus' log simply lack the information necessary to determine whether a privilege applies. For instance, respecting the work product doctrine, many entries on Rambus' privilege log do not state whether an attorney was involved in the creation of the document or whether the document was created in anticipation of litigation. Moreover, as to those entries asserting the attorney client privilege, many do not even state whether the communication involved legal advice. Furthermore, the three-page supporting memorandum filed by Rambus was a general boilerplate recitation of the attorney-client privilege and the work-product doctrine. Hence, the memorandum in no way remedied the inadequacy of the privilege log. Rambus responds to Infineon's complaints about the adequacy of the privilege showing by making the rather remarkable argument that Infineon has not carried the burden of showing that the documents are not privileged. That argument, of course, turns the applicable law on its head. The burden is on Rambus to show the validity of its claims of privilege." (Citations omitted.)

■ *See also Rambus, Inc. v. Infineon Techs. AG.*, 222 F.R.D. 280 (E.D. Va. 2004). The court finally found that the documents reviewed *in camera* were not privileged because of Rambus's systematic spoliation of documents, which the court held to be encompassed under the fraud/crime exception.

So much for the theory that the attorney-client privilege is necessary to help clients conform to the law.

5. Sanction of Loss of Work-Product Protection for Ethical Lapse

Attorney ethical violations will also result in waiver of work-product protection that otherwise would be applicable. Unexplained foot-dragging, a cavalier attitude toward adhering to court orders and the discovery rules, and misrepresentations about the nature of the documents either singly or in combination will result in waiver. This probably should apply less to attorney-client privilege, which is the client's rather than the attorney's work product. Since waiver of either the attorney-client privilege or the work-product protection ultimately redounds to the detriment of the client, the distinction may not make optimal logical sense. And in all events, attorney litigation carelessness, whether by inadvertent disclosure or by failure to provide timely privilege logs, also is not the fault of the client, but redounds to the client's detriment.

■ *Ritacca v. Abbott Labs.*, 203 F.R.D. 332, 336 (N.D. Ill. 2001). Plaintiff aggressively pursued discovery while defendant was recalcitrant. The missing documents came to light not because they were listed in a privilege log but because of a gap in the Bates-stamped production that defendant even then did not identify as privileged. A delay in responding to document requests and detailing privilege claims along with "the fact that Abbott misrepresented to Ritacca that the documents at issue were mere duplicates rather than attorney-client communications for over three months compels a finding of waiver. This gives the appearance of a stalling tactic, a measure undertaken to hide information from Ritacca as long as possible. Fairness requires that we hold Abbott to its misrepresentation."

And finally, even Abbott's belated and slipshod attempt at complying with Rule 26(b)(5) supports a finding of waiver. Rule 26(b)(5) expressly indicates that its purpose is to "enable other parties to assess the applicability of the privilege [asserted]." "As evidenced by Ritacca's frustration with trying to assess Abbott's claims of privilege, which was shared by this Court, Abbott's List of Documents Not Produced comes nowhere close to hitting this mark."

- *Haid v. Wal-Mart Stores, Inc.*, 2001 U.S. Dist. LEXIS 15155 (D. Kan. Jan. 11, 2001), *aff'd*, 2001 U.S. Dist. LEXIS 10564 (D. Kan. June 25, 2001). Not only did the court find a waiver of the privilege where no privilege log was submitted, but it also refused counsel time to file such a log and granted plaintiff's motion for sanctions in bringing the motion to compel while denying defendant's counter-motion for sanctions as frivolous and harmful to defendant's position. The court of appeals affirmed finding no abuse of discretion, remarking that the privilege holder did not even proffer and excuse for its failure to provide a privilege log other than the fact that it believed the documents to be privileged.

On rare occasions, a lawyer's ethical violation may act to defeat an otherwise valid assertion of work-product protection. The situation has arisen in litigation between counsel and a former client. Although the argument was that the lawyer had a conflict of interest, which then trumped the work-product protection, in fact the lawyer simply showed poor judgment by ignoring a continuing obligation of confidentiality to a former client in favor of a desire to get even.

- *Nesse v. Shaw Pittman*, 202 F.R.D. 344, 351, 354 (D.D.C. 2001). The law firm withdrew from representation of a client in part for its failure to pay legal bills, and then did not represent the client at a scheduled hearing that resulted in a bankruptcy trustee being appointed to handle the client's affairs at the behest of the client's adversary. The court allowed an extensive claim of work-product protection to the law firm in respect to many documents created by the firm to assess its own potential liability to the client, brushing aside overly facile claims of a fraud or an intended cover-up with the statement: "If legal advice loses its privileged status merely because the opponent claims that the advice was sought to conceal a fraud, the privilege quickly evaporates. If that were the law, few clients would dare talk to lawyers, because the privilege would disappear the moment their opponent charged a cover-up." Nonetheless, the court found that when a lawyer provided information to the adversary's lawyer regarding the circumstances of the withdrawal, an ethical lapse had occurred, which justified trumping the protection not in its entirety but in respect to the conversation between the former client's lawyer and the adversary's lawyer. The adversary used the information to claim that the trusteeship should not be lifted because the affidavit filed by the former client in support thereof smacked of perjury. "In my view, Webster's failure to secure such advice before providing Wick with information later used against Blair requires the forfeiture by SP of any privilege it could claim as to the work product Webster and SP generated relating to the communications between Wick and Webster." The court put particular emphasis on the lawyer's failure to seek independent counsel prior to making any disclosure to the adversary's counsel. Moral: Don't try to get even with former clients. Your ethical obligations to them persist.

Q. *Requisite Findings for Valid Order*

It seems self-evident, but bears repeating, that courts when ruling on privilege/protection issues, themselves are generally held by courts of appeal to a high standard of specificity of fact-findings as predicates for either the protection or the privilege. Many are the cases remanded to the trial court for clearer findings of fact on which to predicate either a finding that a document is subject to a claim of privilege or protection.

- *United States v. Rockwell Int'l*, 897 F.2d 1255 (3d Cir. 1990). The government subpoenaed a corporation's reserve file. The corporation claimed both the privilege and the protection with respect to the file. The appeals court held that the district court must make specific findings of fact for either privilege or protection to be applicable. The unanswered questions were: What was the nature of the material in the free reserve file? By whom had the materials been prepared? For what purpose? Had there been an intended disclosure to third parties (the SEC)? For what purpose? What was the motivation behind the creation and the maintenance of the file?

Only once these questions were answered by the trial court and only if the privilege/protection was asserted document by document, could a valid determination of either be made.

R. *Judicial* Sua Sponte *Review*

When parties submit documents for review to a court, does the court have the *sua sponte* right to examine documents for privilege? It is hard to imagine that documents submitted for judicial review of privilege issues could be argued to be exempt from such review, but whatever is imaginable, some daft attorney has done. Obviously, courts have held that they have the right *sua sponte* to review documents submitted to the court, even when the issue is whether a *prima facie* case of fraud has first to be established to permit such review.

- *FEC v. Christian Coalition*, 178 F.R.D. 456 (E.D. Va. 1998). While it is necessary for a party to make a *prima facie* showing of fraud before a court will review attorney-client documents under the crime/fraud exception, there is no basis for such a showing under ordinary circumstances. "The Supreme Court in *Zolin* did not directly address whether a court should review all claims of privilege, or just those documents specifically opposed by the requesting party. However, the Court noted that courts are generally thought to have broad discretion to determine whether a privilege is properly asserted." The court found no error in the magistrate having decided to review documents other than those in dispute. What is perplexing about the decision and the position taken by the party contesting disclosure is that obviously all the documents were submitted for judicial review. The magistrate did not go foraging in the attorney's office files *sua sponte*. Thus, the argument that a court may not *sua sponte* review all documents submitted to it for review is simply not comprehensible. Understandable or not, the issue of whether a court has the right *sua sponte* to review documents for privilege has been vetted and not surprisingly found wanting.

Improbable as it may seem, at times it is the court rather than the litigant that raises privilege concerns and orders redacted production subject to a confidentiality order.

- *Wright v. Touhy*, 2003 U.S. Dist. LEXIS 15713 (N.D. Ill. Sept. 8, 2003). Court ordered production of attorney billing statements, redacted to protect any privileged materials. The court also crafted a confidentiality order.

S. *Appeals*

1. From Magistrate's Ruling

With increasing frequency, the federal district court judges are relegating disputed discovery matters, including disputes about which documents are attorney-client privileged and work-product protected, to the federal magistrates.

Appeal from a discovery ruling by a magistrate lies to the very district court that often relegated the matter to the magistrate and has little stomach for the minutia of discovery disputes and their attendant *in camera* review of supposedly privileged documents.

The standard of review from the magistrate to the district court is governed and is set forth in Rule 72(a) of the Federal Rules of Civil Procedure and the Federal Magistrates Act, *28 U.S.C. 636(b)(1)(A) (2002)*. Pretrial discovery matters are generally considered non-dispositive of the litigation. Both the rule and the statute state that, as to non-dispositive matters, a district court shall reverse a Magistrate Judge's order only where it has been shown that the order is "clearly erroneous or contrary to law." That standard is a high one indeed. In effect, the standard is predicated on an abuse of discretion standard, which is also susceptible to be overruled "only if no reasonable person would take the view adopted by the magistrate . . . or if the magistrate's order was arbitrary and capricious." *Devore & Sons, Inc. v. Aurora Pac. Cattle Co.*, 560 F. Supp. 236, 239 (D. Kan. 1983). High standards indeed!

Thus, as a practical matter a magistrate's ruling on privilege is hard to overturn. However, although a magistrate's discovery order dealing with privilege issues is hard to overturn, when the consequences are far-reaching it is possible.

- *Harter v. Univ. of Indianapolis*, 5 F. Supp. 2d 657 (S.D. Ind. 1998). The district court overturned the magistrate's ruling that there was no privilege with respect to client communications where an attorney negotiated with the defendant on the issue of fair accommodation in a case brought under the Americans with Disabilities Act. The consequences of the magistrate's ruling were far-reaching. By transforming the attorney into a necessary witness, the defendant also sought, successfully, to disqualify the attorney from representing the plaintiff. The district court obviously thought that such a litigation stunt would preclude any attorney from trying to negotiate a settlement prior to bringing suit. All one would have to do is inject good faith into the case, call the attorney as a necessary witness, and disqualify the attorney from continued representation of the client.

- *Ami/Rec-Pro, Inc. v. Illinois Tool Works*, 1998 U.S. Dist. LEXIS 1829 (N.D. Ill. Feb. 9, 1998). The district court repeatedly reversed a magistrate's order protecting multiple documents as privileged or work-product protected on the ground that too facile and broad an interpretation of privilege and doctrine had been applied as to communications that contained no confidential information and that were not prepared in anticipation of litigation. "Look. I looked at the documents. . . . I know exactly how lawyers work. And when lawyers make notes of what's going on, it's either attorney work product or it's attorney-client privilege," the court quoted the magistrate judge's opinion before concluding that the opinion was "clearly erroneous" and, therefore, reversing almost in toto the magistrate's holding protecting documents from compelled disclosure.

- *In re Buspirone Patent & Antitrust Litig.*, 210 F.R.D. 43 (S.D.N.Y. 2002). The court refused to set aside a magistrate's ruling that an election had to be made by a certain date as to whether a reliance on advice of counsel defense would be made so discovery could go forward. It also did not set aside the magistrate's refusal to carve out a block of documents as privileged in the event that such a defense would be raised. Obviously, the party was seeking an advisory ruling to determine its downside risk of asserting such a defense. It is hardly surprising that the court refused to accommodate such a desire. "It is not reasonable to request the kind of blanket clarifications that BMS seeks because the answer to whether certain documents fall within the scope of any waiver will likely depend in part on the kind of advice-of-counsel defense that BMS raises, if any, the particularized documents responsive to any such defense, and/or review, in some instances, of the requested documents themselves within the context of the actual factual disputes that are placed at issue. . . . Those determinations must be made on a particularized basis and not, as BMS attempts to do, by some blanket exclusion."

2. From Special Master's Ruling

Occasionally, when discovery disputes are especially protracted and complex, a Special Master may be appointed to review the documents in lieu of a magistrate or the district court undertaking the labor itself. With many federal judges retiring from the bench to continue the lucrative practice of law, they are often available for such duty. In such an instance, the likelihood of any kind of *de novo* review of the documents by the district court is remote.

- *Katz v. AT&T*, 191 F.R.D. 433 (E.D. Pa. 2000). A Special Master was appointed to oversee discovery disputes in complex patent litigation. The court held that the Special Master's decisions with respect to privilege issues was entitled under the Federal Rules of Civil Procedure 53(c) and (d) to the same deference as that of a magistrate and was, thus, subjected to a "clearly erroneous or contrary to law" standard of review. Needless to say, the rulings were sustained.

- *Avery Dennison Corp. v. UBC Films PLC*, 1998 U.S. Dist. LEXIS 15727, at *4 (N.D. Ill. Sept. 30, 1998). When a Special Master had already reviewed, *in camera*, over 800 documents withheld on the grounds of attorney-client privilege and the work-product protection, the court deferred to the special master's determinations on the appropriateness of Avery's privilege claims and refused to conduct an independent review of the withheld documents.

3. From Ruling by the District Court

Any appeal from a discovery order is not final but interlocutory in nature. Certification that a matter is appealable on an interlocutory basis is possible but must be certified by the district court pursuant to 28 U.S.C. § 1292(b).

Judicially devised rules have also evolved regarding when discovery matters may be appealed. As a general rule, discovery orders— such as most rulings on attorney-client privilege and work-product protection issues—are not final orders and, therefore, not immediately appealable unless a party is willing to conform to the *Cobbledick* rule

(*Cobbledick v. United States*, 309 U.S. 323, 328 (1940)), which requires disobedience of an order, followed by a citation for contempt as a condition precedent for appellate review. The *Cobbledick* rule purportedly serves judicial efficiency interests. By requiring the party seeking review to put itself in jeopardy with a contempt finding, it purportedly encourages more thorough reflection both by the party seeking discovery and by the party resisting it, thereby making frivolous appeals less likely. You have to be fairly certain you are right to go the whole mile.

Third parties are generally not required to abide by the *Cobbledick* rule. The reasoning is that third parties have less at stake in protecting the privileged documents that are not their own and, thus, will not court a contempt citation by disobeying a discovery order in order to permit appeal. Hence, discovery orders addressed to third parties when attorney-client issues are raised have been deemed to be immediately appealable without conformity with the *Cobbledick* rule.

An alternative to the *Cobbledick* approach has evolved. It treats discovery orders as immediately appealable under a "collateral order" doctrine. *Cohen v. Beneficial Indus. Loan Corp.*, 337 U.S. 541, 546–47 (1949). The collateral order doctrine allows appeals from the "small category" of decisions "that are conclusive, that resolve important questions separate from the merits, and that are effectively unreviewable on appeal from the final judgment in the underlying action." *Swint v. Chambers County Comm'n*, 514 U.S. 35 (1995).

Some courts of appeal have now held that orders which find that no privilege is applicable fit under the collateral order doctrine.

- *In re Lott*, 424 F.3d 446, 448 n.2 (6th Cir. 2005), *cert. denied*, 126 S. Ct. 1772 (2006). The court discussed the contours of the collateral order doctrine, the courts which have determined it to be applicable, but then concluded that since the case fitted all the criteria for granting mandamus it was not necessary to determine whether it would also have fit under the collateral order doctrine. At issue was a district court order that by claiming actual innocence, a *habeas corpus* petitioner had waived any privilege. Of course not concluded the appellate court.

- *United States v. Philip Morris Inc.*, 314 F.3d 612, 618 (D.C. Cir. 2003). The court of appeals analyzed whether the collateral order doctrine provided appellate jurisdiction to hear an interlocutory appeal challenging denial of an attorney-client privilege claim. The court held that the attorney-client privilege was "important" under *Cohen*, concluding that "the institutional benefits of allowing interlocutory review of attorney-client privilege claims outweigh the costs of delay and piecemeal review that may result."

- *In re Ford Motor Co.*, 110 F.3d 954, 964 (3d Cir. 1997).

- *International Bus. Machs. Corp. v. United States*, 471 F.2d 507, 511 (2d Cir. 1972), *vacated on other grounds*, 480 F.2d 293 (2d Cir. 1973). "We reject the suggestion that an appeal can properly come before us only if some officer of IBM refuses to deliver the 1,200 documents, subjects himself to the consequences of contempt, and appeals from the contempt judgment. The law today must be more ingenious, flexible and resourceful in its ability to avoid any such old-fashioned and semi-barbaric procedure."

Under what has been termed the *Perlman* rule, a discovery order addressed to a non-party sometimes may be treated as an immediately appealable final order vis-à-vis a party who claims to hold an applicable privilege. *Perlman v. United States*, 247 U.S. 7 (1918). Courts frequently have invoked *Perlman* when a client (who is herself a party or a grand jury target) seeks to appeal an order compelling her attorney (who is neither a party nor a target) to produce allegedly privileged materials. The theory behind the *Perlman* doctrine is that a non-party is not likely to risk a civil contempt citation by failing to obey a disclosure order merely to protect the privilege of another.

Under either the *Perlman* or the *Cohen* "collateral order" doctrine, a substantial privilege claim that cannot effectively be tested by the privilege-holder through a contemptuous refusal to produce will qualify for immediate review if the claim otherwise would be lost. The principal difference between the two is that the *Perlman* rule arguably contains no limitation on the scope of review whether the challenge seeks to test either the factual determinations or the application of a settled legal rule to particular facts. Review under the *Cohen* "collateral order" doctrine arguably is limited to "clear-cut legal error" and allows for no review of those decisions that are based on an erroneous reading of the facts.

- *Cobbledick v. United States*, 309 U.S. 323 (1940). The case enunciated the general rule that one to whom a subpoena is directed may not appeal the denial of a motion to quash that subpoena, but must either obey its commands or refuse to do so and contest the validity of the subpoena if the individual is subsequently cited for contempt on account of a failure to obey.

- *Perlman v. United States*, 247 U.S. 7 (1918). The Supreme Court held that when the party subject to the subpoena indicates that it will comply with the court order upon a final adjudication of its validity, an interlocutory appeal sought by an intervenor who claims a justiciable interest in preventing the disclosure should be heard.

Whether an immediate appeal is allowed, however, varies from circuit to circuit.

- *Ross v. City of Memphis*, 423 F.3d 596, 604 (6th Cir. 2005). The court reiterates that it does not allow appeals under the Cohen exception, but does under Perlman. It proceeded to grant an interlocutory appeal by a Municipality which had found that a former employee was held to have waived the Municipality's attorney-client privilege by claiming in a Title VII action that he took certain actions upon advice of counsel. The former employee was the beneficiary of a qualified immunity, being sued in all events in his official, not his personal capacity. Because the Municipality could not prevent the former employee from complying with the District Court's discovery order and because the Sixth Circuit found it untoward that the former employee could waive the Municipality's attorney-client privilege granted an interlocutory appeal and reversed.

- *Grand Jury Proceedings v. United States*, 156 F.3d 1038 (10th Cir. 1998). Based on assertions of attorney-client and work-product protection, a former employee of a hospital intervened to quash a subpoena addressed to the hospital. The motion to quash was denied by the district court and the Tenth Circuit held that the denial was subject to an immediate interlocutory appeal. The denial of the motion was affirmed.

- *Silva v. United States (In re Grand Jury Subpoena issued to Bailin)*, 51 F.3d 203, 205 (9th Cir.), *cert. dismissed*, 515 U.S. 1189 (1995). "The denial of a motion to quash a subpoena directed at the movant's former attorney is appealable."

- *United States ex rel. Pogue v. Diabetes Treatment Ctrs of Am., Inc.,* 444 F.3d 462, 474 (6th Cir. 2006.) The Ninth Circuit stated that it followed neither the "collateral order" nor the Perlman doctrine for a party seeking to appeal an order compelling discovery of its own privileged documents. Nor would mandamus lie because an alternative route for appeal lay in accepting a civil contempt citation and then appealing from that. The rationale, said the Ninth Circuit, was that by requiring such a high level of risk, a party would only seek to protect matters it considered genuinely important. "Indeed, the discovery appeals that arise from that calculus will most likely be those of the greatest significance to both parties—the party resisting discovery must risk a citation for contempt, while the party seeking discovery must move for contempt and thereby risk an interlocutory appeal. The alternative to the contempt route, by contrast, is one that encourages appeal of every unpalatable discovery ruling." The Ninth Circuit concluded that although it was not a party to the *Pogue* litigation, HCA's status as both the privilege-holder and document-possessor seeking to prevent disclosure gives it powerful incentives to suffer such a contempt citation. Accordingly, the Ninth Circuit refused to grant mandamus and allowed the district court's order that inadvertent disclosure of two privileged documents entrained subject matter privilege waiver to stand.

- *Peck v. United States,* 680 F.2d 9, 11–12 (2d Cir. 1982). The court made clear that a discovery order is not subject to the "collateral order" exception to the final judgment rule of 28 U.S.C. § 1291. "We refuse to make an exception to the traditional final judgment rule simply because the Attorney General was the contemnor. . . . Without question, as we have repeatedly noted in dismissing Government appeals of similar orders, the discovery order will be reviewable upon appeal from judgment."

- *United States v. Ryan,* 402 U.S. 530 (1971). The Supreme Court concluded that a third-party custodian of documents "could hardly have been expected to risk a citation for contempt in order to secure [the appealing party] . . . an opportunity for judicial review."

Nine circuits allow an immediate appeal from a denial of a motion to quash a subpoena for privileged documents, regardless of who is the custodian.

- *In re Grand Jury Subpoenas*, 123 F.3d 695, 698 (1st Cir. 1997). The First Circuit reviewed the status of the law in other circuits and expressly overruled its prior law that required an attorney to accept a contempt citation when ordered to testify about privileged matters in order to appeal the ruling. "Mindful that it would be unduly optimistic to anticipate that all attorneys will accept contempt rather than compromise their clients' appeal, we think it unwise to require such an action before permitting an appeal." The court also pointed out that requiring an attorney to face contempt before his client's appeal could ripen, necessarily created a conflict of interest between the client's and the attorney's interests that was not conducive to the best possible representation for the client.

- *Conkling v. Turner*, 883 F.2d 431 (5th Cir. 1989). An order directing the testimony of the client's attorney was immediately appealable.

- *In re Grand Jury Subpoena*, 784 F.2d 857 (8th Cir. 1986), *cert. dismissed*, 479 U.S. 1048 (1987) (same).

- *In re Klein*, 776 F.2d 628, 630 (7th Cir. 1985). "Like several other courts, this one has always treated *Perlman* as a holding that clients always are entitled to appeal as soon as their attorneys are required to produce documents."

- *United States v. (Under Seal)*, 748 F.2d 871, 873 n.2 (4th Cir. 1984). The intervenor or movant may immediately appeal an order requiring disclosure of his privilege.

- *In re Grand Jury Proceedings*, 722 F.2d 303 (6th Cir. 1983), *cert. denied*, 467 U.S. 1246 (1984). Immediate appeal was allowed from an order compelling an attorney's testimony on allegedly privileged matters.

- *In re Grand Jury Proceedings*, 689 F.2d 1351 (11th Cir. 1982) (same).

- *In re Grand Jury Subpoena Served upon Doe*, 759 F.2d 968 (2d Cir. 1985) (same).

- *In re Grand Jury Proceedings*, 604 F.2d 798 (3d Cir. 1979) (same).

So too, the Fifth Circuit has ruled that when a deposition of counsel is ordered, the client can effect an immediate appeal without requiring counsel to refuse to comply with the order and be cited for contempt and then appeal from the finding of contempt.

- *Nguyen v. Excel Corp.*, 197 F.3d 200, 204 (5th Cir. 1999). "When a subpoenaed third party does not have a direct and personal interest in suppression of the requested information, however, the third party is not likely to risk a contempt citation. Some attorneys may be willing to submit to a contempt citation to protect a client's confidences; some client-intervenors might find themselves denied meaningful review by attorneys unwilling to make such a sacrifice. We therefore have treated as an appealable final decision a trial court's order directing the testimony of counsel regarding a client's knowledge."

- *In re Sealed Case*, 146 F.3d 881, 883 (D.C. Cir. 1998). An appeal was allowed when a lawyer filed an affidavit stating an intention to obey a discovery order rather than incur contempt.

Only three circuits have held that an order directing an attorney to testify regarding allegedly privileged material is not immediately appealable.

Among them, the Ninth Circuit draws a bizarre distinction between current and former counsel by applying the *Perlman* exception, which permits immediate appeal by an interested third party of a ruling enforcing a subpoena addressed to current counsel but not to one directed to prior counsel.

- *In re Grand Jury Subpoenas Dated Dec. 10, 1987*, 926 F.2d 847, 853 (9th Cir. 1991). An immediate appeal is granted only if the prior attorney complies with a subpoena by producing documents. "In several cases, we have refused to extend the doctrine to attorneys who were still actively representing the person whose papers were seized."

Others allow immediate appeal to hinge on whether it is unlikely that the attorney would risk a contempt citation to vindicate the privilege without suggesting how that likelihood is to be determined.

- *In re Sealed Case*, 754 F.2d 395, 399 (D.C. Cir. 1985). When two attorneys submitted affidavits stating that they would produce documents rather than risk contempt, an immediate appeal was allowed.

- *In re Grand Jury Proceedings, Subpoena to Vargas*, 723 F.2d 1461, 1464–66 (10th Cir. 1983). An immediate appeal is allowed only if the attorney has accepted a contempt citation or the holder of the privilege can show that the attorney will produce records rather than risk a contempt citation.

But see:

- *In re Grand Jury Subpoena Served upon Niren*, 784 F.2d 939, 941 (9th Cir. 1986) (*per curiam*). In-house counsel was expected to obtain a contempt citation for failure to testify before a grand jury prior to being able to appeal the ruling that the testimony was required in the first instance. The court held that the exception was only applicable when the subpoenaed party could not be expected to risk a contempt citation to protect the interests of a powerless third party. Here counsel was appellant's employee and thus subject to appellant's control.

Tangential matters, such as whether a record can be unsealed, that touch upon attorney-client issues have, on occasion, been held to be immediately subject to appeal.

- *Siedle v. Putnam Invs.*, 147 F.3d 7 (1st Cir. 1998). An order unsealing documents as to which an attorney-client privilege claim had been asserted was immediately appealable. The order unsealing the documents was reversed. "In this instance, we discern no evidence that the district court identified and balanced the interests at stake, or that the court endeavored to determine whether any information contained in Siedle's filings actually fell within the ambit of the attorney-client privilege. In the circumstances at hand, these omissions amount to an abuse of discretion." Redacted versions of the privileged material, disclosing what is not privileged and keeping under seal what is subject to the privilege, can balance the competing interests of public proceedings and the confidentiality protected by the privilege from disclosure.

Appeals can be taken from a district court's rulings on evidentiary matters after a trial or on an interlocutory basis from the grant or denial of a discovery motion. As discussed in the text, appeals from discovery orders, although definitive for most real-life purposes, are not generally considered final and appealable orders. Interlocutory in nature, they must either be certified or accepted for appeal.

Where, however, the privileged material is not subject to a discovery order addressed to one of the parties, but is responsive to a subpoena issued to a third party, a different rule applies. While parties wishing to test by an immediate appeal the validity of a discovery order by refusing to comply and thus subject themselves to a contempt finding before they are assured an immediate appeal, third parties are not similarly expected to place themselves at risk to protect a claim of privilege that may not be their own.

- *Fausek v. White*, 965 F.2d 126, 130 (6th Cir. 1992), *reh'g denied*, 1992 U.S. App. LEXIS 16895 (6th Cir. July 23, 1992), *cert. denied*, 506 U.S. 1034 (1992). The court granted an interlocutory appeal of an order piercing the privilege of a nonparty corporation by subpoena served on the corporation's attorneys.

- *United States v. Jones*, 696 F.2d 1069 (4th Cir. 1982). When there is a substantial risk that a third party will not risk a contempt citation by failing to comply with a subpoena, the client affected by the ordered disclosure may file an immediate appeal.

So too, when the compelled party is not the holder of the privilege (*i.e.*, the client), but is the attorney being compelled to breach the privilege by giving testimony or producing documents, then courts have said that the client has a right to immediate appeal without requiring the attorney to court an actual contempt citation to make the issue on appeal justiciable. A client thus has a right to appeal from an order requiring his or her counsel to breach the privilege without waiting and hoping that counsel will allow the wrath of contempt to fall.

- *In re Sealed Case (Synanon Church)*, 754 F.2d 395 (D.C. Cir. 1985). When attorneys indicated a willingness to testify in response to a grand jury subpoena on a claim that their client had used counsel to destroy documents and engage in a cover-up, the client had a sufficient interest to be able to perfect an appeal.

- *Montgomery County v. Microvote Corp.*, 175 F.3d 296, 300 (3d Cir. 1999). The court stated that it follows the "bright-line rule permitting appeals from discovery orders requiring the disclosure of content putatively privileged by the attorney-client and work-product privileges."

There is no exception for a third party from the *Cobbledick* rule, which requires a willingness to be held in contempt in order to appeal from a discovery ruling requiring the turnover of materials the third party believes are properly privileged.

- *In re Flat Glass Antitrust Litig.*, 288 F.3d 83 (3d Cir. 2002). Appeal dismissed for want of jurisdiction where third party that was ordered to produce documents it contended were both privileged and work-product protected had not incurred a finding of contempt for failure to produce.

On the other hand, when the subpoena is issued to counsel to testify before the grand jury, an immediate appeal by the client is permitted without requiring counsel to be held in contempt for failure to honor the subpoena or, in honoring it, for refusing to testify.

- *In re Witness before the Special Grand Jury 2000–2*, 288 F.3d 289, 291 (7th Cir. 2002). "We permit clients to immediately appeal a court order that their attorney testify before a grand jury under the exception recognized in *Perlman v. United States*, 247 U.S. 7, 62 L. Ed. 950, 38 S. Ct. 417 (1918)."

4. From Ruling by Administrative Law Judge

District courts can review privilege rulings made by administrative law judges. The standard of review under the Administrative Procedure Act is not de novo review. Review is based entirely on the existing record and the standard is abuse of discretion. 5 U.S.C. § 706.

- *Arizona Rehabilitation Hosp., Inc. v. Shalala*, 185 F.R.D. 263 (D. Ariz. 1998). Parties did not dispute the standard of review but did argue about what constituted the record for purposes of ruling on privilege issues.

T. *Availability of Mandamus*

Writs of mandamus and/or prohibition are extraordinary writs, issued against a legally constituted official. Occasionally, they are used as a route to seek judicial review of a court order that is not otherwise immediately appealable. As an extraordinary writ, the route is not favored by the appellate courts and is frequently denied.

- *Peck v. United States*, 680 F.2d 9, 13 (2d Cir. 1982). Although the attorney general was willing to be held in contempt to test a claim of privilege in this case, the appellate court was not thereby persuaded that the issue presented went to the heart of the controversy or was of sufficient magnitude to warrant the extraordinary writ. "[T]his case really presents only a variation of the much litigated question of whether, and what kind of, publication waives a privilege."

Nonetheless, because discovery orders are not immediately appealable, mandamus under the All Writs Act, 28 U.S.C. § 1851(a), will lie from an order compelling disclosure. To comply with the discovery order would defeat the privilege without appealability.

- *In re Regents of the Univ. of California*, 101 F.3d 1386, 1387 (Fed. Cir. 1996), *cert. denied*, 520 U.S. 1193 (1997). The court spelled out when and why a writ of mandamus is appropriate from a ruling finding that privilege does not apply to a particular communication. "[M]aintenance of the attorney-client privilege up to its proper limits has substantial importance to the administration of justice, and because an appeal after disclosure of the privileged communication is an inadequate remedy." "In addition, the immediate resolution of this issue will avoid the development of discovery practices with respect to invention records that might undermine the proper maintenance of the attorney-client privilege."

- *Admiral Ins. Co. v. United States Dist. Court*, 881 F.2d 1486, 1491 (9th Cir. 1989). The court reviewed, on mandamus, a non-final order [no one had as yet been held in contempt] of the district court requiring the production of statements claimed to be protected by the attorney-client privilege. The court concluded that mandamus was appropriate "because maintenance of the attorney-client privilege up to its proper limits has substantial importance to the administration of justice, and because an appeal after disclosure of the privileged communication is an inadequate remedy, the extraordinary remedy of mandamus is appropriate."

- *In re Burlington Northern, Inc.*, 822 F.2d 518, 522 (5th Cir.), *reh'g denied*, 827 F.2d 768 (5th Cir. 1987), *cert. denied*, 484 U.S. 1007 (1988). The court adopted the position that mandamus is an appropriate method of review of orders compelling discovery against a claim of privilege.

- *United States Dep't of Energy v. Brimmer*, 776 F.2d 1554, 1559 (Temp. Emer. Ct. App. 1985), *cert. denied*, 475 U.S. 1045 (1986). "Where substantial claims of privilege are overruled at the discovery stage . . . this court possesses the discretion to review the production order by writ of mandamus."

Ordinarily the writ of mandamus, being a prerogative and extraordinary writ, is not available to obtain appellate review of interlocutory discovery orders. When a claim of attorney-client privilege or the applicability of the work-product protection has been raised and has been rejected by the trial court, however, mandamus is available to obtain immediate appellate review in certain limited instances.

The issue arises frequently as to who has the right to seek the writ. Clearly, the party ordered to make production has that right. Thus, if the client is ordered to produce its documents it has standing to seek mandamus. An attorney ordered to produce documents in his or her possession has standing to seek mandamus. A client harmed by a production order issued against his or her attorney to produce privileged documents does not necessarily have standing. Only if the denial of the review would foreclose any possibility of review altogether would the client have standing.

Thus, some courts have suggested that a factual review must be undertaken as to whether the attorney has an ethical obligation to risk contempt to ripen the review and whether the attorney has an independent self-interest to preserve that makes it likely that the attorney will seek review of a production order in all events.

- *In re Vargas*, 723 F.2d 1461, 1465–66 (10th Cir. 1983). A client had no right to bring a writ of mandamus from an order requiring his attorney to produce privileged documents. The facts of the case indicated that the attorney had raised a Fifth Amendment privilege on his own behalf and, therefore, would have a personal interest in appealing the order. In addition, "[g]enerally an attorney might be expected to defy a court order and risk contempt to preserve his client's interests and prove his reliability as an advocate."

1. Mandamus Issued

Several courts, while granting mandamus from orders compelling production of matters with respect to which a claim of privilege is asserted, have also suggested that some other factor, such as a clearly erroneous ruling, irreparable harm, or a novel issue of law, must be present for the writ to issue. Although courts have been known to grant mandamus and then affirm the ruling of the trial court on privilege issues.

- *In re Powerhouse Licensing, LLC*, 441 F.3d 467 (6th Cir. 2006), *reh'g denied*, 2006 U.S. App. LEXIS 9225 (6th Cir. Apr. 3, 2006). Mandamus issued to review *de novo* scope of waiver for attorney deposition and attorney files. The district court was affirmed nonetheless in allowing discovery of work papers dealing with issues attorney put forth in an affidavit.

In the patent area, which so lacks uniformity as to the extent of the work product waiver when the defendant relies on an advice of counsel defense to ward off a finding of willful infringement, the Federal Court of Appeals has finally spoken, hopefully to bring some order out of the current mess.

- *In re Echostar Communs. Corp.*, 448 F.3d 1294 (Fed. Cir. 2006), *cert. denied*, 2006 U.S. LEXIS 9478 (U.S. Dec. 11, 2006). The law of the Federal Circuit was applied (rather than regional circuit law) to determine the scope of the waiver in an advice of counsel defense against willful infringement. The waiver did not reach work product not communicated to the client. Instead two categories of documents were reached: 1). Anything communicated to the client; 2) Any communications about communications with the client.

- *Dade Eng'g Corp. v. Reese*, 2006 U.S. Dist. LEXIS 32639 (D.V.I. Apr. 13, 206). The court granted mandamus and found that the district court's finding of waiver for failure to supply a privilege log for documents created after the filing of suit was clearly erroneous. The grounds used by the court were that the trial court should have applied Virgin Island statutes not federal law and the former do not recognize such a grounds for waiver. In respect to the finding of waiver for work product, the court had made no distinction between fact and opinion work product.

- *In re Lott*, 424 F.3d 446 (6th Cir. 2005), *cert. denied*, 126 S. Ct. 1772 (2006). Mandamus was issued to stop the compelled disclosure of privileged communications between a convicted man, claiming innocence in a *habeas corpus* proceeding and his lawyer. The court of appeals stated that there was no implied waiver of the privilege entailed in a claim of innocence and resoundingly reversed the District Court, but did so over the equally resounding dissent of Chief Justice Boggs who claimed that the issuance of the writ of mandamus was totally inappropriate since no harm would result that would not be remedial on appeal Apparently the case had already been in litigation in one form or another in the courts over the verdict of guilt and the imposition of the death penalty for over 20 years!

- *In re General Motors Corp.*, 153 F.3d 714, 715 (8th Cir. 1998). "Where the district court has rejected a claim of attorney-client privilege, we will issue a writ of mandamus when the party seeking the writ has no other adequate means to attain the desired relief and the district court's ruling is clearly erroneous."

- *In re Perrigo Co.*, 128 F.3d 430, 437 (6th Cir. 1997). "We find, as have several courts, that forced disclosure of privileged material may bring about irreparable harm."

- *In re Regents of the Univ. of California*, 101 F.3d 1386, 1391 (Fed. Cir. 1996), *cert. denied*, 520 U.S. 1193 (1997). The court granted a writ of mandamus when a discovery order sought production of communications protected by the attorney-client privilege.

- *Rhone-Poulenc Rorer, Inc. v. Home Indem. Co.*, 32 F.3d 851, 861 (3d Cir. 1994). "We find that the petitioners have no other adequate means to attain relief from the district court's order that compels the disclosure of privileged information and work product. In addition . . . the district court has committed clear errors of law. . . . The petitioners' right to the writ [of mandamus] is . . . indisputable."

- *Boughton v. Cotter Corp.*, 10 F.3d 746, 750–51 (10th Cir. 1993). The court noted that "on four occasions we have granted writs of mandamus to review claims of privilege," but declined to do so here because the case involved a dispute between private litigants and did not present a question of "substantial importance."

- *Haines v. Liggett Group Inc.*, 975 F.2d 81, 1992 U.S. App. LEXIS 21069 (3d Cir.), *reh'g denied*, 975 F.2d 81, 1992 U.S. App. LEXIS 26004 (3d Cir. 1992). A district court failed to comply with the Federal Magistrate Act in considering new evidence in reversing a magistrate's ruling protecting 1,500 documents created by the tobacco companies from disclosure. Mandamus from the district court was an appropriate appeal route.

- *Westinghouse Elec. Corp. v. Republic of Philippines*, 951 F.2d 1414 (3d Cir. 1991). Mandamus is the proper vehicle for review of a discovery order compelling disclosure.

- *In re Burlington Northern, Inc.*, 822 F.2d 518, 522 (5th Cir.), *reh'g denied*, 827 F.2d 768 (5th Cir. 1987), *cert. denied*, 484 U.S. 1007 (1988). The court adopted the position of "several courts [that] have concluded that mandamus is an appropriate method of review of orders compelling discovery against a claim of privilege."

- *United States Dep't of Energy v. Brimmer*, 776 F.2d 1554, 1559 (Temp. Emer. Ct. App. 1985), *cert. denied*, 475 U.S. 1045 (1986). The court concluded that "where substantial claims of privilege are overruled at the discovery stage . . . this court possesses the discretion to review the production order by writ of mandamus."

- *Bogosian v. Gulf Oil Corp.*, 738 F.2d 587 (3d Cir. 1984). The court accepted the writ of mandamus to review a discovery order requiring disclosure of documents that were admittedly work product and that formed the basis of an expert's opinion. The appellate court issued an opinion reversing the trial court but forbore from issuing the writ, confident that the trial court would comply with the substance of the opinion rendered by the court of appeals. Judge Becker, dissenting, pointed out that such judicial "courtesy" precluded the losing party from seeking any higher appeal.

- *Jenkins v. Weinshienk*, 670 F.2d 915, 917 (10th Cir. 1982). "[W]hen a district court orders production of information over a litigant's claim of privilege not to disclose, appeal after a final decision is an inadequate remedy; in these circumstances, an appellate court may exercise its mandamus power and consider the merits of the claimed privilege."

- *Diversified Indus., Inc. v. Meredith*, 572 F.2d 596 (8th Cir. 1977). When a claim of the attorney-client privilege has been raised and rejected, mandamus is available as a relief.

- *Pfizer, Inc. v. Lord*, 456 F.2d 545 (8th Cir. 1972). Mandamus was used to determine whether the trial court had properly applied the crime/fraud exception to defeat the attorney-client privilege.

- *Harper & Row Publishers, Inc. v. Decker*, 423 F.2d 487, 492 (7th Cir. 1970) (per curiam), *aff'd by an equally divided Court*, 400 U.S. 348 (1971), *reh'g denied*, 401 U.S. 950 (1971). Mandamus was used to obtain review of a claim of attorney-client privilege. The court found that "because maintenance of the attorney-client privilege up to its proper limits has substantial importance to the administration of justice . . . the extraordinary remedy of mandamus is appropriate."

2. Mandamus Not Issued

There are instances, obviously, where even though the privilege was invaded by a discovery order, a court of appeals has refused to grant a writ of mandamus. Usually what is involved in a denial of mandamus is a tacit finding that order requiring disclosure is not clearly erroneous and therefore it is allowed to stand.

- *In re Powerhouse Licensing*, 441 F.3d 467 (6th Cir. 2006), *reh'g denied*, 2006 U.S. App. LEXIS 9225 (6th Cir. Apr. 3, 2006). "The decision to include Shefferly's affidavit represents a litigation strategy fraught with obvious risks; surely, counsel must have realized that it would be 'pushing the envelope' with respect to the attorney-client privilege to introduce an affidavit from an attorney intimately involved in structuring the very transactions alleged to have been fraudulent. Presumably, a conscious decision was made that the rewards outweighed the risks. In the end, perhaps they will. However, we find that certain statements contained in the affidavit represented opinions, based upon confidential communications between attorney and client, that go to the heart of the legal claims at issue. By including these communications in the affidavit, counsel for petitioners effectively waived the attorney-client privilege."

The court said that it did not see how the claim of work-product protection for the documents was a valid one since they were not prepared for the instant litigation. In all events the injection of the affidavit waived any work product protection as well.

- *United States v. Amlani*, 169 F.3d 1189 (9th Cir. 1999), *appeal dismissed*, 239 F.3d 431 (9th Cir. 2000). Applying the general criteria for granting a writ of mandamus, the Ninth Circuit denied the writ of mandamus addressed to review the district court's refusal to quash subpoenas addressed to a client's current and former attorneys designed to allow discovery into the reasons for the change of counsel where the client claimed he was induced to do so by the prosecutor and thus was denied effective assistance of counsel. Nonetheless, in the process the appellate court extensively reviewed the district court's ruling that granted discovery of privileged materials. The appellate court also suggested that the district court review the materials to be produced *in camera* to assure itself that the privilege was not invaded as to matters other than those that had been waived. The five factors may well become a standard to which other courts turn before granting writs of mandamus from orders compelling disclosure of privileged matters. While denying the writ, the appellate court nonetheless reviewed and expressly affirmed the district court's decision that an implied waiver of the privilege had occurred when the client asserted his underlying claim.

The Second Circuit has observed that it rarely, if ever, issues mandamus to remedy discovery disputes. A recent case had a vigorous dissent while the majority stated the record was not sufficient to permit any review. Thus it is difficult to say in the Second Circuit whether no discovery order will ever be reviewed via mandamus or whether the proper case has yet to be properly presented.

- *In re Dow Corning Corp.*, 261 F.3d 280 (2d Cir. 2001). Over a dissent, the court refused to issue a mandamus to preclude the deposition of in-house counsel concerning corporate board minutes he had prepared even though the majority conceded that the court had probably been wrong to have permitted discovery of what it deemed privileged documents. The court said that the record was too incomplete, not even containing the disputed corporate minutes, to permit a meaningful review.

- *In re FCC*, 217 F.3d 125, 134 (2d Cir.), *cert. denied sub nom.*, *NextWave Personal Communs., Inc. v. FCC*, 531 U.S. 1029 (2000). "This Court will grant a mandamus petition only where the petitioner's right to relief is clear and indisputable." (Citations and internal quotation marks omitted.)

- *In re W. R. Grace & Co.-Conn.*, 984 F.2d 587, 589 (2d Cir. 1993). The court noted that "on rare occasion . . . we have used mandamus petitions to review discovery orders alleged to impair claims of attorney-client privilege," but declined to do so here because there was no novel issue.

- *Chase Manhattan Bank, N.A. v. Turner & Newall, PLC*, 964 F.2d 159, 163 (2d Cir. 1992). "Unlike other circuits, we have rarely used the extraordinary writ of mandamus to overturn a discovery order involving a claim of privilege."

The Federal Circuit, on the other hand, will review under mandamus discovery orders that require disclosure of privileged matters even though upon such review mandamus rarely issues.

- *In re Visx, Inc.*, 18 Fed. Appx. 821 (Fed. Cir. 2001). Reviewed *de novo* whether privilege had been waived, found that it had, and refused to issue mandamus.

- *In re Clemente*, 17 Fed. Appx. 968 (Fed. Cir. 2001). No mandamus issued where court declared privilege waiver for failure to provide timely log.

- *In re Rambus Inc.*, 7 Fed. Appx. 925, 927 (Fed. Cir. 2001). The court concluded that Rambus had not shown entitlement to a writ of mandamus to overturn the district court's determination that a *prima facie* case of fraud was established in the filing of a patent application.

- *In re Santa Fe Int'l Corp.*, 272 F.3d 705, 709 (5th Cir. 2001). The court of appeals denied mandamus, in the process remarking that the district court correctly "concluded that documents falling within the third category of communications . . . were not privileged because there had been no showing that at the time the communications were made—many years before the present litigation—the employers were potential co-defendants acting under an actual or perceived threat of litigation."

U. *Standard of Review for Discovery Orders*

Few areas of privilege law seem to be as divergent among the circuits as is the standard of review to be used in rulings on privilege. Many circuits, deeming the area to be one of law, will apply *de novo* review. Others, concluding that any ruling is necessarily predicated on a factual finding, will only reverse if the district court was clearly erroneous and thus "abused its discretion." A uniform standard is devoutly to be wished in the interest of predictability, which is a necessary concomitant of any rule of law.

The First Circuit has stated that the standard of review applied depends on the nature of the issue litigated. For questions of privilege law, it is *de novo* review. For factual findings, it is clear error and for evidentiary rulings, it is abuse of discretion. Of course since all three are generally involved in any litigated privilege issue, it leaves an appellate court with substantial flexibility as to its standard of review. It will vary depending on how the appellate court chooses to cast the privilege issue: is it a matter of law, a factual dispute, or merely an evidentiary ruling?

- *Cavallaro v. United States*, 284 F.3d 236, 245 (1st Cir. 2002). "We review rulings on questions of law *de novo*, findings of fact for clear error, and judgment calls—such as evidentiary determinations—for abuse of discretion."

- *United States v. MIT*, 129 F.3d 681, 683 (1st Cir. 1997) (same).

The Fourth Circuit has said it will apply a *de novo* standard when reviewing a district court's ruling that either the privilege or the protection does not apply. It applied an abuse of discretion standard to determine whether the crime/fraud exception applies.

- *In re Grand Jury Proceeding*, 33 F.3d 342, 353, 349 (4th Cir. 1994). The court held that the *de novo* standard governed its review of a district court's determination that documents are not privileged because they do not meet the definition of attorney-client communications or work product. The abuse of discretion standard governed when it reviewed a district court's decision that the government presented *prima facie* evidence that the crime-fraud exception applied.

The Sixth Circuit has said it applied a *de novo* standard for issues of waiver. A *fortiori* the same standard should apply for other privilege issues.

- *In re Powerhouse Licensing, LLC*, 441 F.3d 467, 472 (6th Cir. 2006), *reh'g denied*, 2006 U.S. App. LEXIS 9225 (6th Cir. Apr. 3, 2006). "A district court's decision regarding the waiver of the attorney-client privilege is reviewed *de novo*."

Most courts do not distinguish as neatly the standard of review to be applied based on how the privilege issue is defined: legal, factual or evidentiary.

The following cases have applied a *de novo* standard of review to issues regarding the applicability of the attorney-client privilege.

- *United States v. John Doe*, 429 F.3d 450 (3d Cir. 2005). The court said it exercised *de novo* review over the issues of law underlying the application of the attorney-client privilege and the abuse of discretion standard as to other issues.

- *In re Grand Jury Proceeding Impounded*, 241 F.3d 308, 312 (3d Cir. 2001) (same).

- *Chaudhry v. Gallerizzo*, 174 F.3d 394 (4th Cir.), *cert. denied*, 528 U.S. 891 (1999). Decisions as to privilege are reviewed under a *de novo* standard of review because they contain mixed questions of fact and law.

- *United States v. Collis*, 128 F.3d 313, 320 (6th Cir. 1997). "This court reviews *de novo* a district court's decision regarding waiver of the attorney-client privilege."

- *In re Grand Jury Proceedings*, 78 F.3d 251 (6th Cir. 1996). The court did not decide generally what standard of review should be applicable to privilege waiver issues, but concluded that the issues presented for review in this case involved legal issues and were thus subject to a *de novo* standard of review.

- *United States v. Blackman*, 72 F.3d 1418, 1423 (9th Cir. 1995), *cert. denied*, 519 U.S. 911 (1996). Whether the party has established the existence of an attorney-client relationship, as well as the scope of the privilege that then applies, is reviewed *de novo*.

- *Tennenbaum v. Deloitte & Touche*, 77 F.3d 337, 340 (9th Cir. 1996). Whether a party has waived the attorney-client privilege is a mixed question of law and fact that is reviewed *de novo*.

- *United States v. Plache*, 913 F.2d 1375, 1379 (9th Cir. 1990). The court reviewed *de novo* whether a party had waived the attorney-client privilege.

- *United States v. Mendelsohn*, 896 F.2d 1183 (9th Cir. 1990). The court said, without reconciling, that it reviews issues of the waiver of privilege *de novo* and evidentiary rulings under an abuse-of-discretion standard.

Other courts, such as the Fourth and Sixth Circuits, may bifurcate the standard of review, applying clear error or the abuse-of-discretion standard to the extent that they review factual issues that form the basis of any privilege determinations, but *de novo* review if the court's decision rests on legal principles.

- *Frontier Ref., Inc. v. Gorman-Rupp Co.*, 136 F.3d 695 (10th Cir. 1998). The court held that it would review waiver of attorney-client privilege for abuse of discretion, factual findings for clear error, and purely legal questions *de novo*.

- *Better Gov't Bureau v. McGraw*, 106 F.3d 582, 601 (4th Cir. 1997), *cert. denied*, 522 U.S. 1047 (1998). A dual standard is applied to privilege rulings: clear error to the extent that they rest on evidentiary findings, and *de novo* review to the extent that legal principles are applied.

- *Sandberg v. Virginia Bankshares, Inc.*, 979 F.2d 332, 348 (4th Cir. 1992), *amended*, LEXIS Slip Op. (4th Cir. Nov. 17, 1992), *unopposed mot. to vacate granted*, 1993 U.S. App. LEXIS 33286 (4th Cir. Apr. 7, 1993). A mixed standard is generally applied, depending on whether the trial court's decision was essentially predicated on a finding of fact or on the application of a legal theory. Here, *de novo* review was given to a privilege issue because the district court's ruling was largely predicated on the application of legal theory to facts not in dispute.

- *In re Grand Jury Proceedings 88–9*, 899 F.2d 1039, 1042 (11th Cir. 1990). Privilege and protection issues present a mixed question of law and fact that should be given *de novo* review.

- *Tornay v. United States*, 840 F.2d 1424, 1426 (9th Cir. 1988). Privilege issues are subject to *de novo* review.

- *In re Bevill, Bresler & Schulman Asset Mgmt. Corp.*, 805 F.2d 120, 124 (3d Cir. 1986). "The applicability of a privilege is a factual question" and the determination of "the scope of the privilege is a question of law."

Others seem to apply an abuse-of-discretion standard with respect to privilege issues in their entirety.

- *In re Echostar Communs. Corp.*, 448 F.3d 1294 (Fed. Cir. 2006), 2006 U.S. LEXIS 9478 (U.S. Dec. 11, 2006). The Federal Circuit applied an abuse of discretion standard and then found that the district court had abused its discretion in extending the scope of the waiver in an advice of counsel defense to a patent willful infringement suit to encompass attorney work product which had never been communicated to the client.

- *John Doe Co. v. United States*, 79 Fed. Appx. 476 (2d Cir. 2003). In a summary order, the appellate court held that a district court's finding that a document was not governed by the privilege was appealable under an abuse of discretion standard.

- *United States v. Workman*, 138 F.3d 1261 (8th Cir. 1998). The exclusion of evidence is reviewed under an abuse-of-discretion standard.

- *Sprague v. Thorn Ams., Inc.*, 129 F.3d 1355, 1368 (10th Cir. 1997), *corrected*, 1997 Colo. J. C.A.R. 3234 (10th Cir. 1997). "We review rulings related to discovery under an abuse-of-discretion standard."

- *Livingstone v. North Belle Vernon Borough*, 91 F.3d 515 (3d Cir. 1996), *cert. denied*, 520 U.S. 1142 (1997). The court reviewed waiver of attorney-client privilege for abuse of discretion.

- *United States v. Neal*, 27 F.3d 1035 (5th Cir. 1994), *cert. denied*, 513 U.S. 1179 (1995). The court described the privilege issue to be a question of fact, but did not clearly state whether waiver of the attorney-client privilege is subject to a clearly erroneous standard of review.

- *Greater Newburyport Clamshell Alliance v. Public Serv. Co.*, 838 F.2d 13 (1st Cir. 1988). The court reviewed waiver of attorney-client privilege for abuse of discretion.

Another curious wrinkle is that some courts have held that allowing an attorney to testify against a client does not amount to a constitutional error, and is generally reviewed under a harmless-error standard. Nonetheless, convictions that are predicated on the testimony of a defendant's attorney, when such testimony rebuts an essential defense, will be reversed, provided the content of the communication goes to legal advice and the attorney was not acting merely as a messenger for a matter of public record. As a practical matter, such reversal may then permit a claim of double jeopardy to be asserted.

- *United States v. Bauer*, 132 F.3d 504 (9th Cir. 1997). "We view the district court's conclusion that Rivera's communication to Bauer is not protected by the attorney-client privilege as a mixed question of law and fact which this court reviews independently and without deference to the district court."

This profusion of various standards of review of privilege issues makes neither for clarity nor consistency—values devoutly wished for in the law. Thus, it would be advisable if the Supreme Court were to accept a case on certiorari and establish a single standard of review in the area of privilege law.

The Eighth Circuit has continued to apply an "abuse of discretion" standard to review discovery orders dealing with privilege and work-product protection issues after trial. Indeed, it has elevated the standard to one involving "gross abuse of discretion."

- *Gagnon v. Sprint Corp.*, 284 F.3d 839 (8th Cir.), *cert. denied*, *Gagnon v. Sprint Corp.*, 537 U.S. 1014 (2002), *cert. denied*, *Spring Corp. v. Gagnon*, 537 U.S. 1001 (2002). "A district court's refusal to compel discovery is reversed upon a showing of gross abuse of discretion. . . . We find no abuse of the court's discretion concerning the motion to compel the documents protected by the work-product privileges asserted by Sprint PCS. The district court conducted an *in camera* review of specific documents and twice entertained substantial briefing by both parties. Even though Gagnon argues that these documents are not subject to the work-product privilege because they were created in the ordinary course of Sprint PCS's business, the district court found they were prepared in anticipation of litigation and therefore protected from discovery. The district court's holding, based upon a careful review of the documents, as well as both parties' briefing on the matter, is not a gross abuse of discretion, and we therefore affirm." (Citations omitted.)

A different standard of review may be applicable in appeals than applies in mandamus actions. When the issue of waiver of the attorney-client privilege arises on appeal, rather than through a petition for writ of mandamus, there is a conflict among courts of appeals on whether review of the district court's decision is de novo or for abuse of discretion.

Compare:

- *Chaudhry v. Gallerizzo*, 174 F.3d 394, 402 (4th Cir.), *cert. denied*, 528 U.S. 891 (1999). "We review the district court's decision that certain documents are subject to privilege *de novo*. . . ."

- *In re Grand Jury Proceedings*, 219 F.3d 175, 182 (2d Cir. 2000). "We review a district court's finding of waiver of the attorney-client and work-product privileges for abuse of discretion."

However, it appears that virtually all circuits review the decision of a district court underlying a petition for writ of mandamus for abuse of discretion.

- *In re Pioneer Hi-Bred Int'l, Inc.*, 238 F.3d 1370, 1373 (Fed. Cir. 2001). "The remedy of mandamus is available only in extraordinary situations to correct a clear abuse of discretion or usurpation of judicial power."

V. Stay Orders Pending Appeal

Stay orders are not automatically granted pending appeal. In fact, the criteria for granting a stay pending appeal are as high as those for the granting of injunctive relief. There must be a substantial showing that the party challenging the discovery order is likely to prevail. In addition, the courts of appeal tend to make a preliminary assessment whether the materials sought are facially privileged and/or protected. When there is a determination that the materials subject to the disclosure order are not either privileged or protected, obviously a stay pending appeal is not likely to be granted by the reviewing court.

- *In re Grand Jury Proceedings (Twist)*, 689 F.2d 1351 (11th Cir. 1982). The court refused to grant a stay pending appeal based on criteria that mirror those required for obtaining a preliminary injunction: 1) likelihood of prevailing on the merits; 2) irreparable injury unless stay granted; 3) no substantial harm to other interested party; and 4) no harm to the public interest. The court did not grant a stay because it determined that the requested information was not privileged in all events. What was called for was records of dates, places, or times of meetings with attorneys.

When an interlocutory appeal is granted at the behest of a client, of a subpoena served upon an attorney, a stay of the discovery order pending appeal is also likely to be granted. Without the stay, there would be little if any point in granting the interlocutory appeal.

- *Fausek v. White*, 965 F.2d 126, 130 (6th Cir. 1992), *reh'g denied*, 1992 U.S. App. LEXIS 16895 (6th Cir. July 23, 1992), *cert. denied*, 506 U.S. 1034 (1992). Interlocutory appeal of order piercing privilege of non-party corporation by subpoena served on corporation's attorneys was granted and order compelling production was stayed.

A trial court would have the power itself to grant a stay because it retains jurisdiction over the entirety of the case. Nonetheless, a trial court that has already determined that the matters at issue are neither subject to a privilege nor work-product protected, is not likely to grant a stay of its own discovery order, unless it believes that a novel or close issue is being presented.

As a general rule, an order to produce will not be stayed pending appeal, unless the interests of a non-party are threatened. The only relief a party is likely to obtain from discovery of privileged and protected materials erroneously granted is a new trial, if and only if the result in the case is deemed to have been affected by the introduction of the privileged or protected materials. The bell of disclosure having been rung, it cannot easily be unrung.

W. Reversal of Trial Verdict

On occasion, when privileged materials are admitted erroneously in trials, the verdict and/or conviction in the case of a criminal proceeding will be reversed and remanded for a new trial without use of the privileged material. Query whether a motion to bar retrial on double jeopardy grounds should not lie.

- *United States v. Mett*, 178 F.3d 1058 (9th Cir. 1999). A conviction for pension fraud was reversed because attorney-client matters were erroneously admitted into evidence.

- *Frontier Ref., Inc. v. Gorman-Rupp Co.*, 136 F.3d 695 (10th Cir. 1998). The case was remanded for a new trial when attorney-client privileged and work-product protection materials were held to have been improperly admitted into evidence at a trial. Former counsel for one of the parties was even called as an adversary witness in this indemnity case.

Increasingly, federal prosecutors are calling attorneys to testify against their clients on a variety of theories, the full scope of which is beyond the confines of this book. It is clear, however, that the client must be given a complete chance to demonstrate that such testimony violates the attorney-client privilege.

- *United States v. Fortna*, 796 F.2d 724, 732–33 (5th Cir.), *cert denied*, 479 U.S. 950 (1986). On a motion to review the district court's refusal to quash an indictment on the ground of the admission of evidence from an attorney of the defendant, the court of appeals reversed for a full hearing as to the circumstances of the representation, concluding that the district court abused its discretion by accepting statements made in affidavits that no privileged relationship existed and that no privileged communications were conveyed. The attorney had accepted a retainer of $1,000 from the defendant while representing a cooperating witness. "Accordingly, because of its refusal, without any good cause having been shown, to permit Harnage [the client] to consummate the subpoena of Smith [the attorney] for the hearing on the motion to quash as requested, we are unable to at this time accept the district court's determination that Smith did not furnish the government information received by him from Harnage which was confidential and privileged by virtue of an attorney-client relationship between them. We therefore direct the district court to reopen the hearing on Harnage's motion to quash the indictment to allow Harnage the opportunity to call Smith as a witness in respect to that matter, to make supplemental findings in light of any additional testimony, and to certify the transcript of the additional testimony and the supplemental findings in a supplemental record to be furnished this Court. We retain jurisdiction of Harnage's appeal pending receive[sic] of the supplemental record."

Similarly, if a claim of privilege is improperly sustained and evidentiary material is thereby excluded from trial, that result too is susceptible to reversal.

- *Reed v. Baxter*, 134 F.3d 351 (6th Cir.), *reh'g denied*, 1998 U.S. App. LEXIS 4958 (6th Cir. Mar. 5, 1998), *cert. denied*, 525 U.S. 820 (1998). In an appeal from a bench trial where the court dismissed the action based on a claim of reverse race discrimination, plaintiffs' argument that crucial evidence was erroneously excluded based on an erroneously broad application of the attorney-client privilege prevailed. The plaintiffs had sought and been denied an interlocutory appeal, based on the lack of a final and appealable order.

Y. *Mootness*

Increasingly, courts are holding that even when another party has obtained privileged documents, and the cat of confidentiality is out of the bag of protection, the matter is not moot because other relief can be fashioned to protect the principle of the privilege. Privileged documents can be subject to return orders, as well as orders precluding their evidentiary use.

- *Church of Scientology v. United States*, 506 U.S. 9, 18 n.11 (1992). The United States Supreme Court held that although privileged documents had been turned over to the IRS, the court of appeals had erred in dismissing the appeal therefrom as moot on the ground that relief could still have been fashioned, such as requiring a return of the privileged materials or barring their use.

- *Grand Jury Proceedings v. United States*, 156 F.3d 1038 (10th Cir. 1998). The fact that certain documents had been provided to the grand jury did not render the appeal moot because some relief was still possible.

Z. *Preclusive Effect of Prior Discovery Orders*

Clearly a trial court may revisit its own discovery orders. May it also do so when a case is removed from a state to a federal court? The answer would seem to be necessarily yes. Cases so hold.

- *Melhelm v. Meijer, Inc.*, 206 F.R.D. 609, 614 (S.D. Ohio 2002). "The Court finds that it is not bound to the prior discovery ruling issued by the state court, under either the issue preclusion or the law of the case doctrine. This is not to say that all deference to the state court, and all matters of comity in general, should be disregarded when a case is removed. . . . It is only to say that the court to which removal is had has the discretion to revisit a discovery issue." Moreover, the court found that after removal, the parties were subject to the different federal privilege rules that applied in the federal courts.

III. DEPOSING AND TESTIFYING COUNSEL

Increasingly, parties are attempting to depose an opponent's attorney or former attorney. Courts generally refuse such requests both on privilege grounds and also as too disruptive of the litigation process and the attorney-client relationship even when a privilege may have been waived.

For a long time the standard for whether attorneys involved in the case *sub judice* could be deposed was set by the Eighth Circuit in *Shelton*, which frowned upon the practice, but also set out under what limited conditions it might be acceptable.

- *Shelton v. American Motors Corp.*, 805 F.2d 1323, 1327 (8th Cir. 1986), *reh'g denied*, 1987 U.S. App. LEXIS 2002 (8th Cir. Jan. 30, 1987). A party sought to depose in-house counsel of its opponent in order to determine whether document production was complete by checking documents she had reviewed in her capacity as an attorney. The Eighth Circuit, reversing the district court, did not permit the deposition to go forward. In refusing to permit the deposition, the court formulated various factors to be used in determining whether to permit an opposing current or former attorney to be deposed.

In denying the motion to depose opposing counsel, the *Shelton* court set forth policy reasons why such depositions are disfavored. "Taking the deposition of opposing counsel not only disrupts the adversarial system and lowers the standards of the profession, but it also adds to the already burdensome time and costs of litigation. It is not hard to imagine additional delays to resolve work-product and attorney-client objections, as well as delays to resolve collateral issues raised by the attorney's testimony. Finally, the practice of deposing counsel detracts from the quality of client representation. Counsel should be free to devote his or her time and efforts to preparing the client's case without fear of being interrogated by his or her opponent."

What came to be known as the *Shelton* factors are:

(1) No other means exist to obtain the information;

(2) The information sought is relevant and non-privileged; and

(3) The information is crucial to the preparation of the case.

The *Shelton* factors, as they are generally known, have been widely followed in the district courts as the touchstone for whether opposing counsel can be deposed. Only the Sixth Circuit has expressly adopted the *Shelton* factors for determining whether counsel in current litigation can be deposed.

- *Nationwide Mut. Ins. Co. v. Home Ins. Co.*, 278 F.3d 621, 628 (6th Cir. 2002) (adopting Shelton).

- *Waugh v. Pathmark Stores, Inc.*, 191 F.R.D. 427 (D.N.J. 2000). Plaintiff's attempt to depose in-house counsel and obtain his documents failed, although plaintiff's complaints had been forwarded to him and he attended meetings where remediation efforts were discussed. In-house counsel filed an affidavit stating that he had only provided legal advice with respect to the complaint and the defendant contended it would not rely on advice of defense counsel. "[A]n employer must strive to respond to charges of discrimination and take reasonable corrective measures promptly. This court would work a disservice upon both the statutory scheme, as interpreted by the courts, and the employer's efforts to adhere to that scheme, if this court prevented an employer from allowing its in-house counsel to attend factual discussions related to charges of discrimination."

- *Sparton Corp. v. United States*, 44 Fed. Cl. 557 (Ct. Cl. 1999). The deposition of an attorney representing the Navy in settlement negotiations on a patent infringement claim was not allowed because the parties conceded that the attorney did not have independent or firsthand knowledge of the facts, nor had he been directly involved in the events giving rise to the alleged patent infringement. Rather, any information the attorney might have would have been conveyed to him by his client, the Navy, or learned in the course of investigating the alleged patent infringement in preparation for litigation.

- *Boughton v. Cotter Corp.*, 65 F.3d 823, 830 (10th Cir. 1995). The court utilized the *Shelton* test to preclude the deposition of counsel who plaintiffs contended acted in a decision-making role, a contention that the attorney's client disputed.

- *Dunkin' Donuts, Inc. v. Mandorico, Inc.*, 181 F.R.D. 208, 210 (D.P.R. 1998). The presumption that good cause exists to preclude discovery is implicit and does not have to be expressly shown when a party seeks to preclude the deposition of its attorney. The court required a showing that other available sources of information had been explored but were not adequate before permitting deposition of the attorney.

- *American Cas. Co. v. Krieger*, 160 F.R.D. 582, 589–90 (S.D. Cal. 1995). The insurance company brought a declaratory judgment to construe an insurance company. The defendants were the insured and a personal injury plaintiff who after a default judgment in state court had accepted an assignment of the policy. The insurance company was permitted to depose counsel for all the defendants, who had represented the insured in state court and had negotiated the assignment of the claim. The court found that the insurance company had met all three factors for taking an opposing party's deposition: (1) no other means exist to obtain the information than to depose opposing counsel; (2) the information sought was relevant and non-privileged; and, (3) the information was crucial to the preparation of the case. A key fact that tipped the scales in allowing this deposition to go forward was that the default judgment was amended from $1,785,533.77 to $6,391,822.21, which the defendants then sought to enforce against the insurance company. Small wonder that a suspicion of collusion was thereby raised and that the conduct of the attorney became a factor in the underlying dispute. The court found that neither interrogatories nor document requests would be sufficient to answer the questions raised by this conduct.

- M & R Amusements Corp. v. Blair, 142 F.R.D. 304, 305 (N.D. Ill. 1992)(Norgle, J.). The insurance company was sued for failure to pay two claims. It defended on the grounds that it was not notified of the claims within the requisite two-year period. The insured countered by claiming that the insurance company's registered agent waived that requirement in conversations with the insured's attorney. Whereupon the insurance company sought to depose the insured's attorney and subpoena any privileged communications or work product on that alleged conversation. The attempt to depose the attorney was denied on the grounds that there were two parties to that conversation—the insured's attorney and the insurance company's registered agent and that the insurance company had made no showing that it had interviewed or deposed the registered agent or that his testimony would contradict the insured's claim. In a blessedly brief and to the point decision, the court concluded that: "Deposing an opponent's attorney is a drastic measure. It not only creates a side-show and diverts attention from the merits of the case, its use also has a strong potential for abuse. Thus, a motion to depose an opponent's attorney is viewed with a jaundiced eye and is infrequently proper." Since the insurance company had not even bothered to question its own counsel/registered agent, the court dismissed its attempt to depose opposing counsel. Of such lack of common sense are lawsuits made.

- *West Peninsular Title Co. v. Palm Beach County*, 132 F.R.D. 301, 302 (S.D. Fla. 1990). "[T]he party seeking the deposition can show both the propriety and need for the deposition," thereby rebutting the presumption that good cause exists to prevent the deposition.

- *Harriston v. Chicago Tribune Co.*, 134 F.R.D. 232, 233 (N.D. Ill. 1990). The court stated that the deposition of opposing counsel should be limited to situations where it was shown that no other means existed to obtain the information than to depose opposing counsel, the information sought was relevant and non-privileged, and the information was crucial to the preparation of the case. The court found that the plaintiff had not met that burden in respect to any of the three factors and thus the attempt to depose defendant's attorney was denied.

- *Bio-Rad Lab., Inc. v. Pharmacia, Inc.*, 130 F.R.D. 116, 124–25 (D. Cal. 1990). The court determined that in situations in which a patent attorney is made an expert witness, the deposition of that attorney must be allowed.

■ *N.F.A. Corp. v. Riverview Narrow Fabrics, Inc.*, 117 F.R.D. 83, 85–86 (M.D.N.C. 1987).

The Second Circuit in a case rendered moot when the attorney resisting a subpoena agreed to be deposed, stated in language which was necessarily merely dicta, that the *Shelton* factors were not controlling in the Second Circuit in determining whether an attorney could be deposed.

■ *In re Friedman*, 350 F.3d 65, 71-71 (2d Cir. 2003). "Although we have cited *Shelton* for the proposition that depositions of 'opposing counsel' are disfavored, *see United States v. Yonkers Bd. of Educ.*, 946 F.2d 180, 185 (2d Cir. 1991), we have never adopted the *Shelton* rule and have stated specifically that the disfavor with which the practice of seeking discovery from adversary counsel is regarded is not a talisman for the resolution of all controversies of this nature. *Gould Inc. v. Mitsui Min. & Smelting Co., Ltd.*, 825 F.2d 676, 680 (2d Cir. 1987). Indeed, only the Sixth Circuit has followed the Eighth in adopting the *Shelton* rule. *See Nationwide Mut. Ins. Co. v. Home Ins. Co.*, 278 F.3d 621, 628 (6th Cir. 2002) (adopting *Shelton*). Rather, as we implicitly recognized in *Gould*, 825 F.2d at 680, the standards set forth in *Rule 26* require a flexible approach to lawyer depositions whereby the judicial officer supervising discovery takes into consideration all of the relevant facts and circumstances to determine whether the proposed deposition would entail an inappropriate burden or hardship. Such considerations may include the need to depose the lawyer, the lawyer's role in connection with the matter on which discovery is sought and in relation to the pending litigation, the risk of encountering privilege and work-product issues, and the extent of discovery already conducted. These factors may, in some circumstances, be especially appropriate to consider in determining whether interrogatories should be used at least initially and sometimes in lieu of a deposition. Under this approach, the fact that the proposed deponent is a lawyer does not automatically insulate him or her from a deposition nor automatically require prior resort to alternative discovery devices, but it is a circumstance to be considered. Several district courts in this Circuit have properly applied a flexible approach to the issue of lawyer depositions." (Footnotes omitted.)

More recently, however, the Second Circuit went out of its way to suggest that the *Shelton* criteria may be too rigid.

- *In re Friedman*, 350 F.3d 65 (2d Cir. 2003). The appeal was dismissed as moot when the attorney agreed to have his deposition taken. Nonetheless the Second Circuit went out of its way to state: "The district court ruled, relying on the rule set forth in *Shelton v. American Motors Corp.*, 805 F.2d 1323 (8th Cir. 1986), that plaintiff-appellant must exhaust all practical alternative means of obtaining the information sought from Friedman before it would consider allowing the proposed deposition and ordered plaintiff-appellant to proceed first by written interrogatories. We conclude that the deposition-discovery regime of the Federal Rules of Civil Procedure requires a more flexible approach to attorney depositions than the rigid *Shelton* rule, which improperly guided the District Court's exercise of discretion in quashing the subpoena."

The *Shelton* standard was urged, but not followed, by the Fifth Circuit in a recent case where depositions of defendant's counsel, rather than defendant's executives, were allowed on the grounds that the executives had been vague in their responses and fell back on claims of reliance of counsel.

- *Nguyen v. Excel Corp.*, 197 F.3d 200 (5th Cir. 1999). The trial court did not abuse its discretion in permitting depositions of counsel rather than defendant's executives when the responses of counsel on the issue had already been vague and required conferring with their attorneys.

- *Hawthorne Land Co. v. Occidental Chemical Corp.*, 2003 U.S. Dist. LEXIS 16767 (E.D. La. Sept. 19, 2003). Deposition of counsel for plaintiffs allowed where alternative means of discovery had been sought and where communications to client for legal advice and attorney's mental impressions were to be out of bounds. Attorney's involvement into other matters was a permissible area of inquiry.

The fact that an attorney is a former, rather than a current, attorney or has been disqualified may obviate the concern that the attorney-client relationship will be disrupted by virtue of the deposition.

- *Blanchard v. Edgemark Fin. Corp.*, 192 F.R.D. 233 (N.D. Ill. 2000). The fact that an attorney had been disqualified did not obviate the privilege, although the taking of his deposition was permitted. "Court is not convinced that the remedy sought here (a finding that the attorney-client privilege is waived as to Mr. Gravelyn's [the former disqualified attorney's] deposition), is meaningfully related to the unethical behavior, particularly in light of the remedies already awarded for Mr. Gravelyn's behavior."

In certain instances, attorney depositions and grand jury testimony have been allowed, most notably where an exception to the privilege rules would apply in all events.

- *In re Grand Jury Proceedings*, 162 F.3d 554 (9th Cir. 1998). The United States sought the grand jury testimony of the attorney for one pension fund trustee in an investigation of whether that trustee had insisted on a particular investment advisor in order to obtain kickbacks. Since Doe did not contest the fact that the attorney only represented Doe in his role as trustee for the fund and that the communications at issue concerned the administration of the fund it was not necessary to establish the fraud/crime exception to obtain the testimony of the attorney.

- *United States v. Evans*, 796 F.2d 264, 265 (9th Cir. 1986) (*per curiam*). A trustee of a pension plan was convicted of embezzling from the plan. During the trial, the district court admitted the testimony of an attorney "hired by Evans in his capacity as trustee" despite Evans' assertion of the attorney-client privilege.

- *Rainbow Investors Group, Inc. v. Fuji Trucolor, Inc.*, 168 F.R.D. 34, 36 (W.D. La. 1996). The court permitted the deposition of an attorney due to his involvement as a negotiator in business activity prior to litigation.

- *United Phosphorus, Ltd. v. Midland Fumigant, Inc.*, 164 F.R.D. 245, 248 (D. Kan. 1995). "Attorneys with discoverable facts, not protected by attorney-client privilege or work product, are not exempt from becoming a source for discovery by virtue of their license to practice law or their employment by a party to represent them in litigation." The court allowed the deposition of an attorney because he was involved in underlying facts that led to litigation.

- *Frazier v. Southeastern Pa. Transp. Auth.*, 161 F.R.D. 309, 313 (E.D. Pa. 1995). The deposition of opposing counsel concerning his own involvement in the surveillance of his client was allowed in light of allegations that such surveillance was illegal.

- *Kaiser v. Mut. Life Ins. Co.*, 161 F.R.D. 378, 382 (S.D. Ind. 1994). The court held that the deposition of an attorney was appropriate after determining that he was involved in the underlying facts as either an actor or a witness.

- *Bogan v. Northwestern Mut. Life Ins. Co.*, 152 F.R.D. 9, 14 (S.D.N.Y. 1993). The court permitted the deposition of opposing counsel because that attorney had participated in disputed pre-litigation events that related to the issues raised in litigation.

- *Qad. Inc. v. ALN Assocs., Inc.*, 132 F.R.D. 492, 495 (N.D. Ill. 1990). The court ordered the deposition of opposing counsel after determining that none of the items sought from counsel were likely to reveal privileged material.

- *Johnston Dev. Group, Inc. v. Carpenters Local Union No. 1578*, 130 F.R.D. 348, 352–53 (D.N.J. 1990). The court concluded that a deposition was warranted because the attorney's participation in disputed events was the focus of the litigation.

- *Harding v. Dana Transport Co.*, 914 F. Supp. 1084 (D.N.J. 1996). The court concluded that an attorney, hired by an employer to both investigate internal complaints of discrimination and defend the employer against those complaints in related litigation, must submit to both a deposition and disclosure of his documents where the defendant asserted a defense of reasonable and prompt investigation against a complaint of sexual harassment discrimination. By placing the defending attorney's knowledge into issue, the defendant-employer had waived a claim of privilege.

Another tactic which counsel have sought to use to obtain depositions of counsel is a Rule 30(b)(6) notice of depositions which would require designating either trial counsel or someone with equivalent knowledge. Despite the very dim view which virtually every court confronted with the request has expressed of the tactic, counsel keep trying. And in denying the request, courts generally look to the *Shelton* factors.

- *Nocal, Inc. v. Sabercat Ventures, Inc.*, 2004 U.S. Dist. LEXIS 26974 (N.D. Cal. Nov. 15, 2004). The deposition of case counsel was denied where none of the three *Shelton* factors were met.

- *FTC v. U.S. Grant Res., LLC*, 2004 U.S. Dist. LEXIS 11769, at *11 (E.D. La. June 24, 2004). *Shelton* factors were used to grant FTC's motion for a protective order quashing a Rule 30(b)(6) deposition notice which effectively would have required designating trial counsel to respond and thus would have invaded work-product privileges. "The FTC suggests that the defendants have availed themselves of this mode of discovery in an attempt to crawl into the mind's of plaintiff's counsel and tap into opinion work product. Essentially, the requests require that counsel retrace the steps taken in the process of their investigation and evaluation of claims at issue. Simply stated, the FTC urges the Court to close the "back door" as the defendants are not otherwise entitled to discovery of counsel's opinion, work product, or the deliberative process. The plaintiff highlights that counsel's choices, counsel's arrangement of factual material upon which the claims are based, and information as to how the particular documentation in this case was compiled in preparation for litigation necessarily reveals the attorney's thought processes and his theories of the case or mental impressions, *i.e.*, protected work product and the deliberative process." The court closed that "back door."

- *SEC v. Buntrock*, 2004 U.S. Dist. LEXIS 12036 (N.D. Ill. June 25, 2004). A Rule 30 (b)(6) notice of deposition calling for a witness to be designated by the SEC with knowledge of the issue *sub judice* was quashed by the Magistrate Judge and affirmed by the District Court, on *Shelton* grounds that it effectively would have required preparation by counsel and an indirect way of prying into their mental processes.

- *SEC v. Rosenfeld*, 1997 U.S. Dist. LEXIS 13996, 1997 WL 576021 (S.D.N.Y. Sept. 12, 1997). Court quashed a Rule 30(b)(6) to depose SEC official deemed to implicitly require delving into mental processes of trial attorneys.

- *Marco Island Partners v. Oak Dev. Corp.*, 117 F.R.D. 418 (N.D. Ill. 1987).

- *Gould, Inc. v. Mitsui Mining & Smelting Co.*, 825 F.2d 676, 680 n.2 (2d Cir. 1987). The court noted that the tactic of seeking discovery from opposing counsel is generally disfavored.

Where alternative means of obtaining information sought exist, no good reason exists to allow depositions of attorneys.

- *Desert Orchid Partners, LLC v. Transaction Sys. Architects, Inc.*, 227 F.R.D. 215 (D. Neb. 2006). A protective order was entered precluding the taking of the deposition of former in-house counsel or one of the parties. The party desiring the deposition contended that in-house counsel was an essential fact witness involved in some of the disputed transactions. "This case falls somewhere between *Shelton* and *Pamida*. However, the court concludes the *Shelton* test does apply. Here, Mr. Stokes was never trial counsel; however, he was involved with the defense strategy and the litigation of this case and similar actions against the defendants. The plaintiffs have failed to show that Mr. Stokes has relevant, non-privileged information. Mr. Stokes denies he participated in the business transactions described by the plaintiffs and the plaintiffs' evidence does not contradict the denial. Further, the plaintiffs fail to establish either (1) no other means exists to gain the desired evidence or (2) the information is crucial to the preparation of the case. In any event, the defendants have met their burden of showing good cause exists to quash the subpoena and protect Mr. Stokes from a deposition in this matter on the topics described by the plaintiffs."

- *Archuleta v. City of Santa Fe*, 2005 U.S. Dist. LEXIS 21924 (D.N.M. Aug. 10, 2005). The court required the party seeking to depose counsel to exhaust alternative means first: depose two of the investigators instead and serve written interrogatories on counsel.

- *Allergan Inc. v. Pharmacia Corp.*, 2002 U.S. Dist. LEXIS 19811 (D. Del. Mar. 1, 2002). Protective order precluding deposition of patent counsel to demonstrate that there were other inventors was entered. The predicate—namely, the existence of other inventors—had not been demonstrated but could be demonstrated by other means.

- *Doubleday v. Ruh*, 149 F.R.D. 601, 612–614 (E.D. Cal. 1993). This is a Section 1983 excessive force case in which defendants' motion to quash deposition of deputy district attorneys was granted because plaintiff's criminal prosecution was completed and "disclosure of the prosecutorial file is not only a good alternate means, but may also be more complete and accurate."

Depositions of former rather than current attorneys, engaged in the litigation *sub judice* are not likely to be as disruptive and thus may be obtained with slightly greater ease.

- *Carey v. Textron, Inc.*, 224 F.R.D. 530 (D. Mass. 2004). Where former counsel for plaintiff was the last one to have seen a crucial piece of evidence and which could no longer be located, thereby giving defendants a possible spoliation defense, his deposition would be allowed but limited to the issue of what he knew about aforesaid missing item.

- *Bell v. Bd. of Educ. of the County of Fayette.*, 225 F.R.D. 186 (S.D. W. Va. 2004). The deposition of a prosecuting attorney who had represented one of the defendants (a sheriff) at his own deposition was allowed. He was not currently representing any party in the litigation and the claims made was that he might have knowledge regarding the claims asserted. The action was a wrongful death action against various sheriffs for purportedly having knowledge of the pedophilic tendencies of a school teacher who killed a student with an injection of drugs during a sexual assault. The court reasoned that the attorney's office had successfully prosecuted the offender for sexual assault and was prosecuting his for murder and might be expected to have knowledge of the investigative findings of the officers who were defendants in the civil wrongful death suit and that he was thus a "fact" witness. The court did not consider or discuss whether any of the prosecuting attorney's knowledge might be privilege protected.

Needless to say, since courts now will countenance depositions of even litigation counsel, in the appropriate circumstances, utterly frivolous motions seeking such depositions have been sought with a warning that such further silliness would result in sanctions.

- *Ganan v. Martinez Mfg, Inc.*, 2003 U.S. Dist. LEXIS 13990 (N.D. Ill. Aug. 12, 2003). Defendant sought the deposition of plaintiff's litigation counsel to determine plaintiff's motivation in bringing a prior suit wherein different counsel represented plaintiff. The illogic of the request was nothing short of stunning. The court suggested that other less intrusive means were available to obtain such information prior to issuing its warning regarding future sanctions.

Federal Rule of Criminal Procedure 17(c) empowers a court to quash a subpoena if it is "unreasonable or oppressive." Thus when attorneys seek to quash a subpoena served upon them and when courts grant such motions, both would be well advised to rely explicitly on the wording of the rule. Failure to do so may result in time-consuming and costly remands.

- *In re Grand Jury Proceeding Impounded*, 241 F.3d 308 (3d Cir. 2001). The appellate court reversed the district court, which had quashed a grand jury subpoena served upon an attorney on the grounds that the district court failed to cite the appropriate federal criminal rule as the basis of its decision. "We recognize the District Court was concerned with the effect of this subpoena on the attorney-client relationship. But the proper course under Fed. R. Crim. P. 17(c) was to rule on whether the lawyer's testimony was protected under the attorney-client privilege. By employing 'a different analysis' based on 'fundamental fairness' the District Court deviated from the established procedures, which ensure the institutional independence of the grand jury. Therefore, the District Court abused its discretion." The dissent saw little difference in what the district court had done and what the majority believed that the district court should have done. "The District Court in this case considered the specific facts and circumstances before it and found that it was 'fundamentally unfair for the U.S. Attorney's Office to seek [the attorney's] testimony.' Rule 17(c) empowers a court to quash a subpoena if it is 'unreasonable or oppressive.' Presumably, the Majority believes that a finding of 'fundamental unfairness' is insufficient to satisfy this standard. In contrast, I fail to see a difference. A subpoena described as 'fundamentally unfair' could just as easily be described as 'unreasonable and oppressive.'" *Id.* at 319.

If means alternative to deposing counsel exist for obtaining the information sought, depositions of opposing counsel will and should be disallowed.

Nonetheless, courts increasingly allow depositions of counsel while distinguishing between privileged areas involving the giving of legal advice and personal participation as an agent of the client or as an investigator of the validity of some underlying claim, which are not similarly privileged.

Moreover, when ruling either on motions to quash such a deposition or on a protective order to preclude such a deposition, courts will frequently give some advance direction as to what areas of inquiry are to be allowed and which are to be considered off limits. Generally they will state that within those parameters, it is best to see how the deposition unfolds and to allow privilege/protection claims to specific questions. Finally, they will often state their availability by telephone to resolve disputed area of inquiry which may arise in the course of the deposition so that the deposition does not have to be completed subject to objections and then resumed if the ruling goes against the privilege claim.

- *Stanley v. Trinchard*, 2004 U.S. Dist. LEXIS 12983 (E.D. La. July 12, 2004). Counsel was to be deposed regarding his efforts to determine insurance coverage by agreement of the parties. Privilege/protection objections as to other areas of inquiry were preserved. If improperly raised, the matter would become the subject of a motion to compel and the deposition would have to be resumed after a ruling thereon.

- *Chivers v. Central Noble Cmty. Schs*, 2005 U.S. Dist. LEXIS 16057, at *10–11 (N.D. Ind. Aug. 4, 2005). In this claim of sexual harassment by a student against a school district, the deposition of an attorney from the same firm as the litigating attorney was allowed. The school district argued that they would not be relying on an advice of counsel defense, therefore the deposition should not be permitted to go forward. The court did not buy the argument. "[I]t was counsel who assembled the facts, drew the conclusions, and constructed the remedial response. (See Stone Dep. at 73–74; Reply Brief, Ex. 18.)" To prevent Plaintiffs from discovering what was done by counsel and why would be tantamount to giving CNCS and Wellman both the "sword" (i.e., the argument that "we were reasonable because we had our attorney's investigate the [*11] charge and craft a response") and the "shield" (i.e., "what our attorneys did, and why they did it, is privileged"). The court *sua sponte* limited the permissible scope of the inquiry to the attorney's knowledge of the conduct of the investigation and the actions of the school board in response to the complaint. . . .

- *Environ Prods. v. Total Containment, Inc.*, 1996 U.S. Dist. LEXIS 12336 (E.D. Pa. Aug. 22, 1996). The court allowed the deposition of trial counsel, stating: "A party is entitled to discover relevant, non-privileged information from any individual with access to such information," even when that individual is the opposing party's trial counsel. "Nonetheless, Reilly brought this problem on itself by choosing to retain the same counsel to litigate this matter that gave the advice-of-counsel opinion." (Citations omitted.)

- *Carey v. Textron, Inc.*, 224 F.R.D. 530 (D. Mass. 2004). Where counsel for one of the parties was the last person to have seen a crucial piece of evidence which had then gone missing, her deposition would be allowed.

- *New York v. Oneida Indian Nation of N.Y.*, 2001 U.S. Dist. LEXIS 21616, at *17–18 (N.D.N.Y. Nov. 9, 2001). "Lastly, depositions of attorneys are generally frowned upon. The concern is that they are fraught with peril in that there will be attempts to invade the sacrosanct protected relationship between a lawyer and her client. Yet it is not an iron-clad rule that depositions of counsel cannot be held. The Court needs only to satisfy itself before compelling counsel to be deposed that no other means exist to obtain this information, the information is relevant and the information is crucial to the preparation of the case. *Pereira v. United Jersey Bank*, 201 B.R. 644, 678

(S.D.N.Y. 1996). This Court finds that these three elements are satisfied for this attorney to be deposed. If Ms. Hard is to be deposed, the inquiry party must be very careful not to intrude into those conversations, no matter how many, in which the communications sought and received legal advice. Her observations, nonlegal conversations, her personal statements and statement of others that she heard on behalf of the State on this Compact matter are relevant and critical."

If counsel interjects himself to litigation, for instance by giving an affidavit on some point in dispute, the likelihood that his deposition will be allowed and that discovery will be permitted of work product within the subject matter of the affidavit, are extremely high. Accordingly, care should be taken both as to whether the affidavit is really necessary and as to whether someone else could provide the same requisite information. Arguments that such an affidavit merely covered factual issues and thus did not entail any privilege or work product waiver may be difficult to sustain.

- *In re Powerhouse Licensing, LLC*, 441 F.3d 467 (6th Cir. 2006), *reh'g denied*, 2006 U.S. App. LEXIS 9225 (6th Cir. Apr. 3, 2006). The Sixth Circuit granted mandamus, applied *de novo* review to the scope of the waiver committed by an attorney when he submitted an affidavit as to the purport of certain transactions and the intent of the parties. The trial court's ruling, allowing his deposition and allowing discovery of his work product on the subject matter of the affidavit, was affirmed.

And increasingly, there is the rather unseemly spectacle of courts allowing the testimony of counsel against clients provided that no attorney-client privileged communications are implicated in the testimony. Because it is so unseemly and seemingly so counter to expectations of confidentiality and loyalty, which surely should be broader than the privilege, it is respectfully suggested that courts rethink this trend. It is particularly unseemly when a criminal conviction is in any way attributable to the testimony of former counsel. Yet such is not in the least unusual any longer.

- *United States v. Meyers*, 38 Fed. Appx. 99, 101 (3d Cir. 2002). The defendant appealed his conviction of fraud on the grounds that it was wrongfully procured by allowing testimony from his attorney. The appellate court found nothing untoward in that cause or result and affirmed the conviction, stating: "Meyers contends Robinson's testimony violated his attorney-client privilege and the attorney-work-product doctrine. But Robinson testified only to Meyers's prior business practices and history, not 'private communications.' That Meyers had filed for bankruptcy and been involved in lawsuits were matters of public record. Neither the attorney-client privilege nor the work-product doctrine was implicated in Robinson's testimony. . . . We review for abuse of discretion. . . . Robinson's testimony demonstrated Meyers misled potential clients about his past qualifications and experience. Investors detrimentally relied on Meyers's representations. We see no error in admitting Robinson's testimony." (Citations omitted.)

IV. WAIVER OF PRIVILEGE IN GOVERNMENT PROSECUTIONS OR INVESTIGATIONS

There are two areas of substantial developing concern when the government investigates or prosecutes. One is when the government requires a waiver of privilege in order to obtain full pre-indictment discovery as a sign of full cooperation. Whether the government may do so has not yet been substantially litigated.

Another is what is to be done when the government seizes either a lawyer's or a client's files and/or computers in order to preserve any privileges which might be available.

If a valid search warrant has been issued, generally the courts will not do much to protect privileges before the fact of the seizure although they will set up procedures to screen for privilege, often by allowing a screening team in the prosecutors office, which is separate from and "Chinese Walled" from the prosecutorial team.

On occasion criminal defendants whose documents and computer files have been seized pursuant to a validly issued search warrant have sought the appointment of Special Masters or delegation to a Magistrate Judge to review the documents for privilege. Sometimes the request is denied and the court allows the prosecutor's office to review the documents or computer files by a privilege "review team" and to turn over to a trial team after disputed issues have been litigated on the grounds that only so can the government argue effectively why the privilege should not apply.

- *United States v. Grant*, 2004 U.S. Dist. LEXIS 9462 (S.D.N.Y. May 25, 2004). Review of seized documents by a special "privilege team" in the United States Attorney's Office would not constitute a waiver of any privileges which might otherwise be available.

But see:

- *United States v. Griffin*, 440 F.3d 1138 (9th Cir.), *cert. denied*, 127 S. Ct. 259 (2006). A Special Master had been appointed to review for privilege and to redact the documents. The issue on appeal was the scope of the spousal privilege since the documents were sent to a prisoner's wife who was also his lawyer.

- *In re the Seizure of All Funds on Deposit in Accounts in the Names of Nat'l Elecs., Inc.*, 2005 U.S. Dist. LEXIS 19490 (S.D.N.Y. Sept. 6, 2005). The court stated that it did not find a "Chinese wall" within a prosecutorial office solution to reviewing seized documents for privileges a good solution and accordingly appointed a Special Master to conduct the review.

- *United States v. Stewart*, 2002 U.S. Dist. LEXIS 10530, 2002 WL 1300059, at *5 (S.D.N.Y. June 11, 2002). The attorney client privilege "is based in policy, rather than in the Constitution, and therefore cannot stand in the face of countervailing law or strong public policy and should be strictly confined within the narrowest possible limits underlying its purpose." A Special Master was appointed to review for privileges.

If you want to subpoena a government lawyer for a deposition or to testify, you had best check whether some statute requires you to exhaust administrative remedies before asking a district court to enforce the subpoena.

- *In re SEC ex rel. Glotzer*, 374 F.3d 184 (2d Cir. 2004), *reversing United States v. Stewart*, 317 F. Supp. 2d 426 (S.D.N.Y. 2004). The court of appeals granted mandamus and quashed a subpoena for the deposition testimony of two attorneys from the Securities and

Exchange on the grounds that the district court lacked jurisdiction where the attorney for Martha Stewart failed to exhaust administrative remedies seeking such depositions. Federal regulations delegated to the General Counsel for the SEC the authority to review such requests, with an appeal to the full Commission within 10 days of such refusal.

V. ATTORNEY-CLIENT PRIVILEGE AND WORK-PRODUCT PROTECTION IN THE ELECTRONIC AGE

A. *Costs of Privilege Review and Cost Shifting*

The electronic age has added exponentially to the number of documents that businesses can create and store virtually indefinitely. Potentially it has made document production easier. Just throw the endless computer tapes at the other side and let them wade through the morass to find what they want. Argue to the judge that since they want the tapes, they and not your client should bear the burden and costs of shifting through the computer tapes. Since the cost of shifting through such electronically stored data is generally far more costly than plowing through paper documents (except in the mega case) courts might be more willing to shift the cost of organizing the data to be mined for what it is that the adversary may be seeking.

But what do you do about privilege/work product screening? And how do you produce the documents in a reasonable time if such screening has to be conducted?[6]

---

6. The source that courts are beginning to turn to when dealing with issues involving electronic document production is The Sedona Guidelines: Best Practice Guidelines & Commentary for Managing Information & Records in the Electronic Age. (The Sedona Conference Working Group Series, Sept. 2005 Version), available generally at http://www.thesedonaconference.org and more specifically at http://www.thesedonaconference.org/content/miscFiles/TSG9_05.pdf. The Sedona conference is a group of judges, lawyers and electronic technicians knowledgeable about electronic issues in document production. The Sedona Conference, however, has made no recommendations as to how privilege/work product issues are to be handled in the electronic context. Indeed, all the Sedona Conference does state in that regard is what is inanely obvious. Guideline 10: "A responding party should follow reasonable procedures to protect privileges and objections to production of electronic data and documents."

The cost estimates reported in some of the cases may be vastly exaggerated but even so they are surely sobering.

- *Rowe Entm't, Inc. v. William Morris Agency, Inc.*, 205 F.R.D. 421 (S.D.N.Y. 2002). The court was faced with motions by defendants that sought to be protected from the burden and expense of producing e-mail that had been requested by the plaintiffs during discovery in a civil case. One defendant supported its motion with an estimate from a computer consultant that it would cost $395,944 to select, catalogue, restore, and process a limited sampling of the e-mails sought, and $9,750,000 to do the same for all e-mail requested. Another defendant produced cost estimates ranging from $43,110 to $84,060 to produce requested e-mail, with an estimated cost of $247,000 to review the e-mail for privilege and work-product prior to production. A third estimated that it would take more than two years to retrieve and catalogue the e-mails requested by the plaintiff at a cost of $395,000, with an additional cost of $120,000 to conduct privilege review which would take a full-time employee two years to complete.

- *Zubulake v. UBS Warburg LLC*, 216 F.R.D. 280, 283 (S.D.N.Y.), *recons. denied*, 220 F.R.D. 212 (S.D.N.Y. 2003). The defendant submitted cost estimates in support of its request to shift the production costs to the plaintiff of $165,954.67 to search for and restore responsive electronic information, with an additional estimated expense of $107,694.72 for attorney and paralegal review costs.

And the costs of privilege review if all the metadata have to be reviewed for privilege as well are truly sobering. Small wonder that some companies with repeat litigation are beginning to out-source document review to places such as India and the Philippines, much to the dismay of law firm which themselves out-source document production to contract attorneys which provides a nice profit center for the law firm. We will no doubt see claims that such client-run document production centers constitute practicing law without a license.

Some courts also seem to be extraordinarily cavalier about either the costs involved in the danger to proprietary software if data is produced in the manner in which it is kept in the ordinary course of business, when that data is often only accessible through proprietary software. It would be advisable if judges were more educated both as to the reality of these costs and as to cost effective alternatives. Perhaps the Judicial Conference could take on such a project or the Sedona Conference could address these issue.

- *In re Honeywell Int'l, Inc. Sec. Litig.*, 230 F.R.D. 29 (S.D.N.Y. 2003). A third party accounting firm in response to a subpoena produced hard copies of its documents with a guide as to what attachments went with the work papers. The court dismissed these as "hieroglyphics" and ordered production of the documents in electronic form, since that was the way they were kept in the ordinary course of business. In doing so the court brushed aside the accounting firms concerns that doing so would either force it to disclose its proprietary software or cost it $30,000 to translate into neutral form. The court refused to require the party demanding the documents to help defray those costs and "declines plaintiffs' invitation to rule on whether PWC [the accounting firm] may convert some of its workpapers to a PDF file format to protect their integrity."

It is quite incomprehensible how a court can "decline" to rule on so reasonable a request or whether a party must proceed at its own peril to do what it makes economic sense to do.

B. *Non-Waiver Agreements*

What's to be done?

First and foremost. Try to get the court to order that there will be no waiver of privilege if the hard drive or tape backup is produced intact. It will save your client a ton of money in reviewing for privilege without the possibility of having privileged materials used as evidence. There is precedent for such a procedure and it is the most rational way of dealing with the potential costs.

Proposed Rule 502(c) of the Federal Rules of Evidence foresees the entry of such orders and furthermore would make them binding in other proceedings and for non-parties.

> Proposed Rule 502(c) Controlling effect of court orders. — Notwithstanding subdivision (a) [waiver by disclosure], a court order concerning the preservation or waiver of the

attorney-client privilege or work-product protection governs its continuing effect on all persons or entities, whether or not they were parties to the matter before the court.

One seminal reason for the entry of such orders, state the committee comments, is the costs attendant upon review of documents for privilege in the day of electronic evidence.

There are risks to dispensing with privilege review in the expectation that any privileged documents will be returned. It may give your adversary a bird's-eye view of documents your client desperately wants to keep confidential.

As for the courts, they may well conclude that there is precious little worthy of really preserving in the privilege if clients think so little of it once the technological means for its preservation become more problematic.

In an increasingly digitalized world, what is to be done to protect privilege if a court orders production of a hard drive or backup tapes? In a reported case, the court ordered production of the backup tapes, allowed the party seeking production to review the tapes at its cost for relevant documents, and the court also provided that the privilege would not thereby be lost.

- *Rowe Entm't. Inc. v. William Morris Agency, Inc*, 205 F.R.D. 421, 433 (S.D.N.Y. 2002). The court shifted the cost of retrieval of the documents to the party seeking production, established a procedure for culling documents to be used, and permitted them to be reviewed by the party making production for privilege without any waiver thereof by virtue of the fact that they had been seen by the other party's computer expert and attorney.

Report to the Standing Committee on Rules of Practice and Procedure, Judicial Conference of the United States by the Advisory Committee on the Federal Rules of Civil Procedure, September 2005 which proposed rule amendments have now been forwarded to both the Supreme Court and Congress does not come up with suggestions which definitely address the issue of what is to be done in the event of inadvertent production of privileged material. All that Proposed Rules 16 and 26 do is little more than encourage parties engaging in and receiving the electronic discovery to agree not to assert waiver of privilege/work-product protection against an opposing party that agrees to provide expedited production of electronically stored information without first doing a review for privilege and work-product-protected documents. Both Proposed Rules are silent as to whether inadvertent production will be deemed to constitute a waiver and what the scope of that waiver will be. That is still left to case law development—a most sobering thought in light of how harshly some courts have dealt with inadvertent disclosure of privileged matters.

Thus the proposed rules do little more than bless what has become an increasingly frequent practice: non-waiver or "claw back" agreements entered into by the parties and incorporated into either a discovery scheduling order or an independently entered stipulated protective order. Certainly when both parties have similar burdens in reviewing for privilege, neither has any reason not to enter into such non-waiver agreements. When the burdens of privilege review are very different for the two parties, then the party with the substantially lesser burden may have far less interest in entering into a non-waiver agreement. And without agreement, a court will rarely provide for a non-waiver agreement except if discovery is put on an accelerated schedule and involves a truly massive amount of material. Yet even so, it is to the advantage of the party with the lesser burden to know the other's privileged communications since it may aid in the development of its case even if ultimately the document can not be put to testimonial use. Thus the odds are that a non-waiver agreement will be reachable.

Indeed, courts have taken the initiative and begun to suggest that the parties would be well advised to enter into non-waiver agreements, which are frequently called "claw back" agreements. Courts are even in some instances beginning to back off some of the more draconian interpretations of waiver by virtue of inadvertent production. But not all by a long shot. *See* Sections on Inadvertent Disclosure Excused and Inadvertent Disclosure Not Excused.

- *Zubulake v. UBS Warburg LLC*, 216 F.R.D. 280, 290 (S.D.N.Y.), *recons. denied*, 220 F.R.D. 212 (S.D.N.Y. 2003). "Indeed, many parties to document-intensive litigation enter into so-called "claw back" agreements that allow the parties to forego privilege review altogether in favor of an agreement to return inadvertently produced privileged documents. The parties here can still reach such an agreement with respect to the remaining seventy-two tapes and thereby avoid any cost of reviewing these tapes for privilege."

D. *Precautions Against Waiver*

The precautions which must be taken to protect computerized files from inadvertent production invariably involve asking information technology experts to set up systems so that such files are protected. Lawyers have to rely on such "IT" technicians and hope that they know what they are doing since few attorneys have the technical know how to set up such systems themselves or to even know if they have been adequately set up.

Everyone communicates by e-mail these days over public networks. Most attorneys would be amazed to learn that do so is pretty much the equivalent of leaving your office door unlocked and all your client files open for viewing with all the lights on. How far do you think such a lawyer would get with a judge if he then tried to argue that he had taken reasonable precautions and any actual disclosure should not be accounted a privilege waiver? If one wanted to actually protect privileged communications, then all e-mail sent to and from attorneys would have to be encrypted if one wanted to be sure that access is in fact restricted to just those sending and receiving the e-mail. A technologically sound alternative is putting privileged communications on a secure network that is only password accessible. Or, heresy, if one is serious about preserving privileges, snail mail may be preferable or even the spoken word. But that horse has probably fled the barn for good. What is not in fact protected from a technological point of view is sending communications over a public network in the manner we all do every day.

Consistent with the trend of nearly universal e-mail communication, New York and California have enacted laws that provide some protection to e-mail communications. New York C.P.L.R. § 4548 (McKinney 1999) states that a privileged communication does not lose its privileged character for the sole reason that it was sent by e-mail or because persons necessary for the delivery or facilitation of the e-mail may have access to its content. Accord *Cal. Evid. Code* § 917(b) (West 2004). Accordingly, while disagreement exists, *see* NYSBA *Eth. Op. 709, 1998 WL 957924* (September 16, 1998)(citing opinions), the transmission of a privileged communication through unencrypted e-mail does not, without more, destroy the privilege.

Despite the technological reality that such communications are not in fact secure, the prevailing judicial view is that lawyers and clients may communicate confidential information through unencrypted e-mail with a reasonable expectation of confidentiality and privacy. *E.g.*, ABCNY Formal Op. 2000-1, 2000 WL 704689 (January, 2000); ABA Formal Ethics Op. 99-413 (March 10, 1999); NYSBA Eth. Op. 709, 1998 WL 957924 (September 16, 1998); see *City of Reno v. Reno Police Protective Ass'n*, 118 Nev. 889, 59 P.3d 1212, 1218 (Nev. 2002); *see generally* Audrey Jordan, "Note, Does Unencrypted E-Mail Protect Client Confidentiality?", 27 *Am. J. Trial Advoc.* 623, 626 n.25 (Spring 2004)(referencing ethical opinions from twenty-three State bar associations).

At a bare minimum password protection is essential and limited computer access and perhaps even physically limited access to hard drives on which attorney client privileged and work product materials are stored.

What may be entailed in such setups has been well set forth in a recent opinion that described the computerized network and the precautions taken by an assistant district attorney's office where documents would have to be made available to defense counsel as a matter of course in criminal discovery and where in the course thereof inadvertently work-product-protected materials (it is rare that district attorneys office create their own attorney-client protected materials as opposed to materials that are work-product protected or deliberative privilege protected) were also made available. The court excused the inadvertent production in light of the precautions which were taken. One is tempted to say that the court really did not understand the technology involved at all and was gulled by comparing the precautions taken to those which would have been adequate in the paper world but are stunning inadequate in the electronic world. The precautions taken provide some guidance to litigating attorneys as to what is involved in designing systems that will stand the test of inadvertent disclosure if local rules that excuse such disclosure and require immediate return of inadvertently disclosed privileged materials do not. But a key element was left out. There are technological ways to make such files readable only and thus the copying to a consultant's hard drive could easily have been avoided and should have been so done.

- *United States v. Rigas*, 281 F. Supp. 2d 733 (S.D.N.Y. 2003). The entire file of one of the paralegals working for the United States District Attorney's Office were copied on to a hard drive made available to a computer consultant for the defendants' counsel.

The court reviewed the precautions which had been taken in the course of setting up and operating the system and ruled that the inadvertent disclosure was excusable and did not waive the work product.

"The AUSAs provided specific instructions to IT staff members that the drives should be installed in such a way as to prevent additions to or deletions from those drives. They emphasized that the drives were evidence in a criminal matter and that copies of them would be provided to the defense. Lacking the necessary expertise themselves, the legal team relied in good faith on the assurances of IT personnel that the hard drives could be viewed without the risk of alteration. Moreover, the IT staff themselves believed that the drives were safe from the addition or deletion of files as installed, and did not anticipate the replication of an entire user network account on to an Adelphia drive, as occurred in this case. . . .

"Further, when it came time for defense counsel's consultant to copy the hard drives at the USAO's main office, the Government took additional steps to prevent the disclosure of privileged materials. These precautions included an interview with the consultant regarding the security measures employed by his firm, as well as the creation of a log that recorded all drives provided to the consultant during his visit. AUSA Clark reviewed that log to ensure that only Adelphia hard drives were copied. . . .

"With the benefit of hindsight, it now appears that the Government could have avoided the inadvertent disclosure of USAO work product by producing a "pristine" version rather than a working copy of the Adelphia hard drives to defense counsel's computer consultant. . . . Nonetheless, this Court emphasizes that the reasonableness of a party's actions to protect privileged information should be measured in light of the risks foreseeable to that party at the time the precautions were taken. The mere fact of an accidental disclosure does not automatically render the precautionary measures unreasonable at the time they were performed."

Often massive inadvertent disclosure can occur with merely a tap of a finger on the wrong file to be sent or the wrong distribution list. Some courts will forgive such inadvertent production. Others would not. What is to be done? Since to err is human mistakes of inadvertent will happen. It is a good idea to build in at least a sample check by eye and hand rather than relying on doing the entire process on a computer. If only because courts seem to think that is more careful and more thorough.

- *Carda v. E.H. Oftedal & Sons, Inc.*, 2005 U.S. Dist. LEXIS 26368, at *7–8 (D.S.D. Apr. 28, 2005). Where a privileged document was produced as part of a computer disk of documents and court concluded a simple review of the title of the files would have obviated the production, it was not excused, despite that other factors considered by the court tipped the scales to a finding of no waiver. The privilege holder's motion to exclude the document as evidence in the adversary's case was denied.

"Jason M. Smiley, one of Carda's attorneys, stated under oath that he reviewed the CD before sending it to Oftedal's attorney, Ron Schmidt. Smiley stated that he did not recall seeing Carda's letter on the CD. Myrna Meyers, who is Schmidt's legal secretary, stated under oath that when she inserted the disc into her computer and opened the "E" drive, she saw that the disk contained two items, one labeled "Don_K.doc" under the icon of a piece of paper with the symbol for "Word," and the other labeled "Salaried" under the icon of a yellow folder. The Microsoft Word document is the privileged letter from Carda to his attorney Donald Knudsen. The yellow folder document contains hundreds of subfolders which each contain a photograph of a time card. Oftedal also submitted a printout that depicts the CD menu that shows the folder and the Microsoft Word document. Carda did not contest the validity of Meyers' testimony. A quick glance at the CD menu would have revealed the presence of the letter. Furthermore, Smiley did not have another person double-check the discovery materials to ensure that he did not disclose privileged documents. Accordingly, the court finds that counsel for Carda did not take reasonable precautions to prevent the disclosure of privileged material."

- *F.H. Chase, Inc. v. Clark/Gilford*, 341 F. Supp. 2d 562 (D. Md., 2004). A substantial production of privileged documents was inadvertently produced (569 out of 7,155 documents) when the individual designated to cull privilege from non-privileged documents for Internet transmission to a litigation support firm by mistake transmitted the entire document data base rather than the culled file only. The litigation support firm which was hired only to Bates stamp and photocopy the documents did so, in the process of course producing all the documents. The court excused the inadvertent production, basically influenced by the fact that the error was a single one. The error was literally one of the wrong document file attached and transmitted by e-mail. Another judge might not excuse since no sample check was done before production was made.

Another problem arises because so many employees may have readier access to privilege protected information in electronic form that otherwise would be locked away in a private file cabinet. Is there waiver if such documents are disclosed without being able to trace whether the disclosure was authorized? In one reported case the court held there was no waiver and allowed retrieval of the document.

- *Baptiste v. Cushman & Wakefield, Inc.*, 2004 U.S. Dist. LEXIS 2579 (S.D.N.Y. Feb. 20, 2004). A packet of e-mail communications containing privileged content was left on the desk of the plaintiff by someone who was obviously trying to assist her in her claim. Disclosed in discovery, the defendant was unable to determine which employee left the e-mail on the plaintiff's desk or how access was obtained to the e-mail in question. It waited to bring a motion to retrieve until the plaintiff had been fully deposed on the issue. The court found both that the disclosure was not authorized and allowed retrieval of the privileged portion of the e-mail.

E. *Personal Use of Employer's Computer System— Is It Privilege Protected?*

The Supreme Court has suggested that an employee has a reasonable expectation of privacy in his office, desk and files. That reasonable expectation may be reduced by virtue of actual office practices and procedures, or by legitimate regulation. In light of the variety of work environments, the Supreme Court suggested that whether the employee has a reasonable expectation of privacy must be decided on a case-by-case basis.

- *O'Connor v. Ortega*, 480 U.S. 709, 718 (1987).

Nothing is more common than for employees to use an employer's e-mail for personal communications. If such communications are with a personal attorney for an employee, is there a waiver of the privilege by virtue of such use alone? Not necessarily.

- *In re Asia Global Crossing, Ltd.*, 322 B.R. 247, 251 (S.D.N.Y. 2005). "Assuming a communication is otherwise privileged, the use of the company's e-mail system does not, without more, destroy the privilege."

The opinion ultimately holds only that there is no *ipso facto* waiver by virtue of the use of the employer's e-mail system, any more than there would be one by virtue of using an employer's mail system. It says nothing about whether waiver would occur if there were breaches in the security of the e-mail system or what types of breaches would entail waiver.

In general, when it comes to computer use for private matters courts usually ask whether an employee had a reasonable expectation of privacy in his use of the company's computer. If a court finds that such a reasonable privacy expectation existed, privilege protection would flow therefrom for personal communications. The converse is also so. No reasonable expectation of privacy, no privilege protection. In determining whether there was a reasonable expectation of privacy a court may consider the following factors:

(1) Does the corporation maintain a policy banning personal or other objectionable use;

(2) Does the company monitor the use of the employee's computer or e-mail;

(3) Do third parties have a right of access to the computer or e-mails; and

(4) Did the corporation notify the employee, or was the employee aware, of the use and monitoring policies?

(5) Does the company in fact enforce any no personal use policy or is such a policy there for cosmetic reasons only?

1. No Reasonable Expectation of Privacy

- *Muick v. Glenayre Elecs*, 280 F.3d 741, 743 (7th Cir. 2002). The court found that there was no reasonable expectation of privacy in workplace computer files where employer had announced that he could inspect the computer.

- *United States v. Simons*, 206 F.3d 392 (4th Cir. 2000). The court found that there was no reasonable expectation of privacy in office computer and downloaded Internet files where employer had a policy of auditing employee's use of the Internet, and the employee did not assert that he was unaware of or had not consented to the policy.

- *Thygeson v. U.S. Bancorp*, 2004 U.S. Dist. LEXIS 18863, 2004 WL 2066746, at *20 (D. Or. Sept. 15, 2004). The court found there to be no reasonable expectation of privacy in computer files and e-mail where employee handbook explicitly warned of employer's right to monitor files and e-mail.

- *Kelleher v. City of Reading*, 2002 U.S. Dist. LEXIS 9408, 2002 WL 1067442, at *8 (E.D. Pa. May 29, 2002). The court found no reasonable expectation of privacy in workplace e-mail where employer's guidelines "explicitly informed employees that there was no such expectation of privacy."

- *Garrity v. John Hancock Mut. Life Ins. Co.*, 2002 U.S. Dist. LEXIS 8343, 2002 WL 974676, at *1–2 (D. Mass. May 7, 2002). The court found that the employee had no reasonable expectation of privacy where, despite the fact that the employee created a password to limit access, the company periodically reminded employees that the company e-mail policy prohibited certain uses, the e-mail system belonged to the company, although the company did not intentionally inspect e-mail usage, it might do so where there were business or legal reasons to do so, and the plaintiff assumed her e-mails might be forwarded to others.

- *Smyth v. Pillsbury Co.*, 914 F. Supp. 97, 101 (E.D. Pa. 1996). The court found there to be no reasonable expectation of privacy where employee sent an e-mail over the employer's e-mail system.

2. Reasonable Expectation of Privacy

- *Leventhal v. Knapek*, 266 F.3d 64, 74 (2d Cir. 2001). The court found that an employee did have a reasonable expectation of privacy in contents of workplace computer where the employee had a private office and exclusive use of his desk, filing cabinets and computers, the employer did not have a general practice of routinely searching office computers, and had not "placed [the plaintiff] on notice that he should have no expectation of privacy in the contents of his office computer."

- *United States v. Slanina*, 283 F.3d 670, 676–77 (5th Cir.), *vacated on other grounds*, 537 U.S. 802 (2002). The court found that the employee had reasonable expectation of privacy in his computer and files where the computer was maintained in a closed, locked office; the employee had installed passwords to limit access; and the employer "did not disseminate any policy that prevented the storage of personal information on city computers and also did not inform its employees that computer usage and Internet access would be monitored."

- *Haynes v. Office of the Attorney General*, 298 F. Supp. 2d 1154, 1161–62 (D. Kan. 2003). The employee had a reasonable expectation of privacy in private computer files, despite computer screen warning that there shall be no expectation of privacy in using employer's computer system, where employees were allowed to use computers for private communications, were advised that unauthorized access to user's e-mail was prohibited, employees were given passwords to prevent access by others and no evidence was offered to show that the employer ever monitored private files or employee e-mails.)

- *Curto v. Medical World Comms., Inc.*, 2006 U.S. Dist. LEXIS 29387 (E.D.N.Y. May 15, 2006). The court upheld the ruling of the magistrate judge that plaintiff had not waived the attorney-client privilege when she made use of defendant's computers while in their employ for such communications. Defendant had a policy, articulated in an employee handbook and signed by plaintiff that the laptop computer which she had been given to perform her functions was for business use only and that there was no expectation of privacy. Before turning in her computer upon her termination, the employee had deleted all personal e-mails which the former employer managed to retrieve by the use of a forensic expert. Obviously, the court held there was no waiver by inadvertent production. One of the "subfactors" considered was that the employer had not enforced its no private use policy.

F. *Seizure of Entire Hard Drives*

Increasingly in the criminal context, the United States is seizing entire hard drives as to which the party from whom they are seized then makes claims that extensive privileged documents were on the computer hard drives. Courts will enter protective orders to protect from review documents in respect to which privilege is claimed. We can expect to see more *in camera* reviews, screening teams separate from prosecution teams within a prosecutor's office, and in the case of judges who do not feel sufficiently comfortable with such Chinese Walls, the appointment of Special Masters to screen out the privileged from the non-privileged documents. Arguments that the entire prosecution must itself be dismissed as the tree from the poisoned fruit are going nowhere. The privilege is an evidentiary one not a constitutional one.

- *United States v. Segal*, 313 F. Supp. 2d 774 (N.D. Ill. 2004). No dismissal of indictment granted where computer files allegedly containing 13,000 privileged documents were seized. Documents were also seized from Near North Insurance Company's general counsel's office. The court instructed the prosecution not to review documents as to which privilege had been asserted in a privilege log or to make evidentiary use thereof at trial until the privilege claim could be tested by the court.

VI. "TWO STRINGS TO THE BOW" RAISING BOTH PRIVILEGE AND PROTECTION

It is frequent and usually good practice to assert both the attorney-client privilege and the work-product protection, because the two are not coextensive. Nor should they be conflated since the results vary under each.

Obviously, neither should be asserted frivolously and without a basis. But it is wise not to overlook the fact that even if the privilege fails, because it applies to a far smaller scope of communications, the work-product protection, which is broader albeit less absolute in its applicability, may nonetheless be available.

- *FTC v. TRW, Inc.*, 628 F.2d 207 (D.C. Cir. 1980). Although counsel tried to protect a study done of a computerized credit reporting system under both the privilege and the work-product protection, the latter was abandoned on appeal without an explanation in the opinion as to why or whether the position was abandoned for want of a factual predicate. The privilege claim was not sustained. One cannot determine from the opinion whether the work-product protection would have been sustainable.

Even though the work product protection applies to a potentially broader scope of documents, on occasion it is the claim of work-product protection that may fail, while the attorney-client privilege might be available—all the more reason why the possibility of asserting both should not be overlooked.

- *In re OM Group Sec. Litig.*, 226 F.R.D. 579 (N.D. Ohio 2005). An investigatory report prepared for the audit committee of the board of directors designed to assess whether inventory was properly reported failed to meet the criteria for work-product protection because the court found that there was an independent business reason for the creation of the investigatory report—the correct statement of inventory in a public company. On the other hand the court also said that the report would have qualified for attorney-client protection but for the fact that a Power Point detailed summary of the investigatory report, prepared for the full Board of Directors had been produced in the course of discovery and thus any privilege that would have attached had been waived.

But for the waiver, however, the privilege would have been available even though the work-product protection was not.

On the other hand, frivolously raising both attorney-client privilege and work-product protection on the grounds that it "can't hurt," is misplaced. It can indeed hurt, undercutting a party's credibility and annoying a court that must guess which of the two is in fact properly asserted.

- *United Investors Life Ins. Co. v. Nationwide Life Ins. Co.*, 233 F.R.D. 483, 488 (N.D. Miss. 2006). "In preparing a privilege log, a party must not invoke several protections or privileges where only one applies. Erroneous assertions undercut the invoking party's credibility. For instance, when asserting a right to nondisclosure, an attorney should not state "attorney-client privilege and/or work product." Either the attorney-client privilege and the work-product doctrine protect the document or not; opposing counsel and the court should not be left with deciphering that which is the asserting party's burden. Counsel should be aware of the elemental differences between those assertions and choose accordingly."

If both theories are not raised, the court is not likely to do so *sua sponte*. An attorney thus may find documents that discuss trial strategy under an order of disclosure for want of having asserted the proper category of protection sought.

- *Midwestern Univ. v. HBO & Co.*, 1998 U.S. Dist. LEXIS 20550 (N.D. Ill. Jan. 4, 1999). At *11–12 "Documents G14316–G14319 are not privileged because they are notes of the attorney which reflect his strategy. Counsel for Midwestern does not state in its privilege log that Midwestern [the client] contributed to the notes nor is it stated that the notes contain any confidential information from the client. Again, these documents are at best work product, and because of the traditionally narrow application of the attorney-client privilege, this court will neither allow documents to be protected under an inappropriate privilege nor allow a privilege which has not been claimed." The court did protect a letter from the attorney to the client discussing strategy as protected under the attorney-client privilege that had been properly asserted.

- *National Educ. Training Group, Inc. v. SkillSoft Corp.*, 1999 U.S. Dist. LEXIS 8680, at *13 (S.D.N.Y. June 9, 1999). The notes taken by an associate of a director attending a board meeting in the director's stead were not protected from disclosure under the attorney-client privilege because her presence at the meeting as a third party was not necessary for the rendering of the legal advice but was merely for the convenience of the director, allowing him to absent himself. The notes were, nonetheless, protected from compelled disclosure under the work-product protection because they contained the attorney's legal advice about pending litigation being discussed at the meeting of the board of directors.

Thus, if either the protection of privilege or work product is not expressly claimed, it may well be deemed to have been waived.

- *Sonnino v. Univ. of Kansas Hosp. Auth.*, 220 F.R.D. 633, 647 (D. Kan. 2004). "The Hospital Defendants never asserted the attorney-client privilege or work-product doctrine in response to this request for production. It is well settled that a party may not assert a privilege for the first time in its response to a motion to compel; a privilege not timely asserted in the initial response to a request for production is deemed waived. As the Tenth Circuit has stated: 'It is not enough that a document would have been privileged if an adequate and timely showing had been made. The applicability of the privilege turns on the adequacy and timeliness of the showing as well as on the nature of the document.' Thus, the Court finds that the Hospital Defendants have waived any claim to attorney-client privilege or work product immunity that they may have in response to First Request No. 29. The Hospital Defendants shall therefore produce all documents that are responsive to this request that they have previously withheld on the basis of attorney-client privilege or work-product immunity." (Footnotes omitted.)

- *Smith v. Conway Org., Inc.*, 154 F.R.D. 73, 75 (S.D.N.Y. 1994). The failure to assert work-product immunity or attorney-client privilege with respect to the production of certain documents results in waiver of protection.

- *Carte Blanche (Singapore) PTE, Ltd. v. Diners Club Int'l, Inc.*, 130 F.R.D. 28 (S.D.N.Y. 1990). The attorney's failure to specify work product as the particular privilege protecting documents waived work-product immunity for those documents.

But see:

- *BASF Aktiengesellschaft v. Reilly Indus., Inc.*, 224 F.R.D. 438 (S.D. Ind. 2004). Change of theory for basis of privilege/work-product protection not fatal to effectively maintaining its existence.

Where both theories are presented as possible grounds, courts generally consider the privilege claim first and if they find the protection applies may not bother to analyze whether the document would also be protected under the work-product doctrine. Because the work-product protection is far broader and more extensive than the attorney-client privilege, it is a mistake not to always consider its possible availability to protect matters not subject to protection under the privilege, despite the annoyance expressed by one court over the fact that both privilege and protection were asserted in a privilege log indiscriminately. The operative words are *indiscriminately* and *without basis.*

- *Coltec Indus., Inc. v. American Motorists Ins.*, 197 F.R.D. 368, 371 (N.D. Ill. 2000). The attorney work-product doctrine is "distinct from and broader than the attorney-client privilege."

- *In re Pfohl Bros. Landfill Litig.*, 175 F.R.D. 13, 21 (W.D.N.Y. 1997). "The two privileges must be separately asserted as they are grounded in different policies, and waiver of the attorney-client privilege will not result in automatic disclosure of a communication that still enjoys work-product immunity."

VII. INTERPLAY BETWEEN FOIA AND PRIVILEGE/PROTECTION[7]

Exemption 5 under FOIA incorporates a deliberative process privilege, a work-product protection and an attorney-client privilege. At times Exemption 5 deliberative process privilege has been called a "subspecies" of the work product protection. Nonetheless they are not one and the same, nor are the applicable principles co-extensive.

- *Judicial Watch, Inc. v. Department of Justice*, 432 F.3d 366, 372 (Fed. Cir. 2005). The Federal Circuit reversed an order requiring the Department of Justice to produce certain documents in redacted form so that plaintiff had the factual aspect of the documents available. The entirety of the documents were protected under work-product principles said the Federal Circuit. The District Court's principal error was in conflating the deliberative process privilege and the attorney work-product doctrine. It is clear that the privilege and the doctrine are not coterminous in

---

7. No attempt is here made to undertake an exhaustive survey of FOIA law. That would require an entire tome to itself. Merely those elements that bring it into the most obvious interplay with privilege/work product protection doctrine principles are here very briefly addressed.

their sweep. Factual material is not protected under the deliberative process privilege unless it is "inextricably intertwined" with the deliberative material, whereas no such showing is required under the attorney work-product doctrine, . . . [T]he District Court's "blurring of the two privileges led it to hold . . . that 'defendants do have a duty to release segregable information—that is, information that is not inextricably intertwined with protected information.'"

Governmental agencies in civil litigation have tried to rely on FOIA to resist discovery. It is not available for such purposes, but only to determine what must be disclosed to the public pursuant to a request for disclosure of government papers. If the government wishes to resist discovery in civil litigation, it must do so on attorney-client privilege and work-product protection grounds.

- *Kerr v. United States Dist. Court for N. Dist. of Cal.*, 511 F.2d 192, 197–98 (9th Cir. 1975), *aff'd*, 426 U.S. 394 (1976). Prison authorities resisted discovery in a prisoner civil rights action on FOIA grounds. It was held that the FOIA claim is not available to a state governmental agency, but even had they been applicable, that would not have been a sufficient basis on which to resist discovery. "[T]he exceptions to the disclosure in the Act were not intended to create evidentiary privileges for civil discovery. . . . They were intended only to permit withholding of certain types of information from the public generally."

- *Moore-McCormack Lines, Inc. v. ITO Corp.*, 508 F.2d 945 (4th Cir. 1974). The plaintiff in an indemnity action sought disclosure of an accident report prepared by the Department of Labor of a longshoreman injured while unloading a ship. The trial court refused to compel disclosure in response to a third-party subpoena on the department as to its conclusion of what caused the accident on FOIA grounds. The court of appeals reversed. The department could not refuse to produce a portion of a report in civil litigation that would in all events not be subject to an exception and would be discoverable under an FOIA request.

- *Pleasant Hill Bank v. United States*, 58 F.R.D. 97 (W.D. Mo. 1973). The government's reliance on an FOIA exemption, even where validly asserted, was not sufficient to resist discovery in litigation.

- *Verrazzano Trading Corp. v. United States*, 349 F. Supp. 1401, 1403. (Cust. Ct. 1972). The FOIA shield was pierced in an action regarding the classification of imported fabrics.

Objection to production of work-protected materials in the FOIA context is often asserted under 5 U.S.C. § 552(b)(5), which provides that FOIA requests may be denied if the information consists of "inter-agency memorandums or letters that would not be available by law to a party other than an agency in litigation with the agency." This provision has been interpreted to encompass work-product-protected materials.

- *Raytheon Aircraft Co. v. U.S. Army Corps of Eng'rs*, 183 F. Supp. 2d 1280 (D. Kan. 2001). The court concluded that two reports were produced by inside counsel for the Army Corps of Engineers with specific CERCLA litigation in mind and thus were protected. The underlying information upon which the reports were based was not similarly protected despite competing lines of cases—some according protection, others not—because revealing the documents would not compromise the attorney's mental processes in compiling the work-product-protected reports.

The deliberative process privilege has also on occasion been deemed a sub-species of the work product privilege, although it certainly does not fit into the traditional definition of it as provided by federal rule and often is not prepared in anticipation of litigation at all.

- *DiPace v. Goord*, 218 F.R.D. 399, 403 (S.D.N.Y. 2003). "The deliberative process privilege is a "sub-species" of the work product doctrine. *See Tigue v. United States Dep't of Justice*, 312 F.3d 70, 76 (2d Cir. 2002), *cert. denied*, 538 U.S. 1056 (2003). It has also been called the "official information" privilege, the "intra governmental opinion" or "governmental opinion" privilege, and the "executive" privilege."

Where the more traditional aspect of work product protection is claimed under Exemption 5, namely that a document was prepared in anticipation of litigation, it has been held that the government can not make a blanket assertion of that nature, but must identify the litigation for which it was prepared.

- *Church of Scientology Int'l v. United States Dep't of Justice*, 30 F.3d 224, 237 (1st Cir. 1994). The First Circuit has stated that "at a minimum, an agency seeking to withhold a document in its entirety [by invoking the work-product doctrine under 5 *U.S.C.* § *552(b)(5)*] must identify the litigation for which the document was created (either by name or through factual description) and explain why the work-product privilege applies to all portions of the document."

Courts have not been willing to give dual-purpose documents protection even when the documents encompass work-product-protected materials. Thus if a document is prepared by the government, for instance, primarily for purposes of rule making, even though litigation may be foreseen, the document will not thereby be protected. The courts have said it would eviscerate the purposes of FOIA, which is to make government business and rule making as transparent as possible.

- *Maine v. United States Dep't of the Interior*, 285 F.3d 126, 134 (1st Cir.), *op. withdrawn* (Apr. 5, 2002), *substituted op.*, 298 F.3d 60 (1st Cir. 2002). "However sound the reasoning in *Adlman* may be in the civil discovery context, we are not persuaded that it should apply in an action seeking disclosure of documents pursuant to FOIA. As the district court observed, agency decision making on controversial regulations, as this case highlights, usually involves the prospect of litigation and in many cases does lead to litigation. The standard adopted by *Adlman* would hinder the openness that Congress envisioned in enacting FOIA and shield from disclosure documents that would aid in understanding the decision-making process of an agency. Indeed, the Supreme Court has cautioned that the discovery rules can only be applied under Exemption 5 by way of rough analogies. . . . The use of FOIA, as the DOI alleges Maine is doing here, to expand discovery that otherwise would not be available in a civil action, is permissible in light of the Congressional purpose and policy of the Act. Thus, we cannot say that the district court erred in this case in requiring the DOI to demonstrate that the withheld documents were created primarily for litigation purposes in order to claim the work-product privilege under 5 U.S.C. Sec. 552(b)(5)."

- *Federal Open Market Comm. v. Merrill*, 443 U.S. 340, 360 n.23 (1979). The Supreme Court stated that "a memorandum subject to the affirmative disclosure requirement of [Section] 552(a)(2) [(the FOIA provision that requires disclosure of agency's working law)] is nevertheless shielded from disclosure under Exemption 5 [if] it contain[s] a privileged attorney's work product." The Supreme Court distinguished between the deliberative process privilege and the attorney work-product privilege, explaining that the former does not trump the mandatory disclosure requirement under Section 552(a)(2), but the latter does.

- *Tax Analysts v. IRS (Guidance II)*, 294 F.3d 71, 76 (D.C. Cir. 2002), *reh'g denied*, 2002 U.S. App. LEXIS 15955, 15956 (D.C. Cir. Aug. 5, 2002), *affirming in part Tax Analysts v. IRS (Guidance I)*, 152 F. Supp. 2d 1, 18 (D.D.C. 2001). Tax Analysts sought full disclosure under FOIA of several categories of documents prepared by OCC, including intra-divisional Technical Assistance memoranda ("TAs") prepared by Chief Counsel attorneys in preparation for trial and withheld in their entirety pursuant to FOIA Exemption 5. The plaintiff disputed the scope of the attorney work-product privilege, arguing that the privilege protects only the "mental impressions, conclusions, opinions, or legal theories of an attorney," or "factual materials prepared in anticipation of litigation," but not "agency working law, legal analysis and conclusions."

The district court had rejected plaintiff's argument, that "as long as the eight TAs in dispute are documents that were prepared in anticipation of litigation or for trial, they can be withheld, including any agency working law that they may contain." Id. at 19. (Emphasis added.)

The Court of Appeals affirmed the reasoning and conclusions of the district court on this point, holding that: "The District Court correctly determined that IRS need not segregate and release agency working law from TAs withheld in their entirety pursuant to the attorney work-product privilege. Because the District Court's analysis and conclusions on these points are eminently sound, no further elaboration is necessary. We therefore affirm the District Court's judgment on these issues and adopt its reasoning and conclusions."

"The District Court correctly determined that IRS need not segregate and release agency working law from TAs withheld in their entirety pursuant to the attorney work-product privilege. Because the District Court's analysis and conclusions on these points are eminently sound, no further elaboration is necessary. We therefore affirm the District Court's judgment on these issues and adopt its reasoning and conclusions."

- *Tax Analysts v. IRS*, 391 F. Supp. 2d 122 (D.D.C. 2005). The Federal Circuit followed the reasoning of the Tax Analysts court in respect to the interplay of FOIA and work-product protection and applied it in the context of Section 6110 (c) of the Internal Revenue Code's requirements. At issue were memoranda prepared by attorneys in the IRS Office of Chief Counsel ("OCC") in response to requests from IRS field offices for guidance on legal interpretations and IRS policy with respect to provisions of the tax laws. The IRS is required to keep its "written determinations" available for public inspection. Exemptions comparable to those of FOIA apply.

The above two cases thus reverse prior precedent of *Tax Analysts v. IRS*, 1998 WL 419755, at 3 (D.D.C. 1998), where the court held that however work product was defined, and therefore redacted, the requester was entitled to the agency working law. This case thus should no longer be relied upon.

Astonishingly, a member of Congress had recourse to FOIA when the Veterans Administration refused to supply him with an internal memo which it relied upon for the administration of veteran's benefits. The Veterans Administration lost its FOIA Exemption 5 (work product) claim.

- *Evans v. United States Office of Personnel Mgmt.*, 276 F. Supp. 2d 34, 39 (D.D.C. 2003). The court used the precedent of Tax Analysts II to grant the eleventh term Congressman's FOIA request for a memo that served as guidance for the administration of veteran's benefits. The Congressman was the ranking Democratic Member on the House Veteran's Affairs Committee. In sum, a "strong theme" of this Circuit's deliberative process opinions "has been that an agency will not be permitted to develop a body of 'secret law,' used by it in the discharge of its regulatory duties and in its dealings with the public, but hidden behind a veil of privilege because it is not designated as 'formal,' 'binding,' or 'final.'" Coastal

States, 617 F.2d at 867. The present case fits this pattern perfectly. Because the memo at issue describes OPM's [Office of Personnel Management] legal position in terms and under circumstances strongly suggestive of finality, the agency may not claim deliberative process to shield its articulation of that position.

The question of whether a disclosure of privileged or work-product protected was or was not authorized arises rarely in the context of private parties. It arises with some frequency in the governmental context. Not surprisingly, courts are much likely to find waiver unless the "leak" or disclosure was clearly an authorized one.

- *DiPace v. Goord*, 218 F.R.D. 399 (S.D.N.Y. 2003). The court found that whatever public disclosure had been made of a work product document was not authorized and hence entailed no waiver. "While disclosure of otherwise privileged material to a non-governmental recipient may result in a waiver," no waiver will be found unless that disclosure was "authorized" by the governmental agency and "voluntary."

- *Overby v. United States Fid. & Guar. Co.*, 224 F.2d 158, 163 (5th Cir. 1955). Bank directors authorized to see a government report made an unauthorized disclosure to their attorneys and auditors. In concluding that the government's "official information" privilege had not been waived, the court held that "the privilege belongs to the Government and . . . can neither be claimed nor waived by a private party." (Internal quotation marks and citation omitted.)

- *Safeway Stores Inc. v. FTC*, 428 F. Supp. 346, 347 (D.D.C. 1977). The court found that no waiver occurred when an FTC staff report, after having been transmitted to certain congressional committees, was "leaked" to the *Washington Post*. The court rejected the argument that the newspaper's publication of an article on the report waived the applicability of the privilege.

- *United States v. Alex. Brown & Sons, Inc.*, 169 F.R.D. 532, 543–44 & n.6 (S.D.N.Y. 1996). The court found no waiver of privileges, including deliberative-process privilege, even though a privileged document was apparently shared with members of the press where it was not possible to identify the parties responsible for this disclosure. The court concluded that as far as it was aware, in each case where a finding of waiver was reached in respect to an otherwise privileged document evidence existed that the agency had actually authorized the document's release.

- *North Dakota ex rel. Olson v. Andrus*, 581 F.2d 177, 179, 182 n.9 (8th Cir. 1978). Waiver occurred when a document voluntarily disclosed in discovery to opposing counsel.

- *Shell Oil Co. v. IRS*, 772 F. Supp. 202, 211 (D. Del. 1991). Where an agency employee read aloud the contents of privileged document at a meeting attended by non-governmental entities waiver occurred.

- *Education/Instruccion, Inc. v. United States Dep't of Hous. & Urban Dev.*, 471 F. Supp. 1074, 1081 (D. Mass. 1979). Where a document was provided voluntarily to outside entity and there was no contention that the disclosure was unauthorized waiver occurred.

VIII. CONCLUSION: WHITHER THE PRIVILEGE

More than a quarter of a century has elapsed since the first edition of this book was first presented at a American Bar Association's annual meeting where one of the panels discussed the attorney-client privilege. The looseleaf bound notebook there distributed, which collected most of the significant cases on the subject matter at the time, amounted to no more than some 100 pages or so.

Since then an entire body of law has evolved around and about the attorney-client privilege and the work-product doctrine. This fifth edition reflects that change, not only in the number of pages—now close to 1,000 rather than a mere tenth the size—but also the sheer scope of the law in this area. Do a LEXIS search and you will find approximately 300 decisions a month issued dealing with attorney-client and work-product protection disputes in the federal courts. The disease does not seem to have spread with like virulence in the state courts, which raises interesting anthropological questions about the differences between the two.

As is wont in virtually anything subject to common law development, virtually every imaginable situation that could arise has arisen and required adjudication. In the process the attorney-client privilege protects far less than many practitioners and their clients believe it does.

Lawyers fret that the protections of the attorney-client privilege and the work-product protection are being eroded. That concern is hardly surprising. Of all the evidentiary and discovery rules, these two go to the heart of both the attorney's relationship with a client and with the attorney's jealously guarded right to develop litigation strategies without fear of compelled disclosure to an adversary.

Yet as one who has watched over the years this explosive development of attorney-client privilege law and the legal and judicial resources which adjudication of these issues has come to consume, I cannot resist posing a challenge to the profession.

Granted, litigating privilege issues is most financially rewarding for the legal profession. Many youthful bodies can be thrown into reviewing paper documents (with more to come now as we fully enter the electronic age). Privilege logs are time consuming and exceedingly costly to prepare, although some courts and even litigators deem them to be near worthless. So do all good intentions produce untoward bureaucratizing results. And good intentions indeed initially surrounded the creation of privilege logs, initially on a voluntary and subsequently on a Rule mandated basis. Moreover, privilege logs, as we have seen, hardly obviate, in most instances, *in camera* review which once upon a time was the exception and has now become the rule, subject occasionally even to a rebuke by an appellate court that the trier of fact has abused his or her discretion in failing to conduct such a review. And so are yet more judicial resources swallowed up in something that has not only grown like topsy, but perhaps like kudzu weed as well.

But as the ancient Romans were wont to ask when considering a legal matter in dispute, *Qui bonum?* Is all of this review for privilege and litigation about privilege in the client's real interests or the lawyer's?

Now don't get me wrong. I think the privilege has a real role to play in the criminal context. And practitioners and businessmen vehemently assure one and all that to properly abide by the law corporations too must be free to ask an attorney how to right a wrong or illegality that they discover or seek to avoid without fear that the attempt will become usable against the corporation either in the civil litigation or the criminal context.

Nonetheless there are days when I wonder if perhaps the Elizabethans and not we had it right on the privilege. For them it was the lawyer's privilege and not the client's. A lawyer was a gentleman and a gentleman did not squeal on his client. Thus some cases which allow lawyers to cut deals on their own behalf and thereafter testify against clients are shocking. Yet the courts have allowed it.

A case that surely shocks or should shock a self-respecting professional attorney's conscience is *United States v. White*, 970 F.2d 328 (7th Cir. 1992), and 950 F.2d 426 (7th Cir. 1991). The prosecutor induced informal cooperation and grand jury testimony from the former bankruptcy counsel for two grand jury targets, the attorney's former clients. The attorney had himself been convicted on a collateral matter. It was sentencing time. Afraid that he would be blamed for his clients' failure to disclose assets on their bankruptcy petition, the lawyer agreed to cooperate with the prosecution by ratting on his clients to the prosecutor and the grand jury.

The Seventh Circuit remanded the issue for a full evidentiary hearing on the clients' claim that they had been convicted on the testimony of their former counsel out to save his own neck. After a full hearing, the district court concluded, and the Seventh Circuit agreed, that no violation of the privilege had occurred because the documents and information provided by the convicted attorney were conveyed to him with the intention of being placed on a bankruptcy petition in all events. Thus, the Seventh Circuit strictly and correctly applied the privilege and ruled that no privilege had attached to the communications *ab initio* because they were never invested with the requisite intention of confidentiality.

The clients were convicted of fraud when the attorney exculpated himself by turning over documents provided by his clients. Moreover, the government joined in the attorney's motion to reduce the lawyer's sentence, a bargain received in return for having turned in the clients.

Nonetheless, as the Seventh Circuit and Judge John Koeltl have remarked, the attorney-client privilege is a testimonial not a constitutional privilege, and even a shocking violation of an attorney's ethical obligations to the attorney's client will not necessarily lead to a reversal of an otherwise valid conviction. No poisoned fruit of a poisoned tree here. When the privilege is really essential, the moral may well be: Caveat client lest you pick a co-crook for an attorney because when the prosecutor comes calling it is every man to the lifeboats. He who reaches them first will be saved by tossing overboard the newcomers. Or it may well be that the former clients here sought an unavailable remedy: overturning their conviction. Query whether a claim for malpractice damages based on a breach of client confidence resulting in substantial harm to the clients might not, however, lie.

And I once represented a lawyer, sued for malpractice by his former clients, because he wore a wire on his drug supplier/clients. The state court judge who tried the malpractice claim did not dismiss it and in his own inimitable way assured settlement.

But how much is in fact left of the privilege once one takes into account all the situations for which privilege is claimed where it does not apply? Mind I am speaking only in the context of organizations, not individuals, which context by the way is where the great bulk of the very costly adjudication takes place. Is what lawyers are so assiduously protecting and litigating until the cows have long since come home and been milked, fed and stabled in fact worthy of all that cost and effort, as Judge Posner and the University of Chicago cost/benefit school of legal reasoning would ask? Something has surely gone totally disproportionate although the remedy is not self-evident.

How many of those documents, so assiduously battled over, must in fact be kept confidential lest they harm the client? And if that is the case, an exception or one of the infinite varieties of waiver are likely to kick in and compel disclosure. But most telling is the alacrity with which parties are entering into "claw back" agreements, agreements which provide for a contractual lack of waiver if a privileged document is inadvertently produced. Or given the costs, parties are making discovery without privilege review, in the expectation that privileged documents will not be admissible as evidence even if produced. In a sense, I would suggest, lawyers are *de facto* answering my question with these agreements. Namely at the end of the day, there is precious little that must be zealously guarded by means of the privilege lest harm result to an organizational client.

Bibliography

Alexander, Vincent C., *The Corporate Attorney-Client Privilege: A Study of the Participants*, 63 ST. JOHN'S L. REV. 191 (1989).

Annotation: *Fraud Exception to Work Product Privilege in Federal Courts*, 64 A.L.R. Fed 470 (1983).

Annotation, *Applicability of Attorney-Client Privilege to Communications Made in the Presence of or Solely to or by Third Persons*, 14 A.L.R. 4th Ed. 594 (1982).

Bahner, T. Maxfield & Michael L. Gallion, *Waiver of Attorney-Client Privilege Via Issue Injection: A Call for Uniformity*, 65 DEF. COUNS. J. 199, 204 (1998).

Bartell, Laura B., THE ATTORNEY-CLIENT PRIVILEGE AND WORK PRODUCT DOCTRINE, ALI/ABA Resource Materials Civil Practice and Litigation in the Federal and State Courts 583 (2d ed. 1984).

Battersby, Gregory J. & Charles W. Grimes, *The Attorney-Client Privilege and the Work Product Immunity in the Eye of the Accused Infringer*, AM. INTELL. PROP. L. ASS'N Q.J. 236 (1987).

Becker, Susan J., *Conducting Informal Discovery of a Party's Former Employees: Legal and Ethical Concerns and Constraints*, 51 MD. L. REV. 239, 308 (1992).

Blakely, Alan F. *Privilege Log Dilemma*, THE FEDERAL LAWYER, Nov./Dec. 2005.

Bruckner-Harvey, Anne G., Comment, *Inadvertent Disclosure in the Age of Fax Machines: Is the Cat Really Out of the Bag?* 46 BAYLOR L. REV. 385, 394 (1994).

Calamari, Peter E., *Failing Financial Institution Investigations: Privilege Considerations*, 466 PLI/COMM 305, 315 (1988).

Callan, J. Michael & Harris David, *Professional Misconduct and the Duty of Confidentiality: Disclosure of Client Misconduct in an Adversary System*, 29 RUTGERS L. REV. 332 (1976).

Capra, Daniel J., *The Attorney-Client Privilege in Common Representations*, 20 TRIAL LAW. Q., Summer 1989.

Comment, *The Attorney-Client Privilege, Ethical Rules of Confidentiality, and Other Arguments Bearing on Disclosure of a Fugitive Client's Whereabouts*, 68 TEMP. L. REV. 307 (1995).

Comment, *The Attorney-Client Privilege in Multiple Party Situations*, 8 COLUM. J.L. & SOC. PROBS. 179 (1972).

Comment, *Discoverability of Attorney Work Product Reviewed by Expert Witnesses: Have the 1993 Revisions to the Federal Rules of Civil Procedure Changed Anything?* 69 TEMP. L. REV. 451, 478–79 (1996).

Comment, *Issues of Waiver In Multiple-Party Litigation: The Attorney-Client Privilege and the Work Product Doctrine*, 61 UMKC L. REV. 757 (1993).

Comment, *Patent Attorneys and the Attorney-Client Privilege*, 35 SANTA CLARA L. REV. 611, 625 (1995).

Comment, *Stuffing the Rabbit Back into the Hat: Limited Waiver of the Attorney-Client Privilege in an Administrative Agency Investigation*, 130 U. PA. L. REV. 1198 (1982).

Comment, *Privileged Communications with Accountants: The Demise of United States v. Kovel*, 86 MARQ. L. REV. 977 (2003).

Davidson, George A., *Judicial Procedures for Resolving Claims of Privilege*, 8 LITIGATION 36 (Summer 1982).

Davis, Stanley D. & Thomas D. Beisecker. *Discovering Trial Consultant Work Product: A New Way to Borrow an Adversary's Wits?* 17 AM. J. TRIAL ADVOC. 581, 619 (1994).

Developments in the Law—*Privileged Communications*, 98 HARV. L. REV. 1450 (1985).

DeVito, Daniel A. & Michael P. Dierks, *Exploring Anew the Attorney-Client Privilege and Work-Product Doctrine in Patent Litigation: The Pendulum Swings Again, This Time in Favor of Protection*, 22 AIPLA Q.J. 103 (1987).

DeWitt, Timothy R., *Defendants Beware: Raising the Defense of Estoppel May Waive the Attorney Client Privilege*, 7 FED. CIR. B.J. 55 (1997).

Dragseth, John, *Coerced Waiver of the Attorney-Client Privilege for Opinions of Counsel in Patent Litigation*, 80 MINN. L. REV. 167, 174–75 (1995).

Easton, Stephen D., *Ammunition for the Shoot-Out With the Hired Gun's Hired Gun: A Proposal for Full Expert Witness Disclosure*, 32 ARIZ. ST. L. J. 465 (2000).

Fischer, James M., *The Attorney-Client Privilege Meets the Common Interest Arrangement: Protecting Confidences While Exchanging Information for Mutual Gain*, 16 REV. LITIG, 631 (1997).

Flaum, Douglas H. and Rachel Sims, *Using the Common Interest Doctrine to Prevent a Waiver of Privilege*, N.Y.L.J., Jul. 25, 2003.

Fried, *Too High a Price for Truth: The Exception to the Attorney-Client Privilege for Contemplated Crimes and Frauds*, 64 N.C.L.REV. 443, 467 (1986).

Fulmer, Amy M. *Making a Wrong Turn on the Information Superhighway: Electronic Mail, The Attorney-Client Privilege and Inadvertent Disclosure*, 26 CAP. U. L. REV. 347 (1997).

Galanek, Christopher P., *The Impact of the Zolin Decision on the Crime-Fraud Exception to the Attorney-Client Privilege*, 24 GA. L. REV. 1115, 1124 (1990).

Gardner, J., *The Crime or Fraud Exception to the Attorney-Client Privilege*, 47 A.B.A. J. 708 (1961).

Gergacz, John W., ATTORNEY-CORPORATE CLIENT PRIVILEGE (2d ed. 1990).

Gibbs, Charles F. & Cindy D. Hanson, *The Fiduciary Exception to a Trustee's Attorney/Client Privilege*, 21 ACTEC NOTES 236 (1995).

Goff, Jared. Comment. *The Unpredictable Scope of the Waiver Resulting from the Advice-of-Counsel Defense to Willful Patent Infringement*, 1998 B.Y.U. L. Rev. 213 (1998).

Goode-Trufant, Muriel, *Privileges in Federal Court*, 738 PLI/Lit. 77 (2006).

Graham, Michael, H. *Discovery of Experts under Rule 26(b)(4) of the Federal Rules of Civil Procedure: Part Two, An Empirical Study and a Proposal*, 1977 U. ILL. L.F. 169, 172.

Graham, Michael H., *Expert Witness Testimony and the Federal Rules of Evidence: Insuring Adequate Assurance of Trustworthiness*, 1986 U. Ill. L. Rev. 43.

Grippando, James M., *Attorney-Client Privilege: Implied Waiver Through Inadvertent Disclosure of Documents*, 39 U. MIAMI L. REV. 511, 514–15 (1985).

Hajek., Luther, *Guise, Contrivance, or Artful Dodging?: The Discovery Rules Governing Testifying Employee Experts*, 24 REV. LITIG. 301, 315 (2005).

Halfenger, G. Michael, *The Attorney Misconduct Exception to the Work Product Doctrine*, 58 U. CHI. L. REV. 1079, 1090 (1991).

Harnisch, *Confidential Communications Between Clients and Patent Agents: Are They Protected Under the Attorney-Client Privilege?* 16 HASTINGS COMM. & ENT. L.J. 433 (1994).

Hazard, Geoffrey C., Jr., *An Historical Perspective on the Attorney-Client Privilege*, 66 CAL. L. REV. 1061 (1978).

Higgason, Robert W., *The Attorney-Client Privilege in Joint Defense and Common Interest Cases*, 34-AUG HOUS. LAW. 20, 24 (1996).

Hundley, John T., *"Inadvertent Waiver" of Evidentiary Privileges: Can Reformulating the Issue Lead to More Sensible Decisions?* 19 S. ILL. U. L.J. 263 (Winter 1995).

Jones, Trina, *Inadvertent Disclosure of Privileged Information and the Law of Mistake: Using Substantive Legal Principles to Guide Ethical Decision Making*, 48 EMORY L.J. 1255 (1999).

Kayle, *The Tax Advisor's Privilege in Transaction [*19] Matters: A Synopsis and a Suggestion*, 54 TAX LAW 509, 521 (2001).

Klopfenstein, Christa L., Note, *Discoverability of Opinion Work Product Materials Provided to Testifying Experts*, 32 IND. L. REV. 481 (1999).

Leary, Thomas B., *Is There a Conflict in Representing a Corporation and Its Individual Employees?* 36 BUS. LAW. 591 (1981).

Levine, Henry D., *Self-Interest or Self-Defense: Lawyer Disregard of the Attorney-Client Privilege for Profit and Protection*, 5 HOFSTRA L. REV. 783 (1987).

Lewis, Donald B., *The Availability of the Attorney-Client and Work-Product Privileges in Shareholder Litigation*, 32 CLEVE. ST. L. REV. 189 (1984).

Marcus, Richard L., *The Perils of Privilege: Waiver and the Litigator*, 84 MICH. L. REV. 1605 (1986).

McSherry, William J., Jr., *Attorney-Client Privilege Waiver in Second Circuit*, N.Y. L.J., July 20, 1998.

Mickus, Lee, *Discovery of Work Product Disclosed to a Testifying Expert Under the 1993 Amendments to the Federal Rules of Civil Procedure*, 27 CREIGHTON L. REV. 773(1994).

Mitchelson, William R., Jr., Comment, *Waiver of the Attorney-Client Privilege by the Trustee in Bankruptcy*, 51 U. CHI. L. REV. 1230, 1258–59 (1984).

Nash, *Upjohn: A New Prescription for Attorney-Client Privilege and Work Product Defenses in Administrative Investigations*, 30 BUFFALO L. REV. 11, 68–78 (1981).

Nielsen, Joseph W., Note, *Privileged Communications*, 27 SETON HALL L. REV. 1123, 1123–26 (1997).

Note, *The Attorney-Client Privilege: Fixed Rules, Balancing, and Constitutional Entitlement*, 91 HARV. L. REV. 464 (1977).

Note, *The Future Crime or Tort Exception to Communications Privileges*, 77 HARV. L. REV. 730 (1964).

Note, *The Attorney-Client Privilege in Multiple Party Situations*, 8 COLUM. J.L. & SOC. PROBS. 179 (1972).

Note, *Attorney Liabilities Under ERISA*, 82 W. VA. L. REV. 129 (1981).

Note, *Waiver of the Attorney-Client Privilege on Inter-Attorney Exchange of Information*, 63 YALE L.J. 1030 (1954).

Oishi, Duke, *A Piece of Mind for Peace of Mind: Federal Discoverability of Opinion Work Product Provided to Expert Witnesses and Its Implications in Hawaii*, 24 U. HAW. L. REV. 859, 868 (2002) (addressing differences between pre-1993 expert discovery rules and post-1993 expert discovery rules).

Peterson, Gene A., *Attorney-Client Privilege in Internal Revenue Service Investigations*, 54 MINN. L. REV. 67 (1969).

Plunkett, Michael E., *Discoverability of Attorney Work Product Reviewed by Expert Witnesses: Have the 1993 Revisions to the Federal Rules of Civil Procedure Changed Anything?* 69 TEMPLE L. REV. 451, 479 (1996).

Porter, Richard H. *Voluntary Disclosures to Federal Agencies—Their Impact on the Ability of Corporations to Protect From Discovery Materials Developed During the Course of Internal Investigations*, 39 CATH. U.L. REV. 1007, 1016 (1990).

Reid, Rust E., William R. Mureiko & D'Ana H. Mikeska, *Privilege and Confidentiality Issues When a Lawyer Represents a Fiduciary*, 30 REAL PROP. PROB. & TR. J. 541 (1996).

Rice, Paul R., ATTORNEY-CLIENT PRIVILEGE IN THE UNITED STATES § 8.12 (1993 & Supp. 1997).

Rushing, Susan K., Note, *Separating the Joint-Defense Doctrine from the Attorney-Client Privilege*, 68 TEX. L. REV. 1273, 1299–1300 (May 1990).

Saltzburg, Stephen A., *Corporate and Related Attorney-Client Privilege Claims: A Suggested Approach*, 12 HOFSTRA L. REV. 279 (1984).

Saltzburg, Stephen A., et al., FEDERAL RULES OF EVIDENCE MANUAL (6th ed. 1994).

The Sedona Conference, *The Sedona Principles: Best Practices Recommendations & Principles for Addressing Electronic Document Production*, March, 2003, comment 10a, http://www.thesedonaconference.org.

Sexton, John E., *A Post-Upjohn Consideration of the Corporate Attorney-Client Privilege*, 57 N.Y.U. L. REV. 443 (1982).

Simon, David, *The Attorney-Client Privilege as Applied to the Corporation*, 65 YALE L.J. 953 (1956).

Snider & Ellins, *Corporate Privilege and Confidential Information* (2004).

Spiro, Edward & Caroline Rule, *'Kovel' Experts Cloaked by Attorney-Client Privilege*, N.Y. L.J. (Feb. 22, 1994).

Stone, Scott N. & Robert K. Taylor, TESTIMONIAL PRIVILEGES (2d ed. 1996).

Voth, William H., *Waiver of the Attorney-Client Privilege*, 64 OREGON L. REV. 737 (1986).

Welles, Patricia, *A Survey of Attorney-Client Privilege in Joint Defense*, 35 U. MIAMI L. REV. 321, 331–32 (1981).

Yoshida, Daiske, Note, *The Applicability of the Attorney-Client Privilege to Communications with Foreign Legal Professionals*, 66 FORDHAM L. REV. 209, 226 (1997).

Zwerling, Matthew, *Federal Grand Juries v. Attorney Independence and the Attorney-Client Privilege*, 27 HASTINGS L.J. 1263 (1976).

Table of Cases

L

About the Author

Edna Selan Epstein has had her own law firm since May of 1989. She handles a wide variety of litigated matters, including employment discrimination, pension fraud class actions, medical and legal malpractice, and business torts. She does so generally on the plaintiff's side. Epstein also represents defendants in multidefendant conspiracy blockbusters in the United States District Court.

Until starting her own law firm, Epstein was first an associate and then a partner at the law firm of Sidley & Austin in Chicago, where she spent thirteen years, from 1976 to 1989.

Epstein began her legal career, after graduating cum laude and Order of the Coif from the University of Chicago Law School in 1973, at the Cook County State's Attorney's Office. She served first in the civil division, then in the criminal division, where she headed up a newly established bureau dedicated to the prosecution of sex felonies.

Before going to law school, Epstein had embarked upon an academic career in the study of Romance languages and literature, obtaining her Ph.D from Harvard University in 1967. She taught for three years as an assistant professor in the French department at the University of Illinois in Chicago and published articles on 19th Century French poetry in various academic journals.

Epstein has taught courses in trial practice and negotiations at NITA, the University of Chicago Law School, and IIT-Kent Law School. She has been on any number of panels dealing with a wide range of legal issues and has written articles on various areas of the law.

Currently she serves as an editor of Litigation magazine and is also active with the Book Publishing Board of the American Bar Association's Section of Litigation. In the past she served as chairperson of the Trial Evidence Committee and was a member of the Council of the Litigation Section.

Epstein has been married to Wolfgang Epstein for forty years. She is the mother of three adult children and the dotingly proud grandmother of seven grandchildren.